Human-Computer Interaction Series

Human-Computer Interaction is a multidisciplinary field focused on human aspects of the development of computer technology. As computer-based technology becomes increasingly pervasive – not just in developed countries, but worldwide – the need to take a human-centered approach in the design and development of this technology becomes ever more important. For roughly 30 years now, researchers and practitioners in computational and behavioral sciences have worked to identify theory and practice that influences the direction of these technologies, and this diverse work makes up the field of human-computer interaction. Broadly speaking, it includes the study of what technology might be able to do for people and how people might interact with the technology.

In this series, we present work which advances the science and technology of developing systems which are both effective and satisfying for people in a wide variety of contexts. The human-computer interaction series will focus on theoretical perspectives (such as formal approaches drawn from a variety of behavioral sciences), practical approaches (such as the techniques for effectively integrating user needs in system development), and social issues (such as the determinants of utility, usability and acceptability).

For further volumes:
http://www.springer.com/series/6033

Emmanuel Dubois · Philip Gray · Laurence Nigay
Editors

The Engineering of Mixed Reality Systems

Springer

Editors
Dr. Emmanuel Dubois
Université Toulouse III - Tarbes
Institut de Recherches en
Informatique de Toulouse (IRIT)
France

Philip Gray
University of Glasgow
Dept. Computing Science
UK

Pr. Laurence Nigay
Université Grenoble I
Labo. d'Informatique de
Grenoble (LIG)
France

ISSN 1571-5035
ISBN 978-1-4471-2522-8 e-ISBN 978-1-84882-733-2
DOI 10.1007/978-1-84882-733-2
Springer London Dordrecht Heidelberg New York

British Library Cataloguing in Publication Data
A catalogue record for this book is available from the British Library

Printed on acid-free paper

Springer is part of Springer Science+Business Media (www.springer.com)

Contents

Contributors

Minoru Asada Graduate School of Engineering, Osaka University, Osaka, Japan, asada@ams.eng.osaka-u.ac.jp

Benjamin Avery Wearable Computer Laboratory, University of South Australia, Mawson Lakes, SA, Australia, 5095, ben@benavery.net

Cédric Bach University of Toulouse, IRIT, 118 route de Narbonne, 31062 Toulouse Cedex 9, France, Cedric.Bach@irit.f

Sergi Bermúdez i Badia SPECS@IUA: Laboratory for Synthetic Perceptive, Emotive, and Cognitive Systems, Universitat Pompeu Fabra, Tànger 135, 08018 Barcelona, Spain

Ulysses Bernardet SPECS@IUA: Laboratory for Synthetic Perceptive, Emotive, and Cognitive Systems, Universitat Pompeu Fabra, Tànger 135, 08018 Barcelona, Spain, bernuly@gmail.com

Margit Biemans Novay, 7500 AN Enschede, The Netherlands, Margit.Biemans@novay.nl

Matthias Bohnen University Koblenz-Landau, Koblenz, Germany, mbohnen@uni-koblenz.de

Christophe Bortolaso University of Toulouse, IRIT, 118 route de Narbonne, 31062 Toulouse Cedex 9, France, Christophe.Bortolaso@irit.fr

Syrine Charfi University of Toulouse, IRIT, 118 route de Narbonne, 31062 Toulouse Cedex 9, France, Syrine.Charfi@irit.fr

Adrian David Cheok Mixed Reality Lab, 21 Lower Kent Ridge Rd, National University of Singapore, Singapore 119077, Singapore, adriancheok@mixedrealitylab.org

Céline Coutrix Grenoble Informatics Laboratory, 385 avenue de la Bibliothèque, Domaine Universitaire, B.P. 53, 38 041 Grenoble cedex 9, France, Celine.Coutrix@imag.fr

Nadine Couture ESTIA-RECHERCHE, Technopole Izarbel, 64210 Bidart, France; LaBRI, 351, cours de la Libération, 33405 Talence, France, n.couture@estia.fr

Vincent Delfosse LUCID-ULg: Lab for User Cognition and Innovative Design – University of Liège – Belgium, Vincent.Delfosse@ulg.ac.be

Emmanuel Dubois University of Toulouse – Tarbes, IRIT, 118 route de Narbonne, 31062 Toulouse Cedex 9, France, Emmanuel.Dubois@irit.fr

Armin Duff SPECS@IUA: Laboratory for Synthetic Perceptive, Emotive, and Cognitive Systems, Universitat Pompeu Fabra, Tànger 135, 08018 Barcelona, Spain

Sophie Dupuy-Chessa Laboratory of Informatics of Grenoble, Grenoble Université, 385 rue de la bibliothèque, B.P. 53, 38041 Grenoble Cedex 9, France, Sophie.Dupuy-Chessa@imag.fr

Florian Echtler Technische Universität München, München, Germany

Martin Flintham Mixed Reality Lab, Computer Science, University of Nottingham, Jubilee Campus, Nottingham, NG8 1BB, UK, mdf@cs.nott.ac.uk

Areti Galani International Centre for Cultural and Heritage Studies, Newcastle University, Bruce Building, Newcastle upon Tyne, NE1 7RU, UK, areti.galani@ncl.ac.uk

Guillaume Gauffre University of Toulouse, IRIT, 118 route de Narbonne, 31062 Toulouse Cedex 9, France, Guillaume.Gauffre@irit.fr

Reinhard Gerndt University of Applied Sciences Braunschweig/Wolfenbuettel, Wolfenbuettel, Germany, r.gernd@fh-wolfenbuettel.de

Martin R. Gibbs Interaction Design Group, Department of Information Systems, The University of Melbourne, Parkville, VIC, Australia, martin.gibbs@unimelb.edu.au

Guillaume Godet-Bar Laboratory of Informatics of Grenoble, Grenoble Université, 385 rue de la bibliothèque, B.P. 53, 38041 Grenoble Cedex 9, France, Guillaume.Godet-Bar@imag.fr

T.C. Nicholas Graham School of Computing, Queen's University, Kingston, Canada K7L3N6, graham@cs.queensu.ca

Phil Gray University of Glasgow, DCS, Glasgow G12 8QQ, Scotland, UK, pdg@dcs.gla.ac.uk

Timber Haaker Novay, 7500 AN Enschede, The Netherlands, timber.haaker@telin.nl

Manuel Huber Technische Universität München, München, Germany, huberma@in.tum.de

Martin Inderbitzin SPECS@IUA: Laboratory for Synthetic Perceptive, Emotive, and Cognitive Systems, Universitat Pompeu Fabra, Tànger 135, 08018 Barcelona, Spain

Björn Johansson Department of Computer and Information Science, Linköping University, SaabSecurity, Santa Anna IT Research Institute AB, Linköping, Sweden, bjorn.j.e.johansson@saabgroup.com

Arne Jönsson Department of Computer and Information Science, Linköping University, SaabSecurity, Santa Anna IT Research Institute AB, Linköping, Sweden, arnjo@ida.liu.se

David Juras Laboratory of Informatics of Grenoble, Grenoble Université, 385 rue de la bibliothèque, B.P. 53, 38041 Grenoble Cedex 9, France, David.Juras@imag.fr

Peter Keitler Technische Universität München, München, Germany, keitler@in.tum.de

Eng Tat Khoo Mixed Reality Lab, 21 Lower Kent Ridge Rd, National University of Singapore, Singapore 119077, Singapore, khooet@mixedrealitylab.org

Mendel Kleiner Department of Applied Acoustics, Chalmers University of Technology, SE-412 96, Göteborg, Sweden, mendel.kleiner@chalmers.se

Gudrun Klinker Technische Universität München, München, Germany, klinker@in.tum.de

Pontus Larsson Department of Applied Acoustics, Chalmers University of Technology, SE-412 96, Göteborg, Sweden; Volvo Technology Corporation, SE-405 08 Göteborg, Sweden, pontus.larsson@chalmers.se

Pierre Leclercq LUCID-ULg: Lab for User Cognition and Innovative Design – University of Liège – Belgium, Pierre.Leclercq@ulg.ac.be

Sylvain Le Groux SPECS@IUA: Laboratory for Synthetic Perceptive, Emotive, and Cognitive Systems, Universitat Pompeu Fabra, Tànger 135, 08018 Barcelona, Spain

Jônatas Manzolli Interdisciplinary Nucleus for Sound Communications (NICS), State University of Campinas, Rua da Reitoria, 165 – Cidade Universitária "Zeferino Vaz" Campinas, São Paulo, Brasil

Zenon Mathews SPECS@IUA: Laboratory for Synthetic Perceptive, Emotive, and Cognitive Systems, Universitat Pompeu Fabra, Tànger 135, 08018 Barcelona, Spain

Tim Merritt Mixed Reality Lab, 21 Lower Kent Ridge Rd, National University of Singapore, Singapore 119077, Singapore, tim@mixedrealitylab.org

Jan M.V. Misker V2_ Institute for the Unstable Media, Eendrachtsstraat 10, 3012 XL, Rotterdam, The Netherlands, jan@v2.nl

Florian 'Floyd' Mueller Interaction Design Group, Department of Information Systems, The University of Melbourne, Parkville, VIC, Australia, floyd@floydmueller.com

Anna Mura SPECS@IUA: Laboratory for Synthetic Perceptive, Emotive, and Cognitive Systems, Universitat Pompeu Fabra, Tànger 135, 08018 Barcelona, Spain

Roderick Murray-Smith University of Glasgow, Glasgow, UK, rod@dcs.gla.ac.uk

Laurence Nigay Grenoble Informatics Laboratory, 385 avenue de la Bibliothèque, Domaine Universitaire, B.P. 53, 38 041 Grenoble cedex 9, France, Laurence.Nigay@imag.fr

Susanna Nilsson Department of Computer and Information Science, Linköping University, SaabSecurity, Santa Anna IT Research Institute AB, Linköping, Sweden, susni@ida.liu.se

J.-L. Pérez-Medina Laboratory of Informatics of Grenoble, Grenoble Université, 385 rue de la bibliothèque, B.P. 53, 38041 Grenoble Cedex 9, France, Jorge-Luis.Perez-Medina@imag.fr

W. Greg Phillips Department of Electrical and Computer Engineering, Royal Military College of Canada, Kingston, Canada K7K7B4, greg.phillips@rmc.ca

Wayne Piekarski Wearable Computer Laboratory, University of South Australia, Mawson Lakes, SA 5095, Australia, wayne@tinmith.net

Daniel Pustka Technische Universität München, München, Germany

Andrea Resmini University of Bologna, Via Carboni 2, 43100 Parma, Italy, root@resmini.net

Patrick Reuter LaBRI, 351, cours de la Libération, 33405 Talence, France; INRIA Bordeaux – Sud Ouest, 351, cours de la Libération, 33405 Talence France; Université Bordeaux 2, 146 rue Léo Saignat, 33076 Bordeaux, France, preuter@labri.fr

Dominique Rieu Laboratory of Informatics of Grenoble, Grenoble Université, 385 rue de la bibliothèque, B.P. 53, 38041 Grenoble Cedex 9, France, Dominique.Rieu@imag.fr

Guillaume Rivière ESTIA-RECHERCHE, Technopole Izarbel, 64210 Bidart, France; LaBRI, 351, cours de la Libération, 33405 Talence, France, g.riviere@estia.fr

Luca Rosati University for Foreigners of Perugia, via XX settembre 25, 06124 Perugia, Italy, luca@lucarosati.it

Stéphane Safin LUCID-ULg: Lab for User Cognition and Innovative Design – University of Liège – Liège, Belgium, Stephane.Safin@ulg.ac.be

Holger Schnädelbach Mixed Reality Lab, Computer Science, University of Nottingham, Jubilee Campus, Nottingham, NG8 1BB, UK, hms@cs.nott.ac.uk

Rodrigo da Silva Guerra Graduate School of Engineering, Osaka University, Osaka, Japan, rodrigo.guerra@ams.eng.osaka-u.ac.jp

J. David Smith School of Computing, Queen's University, Kingston, Canada K7L3N6, smith@cs.queensu.ca

Ross T. Smith Wearable Computer Laboratory, University of South Australia, Mawson Lakes, SA 5095, Australia, ross@r-smith.net

Vladimir Stantchev Public Services and SOA Research Group, Berlin Institute of Technology and Fachhochschule für Ökonomie und Management, Berlin, Germany, vstantch@cs.tu-berlin.de

Jelle van der Ster V2_ Institute for the Unstable Media, Eendrachtsstraat 10, 3012 XL, Rotterdam, The Netherlands, jelle@v2.nl

Ellen Szwajcer Novay, 7500 AN Enschede, The Netherlands, Ellen.Szwajcer@telin.nl

Ana Tajadura-Jiménez Department of Applied Acoustics, Chalmers University of Technology, SE-412 96, Göteborg, Sweden, ana.tajadura@gmail.com

Bruce H. Thomas Wearable Computer Laboratory, University of South Australia, Mawson Lakes, SA 5095, Australia, bruce.thomas@unisa.edu.au

Aleksander Väljamäe Department of Applied Acoustics, Chalmers University of Technology, SE-412 96 Göteborg, Sweden; Research Laboratory for Synthetic Perceptive, Emotive and Cognitive Systems (SPECS), Institute of Audiovisual Studies, Universitat Pompeu Fabra, Barcelona, Spain, aleksander.valjamae@iua.upf.edu

Daniel Västfjäll Department of Applied Acoustics, Chalmers University of Technology, SE-412 96, Göteborg, Sweden; Department of Psychology, Göteborg University, Göteborg, Sweden, daniel@ta.chalmers.se

Paul F.M.J. Verschure SPECS@IUA: Laboratory for Synthetic Perceptive, Emotive, and Cognitive Systems, Universitat Pompeu Fabra, Tànger 135, 08018 Barcelona, Spain; ICREA, Technology Department, Universitat Pompeu Fabra, Tànger 135, 08018 Barcelona, Spain, paul.verschure@iua.upf.edu

Frank Vetere Interaction Design Group, Department of Information Systems, The University of Melbourne, Parkville, VIC, Australia, fv@unimelb.edu.au

John Williamson University of Glasgow, Glasgow, UK, jhw@dcs.gla.ac.uk

Christopher Wolfe School of Computing, Queen's University, Kingston, Canada K7L3N6, wolfe@cs.queensu.ca

Chapter 1
Introduction

Emmanuel Dubois, Phil Gray, and Laurence Nigay

1.1 Mixed Reality Systems: A Booming Domain

Human–Computer Interaction (HCI) is no longer restricted to interaction between users and computers via keyboard and screen: Currently one of the most challenging aspects of interactive systems is the integration of the physical and digital aspects of interaction in a smooth and usable way. The design challenge of such mixed reality (MR) systems lies in the fluid and harmonious fusion of the physical and digital worlds. Examples of MR systems include tangible user interfaces, augmented reality, augmented virtuality and embodied interfaces. The diversity of terms highlights the ever growing interest in MR systems and the very dynamic and challenging domain they define.

1.1.1 Variety of Mixed Reality Systems

The growing interest of designers and developers for mixed reality systems is due to the dual need of users to both benefit from computers and stay in contact with the physical world. A first attempt to satisfy this requirement consists of augmenting the real world with computerized information: This is the rationale for augmented reality (AR). Another approach consists of making the interaction with the computer more realistic. Interaction with the computer is augmented by objects and actions in the physical world. Examples involve input modalities based on real objects, such as bricks also called tangible user interfaces and more generally augmented virtuality (AV).

E. Dubois (✉)
University of Toulouse, IRIT, 118 route de Narbonne, 31062 Toulouse Cedex 9, France
e-mail: emmanuel.dubois@irit.fr

E. Dubois et al. (eds.), *The Engineering of Mixed Reality Systems*, Human-Computer Interaction Series, DOI 10.1007/978-1-84882-733-2_1,

This anthology contains these two types of mixed reality systems. For example, Chapter 6 considers tangible interaction, while Chapter 11 focuses on augmented reality in the case of a mobile user.

1.1.2 Variety of Application Domains

There are many application domains of mixed reality, including game, art, architecture and heath care. The variety of application domains makes it difficult to arrive at a consensus definition of mixed reality systems, i.e. different people having distinct goals are using the term "Mixed Reality".

This anthology is an attempt to highlight this variety. The last part of the anthology is dedicated to applications of mixed reality.

1.2 Mixed Reality Engineering

In this very dynamic research and industrial context, the goal of this anthology is to go one step ahead to gain understanding of this challenging domain. The book covers topics on mixed reality engineering by addressing the design and development of such systems: it includes chapters on conceptual modelling, design and evaluation case studies, prototyping and development tools, and software technology.

The book brings together papers on a broad range of mixed reality engineering issues organized into three main sections:

- Interaction design
- Software design and implementation
- Applications of mixed reality.

1.2.1 Interaction Design

The first section dedicated to interaction design includes nine chapters.

1.2.1.1 Elements of Design

- *Chapter 2: An Integrating Framework for Mixed Systems.* This chapter presents a framework for comparing Mixed Reality Systems and exploring the design space. It proposes the concept of mixed object as a unified point of view on MRS. Based on intrinsic and extrinsic characteristics of mixed objects, this chapter illustrates the use of this framework on several mixed systems.
- *Chapter 3: A Holistic Approach to Design and Evaluation of Mixed Reality Systems.* This chapter focuses on the usefulness of a mixed reality system that is complementary to the usability of the system. As part of an iterative user-centred design approach, this chapter highlights the value of qualitative methods in natural setting for evaluating the usefulness of a mixed reality system. Two case studies of mixed reality systems and their qualitative experimental results are presented.
- *Chapter 4: Embedded Mixed Reality Environments.* This chapter describes, analyses and compares the context of the use of three different mixed reality environments in terms of interaction space, asymmetries between physical and digital worlds and social interaction triggered by these MRE before discussing potential impacts of these dimensions on the interaction with such MRE.
- *Chapter 5: The Semantic Environment: Heuristics for a Cross-Context Human–Information Interaction Model.* This chapter addresses the challenge of how to support activities that involve complex coordination between digital and physical domains, such as shopping experiences that combine both online and store-based aspects. The authors present an information-oriented model that offers a framework for the analysis of such mixed environments in terms of information and product design, and spatial layout.

1.2.1.2 Specific Design Issues

- *Chapter 6: Tangible Interaction in Mixed Reality Systems.* This chapter discusses the design of tangible interaction techniques, a particular form of mixed reality environments. An engineering-oriented software/hardware co-design process is introduced and illustrated with the development of three different tangible user interfaces for real-world applications. Feedback collected from user studies raised discussion about the use of such interaction techniques.
- *Chapter 7: Designing a Mixed Reality Intergenerational Entertainment System.* This chapter focuses on the particular design issue of mixed reality for intergenerational family members (grandparents, parents and grandchildren simultaneously using the mixed system). The focus is on intergenerational family entertainment and the chapter presents a user-centred design process for designing a collaborative Space Invaders mixed game.
- *Chapter 8: Auditory-Induced Presence in Mixed Reality Environments and Related Technology.* This chapter explores how audio-based techniques can be used to develop MR systems that enhance the sense of presence, one element of comparison between the multiplicity and the heterogeneity of MR systems.

- *Chapter 9: An Exploration of Exertion in Mixed Reality Systems via the "Table Tennis for Three" Game*. This chapter explores dimensions relevant for the design of MR systems that involve a user's body in the interaction. A case study is used through the chapter to illustrate the different dimensions of the design of such interaction.

1.2.1.3 Structuring the Design

- *Chapter 10: Developing Mixed Interactive Systems: A Model-Based Process for Generating and Managing Design Solutions*. Using a classic model-based transformational approach, the authors demonstrate via a worked example how the ASUR family of models can be used to support the progressive refinement of a mixed reality system design from conceptual model to software realization.

1.2.2 Software Design and Implementation

The second section addresses technical platforms and solutions for interaction techniques, development tools and a global view on the software development process. This section includes six chapters.

1.2.2.1 Technical Solutions and Interaction Techniques

- *Chapter 11: Designing Outdoor Mixed Reality Hardware Systems*. This chapter presents the design of an outdoor mixed reality system from the point of view of the involved hardware for localization, I/O interaction, computer systems and batteries, and finally raises a set of lessons learnt related to technical considerations, computing system management and I/O interactions.
- *Chapter 12: Multimodal Excitatory Interfaces with Automatic Content Classification*. This chapter presents a technical solution supporting the "active perception" concept: the goal is to encode information descriptor through the use of vibrotactile and sonic feedback in response to user's action on a device that contains the information.

1.2.2.2 Platform: Prototyping, Development and Authoring Tools

- *Chapter 13: Management of Tracking for Mixed and Augmented Reality Systems*. This chapter describes a platform, namely trackman built on top of the UbiTrack middleware, that allows us to model a constellation of sensors for quickly defining a tracking setup based on a spatial relationship graph and a data flow diagram. This is done in a graphical editor.
- *Chapter 14: Authoring Immersive Mixed Reality Experiences*. This chapter presents a platform for authoring immersive mixed reality experiences for artistic

use. The platform enables artists and designers to create the content for immersive mixed reality environments. An example of a production, an art game done by an artist along with a programmer, is presented.

- *Chapter 15: Fiia: A Model-Based Approach to Engineering Collaborative Augmented Reality.* This chapter presents and illustrates a platform supporting the implementation of a collaborative and distributed augmented reality system on the basis of a high-level notation that models the system and abstracts the distribution and software implementation considerations.

1.2.2.3 Life Cycle

- *Chapter 16: A Software Engineering Method for the Design of Mixed Reality Systems.* Like the approach described in Chapter 10, the software engineering process model presented here proposes that mixed reality systems are developed via the progressive refinement of a set of linked models. Here the Symphony development method has been augmented to accommodate mixed reality concerns, including the physical aspects of interaction and the richer representational options of mixed systems.

1.2.3 Application of Mixed Reality

The final section consists of a set of detailed case studies that highlight the application of mixed reality in a number of fields, including emergency management, games, and health care. The section includes five chapters.

- *Chapter 17: Enhancing Health-Care Services with Mixed Reality Systems.* This chapter presents the steps of a development approach for enhancing health-care services with mixed reality systems. The steps of the development approach are illustrated by considering the design and development of a location-aware system in the surgical sector of a hospital.
- *Chapter 18: The eXperience Induction Machine: A New Paradigm for Mixed-Reality Interaction Design and Psychological Experimentation.* The eXperience Induction Machine is a novel and rich mixed reality environment that offers a test bed for immersive applications. The authors describe the environment, present a justification for their system in terms of its role in exploring the psychological and social aspects of mixed reality interaction and give two examples of experiments performed using it.
- *Chapter 19: MyCoach: In Situ User Evaluation of a Virtual and Physical Coach for Running.* The work presented in this chapter is rather different than others in this anthology. MyCoach is a mobile system designed to work in concert with a human coach in delivering assistance to amateur runners in improving their performance. This study examines the potential of such an approach compared to the non-augmented approach using a conventional human coach alone.

- *Chapter 20: The RoboCup Mixed Reality League – A Case Study*. This chapter describes a mixed reality platform where robots are involved. It provides a way to tightly couple real and virtual worlds in a two-way interaction. The case study is a soccer game where micro-robots on a table are playing soccer.
- *Chapter 21: Mixed-Reality Prototypes to Support Early Creative Design*. This chapter discusses EsQUIsE, a mixed reality system that supports early stage architectural design. The system and its rationale are given, followed by the description of user-based evaluation and a discussion of the results of the evaluation in terms of the system's mixed reality features.

Part I
Interaction Design

Chapter 2
An Integrating Framework for Mixed Systems

Céline Coutrix and Laurence Nigay

Abstract Technological advances in hardware manufacturing led to an extended range of possibilities for designing physical–digital objects involved in a mixed system. Mixed systems can take various forms and include augmented reality, augmented virtuality, and tangible systems. In this very dynamic context, it is difficult to compare existing mixed systems and to systematically explore the design space. Addressing this design problem, this chapter presents a unified point of view on mixed systems by focusing on mixed objects involved in interaction, i.e., hybrid physical–digital objects straddling physical and digital worlds. Our integrating framework is made of two complementary facets of a mixed object: we define intrinsic as well as extrinsic characteristics of an object by considering its role in the interaction. Such characteristics of an object are useful for comparing existing mixed systems at a fine-grain level. The taxonomic power of these characteristics is discussed in the context of existing mixed systems from the literature. Their generative power is illustrated by considering a system, Roam, which we designed and developed.

Keywords Mixed systems · Mixed object · Interaction model · Characterization space · Taxonomy

2.1 Introduction

The growing interest for mixed interactive systems is due to the dual need of users to both benefit from computers and stay in contact with the physical world. Mixed systems can take various forms and include augmented reality, augmented

C. Coutrix (✉)
Grenoble Informatics Laboratory, 385 avenue de la Bibliothèque, Domaine Universitaire, B.P. 53, 38 041, Grenoble cedex 9, France
e-mail: Celine.Coutrix@imag.fr

E. Dubois et al. (eds.), *The Engineering of Mixed Reality Systems*, Human-Computer Interaction Series, DOI 10.1007/978-1-84882-733-2_2,

virtuality, and tangible systems. Although mixed systems are becoming more prevalent, we still do not have a clear understanding of this interaction paradigm. In particular, we lack capitalization of our experience, comprehension of problems when explaining the choice of a design to other designers. In addition, we are not able to explore the design space in a systematic way and as a result quite often find a better solution after the development is finished. Even though several conceptual results exist for understanding and designing such systems, they do not address the entire design and remain local and are not related to each other. As a consequence, it is difficult to compare existing mixed reality systems and explore new designs.

Rather than presenting yet another taxonomy that would not improve the clarity of this domain, we capitalize on existing research in our framework:

- We encapsulate related works in order to provide a coherent, integrating, and unifying framework.
- We identify overlaps between existing studies, so that we can contribute to a better comprehension of the domain.
- We refine existing taxonomies as well as identify new characteristics and uncover areas to be explored in the design space.

The basis of our integrating framework is that we take the viewpoint of the objects involved in interaction with mixed systems, namely mixed objects, i.e., hybrid physical–digital objects straddling physical and digital worlds. Our framework is therefore made of characteristics of mixed objects. The characteristics are useful for analysis and comparison of existing systems as well as for design: indeed the characteristics allow generation of ideas and choice of design alternatives. Since these characteristics are also used for design, we organized them according to two points of view of a mixed object that make sense for design: intrinsic and extrinsic characteristics. These two sets of characteristics enable designers to study the reusability of their design for different application contexts. Indeed intrinsic characteristics of a mixed object are not modified from one context to another, whereas extrinsic characteristics are modified.

In this chapter, we first recall our definition of a mixed object [8, 9] and then present the corresponding intrinsic characterization space of a mixed object while demonstrating its taxonomic power. We then focus on interaction with mixed objects [8]: we present the resulting extrinsic characterization space of a mixed object and study its taxonomic power. The taxonomic power of our intrinsic and extrinsic characteristic framework is studied in the light of several existing mixed systems that we present in the following section. Finally, in the last section, we show how our characteristic framework is useful for the design, in the context of a new mixed system that we designed and developed.

2.2 Illustrative Examples

For demonstrating the taxonomic power of our framework, we rely on existing mixed systems. We purposely chose mixed systems that seemed similar at first glance. Indeed, the selected mixed systems support interaction with objects on a horizontal surface. These systems are from the literature (i.e., not designed using our framework) and are therefore unbiased examples for evaluating the taxonomic power of our framework.

NavRNA [2] is a system for interacting with RNA molecules. As shown in Fig. 2.1 (left), biologists are gathered around a table equipped with a camera and a projector. The camera captures the positions of the blue tokens that the users hold and move in order to explore (i.e., move, turn, resize) the 2D view of RNA.

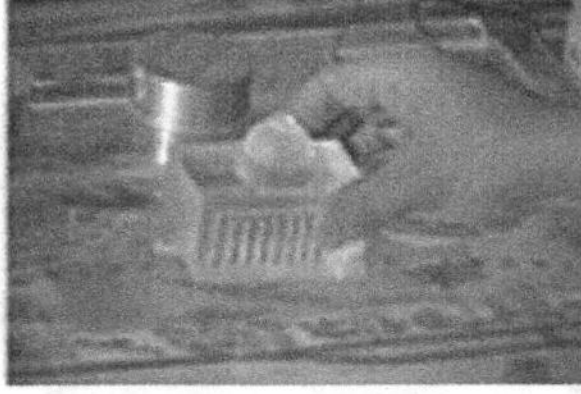

Fig. 2.1 NavRNA (*left*), the MIT Great Dome Phicon in the Tangible Geospace (*center*), the reacTable (*right*)

Phicon [22] stands for Physical Icons. In the Tangible Geospace [22] (Fig. 2.1, center), the Phicon is a tool shaped as the MIT Great Dome. Users hold and move it on the table, where a map of the campus is projected. In this way, the location of the Phicon on the table always corresponds to the location of the Dome on the map.

The reacTable [16] (Fig. 2.1, right) is used as a music synthesizer, where mixed cubes and tokens represent the synthesizer modules. Users can directly touch the surface with several fingers in order to interact. They can also hold and move, change the relative distance, orientation, and relation of the objects on the table in order to control the synthesizer. When studying reactTable, we consider only the interaction with the objects. The table is augmented by a camera, which tracks the nature, location, and orientation of the objects, and by a projector for displaying animation corresponding to the state of the objects onto the surface.

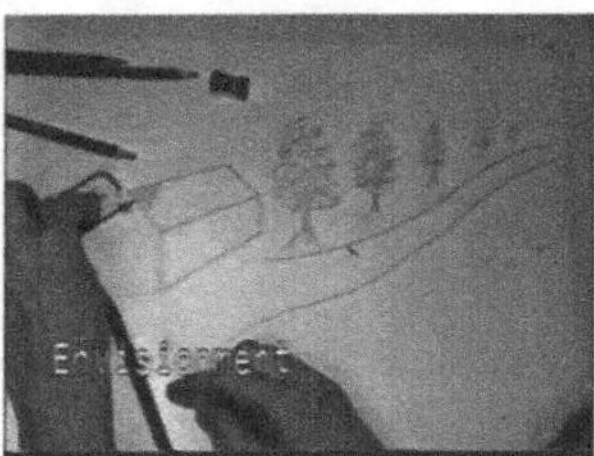

Fig. 2.2 The music bottles (*left*) filling a drawing (a roof with tiles) with the Digital Desk (*center*) and erasing a part of the drawing with the Digital Desk (*right*)

The music bottles (Fig. 2.2, left) are objects that are part of a music player system. Each bottle contains a musical part. When a music bottle [15] is put on the table and opened, the corresponding music part is played. In addition, rear-projected light corresponding to pitch and volume is displayed underneath the bottle on the table.

The Digital Desk [25] is one of the first mixed systems and was partially developed. We consider the seminal drawing scenario (Fig. 2.2, center and right). The user draws a house with a regular pen on a regular sheet of paper on a table equipped with a camera and a projector. In Fig. 2.2 (center), the user starts drawing tiles on the roof and then decides to use a "fill" paper button by pointing it toward the roof. She then presses the paper button, which is sensed by the camera. Then the roof is filled with tiles displayed by the projector. The resulting drawing is mixed with physical parts, made by a pen, and a projected digital part. In Fig. 2.2 (right), the user erases projected tiles with a regular eraser, thanks to the camera.

Fig. 2.3 Digital pointing using an interaction device and a hand held display

The actuated workbench [19] is a table that embeds magnets. On this table, the user or the system can manipulate pucks. The manipulation of a puck can be indirect by using a trackball (Fig. 2.3, left) or direct by holding the puck (Fig. 2.3, center).

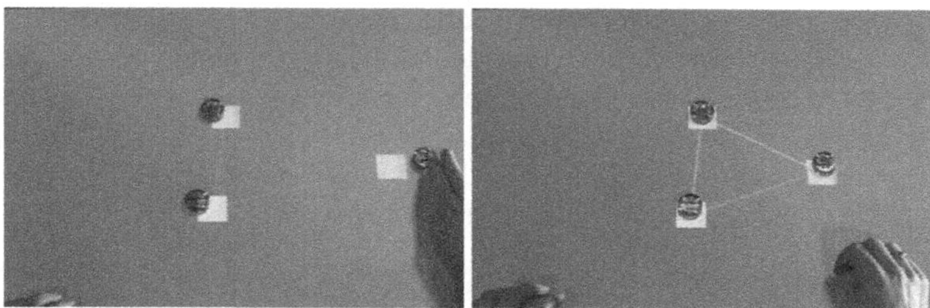

Fig. 2.4 The PICO system tries to have an equilateral triangle: as the user moves one puck, the system changes its position in order to form an equilateral triangle

PICO [20] stands for "physical intervention in computational optimization." The system [20] is similar to the actuated workbench, with a table embedding magnets and augmented by a camera and a projector above. The system computes the ideal positions of the pucks on the table and the magnets automatically move them toward these positions (Fig. 2.4). Furthermore the user can add physical constraints: For example, in Fig. 2.3 (right), the puck cannot access the entire surface of the table.

2.3 Integrating Framework for Describing and Classifying Mixed Systems

Focusing on mixed objects involving a mixed system, our integrating framework is made of intrinsic and extrinsic characteristics of a mixed object. We first present the modeling of a mixed object and the induced intrinsic characteristic framework. We then put the mixed objects into interaction context and we expose the modeling of interaction with mixed objects. From this modeling of mixed interaction, we finally describe the extrinsic characteristic framework.

2.3.1 *Modeling of a Mixed Object*

Mixed objects are hybrid objects with a physical part, like a physical object, in addition to a digital part like a digital object. For describing mixed objects, we consider its physical and digital parts as well as the link between them. On the one hand, the user interacts with the physical part, because users belong to the physical world. On the other hand, the system can interact with the digital part of the object. Physical–digital properties are properties like shape, color, weight, etc. for physical properties and a digital image, a boolean value, etc. for digital properties.

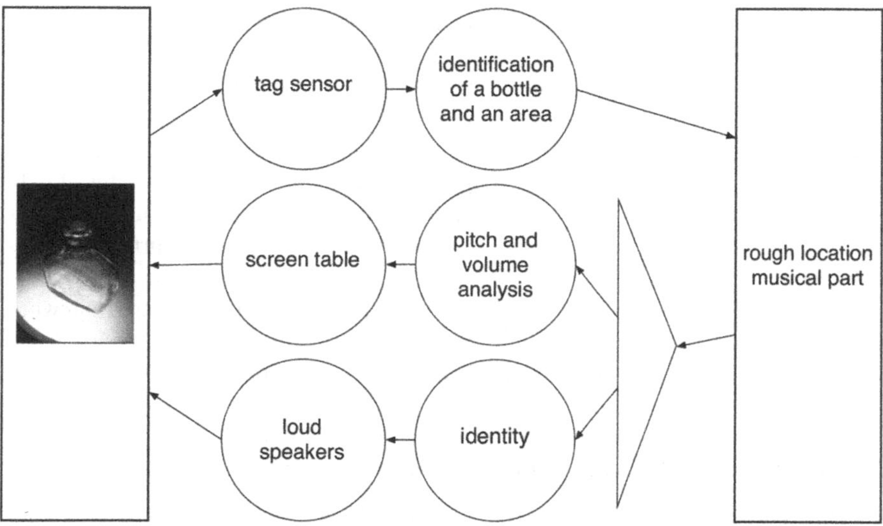

Fig. 2.5 Our description of the music bottle

We describe the link between these properties with linking modalities and draw the definition of a linking modality from that of an interaction modality [24]: given that *d* is a physical device that acquires or delivers information and *l* is an interaction language that defines a set of well-formed expressions that convey meaning, an interaction modality is a pair *(d,l)*, such as (*camera, computer vision*). The two levels of abstraction (*device, language*) constitute the basis of the definition of a linking modality. But in contrast to high-level interaction modalities used by the user to interact with mixed environments, the low-level modalities that define the link between physical and digital properties of an object are called linking modalities. Figure 2.5 shows the two types of linking modalities (i.e., input/output linking modalities) in the example of the music bottle. An input linking modality allows the system to compute the presence and placement of the bottle on the table. The musical part is made perceivable by the user, through two combined output linking modalities. For the composition of the linking modalities we reuse the CARE (complementarity, assignment, redundancy, and equivalence [24]) properties: in the music bottle example, the composition of the two different output linking modalities corresponds to a case of partial redundancy.

2.3.2 *Mixed Object: Intrinsic Characterization*

Based on the modeling of a mixed object, our intrinsic characteristic framework applies to a mixed object without considering its context of use in a particular interactive mixed system. We consider related studies and show how our characterization scheme unifies such approaches. Existing characteristics including affordance [18], expected and sensed actions [4], characteristics of devices [6, 17] and languages [5, 24], bounce-back physical properties [10], and some aspects of composition of physical properties [13, 11] fit in our modeling of a mixed object. More interestingly, this modeling leads us to identify new characteristics, such as generated physical properties, acquired and materialized digital properties, bounce-back digital properties, and some aspects of composition of physical properties. This clearly states our contribution: we provide a unifying framework that organizes various existing characteristics into a single unifying framework and we further identify new characteristics.

Based on our modeling of a mixed object, we present our integrating framework by starting with the characteristics of the linking modalities. We then consider the characteristics that apply to the physical and digital properties.

2.3.2.1 Characteristics of the Linking Modalities (Devices and Languages)

As our approach capitalizes on existing studies, we reuse the results from multimodal interaction studies for characterizing the two levels of abstraction of a linking modality. Taxonomies of devices [6, 17] are applied to characterize input and output linking devices. Frameworks described in [5, 24] can be applied for the linking languages also: a language can be static or dynamic, linguistic or not, analogue or not (similarity with the real world or not), arbitrary or not (need to be learned or not), deformed or not (like "how r u?" as opposed to "how are you?"), local or global (only a subset of the information or all the information are conveyed). Our framework also allows study of the relationship between devices and languages [12]. For example, is the precision of the device lost through the language? Finally, we also capitalize on research on multimodality to characterize composition of modalities with the CARE properties (complementarity, assignation, redundancy, equivalence) [24]. For example, we can immediately make the difference between the eraser in the Digital Desk (Fig. 2.2, right) and the music bottle (Fig. 2.2, left): the latter has a multimodal output link, whereas the first one does not.

Focusing on the relationships between input and output linking modalities of a mixed object, our model generalizes the temporal relationships identified in [14]. Indeed we refine the temporal coupling characterization from tightly/loosely coupled [14] to five possibilities: linking modalities can be asynchronous, in sequence, concomitant, coincident, or in parallel [24]. Moreover, spatial coupling of input and output linking modalities has been studied as Continuity in [11], Embodiment in [13], or as Physical and Virtual Layers in [14]. As for temporal relationships, we extend these existing frameworks by considering five spatial relationships [24]: the input and output space of a mixed object can be either separate, adjacent, intersecting, overlaid, or collocated.

2.3.2.2 Characteristics of the Physical Properties

We use four intrinsic characteristics for physical properties, namely affordance of, bounce-back, sensed/generated, and aspects of composition of physical properties.

Affordance and Expected Changes

Affordance [18] is defined as the aspect of an object that suggests how the object should be used. A flat object can be translated on a table. Expected/nonexpected actions [4] are also those we expect the user to do with an interface. Considering the physical properties, these characteristics allow us to identify a simple difference between the examples of Section 2.2: if we consider the symmetry of rotation of the objects, we have on the one hand objects like the tokens in NavRNA, the pucks in the actuated workbench and PICO that are invariant when rotated. On the other hand, we find the Dome Phicon, the cubes of the reacTable, the music bottles, and the objects used in the Digital Desk that are not symmetrical. Based on this absence of symmetry, we expect the user to rotate the objects of the second category more often.

Bounce-Back Physical Properties

A bounce-back button, introduced in [10], is a button that rebounds, like a spring or a rubber band, and goes back to its initial position. Some objects have this physical property, like a simple light switch. Within our model, a physical property can be bounce-back, like the physical location in PICO: even if the user puts it in a particular position, it tries to go back to its ideal position.

Sensed/Generated Physical Properties

Sensed actions [4] are those that can be captured by the system. Sensed actions and sensed physical properties are related: a sensor does not sense an action but some physical properties from which the system can identify actions. In our framework, sensed physical properties are properties that are captured by any input linking modality. We draw on our capitalization of sensed actions into our description of mixed objects in order to characterize generated physical properties also (those that are made physical by any output linking modality). We characterize physical properties with two orthogonal sensed/generated axes as schematized in Fig. 2.6. The sensed/generated characteristics of physical properties correspond to the "Input&Output" axis described in [14] ["what properties can be sensed and displayed back to the user (or system)?"].

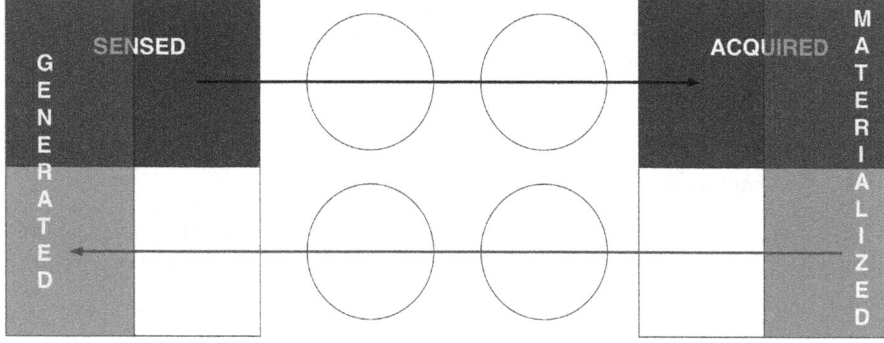

Fig. 2.6 Characterization of the sensed/generated physical and acquired/materialized digital properties of a mixed object

If we consider the physical location of the mixed objects presented in Section 2.2, we obtain the classification presented in Table 2.1. All these objects share this physical property: they all have a physical location. For almost all these objects, their location is sensed, but it is also generated for two types of objects: those in PICO and actuated workbench. Studying the location of the objects in light of our framework leads us to three main classes of mixed systems.

Table 2.1 Studying the physical location of mixed objects in light of our framework

Physical location	Generated	Nongenerated
Sensed	PICO Actuated workbench (in computer vision mode)	NAVRNA Tangible Geospace reacTable Music bottle Digital desk
Nonsensed	Actuated workbench (in mouse mode)	

Table 2.2 Studying the color of mixed objects in light of our framework

Color	Generated	Nongenerated
Sensed		NAVRNA reacTable
Nonsensed	Music bottle PICO Actuated workbench (in computer vision mode)	Tangible Geospace Actuated workbench (in mouse mode)

Toward a more detailed classification, we consider another physical property: the color. In examples like NavRNA or reacTable, the color is sensed by the camera and is used by the language of the input linking modality to compute the location of the object. In the case of the reacTable, the modality tracks markers, so their color cannot be changed at all or can be changed in a very limited way. Similarly for NavRNA, the color cannot be changed. In examples like the Music bottles, PICO, and actuated workbench, the color is not sensed: the system senses the infrared light emitted by the objects for the later, and an electromagnetic resonator tag is used for the music bottles. Contrastingly, color is generated for these three systems. Finally, in the case of the Tangible Geospace, the color is neither generated nor sensed – infrared is used instead. Note that we do not consider the Digital Desk example for this physical property since this part of the system was not developed. By considering the color property, we then obtained three classes of systems as shown in Table 2.2.

Aspects of the Composition of Physical Properties

Based on the spatial and temporal composition of linking modalities, we can characterize the coupling between sensed and generated physical properties at the physical level. More interestingly, we can also consider the spatial and temporal compositions of those sensed/generated physical properties with the nonsensed/nongenerated physical properties. This relation has five possibilities: properties can be asynchronous, in sequence, concomitant, coincident, or in parallel (temporal aspects) or either separate, adjacent, intersecting, overlaid, or collocated (spatial aspects) [24]. For example, the generated display of the reacTable cube is adjacent to the nongenerated part of the object (Fig. 2.1, right), whereas in the actuated workbench in computer vision mode (Fig. 2.3, center), the generated display is collocated with the nongenerated part of the object.

2.3.2.3 Characteristics of the Digital Properties

We use two intrinsic characteristics for digital properties, namely acquired/ materialized and bounce-back digital properties.

Acquired/Materialized Digital Properties

By considering the digital properties symmetrically to the sensed/generated physical properties, we can characterize digital properties with two orthogonal acquired/materialized axes as schematized in Fig. 2.6. A digital property can be acquired and/or materialized by any input/output linking modality. This set of characteristics is independent of the types of linking modalities.

We consider the example of the digital property corresponding to the location. For most of our examples, this property is a pair of coordinates (x, y). The music bottle is the only object that does not need such a precise location. The system needs to know only the area (one of the three defined parts of the table). If we consider the actuated workbench in mouse mode (Fig. 2.3, left) in Table 2.3, in this case the digital location is not acquired; it is updated indirectly through a tool, and therefore the object has no input linking modality acquiring this digital location. The other examples in Table 2.3 show that the digital location of the mixed object is acquired. Yet, for example, like the actuated workbench in computer vision mode, the reacTable, and PICO, the digital location is materialized through a projection on the table. In contrast to the others, the system does not provide observability of the state of the object: the acquired digital location is not materialized. Through this example, we are then able to more finely classify the examples of Section 2.2: for example, the difference between the NavRNA and the reacTable tokens is based on the affordance of the physical properties and whether the digital location is materialized or not.

Table 2.3 Studying the digital location in light of our framework

Digital location	Materialized	Nonmaterialized
Acquired	Actuated workbench (in computer vision mode) reacTable PICO	NAVRNA Tangible Geospace Music bottle Digital desk
Nonacquired	Actuated workbench (in mouse mode)	

Bounce-Back Digital Properties

We generalize the bounce-back characteristic to the case of digital properties. Digital properties can also behave like a spring and when modified go back to their initial value after a specified time. For example, we previously explained that the physical location of the mixed objects in PICO was a bounce-back physical property. This can be explained by the fact that the physical position of the pucks is generated from the digital location. The digital location corresponds to the stability value and is therefore a bounce-back digital property. This implies that the corresponding generated physical property is also characterized as a bounce-back physical property.

As a conclusion, Table 2.4 summaries the intrinsic characteristics of a mixed object. By characterizing a mixed object, we have shown that our framework generalizes and refines several existing frameworks and identifies overlaps between them. We therefore showed that our description of a mixed object provides a unifying framework for capitalizing existing studies. We also showed that it enables us to identify new characteristics. We demonstrated that these new characteristics of a mixed object are useful elements to finely classify existing systems.

Table 2.4 Summary of intrinsic characteristics (our new characteristics are underlined)

Level	Characteristic	Possible values
Physical properties	Affordance, expectations	
	Sensed	Yes/No
	<u>Generated</u>	Yes/No
	Bounce-back	Yes/No
	<u>Compositions</u>	Five schemas for the spatial aspects as well as for the temporal aspects
Link	Multimodality	– Direction: in/out – Number: integer – CARE characterization
	Precision of device	
	...	
	Dynamicity of language	Yes/No
	...	
Digital Properties	<u>Acquired</u>	Yes/No
	<u>Materialized</u>	Yes/No
	<u>Bounce-back</u>	Yes/No

2.3.3 Modeling Mixed Interaction: Putting Mixed Objects into Interaction Context

A mixed interaction involves a mixed object. An object is either a tool used by the user to perform her/his task or the object that is the focus of the task. To model mixed interaction, we enrich the instrumental interaction model [3] with the notion of *interaction* modality (d, l) [24]. We study the two types of mixed objects, namely *mixed tool* and *mixed task object*, involved in the interaction in light of a definition of an interaction modality [24] as the coupling of a physical device d with an interaction language l:

- *A mixed tool* is a device of a given modality. In Fig. 2.7 (in gray) the mixed tool is a device d coupled with an *interaction* language l that will translate the action into an elementary task.
- *A mixed task object* is manipulated by the user by means of an interaction modality.

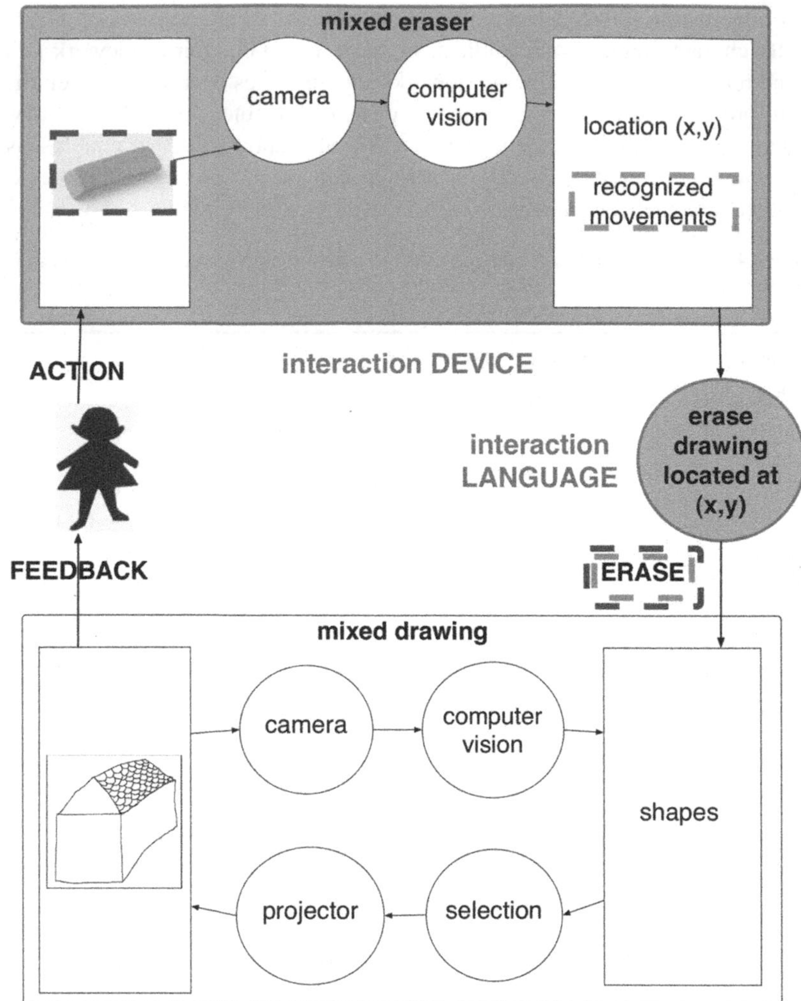

Fig. 2.7 Interaction between the user, the mixed tool in *gray* (*eraser*) and the mixed task object (*drawing*) in the Digital Desk, the and assessment of the noun (*dotted dark gray*) and verb (*dotted light gray*) metaphors

For example, in Fig. 2.7, we consider the example of the Digital Desk of Fig. 2.2 (left). The user is handling and moving the eraser – the mixed tool. This action on the physical properties of the object is sensed by the input linking modality (*camera, computer vision*) in order to update the digital properties <location> and <recognized movements>. The changes in the digital properties of the mixed tool are interpreted by the interaction language into an elementary task: (x, y) location is translated into "erase drawing located at (x, y) on the table." This elementary task is applied to the task object and the digital properties of the mixed drawing are consequently modified. The mixed drawing shows its internal digital changes by updating its display through its output linking modality – the feedback.

2.3.4 Mixed Object: Extrinsic Characterization

Extrinsic characterization concerns the aspects of a mixed object specific to its use in a particular application. We first consider the object as a whole in the interaction and show how we can characterize its role. We then focus on the part of a mixed object that serves as an interface to its outside environment: the physical and digital properties. As for the intrinsic characterization framework, we show how related studies fit in our description of a mixed interaction. We capitalize on existing characteristics (roles [12, 3], metaphors [13], physical constraints [21, 23], desired actions for an application [4]) in our characterization framework. Moreover, our description leads us to identify new characteristics, such as a new dimension for metaphors, output physical ports, and input digital ports.

2.3.4.1 Characteristics of the Roles

As identified in the ASUR (Adapter, System, User, Real object) design notation for mixed systems [12] and in the instrumental interaction model [3], an object can play two roles in interaction: it is either a tool used by the user to perform her/his task or the object that is the focus of the task (i.e., task object). In our examples of Section 2.2, this enables us to distinguish two categories of objects. On the one hand, the tokens in NavRNA and the Dome Phicon are tools. On the other hand, the music bottle is the object of the task.

2.3.4.2 Characteristics of the Physical Properties

We use three extrinsic characteristics for physical properties, namely noun metaphor of, ports of, and aspects of composition of the physical properties of mixed objects.

Noun Metaphor

In [13], the noun metaphor is defined as "an <X> in the system is like an <X> in the real world." To assess the noun metaphor based on the modeling of mixed interaction, we study how the physical properties reflect the task performed with the mixed object. For example in Fig. 2.7 (dotted dark gray), the physical properties of the eraser reflect the task: erasing. The Dome Phicon belongs to the same category, as opposed to the tokens of NavRNA, the cubes of the reacTable, and the pucks of PICO.

Instead of considering only the metaphor with the "real" natural world, we consider a continuum from this real-world metaphor to digital practice-based metaphors, putting thus on equal footing physical and digital worlds. For example, in the Digital Desk [25], the user interacts with a mixed tool made of paper that looks like a digital button in GUI.

Moreover, we also consider the command and its parameters as two different metaphors. For example, for the case of the Dome Phicon, the physical properties reflect the parameter of the task "*move* the location of the *dome* of the map to (x,y)." In contrast, the digital properties of the eraser reflect the command itself.

Ports

Physical input ports are related to the affordance of the object. Affordance [18] is defined by the physical properties that the user can act on. Some of these actions might be impossible because of external constraints, as defined in [21, 23, 20]: the corresponding physical ports are closed (i.e., not fully open). As explained in [20],

- On the one hand, some physical input ports can be closed in order to guarantee data that can be processed by the input linking modality. This can be done to overcome some technological limitations. For example, in most of our examples, the position of an object on a table is constrained so that it does not get out of range of the camera.
- On the other hand, the user can close some physical input ports explicitly in the interaction process, as in [20], when the user puts an object filled with sand on a mixed puck in order to prevent it from moving.

We extend this characterization of physical ports by also considering the output physical ports. Output ports define properties exported by a mixed object. For example, if we consider the generated physical property corresponding to the display projected onto the table of the systems of Section 2.2, the output ports can be partially closed according to the kinds of projection (from the top, from behind). Indeed with a projection from the top, as in the Digital Desk, the actuated workbench, and PICO, the users' hands or head may hide some parts of the projection. In contrast, with a rear projection, as for the reacTable and the music bottle, the output ports are always open.

Aspects of the Composition of Mixed Objects

As part of the intrinsic characterization framework of a mixed object, we described the spatial and temporal coupling of a mixed object by focusing on the relationships between its physical properties. Symmetrically, at the extrinsic level, we also study the spatial and temporal relationships between properties of different mixed objects. For example, we can study the spatial relationships between the physical properties of the mixed drawing and the mixed eraser in the Digital Desk and compare it with the relationships between the physical properties of the NavRNA tokens and the projected RNA molecule, or with the relationships between the Dome Phicon and the map. All pairs of objects are adjacent, in contrast to the reacTable cubes: indeed the cubes and the synthesized sound are spatially overlaid – where we can perceive the cubes, we can perceive the sound, but the reverse is not always true.

2.3.4.3 Characteristics of the Digital Properties

We use two extrinsic characteristics for digital properties, namely verb metaphor of and ports of the digital properties of a mixed object.

Verb Metaphor

In [13], the verb metaphor is represented by the phrase "<X>-ing the object in the system is like <X>-ing in the real world." To assess the verb metaphor, we study if the acquired digital properties reflect the task performed with the mixed object. For example, in Fig. 2.7 (dotted light gray), the acquired digital property <recognized movements> of the mixed eraser reflects the task. Note that in this particular example, there is both a noun and a verb metaphor, but we can consider them independently. For example, the eraser in the Digital Desk could be used without the verb metaphor by putting the eraser on the drawing in order to erase the designated area, without moving it like an eraser. The mixed cork of a music bottle belongs to the same category.

Ports

Output digital ports define digital properties exported by a mixed object toward an interaction language. For example, in Fig. 2.7, the mixed eraser exports the location of the eraser (x, y), that is then transformed by the interaction language to obtain the final task. The output digital port corresponds to the notion of "desired actions" in [4].

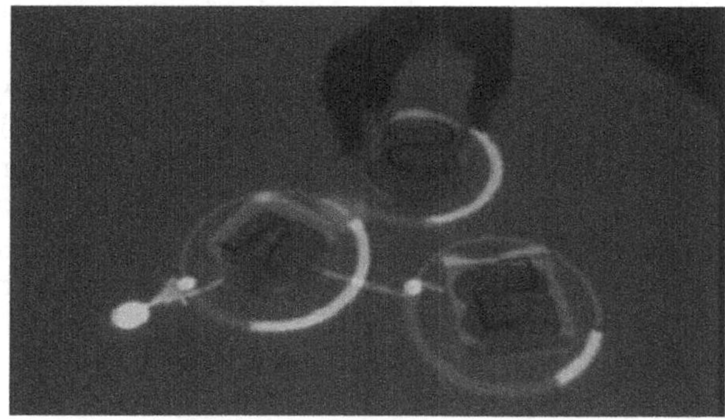

Fig. 2.8 A token of the reacTable with a digital property controlled by another circular tool

We further identify input digital ports. Indeed the application context can modify and/or prevent possible values of a digital property through the interaction language. The input digital port is then open or closed. For example, the blue tokens in NavRNA and the Dome Phicon in Tangible Geospace have no input digital port, whereas the cubes in the reacTable do; the system can modify digital properties of some cubes by adding an extra circular tool on the table that controls one of its digital properties. Figure 2.8 shows this case with a sinusoidal low-frequency oscillator controlling a band-pass sound filter.

As a conclusion, by extrinsically characterizing a mixed object based on our modeling of mixed interaction, we have shown that our framework encompasses and extends existing frameworks. Table 2.5 summaries our extrinsic characteristic framework.

Table 2.5 Summary of extrinsic characteristics (our new characteristics are underlined)

Level	Characteristic	Possible values
Mixed object	Role	Tool/task object
Physical properties	Noun metaphor	Absence/<u>related to a command/related to a parameter</u> and <u>related to natural to digital world</u>
	Input ports	Open/closed
	<u>Output ports</u>	Open/closed
	<u>Compositions</u>	Five schemas for the spatial aspects as well as for the temporal aspects
Digital properties	<u>Input ports</u>	Open/closed
	Output ports	Open/closed
	Verb metaphor	Absence/related to command and <u>related to natural to digital world</u>

Our integrating framework is made of both intrinsic and extrinsic characteristics of a mixed object. Tables 2.4 and 2.5 list the identified intrinsic and extrinsic characteristics, respectively. Based on this integrating framework, we are able to classify the existing mixed systems. To conclude on the taxonomic power of our framework, Table 2.6 shows how the examples of Section 2.2 differ from each other based on the identified intrinsic and extrinsic characteristics. In this table, we see that the framework allow us to find at least one characteristic to make a difference between systems. Finally, each system belongs to a single category, even if they were chosen similar at the beginning.

2.4 Integrating Framework for Designing Mixed Systems: The Case of Roam

Having presented our framework and studied its taxonomic power, we now focus on the design and illustrate the generative power of our framework. We purposely choose for our design example an application that is of a radically different type than the considered existing mixed systems of the previous section. The considered mixed system that we designed and developed is Roam, a mobile recording system.

We designed and developed Roam as part of a multidisciplinary project involving a designer and computer scientists. Roam is a mobile mixed system for recording

Table 2.6 Classification of the existing systems of Section 2.2

	NavRNA	Phicon	PICO	Bottle	Drawing	Eraser	reacTable	Puck (vision)	Puck (trackball)
Puck (trackball)	(3)	(3)	(2)	(1)	(1)	(1)	(1)	(1)	
Puck (vision)	(3)	(1)	(1)	(10)	(1)	(1)	(6)		
reacTable	(9)	(9)	(10)	(2)	(3)	(3)			
Eraser	(5)	(8)	(1)	(4)	(7)				
Drawing	(7)	(7)	(1)	(4)					
Bottle	(2)	(2)	(10)						
PICO	(3)	(1)							
Phicon	(2)								
NavRNA									

In this table, for clarity purposes, we show only one difference based on a given characteristic between each system, while several characteristics can be applied to distinguish them. Our new characteristics are underlined. Differences are made by characterizing (1) sensed/generated physical location, (2) sensed/generated color, (3) materialized/nonmaterialized digital location, (4) simple/multimodal output link, (5) affordance, (6) adjacent/collocated generated and nongenerated parts, (7) tool/task object role, (8) command/parameter noun metaphor, (9) digital input port, and (10) physical output port (display can be hidden or not).

(pictures, sounds). Even if users already use camera for recording images as keepsakes, the intention during the design of Roam is to have a tool that does not distract user's attention from the world. With commonly used recording tools, like camera, people focus on the tool in order to record a souvenir. In contrast, Roam is intended to stay in the background of the focus of attention and not to distract the user from the facts of interests.

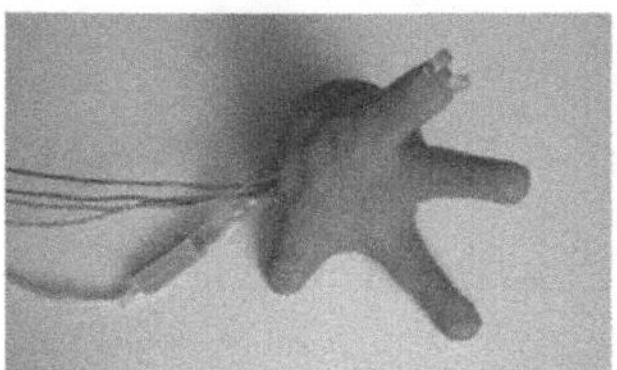
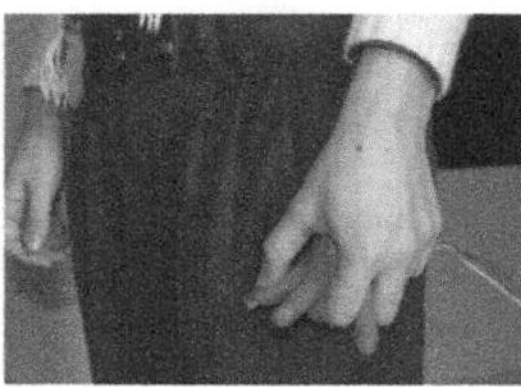
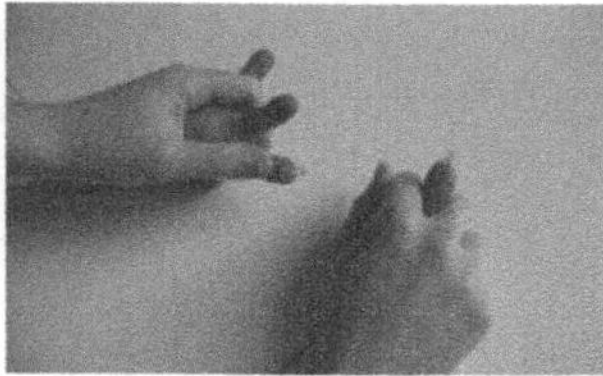

Fig. 2.9 Roam tool prototypes: close-up of final prototype with bend sensors and green/yellow LEDs (*left*) in the hand of the user (*center*). Another prototype of the Roam tool with separated physical properties (*right*)

Figure 2.9 (left and center) shows the pictures of our prototype of the Roam tool for recording sound souvenirs. It fits in the hand of the user in an unobtrusive way. She can bend a part in order to start recording and release to stop recording. A yellow LED enables her to know if she bent or released enough to start or stop recording. A green LED allows her to know if the tool is actually recording. Playback of the record is not planned in Roam but can be done using a computer (i.e., after using Roam).

We focus on the design of Roam and show how our framework helps in exploring the design space by considering examples during the design process. Since we know the application context of the tool, we first focus on extrinsic design exploration of the Roam tool. We then present examples of intrinsic design exploration.

2.4.1 Extrinsic Design

This tool is to be used in a mobile context. We therefore need to avoid obtrusiveness. Apart from its role, some extrinsic characteristics are yet to be explored. We selected examples from the characteristics of our framework: the noun metaphor and the digital/physical ports.

We first present the example of exploring the different types of noun metaphors. A noun metaphor can be related to a command such as the eraser of the Digital Desk or to a parameter of the command such as the Dome Phicon of the Tangible Geospace. We also identify a continuum from the real-world metaphor to digital practice-based metaphors. For the Roam tool, this helped us to generate six ideas, presented in Table 2.7. We chose the octopus because it fitted better in the hand of the user.

Table 2.7 Exploring the design of the Roam tool thanks to the noun metaphor dimensions: the task is "record the sound" in contrast to "record the image"

	"Natural" practice	↔	Digital practice
Command (record)	Octopus (record as taking/eating: the octopus eats through the beak and takes things from the environment with tentacles)	Crank handle as with old cameras (record as unwinding of a film)	Red dot (record icon usually used in systems)
Parameter (sound)	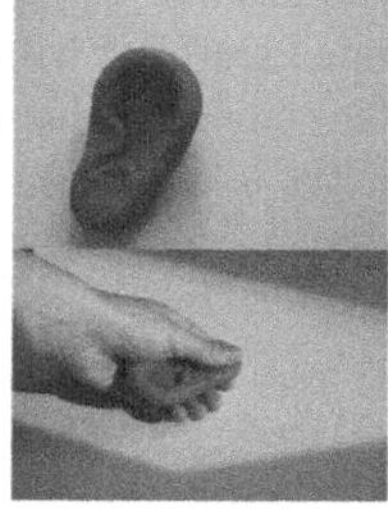 Ear	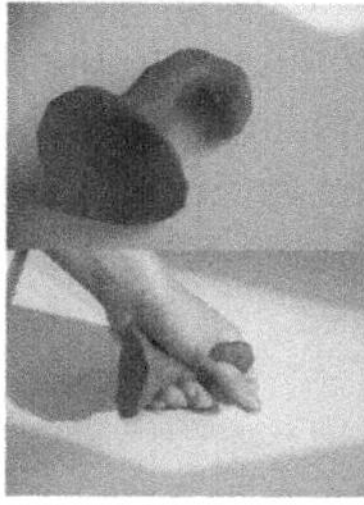 Horn of the early phonographs	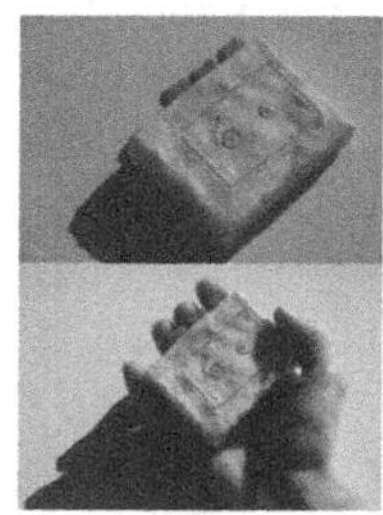 Tape recorder

We now consider the input digital ports. Exploring the design space along our characterization framework, we identified the need for an output digital port – isOn. Apart from this required output port, our design space drove our attention to the possibility of having a digital input port in our tool. It inspired us to come up with the idea of a response from the task object (the record) toward this tool: the tool contains a digital property that conveys the success of the record action. If this input digital property is then materialized, this enforces the observability principle as we argued in [8]. We chose to have an input digital port, named isOk.

We now consider the examples of exploring the physical properties of the tool and its output physical ports. The framework enabled us to explore physical properties that can be output ports. We explored alternatives and found sound and light: beeping (Fig. 2.10, left) and blinking (Fig. 2.10, center and right).

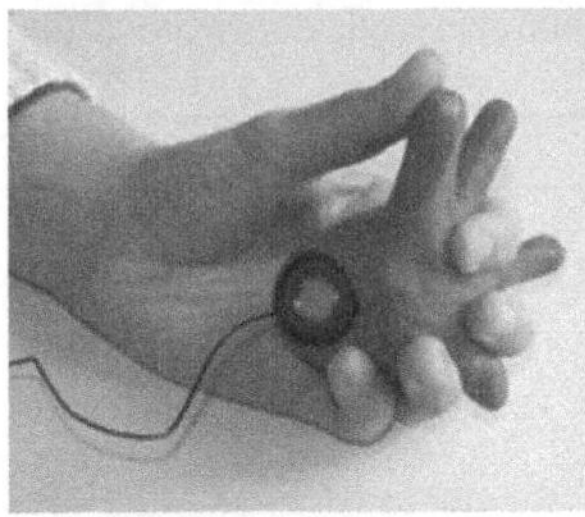

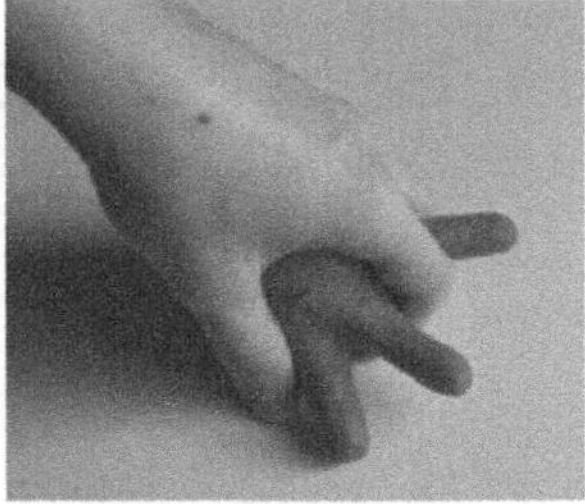

Fig. 2.10 Design alternatives for output ports: sound (*left*), light (LEDs in *center* and *right*). Focusing on the output ports: according to the way the tool is handled by the user, the lights may be hidden or not

For our mobile tool, this also highlights which and how physical properties are going to be perceivable in the context of use. For example, the sound of the loudspeakers can be too intrusive according to the environment: the others can hear it. Moreover, depending on how the tool is handled by the user, the physical properties generated by the LEDs can be hidden (Fig. 2.10, right). Thus we studied the placement of the LED as shown in Figs. 2.9 (left and center) and 2.10 (center).

Exploring the design space, thanks to the dimensions identified with our framework, gave rise to the design of alternatives that were not envisioned at first sight. It thus assisted us in exploring the extrinsic design space. We now present the intrinsic design of this tool.

2.4.2 Intrinsic Design

We first consider the example of the bounce-back characteristic for digital properties. We already identified, thanks to extrinsic design, two digital properties: an output port isOn and an input port isOk. From the intrinsic viewpoint on design, we can study if the two properties are bounce-back or not. Given that the output linking language turns the yellow LED on as long as isOn is true, if isOn is bounce-back, then the yellow LED blinks only once. If isOn is not bounce-back, then the yellow LED is on as long as isOn is true. In our design, we chose isOn not to be bounce-back. On the contrary, we chose isOk to be bounce-back; according to the output linking language, if the user wants to be sure the system is recording, she has to have a quick look at the green LED when she bends the tentacle.

We can also consider the composition of the physical properties. Thanks to our framework, we can envision multiple spatial compositions of the physical properties of the tool. They can be collocated and adjacent (Fig. 2.9, left and center) or separated, manipulated by the two hands (Fig. 2.9, right).

In this section we showed how the new characteristics we identified, thanks to our framework, were useful for the design of a tool. The characteristics allow generation of ideas by suggesting different types of alternatives. We chose to illustrate only the new characteristics identified with the framework, but the complete framework was used to design Roam. We studied the reusability of our intrinsic design for a different application context. Indeed the Roam tool can be used for interaction with Google Earth, which is a completely different application. However, in this context, intrinsic characteristics of the tool are not modified. For example, the digital property isOn is still not bounce-back. On the contrary, some extrinsic characteristics are modified: Google Earth does not enable the property isOk to be an input digital port. These ideas show the benefits of using the framework for design.

2.5 Conclusion

This chapter has introduced a new way of thinking of interaction design of mixed systems in terms of mixed objects. We presented intrinsic and extrinsic characteristics of a mixed object, the object being a tool or a task object. By showing how this characteristic framework enables us to classify existing similar systems, we demonstrated the taxonomic power of our framework. We also illustrate the generative power of our framework by considering the design of a mixed system, Roam. In addition to Roam, the framework has also been used to design other mixed systems such as ORBIS [9], RAZZLE [8], and Snap2Play [7]. Moreover, we are currently conducting an evaluation of our framework by considering the design of objects for exhibits in museums.

Several characteristics of our framework come from related work. Our contribution lies in the capitalization of these results into a single unifying/integrating framework and in the identification of new characteristics. However, a more thorough analysis of mixed systems could lead to extensions of the framework with new intrinsic or extrinsic characteristics of mixed objects and to a better assessment of its limitations.

As ongoing work, we are focusing on the design of mixed objects based on our framework. Design relies on both "thinking it through" and "working it through." We are working on putting the conceptual framework in operation for designing by prototyping. A toolkit for building mixed objects explicitly based on the underlying concepts of the framework is under development. The toolkit covers existing development frameworks and toolkits and provides modularity and extensibility. This toolkit will enable us to quickly develop prototypes that look like and work like the intended designed mixed object, as illustrated with the Roam system.

Acknowledgments We would like to thank the authors of the example systems for using their illustrations, Jérôme Drouin, designer, for his participation in the Roam project, and George Serghiou for reviewing the paper. The work presented in the article is partly funded by the "Plan Pluri-Formation" on Multimodal Interaction (financed by four Universities in Grenoble), by the French Research Agency under contract CARE (CulturalExperience: Augmented Reality and Emotion) – www.careproject.fr – and by the European Commission under contract OpenInterface (FP6-35182), www.oi-project.org.

References

1. Abowd, G., Coutaz, J., Nigay, L., 1992. Structuring the Space of Interactive System Properties. In Proceedings of EHCI'92, 113–130.
2. Bailly, G., Nigay, L., Auber, D., 2006. NAVRNA: Visualization – Exploration – Edition of RNA. In Proceedings of AVI'06, ACM Press, New York, NY, 504–507.
3. Beaudoin-Lafon, M., 2004. Designing Interaction, not Interfaces. In Proceedings of AVI'04, ACM Press, New York, NY, 15–22.
4. Benford, S. et al., 2005. Expected, Sensed, and Desired: A Framework for Designing Sensing-Based Interaction. ACM Transactions on Computer–Human Interaction, 12, 1 (March 2005), 3–30.
5. Bernsen, N., 1993. Taxonomy of HCI Systems: State of the Art. ESPRIT BR GRACE, Deliverable 2.1.
6. Buxton, W., 1983. Lexical and Pragmatic Considerations of Input Structures, Computer Graphics, 17, 1 (January 1983), 31–37.
7. Chin, T., Chevallet, J.-P., Coutrix, C., Lim, J., Nigay, L., You, Y., 2008. Snap2Play:A Mixed-Reality Game based on Scene Identification. In Proceedings of MMM'08, Springer-Verlag, LNCS (Lecture Notes in Computer Science), Volume 4903/2008, pp. 220–229.
8. Coutrix, C., Nigay, L., 2006. Mixed Reality: A Model of Mixed Interaction. In Proceedings of AVI'06, ACM Press, New York, NY, 43–50.
9. Coutrix, C., Nigay, L., 2008. Balancing Physical and Digital Properties in Mixed Objects. In Proceedings of AVI'08, ACM Press, New York, NY, pp. 305–308.
10. Dix, A., et al., 2007. Modeling Devices for Natural Interaction. In Electronic Notes in Theoretical Computer Science. FMIS 2007.
11. Dubois, E., Nigay, L., Troccaz, J., 2001. Consistency in Augmented Reality Systems. In Proceedings of EHCI'01, LNCS, Springer, 117–130.
12. Dubois, E. Gray, A Design-Oriented Information-Flow Refinement of the ASUR Interaction Model, EIS'07.
13. Fishkin, K., 2004. A Taxonomy for and Analysis of Tangible Interfaces. Personal Ubiquitous Computing, 8, 5 (September 2004), 347–358.
14. Fitzmaurice, G., Ishii, H., Buxton, W., 1995. Bricks: Laying the foundations for Graspable User Interfaces. In Proceedings of CHI'95, ACM Press, New York, NY, 442–449.
15. Ishii, H., Mazalek, A., Lee, J., 2001. Bottles as a Minimal Interface to Access Digital Information. In CHI'01 Extended Abstracts, ACM Press, New York, NY, 187–188.
16. Jordà, S., Geiger, G., Alonso, M., Kaltenbrunner, M., 2007. The reacTable: Exploring the Synergy between Live Music Performance and Tabletop Tangible Interfaces. In Proceedings of TEI'07, ACM Press, pp. 139–146.
17. Mackinlay, J., Card, S., Robertson, G., 1990. A Semantic Analysis of the Design Space of Input Devices, Human Computer Interaction, 5, 2&3 (1990), Lawrence Erlbaum, 145–190.
18. Norman, D., 1999. Affordance, Conventions and Design. Interactions, 6, 3 (May, June 1999), 38–43.
19. Pangaro, G., Maynes-Aminzade, D., Ishii, H., 2002. The Actuated Workbench: Computer-Controlled Actuation in Tabletop Tangible Interfaces. In Proceedings of UIST'02, ACM Press, New York, NY, 181–190.
20. Patten, J., Ishii, H., 2007. Mechanical Constraints as Computational Constraints in Tabletop Tangible Interfaces. In Proceedings of CHI'07, ACM Press, New York, NY, 809–818.
21. Shaer, O., Leland, N., Calvillo, E., Jacob, R., 2004. The TAC Paradigm: Specifying Tangible User Interfaces, Personal and Ubiquitous Computing, 8, 5 (September 2004), 359–369.
22. Ullmer, B., Ishii, H., 1997. The metaDESK: Models and Prototypes for Tangible User Interfaces. In Proceedings of UIST'97, ACM Press, New York, NY, 223–232.

23. Ullmer, B., Ishii, H., Jacob, R., 2005. Token+constraint systems for tangible interaction with digital information, ACM Transactions on Computer–Human Interaction, 12, 1 (March 2005), 81–118.
24. Vernier, F., Nigay, L., 2000. A Framework for the Combination and Characterization of Output Modalities. In Proceedings of DSVIS′00, LNCS, Springer, 32–48.
25. Wellner, P., 1993. Interacting with paper on the DigitalDesk, Communications of the ACM, 36, 7 (July 1993), 87–96.

Chapter 3
A Holistic Approach to Design and Evaluation of Mixed Reality Systems

Susanna Nilsson, Björn Johansson, and Arne Jönsson

Abstract This chapter addresses issues related to usability and user experience of mixed reality (MR) systems based on a naturalistic iterative design approach to the development of MR applications. Design and evaluation of MR applications are still mostly based on methods used for development of more traditional desktop graphical user interfaces. MR systems are in many aspects very different from desktop computer applications, so these traditional methods are not sufficient for MR applications. There is a need for new approaches to user-centred design and development of MR systems. One such approach is based on the concepts of cognitive systems engineering (CSE). In this chapter we show how this approach can be applied to the development of MR systems. Two case studies are described, where a holistic CSE approach to design, implementation and evaluation has been used. The results show that allowing real end users (field/domain experts) to interact in a close to naturalistic setting provides insights on how to design MR applications that are difficult to attain otherwise. We also show the importance of iterative design, again involving real end users.

keywords Mixed reality systems · Augmented reality · User study · User evaluation

3.1 Introduction

Mixed reality (MR) systems are still, 40 years after Ivan Sutherland's [35] first descriptions of a head-mounted display, mainly used and studied in the research domain. There are no practical and easy-to-use commercial off-the-shelf MR applications or widely used systems in the same way that many other computer-based

---

S. Nilsson (✉)
Department of Computer and Information Science, Linköping University, Linköping, Sweden
e-mail: susni@ida.liu.se

E. Dubois et al. (eds.), *The Engineering of Mixed Reality Systems*, Human-Computer Interaction Series, DOI 10.1007/978-1-84882-733-2_3,

applications have become a natural part of everyday working life in the industrialised world. New applications are developed every year, but to a large extent they remain in the research community, seemingly far away from the potential end users.

There can of course be many reasons for this development, but one issue that contributes to this fact is that so few of the designs are actually based on explicit user needs and requirements. There are few examples of MR applications that have been developed solely as a way to solve a real end user problem. Instead many applications are developed mainly because the technical resources and skills to develop them exist, alongside researchers with creative ideas. This type of research is important, but the resulting applications and designs are then not necessarily related to real end users and their needs [11]. Furthermore, these systems are often at best tested on a number of more or less randomly chosen people and evaluated based on participant comments, statistical measurements or technical findings [36, 7].

The methods used for user evaluation of MR applications are in general based on usability methods for graphical user interfaces, sometimes in combination with usability for virtual reality (VR) applications [37]. Currently most papers in the field of MR which include evaluation of some kind (not necessarily user evaluation) are quantitative, and of the ones referred to as user evaluations the vast majority make use of objective measurements such as error rate, task completion time [7] and the participants tend to be randomly chosen students. These studies stem from a more traditional view of cognition where the use of structured experiments and quantitative measurements is common. This approach, although the most commonly used, may not be the most appropriate. We do, however, not claim that studies on performance and economic relevance are unnecessary, but that such studies are not enough to understand how users experience and use MR systems.

As noted by Livingston [22] and Nilsson and Johansson [26] there are problems addressing human factors in MR systems. MR systems and applications differ from standard desktop applications in many ways and these differences between MR systems and desktop computer display-based systems create a need for a different approach to both development and evaluations of these systems. To understand the potential of MR systems in real-world tasks the technology must be designed based on investigations in real-world scenarios.

This chapter will describe and discuss two user applications where the studies to some extent represent examples of traditional qualitative user studies. The first study illustrates the approach applied to a single user application. This study has been published previously to varying extent [27, 28]. The second study illustrates the approach in a collaborative setting. This study has not been reported previously. The participants involved in both studies are real end users – in the first study medical staff at a hospital and in the second study personnel from three civil service organisations – and the applications have been built after explicit requirements and involvement from the particular end user groups. The focus of the result analysis is not traditional quantitative values but rather qualitative values such as user experience and acceptance [5].

3.2 Related Work

In this section we describe properties of MR systems and important aspects on how to evaluate and design these systems.

3.2.1 Mixed Reality Systems

The general aim of mixed reality systems is the merging of worlds by adding virtual information to the real world. The field of mixed reality is a relatively new field in terms of commercially and publicly available applications. As a research field, however, it has existed for a considerably longer time with applications in diverse domains, such as medicine, military applications, entertainment and infotainment, technical support and industrial applications, distance or remote operation and geographic applications [2, 1].

Milgram and Kishino's [23] virtual continuum is often used to describe the relation between augmented reality, virtual reality and the stages in between. Mixed reality is the collective name for all the stages (see Fig. 3.1).

The systems used in the case studies in this chapter can be defined as MR systems as they hold the possibility of being completely immersive. We use head-mounted displays that can be used to display only virtual information, shielding the user off from the surrounding world. However, they can also be used as AR systems; the applications described in this chapter are not immersive, but rather augments the users normal sight with virtual elements. To be considered an AR system, the system has to fulfil three criteria according to Azuma [1]: they all combine the real and the virtual, they are supposedly interactive in real time and they are registered and aligned in 3D [2, 1]. These three criteria are fulfilled in the systems described in this chapter.

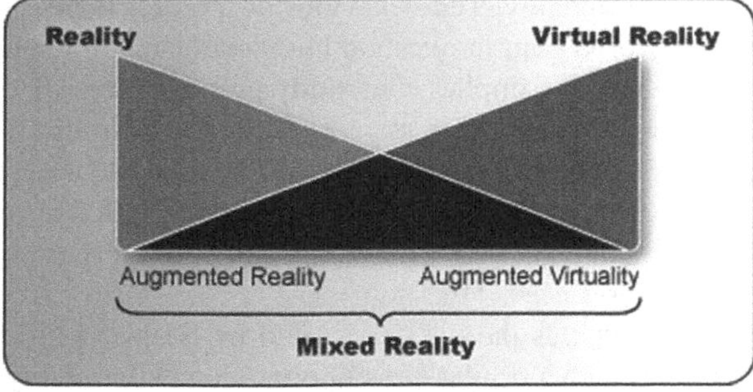

Fig. 3.1 The virtual continuum (after Milgram and Kishino)

3.2.2 Usefulness

To successfully integrate new technologies into an organisation or workplace means that the system, once in place, is actually used by the people it is intended for. There are many instances where technology has been introduced in organisations but not been used for a number of different reasons. One major contributor to the lack of usage is of course the usability of the product or system in itself. But another issue is how well the system operates together with the users in a social context – are the users interested and do they see the same potential in the system as the people (management) who decided to introduce it in the organisation? Davis [5] describes two important factors that influence the acceptance of new technology, or rather information systems, in organisations: the perceived usefulness of a system and the perceived ease of use. Both influence the attitude towards the system, and hence the user behaviour when interacting with it, as well as the actual use of the system. If the perceived usefulness of a system is considered high, the users can accept a system that is perceived as harder to use than if the system is not perceived as useful. For example, in one study conducted in the field of banking the perceived usefulness of the new technology was even more important than the perceived ease of use of the system, which illustrates the need to analyse usability from more than an ease-of-use perspective [20]. For an MR system this means that even though the system may be awkward or bulky, if the applications are good, i.e. useful enough, the users will accept and even appreciate it. Equally, if the MR system is not perceived useful, the MR system will not be used, even though it may be *easy* to use.

3.2.3 Technology in Context

Introducing new technology in a specific domain affects not only the user but also the entire context of the user, and most noticeably the task that the user performs. Regardless of whether the technology is only upgraded or if it is completely new to the user, the change as such will likely have an effect on the way the user performs his/her tasks. What the effects may be is difficult to predict as different users in different contexts behave differently. The behaviour of the user is not only related to the specific technology or system in question but also related to the organisational culture and context [38]. This implies that studying usefulness of technology in isolation from the natural context (as in many traditional, controlled usability studies) may not actually reveal how the technology will be used and accepted in reality. Understanding and foreseeing the effects of change on user, task and context require knowledge about the system, but perhaps even more importantly, an understanding of the context, user and user needs [16].

Usability guidelines such as the ones presented by Nielsen [25], Shneiderman [33] or other researchers with a similar view of cognition and usability are often the main sources of inspiration for usability studies of MR and AR systems. Several examples of such studies are listed in the survey of the field conducted by Dünser et al. [7]. The guidelines used in these studies are sensible and purposeful in many ways but they often fail to include the context of use, the surroundings and the effect the system or interface may have in this respect. Being contextually aware in designing an interface means having a good perception of not only *who* the user is but also *where* and *how* the system can and should affect the user in his/her tasks.

In many usability studies and methods the underlying assumption is that of a decomposed analysis where the human and the technical systems are viewed as separate entities that interact with each other. This assumption can be accredited the traditional idea of the human mind as an information processing unit where input is processed internally followed by some kind of output [24]. In this view, cognition is something inherently human that goes on inside the human mind, more or less isolated. The main problem with these theories of how the human mind works is not that they necessarily are wrong, the problem is rather that they, to a large extent, are based on laboratory experiments investigating the internal structures of cognition, and not on actual studies of human cognition in an actual work context [24, 6].

Another issue that complicates development and evaluation of systems is what is sometimes referred to as the "envisioned world problem" which means that even if a good understanding of a task exists, the new design, or tool, will change the task, making the first analysis invalid [17, 40].

As a response to this, a general and approach to human–machine interaction has been suggested by Hollnagel and Woods called *cognitive systems engineering* (CSE) [16, 17]. The main idea in the CSE approach is the concept of cognitive systems, where the humans are a part of the system, and not only users of that system. The focus is not on the parts and how they are structured and put together, but rather the purpose and the function of the parts in relation to the whole. This means that rather than isolating and studying specific aspects of a system by conducting laboratory studies or experiments under controlled conditions, users and systems should be studied in their natural setting, doing what they normally do. For obvious reasons, it is not always possible to study users in their normal environment, especially when considering novel systems. In such cases, CSE advocates studies of use in simulated situations [16]. Thus, the task for a usability evaluator is not to analyse only details of the interface, but rather allowing the user to perform meaningful tasks in meaningful situations. This allows for a more correct analysis of the system as a whole. The focus of a usability study should be the user performance with the system rather than the interaction between the user and the system. Comprising the concepts derived from the CSE perspective and Davis (presented above), the design of a system should be evaluated based on not only how users actually perform with a specific artefact but also how they experience that they can solve the task with or without the artefact under study.

CSE is thus in many respects a perspective comprising several theories and ideas rather than a single theory. A central tenant in the CSE perspective is that a cognitive system is a goal-oriented system able to adjust its behaviour according to experience [16]. Being a child of the age of expert systems, CSE refers to any system presenting this ability as a "cognitive system". Later, Hollnagel and Woods [16] introduced the notion of "joint cognitive system" pointing to a system comprised of a human and the technology that human uses to achieve a certain task in a certain context.

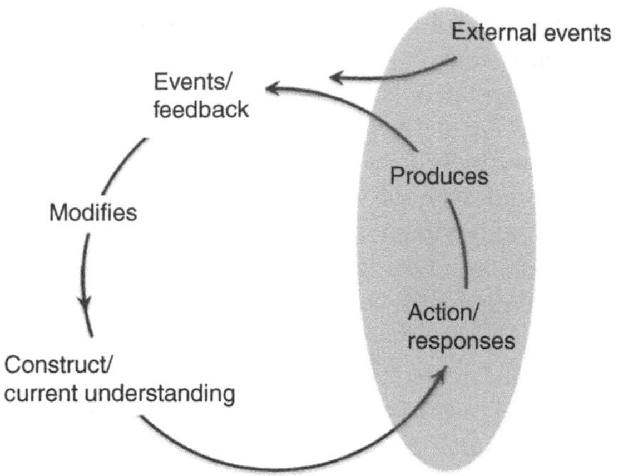

Fig. 3.2 The basic cyclical model as described in CSE

Several other cognitive theories such as situated cognition [34], distributed cognition [18] and activity theory [39, 8] advocate similar perspectives. What all of these approaches share is that they mostly apply qualitative methods such as observation studies, ethnography, conversational analysis. Grounded in the perspective that knowledge can be gained in terms of patterns of behaviour that can be found in many domains, strictly quantitative studies are rarely performed. A basic construct in the CSE movement is the cyclic interaction between a cognitive system and its surroundings (see Fig. 3.2). Each action performed is executed in order to fulfil a purpose, although not always founded on an ideal or rational decision. Instead, the ability to control a situation is largely founded on the competence of the cognitive system (the performance repertoire) and the available information about what is happening and the time it takes to process it.

From the basic cyclical model, which essentially is a feedback control loop operating in an open environment, we can derive that CSE assumes that a system has the ability to shape its future environment, but also that external influence will shape the outcome of actions, as well as the view of what is happening. The cognitive system must thus anticipate the outcomes of actions and interpret the actual outcome of actions and adjust in accordance to achieve its goal(s). Control from this perspective is the act of balancing feed forward with feedback. A system that is forced into reactive feedback-driven control mode due to lack of time or an adequate model of the world is bound to produce short-sighted action and is likely to ultimately loose control. A purely feed forward-driven system would conversely get into trouble since it has to rely solely on world models, and these are never complete. What a designer can do is create tools that support the human agent in such a way that it is easier to understand what is happening in the world or amplify the human ability to take action, creating a joint cognitive system that can cope with its tasks in a dynamic environment. This is particularly important when studying MR systems as the outspoken purpose of MR is to manipulate perceptual and cognitive abilities of a human by merging virtual elements into the perceived real world. From the very same point of view a number of risks with MR can be identified; a poorly designed MR system will greatly affect the joint human–MR system's performance.

Most controlled experiments are founded on the assumption of linear causality, i.e. that external variables are controlled and that action A always leads to outcome B. In most real-world or simulated environments with some level of realism and dynamics, this is not the case. Depending on circumstances and previous actions, the very same action may yield completely different outcomes. Taking this perspective, *process* becomes the focus of study, suggesting that it is more important to produce accurate descriptions than using pre-defined measures. The pre-defined measures demand that a number of assumptions about the world under study stay intact, assumptions that rarely can be made when introducing new tools such as MR systems in a real working environment.

Although some social science researchers [21] perceive qualitative and quantitative approaches as incompatible, others [29, 31] believe that the skilled researcher can successfully combine approaches. The argument usually becomes muddled because one party argues from the underlying philosophical nature of each paradigm and the other focuses on the apparent compatibility of the research methods, enjoying the rewards of both numbers and words. Because the positivist and the interpretivist paradigms rest on different assumptions about the nature of the world, they require different instruments and procedures to find the type of data desired. This does not mean, however, that the positivist never uses interviews nor that the interpretivist never uses a survey. They may, but such methods are supplementary, not be dominant. Different approaches allow us to know and understand different things about the world. Nonetheless, people tend to adhere to the methodology that is most in accordance with their socialised worldview [12, p. 9].

3.3 User Involvement in the Development Process

A long-term goal of MR research is for MR systems to become fully usable and user-friendly, but there are problems addressing human factors in MR systems [22, 28]. As noted, research in MR including user studies usually involves mainly quantifiable measures of performance (e.g. task completion time and error rate) and rarely focuses on more qualitative performance measures [7]. Of course there are exceptions such as described by Billinghurst and Kato [3] where user performance in collaborative AR applications is evaluated by not only quantitative measures but also with gesture analysis and language use. Another example is the method of domain analysis and task focus with user profiles presented by Livingston [22]. However these approaches are few and far between. For most instances the dominating method used is quantitative.

To investigate user acceptance and attitude towards MR technology, this chapter describes two case studies, one single user application and one collaborative multiuser application. The MR applications were developed iteratively with participation from the end user group throughout the process of planning and development.

In the first study the participants received instructions on how to assemble a relatively small surgical instrument, a trocar, and the second study focused on a collaborative task, where participants from three different organisations collaborated in a command and control forest fire situation. While the first case study is an example of a fairly simple individual instructional task, the second case study is an example of a dynamic collaborative task where the MR system was used as a tool for establishing common ground between three participating organisations.

3.3.1 The Method Used in the Case Studies

Acknowledging the "envisioned world" problem, we have adapted an iterative design approach where realistic exercises are combined with focus groups in an effort to catch both user behaviour and opinions. The studies have a qualitative approach where the aim is to iteratively design an MR system to better fit the needs of a specific application and user group.

As noted, the CSE approach to studying human–computer interaction advocates a natural setting, encouraging natural interaction and behaviour of the users. A fully natural setting is not always possible, but the experiments must be conducted in the most likely future environment [11, 16]. A natural setting makes it rather meaningless to use metrics such as task completion time, cf. [14] as such studies require a repeatable setting. In a natural setting, as opposed to a repeatable one, unforeseen consequences are inevitable and also desirable. Even though time was recorded through the observations in the first case study presented in this chapter, time was not used as a measurement, as time is not a critical measure of success in this setting. In the second setting task completion could have been used as a measurement but the set-up of the task and study emphasised collaboration and communication rather than task performance. The main focus was the end users' experience of the system's usefulness rather than creating repeatable settings for experimental measurements. Experimental studies often fail to capture how users actually perceive the use of a system. This is not because it is impossible to capture the subjective experience of use, but rather because advocates of strict experimental methods often prefer to collect numerical data such as response times, error rates. Such data are useful but it is also important to consider qualitative aspects of user experience.

3.3.2 The Design Process Used in the Case Studies

The method used to develop the applications included a pre-design phase where field experts took part of a brainstorming session to establish the initial parameters of the MR system. These brainstorming sessions were used to define the components of the software interface, such as what type of symbols to use and what type of information is important and relevant in the different tasks of the applications. In the single user application this was, for instance, the specifics of the instructions designed and in

Fig. 3.3 Digital pointing using an interaction device and hand-held displays

the multiuser application the specifics of the information needed to create common ground between the three participating organisations. Based on an analysis of the brainstorming session a first design of the MR system as well as of the user task was implemented. The multiuser application was designed to support cooperation as advocated by Billinghurst and Kato [3] and thus emphasised the need for actors to see each other. Therefore, we first used hand-held devices that are easier to remove from the eyes than head-mounted displays, see Fig. 3.3.

The first design and user task was then evaluated by the field experts in workshops where they could test the system and give feedback on the task as well as on the physical design and interaction aspects of the system. In the single user application the first system prototype needed improvements on the animations and instructions used, but the hardware solutions met the needs of the field experts. The evaluation of the multiuser application, however, illustrated several problematic issues regarding physical design as well as software-related issues, such as the use of the hand-held display which turned out to be a hindrance for natural interaction rather than an aid.

For the multiuser application we further noticed that when a user points at things in the map, the hand is occluded by the digital image of the map in the display. Thus, hand pointing on the digital map was not possible due to the technical solution. This problem was solved by using an interaction device to point digitally (see Fig. 3.3). The virtual elements (the map and symbols) and interaction device also had several improvement possibilities.

Based on this first prototype evaluation another iteration of design and development took place where the MR system went through considerable modifications. Modifications and improvements were also made on the user task. As mentioned the single-user application and task only had minor changes made, while the multiuser application went through considerable changes. The hand-held displays were replaced with head-mounted displays, the interaction device was transformed and the software was upgraded considerably to allow more natural gestures (hand pointing on the digital map). Besides these MR system-related issues several changes were also made to the user task to ensure realism in the setting of the evaluation.

After the changes to the MR system and user task were made, another participant workshop was held to evaluate the new system design and the modified user task and scenario. This workshop allowed the field experts to comment and discuss the updated versions of the applications and resulted in another iteration of minor changes before the applications were considered final and ready for the end user studies. The final applications are described in detail in the following case study descriptions.

3.4 The First Case Study – An Instructional Task

The public health-care domain has many challenges and among them is, as in any domain, the need for efficiency and making the most of available resources. One part of the regular activities at a hospital is the introduction and training of new staff. Even though all new employees may be well educated and professionally trained, there are always differences in tools and techniques used – coming to a new work place means learning the equipment and methods used in that particular place. In discussions following a previous study [26] one particular task came up as something where MR technology might be an asset in terms of a training and teaching tool. Today when new staff (physicians or nurses) arrive it is often up to the more experienced nurses to give the new person an introduction and training to tools and equipment used. One such tool is the trocar (see Fig. 3.4), which is a standard tool used during minimal invasive surgeries. There are several different types and models of trocars and the correct assembly of this tool is important in order for it to

Fig. 3.4 The fiducial marker on the index finger of the user, *left*, and the participants view of the trocar and MR instructions during the assembly task, *right*

work properly. This was pointed out as one task that the experienced staff would appreciate not having to go through in detail for every new staff member. As a result MR instructions were developed and evaluated as described in this section.

3.4.1 Equipment Used in the Study

The MR system included a Sony Glasstron head-mounted display and an off-the-shelf headset with earphones and a microphone. The MR system runs on a laptop with a 2.00 GHz Intel®Core^{TM} 2 CPU, 2 GB RAM and a NVIDIA GeForce 7900 graphics card. The MR system uses a hybrid tracking technology based on marker tracking; ARToolKit (available for download at [15]), ARToolKit Plus [32] and ARTag [9]. The marker used can be seen in Fig. 3.4. The software includes an integrated set of software tools such as software for camera image capture, fiducial marker detection, computer graphics software and also software developed specifically for MR-application scenarios.

As a result of previous user studies in this user group [26, 28] the interaction method chosen for the MR system was voice control. The voice input is received through the headset microphone and is interpreted by a simple voice recognition application based on Microsoft's Speech API (SAPI).

3.4.2 The User Task

The participants were given instructions on how to assemble a trocar (see Fig. 3.4). A trocar is used as a gateway into a patient during minimal invasive surgeries. The trocar is relatively small and consists of seven separate parts which have to be correctly assembled for it to function properly as a lock preventing blood and gas from leaking out of the patient's body. The trocar was too small to have several different markers attached to each part. Markers attached to the object would also not be realistic considering the type of object and its usage – it needs to be kept sterile and clean of other materials. Instead the marker was mounted on a small ring with adjustable size which the participants wore on their index finger (see Fig. 3.4).

As described above, instructions on how to put together a trocar are normally given on the spot by more experienced operating room (OR) nurses. Creating the MR instructions was consequently somewhat difficult as there are no standardised instructions on how to put a trocar together. Instead we developed the instructions based on the instructions given by the OR nurse who regularly gives the instructions at the hospital. This ensures some realism in the task. The nurse was video recorded while giving instructions and assembling a trocar. The video was the basis for the sequence of instructions and animations given to the participants in the study. An example of the instructions and animation can be seen in Fig. 3.4. Figure 3.5 shows a participant during the task.

Before receiving the assembly instructions the participants were given a short introduction to the voice commands they can use during the task; *OK* to continue to the next step and *back* or *backwards* to repeat previous steps.

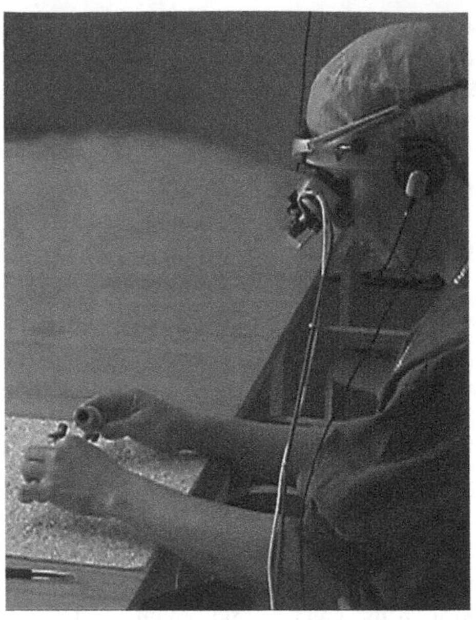

Fig. 3.5 A participant in the user study wearing the MR system and following instructions on how to assemble the trocar

3.4.3 Participants and Procedure

As the approach advocated in this chapter calls for real end users the selection of participants was limited to professional medical staff. Twelve professional (ages 35–60) operating room (OR) nurses and surgeons at a hospital took part in the study. As medical staff, the participants were all familiar with the trocar, although not all of them had actually assembled one prior to this study. None of them had previously assembled this specific trocar model. A majority of the participants stated that they have an interest in new technology and that they interact with computers regularly; however, few of them had experience of video games and 3D graphics. The participants were first introduced to the MR system. When the head-mounted display and headset were appropriately adjusted they were told to follow the instructions given by the system to assemble the device they had in front of them. After the task was completed the participants filled out a questionnaire about their experience. The participants were recorded with a digital video camera when they assembled the trocar. During the task, the participants' view through the MR system was also logged on video. Data were collected both through direct observation and through questionnaires.

The observations and questionnaire were the basis for a qualitative analysis. The questionnaire consisted of 10 questions where the participants could answer freely on their experience of the MR system. The questions were related to overall impression of the MR system, experienced difficulties, experienced positive aspects, what they would change in the system and whether it is possible to compare receiving MR instructions to receiving instructions from a teacher.

3.4.4 Results of the Study

All users in this study were able to complete the task with the aid of MR instructions. Issues, problems or comments that were raised by more than one participant have been the focus of the analysis. The responses in the questionnaire were diverse in content but a few topics were raised by several respondents and several themes could be identified across the answers of the participants. None of the open-ended questions were specifically about the placement of the marker, but the marker was mentioned by half of the participants (6 of the 12) as either troublesome or not functional in this application:

> It would have been nice to not have to think about the marker.[1] (participant 7)

Concerning the dual modality function in the MR instructions (instructions given both aurally and visually) one respondent commented on this as a positive factor in the system. But another participant instead considered the multimedia presentation as being confusing:

> I get a bit confused by the voice and the images. I think it's harder than it maybe is. (participant 9)

Issues of parallax and depth perception are not a problem unique to this MR application. It is a commonly known problem for any video-see-through system where the cameras angle are somewhat distorted from the angle of the users eyes, causing a parallax vision, i.e. the user will see her/his hands at one position but this position does not correspond to actual position of the hand. Only one participant mentioned problems related to this issue:

> The depth was missing. (participant 7)

A majority among the participants (8 out of 12) gave positive remarks on the instructions and presentation of instructions. One issue raised by two participants was the possibility to ask questions. The issue of feedback and the possibility to ask questions are also connected to the issue of the system being more or less comparable to human tutoring. It was in relation to this question that most responses concerning the possibility to ask questions and the lack of feedback were raised. The question of whether or not it is possible to compare receiving instructions from the MR system with receiving instructions from a human did get an overall positive response. Four out of the twelve gave a clear yes answer and five gave more unclear answers like

> Rather a complement; for repetition. Better? Teacher/tutor/instructor is not always available – then when a device is used rarely – very good. (participant 1)

Several of the respondents in the yes category actually stated that the AR system was better than instructions from a teacher, because the instructions were objective in the sense that everyone will get exactly the same information. When asked about

[1] All participant excerpts are translated from Swedish to English.

their impressions of the MR system, a majority of the participants gave very positive responses:

> Very interesting concept. Easy to understand the instructions. Easy to use. (participant 3)

Others had more concerns:

> So and so, a bit tricky. (participant 6)

One question specifically targeted the attitude towards using MR in their future professional life and all participants responded positively to this question. This is perhaps the most important result and also the most obvious from a developer point of view – if people from the target user group actually state that they want to use it in their work, the system has a much higher promise than a perfectly good system which the target users have not requested or do not consider useful [5].

3.5 The Second Case Study – A Collaborative MR Application

Collaborative work has been studied extensively in many different research domains, from sociological, psychological as well as organisational perspectives. Technological tools that aid collaboration have also been developed within the broad range of research on computer-supported collaborative work, such as decision support systems combined with teleconferencing systems.

Virtual environments have been used as tools for training and simulating collaborative work (for instance, the CAVE system and the Virtual Workbench [10]), but few, if any, systems have actually been aimed for use in real crisis management situations. When personnel from different organisations work together under stress, as in many crisis situations, there is always a risk that misunderstandings emerge due to differences in terminology or symbol use. In linguistics, it is common knowledge that time has to be spent on establishing a "common ground", or a basis for communication, founded on personal expectations and assumptions between the persons communicating with each other [4, 19]. Thus, providing means to facilitate establishing a common ground is important for efficient collaboration.

In addition to this, there are situation-specific problems that emerge in collaborative command and control tasks. Such tasks often circle around a shared representation of the current activities, as in the case of a situational map. Most organisations involved in such tasks, like the military or rescue services, have developed a library of symbols that can be utilised for representing units and events. Problems arise when representatives from different organisations are to work together, since they are used to working with their own, organisation-specific, symbols and conventions. This means that time has to be spent explaining and negotiating meaning when jointly creating and manipulating a shared representation, a tedious task to undertake when there is little time, as, for example, in the case of forest fire fighting in, or close to, urban areas.

Furthermore, for each organisation there is information that is only interesting for the representatives from that organisation. Thus, commanders from different organisations need personalised views of the same situational map, for instance, using MR.

3.5.1 Equipment Used in the Study

A multiuser collaborative MR application was developed through the iterative design process described previously in this chapter.

The MR system was an early high fidelity prototype, which allowed the users to interact with virtual elements. It includes a Z800 3DVisor from eMagin[2] integrated with a firewire camera. The mixed reality system runs on a 2.10 GHz laptop with 3 GB RAM and a 128 MB NVIDIA GeForce 8400 M GS graphics card. In order to interact with the MR system the users had a joystick-like interaction device allowing them to choose objects and functions affecting their view of the digital map (see Fig. 3.6).

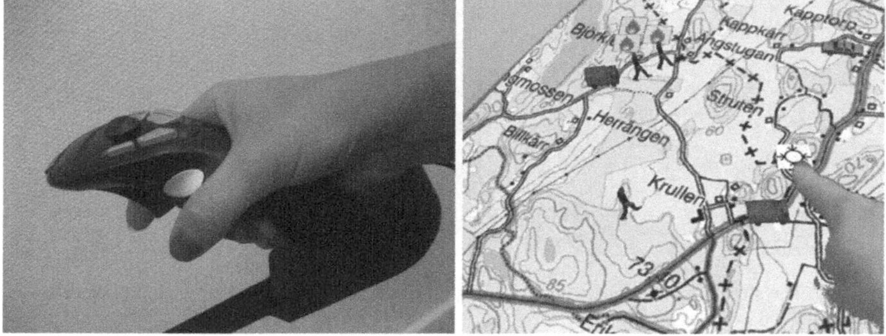

Fig. 3.6 Interaction device, *left*, and the users display, *right*, with symbols and pointing used in the collaborative MR application

3.5.2 The User Task

The study was conducted with the purpose of evaluating the MR system and application design in order to improve it as a tool for collaboration between organisations. It is not possible to conduct experiments in real fire-fighting situations. Instead, to create a realistic study, we used a scenario where the groups had to collaborate, distribute resources and plan actions in response to a simulated forest fire and other related or non-related events. In the scenario the participants act as they would as

[2]http://www.3dvisor.com/

on-scene commanders in their respective organisation. This means that they together have to discuss the current situation and decide how to proceed in order to fight the fire, evacuate residents, redirect traffic, coordinate personnel as well as dealing with any unexpected events that may occur during such incidents. The MR system was used as a tool for them to see and manipulate their resources and as a way to have an overall view of the situation (see Fig. 3.6).

In order to create a dynamic scenario and realistic responses and reactions to the participants decisions in the final study, we used a gaming simulator, C3 Fire [13]. The simulator was run in the background by the research team (see Fig. 3.7), where one member inserted information into the gaming simulator, for instance, that several police cars have been reallocated to attend to a traffic incident. The exercise manager acted as a feedback channel to the participants in order for them to carry out their work. For instance, when the reallocated police cars had reached their new destination the exercise leader returned with information to the participants. Other examples of information from the gaming simulator are weather reports, status of personnel and vehicles, the spread of the fire.

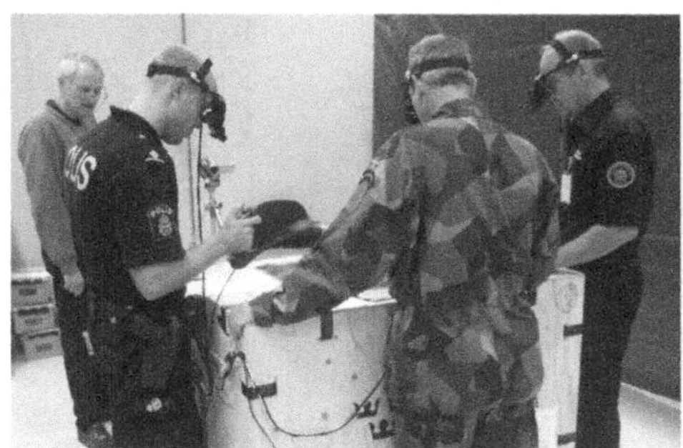

Fig. 3.7 The simulated natural setting (a helicopter base), *left*, and the gaming simulator that was controlling the experiment, *right*

3.5.3 Participants and Procedure

The MR application was evaluated in a study where nine groups with three participants in each group used the system in a simulated scenario of a forest fire. To promote realistic results, the participants were representatives from the three organisations in focus; the fire department, the police and the military. All participants were novices to the application and scenario, none of them were involved during the developing phase of the application. The setting was at a military helicopter base (see Fig. 3.7).

The application was designed around an exercise in which the participants, one from each organisation (the fire and rescue services, the police department and the military), had to interact and work together to complete tasks in a dynamic scenario. The exercise was observed and the participants also answered questionnaires pertaining to the MR system design, and finally a focus group discussion was held where the participants could reflect on and discuss a series of topics relating to the exercise, the scenario and the MR system. The tools used for data gathering were mainly qualitative; observation, focus groups and questionnaires.

3.5.4 Results of the Study

The results from the previously described design phase studies were very useful for improving the application scenario as well as the system. The head-mounted display was a big improvement which allowed the participants to move around and interact more freely. The new interaction device was also appreciated and the participants found it very easy to use and quick to learn.

The added possibility to see hand gestures such as pointing on the digital map has simplified the interaction considerably and also resulted in a more natural interaction and better communication between the participants. In the redesigned application the participants had exactly the same view allowing them to alter their personal image but still seeing the same map, and not as previously an organisation-specific map. As noted by one of the participants during a group discussion:

> A common picture, everything is better than me telling someone what it looks like...you need to see the picture and not to hear my words. (pilot, pre-study workshop)

The main results of the study are not limited to the actual evaluation of the MR system and the application in itself. Even more importantly, the results are an indication that the naturalistic approach brought out comments that would be impossible had the task not been a relatively realistic task, and the participants not been professionals with experience from these types of tasks.

> What I would want, it's a bit reactionary but I would like to have only a small red dot with an identifier on the unit that I have. I think that the vehicles were to big and that's charming and nice visually but I would prefer working with tactical units and then add their designation, regardless of what vehicle it is, what it looks like I don't care...That would increase my efficiency in this system even though it will be a more dull environment... (fire department, day 2)

This quote illustrates the importance of real participants, iterative design and a holistic approach. As a representative from the fire department he is not impressed by the neat 3D graphics vehicles, instead he prefers tactical units. As he has been using the system in a close to natural setting he also provides additional information on how to make the interface more efficient (using red dots). The tactical unit can, as the participant suggests, be used for each individual organisation; however, as another quote illustrates, the participants do not necessarily need to see more than a 3D object of the other organisations information:

> It's good, maybe more 'nice' than 'need', but I think it's good because it's quick for those who are not familiar. If I would put up a lot of symbols otherwise maybe no one would know, because everyone has different symbols, but you see quickly what is a fire truck and what is a tanker, everybody understands what a helicopter is rather than me drawing if it is a medium heavy or heavy, you don't know if that's a transport helicopter or...so if you have an image it is easier (pilot, day 1)

As a lesson learned the design could be enhanced by making the symbols on an individual level, meaning that the symbols representing other organisations could be pictorial objects, while the own organisations' objects are represented in much more detail, as tactical units with identifiers rather than as visual 3D objects.

It is also important to note that to do a fair evaluation of the MR system the participants need some training. In any organisation a new type of technology or system is not expected to function perfectly on the very first day of use. This study was the first time any of these participants had any contact with MR technology and therefore the participants did find the second session with the MR system easier:

> I thought it went very well the last time. We are beginners and we had learned the talk, we had learned to point on the map. My opinion is that we passed (fire department, day 2)

So basing a system evaluation on first time user experiences may not be very relevant since in real life people are actually trained, and after some time the use of the system will most likely be considerably more efficient and meaningful.

Another result of the study (including the pre-user study workshops) was the participants ability to see what possibilities MR technology hold for their professions. One organisation remarked that MR would be very useful as a tool to distribute situational pictures to command and control functions elsewhere in the organisational structure. This means that the command and control function on the field has the opportunity to convey what's going on to the command and control out of the field, that is, functions in the organisational hierarchy with responsibility for general planning of the operation. This, however, does not affect the purpose of the use of MR as a collaborative tool as this would merely be a form of information transmission or distribution rather than part of an ongoing collaborative task such as the one studied here. One participant saw the possibilities of distributed collaboration between the organisations, where one organisations' view can be shared with others while discussing the problem at hand and being able to point in each others field of view regardless of where the actors are situated geographically. This possibility was greatly appreciated:

> So you can be completely distributed but still see the hands of people? That's fantastic. (fire department, pre-study workshop)

The participants did not only appreciate the new design, it also gave them ideas on how to further develop the MR system and see the potential of its following applications. Even though the participants in many respects are very positive towards the new technology and the possibilities it may hold for their organisation, they are also realists and they are fully aware of the demands placed on new technology in their natural environment:

> I only have a hard time seeing it in a real large fire in reality. In a situation where you are supposed to practice like we have done here, where you practice making decisions, where you practice cooperating, where you are supposed to get the picture of what you need to talk about, and what decisions have to made, then it is perfect. But take this out in the forest, and then run out and give directions to someone else where I need a paper map anyway because

he's not supposed to hang around, he's supposed to go there and he needs to know what to do, he needs to bring an operational picture when he leaves, then I don't see it yet. (pilot, day 2)

The main goal of the study was to evaluate the potential of the technology and not to evaluate a finished design, and as such the study was successful. Even though the MR system is not yet final in design and implementation the professional opinions and comments received through this study are imperative for future design and implementation. The results also clearly show the importance of an iterative design process of MR applications.

3.6 Discussion

Both MR studies presented in this chapter share two qualities that make them stand out in comparison to most current MR research; all users were professionals, and an iterative design process with end user involvement was used. Furthermore, the underlying theoretical approach utilised was cognitive systems engineering which provides a view on design that differs from traditional cognitive theories, in some important respects. Cognitive systems engineering postulates that the user and his/her tools should be seen as a joint system, acting with a purpose. Most traditional human–computer interaction study methods, which are the basis for most usability studies in the MR domain, are based on theories of cognition. They are therefore also based on a decomposed view of humans and the tools they use.

To apply a decomposed view of a human and an MR system is in many respects a difficult task since the actual purpose of the MR system is to manipulate the perception of the user.

Another important aspect is that the designs used in the two studies have, as far as possible, tried to free themselves from design principles based on desktop systems. Already in the early stages of the first study, we discovered that such principles have little value for designing MR applications. The reason for this lays in the fact that presentation and interaction with MR objects differ greatly from systems based on the desktop metaphor.

The method used in these case studies included a long development phase with several design iterations and end user representatives were involved throughout the entire process. This method is invaluable in terms of the final outcome – these experts found issues in the system that would be very difficult for non-experts in the field to spot. For instance many user development methods involve students during the design phases. However, for many domains, such as health care and civil service, involving expert users is imperative. The participants in the design iterations gave invaluable insight into what information is actually useful in the field and what information is not as important. This gives meaningful and relevant feedback on what changes should be prioritised. Real expert users also have knowledge and experience allowing them to interpret the information in context. For instance, the information displayed in relation to objects in the collaborative task is useful to professionals in the field but may appear meaningless to someone without domain expertise.

Real end users in the evaluation also provided new insights on the use of MR systems and future research and development. Where many other studies result in findings where tracking optimisation and better resolution displays are the most important issues, the results from our end user case studies actually show that the resolution and tracking are of minor importance to the end user, cf. Gabbard and Swan, 2008 [11]. What is of importance, however, is the interaction possibilities and the content of the presented information. One negative aspect of end user involvement is of course the risk of bias – if the user is part of the development team there is the risk that no matter what the design result is they will be positive. However, this can to some extent be controlled in that the users actually taking part in the study and evaluation of the application are not involved in the development phase. In our studies the participants in the end studies had no previous involvement in the project and were informed that the results of the study would be used solely for research and development purposes, and that their individual performance and opinions were confidential. Despite this there can of course be reasons out of our control for them to be positively or negatively biased as representatives from the end user group. No matter what study, when involving users the potential bias in one way or another will be present, but the advantages and possible gain from their involvement definitely outweigh the potential risks.

3.7 Conclusions and Future Direction

New designs, based on novel technologies, like the ones presented in this chapter naturally lacks in maturity. There are child diseases in terms of technical limitations, various bugs due to experimental software, and the mere fact that the users are not acquainted with the way of interacting. This leads to problems in applying traditional evaluation methods that, for example, focus on efficiency. Instead, when introducing new systems, like MR, in an activity, user acceptance and perspectives are crucial evaluation criteria. The overall results from both case studies presented in this chapter show a system that the participants like rather than dislike, although both need specific improvements before they can be implemented into the context of use. Both user groups clearly see a future for the MR technology in their work domains. By allowing professional users to test the applications new ideas are generated, both on behalf of the users and the designers. The "envisioned world problem" described above certainly manifests itself. However, the word "problem" may be an inappropriate notion. When working with novel systems like these, we should perhaps rather talk about possibilities. Even if the actual use differs from the envisioned, every iteration has so far provided very important input that definitely has led to large improvements and innovation.

Interactivity is an important part of direct manipulation user interfaces and also seems to be of importance in an MR system of the kind investigated in these studies. In the first case study, a couple of the participants who responded negatively on the question regarding comparability between the MR system instructions and human instructions motivated their response in that you can ask and get a response from a human, but this MR system did not have the ability to answer random questions from the users. Adding this type of dialogue management and/or intelligence in the system would very likely increase the usability and usefulness of the system, and also make it more human-like than tool-like [30]. In the second study we found that showing real-time status of vehicles and resources is one important output improvement. Connecting the MR interface with other technological systems already in use in the organisations, GPS for instance, would enhance the MR system. We also found that the interaction device could be used more efficiently if buttons and menu items were organised differently.

We believe that our iterative design method gave us MR systems that were appreciated by our subjects. However, the experiences from our case studies also show the need for further research on user perspectives on interaction and output in MR systems.

Acknowledgements This research is funded by the Swedish Defence Materiel Administration (FMV). The MR system was developed in close cooperation with XM Reality AB. We are deeply indebted to all the participants in our studies who volunteered their time and expertise to these projects.

References

1. Azuma, R.: A survey of augmented reality. Presence **6**(4), 355–385 (1997)
2. Azuma, R., Baillot, Y., Behringer, R., Feiner, S., Julier, S., MacIntyre, B.: Recent advances in augmented reality. IEEE Computer Graphics and Applications **21**(6), 34–47 (2001). http://computer.org/cga/cg2001/g6034abs.htm
3. Billinghurst, M., Kato, H.: Collaborative augmented reality. Communications of the ACM **45**(7), 64–70 (2002)
4. Clark, H.H.: Using Language. Cambridge University Press, Cambridge (1996)
5. Davis, F.D.: Perceived usefulness, perceived ease of use, and user acceptance of information technology. MIS Quarterly **13**(3) (1989)
6. Dekker, S., Hollnagel, E.: Human factors and folk models. Cognition Technology Work **6**(2), 79–86 (2004). DOIhttp://dx.doi.org/10.1007/s10111-003-0136-9
7. Dünser, A., Grasset, R., Billinghurst, M.: A survey of evaluation techniques used in augmented reality studies. Tech. Rep. Technical Report TR2008-02, Human Interface Technology Laboratory New Zealand (2008)
8. Engeström, Y., Miettinen, R., Punamaki, R. (eds.): Perspectives on activity theory (Learning in doing social, cognitive and computational perspectives). Cambridge University Press, Cambridge (1999)
9. Fiala, M.: Artag rev2 fiducial marker system: Vision based tracking for AR. In: Workshop of Industrial Augmented Reality, Wienna Austria (2005)
10. Fuhrmann, A., Löffelmann, H., Schmalstieg, D.: Collaborative augmented reality: Exploring dynamical systems. In: R. Yagel, H. Hagen (eds.) IEEE Visualization 97, pp. 459–462. IEEE (1997)
11. Gabbard, J.L., Swan II, J.E.: Usability engineering for augmented reality: Employing user-based studies to inform design. IEEE Transactions on Visualization and Computer Graphics **14**(3), 513–525 (2008)
12. Glesne, C., Peshkin, A.: Becoming qualitative researchers: An introduction. Longman White Plains, New york (1992)

13. Granlund, R.: Web-based micro-world simulation for emergency management training. Future Generation Computer Systems **17**, 561–572 (2001)
14. Grasset, R., Lamb, P., Billinghurst, M.: Evaluation of mixed-space collaboration. In: ISMAR '05: Proceedings of the 4th IEEE/ACM International Symposium on Mixed and Augmented Reality, pp. 90–99. IEEE Computer Society, Washington, DC, USA (2005). DOI http://dx.doi.org/10.1109/ISMAR.2005.30
15. HITLAB: http://www.hitl.washington.edu/artoolkit/ (2007)
16. Hollnagel, E., Woods, D.D.: Cognitive systems engineering: New wine in new bottles. International Journal of Man-Machine Studies **18**(6), 583–600 (1983)
17. Hollnagel, E., Woods, D.D.: Joint cognitive systems: Foundations of cognitive systems engineering. CRC Press, Boca Raton, FL (2005)
18. Hutchins, E.: Cognition in the wild. MIT Press, London, England (1995). URL http://www.netlibrary.com/summary.asp?id=1687
19. Klein, G., Feltovich, P.J., Bradshaw, J.M., Woods, D.D.: Common ground and coordination in joint activity, vol. Organizational Simulation, Chap. 6, pp. 139–184. John Wiley & Sons, New York (2005). http://dx.doi.org/10.1002/0471739448.ch6
20. Liao, Z., Landry, R.: An empirical study on organizational acceptance of new information systems in a commercial bank. In: HICSS (2000). URL http://computer.org/proceedings/hicss/0493/04932/04932021abs.htm
21. Lincoln, Y.S., Guba, E.G.: Naturalistic Inquiry. Sage, Beverly Hills, CA (1985)
22. Livingston, M.A.: Evaluating human factors in augmented reality systems. IEEE Computer Graphics and Applications **25**(6), 6–9 (2005). URL http://doi.ieeecomputersociety.org/10.1109/MCG.2005.130
23. Milgram, P., Kishino, F.: A taxonomy of mixed reality visual displays. IEICE Transactions on Information Systems **E77-D**(12) (1994)
24. Neisser, U.: Cognition and reality. W.H. Freeman, San Francisc, CA (1976)
25. Nielsen, J.: Usability Engineering. Academic Press, Boston, MA (1993)
26. Nilsson, S., Johansson, B.: User experience and acceptance of a mixed reality system in a naturalistic setting – A case study. In: ISMAR, pp. 247–248. IEEE (2006). URL http://dx.doi.org/10.1109/ISMAR.2006.297827
27. Nilsson, S., Johansson, B.: Fun and usable: augmented reality instructions in a hospital setting. In: B. Thomas (ed.) Proceedings of the 2007 Australasian Computer-Human Interaction Conference, OZCHI 2007, Adelaide, Australia, November 28–30, 2007, *ACM International Conference Proceeding Series*, vol. 251, pp. 123–130. ACM (2007). http://doi.acm.org/10.1145/1324892.1324915
28. Nilsson, S., Johansson, B.: Acceptance of augmented reality instructions in a real work setting. In: M. Czerwinski, A.M. Lund, D.S. Tan (eds.) Extended Abstracts Proceedings of the 2008 Conference on Human Factors in Computing Systems, CHI 2008, Florence, Italy, April 5-10, 2008, pp. 2025–2032. ACM (2008). http://doi.acm.org/10.1145/1358628.1358633
29. Patton, M.Q.: Qualitative evaluation and research methods, (2nd edn). Sage Publications, Thousand Oaks, CA (1990)
30. Qvarfordt, P., Jönsson, A., Dahlbäck, N.: The role of spoken feedback in experiencing multimodal interfaces as human-like. In: Proceedings of ICMI03, Vancouver, Canada (2003)
31. Reichardt, C., Cook, T.: Beyond qualitative versus quantitative methods. Qualitative and Quantitative Methods in Evaluation Research pp. 7–32 (1979)
32. Schmalstieg, D.: Rapid prototyping of augmented reality applications with the studierstube framework. In: Workshop of Industrial Augmented Reality, Wienna, Austria (2005)
33. Shneiderman, B.: Designing the user interface (3rd edn). Addison Wesley (1998)
34. Suchman, L.A.: Plans and situated actions. Cambridge University Press, Cambridge (1987)
35. Sutherland, I.E.: A head-mounted three-dimensional display. In: AFIPS Conference Proceedings, vol. 33, pp. 757–764 (1968)
36. Swan II, J.E., Gabbard, J.L.: Survey of user-based experimentation in augmented reality. In: 1st International Conference on Virtual Reality, Las Vegas, NV (2005)

37. Träskbäck, M.: Toward a usable mixed reality authoring tool. In: VL/HCC, pp. 160–162. IEEE Computer Society (2004). URL http://doi.ieeecomputersociety.org/10.1109/VLHCC.2004.60
38. Tushman, M.L., OReilly III, C.A.: Ambidextrous organizations: Managing evolutionary and revolutionary change. California Management Review **38**(4), 8–30 (1996)
39. Vygotsky, L.S.: Mind in society. Harvard University Press, Cambridge (1978)
40. Woods, D.D., Roth, E.M.: Cognitive engineering: human problem solving with tools. Human Factors **30**(4), 415–430 (1988)

Chapter 4
Embedded Mixed Reality Environments

Holger Schnädelbach, Areti Galani, and Martin Flintham

Abstract The deployment of mixed reality environments for use by members of the public poses very different challenges to those faced during focused lab studies and in defined engineering settings. This chapter discusses and presents examples from a set of case studies that have implemented and evaluated fully functioning mixed reality environments in three different organisational settings. Based on these case studies, common themes that are critical in the engineering of publicly deployed mixed reality are drawn out. Specifically, it is argued how the creation of a mixed reality interaction space depends on the technology as well as the environment, how asymmetric access provided to different sets of participants can be desirable and how social interaction reflects the particulars of the embedded technology, the length of deployment and the existing social organisation.

Keywords Mixed reality environments · Public deployment · Case study · Embeddedness · Interaction space · Asymmetry · Social interaction

4.1 Introduction

The engineering of mixed reality (MR) systems poses significant technical challenges, for example, with regard to the registration of real and virtual environments, the portability of computing devices and the real-time processing of data to allow for interaction. Early work by Billinghurst et al. addresses these issues in the realm of computer-supported collaborative work [3, 4]. The Studierstube set of projects investigated the application of MR in a variety of work environments, from maths education to surgery [6, 27, 28]. The technical challenges highlighted there and elsewhere have been substantial, even for MR systems used in controlled research

H. Schnädelbach (✉)
Mixed Reality Lab, Computer Science Department, University of Nottingham, Nottingham NG8 1BB, UK
e-mail: hms@cs.nott.ac.uk

E. Dubois et al. (eds.), *The Engineering of Mixed Reality Systems*, Human-Computer Interaction Series, DOI 10.1007/978-1-84882-733-2_4,

environments or work settings in industry. As is evident in the ISMAR series of conferences [12], interest in the area of mixed reality remains strong, and there is a growing number of tools that are designed to make the authoring of MRE more widely available [32]. However, it is also clear that a better understanding of interactions within MR systems is needed to take the concept further [22].

Moreover, in current research, other terms such as Ubiquitous and Pervasive Computing are used alongside mixed reality and augmented reality to describe work in this area, and the separation between terms is not always very clear (for example, in [33], an ubiquitous computing urban game is also called a mixed reality game). In fact, different researchers use different terms to refer to similar types of environments or experiences, which also reflects the recent use of MR technology in large-scale installations that involve several spaces and multiple users [12].

Milgram's virtuality continuum already suggests that there is clearly more than technology in the design, development, implementation and use of MR systems. Even this very concise model suggests that the "virtual" and "physical" environments that MR is placed in are clearly very important [20]. The deployment of mixed reality environments (MREs) into real settings then, on the one hand, poses new technical challenges and this has been a long-standing concern in this research field. For example, Azuma has detailed the practical issues that need to be faced when working with relevant technologies outdoors [1]. On the other hand, as previous research in the field of CSCW has shown, there are also entirely different context-related challenges linked to the environment that specific technologies become deployed in. These are concerned with the associated existing technological and social circumstances at the particular settings [7, 8].

In this chapter, we will draw on examples from three MREs, all emanating from the UK EQUATOR project [24]. These were implemented in a museum exhibition, a series of office spaces and a cityscape. We discuss the design and deployment of those environments and the ways in which they support medium- to large-scale groups of people in their activities. Here, the emphasis is on those activities that are not primarily task-driven but occur in the realm of people's social engagement with colleagues, friends and strangers in the context of work and leisure. The three case studies are sufficiently diverse in their spatial, temporal and social functions – spanning both short- and long-term deployments, private and public settings, and medium to large usage capacity, and this allows us to observe recurring themes in terms of design and usage, and establish design propositions with regard to their physical and social embeddedness. This informs a wide-ranging discussion of the relevant issues in this context, related to the spatial, social and organisational properties of the cases presented and the day-to-day interaction that they support.

The remainder of this chapter will initially outline the three case studies, their motivation, design and brief summary of outcomes. Drawing on examples from the case studies, it will then focus on common design themes and challenges, more widely relevant for the deployment of MREs. These include the creation of interaction spaces, the role of asymmetries in the design of MREs and the key social interactions afforded. In remaining close to our case study material, we will not cover all possibilities but rather reflect on issues that we have observed in practice. The chapter will conclude with a reflection on the lessons learned.

4.2 Three Embedded Mixed Reality Environments

In what follows, we reflect on the design and study of three specific MREs that the authors themselves have been closely involved with. The MackRoom experience brought local and remote museum visitors together to co-visit an exhibition; mixed reality architecture (MRA) flexibly extends office environments to allow distributed team members to collaborate; Uncle Roy All Around You (URAAY) is a touring performance bringing together players online and on the street. The three case studies involved the development and deployment of diverse technologies such as sensors, hypermedia, 3D spaces and communication technologies to create complementary environments that permitted both synchronous and asynchronous interactions across physical and digital spaces. All three case studies were developed in fully working prototypes and systems that had the capacity to engage several users at any given time and were deployed and studied "in the wild", i.e. in physical and social settings appropriate to the activity at hand. They also aimed to fit in with those activities that are not primarily task-driven but happen in the realm of people's everyday social engagement with colleagues, friends and strangers in the context of work and leisure.

4.2.1 The MackRoom: Co-visiting an Exhibition from Different Physical Locations

The MackRoom MRE was designed for the *Mack Room* in The Lighthouse in Glasgow, UK, which exhibits some artefacts as well as extensive documentation about the artist and architect C. R. Mackintosh. The system aimed to support simultaneous visiting of the *Mack Room* by at least three participants. One of the participants was in the gallery and the other two were visiting remotely from separate locations. This approach was informed by current museological literature that indicates the importance of social context [13] in the visiting experience. The MackRoom MRE also aimed to explore the role of sociality in the visiting experience, especially in a situation where traditional social cues, such as talking and gestures were mediated through technology. Furthermore, it responded to the broader concerns for accessibility to collections and museum experiences for remote visitors, pertinent to the museum and heritage sector.

In the MackRoom MRE, the on-site participant carried a handheld device (iPaq, Hewlett Packard) that was location aware and displayed the ongoing positions of all three visitors on a map of the gallery (Fig. 4.1 (left)). The tracking of the device that was installed in the gallery was done through ultrasound technology [23]. The two off-site participants used two different environments: a hypermedia-only environment and a virtual environment (VE) combined with hypermedia. The hypermedia participant used a desktop with a standard web browser with an applet that displayed the gallery map (Fig. 4.1 (right)). All participants were represented on the gallery map by different colour icons and their locations were updated upon movement. The VE participant used a laptop that displayed a first-person 3D model of the *Mack Room* with avatars representing the other visitors (Fig. 4.2) in combination with hypermedia for the delivery of relevant information. All devices were connected via a wireless communications network that was installed in The Lighthouse and they were coordinated through Equator's shared tuple space infrastructure, EQUIP [19]. All participants shared an open audio channel and wore headphones and microphones.

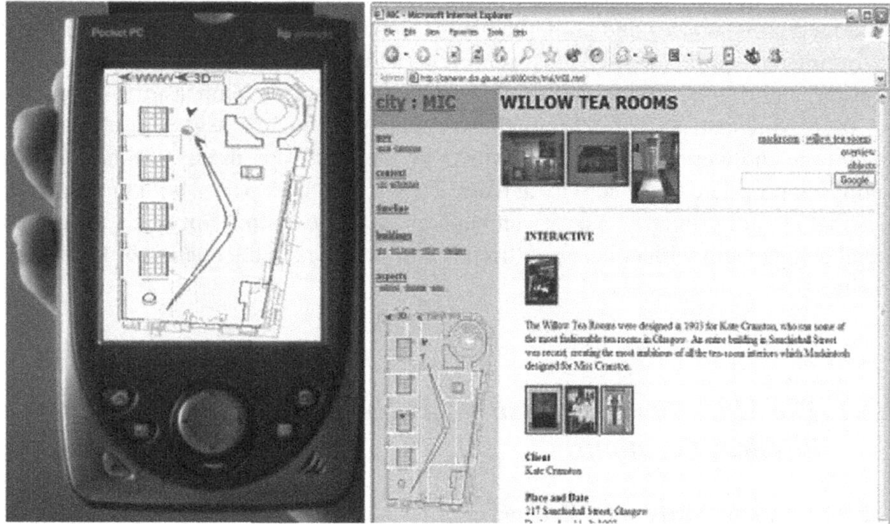

Fig. 4.1 The handheld device with the display of the floor plan (*left*) and the hypermedia environment with the floor plan and museum content (*right*)

While the handheld device presented only the dynamic map of the gallery, the system supported multimedia information for the off-site visitors in the form of web pages that were dynamically presented upon movement in the map or the VE. This information was similar but not identical to the information presented on labels and panels in the gallery, for example, the content of the touch screens was not available to the off-site visitors. The presentation of information schematically followed the spatial organisation of the exhibition so that all visitors were able to "look" at the same display when in the same "location". This was afforded by the segmentation of the gallery map and 3D model into information zones according to the thematic topics of the exhibition. In that respect, the system supported synchronous interaction around corresponding exhibition displays in the gallery and in digital form.

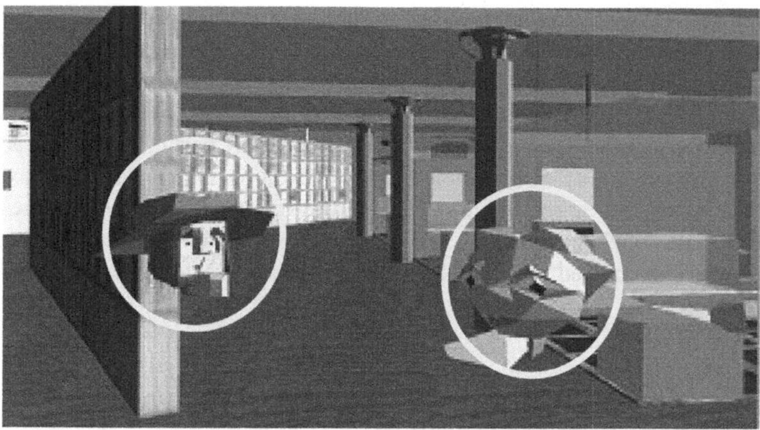

Fig. 4.2 The avatars of the hypermedia participant (*left*) and the local participant (*right*) as seen by the VE participant (both highlighted for clarity)

4.2.1.1 MackRoom in Use and Experience

The MackRoom MRE was implemented for a short period of time in The Lighthouse. Data regarding the co-visiting activity in the MRE were collected during informal pre-trial sessions, designed to fine-tune the system and study, as well as structured trial sessions. The user trials of the mixed reality environment took place in The Lighthouse in summer 2002. Nine groups of three and two groups of two (15 male and 16 female, age range 18–45 years) were recruited as friends and museum–goers through poster advertisements in both the university campus and the centre of Glasgow. The participants' knowledge of C. R. Mackintosh varied considerably, from experienced visitors who had visited the majority of the Mackintosh-related attractions in the city to complete novice viewers. Their technological experience also varied. However, all participants had used a computer before and they were familiar with web browsing.

Each visiting session lasted approximately 1 hour and was composed of an explorative part and an activity-based part, in which participants were given a mixture of open-ended and focused questions about Mackintosh's work and were asked to come up with answers based on evidence from the gallery or their personal experience of the exhibition. The activity of the local participant was video recorded; the discussions of the whole group were also recorded and all participants' movements were logged. Semi-structured debriefing interviews followed each visit, focusing on the participants' overall experience and on specific aspects such as navigation issues and engagement with the displays. As all sessions ran in regular opening times of the gallery, the participant in the gallery was constantly confronted with the local organisation of the environment and the ordinary visiting activity of the setting.

Overall, the MackRoom trials enabled rich interactions between individual visitors and the exhibition (a detailed account of the participants' experience can be found in [14]). Well-reported museum behaviours, such as reproducing the content of the labels for fellow visitors and managing ones' own pace according to the pace of the group, indicated that local and remote visitors had a shared social visit. However, different interactional resources within the environment, e.g. the map, had different effects on the experience [9]. Particularly, participants took advantage of the mixed reality information space to explore the displays and express personal opinions; conversely, asymmetries in the availability of spatial and gestural resources, on the one hand, challenged their navigation around the environment but, on the other hand, enabled some creative use of the space, as will be discussed later in this chapter.

4.2.2 Mixed Reality Architecture: Flexible Audio-Visual Connections Between Distributed Offices

Mixed reality architecture (MRA) was designed to extend standard office environments to flexibly and easily integrate remote spaces, with the aim to support interaction among distributed members of a team. This was achieved by linking multiple physical offices through the medium of a shared 3D virtual environment via embedded audio-visual connections into a large, persistent and distributed mixed reality environment. In each of the connected offices, MRA was displayed on a large screen (projected or LCD) connected to a standard PC, which also supported an echo-cancelled microphone and a set of stereo speakers, as shown in Fig. 4.3.

Fig. 4.3 An office installation (*left*) and the MRA on-screen view (*right*)

Using a standard joystick, users could freely position their office, "steering" it through the virtual world so as to align themselves with others with whom they wished to collaborate for a while. The distance within the virtual space determined how large the video appeared as well as the volume of the audio, spatially mediating the quality of communication, similar to physical space. To support social interaction, the boundaries of the interaction space were made explicit: the virtual offices represented the view of the virtual camera through their shape (see Fig. 4.3 (right)), the range of virtual audio was delineated (see circles on the floor in Fig. 4.3 (right)) and the view of the physical camera was mirrored in the interface so that participants could establish whether they were in view or not (see Fig. 4.4 (left) – "my video").

Fig. 4.4 Two offices close to each other (*left*) and the view across (*right*)

Once two or more offices were in range of each other (see Fig. 4.4), it was easy to walk up, see who was available and start to communicate with remote team members as if they were working in the same physical office. There was no requirement for meeting preparation, booking of software or meeting rooms. To ensure privacy, users could move their office away from others so that audio was not transmitted or they could close their virtual door to indicate that they were not available. Finally, they could also mute their microphone.

MRA's design reflects concerns from physical architecture, representing real offices with virtual offices that the inhabitants have a certain level of control over. By reconfiguring the virtual topology of the mixed reality office, environment inhabitants could encourage or discourage different types of social interaction. This could be further re-enforced by the afforded level of control over the "door" to the virtual office representation, which allowed the MRA node to appear as open, semi-open and unavailable. In addition, the physical placement and orientation of the MRA technology within active office environments responded to the individual concerns of office inhabitants, e.g. privacy and social interaction desired, and the ongoing activities and processes that were already present before deployment. In particular, the aim was to enable informal social interaction between dispersed groups of people in a fashion similar to the interaction taking place within the same building. MRA was deployed on standard PC hardware using the MASSIVE3 Collaborative Virtual Environment [15] to render the connecting virtual environment. Video and audio were streamed and rendered into this environment in real time and associated with the virtual position of the representation of the connected physical office.

4.2.2.1 MRA in Use and Experience

MRA has been used to support research collaborations within the EPSRC-funded EQUATOR project. This included installations at UCL as well as Nottingham, Salford and Bath universities, which were used over a period of more than 3 years. Within these organisations, a sub-group of researchers were the people who used MRA most. They were mostly from an IT background, while there were also architects and psychologists. This trial was extensively studied using a combination of data log analysis, diaries and interviews and an observational study drawing on video recordings of the system in use. In terms of the underlying concept, the support it provided for team work and the excitement MRA generated, the trials were very successful. Full evaluation details can be found in [30] and [31]. The following briefly reflects on those results that are relevant in the context of this chapter.

In contrast to conventional video and audio conferencing, MRA was always on, providing team awareness across sites and the opportunity for spontaneous as well as planned meetings. Its long-term deployment has then demonstrated how it became embedded in the physical architecture as well as with the ongoing work and social processes at the various organisations. Office workers could flexibly reconfigure their office environment by combining the privacy of a single office with the stimulation and professional contact associated with an open-plan office. MRA provided an integrated *awareness and communication environment* that supported spontaneous and planned meetings between individuals and groups of people over both short and long timescales. In this way, it enabled the trial partners to better support distributed teams, allowing people to socially and professionally interact.

4.2.3 Uncle Roy All Around You: A Mobile Mixed Reality Performance

Uncle Roy All Around You (URAAY) was a mixed reality experience that brought together mobile with online players. Mobile players undertook a journey through the streets of a real city, in search of an elusive character called Uncle Roy, while online players explored a parallel three-dimensional virtual city, both inhabiting a shared mixed reality environment. Online players followed the progress of individual mobile players, communicating and collaborating with them, and choosing to help or hinder them. The main objective of the experience was to question the anonymity of the digital world and a mobile player's trust in strangers, whether they be online players, the mysterious figure of Uncle Roy or people encountered by chance on the streets of the real city [2].

Mobile players purchased a ticket for the experience, which lasted for up to 1 hour. They handed over all of their personal possessions in exchange for a handheld computer, an act that was intended to increase their sense of isolation and disconnection from the everyday experience of the city. The handheld computer revealed a map of the surrounding area, with the mobile player's location indicated by an icon, as shown in Fig. 4.5 (right).

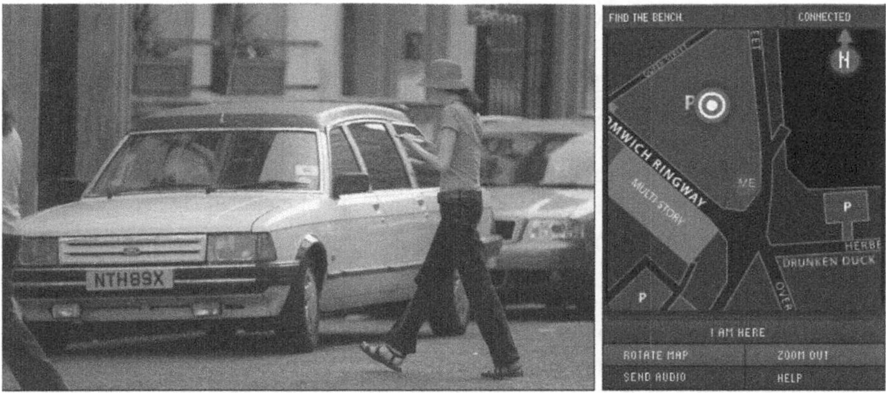

Fig. 4.5 A mobile player (*left*) and the mobile interface (*right*)

As the player moved through the city, they self-reported their changing location by dragging the icon on the map. Clicking a button marked "I am here" reported their location to Uncle Roy, the voice of the experience, which responded with a short text message indicating where to go next. Some were direct and useful, while others were misleading to the point of being mischievous, encouraging mobile players to follow diversions, drawing on the history of the local environment or even implicating passers-by in the experience. In this way the player moved through the city searching for Uncle Roy's office – a real office somewhere in the city.

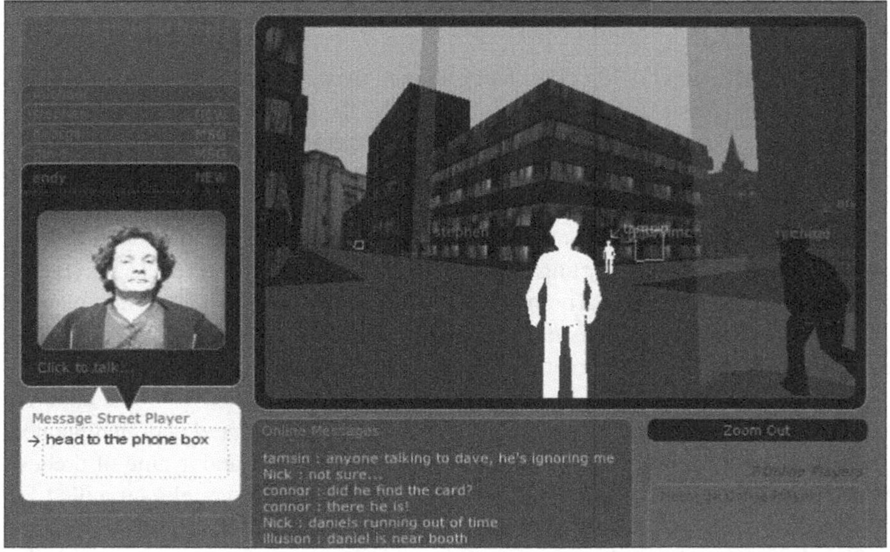

Fig. 4.6 Assisting a mobile player online

Online players, connected to the experience over the Internet, explored a parallel 3D model of the same city space, as shown in Fig. 4.6. They moved their avatar through the virtual city using the arrow keys, encountered other online players, and they could send them public text messages. Mirroring the mobile experience, they needed to find Uncle Roy's office door by searching through photo objects in the virtual city, each of which revealed a photograph of the real city. In this way, online players could gather useful information to aid mobile players.

The MRE was enabled by revealing the locations of mobile players in the virtual city as walking avatars and the locations of online players as icons on the handheld computers carried by mobile players. Two-way communication was established between the two populations with online players sending text messages to mobile players and in return listening to short audio messages recorded by mobile players. If a mobile player found the office within their allotted time of 50 minutes, they were rewarded with the final performative pay-off of the experience. Their handheld computer switched to a pre-scripted and timed series of instructions. They were asked to press a buzzer by the door, which opened to allow entry into Uncle Roy's deserted office. On the desk was a postcard with the question "when can you begin to trust a stranger?" and the mobile player was invited to fill in their answer to this question and to look into a nearby camera and picture a stranger in mind. Any online players who were in the vicinity were also invited into the virtual equivalent of the office, which revealed a live webcam view of the mobile player sitting in the real office. After leaving the office, mobile players were instructed to wait in a nearby phone box. The phone rang, and they were told to enter a waiting limousine. An actor climbed in behind them, and the limousine took participants back to the starting venue.

4.2.3.1 URAAY in Use and Experience

Uncle Roy All Around You has been shown in three cities to date, London, Manchester and West Bromwich, and the MRE – the trail of clues, the virtual city model and the physical office set – was tailored specifically for each venue. Each staging lasted for 10 days, typically being played for between 6 and 8 hours each day. Each mobile player's experience lasted for a maximum of 1 hour and up to 12 street players were active at any one time, with new players being added as current ones returned to the starting venue. Up to 20 online players were playing at any one time. Around 300 participants played in each of the host cities and players were "self-selecting" members of the general public. An analysis of the experience including an overview of the methodology can be found in [2].

While players had wide agency regarding how they interacted with one another, their progression through the experience was carefully monitored and manipulated throughout by a team of behind-the-scenes crew, performers and a suite of orchestration tools. On leaving the venue, mobile players were discretely surveilled by performers on the streets who could react to technical difficulties or the player getting lost in a manner that attempted to minimise loss of engagement with the experience. A control-room crew member manipulated the automated content of the experience in order to hasten or delay a player in reaching the office, if they were running out of time or there was a backlog of players, respectively. The orchestrators of Uncle Roy played an essential third role in the MRE; as a temporary installation, they had to reconfigure the experience for each new venue; as a performance, they needed to ensure that each player was steered through the experience in a timely manner whilst making the best use of limited resources.

4.3 Designing for Embeddedness

The case studies outlined above are very different in their nature. However, although they were deployed in different settings and developed for different purposes, all three were intended to be embedded in the architectural, social and organisational context of their settings. In this section we draw on their comparison to illustrate key themes for the design of embedded MREs. In particular, we discuss the relationship of MREs to their physical environment and how interactional space was created, the asymmetries in the design of the interface between physical and digital environments and the notable types of social interaction that emerged. To this end, we select appropriate material from one or more of the three case studies.

4.3.1 Creating Space for Interaction

While recognising the significant technological challenges that arise when embedding MR technologies in physical environments and the interactional challenges that concern the direct engagement with that same technology, in what follows we argue that it is critical to understand the locating of MREs in terms of what type of interaction space is desired and appropriate. Arguably, in creating space for interaction, designers of MREs face the dilemma of using technology to support seamless transitions and interfaces, as expressed in Weiser's vision of disappearing computing [34] or, in contrast, to support "proactive people", by enabling participants "to engage more actively in what they currently do" [25]. This section, however, does not intend to reiterate the debate about seamless and seamful design explored in [10] and [11]; instead, similar to [26], it seeks to identify how the observable presence or absence of seams in the interaction space of MREs might affect their embeddedness. Thus, we highlight the set-up of the physical interaction space, its availability to users and its extent.

4.3.1.1 Setting Up the Physical Interaction Space

In MREs, either existing or purpose-built digital infrastructures are used in the physical setting to enable the activity at hand as well as the interaction between participants. The three case studies suggest that the means through which interaction spaces are set up shape the interaction and its availability to diverse participants, in relation to the combination of physical embeddedness and access to the MREs.

In the MackRoom and URAAY MREs, the "technology" used was either carefully concealed in the fabric of the physical space or already in place. For example, the sensor system in MackRoom was deliberately placed out of sight on the ceiling of the room to not disturb the existing gallery setting. Likewise, URAAY relied on the public mobile phone network to connect participants, but also inconspicuously positioned important elements of the interaction space, e.g. the limousine, in the physical environment. In this respect, the physical interaction space of these MREs was seamlessly blended into the environments they occupied. At the same time, access for in-gallery and on-the-street participants to these MREs required explicit actions and customised technologies, which were dedicated to the specific activities only. In both MackRoom and URAAY, mobile devices enabled with the appropriate software were used to facilitate the participation of the users in the activity. Furthermore, the activities themselves were available only at specific times for people who had been either recruited or self-selected through buying a ticket. We argue that conversely to the (relatively) seamless nature of the technologies that enabled the interaction space in these MREs, the movement between the MR spaces and the physical spaces in which they were embedded was clearly defined.

In contrast, the MRA interface was very much visible. This was the result of the quasi-permanent installation of large MRA interfaces (screen, camera, microphone, speakers) in fixed locations. The location and orientation of MRA interfaces was carefully chosen to fit with the existing office layouts and the work practices of the offices' inhabitants. Rather than being hidden or dedicated to specific uses, the MRA interfaces were clearly visible and publicly accessible to anyone with a right to be present in the particular office environment. In this way, the MRA interface installation itself can be described as seamful. However, as no dedicated interface technology had to be appropriated when coming in contact with MRA, activity and conduct moved relatively seamlessly in and out of the designated interaction space.

4.3.1.2 Extent of Physical Interaction Space

The interplay between observable and "hidden" seams in the design of the MREs was particularly prominent in the definition of the extent of the interaction space. Above, we have briefly established that the set-up of interaction spaces inevitably creates boundaries between it and those spaces where interaction cannot take place, i.e. in all three case studies, specific spaces and interactions were considered to occur outside the interaction space. When looking at the detail though, these boundaries were established variously through a combination of technological features and the design of each of the experiences.

In MackRoom and in MRA, the boundaries of the MREs were determined by the technology used, such as the sensors and the audio-visual equipment, respectively. In both cases, this boundary was absolute, in the sense that interaction truly outside the technological interaction space could not be covered, but it was also very fuzzy as we discuss below. In the MackRoom, the implementation of the tracking technology and the architectural elements of the physical space allowed for various degrees of tracking coverage in the exhibition space; in particular, specific areas of the gallery were not covered by sensors, as no visiting activity was expected to take place there. In addition, the lack of signposting of the tracking system boundaries, the pseudo-dynamic nature of those due to the lighting and crowd conditions in the gallery, and the persistent, open audio channel introduced ambiguities. This was perceived both as intriguing and as disruptive in the explorative and the activity-based parts of the visit, respectively (further discussed in [10]).

The boundaries of the interaction space were also fuzzy in MRA. Overall, the MRA topology comprised one shared virtual space, which allowed for its spatially dynamic nature, and a number of physical spaces. For all practical purposes it reached into those physical spaces only in a narrowly defined way: as far and wide as the camera could see, the screen could be seen and the audio could be transmitted to and from. This meant that although it did connect remote physical spaces, only a small part of each connected physical space became the actual interaction space around its interface technology. The technical properties, e.g. field of view of the camera and reach of speakers and microphone, as well as their exact location and orientation then determined the extent and shape of the MRA interaction space, and enabled certain unexpected uses of the MRE, as we will discuss in the forthcoming sections.

For URAAY, technology was not the determining factor for the extent of the interaction space. As communication and interaction among participants relied on mobile technology, no public spaces in the city were off-limits, assuming uniform cover of the mobile phone network. The design, however, of the experience defined the boundaries of the MRE. Similar to the MackRoom and the MRA, this was informed by the architectural elements of the physical environment. For each city that it was staged in, decisions were made about what possible routes participants might take between the various fixed physical points of the experience, and the area was conceptually bounded based on this information. However, this space had no hard boundaries of any kind. Additionally, the ambiguity of the boundaries aided the aim of the experience, i.e. to explore issues of trust and surveillance. In this context, participants could easily leave the designated area but were prompted to remain within to be able to perceive URAAY as intended and within the given time frame of 1 hour. Consequently, the perceived rules of the game rather than the technical and contextual features of the MRE defined the extent of the interaction space.

4.3.2 Asymmetries in the Interface Between Digital and Physical Environments

The interaction space is further constructed through the mapping between physical and digital environments as well as the mapping of available interactional resources. Understanding the role of symmetries and asymmetries in the interface of MREs, especially when the physical environments involved may be as dynamic and changing as a cityscape, is paramount in the design of such environments. This section builds on previous work, which suggested that designed asymmetries may enhance the user experience [10], see also [17]; it further identifies the kind of asymmetries that might be meaningful in MREs that support informal activities. In the three case studies, interactions across physical and digital environments were enabled through both symmetrical and asymmetrical points of reference in the representation of users in the MRE, the spatial elements of the environments and the available content.

4.3.2.1 User Representations

With regard to user representations, MRA aimed at designing symmetrical communication conditions among the connected environments, afforded primarily by an audio-visual stream. Specifically, each physical office connected via MRA was represented with a virtual office as shown in Fig. 4.3. This virtual office projected the live audio-visual stream into the shared 3D environment. Beyond their appearance, the virtual offices were all identical and were designed to provide for reciprocity of awareness [18]. This refers to the fact that inhabitants should be able to see another physical space only if inhabitants of that space were able to see them in return. The form of the virtual MRA nodes, which was shaped to follow the *field of view* of the virtual camera, made this possible. This prevented "visual spying", but on a more positive note it also allowed inhabitants to align their MRA node to be in view of others, as this was usually intended and necessary for social interaction [17].

On the other hand, both the MackRoom and the URAAY MREs presented users with specific asymmetries in terms of their communication and awareness of each other. In MackRoom, all visitors had symmetrical access to each other's audio but asymmetrical awareness of each other's location; the mobile and hypermedia participants had a map view of all users' locations but the VE participant was able to see only the avatars in his/her proximity. Similarly, in most of the parts of the URAAY experience, online players had an awareness of the location of both fellow online and mobile players, whereas mobile players were aware of online players only through other communication channels, such as text messaging. Although in the MackRoom the fragmented reciprocity of awareness led to an overreliance on the audio channel, in URAAY the carefully orchestrated nature of communicative asymmetries carried the subversive nature of the game and enhanced the users' experience. However, in the instances when communicative and awareness-related asymmetries were unexpected due to technology limitations, e.g. unreliable mobile network coverage or delays in the location tracking system, further effort was required by the participants to address the arising confusion, also reported in [33].

4.3.2.2 Spatial Mapping

Particularly challenging for the participants were the spatial asymmetries in the different environments in the three MREs. The examination of the three case studies suggests that symmetry in the representation of the different spatial elements of large-scale MREs is often limited because of the architectural and organisational characteristics of the physical environments and the limitations of the available technologies. For example, in URAAY and in MackRoom, some spatial asymmetries arose due to the movement of gallery furniture between trials. In MRA, spatial asymmetries arose simply through the fact that the connected offices had very different shapes; one space was L shaped with virtually all occupants sitting outside camera view.

Furthermore, the MRA cameras were placed on the screen surface itself facing into the space, leaving substantial parts of the offices unseen by the camera. Unlike within the virtual environment of MRA, this could lead to communication problems when people attempted to interact without being visible to others. Similarly, in MackRoom, the orientation, navigation and alignment of members of the group towards specific displays often utilised spatial features as landmarks, the inconsistent presentation of which led regularly to breakdowns in communication. These asymmetries, however, also allowed some creative and unintended playful uses of the respective MREs; these included a popular prank to be played, when inhabitants took their MRA node to others, deliberately remaining outside camera view, to startle the remote colleagues, and a race inside the *Mack Room*. The latter was instigated by the hypermedia user and required from the on-site user to negotiate the size, height and volume of display cases, which could not be accurately represented on the two-dimensional map.

4.3.2.3 Content Mapping

The creativity of the participants was often fostered by asymmetries in the representation of content in two of the MREs discussed here, MackRoom and URAAY. Both MREs included pre-authored content as part of the experience; in addition, URAAY also supported the creation of content on the fly by participants and performers alike. The pre-authored content in these experiences was designed to be asymmetric across the different environments. In the case of the MackRoom, this reflected the different media and interfaces used in the MRE, with the gallery participant having access to the information displayed in the physical space and the hypermedia and the VE participant accessing the corresponding hypermedia content as well as the Web. In URAAY, the content available to mobile and online players was deliberately asymmetric in terms of its references, sequence and information value. Regardless of their nature and origin, however, content-related asymmetries often proved to stimulate conversation, support individual engagement and exploration alongside group interaction and, according to MackRoom participants, were to some extent anticipated as a means of addressing the perceived imbalance between access to “real” objects and information.

4.3.3 Social Interaction in Embedded Mixed Reality Environment

The different variations in designing the interaction space and the mapping of content, spatial features and participants’ representations in MREs may be further understood through looking at the social interaction and the participants’ encounters within these environments. In what follows, we concentrate on two particular aspects of the interaction observed. Firstly, we discuss the various roles that participants took on during their use of the MRE and the varying degree of influence they had on events. Secondly, we relate behaviours observed in MREs to the social rules and norms associated with the activities and the environments in which MREs were situated. These aspects of conduct are particularly relevant in relation to the aim of the three case studies in supporting informal activities and our discussion on embeddedness.

4.3.3.1 Role Taking

According to our observations, different participants took on different roles when engaging with the three case studies. This can be traced back to two main reasons: the different levels of access provided through different interface technologies and the level of familiarity that participants developed over the course of the deployment.

Within URAAY and MackRoom, different participants had very different levels of access to the MRE. For example, in URAAY, the handheld computer displayed the shared interaction space on a map and participants physically moved through this environment at walking pace. On the contrary, online players had access to a 3D representation; consequently, they could move more freely and gain an overview more quickly, ahead of the player on the street who they were paired up with. This frequently led them to take a leading role over the course of the event. Different participants then used this in different ways, sometimes to be generally helpful to the on-the-street player and other times to be more mischievous, trying to get their paired participant off-course. The interfaces in MackRoom were similar; while the gallery visitor in MackRoom engaged with the exhibits, the hypermedia and VE visitors had access to representations of those only and this via two totally different technological interfaces. However, all three shared the same audio channel; this allowed for the more knowledgeable or enthusiastic participant in the group to take the lead in the visit, as is often the case with co-located visits.

In contrast to the above, people using MRA had access to the same interface technology in principle. Importantly though, MRA was deployed long term in contrast to the other two MREs that were event-based, both lasting for around an hour. For this reason, the office occupants in contact with MRA had the opportunity to engage with the technology over a longer period of time. Our observations then showed how there were two broad types of users who were differentiated by their access to and control over MRA: inhabitants and visitors. Inhabitants were the people who had regular access to an MRA node; usually their main workspace was part of an MRA node itself. Their experience with MRA had often evolved through at least a number of months of exposure and in response to their own interest in using it. Visitors generally had much less direct experience with MRA and had little control over its configuration, as their main office space was located elsewhere in physical space. Their use of MRA became opportunistic and was mostly organised around the pre-existing topological structure as set by the inhabitants. The observations then showed how inhabitants of MRA took control over and ownership of the

MRA topology, actively re-configuring it according to their needs. This had a direct impact on the possible encounters within MRA, between and among the different groups of people using the environment. Consequently, all interaction, and integration of the MRA in people's activities, was fundamentally shaped by the actual real access to the MRA interface.

4.3.3.2 Social Rules and Norms

Regardless of the roles participants may assume, a unique implication of MREs that are deployed in physical environments to enable existing or new collaborative activities is the alignment of the activities happening within the MRE with the norms of the places they are embedded in (see also [16]). Locales such as an exhibition, an office and a city are often associated with behaviours that are shaped by the organisations and the people that inhabit them. For example, one such norm for an exhibition space is the use of discrete voice in conversations. These norms may be unspoken but also signposted.

Participants in the three MREs were aware of the norms of their respective settings and often followed them. This was particularly clear in MRA, in which the configurations of the participants' offices across the shared mediating virtual environment followed accepted norms and rules prevalent in the connected organisations. For example, remaining in someone's audio range for any length of time was not acceptable to inhabitants, similar to the way that it is not acceptable to linger by someone's office door and listen in. The configurations were also the result of the particular preferences of the inhabitants present. When colleagues knew each other well, they would often remain within audio range, being able to generally hear what was going on without being able to pick out any details.

On the other hand, in MackRoom and URAAY, participants were regularly observed to diverge from usual public behaviours or operate on the margins of the social norms of specific places. In MackRoom MRE, this was expressed through regular unexpected gesticulation, particularly greeting gestures addressed to the otherwise "invisible" online participants. In both MREs, participants would also change direction unexpectedly, demonstrate curious behaviour, such as following people on the street, and engage with spaces and objects in an uninhibited manner, such as running in the gallery. Although those behaviours were not considered as problematic or troubling in the course of the activities, they brought to the fore the fact that MREs themselves and their participants may also be subject to intrinsic norms that may or may not be compatible with the environments they reside in.

Our observations during the three case studies suggested that participants in the MREs and the activities those enabled were caught in the tension of handling multiple accountabilities which may well conflict with each other – also reported with reference to mobile phone use in public [21], namely to attend the rules of social conduct traditionally expected in the specific environment and to present oneself as a responsive friend, player or colleague. Those accountabilities were derived from the settings of the activity, the specific activity and the users' relationship with their fellow participants. Although it would be difficult to decipher the balance of the accountabilities, for instance, in MRA and MackRoom, participants appeared keener to respond to their friends and colleagues, whereas in URAAY, they responded more readily to the design of the game; designing for a safe but meaningful negotiation and resolution of participants' accountabilities is paramount in achieving embeddedness.

4.4 Reflection

Through our focus on three diverse MREs, deployed in a gallery, an office environment and an urban setting, we have highlighted a series of significant topics that are relevant to understanding the embedded nature of these environments. In particular, previous sections discussed the construction and extent of the interaction space, with emphasis on the physical environment; the design symmetries and asymmetries in the mapping of content, space and participants' representation; and the conduct of participants with regard to their roles in the MRE and the relationship between emerging behaviours and the existing norms of the environments they are situated in. While the issues raised are not expansive, they are directly derived from practice; and they should be valuable to anyone developing and deploying MREs that are designed to support informal activities and social engagement in the context of work and leisure, in the way that our three case studies did.

In this regard, we would be keen to reiterate Crabtree and Rodden's [11] assertion that designing for "hybrid ecologies", i.e. environments that span and merge diverse digital and physical interfaces, will require further long-term study. This involves the understanding of the balance between the technological, organisational, and social context of activities, enabled by any given MRE. The comparison of the three case studies, however, gave us the opportunity to identify reoccurring conditions that challenge the embeddedness of MREs; specifically, the tension between assumed and actual seamlessness in the design, the access to and ownership of appropriate interactional resources and the emergence of conflicting accountabilities.

Negotiating assumed and actual seamlessness in the design of MREs: The discussion of the three case studies shows that in the creation of a mixed reality interaction space, technological choices and implementations can be understood only within the context of the physical environment that the MRE is embedded in and the context of the activity that a particular MRE is aimed to enable. Arguably, aspects of seamless and seamful design may be seen to be complementary in combining technological infrastructure with architectural elements and organisational patterns of the physical and digital environments [10, 11]. However, the assumed seamlessness (or seamfulness) of the resulting MRE has a significant impact on the experience of the users. As discussed in the previous sections (see also [33]), when the technological infrastructure and communication channels dedicated to the main activity of the MRE were designed to physically and interactionally blend into the setting, participants assumed overall seamlessness in the interaction. If there were then breakdowns in the information and communication flow, this would disrupt the experience. Conversely, very conspicuously placed technology became embedded over time and then allowed for smooth engagement and disengagement with a particular activity – this effect can also be seen in [29]. In contrast, the discrepancy between assumed and actual seamlessness was less challenging in users' appreciation of the extent of the interaction space. Participants in the deployed MREs understood those boundaries through emerging practice over the longer term; furthermore, the ambiguity of the boundaries was also used to engender exploratory and playful behaviours. This aspect may be a powerful design tool in MREs that aim to enable such behaviours in the context of learning, play and leisure.

Access to and ownership of interactional resources: The three case studies made clear that asymmetries in the access to the MREs and in the representation of people, space and content are inherent in the design of distributed MREs due to the diverse nature of the physical and digital media used in the ensemble. The balance between the symmetrical and the asymmetrical availability of these interactional resources needs to be handled with sensitivity to the particular activity at hand. For example, the deployment of particular interface technologies plays an important part, where the differences in access to shared content can provide one group of participants with an elevated sense of control at the expense of his/her co-participants. A developer might then set out to ensure that interface technologies are exactly the same to ensure equal access. It is important, however, to understand that the negative effects of asymmetries in MREs may not necessarily relate to a lack of specific resources but of appropriate resources, and combinations of, for the achievement of communicative actions; this is also supported by findings reported in [5] with regard to asymmetries between wearable and traditional collaborative interfaces. Furthermore, the social organisation around an interface can still yet lead to differences in engagement. Concentrating on aspects of embedded MREs, it is evident in the three case studies that when the interaction space is set up in a space or delivered though media owned by particular users, those participants will naturally take more control over its use.

Negotiating conflicting accountabilities: Our final point highlights the interrelation between the social rules and norms of the setting that an MRE is situated in and the behaviours enabled by it. It is, therefore, particularly relevant to the organisational embeddedness of an MRE. As discussed in previous sections, the creation of MREs within existing environments appeared to facilitate the co-existence of overlaid social contexts in the course of a single activity, which also led to overlaid conflicting accountabilities with regard to user's actions within a setting. In the three case studies, the handling of the tension that arose from conflicting accountabilities was subject to the participants' judgement and appreciation of the situation based on local resources, such as the relationship with fellow participants, the rules of the game, the presence of others, and so forth. Additionally, social accountability, i.e. response to the norms associated with the event or the experience, rather than the norms of the specific setting appeared to be higher in the priorities of the participants in the two leisure-related MREs (also supported by [33] and [26]). This suggests that in the design of embedded MREs, attention is required on how their deployment may alter the rules of engagement in a specific setting and what effect this might have on participants and nonparticipants alike. For instance, continuous breaching of a rule or a norm might render them redundant or force an "organisation", it being a museum, an office occupant or a street officer, to take action for their reinforcement.

4.5 Conclusions

Our focus in this chapter has been the discussion of three example Mixed Reality Environments and how specific design decisions enabled or hindered their technological, spatial, social and organisational embeddedness. The structure of the discussion and the emphasis on selected topics and challenges emanates from the specific MREs, which aimed to support informal interactions among friends, colleagues and strangers in the context of work and leisure. The comparison of the three case studies suggested that the variation of degrees of embeddedness in the physical environment, the activity at hand and the social and organisational context may result in significantly different MREs. As ubiquitous, pervasive and MR technologies become deployed more widely and over longer periods of time, it will be important to consider how they can meaningfully interact. This will have to consider interoperability between those environments but more importantly the careful consideration of how MREs can become embedded not just in physical settings but also within the digital worlds that we increasingly make use of and their technical, social and organisational norms.

Acknowledgments We thank the EPSRC for their support of the case studies through the EQUATOR IRC [GR-N-15986]. This research is also supported by the Leverhulme Trust.

References

1. Azuma R T (1999) The Challenge of Making Augmented Reality Work Outdoors. In: Ohta Y, Tamura H (eds.) Mixed Reality: Merging Real and Virtual Worlds. Springer, New York.
2. Benford S, Flintham M, Drozd A, Anastasi R, Rowland D, Tandavanitj N, Adams M, Row-Farr J, Oldroyd A, Sutton J (2004) Uncle Roy All Around You: Implicating the City in a Location-based Performance. In Proceedings of: ACE 2004, Singapore, ACM Press
3. Billinghurst M, Baldis S, Miller E, Weghorst S (1997) Shared Space: Collaborative Information Spaces. In Proceedings of: HCI International, San Francisco, USA, 7–10
4. Billinghurst M, Kato H (1999) Collaborative Mixed Reality. In Proceedings of: International Symposium on Mixed Reality, Yokohama, Japan, 261–284
5. Billinghurst M, Kato H, Bee S, Bowskill J (1999) Asymmetries in collaborative wearable interfaces. In Proceedings of: 3rd International Symposium on Wearable Computers, San Francisco, USA, IEEE, 134–140
6. Bornik A, Beichel R, Kruijff E, Reitinger B, Schmalstieg D (2006) A Hybrid User Interface for Manipulation of Volumetric Medical Data. In Proceedings of: IEEE Symposium on 3D User Interfaces, 29–36
7. Bowers J, O'Brien J, Pycock J (1996) Practically Accomplishing Immersion: Cooperation in and for Virtual Environments. In Proceedings of: CSCW, Boston, USA, ACM Press, 380–389

8. Bowers J, Rodden T (1993) Exploding the Interface: Experiences of a CSCW Network. In Proceedings of: Interchi, Amsterdam, The Netherlands, ACM Press, 255–262
9. Brown B, MacColl I, Chalmers M, Galani A, Randell C, Steed A (2003) Lessons From the Lighthouse: Collaboration in a Shared Mixed Reality System. In Proceedings of: CHI Ft. Lauderdale, USA, ACM Press, 577–584
10. Chalmers M, Galani A (2004) Seamful Interweaving: Heterogeneity in the Theory and Design of Interactive Systems. In Proceedings of: DIS, Cambridge, USA, ACM Press, 243–252
11. Crabtree A, Rodden T (2008) Hybrid Ecologies: Understanding Cooperative Interaction in Emerging Physical–Digital Environments. Personal and Ubiquitous Computing 12:481–493.
12. Drummond T, Julier S (2008) 7th IEEE and ACM International Symposium on Mixed and Augmented Reality – ISMAR 2008. Vol. 2008. ACM Press, Cambridge, UK Conference web site for ISMAR 2008
13. Falk J H, Dierking L D (1992) The Museum Experience. Whalesback Books, Washington, DC.
14. Galani A, Chalmers M (2007) Blurring Boundaries for Museum Visitors. In: Marty P F, Jones K B (eds.) Museum Informatics. Routledge, New York.
15. Greenhalgh C, Purbrick J, Snowdon D (2000) Inside MASSIVE-3: Flexible Support for Data Consistency and World Structuring. In Proceedings of: CVE, San Francisco, USA, ACM Press, 119–127
16. Harper R H R, Hughes J A (1993) "What a F-ing System! Send 'em all to the same place and then expect us to stop 'em hitting": Making technology work in air traffic control. In: Button G (ed.) Technology in Working Order: Studies of Work, Interaction, and Technology. Routledge, London
17. Heath C, Luff P (1992) Media Space and Communicative Asymmetries: Preliminary Observations of Video-Mediated Interaction. Human Computer Interaction 7:315–346.
18. Koleva B, Schnädelbach H, Benford S, Greenhalgh C (2001) Experiencing a Presentation through a Mixed Reality Boundary. In Proceedings of: Group, Boulder, USA, ACM Press, 71–80
19. MacColl I, Millard D, Randell C, Steed A (2002) Shared visiting in EQUATOR City. In Proceedings of: CVE, Bonn, Germany, ACM Press, 88–94
20. Milgram P, Kishino F (1994) A Taxonomy of Mixed Reality Visual Displays. IEICE Transactions on Information Systems E77:1321–1329.
21. Murtagh G M (2002) Seeing the "Rules": Preliminary Observations of Action, Interaction and Mobile Phone Use. In: Brown B, Green N, Harper R H R (eds.) Wireless World: Social and Interactional Aspects of the Mobile Age. Springer, London
22. Nigay L, Coutrix C (2006) Mixed Reality: A Model of Mixed Interaction. In Proceedings of: AVI, Venezia, Italy, ACM Press, 43–50
23. Randell C, Muller H (2001) Low Cost Indoor Positioning System. In Proceedings of: UbiComp, Atlanta, USA, Springer, 42–48
24. Rodden T (2000–2007) EQUATOR Project. Vol. 2008, Nottingham, UK
25. Rogers Y (2006) Moving on from Weiser's Vision of Calm Computing: Engaging UbiComp Experiences. In Proceedings of: UbiComp, Orange County, USA, Springer, 404–421
26. Rudström Å, Höök K, Svensson M (2005) Social positioning: Designing the Seams between Social, Physical and Digital Space. In Proceedings of: Online Communities and Social Computing at HCII, Las Vegas, USA, Lawrence Erlbaum Associates,
27. Schmalstieg D, Fuhrmann A, Szalavari G H Z, Encarnacao L M, Gervautz M, Purgathofer W (2002) The Studierstube Augmented Reality Project. Presence: Teleoperators and Virtual Environments 11:33–45.
28. Schmalstieg D, Kaufmann H (2003) Mathematics And Geometry Education With Collaborative Augmented Reality. Computers & Graphics 27:339–345
29. Schnädelbach H, Koleva B, Twidale M, Benford S (2004) The Iterative Design Process of a Location-Aware Device for Group Use. In Proceedings of: UbiComp, Nottingham, UK, Springer, 329–346

30. Schnädelbach H, Penn A, Steadman P (2007) Mixed Reality Architecture: A Dynamic Architectural Topology. In Proceedings of: Space Syntax Symposium, Istanbul, Turkey, Technical University Istanbul, 10601–10614
31. Schnädelbach H, Penn A, Steadman P, Benford S, Koleva B, Rodden T (2006) Moving Office: Inhabiting a Dynamic Building. In Proceedings of: CSCW, Banff, Canada, ACM Press, 313–322
32. Seichter H, Looser J, Billinghurst M (2008) ComposAR: An intuitive tool for authoring AR applications. In Proceedings of: ISMAR, Cambridge, UK, IEEE, 177–178
33. Vogiazou Y, Raijmakers B, Geelhoed E, Reid J, Eisenstadt M (2007) Design for emergence: experiments with a mixed reality urban playground game. Personal and Ubiquitous Computing 11:45–58
34. Weiser M (1991) The Computer for the Twenty-First Century. Scientific American 265: 94–104.

Chapter 5
The Semantic Environment: Heuristics for a Cross-Context Human–Information Interaction Model

Andrea Resmini and Luca Rosati

Abstract This chapter introduces a multidisciplinary holistic approach for the general design of successful bridge experiences as a cross-context human–information interaction model. Nowadays it is common to interact through a number of different domains in order to communicate successfully, complete a task, or elicit a desired response: Users visit a reseller's web site to find a specific item, book it, then drive to the closest store to complete their purchase. As such, one of the crucial challenges user experience design will face in the near future is how to structure and provide bridge experiences seamlessly spanning multiple communication channels or media formats for a specific purpose.

Keywords Bridge experience · Human–information interaction · Information architecture · Information seeking · Findability · Internet of Things · Retail design · Ubiquitous computing

5.1 Introduction

> And indeed, for Aldrovandi and his contemporaries, it was all legenda – things to be read. For Aldrovandi was meticulously contemplating a Nature that was, from top to bottom, written. (Foucault [13])

In recent years phenomena like ubiquitous computing [56], the rise of an Internet of Things [54], and issues related to information overload [57, 16] have clearly demonstrated that a proper organization of information is becoming integral not only to computer desktops, libraries, or web sites but to the physical environment as well [33].

A. Resmini (✉)
University of Bologna, Via Carboni 2, 43100 Parma, Italy
e-mail: root@resmini.net

E. Dubois et al. (eds.), *The Engineering of Mixed Reality Systems*, Human-Computer Interaction Series, DOI 10.1007/978-1-84882-733-2_5,

Digital information is bleeding out of cyberspace and back into the real world: Internet access moves into cell phones and hand-held devices; social networks go mobile and constantly connect physically separated users; common daily objects become network enabled; shopping increasingly relies on web sites, brick-and-mortar stores, and related user-generated content in the form of reviews, comments, and personally selected links as common-use tools in a single strategy.

As a consequence, human–information interaction across different environments is increasingly becoming a common day-to-day experience. Communicating successfully; completing a task; eliciting a desired physical, mental, or emotional response: All of these tasks often require users to move back and forth across a variety of environments, interfaces, information architectures, and interaction models.

Boundaries are blurring: Twitter is a micro-blogging application which lets user broadcast 140-character-long messages to and from the Web using a number of different devices. Is twittering friends from a cell phone about one's dinner plans interacting with the digital or the physical?

5.2 A Holistic Framework

Currently, we have no common cognitive frame of reference for the design of seamless interaction across different environments, and often across different experiences inside the same environment. The Web and the store are treated like discreet blocks, and this creates a heavy personal, cultural, and social burden [10]. User experience design can relieve this by providing, structuring, and sustaining bridge experiences: Coherent experiences capable of spanning multiple communication channels, document genres, or media formats for a specific, tactical purpose [17].

This contribution outlines a holistic framework for the general design of successful bridge experiences as a cross-context human–information interaction model for the design of cognitive and informational continuity between digital and physical spaces. We maintain this framework which improves user experience by allowing users to rely on well-known, coherent behavioral, and cognitive patterns and by encouraging their repeated application across environments and across different layers of abstraction [23].

Bridge experiences rely on a synchronic model involving the user, space, and time [50]. To this extent, the model identifies and describes four different ground heuristics which act on the key aspects of the relationship. These are *Resilience*, *Place*, *Choice*, and *Correlation*.

- *Resilience* is defined as the capability of a human–information interaction model to shape and adapt itself to specific users, needs, targets, and seeking strategies.
- *Place* is defined as the capability to help users reduce disorientation and increase legibility and way-finding in digital, physical, and mixed reality spaces.

- *Choice* is defined as the capability to reduce the stress and frustration associated with choosing from an ever-growing set of information sources, services, and goods.
- *Correlation* is defined as the capability to suggest relevant connections between pieces of information, services, and goods to help users achieve explicit goals or stimulate latent needs.

To illustrate how the model works, we will briefly introduce our view on the current shift in design; we will describe in detail the four information architecture principles and heuristics that constitute the framework; we will show how these can be merged within a unified approach; and, finally, we will outline a prototype design scenario for a semantically enhanced retail store, where different contexts like web site, paper catalogs, and brick-and-mortar spaces serve different goals and interfaces but share a common and unique information architecture and strategy to provide seamless user experience and improved interaction.

Within the scope of this contribution, the terms *context*, *domain*, and *environment* will be used interchangeably to describe the place where human–information interaction takes place; the term *semantic layer* or *information layer* will be used to refer to all information in context, provided to users by means of digital technology, signage, or any combination of these. Similarly, the definition of *semantic supermarket* is used for the information-enhanced shopping place where the presence of a semantic information layer is made available to and exploitable by consumers. Although this work is the result of a collaborative effort, Andrea Resmini wrote Sections 5.5, 5.6, 5.7, 5.8, and 5.9; Luca Rosati wrote Sections 5.1, 5.2, 5.3 and 5.4, and 5.5.2.

5.3 From Information Retrieval to Human–Information Interaction

Information architecture (IA) is an emerging discipline and community of practice focused on bringing principles of library science, design, and architecture to information space [46]. Originally considered tightly connected to the World Wide Web, it is now seen as a boundary field whose contributions are crucial where complexity, unfamiliarity, and information overload stand in the way of the user [33, 34]. We consider this evolution of information architecture a strategic part of the general shift from the design of objects to the design of processes [44, 50]. Contemporary culture shows similar convergence patterns [20].

In the history of design, the two separated concepts of information retrieval and interface are the product of a time when computers were limited, slow, and barely able to interact with humans. They were significant when all interaction was in absolute propositions and conveyed through a stand-alone computer screen: This is no longer the case in a world where fast, connected micro-computers are everywhere. Not surprisingly, since the late 1990s the focus has been shifting continually from retrieval and interfaces to interactions and user experience [4, 10, 47].

While interfaces are bound to a specific single artifact, interaction models can span a whole process involving a varying number of artifacts. A very good example is the way Apple designed a common experience throughout the iPod/iTunes line of products and are now actively bringing it to their stores [39]. Since the process itself is a continuum, designing the interaction model globally allows to build global, constant interaction patterns: Users are not forced to learn or relearn diverging behaviors even if individual interfaces differ. This is why in the design of bridge experiences interface design is not enough: Human–information interaction issues have to be addressed throughout the whole process, incorporating the apparent quirks of human behavior into information-seeking strategies [30].

This marks a shift from the traditional view of multichannel strategies [14] as well, as the focus gets moved from optimized, data-driven information flows to stable human–information interaction models [43].

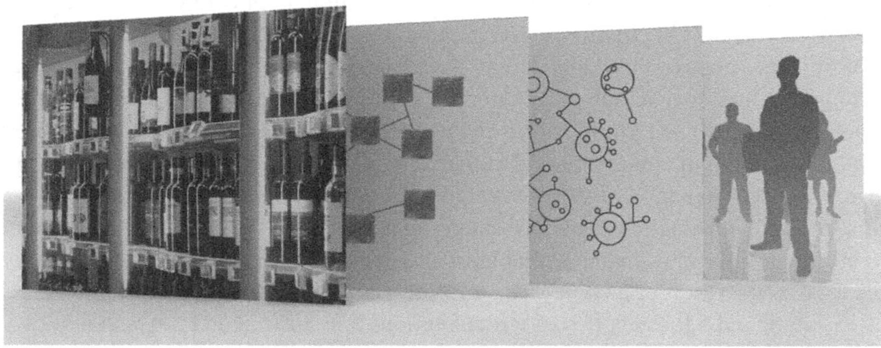

Fig. 5.1 A physical–digital environment where our interactions with items and information are tracked and saved to provide an improved user experience. A digital layer (*middle*) records the interaction between the users (*right*) and the context (*left*). Image: A. Falcinelli

5.4 Resilience

> I've often imagined gazes
> surviving the act of seeing
> as if they were poles,
> measured distances, lances
> in battle.
> Then I think of a room
> just abandoned
> where similar traces remain
> for a time, suspended and intersecting
> in the balance of their design
> intact and overlapping, like
> pick-up-sticks. (Magrelli [28])

Our goals deeply influence our strategies when searching. Furthermore, cognitive, cultural, and social models have a strong impact on behavior: As a result, different individuals browse and search differently because they follow different goals and possess different models [3], and they might modify their patterns according to context, time, and goals.

To work effectively then, an information space has to be able to adapt to changing information-seeking strategies [43]. Through the years, different techniques, strategies, and technologies have been devised to solve or alleviate this issue in specific domains and increase their findability: Faceted classification, ontologies, the Semantic Web, folksonomies, and social classification. We think that these approaches cannot be used as is in the cross-context design though, as they are fundamentally asynchronous in a world becoming synchronic. A synchronic world weaves stories through space and time, and every single noteworthy item generates a story and a very large number of paths, which can be investigated, tracked, and interpreted. These stories and paths do not form a dusty ink and paper archive, but a vast data pool which can be manipulated in real time [50].

Being able to use it to its full extent is a fundamental opportunity and the real challenge awaiting design: By observing and tracking the user's paths and choices inside the digital/physical environment, a system can adapt to their different navigational models (that is, the physical layout of information, goods, and shelves can be tuned and used to provide the correct pieces of information) even in real time, and then leave these patterns available for social or personal reuse (Fig. 5.1). By exploiting these data we can apply to physical spaces the hypertext logic and social contexts which are currently peculiar to the Web (Fig. 5.2).

5.4.1 Scenario: The Resilient Supermarket

If Resilience in digital spaces is the capability of an information system such as a web site to adapt and sustain different information-seeking strategies, when it is applied to the physical context of the supermarket it is immediately apparent that most of its outcome still remains information related and information based.

In this supermarket consumers use cell phones, hand-held devices, or a dedicated reader to access the local information layer. This layer can comprise specialized in-place information channels, as well as the official web site and any number of independent sources. Through this, they can

– refind and retrace tasks and paths, including shopping tasks;
– personalize their tasks and paths;
– optimize their navigation, flow, and time spent shopping;
– create ad hoc paths around aisles, sales, and information; and
– receive suggestions and be informed of possible correlations among items.

The environment is now synchronic: It has not changed much in terms of general layout or appearance, but it is aware of actions, space, and time.

Concretely, one of the possible strategies to acquire and build Resilience is to capitalize on the flows and behavior of customers moving around, browsing, choosing, and choosing not to choose by correlating these data. This is for example what has been done with the EU SHAPE Living Exhibition Project [9]: Participants were able to leave traces that were later used to potentially influence other people's experience of the exhibit [8]. Similarly, by preserving the history of customer interactions with the supermarket, a resilient layer can be offered to customers possessing an appropriate device capable of both registering their shopping patterns and returning them as structured, contextualized, social knowledge.

Resilience is not limited to be experienced through an augmented reality layer, though. The supermarket can easily supplement this approach by empirically applying guidelines originally written for the design of web sites [45] to the physical design of aisles and shelves to reinforce flexibility and adaptivity (Fig. 5.2). Sample correspondences are briefly sketched out in Table 5.1.

Table 5.1 Web site–retail space correspondences map

Web site	Supermarket
Main navigation	Departments and aisles
Site map	Interactive map of the supermarket
Alphabetic order	Alphabetic display of products with their physical location
Shortcuts	Preferred paths for returning users; discounted shopping; healthy shopping; special regimes shopping
What is new	Sales and promotions
Local or special navigation	Theme paths: Pasta; Italian wines; Thai cuisine, etc.

In this scheme, every space and function is identified with a unique chromatic, alphanumeric code:

- icons or geometrical shapes for departments;
- letters for aisles;
- numbers for racks or parts of racks, so that every product can be identified by its letter + number combination code;
- colors for shortcuts and navigational themes, using either rack, shelf, ceiling, or floor signage or any combination of these (Figs. 5.3 and 5.4).

Sales, promotions, and themed navigation are displayed in the main hall as well, so that all options are immediately visible and available and users can simultaneously satisfy different cognitive models and personal search strategies. This favors the passive gathering of information and products (push) as well, in accordance with the *principle of Least Effort* [29] recalled by Bates [3].[1]

[1] Although the "Principle of Least Effort" was first discussed by Zipf in his seminal book *Human Behaviour and the Principle of Least Effort: An Introduction to Human Ecology*, Mann was the first to describe it in relationship with the information sciences.

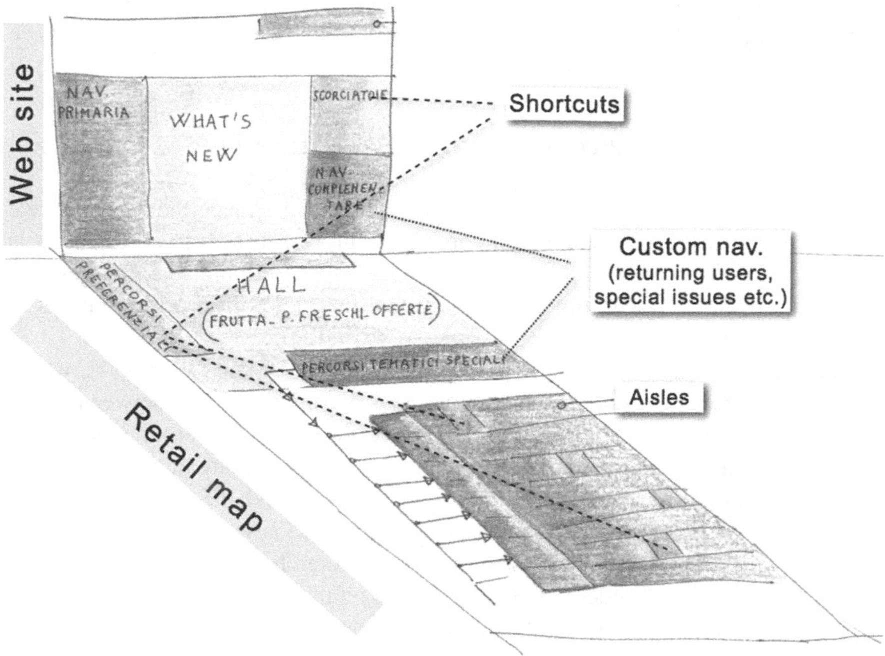

Fig. 5.2 Comparison map of interactions in a web site and in a supermarket

5.5 Place

> "Here is Ts'ui Pên's labyrinth," he said, indicating a tall lacquered desk. [...] "A labyrinth of symbols," he corrected. "An invisible labyrinth of time [...]" (Borges [5]).

> The most important thing to know about Spimes is that they are precisely located in space and time. They have histories. They are recorded, tracked, inventoried, and always associated with a story. Spimes have identities, they are protagonists of a documented process. (Sterling [50]).

Space and place are different: Space is the base experience of our embodiment [37], and it is objective, impersonal, and undifferentiated. Place, on the other hand, involves a particular kind of presence that includes, besides physical space, memories, experiences, and behavioral patterns associated with the locale [8]: It is personal, subjective, and communitarian. In a way, space exists independently of man, while place cannot: And a sense of place is essential to our well-being as men and women [51].

Although semantic space, digital space, or the Web do not map precisely or exhaustively to a single physical representation of space [12], they can be places, and they need to be places if they want to provide satisfying experiences. "People goes where people is" [36]: As our interactions become often mediated by technology and devoid of physical presence, we tend to lose the ability to bond with people, places, workplaces. As a side effect, the value of place has been reinforced and a new longing for community has been aroused. We see that these fuel a thousand successful social networks, and they are successful precisely because they have become places [55].

5.5.1 Hansel and Gretel or Getting Lost in the Woods

Space plays a special role in the way human beings experience the world, as we exist primarily in space: It should not come as a surprise that abstract reasoning is shaped by underlying spatial patterns. This is the case with language, for example [21], and it is the case with time. The traditional fairy tale offers a little insight in this relationship.

Tales of spatial discomfort such as the story of Hansel and Gretel [11], where children are purposely lost in the woods, express a primary tension between place, the house, the small community, and space, the indistinct dangerous void of the forest. Having no place in the world means being lost and risking one's life.

With communities becoming larger, cities boomed and the woods were cut, tamed, and made into tilled fields. Technology provided new means for the objective measuring of time to a new class of time-savvy merchants [25], and discomfort moved. In the story of Cinderella, it is being late on midnight that loses the protagonist, as she effectively runs out of time as the hours pass. Having no place in the world means being out of time.

In these stories and in common perception though, time is still experienced as eminently spatial and linear: Hypertext is neither [42]. Nonetheless, experimental research has shown that space is again the primary and most successful cognitive metaphor used in dealing with digital space [49], and way-finding and spatial knowledge [52] are strategic tools for navigation and place-making in information space as well [35]. But since visual cues are even more important in information space as the constant dynamic evaluation of being on the right track available in physical space is lacking [26, 32], way-finding and spatial knowledge have to be supplemented by berry-picking and information scent.

5.5.2 Berry-Picking

Berry-picking is an information-seeking strategy that is used when performing active and directed information search [2]. Berry-picking differs from classical information retrieval models in that it postulates an evolutionary flow and the use of different seeking strategies at the same time, as the user constantly adjusts and changes ***his strategy as new information is gained or new goals emerge (Table 5.2).

Berry-picking is an eminently empirical and cross-contextual theory, maintaining that similitude, metaphor, and metonymy act as the core mechanisms which enable successful, adjustable information-seeking strategies, and that information-seeking strategies apply to both physical and digital environments without any significant differences [3].

Table 5.2 Comparison of berry-picking strategies in primary and digital sources

Berry-picking strategies	In primary sources (paper, etc.)	In electronic documents
Footnote chasing (or backward chaining)	People follow up footnotes found in books and articles of interest, and therefore move backward in successive leaps through reference lists	People follow up the contextual links inside the main text of a page or the related links near it
Citation searching (or forward chaining)	One begins with a citation, finds out who cites it by looking it up in a citation index, and thus leaps forward	It is useful to be able to both browse through the complete list of citations and jump to each resource in detail
Journal run	As one identifies a central journal in an area, he then locates the run of volumes of the journal and searches straight through relevant volume years	While browsing an electronic journal, accessing by date, subject, author, metadata is important, as it is the possibility to access index and abstracts for each issue
Area scanning	People browse the materials that are physically collocated with/near to materials located earlier in a search	A numerical notation is of the utmost importance because of the correspondence notation–class–shelf
Subject search (in bibliographies, abstracting and indexing services)	Once the subject under which a work is classified is found, other works in the same area are added to the search/browse set	Navigating an electronic catalog using subjects (classes and subclasses) is often not considered and an underestimated feature
Author search	Author names are used as landmarks, as searchers use them to check if any given author has done further work on the same topic	This feature is valuable if connected to the inherent hyperlinking qualities of electronic texts and related to all relevant metadata (author, abstract, etc.)

It seems interesting to point out that book browsing is not an innate human attribute, but rather a learned, skilled, and a recent one as well [3, 7].

5.5.3 Information Scent

The evolutionary search model of berry-picking highlights the importance of providing users with contextual cues. Since the goals change and there is no straight-forward path from start to end, users might get lost in the woods. Information scent, a part of the larger theory of *information foraging* [38], suggests that a common pattern of evolutionary biology is to reuse features adapted for one purpose for a second different purpose when the environment puts different demands on the species. This is called *exaptation* [3].

Information scent maintains that users base their searches on contextual indicators pertaining to the local information space to evaluate the usefulness of a resource or path, in a way human beings and animals are used to when foraging. These indicators provide the information scent: The stronger, so to speak, the better, as it probably suggests the availability of larger quantities of food. In the act of browsing, human beings apply a general propensity to sample and select which has been evolving through millions of years to information space. Foraging behavior might have simply exapted to browsing and other information-seeking behaviors [3].

5.5.4 Scenario: Sense of Place in the Supermarket

> Cyberspace is not a place you go to but rather a layer tightly integrated into the world around us. (Institute For The Future [19]).

What does favoring berry-picking and information scent in a store actually mean?

Even if undoubtedly logistics and marketing have provided copious literature on the subject of organizing consumer way-finding in supermarkets, their stance is ultimately directed toward improving cross-selling and up-selling metrics. Considering Place implies orienting spaces and goods layouts to favor exploratory behaviors along different seamless paths to favor the user experience. This opens up the consumer to serendipity [53], effectively exporting to the physical world one of the most remarkable and significant features of digital spaces and the Web (Fig. 5.2).

In the supermarket, berry-picking is enhanced by favoring it through appropriate techniques such as extending the items listed in Table 5.2 to compare against the store itself (Table 5.3) and providing this additional information to consumers through its semantic layer, either as digital content or proper coloring, labeling, and signage (Figs. 5.3, 5.4, 5.5 and 5.6). It is important to note that these are possible search keys to be implemented at the process level (e.g., the supermarket environment) and not at the object level (e.g., the single product: This does not simply concern better box labels).

Table 5.3 Berry-picking techniques applied to a supermarket

Berry-picking in documents	Berry-picking in the supermarket
Footnote chasing and citation searching	Search/access for ingredients, recipes, coupling
Journal run	Products of the same line
Area scanning	Area/shelf scanning
Subject search	Theme paths
Author search	Products belonging the same brand

Fig. 5.3 Luca is a returning user and the supermarket recognizes him. His phone, PDA, or dedicated reader shows him his home-compiled or web-compiled shopping list. Image: A. Falcinelli

Fig. 5.4 A map, path, or coordinate system guides him to the different shelves. Image: A. Falcinelli

Fig. 5.5 By reading, scanning, or taking a picture of an item, Luca can receive detailed information about it on his device. Image: A. Falcinelli

Fig. 5.6 When choosing an item, Luca receives suggestions concerning related products, current sales, other users' preferences, or his past favorites. Image: A. Falcinelli

These heuristics improve the information scent as well: If finding the shelves themselves is decidedly easier in the physical world, as opposed to what happens on the Web, for instance, actual navigation is hindered by a longer list of personal and environmental constraints, including actual motion from one place to the other or the time at hand, and favoring exploratory behaviors is more difficult. *Resilience* and *Place* allow consumers to have a more complete cognitive map of the supermarket, effectively improving their navigation (see Section 5.6 below as well).

Information scent in the supermarket is also reinforced by means of invitations: When consumers have found the products they are looking for, Correlation (see Section 5.7) is used to suggest other possible choices, Amazon style: "if you like x maybe you would like y as well," or "people buying product x also bought product y" (Figs. 5.5 and 5.6).

5.6 Choice

> "I want a pair of jeans–32-28," I said. "Do you want them slim fit, easy fit, relaxed fit, baggy, or extra-baggy?" she replied. "Do you want them stonewashed, acidwashed, or distressed? [. . .]" I was stunned. A moment or two later I sputtered out something like "I just want regular jeans [. . .]" (Schwarz [48]).

The berry-picking and information scent theories postulate the importance of offering users multiple cues and paths along the way. Current economic theories suggest that under the influence of electronic commerce, markets are moving toward a long tail model: Strong differentiation and personalization, attention to an increasing number of niches, selling few items to many instead of many items to few [1].

In economics, it is maintained that the set of available alternatives or choices has to take into account the costs of economic agents as well as the preferences of the consumers. This may lead to offering more alternatives not always being better for economic agents than offering fewer alternatives. Search costs may induce consumers not to search and not to choose when too many alternatives are offered, as they mean too many evaluations to reach a satisfactory answer [22]. Even when a choice is made, an ever-growing number of possibilities can generate a stressful experience: This is what is known as the *paradox of choice* [48].

We have a conflict: Berry-picking and a long tail economy suggest that users need more information; information overload and the paradox of choice suggest more information is actually less information. Information overload is not (only) an issue of quantity, but rather an issue of quality, as it directly relates to how information is organized, visualized, and finally made accessible: Considerations on place and time, or context are paramount. Ergonomics and Hick's law [24, 31, 41] offer some help.

5.6.1 Hick's Law

Hick's law provides the mathematical model which explains the paradox of choice and suggests some countermeasures as well. Given n equally probable choices, the average reaction time required to choose among them is approximately proportional to the logarithm to base 2 of the number of choices, plus 1. That is,

$$\text{Time} = a + b\ \log_2 (n + 1), \tag{5.1}$$

where a and b depend on context conditions, such as presentation and the user's degree of familiarity with the subject. For example, if choices are poorly presented, both a and b increase, while familiarity only decreases b.

What's worth noticing is that the correlation between reaction time and possible choices is expressed logarithmically, that is, it is non-linear. Every time we choose, we do not consider every available option (linear time), but rather we cluster options in categories, dismissing progressively a part of them (roughly half of the options every time). For a and b constant, if the number of options grows, so does reaction time. Vice versa, given an equal number of choices, a and b influence reaction time.

This is why necessary caution has to be used for instance when applying Hick's law to items in a menu: If a list is unordered, or ordered meaninglessly from the user's point of view, no clustering takes place and the user will probably browse through each item every time. That means that reaction time becomes linear and the formula loses any utility. An ordered list (for example, alphabetically ordered lists such as those in a vocabulary or phone directory) on the other hand allow for such scanning: The user goes to the pertinent letter (e.g., M) and starts reading only the relevant subset (e.g., all words whose name begins with M). This time the law applies and reaction time is non-linear. Hence, choosing once from a significantly ordered eight-item menu is quicker than choosing twice from two four-item menus: Wide structures (less levels) are to be preferred over deep structures (more levels).[2] Furthermore, Hick's law clearly shows that reaction time depends not only on the number of choices but also on the way these choices are presented to users.

5.6.2 Reducing the Load: Organize and Cluster, Focus, and Magnify

Hence, an *organize and cluster* principle could be applied to counter the information and cognitive load brought on by overloaded choices, in two different directions: By listing menu items using meaningful, self-evident rules, so that users can cluster items, according to Hick's law; or by clustering and organizing in levels, since a

[2]Mathematically, with a menu of eight items the law returns: $a + b \log_2 8 = a + 3b$, as $\log_2 8 = 3$. While with two menus each of four items, the law returns: $a + b \log_2 4 = 2a + 4b$, as $\log_2 4 = 2$. For an exhaustive review of Hick's law, see [24].

wide structure offers no advantage over a deep structure when Hick's law does not apply.

Another possible strategy relies on contextualization and customization. This is what the long tail model prescribes: It is not simply about having fewer choices, as fewer choices as well could lead to dismissal and failed searches [22], but about showing choices at the right moment in the right way, where right means appropriate, in context [1]. Amazon's flexible suggestions interface is a good example of this behavior (who bought x also bought y, if you are interested in z you might be also interested in w). This strategy successfully relies on the natural human attitude to sample and select [3] offered by berry-picking: We could describe this procedure as *focus and magnify* – first you focus a niche, an item, and then you magnify and look for similar items around it (Figs. 5.5 and 5.6).

The results are analogous to those obtained with clustering: Choices are made easier and simplified using logical separations.

5.6.3 Scenario: Choice in the Supermarket

The supermarket clusters products and goods.

Everything is initially organized for simplicity: Complexity is available when needed, as establishing a feeling of simplicity in design requires making complexity available in some explicit form [27]. Shelves and aisles work as solution clusters for large task-driven sections such as grocery, kitchenware, or frozen products, but they stream down to complimentary paths leading to specific needs such as sale products, national products, and organic products. This helps to reduce any initial spatial discomfort and sense of disorientation consumers might experience in physical space.

The supermarket focuses and magnifies products and goods as well using aisle and shelf labeling, coloring, and layout. Consumers are supported in their personal goals and not enticed into compulsive shopping behaviors, as these are no longer required to push sales. Findability and serendipity are supported and favored as well, and they are consumer specific. The shopping experience improves and this in turn improves brand perception and goodwill, taking away the sense of frustration and waste of time and money that compulsion on one side and long searches on the other carry along with them [18].

Clustering and magnifying are digitally enhanced by appropriate information architectures, for example using a faceted classification scheme which allows any related products belonging to the same facet (in place, in time, and in context) to be pushed to consumer devices.

5.7 Correlation

You read the Bible? There's a passage I got memorized. Ezekiel 25:17 [...] I been sayin' that shit for years. And if you ever heard it, it meant your ass. (Tarantino, Pulp Fiction)

Quentin Tarantino's movie Pulp Fiction is a very good example of non-linear storytelling. The narrative moves in circles and the beginning and the end of the movie are tied together in what resembles a Moebius strip pattern, with chronologically contiguous events moved away from one another and then reconnected with a twist and some minimal, subtle changes [44].

The world depicted accepts a description of space/time radically different from the one Cinderella lost her shoe in: There is no linearity, but rather circularity, and the story moves freely back and forth in both time and space. Because of its intrinsic fragmentation, the movie can also be considered a tightly integrated series of interconnected episodes: Citations of other movies are plenty, and everything seems to be linked.

Pulp Fiction applies the new model of correlations and semantic ties of hyperlinking to traditional moviemaking and storytelling: Elements belonging to the same or to different physical and digital collections (movies and pop culture, in this case) are connected in one single whole, enriching the narrative with supplementary layers (Fig. 5.1).

5.7.1 Scenario: Correlation in the Supermarket

> Implicit recommendations are relationships formed by social behavior – the traces of many people acting with objects. (Marchionini [30])

In the supermarket all items are correlated, either by agents or by consumers.

Using their cell phones, hand-held devices, or dedicated readers, consumers receive personalized information concerning theme paths, coupling paths (if you bought *a* we suggest *b* and *c* that you can find on shelf *x*), recommended or best-selling products, products on sale.

Since the supermarket is a Place, they receive integrated maps, and GPS-like itineraries as well, highlighting items of interest and correlated products.

Consumers are an integral part of the human–information interaction process; they also have access to a wide array of social, collaborative content shared by the community of people buying in the supermarket. Some consumers have re-cataloged part of the available products using faceted classification, some others provide top tens, reviews, and link to external informational sources on recipes or health-related matters, some others have tagged most of the cereals and bakery products according to their vitamin content. These additional layers are all available and connected to the larger pervasive information layer: Products acquire histories, annotations, and links that strongly affect their finding and use.

Correlations are freely added by all users of the system, allowing opportunities to discover new kind of features and to relate products and opinions in novel ways which allow for more productive, synchronic clustering [30].

5.8 The Semantic Supermarket

In the semantic supermarket, products are classified by using a mixed classification scheme which uses traditional top-down classification, faceted classification, and free-form social classification accordingly. In a niche or specialized retail store selling a more homogeneous range of products, it might be possible to use just one single general faceted scheme, since a pre-requisite for the applicability of faceted classification is that the items to be classified share similar characteristics [15, 40]. Facets allow for easy correlation and favor berry-picking. In the semantic supermarket, this means experimenting with product layouts, for example by having rack sections for *Meals, Times of the day,* or *Kitchen, Bathroom* and *Bedroom,* or *Regional recipes*.

In the semantic supermarket the general layout might even move away from the common linear, sequential layout where a number of straight racks are placed back to back, for example to a radial structure where a core, a main hall, acts as the entry

Table 5.4 Continuity between digital and physical environments

		Web site	Retail shop
	General classification model	Taxonomy implemented as navigation and navigation aids	Taxonomy implemented as department, shelves, and goods layout. Study of paths
Findability 1	Controlled vocabularies	Thesauri, metadata	Product index (with links, variants, and synonyms), RFID or SIM enabled
	Direct search	Search engine using vocabularies	Interactive displays, PDAs, help desks
Findability 2	Shortcuts	Quick links, social navigation, personalization (history, wish list)	Color-coded paths, integration with the web site
	Information circularity	Contextual navigation	Related products highlighted via displays, data transmission to PDAs, etc.
	Navigational aids	Location markers	Color and alphanumerical codes used to map spaces
Home	Home	Homepage	Main hall, start and finish zone, gathering zone

and exit point and is used as a multi-purpose landmark [18]. It is the main physical way-finding hub, so it is easily accessible from every entrance and from every area. This is *home*, and it acts as a one-stop shop which allows fast navigation toward all departments, racks and shelves, cashiers, check-out points: It accommodates all starting points for signage, those marking personalized navigation and those for theme paths, discount sales, maps, interactive indexes, accessible displays, and help desks.

A final correspondence scheme is detailed in Table 5.4.

In the semantic supermarket aisles become lighter artifacts. Showcasing and physically acquiring products, especially for certain kinds of goods, might become two separate activities. The shelves themselves might just as easily be simple displays, with no more than a few items available for direct evaluation: Samples, whose code customers can read into their devices to acquire all necessary information. Later, after they have been confirmed, the real items could be checked out from a larger warehouse area closer to the parking lots [18].

5.9 Conclusions: Toward a Cross-Context Human–Information Interaction Model

> For instance, take the two words “fuming” and “furious.” Make up your mind that you will say both words, but leave it unsettled which you will first. Now open your mouth and speak. If your thoughts incline ever so little towards “fuming,” you will say “fuming-furious”; if they turn, by even a hair’s breadth, towards “furious,” you will say “furious-fuming”; but if you have the rarest of gifts, a perfectly balanced mind, you will say “frumious” (Carroll [6])

Each of the heuristics we described so far is a Lego brick we used to build a complete unified human–information interaction model, and as with Lego bricks the resulting construction might look like nothing similar to the initial disordered pile of single pieces.

We described how these heuristics help solve the general problem of too many diverging interaction models, information overload, and sense of unbelonging, and we applied them to a hypothetical supermarket bridge-experience scenario.

Resilience and *Place* (Sections 5.4 and 5.5) help structure an adaptive and spatially meaningful experience of digital or physical environments. *Choice* strategies (Section 5.6) help reduce the paradox of choice and the costs related to information overload. These three heuristics simplify our experience by taking away the unnecessary or the overly complicated, and provide grounding. *Correlation* (Section 5.7) enriches the user experience by enabling semantic linking through otherwise unrelated items. This final heuristic enriches the user experience by providing more meaningful information and supporting a berry-picking exploration of goods and services – making a fluid upstream/downstream choosing process possible.

Together, these create a human–information interaction continuity between different channels, media, and environments that lays down the foundations for an improved cross-context user experience.

References

1. Anderson C (2006) The long tail: Why the future of business is selling less of more. Hyperion, New York.
2. Bates M (1989) The design of browsing and berrypicking techniques for the online search interface. Online Rev 13:407–424. Also at http://www.gseis.ucla.edu/faculty/bates/berrypicking.html. Accessed 5 January 2008.
3. Bates M (2002) Toward an integrated model of information seeking and searching. Keynote Address, 4th International Conference on Information Needs, Seeking and Use in Different Contexts. http://www.gseis.ucla.edu/faculty/bates/articles/ info_SeekSearch-i-030329.html. Accessed 5 January 2009.
4. Bonsiepe G (1995) Dall'oggetto all'interfaccia: Mutazioni del design (From object to interface: Design mutations). Feltrinelli, Milan.
5. Borges JL (1999) The garden of forking paths. In: Borges: Collected fictions. Penguin, New York.
6. Carroll L (2008) The hunting of the snark. Project Gutemberg. http://www.gutenberg.org/ebooks/13. Accessed 5 January 2009.
7. Casson L (2002) Libraries in the ancient world. Yale University Press, New Haven.
8. Ciolfi L (2004) Understanding spaces as places: Extending interaction design paradigms. Cogn Tech Works 6:37–40.
9. Ciolfi L, Bannon L (2002) Designing interactive museum exhibits: Enhancing visitor curiosity through augmented artifacts. In: Bagnara S et al. (eds) 11th European conference on cognitive ergonomics (ECCE 11).
10. Cooper A (1999) The inmates are running the asylum: Why high tech products drive us crazy and how to restore the sanity. Sams, Indianapolis.
11. Coulton GG (1989) The Medieval Village. Dover Books, New York.
12. Dillon A, Richardson J, McKnight C (1993) Space – the final chapter or why physical representations are not semantic intentions. dLIST. http://dlist.sir.arizona.edu/1184/. Accessed 5 January 2009.
13. Foucault M (1970) The order of things: An archaeology of the human sciences. Routledge, London.
14. Gardner J (2006) Multichannel strategy – two differing views. BankerVision. http://bankervision.typepad.com/bankervision/2006/03/multichannel_in.html. Accessed 5 January 2009.
15. Gnoli C, Marino V, Rosati L (2006) Organizzare la conoscenza: Dalle biblioteche all'architettura dell'informazione per il web (Organising knowledge: From libraries to information architecture for the web). Tecniche Nuove, Milan.
16. Gouveia L (2004) Information overload: The case for e-learning within Gaia Global. http://www.inter-disciplinary.net/ati/education/ioe/ioe3/Gouveia paper.pdf. Accessed 5 January 2009.
17. Grossmann J (2006) Designing for bridge experiences. UX Matters. http://www.uxmatters.com/MT/archives/000105.php. Accessed 5 January 2009.
18. Institute for the Future (2000). The future of retail: Revitalizing bricks-and-mortar stores. Institute for the Future Corporate Associates Program SR-689. http://www.iftf.org/library. Accessed 30 October 2007.
19. Institute for the Future (2008) Blended reality: Reports from the digital/physical future. IFTF. http://www.iftf.org/node/2365. Accessed 5 January 2009.
20. Jenkins H (2006) Convergence culture: Where old and new media collide. New York University Press, New York.
21. Johnson M (1987) The body in the mind: The bodily basis of meaning, imagination, and reason. University of Chicago Press, Chicago.
22. Kuksov D, Villas-Boas JM (2007) When more alternatives lead to less choice. Washington University, St. Louis and University of California, Berkeley. http://www.haas.berkeley.edu/˜market/PAPERS/VILLAS/Alternatives9-25-07.pdf. Accessed 5 January 2009.

23. Lakoff G, Johnson M (1980) Metaphors we live by. University of Chicago Press, Chicago.
24. Landauer TK, Nachbar DW (1985) Selection from alphabetic and numeric menu trees using a touch screen: Breadth, depth, and width. SIGCHI Conference on Human Factors in Computing Systems. http://doi.acm.org/10.1145/317456.317470. Accessed 22 January 2009.
25. Le Goff J (1982) Time, work, and culture in the Middle Ages. University of Chicago Press, Chicago.
26. Lynch K (1960) The image of the city. The MIT Press, Cambridge.
27. Maeda J (2006) The laws of simplicity. The MIT Press, Cambridge.
28. Magrelli V (1991) Nearsights. Graywolf Press, Saint Paul. Also at http://italy. poetryinternationalweb.org. Accessed 5 January 2009.
29. Mann T (1987) A Guide to library research methods. Oxford University Press, New York.
30. Marchionini G (2004) From information retrieval to information interaction. Keynote Address, 26th Annual European Conference on Information Retrieval. http://ils.unc.edu/~march/ECIR.pdf. Accessed 5 January 2009.
31. Menini S (2003) Architettura dell'informazione e struttura dei menu gerarchici (Information architecture and hierarchical menus structure). LucaRosati. http://lucarosati.it /blog/architettura_dellinformazione_e_struttura_dei_menu_gerarchici. Accessed 5 January 2009.
32. Morgenroth L (2004) An intimate geography: Boston neighbourhoods. In: Hiestand E, Zellman A (eds) The Good City. Beacon Press, Bostan.
33. Morville P (2005) Ambient findability. O'Reilly, Sebastopol.
34. Morville P (2006) Information architecture 3.0. Semantic Studios. http://semanticstudios. com/publications/semantics/000149.php. Accessed 5 January 2009.
35. Munro A, Hook K, Benyon D (1999) Social navigation of information space. Springer, London.
36. Nalhan G, Finch E (2004) Place attachment and sense of belonging. Facil 122:120–127.
37. Norberg-Schulz C (1974) Existence, space and architecture. Prager, New York.
38. Pirolli P (2007) Information foraging theory: Adaptive interaction with information. Oxford University Press, New York.
39. Potente D, Salvini E (2008) Apple, Ikea and their integrated information architecture. Europe's 4th Information Architecture Summit. http://www.euroia.org/Programme.aspx. Accessed 5 January 2009.
40. Quintarelli E, Resmini A, Rosati L (2008) The FaceTag engine: A semantic collaborative tagging tool. In: Zambelli M, Janowiak A, Neuckermans H (eds) Browsing architecture: Metadata and beyond. IRB, Stuttgart. Also at http://www.mace-project.eu/files/MACE_complete_book.pdf. Accessed 5 January 2009.
41. Raskin J (2000) The human interface: New directions for designing interactive systems. Addison-Wesley, New York.
42. Resmini A (2007) Appendix. In: Rosati L (2006).
43. Resmini A, Rosati L (2008) Semantic retail: Towards a cross-context information architecture. Knowl Organ 35, 1:5–15.
44. Rosati L (2006) Architettura dell'informazione: Trovabilltà dagli oggetti quotidiani al Web (Information architecture: From everyday things to the web). Apogeo, Milan.
45. Rosenfeld L (2004) Information architecture heuristics. Bloug. http://louisrosenfeld.com / home/bloug_archive/000286.html. Accessed 5 January 2009.
46. Rosenfeld L, Morville P (2006) Information architecture for the world wide web: Designing large-scale web sites. O'Reilly, Sebastopol.
47. Saffo P (1999) Premise. In Cooper (1999)
48. Schwartz B (2004) The paradox of choice: Why more is less. HarperCollins, New York.
49. Stahl E (2005) Is hypertext a book or space? The impact of different introductory metaphors on hypertext construction. Comput Educ 44:115–133.
50. Sterling B (2005) Shaping things. The MIT Press, Cambridge.
51. Tuan Y (1990) Topophilia. Columbia University Press, New York.

52. Tversky B (1991) Spatial mental models. Psychol Learn Motiv 27:109–145.
53. Van Andel P (1994) Anatomy of the unsought finding: Serendipity: Origin, history, domains, traditions, appearances, patterns and programmability. Br J Philos Sci 45:631–648.
54. Van Kranenberg R (2008) The internet of things: A critique of ambient technology and the all-seeing network of RFID. Institute of Network Cultures, Amsterdam.
55. Weinberger D (2007) Everything is miscellaneous: The power of the new digital disorder. Times Books, New York.
56. Weiser M (1996) Ubiquitous computing. Ubic. http://www.ubiq.com/hypertext/weiser/UbiHome.html. Accessed 5 January 2009.
57. Wurman RS (2000) Information anxiety. Que, Indianapolis.

Chapter 6
Tangible Interaction in Mixed Reality Systems

Nadine Couture, Guillaume Rivière, and Patrick Reuter

Abstract In this chapter, we discuss the design of tangible interaction techniques for mixed reality environments. We begin by recalling some conceptual models of tangible interaction. Then, we propose an engineering-oriented software/hardware co-design process, based on our experience in developing tangible user interfaces. We present three different tangible user interfaces for real-world applications and analyze the feedback from the user studies that we conducted. In summary, we conclude that since tangible user interfaces are part of the real world and provide a seamless interaction with virtual words, they are well adapted to mix together reality and virtuality. Hence, tangible interaction optimizes users' virtual tasks, especially in manipulating and controlling 3D digital data in 3D space.

Keywords Tangible user interface · Augmented virtuality · Design process · Case studies

6.1 Introduction

Tangible user interfaces (TUIs) are one of several genres of sensing-based interaction, and they have attracted significant attention during recent years. TUIs were initially defined by [22] as user interfaces that "augment the real physical world by coupling digital information to everyday physical objects and environments." Note, though, that the concept of TUIs is not new and was previously known as passive props [19] or as graspable user interfaces [14].

To get a taste of tangible interfaces, let us consider two examples. First, Urp (urban planning workbench) [43] allows several users together to control an urban simulation with physical-scale models of buildings, manipulating it via a physical workbench. The buildings' shadows or wind flow can be simulated and displayed

N. Couture (✉)
ESTIA-RECHERCHE, Technopole Izarbel, 64210 Bidart, France
e-mail: n.couture@estia.fr

E. Dubois et al. (eds.), *The Engineering of Mixed Reality Systems*, Human-Computer Interaction Series, DOI 10.1007/978-1-84882-733-2_6,

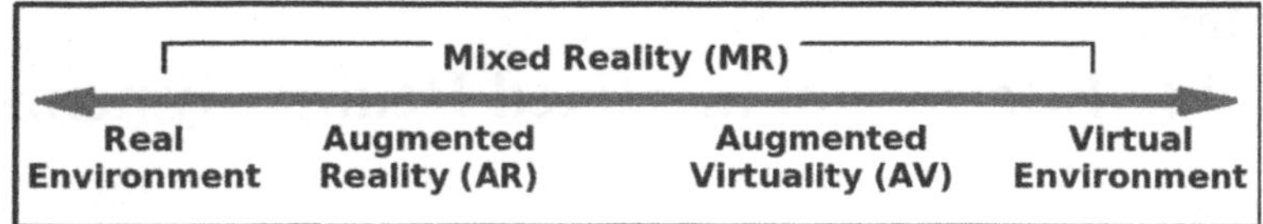

Fig. 6.1 Reality–virtuality continuum [30]

on the workbench, integrated with the scale models. Second, illuminating clay [37] allows road builders, environmental engineers, and landscape designers to modify a terrain relief by modeling with their fingers a physical surface that represents the ground. Analytic data, like slope variation, water flow, or land erosion, can be displayed directly on this surface. Users manipulate the physical terrain model around a workbench and can thus work together in order to design the course of a new roadway, a housing complex, or a parking area that satisfies engineering, environmental, and aesthetic requirements.

We are convinced that real-world physical objects are essential as physical representations and controls of digital information for user interaction. Since TUIs integrate both the physical and digital aspects of interaction, they are as such part of the mixed reality (MR) paradigm.

Let us first study the way how the physical and the digital world are mixed in a mixed reality system. To this end, consider the "virtuality" continuum, introduced in [30] and illustrated in Fig. 6.1. At one extreme of this continuum, the task is embedded in the physical real-world environment of the users and at the other extreme, the task is embedded in the purely digital virtual environment. Between these extremes, *augmented reality* consists of embedding some digital information in the real world and *augmented virtuality* consists of embedding some physical information in a virtual world. According to this continuum, in essence, tangible user interfaces are part of augmented virtuality. According to [40], tangible interfaces "give physical form to digital information, employing physical artifacts both as representations and controls for computational media." Recall that in augmented virtuality, the task takes place in a virtual environment and the user interacts with this digital information by manipulating physical objects. These physical objects can represent either digital information or the control of digital information in the physical world or, even both, the digital information and its control!

An interactor is the abstraction of an entity capable of representing both input and output [5]. Consequently, a tangible interactor (also called tangible objects, tangibles, or props) is a mixed object [8] with a role in both the real world and the virtual world that are linked by the computer. Tangibles allow the user to perceive and/or to modify the state of the digital information. As an example, in the TUI PinWheels [21], rotations of the pinwheels represent a flow, such as car traffic in a street or stock market exchanges. Here, the pinwheels only physically represent the digital information, i.e., a flow, without user control capacity.

Note that a system using physical devices is not necessarily a tangible user interface. Indeed, according to the preceding definitions, "physical" is not a synonym of "tangible." Indeed, work on graspable user interfaces already distinguished graspable devices from graspable functions [12, 13]. The principal characteristic of a TUI is to be a mixed reality system, where the task takes place in the virtual world, which uses augmented virtuality. An interface consisting of physical objects (e.g., mouse, stylus) can be simply considered as neither a TUI nor a mixed reality system. A physical object becomes a tangible object only when it represents and/or controls digital information!

This chapter is organized as follows. First, we present a state-of-the-art review of tangible user interface models. Second, taking an engineering approach, we focus on the design of tangible interaction techniques in mixed reality environments based on our experiences in designing and building TUIs. Then, we illustrate the previous design steps with three TUI examples that we have developed. Finally, we offer some lessons learnt from the analysis of the feedback from the user studies that we have conducted for each of the TUIs. To conclude, by understanding the world as a 3D environment where TUIs are part of the real world, we show how TUIs are well adapted to mix together reality and virtuality in order to optimize the users' virtual tasks and to manipulate and control 3D numerical data in 3D space.

6.2 State of the Art of Tangible User Interface Models

In this section, we initially present the earliest tangible interaction model: the MCRpd [40]. This interaction model is an extension of the classical model view control (MVC) principle for graphical user interfaces. Then, we describe the evolution of this initial tangible interaction model to an extended version [20].

6.2.1 The Seminal Tangible Interaction Model

The MCRpd model, short for *m*odel-*c*ontrol-*r*epresentation *p*hysical and *d*igital, initially introduced by [40, 41] has since 2002 been renamed to MCRit, short for *m*odel-*c*ontrol-*r*epresentation *t*angible and *i*ntangible [39, 42].

By analogy with the MVC model for graphical interfaces, the MCRit model describes the different physical and digital components that occur in a tangible interface. Graphical user interfaces and tangible user interfaces can thus be compared as follows:

- *Graphical user interfaces* (GUIs) represent information with intangible pixels on a bit-mapped display and sound. General-purpose input devices allow users to control those representations (see Fig. 6.2a).
- *Tangible user interfaces* (TUIs) make information directly graspable and easily manipulated with haptic feedback, by giving tangible (physical) representation to

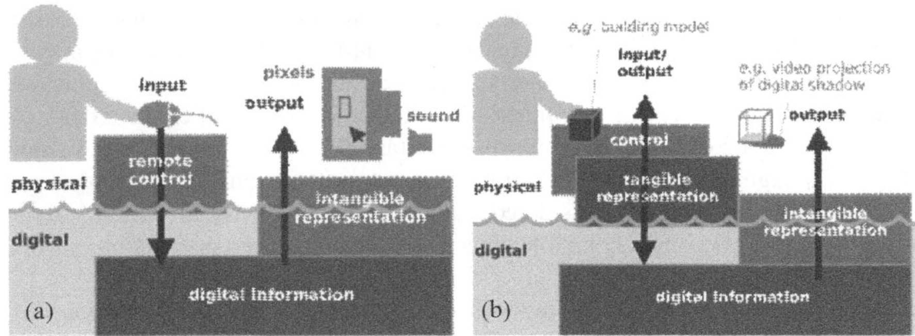

Fig. 6.2 (**a**) Graphical user interface model. (**b**) MCRit. Tangible user interface model (both are reprinted from [20])

the digital information. Intangible representation, such as video projection, for example, may complement tangible representations by synchronizing with it (see Fig. 6.2b).

6.2.2 The Extended Tangible Interaction Model

In 2008, Ishii [20] introduced an extension to the MCRit model. He states that an interaction with a tangible object is always composed of two feedback loops, and he points out that in some cases even a third feedback loop appears.

The first feedback loop is passive haptic feedback (see Fig. 6.3a). This feedback loop provides the user with an immediate confirmation that he or she has grasped and moved the physical object. This loop exists within a physical domain, and it does not require any sensing or processing by a computer.

The second loop is digital feedback loop. This feedback loop provides a visual or an audible response from the movement of the physical object. Therefore, this

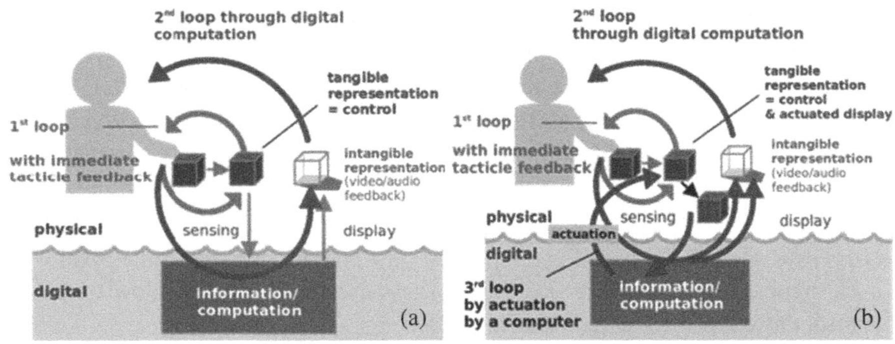

Fig. 6.3 (**a**) TUI's double feedback loops. (**b**) TUI with actuation (both are reprinted from [20])

second feedback loop implies a computational delay and takes longer than the first loop.

The third feedback loop, which can be called the physical actuation[1] loop, can be adjoined to the two preceding loops when the computer gives physical feedback on the status of the digital information as the model changes or responds to internal computation. Hence, the computer generates a physical update (physical actuation) of the tangibles. Figure 6.3b illustrates the third loop introduced into the tangible interaction model by computer-controlled actuation and sensing.

As an example, in PICO [34], the pucks move on a tabletop according to the calculations done by an optimization algorithm so that the user can intervene in computational optimization problems by adding physical constraints on the puck movements (e.g., cell-phone tower placement). Today, in the area of tangible interfaces, there is still a high potential to better exploit the physical actuation loop. The reasons for this are manifold, but they are primarily feasibility (and thus technical) issues. However, there are some promising novel solutions that create physical artifacts that move, animate, or deform themselves: the Actuated Workbench [33], the HoverMesh [29], the Surflex [6], the Sprout I/O [7], the and BounceSlider [15].

6.3 Designing Tangible Interaction Techniques in MR Environments

The objective in tangible user interface design is twofold. First, the designer has to choose an adequate physical form for representing the digital information and/or the control of the digital information. Second, the designer has to integrate this real product in an interactive system. In order to better understand his or her design, it is useful for the designer to have a categorization of the available system elements. Hence we start this section by outlining two major categorizations of TUIs from the literature.

6.3.1 Categorizations of Tangible User Interfaces

In 2004, Fishkin [11] discussed and analyzed existing TUIs and found no useful binary characteristic function that meaningfully includes some of the TUIs while excluding others. Instead, he proposed a taxonomy that unifies previous and various different definitions and categorizations of TUIs. For that, he found it useful to view "tangibility" as a multivalued attribute. Fishkin proposed two axes. The metaphor axis classifies the TUI in terms of the way the system effect of a user action is analogous to the real-world effect of similar actions. The embodiment axis classifies the TUI with respect to how closely the input focus is tied to the output focus. Fishkin's

[1] Actuation means "to put in action," "to move."

taxonomy is the result of unifying various classifications that existed before 2004 into one framework [11].

More recently, in 2008, Ishii [20] introduced an overview of seven types of promising TUI applications based on an analysis of interfaces developed by the research community during the previous 10 years: tangible telepresence, tangibles with kinetic memory, constructive assembly, tokens and constraints, tangible interactive surfaces, continuous plastic TUIs, and augmented everyday objects. We refer the interested reader to [20] for details of each type of TUI application and for examples.

6.3.2 A Multidisciplinary and Participatory Approach

We recommend a design methodology that integrates classical methods of both computer science and product design. In our approach, the key element in the early stage of design of a tangible user interface consists of identifying the users' major needs for a new interaction device, taking into account the users' skills and experience in doing the targeted task. We propose that the next stage is multidisciplinary integrating both the product designer and the software designer, as well as being a participatory approach that also includes the end user. The goal of this process is to design the right interaction technique and the most suitable device. We should note that while GUIs are fundamentally general-purpose interfaces, TUIs are relatively specific interfaces tailored to a certain type of application in order to increase the directness and intuitiveness of the interaction. By taking advantage of existing skills and work practices, the critical task can be identified where TUIs can reveal their best performance.

6.3.3 Taking into Account the Skills of Users

In order to integrate human factors in the design of the user interface under consideration, it is obviously necessary to take into account the end user of the interface during the design. It is also important to take into account the know-how of the user in order to develop tools that are adapted to the targeted tasks.

An example is ESKUA (described below in Section 6.4.2), a tangible user interface for 3D CAD parts assembly. CAD systems are widely used to design parts and to assemble them, and these systems have become more and more powerful. They now provide very high-level functions that allow a user to position many parts with only a few mouse clicks. For example, it is possible to perform a multiple selection on two, three, or more objects with one click. Then, bringing their axis in alignment requires only selecting the matching item in a pop-up menu. Unfortunately, even though these powerful functionalities are very useful from a computer user point of view, they mask real problems that occur only in the final production stage. For example, the operator may not have enough hands to handle all the parts and perform the alignment! Hence, there is obviously a wide gap between the way this action is performed in the CAD system and the way it is in the real world by taking into account the skills of the operators. As a consequence, we designed ESKUA together with professional CAD users, because the handling of real objects makes it possible to "anticipate" some physical aspects of the product assembly phase and thus leads the designer to raise questions by carrying out the gestures related to the assembly in the early design stage.

Another example is ArcheoTUI (described below in Section 6.4.3). ArcheoTUI was initiated by the demand of archaeologists to improve user interaction for the broken fragments assembly task. We designed ArcheoTUI in a direct collaboration with a team of archaeologists, and we proved its efficiency in a case study of the assembly of one of their fractured archaeological findings.

6.3.4 The Design Process

First, the designer of a tangible user interface has to design an adequate physical form for representing the digital information and/or the control of the digital information, and second, he or she has to integrate this real product into an interactive system. In order to make the design process successful, we propose to undertake a multidisciplinary and participatory approach by implementing a classical engineering design process in seven steps. At each step, if necessary, the designer can go back to one of the previous steps. The end user is taken into account at every step, and we recommend that the designers should not consider the end user as he or she imagines them but as he or she actually is! This implies meeting the end users in the early design stage. To this end, we propose the following approach:

Step 1. *Creativity/brainstorming with the end users.* Meetings are organized with the end users in order to determine the context of use, the usage scenarios, the data to manipulate, the main tasks, and difficulties encountered in the previous way of working. It is important to analyze the end users' spontaneous working conditions. Sometimes, these spontaneous conditions are more likely the way they worked before the arrival of computer systems and the usage of graphical interfaces. At this step of the process, the dialogue between designers and end users makes it possible for the designer to understand the skills of the users. After these first meetings, the designers of the TUIs should present the established requirements list to the end users. Subsequently, meetings should be organized again in order to find the best solution to the problem, where the designers propose various solutions of interfaces and interaction techniques.

Step 2. *Intermediate objects/demonstrators.* The designers develop initial mock-ups of the solutions that have been adopted and present them to the end users.

Step 3. *Adaptation of functional specifications and constraints.*

Step 4. *Simulations.* Note that at this step, the first mock-ups do not necessarily use the final technology. Moreover, if the technology is not available, the

Wizard of Oz technique can be used to conduct early user studies (see, for example [9]).

Step 5. *Setting situations.*

Step 6. *Development and test.* The designers develop a working prototype.

Step 7. *User experimentations.* First experimental studies are carried out with the end users on the working prototype, in order to validate the design choices.

In the next sections, we validate the design process described above by comparing the designed product/system to the expected product/system. We show a high level of correspondence between them in terms of characteristics, qualities, and functionalities. We reinforce the validation of our design approach concretely by the investigations with end users that we conducted in three different applications (see below in Section 6.5).

6.4 Case Studies

By following the design process described above, we designed three TUIs for different fields of use. For each of them, we give a rationale for its creation and illustrate its conception. These three TUIs called ESKUA, GeoTUI, and ArcheoTUI are case studies of the so-called augmented virtuality systems.

6.4.1 *A Tangible User Interface for 3D CAD Parts Assembly: ESKUA*

ESKUA is a TUI for interaction with computer-aided design (CAD) software. Thanks to its props, ESKUA provides product designers with a physical simulation of parts assembly operations (see Fig. 6.4a). Each prop is associated with one or more virtual objects, the CAD parts. We have designed and manufactured a set of props made out of 60 elements with holes (see Fig. 6.4b). The actions that the

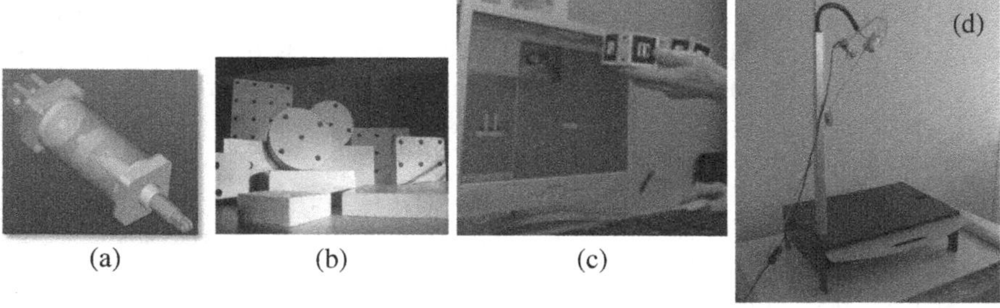

Fig. 6.4 (**a**) CAO assembly. (**b**) ESKUA tangible props. (**c**) The association of the props to CAD parts. (**d**) The setup of ESKUA

user carries out on the props (displacement, assembly, rotation, etc.) are reproduced on the CAD parts on the display screen (see Fig. 6.4c). The capture of the position and the orientation of the props is done by video capture (see Fig. 6.4d). The use of ESKUA gives the product designer a physical perception of the assembly constraints during the "virtual" CAD part manipulation. Indeed, the designer is confronted with real assembly operation constraints such as difficulties in positioning parts or maintaining elements in a joint position. The props set based on functional surface reasoning makes it possible to carry out physical simulations and allows the designers to identify assembly difficulties and to modify the CAD part design.

Note that when assembling two elements [CAD parts, archaeological fragments (see ArcheoTUI below), and so on], the user has to manipulate double 6DOF at the same time, and classical user interfaces such as the 2D mouse or the keyboard are impractical for this assembly task. Using TUIs for assembly is not a new idea. The assembly of numerous Lego-like blocks as props was already done with Active Cubes [25]. Based on the conceptual framework of [17], two-handed manipulation techniques were developed, see for example [19, 28, 35], and a part of their success can be attributed to their cognitive benefits [26]. Our work is inspired by the seminal work of Hinckley et al. [19], where passive real-world interface props are used for neurosurgical visualization.

6.4.2 A Tangible Tabletop for Geoscience: GeoTUI

In the field of energy, a key activity is the search for hydrocarbons by geoscientists. The geophysicists must reconstitute a three-dimensional (3D) model of deep structures by interpreting seismic 3D data (see Fig. 6.5a) based on their expertise and assistance by powerful geological simulation software.

In order to explore a cubic volume of subsoil, the geophysicists perform vertical cutting planes. Cutting planes are vertical in the cube since it is too difficult for the geophysicists to create a mental 3D representation of the subsoil starting from arbitrarily oriented cutting planes. Before GUIs existed, geophysicists used to cut planes on paper sheets in a noninteractive way. GUIs allow the geophysicists to interactively edit splines and the composition of the subsoil from cutting planes. However, the complexity of the interaction makes the work too difficult for many geophysicists. Moreover, to understand the data, geophysicists often work together with geologists – but sharing a mouse and a keyboard in front of a screen does not necessarily promote such collaboration. Our new tangible user interface (see Fig. 6.5b) displays cutting planes and geographical maps on a tabletop and provides tangible props for the manipulation of the data. Our aim is to combine the paper/pen/tools conditions of interaction on a table familiar to geophysicists with the computational power of modern geological simulation software. The tangible tools are directly manipulated on intangible cutting planes and maps. According to the recommendations of Norman [31], GeoTUI system has a perfectly coinciding action and perception space. Consequently, the geophysicists concentrate as much as possible on the actual task at hand. Moreover, we strongly believe that tangible

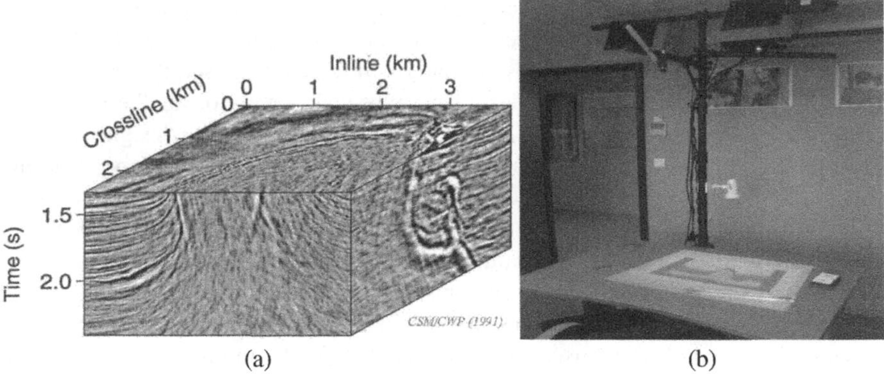

Fig. 6.5 (**a**) Seismic 3D volumetric data (*CSM/CWP 1991*). (**b**) The setup of GeoTUI

interaction for the manipulation of data in the physical world (instead of logical manipulation in the digital world) helps the geophysicists to concentrate more on their actual professional problems.

In order to explore a cube of subsoil and to edit splines and composition, the geologists and geophysicists identify cutting planes. Specifying a cutting line from geographical subsoil maps in order to obtain a cutting plane is a frequent task in the geophysicists' work. We focused on this key task in order to develop a prototype and to prove the relevance of tangible tabletop to geoscience. We implemented four means of interaction for navigation in the subsoil model in order to evaluate the best method of interaction for the cutting line selection task. "The best interaction" has to be understood in terms of speed and, more importantly, in terms of reliability. One is with the mouse on the screen (classical GUI), and three are with tangible props as input and the tabletop as output: one puck, two pucks, and a ruler (see Fig. 6.6a–c). The mouse and the one-puck prop are used to repeatedly control the positions of two logical handles of the cutting line that is drawn on the map. The two-puck props are two physical handles that allow the geophysicist to control the cutting line that is displayed between them. The graded border of the ruler prop represents the cutting line, and the ruler allows the geophysicist to control the position and the orientation of the cutting line.

The 2D cutting planes cannot be calculated on the fly. In the GUI, a graphical button allows the geophysicists to select the cutting line and to engage the calculation of the 2D cutting plane. After the calculation, this 2D cutting plane is displayed instead of the map. In GeoTUI, we propose to couple the use of the props with an additional device: a physical button box (see Fig. 6.6d). Adding buttons on tangibles is not always a good solution [2, 19], so this button box is a solution intended for tangible tabletops. We built this button box consisting of physical buttons in the spirit of Norman [32]. Norman explains the benefits of "physical affordances," not "perceived affordances," and that "people would be better served if we were to return to control through physical objects, to real knobs, sliders, buttons, to simpler,

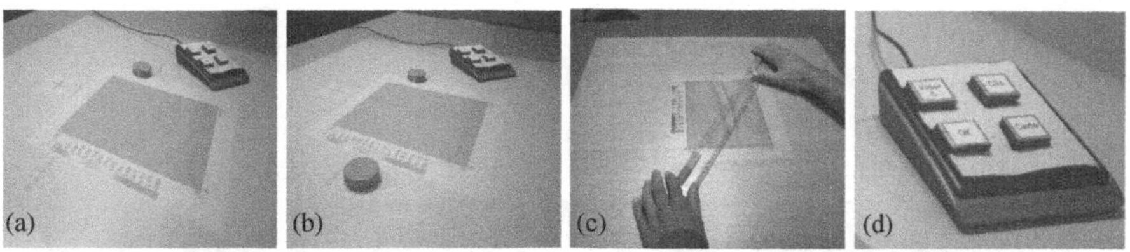

Fig. 6.6 (**a**) The one-puck prop. (**b**) The two-puck prop. (**c**) The ruler prop. (**d**) The button box

more concrete objects and actions." In the prototype, the button box is composed of four buttons that are labeled exactly the same as the button widgets in the GUI that the geophysicists are used to. When the user validates a cutting line on the map, the cutting plane is displayed instead of the map.

In the context of a geographical subsoil model, to the best of our knowledge, the GeoTUI system, specifically designed for geophysicists, is the first work that uses tangibles on a tabletop for the specific task of selecting perpendicular cutting planes from a topographic map. It combines the advantages of the spontaneous user interaction that the geophysicists are commonly used to in their classical paper/pen/ruler environment, with the advantages of the use of powerful geological simulation software.

6.4.3 A Tangible User Interface for the Virtual Reassembly of Fractured Archaeological Objects: ArcheoTUI

Objects found during archaeological excavations are often broken and fractured into a large number of fragments. A common tedious and time-consuming task for archaeologists is to reassemble these fractured objects. Large 3D puzzles have to be solved, so to speak. This task is sometimes made even more difficult because some of the fragments are either very heavy, underwater, deteriorated by erosion and damage, or sometimes even missing.

Various researchers have proposed to scan fragments in 3D in order to use ever-increasing computing power to create a virtual computer-aided assembly (see Fig. 6.7). Once one has figured out how the virtual fragments fit together, the information can be used as a blueprint to reconstruct the real-world object. Even though automatic matching techniques exist, they fail when entire fragments are missing, or when the fragments are seriously deteriorated by, for example, erosion, weathering, or impact damage.

ArcheoTUI is a new tangible user interface for the efficient assembly of 3D scanned fragments of fractured archaeological objects. The key idea of the ArcheoTUI system is to use props as physical representation and control for the scanned virtual fragments. In each hand, the user manipulates an electromagnetically tracked prop, and the translations and rotations are directly mapped to the corresponding virtual fragments on the display. For each hand, a corresponding foot

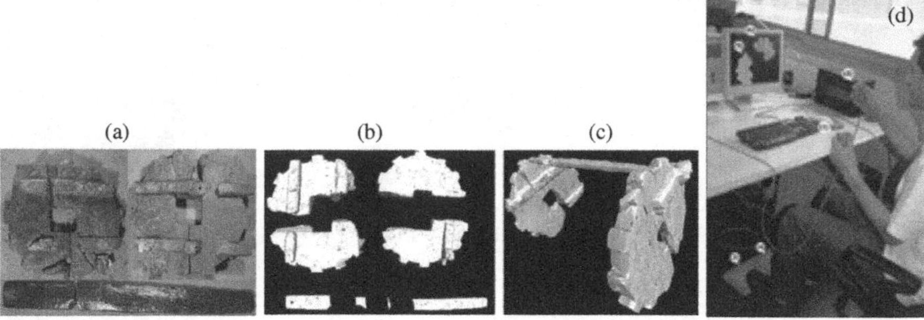

Fig. 6.7 (**a**) Photos of the fractured fountain parts. (**b**) The virtual fragments. (**c**) The assembly of the virtual fragments. (**d**) The setup of ArcheoTUI

pedal is used to clutch the hand movements. Hence, the user's hands can be repositioned or the user can be switched. This declutching mechanism was already used by Hinckley et al. [19] with only one foot pedal, and we extended this metaphor to two foot pedals: the left pedal for the user's left foot is associated with the user's left hand actions and with the right pedal for the right hand's actions, respectively. Foot pedals for two feet were also used by Balakrishnan [2]; however, in contrast to our foot pedals, in their work the role of each foot is not the same. The ArcheoTUI software is designed to enable assembly hypotheses to be changed easily, beyond classical undo/redo, since the reassembly of archaeological findings is a lengthy trial-and-error task. Once the user has figured out how the virtual fragments fit together, the information can be used as a blueprint to reassemble the real-world archaeological object.

6.4.4 Illustration of the Design Approach on Case Studies

The three previous examples of tangible interfaces illustrate the design approach presented in Section 6.3. It is out of the scope of this chapter to detail each step of the design approach for each TUI. Nevertheless, we illustrate the design approach by focusing on the first steps: taking into account the skills of the users (in Step 1) and the building of intermediate demonstrators followed by the adaptation of the functional specifications and constraints (Steps 2 and 3). Step 7 will be illustrated in Section 6.5.

Step 1. *Taking into account the skills of the users, illustrated by ArcheoTUI.* The design approach has to be chosen right from the start by taking into account the skills of the users. For example, several meetings with the archaeologists convinced us that in archaeology, the years of experience of the archaeologists is crucial to solving the 3D assembly puzzle. The archaeologists reason not only bottom-up by pairwise matching but also top-down by considering the assembly problem as a whole and by taking into account the archaeological context. We observed that the user interaction techniques involved in classical existing 3D modeling software hinder the efficient virtual assembly of 3D objects, because the two 3D objects have to be positioned and oriented relative to each other. Since the archaeologists are often inexperienced in user interaction with 3D models by using the 2D metaphor of the mouse, in some laboratories, the virtual assembly is slowed down or even completely abandoned. Note that it is already difficult to position and orientate *one* 3D object with a 2D metaphor such as the trackball metaphor. Consequently, positioning and orientating *two* objects relative to each other is even harder, especially for non-3D experts. ArcheoTUI was designed to overcome this difficulty.

Steps 2 and 3. *Building intermediate objects/demonstrators followed by adaptation of the functional specifications and constraints illustrated by ESKUA.* We defined a typology of these tangibles based on concepts proposed in "Design for Assembly" (DFA) methods [4]. Following this first proposal, we carried out different investigations [27] to test this first set of tangibles with different types of users: designers, assembly experts, CAD users, and ergonomic experts. Our studies highlight that the subjects use different cognitive techniques to associate the CAD parts with the tangibles. Basically, our experiments show that the subjects propose different combinations of tangibles according to two kinds of criteria. The first criterion is the general form of the part (like the DFA principle) and the second one is the functional surface of the part. We then designed a new set of tangibles with specific functional surfaces that are commonly used in the assembly process (such as chamfer on shaft and bore, fillet, flat on shaft).

6.5 User Studies in the Workplace: Feedback

We provide an analysis of feedback from the user studies that we conducted for each of the previously presented TUIs. For each user study, we present the setup, the targeted task, and the overall success of the interaction technique provided. "Overall success" has to be understood in terms of speed and, more importantly, reliability. The particular interest of this feedback lies in the fact that the studies were conducted within the user's respective everyday environments – their workplaces.

6.5.1 Evaluation: Setup, Metrics, Analysis

6.5.1.1 ESKUA

The principal goal of the user study was to verify the following research questions. Does the use of the props cause a reflection on the assembly? Does the link between the prop and the CAD part depend on the shape or on the functional surfaces? Does the user naturally create new props when the parts have more complex shapes? The subjects were two CAD experts, an assembly expert, an experienced CAD user, and an ergonomist. We provided the subject with a 3D visualization of a CAD assembly and the set of props. Then, we asked the subject to create the assembly by using the props. This was done for 10 different assembly tasks. In these 10 different assembly tasks, we could qualitatively identify that the subjects have two ways of associating the assembly of the props with the assembly of the CAD parts. The first association is based on reasoning about the geometric shapes, and the second one is based on reasoning about the functional surfaces of the CAD parts. In particular, it appears that the assembly expert, who is the one we address with our research, tries to identify primarily the functional surfaces in order to analyze and optimize the product as a whole.

The main result (see [16] for details) is that the less the users are specialized in the assembly task, the less they reason about the surfaces and the more they reason about the geometries. Therefore, we produced a state-of-the-art report on the technology components that are mainly used in different mechanical products. Furthermore, we proposed a new set of props with specific functional surfaces that are commonly used in the assembly process (e.g., chamfer on shaft and bore, fillet, flat on shaft). Moreover, new "fastening props" had also been designed for the use of different fastening technologies (e.g., bolt with nut, screw, centring pin, rivet), and we built additional props in order to promote props combinations regarding both functional surface-based reasoning and geometric form reasoning.

6.5.1.2 GeoTUI

We conducted two user studies in succession. First, a cognitive walkthrough-based user study [36] with 10 participants showed the ability of GeoTUI to support the cutting line selection task. The users were in an exploratory learning mode. The subjects received no instructions about the usage of the two interfaces being compared: the GUI and GeoTUI. Both the GUI and the GeoTUI interface controlled the same geoscience software called JOHN [23]. We gave each subject a box containing a ruler, six pucks, and the button box, and we said, "Take them and put them where you want during the exercises [. . .] Place the button box where it will be most comfortable for you to use." When using GeoTUI, the user had to arrange the objects as he or she liked and then had to choose the props that he found the most representative for the task of cutting line selection. Second, a formal comparative user study with 12 participants allowed us to evaluate user performance with respect to the usage of the three tangible props: one-puck, two-puck, and the ruler to specify cutting planes. For the two user studies, the order of using the GUI and TUI was counterbalanced, and when testing several props in the second user study, the interaction order was counterbalanced as well within the TUI conditions.

One of the exercises consisted of the selection of a series of six cutting planes at various given coordinates on the map. Another consisted of the selection of cutting planes on the map, in order to navigate through a model to find marks hidden in the subsoil at random locations. For the last exercise, the user had to locate and identify a 3D geometric form, shaped as a letter of the alphabet and hidden in a cube, and the user can view only the 2D planes of this cube. All exercises were time limited.

In the context of geological applications, these experiments allowed us to validate the hypothesis of [12] by convincing quantitative results: the experiment showed that the specialized space-multiplexed conditions outperform the generic space-multiplexed conditions since the task involves a generic working problem that has to be solved by means of the manipulation of input devices (see results and details in [10]). Hence, the ruler is chosen more often as an input device by geophysicists. It may help them to concentrate more on their actual complex working task. Certainly, being able to work in a space where action and perception are unified, thanks to the tabletop, is crucial.

6.5.1.3 ArcheoTUI

We conducted two user studies on site at the workplace of the archaeologists. The subjects had to accomplish a series of six assemblies of geometrical shapes or archaeological fragments. The first user study revealed that the interface, and especially the foot pedal, was accepted and that all the users managed to solve simple assembly tasks efficiently (see [38] for details on setup and analysis). In a second user study, we replaced the foot pedal declutching mechanism by classical buttons on the props and we compared these two different clutching mechanisms with each other. The conditions were between-subject, and the preference between pedals and buttons was evenly distributed with a slight preference for the foot pedals. This second user study revealed as well that the movement of the hands is more similar to real-world assembly scenarios when using the foot pedals and that the users can keep on concentrating on the actual assembly task.

6.5.2 Lessons Learnt from the User Studies

The method of evaluation of TUIs compared to GUIs is unusual, since the manipulation of the data happens in the real world. Based on the instrumental interaction model, Beaudouin-Lafon [3] explains that TUIs "transfer most of the characteristics usually found in the logical part of the instrument into the physical part." The evaluation of a GUI focuses primarily on the logical aspect of the interface. For GUIs, the set of physical actions is limited (see the UAN notation [18]). For TUIs, the physical part, i.e., the aggregation of several tangible objects, is developed specifically for each interface. Furthermore, the physical manipulation does not deal with the graspable input devices but with physical representations of digital information. Some TUIs are especially designed to exploit bimanual interaction, but users often perform two-handed manipulations with TUIs even if it was not especially designed with that in mind. Having multiple, tangible objects encourages two-handed interaction [12], and experiments should examine how users take advantage of it or if it is sometimes cumbersome to use [24]. The previous analyses allow us to draw some recommendations in order to evaluate TUIs.

6.5.2.1 Recommendations Derived from Our User Studies on Tangible Interaction

During our evaluation, some information was gathered by simple observation, e.g., in the particular case of interactive tangible tabletops, the locations of the tangible objects on the table, as well as the way the user arranges and organizes his or her workspace. By studying the position of the hands of the user on the tangible object, one can discriminate between a single-handed and bimanual interaction with one or two tangibles. It is also interesting to study how the tangible object is held, for example, grasped with the whole hand or only with the fingertips, in the middle or at the ends. The position of the user, e.g., sitting, standing, or alternating between both, provides interesting information about eventual problems concerning accessibility particularly in the case of interactive tables.

For the comparison of two tangible interactors, the respective manipulation times between two delimiting actions can be analyzed. For example, for GeoTUI, in order to measure the time needed to specify a cutting line, we measured the time difference between the visualization and the validation action. As another example, for ArcheoTUI, we measured the time difference between the clutching and the declutching of a fragment to the props, both for the foot pedal mechanism and the buttons on the props.

The 2M conception space [1] analyzes the bimanual interaction according to three axes: the nature of the action (discrete, continuous, or composed), the temporality (anachronistic, sequential, concomitant, coinciding, or simultaneous), and the dependence (lexical fusion, syntactic, semantic, or independence otherwise). This theoretical basis allowed us to analyze the TUIs that use bimanual interaction. For example, for ArcheoTUI, we have analyzed the temporality of the two symmetric and continuous bimanual actions with two independent subtasks. We wanted to determine whether the user really interacts with the two props at the same time and whether one prop was used more frequently than another. It is useful from a design point of view to study the chronology of every single action of the user and to calculate the interlacing of two continuous actions by distinguishing the situations where a unique action is realized from the situations where both actions are done at the same time.

In summary, the most important fact is that physical manipulation is the salient point to be measured during the evaluation.

To this end, in order to collect all these information, we recall some useful techniques: an observer can fill out a form during the experiment or after the experiment by analyzing a video of the experiment, and a log file can be used as well. Moreover, in order to collect a sufficient amount of data to assess the proposed tangible interaction, we recommend conducting two types of investigation successively. First, a cognitive walkthrough-based user study compares the major choices and prepares the second and more precise evaluation. Second, a comparative user study evaluates the user performance.

6.5.2.2 Some Questions as a Guide

The user study protocol has to be constructive with the aim of establishing the relevant criteria for the major points described above. In order to help the evaluator to evaluate the tangible system and to define the criteria, we propose some questions as a guide. By answering these questions, the evaluator follows the previous recommendations.

Q1. Are the tangible props representative of the role they play?
Q2. Can the tangible props be easily seized with the hands?
Q3. Are the tangible props manipulated by one or two hands or even in cooperation by various users at a time?
Q4. Are the tangible props manipulated sequentially or in parallel?
Q5. Does the manipulation of the tangible props influence the actual task?
Q6. Is the use of the tangible props with the digital world intuitive?
Q7. Is the use of the tangible props efficient?

There is no order to these questions; rather, they should be considered in parallel. The first five require simple yes/no answers, whereas the last two questions require some qualitative judgment. It is often useful to fill out an observation form. The user study protocol has to be set up so that the answers to these questions can be clearly identified, with sufficient statistical evidence.

6.6 Conclusion: The Benefits of Tangible Interaction in Mixed Reality Systems

When considering the world as a 3D environment, TUIs are part of the real world, and they interact with digital information. We presented a conceptual analysis of TUI models in order to understand tangible interaction. It is easy to see that TUIs are well adapted to mixing reality and virtuality together in a mixed reality system, especially when they provide two-handed 3D interaction. As we saw in the case studies, the users interact with mixed reality systems by means of TUIs with a minimum of cognitive workload. This is because TUIs provide a seamless interaction with virtual worlds.

Based on the user studies we have conducted, we have provided an analysis of the feedback, and we have offered some recommendations for the evaluation of TUIs. The key point is to measure the physical manipulation during the evaluation. We presented seven questions that we consider useful in order guide the designer in evaluating a tangible system. They deal with the use of tangibles, manual manipulation, the sequential/parallel way of using tangibles, and the affordance of the tangible. In order to collect a sufficient amount of data for the assessment of the proposed tangible interaction and to answer the seven questions, we recommend conducting two forms of evaluation: a cognitive walkthrough-based user study followed by a comparative user study for a more precise evaluation of user performance.

Moreover, based on our experience in building tangible interfaces for different fields of use, we presented a hardware/software co-design for tangible user interfaces. Tangible user interfaces are leaving the conventional computer-generated virtual world behind, moving into the physical world. Obviously, the designer of a TUI has to conceive both the physical part and the logical part of the interface. For this reason, we recommend using a classical engineering design process for mechanical products with an end user participatory approach coupled with a software development method. This results in a multidisciplinary approach straight from the beginning of the conception of TUIs by integrating the end user, the product designer, and the software designer.

This design process could help the designer to choose an adequate physical form for representing the digital information and/or the control of the digital information. This design process helps to integrate the tangible object into an interactive system as well. The salient point is, from our perspective, to take into account the users' skills and users' experience in performing the task in question.

References

1. Bailly, G., Nigay, L., Auber, D.: 2 M: Un espace de conception pour l'interaction bi-manuelle. In: UbiMob'05 the 2nd French-speaking conference on Mobility and ubiquitous computing, pp. 177–184. ACM (2005)
2. Balakrishnan, R., Fitzmaurice, G., Kurtenbach, G., Singh, K.: Exploring interactive curve and surface manipulation using a bend and twist sensitive input strip. In I3D ′99 the 1999 symposium on Interactive 3D graphics, pp. 111–118. ACM (1999)
3. Beaudoin-Lafon, M.: Instrumental interaction: An interaction model for designing post-WIMP user interfaces. In: CHI'00 the 18th SIGCHI conference on Human factors in computing systems, pp. 446–453. ACM (2000)
4. Boothroyd, G., Dewhurst, P.: Product Design for Assembly – A Designer's Handbook. Department of Mechanical Engineering, University of Massachusetts (1993)
5. Calvary, G., Daassi, O., Coutaz, J., Demeure, A.: Des widgets aux comets pour la Plasticité des Systèmes Interactifs. J. RIHM Revue d'Interaction Homme-Machine. 6, 1, 33–53 (2005)
6. Coelho, M., Ishii, H., Maes, P.: Surflex: A programmable surface for the design of tangible interfaces. In: CHI'08 extended abstracts of the 26th SIGCHI conference on Human factors in computing systems, pp. 3429–3434. ACM (2008)
7. Coelho, M., Maes, P.: Sprout I/O: A texturally rich interface. In: TEI'08 the 2nd international conference on Tangible and embedded interaction, pp. 221–222. ACM (2008)
8. Coutrix, C., Nigay, L.: Mixed reality: A model of mixed interaction. In: AVI'06 the 8th International Working Conference on Advanced Visual Interfaces, pp. 43–50. ACM (2006)
9. Couture, N., Minel, S.: TactiMod dirige et oriente un piéton. In: UbiMob ′06 the 3rd French-speaking conference on Mobility and Ubiquitous computing, pp. 9–16. ACM (2006)
10. Couture, N., Rivière, G., Reuter, P.: GeoTUI: A tangible user interface for geoscience. In: TEI'08 the 2nd international conference on Tangible and Embedded Interaction, pp. 89–96. ACM (2008)
11. Fishkin, K.: A taxonomy for and analysis of tangible interfaces. J. PUC Personal Ubiquitous Comput. 8, 5, 347–358 (2004)
12. Fitzmaurice, G.: Graspable User Interfaces. PhD thesis, University of Toronto (1996)

13. Fitzmaurice, G., Buxton, W.: An empirical evaluation of graspable user interfaces: Towards specialized space-multiplexed input. In: CHI'97 the 15th SIGCHI conference on Human factors in computing systems, pp. 43–50. ACM Press (1997)
14. Fitzmaurice, G., Ishii, H., Buxton, W.: Bricks: Laying the foundations for graspable user interfaces. In: CHI'95 the 13th SIGCHI conference on Human factors in computing systems, pp. 442–449. ACM Press/Addison-Wesley Publishing Co (1995)
15. Gabriel, R., Sandsjö, J., Shahrokni, A., Fjeld, M.: BounceSlider: Actuated sliders for music performance and composition. In: TEI'08 the 2nd international conference on Tangible and embedded interaction, pp. 127–130. ACM (2008)
16. Garreau, L., Legardeur, J., Rouillon-Couture, N.: Une plate-forme basée sur les interfaces tangibles pour l'assemblage en CFAO. J. Ingénierie Numérique, Interaction Homme-Machine et CAO. 1, 2, 133–148. Lavoisier-Hermes (2005)
17. Guiard, Y.: Asymmetric division of labor in human skilled bimanual action: The kinematic chain as a model. J. Motor Behavior. 19, 486–517 (1987)
18. Hartson, H.R., Siochi, A.C., Hix, D.: The UAN: A user-oriented representation for direct manipulation interface designs. J. TOIS ACM Trans. Inf. Syst. 8, 3, 181–203 (1990)
19. Hinckley, K., Pausch, R., Goble, J., Kassell, N.: Passive real-world interface props for neurosurgical visualization. In: CHI'94 the 12th SIGCHI conference on Human factors in computing systems, pp. 452–458. ACM (1994)
20. Ishii, H.: Tangible bits: Beyond pixels. In: TEI'08 the 2nd International Conference on Tangible and Embedded Interaction, pp. XV–XXV. ACM Press (2008)
21. Ishii, H., Ren, S., Frei, P.: Pinwheels: Visualizing information flow in an architectural space. In: CHI'01 extended abstracts of the 19th SIGCHI conference Human factors in computing systems, pp. 111–112. ACM (2001)
22. Ishii, H., Ullmer, B.: Tangible bits: Towards seamless interfaces between people, bits and atoms. In: CHI'97 the 15th SIGCHI conference on Human factors in computing systems, pp. 234–241. ACM (1997)
23. Jurado, F., Sinoquet, D., Lailly, P.: Jerry: A 3D reflection tomography designed for complex structures. Technical report, KIM 1996 Annual Report, Institut Français du Pétrole (1996)
24. Kabbash, P., Buxton, W., Sellen, A.: Two-handed input in a compound task. In: CHI '94 the 12th SIGCHI conference on Human factors in computing systems, pp. 417–423. ACM (1994)
25. Kitamura, Y., Itoh, Y., Kishino, F.: ActiveCube: A Bi-directional user interface using Cubes. In: CHI'01 extended abstracts of the 19th SIGCHI conference on Human factors in computing systems, pp. 355–356. ACM (2001)
26. Leganchuk, A., Zhai, S., Buxton, W.: Manual and cognitive benefits of two-handed input: An experimental study. J. TOCHI. 5, 4, 326–359 (1998)
27. Legardeur, J., Garreau, L., Couture, N.: Experiments to evolve toward a tangible user interface for CAD parts assembly. In: SPIE'04 Electronic Imaging'04, pp. 438–445. SPIE (2004)
28. Llamas, I., Kim, B., Gargus, J., Rossignac, J,. Shaw, C.: Twister: A space-warp operator for the two-handed editing of 3D shapes. In: SIGGRAPH '03: ACM SIGGRAPH 2003 Papers, pp. 663–668. ACM (2003)
29. Mazzone, A., Spagno, C., Kunz, A.: The HoverMesh: A deformable structure based on vacuum cells: New advances in the research of tangible user interfaces. In: ACE'04 the 2004 ACM SIGCHI International Conference on Advances in computer entertainment technology, pp. 187–193. ACM (2004)
30. Milgram, P., Kishino, F.: A taxonomy of mixed reality visual displays. J. IEICE Trans. Inf. Syst. E77-D, 12, 1321–1329 (1994)
31. Norman, D.: The Psychology of Everyday Things. Basic Books, New York (1988)
32. Norman, D.: Affordance, conventions, and design. J. Interactions. 6, 3, 38–43 (1999)
33. Pangaro, G., Maynes-Aminzade, D., Ishii, H.: The actuated workbench: Computer-controlled actuation in tabletop tangible interfaces. In: UIST'02 the 15th annual ACM symposium on User Interface Software and Technology, pp. 181–190. ACM (2002).

34. Patten, J., Ishii, H.: Mechanical constraints as computational constraints in tabletop tangible interfaces. In: CHI'07 the 25th SIGCHI conference on Human factors in computing systems, pp. 809–818. ACM (2007)
35. Pierce, J., Stearns, B., Pausch, R.: Voodoo dolls: seamless interaction at multiple scales in virtual environments. In: I3D ′99 the 1999 symposium on Interactive 3D graphics, pp. 141–145. ACM (1999)
36. Polson, P.G., Lewis, C., Rieman, J., Wharton, C.: Cognitive walkthroughs: A method for theory-based evaluation of user interfaces. J. Man-Mach. Stud. 36, 5, 741–773 (1992)
37. Piper, B., Ratti, C., Ishii, H.: Illuminating Clay: A 3-D tangible interface for landscape analysis. In: CHI'02 the 20th SIGCHI conference on Human factors in computing systems, pp. 355–362. ACM (2002)
38. Reuter, P., Rivière, G., Couture, N., Sorraing, N., Espinasse, L., Vergnieux, R.: ArcheoTUI – A tangible user interface for the virtual reassembly of fractured archeological objects. In: VAST2007 the 8th EuroGraphics International symposium on Virtual Reality, Archaeology and Cultural Heritage, pp. 15–22. EuroGraphics Association (2007)
39. Ullmer, B.: Tangible Interfaces for Manipulating Aggregates of Digital Information. PhD thesis, Massachusetts Institute of Technology (2002)
40. Ullmer, B., Ishii, H.: Emerging frameworks for tangible user interfaces. J. IBM Syst. 39, 3/4, 915–931 (2000)
41. Ullmer, B., Ishii, H.: Emerging frameworks for tangible user interfaces In: Human–Computer Interaction in the New Millennium, pp. 579–601. ACM Press/Addison-Wesley Publishing Co. (2001)
42. Ullmer, B., Ishii, H., Jacob, R.: Token+constraint systems for tangible interaction with digital information. J. TOCHI 12, 1, 81–118 (2005)
43. Underkoffler, J., Ishii, H.: Urp: A luminous-tangible workbench for urban planning and design. In: CHI'99 the 17th SIGCHI conference on Human factors in computing systems, pp. 386–393. ACM (1999)

Chapter 7
Designing a Mixed Reality Intergenerational Entertainment System

Eng Tat Khoo, Tim Merritt, and Adrian David Cheok

Abstract This chapter presents steps for designing an intergenerational mixed reality entertainment system, which focuses on physical and social interactions using a mixed reality floor system. The main design goals include the following: facilitating interactions between users with varied levels of skill in utilizing technology, utilizing the familiar physical motions from other activities to make an intuitive physical interface, and encouraging social interactions among families and friends. Detailed implementation of these steps is presented in the design of our intergenerational entertainment system, Age Invaders. Our design process is based on user-centered design. The results of the study help to focus the refinements of the existing platform from a usability standpoint and also aid in the development of new physical entertainment and interactive applications. This study provides insights into user issues including how users interact in a complex mixed reality experience.

Keywords Mixed reality entertainment · Social computing · Family entertainment · Game play · User-centered design

7.1 Introduction

Due to the aging global population [1], intergenerational entertainment is becoming increasingly important. Based on our initial user studies with Singaporean older people between 60 and 80 years old and young students between 10 and 12 years old, none of the older people participated in computer and electronic gaming activities while all the young students engaged in games for a substantial amount of time weekly. Although the older cohort do not object to their grandchildren in playing games, and they are inclined to play together with them, they have failed to do

E.T. Khoo (✉)
Mixed Reality Lab, 21 Lower Kent Ridge Rd, National University of Singapore, Singapore 119077, Singapore
e-mail: khooet@mixedrealitylab.org

E. Dubois et al. (eds.), *The Engineering of Mixed Reality Systems*, Human-Computer Interaction Series, DOI 10.1007/978-1-84882-733-2_7,

so due to the steep learning curve to play the games. The older cohort has elaborated that the steep learning curve is attributed to mouse and keyboard interface, graphic user interface, and language used in the games. Our finding is also consistent with some literature review [2–4], which stated that one of the main reasons that elderly users have been underrepresented in computing is that until recently, hardware and software designs, particularly interfaces, have simply not been designed to accommodate them.

It would be beneficial if the older people could interact actively with the young family members through gaming activities. This could possibly strengthen family bonding and bridge the gap between older people and youth culture. Studies show that greater participation of the older people and young in computer-related activity benefited both parties [5]. In addition, one of the key factors why people play is due to "the people factor," since players use games as mechanisms for social experiences [6]. Players in groups emote more frequently and with more intensity than those who play on their own. However, according to the recent goo research survey results on over 1000 married women in Japan between the ages of 50 and 69 [7], only 6.5% of the users play computer or electronic games with their grandchildren. Furthermore, very little work is found on developing intergenerational computer games, and very few systems facilitate multiplayer physical interaction.

This chapter illustrates the design process of four main prototype iterations of a mixed reality intergenerational family entertainment game. We aim to develop an interactive system that can be played by the grandparents, parents, and grandchildren simultaneously, as shown in Fig. 7.1. Previously we have developed Human Pacman [6], a novel interactive mixed reality entertainment system that ventures to embed the natural physical world seamlessly with a fantasy virtual playground by capitalizing on mobile computing, wireless LAN, ubiquitous computing, and motion-tracking technologies. It emphasizes collaboration and competition between players in a wide outdoor physical area which allows natural wide-area physical movements. We were inspired to develop a family version of Human Pacman, which encourages a high level of social and physical interaction. In designing an interactive system for older people and children, ease of use was one of our main concerns, as we wanted to rely on the physical interactions of the players' movements without the burden of heavy game equipment, for example, the wearable computer and head-mounted display, which can impede movement and reduce the level of enjoyment of the game.

We show the progression through the initial stages of the research to the Age Invaders game prototype, which has been shown worldwide as noted in [9, 10]. We share the overall design process steps and share the design decisions that carried the system through each iteration. We give special attention to illustrating the involvement of children and older people in the design process, as they are critical users of the system. Their technology proficiencies are widely different, and therefore, part of the challenge was in developing a system which was simple enough to be understood by the non-gamers, yet engaging for the skilled gamers as well. We then present discussions about the design options for the next iterations of the system, which will be yet another large step in creating a more flexible, physically

Fig. 7.1 Age Invaders: An intergenerational, social and physical game

interactive, mixed reality system, which brings innovation to group interaction for players of all ages.

7.2 Related Work

Findings from scientific research studies show that playing video games can lead to changes in an individual's pleasure, arousal, dominance, and/or affiliative behavior [11–13]. Furthermore, it has been shown that older people enjoy computer gaming experiences [14]. Participation in an activity helps older people feel better and healthier as they recognize their ability to move and create something [15]. According to a recent report, moderate, regular exercise may be just as helpful in combating serious depression in older people as antidepressant medication [16]. Therefore, it is worthwhile to investigate how we could use digital technology to improve the well-being of older people through social interaction, physical activity, and entertainment.

Commercial arcades have recently seen a growing trend in games that require human physical movement as part of the interaction. For example, dancing games such as Dance Dance Revolution (DDR) and ParaParaParadise by Konami are based on players dancing in time with a musical dance tune and moving graphical objects. Some game systems have offered Exergames [17], which use the electronic game format to promote exercise, but these are often lacking in the ability to motivate the players. These systems still force the person to stand, more or less in the same spot, and focus on a computer screen in front of them.

Recently, the Brain Age games on Nintendo DS have gained huge popularity among older Japanese people [18]. The older players believe that such games can sharpen their thinking and they enjoy playing the games very much. On the other hand, Nintendo Wii has gained tremendous popularity and has sold over 6 million consoles since its launch in late 2006 [19]. To play the games on the console, for example, in Wii Sports, the player physically swings and moves the Wii remote, which goes beyond the micromovements of just pressing buttons. In addition, iGameFloor [20], a recent research project that uses an interactive floor platform for social games and entertainment has shown that children are generally motivated by the use of bodily interaction. Thus, we believe that there is a growing need and trend for video games which promote physical activity and mental stimulation for children, adult, and older people as well. The physical nature of mixed reality games has been explored more in recent years, showing positive benefits of high user motivation to play and to quickly establish bonds between the players [21]. Physical and social interactive systems are of particular interest in the research community and have given rise to new systems to facilitate telepresence and exertion [22, 23]. In the Human Pacman mixed reality game [8], players enjoyed high levels of enjoyment in the context of social and physical interaction. Digital technology has also been shown to motivate individuals when in adopting positive health behaviors for the proactive management of diseases [24].

7.3 Design Methodology

In the design of systems, there can be a focus on various aspects, which can result in a system which meets the expectations of the various stakeholders at differing levels of success. In a traditional model of software development known as the waterfall model, the requirements of the system are defined in the beginning and the development continues following this with the design goal as the most critical issue. In interaction design, it is more widely accepted to involve the users of a system throughout the design process in the hopes that the completed system will efficiently and accurately address the needs of the users. There are various models which follow the user centered approach and involve an iterative design process. Prototypes with few features are built for purposes of validating assumptions about the user needs and reducing the time delays and costs associated with building and rebuilding complete systems with full functionality. The spiral model of software development is another traditional methodology, which has risk reduction as one of its main goals and involves the cyclical process of prototyping [25]. Its strengths are best felt in large-scale business projects.

Our approach is "Design-oriented Research," whereas our efforts are primarily research focused and aim to find an appropriate use of media to understand and address a perceived human problem [26]. The creation of prototypes is secondary to the search for knowledge and understanding of difficult issues. With this in mind, we must also consider that our field of research is not focused on the human alone, but also the role of the machine in mediating communication and providing new situations and contexts of use. The driving force is in improving human issues in the world and understanding how technology can be crafted to be a tool and facilitator of communication. Our problem statement focuses on two groups of users with very different levels of acceptance of technology and tolerance for usability problems. In the design of the system, we had to make a system which was easy enough for the elderly to participate and to hold their confidence in the technology and motivation, yet also challenging and fast paced for the younger players who are technology experts and who are easily bored when faced with simple interactions. We set out to design the system, which is not a simple productivity application, but a system that is an open platform encouraging interaction and promoting fun social gaming. We followed a user-centered design approach in defining the steps for our research prototype development. These steps borrow from existing models [27], yet does not call for in-depth risk analysis as in business application development. This allowed the researchers to more quickly design the interactive system and provide workable prototype iterations. Our process also involved the use of highly proficient game players as advocates for the elderly players before the elderly experienced the game for the first time. We involved these expert players to advocate and facilitate for the older people during and after the game play as well.

The design steps we followed include the following: problem identification, problem exploration, setting the design goals, design requirements of prototype, research user needs, research context of use, design idea generation, prototype creation, and usability studies. These steps are now described with attention given to the considerations needed when designing for intergenerational family entertainment. Each iteration returned to the beginning and followed a subset of the design cycle in attempts to understand the user better or to overcome a technical challenge. In later sections, we also describe the prototype iterations and discuss the results from the user studies.

7.3.1 Problem Identification

Singapore has a rapidly aging population, as in many countries around the world, and the trend shows that the family is a strong source of financial and emotional support to older people. According to census data, the majority of those aged 65 years and above live with their children and grandchildren [28].

There is a growing trend of commercial games that require human physical movement as part of the interaction. However, there is still no entertainment platform that is designed specially for older people and children to play harmoniously together.

The problem was identified as follows: "How can a digital gaming system be created that will encourage intergenerational physical and social interaction, considering the unique needs of the users and the varied proficiency with technology?"

7.3.2 Problem Exploration

We carried out a preliminary user study to understand the users better, in particular, the grandparents and children in the context of Singapore. The results of the study are presented below.

Singapore has many senior citizen-focused community centers, each located among the clusters of high-rise residential apartment buildings. These community centers offer a common place for older people who are living in the vicinity to socialize and participate in activities. The facilities commonly offered include televisions, tables and chairs, exercise equipment. The older people normally gather at these centers during the daytime. We have carried out initial observation-based studies at one of the community centers, "Peace Connect," which serves as a general model. We did the studies twice over a period of 1 month. We observed that there were many older people sitting around the tables. Some were watching TV and playing board games but most of them were idle. There was little social interaction among the older people there and they exhibited little motivation to exercise or move around, even though there were treadmills and other exercise equipment provided. They looked tired and most of the time they rested in their seats. This was explained to us by the support staff as being normal.

We conducted verbal surveys with 10 older people in a focus group session during our second visit and realized that all the older people were illiterate or have very limited command of written English or Mandarin Chinese. They communicated verbally in the Chinese dialects of Hokkien or Cantonese.

In a similar process, we carried out a focus group study with 10 school children aged 10–12, from a neighborhood primary school. Eighty percent of them indicated that they play electronic games, ranging from personal computer games to console games such as Microsoft X-box and Sony Play Station for more than 10 h a week. On the contrary, 100% of the 10 older people aged 60–80 in our focus group study reported that they have never played any form of electronic games although they were aware of them.

From the initial study we observed the following trends:

1. Many of the older people in Singapore live under the same roof with their children and grandchildren. There is strong bonding between the three generations.
2. Besides the student who does not have grandparents in the family (only 1 out of the 10 students), the students reported spending, on average, 10–20 h with their grandparents with common activities including board games, card games, and swimming.
3. Eighty percent of the children indicated that they play electronic games ranging from computer games to console games more than 10 h each week.
4. Older people do not play electronic games and do not have computer-related experience.
5. Older people are supportive of the grandchildren playing the games, although they have no understanding of the content of the games, nor do they understand how to participate.

6. All of the 10 older people did not attempt to understand the games played by their grandchildren, primarily because they are apprehensive about using computer interfaces like the LCD screen, keyboard, and mouse, and do not understand the language used in the game.
7. The older people are interested in playing games similar to DDR which promote their body movements as a form of exercise. The students that had played DDR enjoyed playing it.
8. Older people are hesitant to try DDR because of the fast-paced nature of the dancing game, which is perceived as too demanding for their physical ability. One hundred percent of the older people expressed that an entertainment platform that could allow them to play with children must have an adjustable game speed so that the game pace can be calibrated to suit both parties.
9. Parents are busy at work and often not around at home. They only return home late at night.

From the above observations, in the middle-class Singaporean context, older people and children spend substantial time together as a family. A majority of the students play and enjoy computer gaming experiences. Their familiarity with electronic games and their skill level are much superior to the older generations. There is no widely used computing platform which allows children and older people to play together.

7.3.3 Design Goals

Based on the observations above, we established the design goals for Age Invaders as listed below.

1. Intergenerational family entertainment – We wanted to create an entertainment system that would enable different generations, the grandparents, parents, and children to participate in meaningful game play that could possibly strengthen family bonding.
2. Physical and tangible interaction – Based on the above study, we have identified that the barrier for older users to participate in computer games is attributed to computer interfaces like keyboard and mouse, which seem difficult to use, and a lack of understanding of the language used in games. We propose to use body movements as the interface to the game, replacing the need for a keyboard or joystick to participate in the game. Besides being intuitive, it should also double as a form of exercise and the game controllers should be easy to use tangible interfaces with big buttons that are easy to manipulate.
3. Social interaction – Although there is an emergence of multiplayer games, the interface to the games still remain largely in the form of individual two-dimensional screens to facilitate user interaction. In some cases this is a portable screen, such as with personal game consoles. In either case, it forces the user to

use the media to facilitate the interaction which can cause for a loss of richness in sharing of meaning and emotions. Furthermore, from our initial study, all the older users felt uncomfortable interacting with computer screen interface. Hence, we envisioned a system that would allow players to interact with each other in close physical proximity, while augmenting the experience with the logic of the digital game.
4. Remote interaction – Parents in modern society often have mobile and digital lifestyles. They may be busy at work and go frequently on business trips; hence, it is not always possible to physically interact with their family. To further enhance family interaction and bridge the physical distance between family members, we included a virtual world interface so that parents can join in the game in real time, remotely through the Internet with the players at home.
5. Adjustable game parameters – The older people in the study expressed apprehension to participate in entertainment games because of their incompetence with the technology and the pace of such activities which are perceived as too fast for them, such as the DDR game. Hence, by having adjustable game parameters that could be tailored for users of different levels of physical fitness and competency with the game, we could potentially balance the game play between the older and young players.

7.4 Design Requirements and Ideas Generation

In this step, we identified the design requirements for the prototype. This phase takes into consideration a negotiation of the factors including user needs, context of use, available resources, and time constraints.

7.4.1 Resources and Time Constraints

The research lab takes into account the number of resources and skills available to develop the project. Because the funding of the lab is based on various sources, the tentative dates for the subsequent prototypes were established, but the features to be included remained undefined until the findings from each prototype were released.

7.4.2 User Needs

As older people are hesitant to engage in computer-related activities, the system should support our interaction design goals by not intimidating older people with traditional interfaces, such as keyboard, mouse, and monitor. To support physical interaction, the player's body should become the interface to the system. Instead of fiddling with a keyboard, the players should move their bodies to manipulate the digital elements in the game or entertainment system. Dedicated controllers that are intuitive and simple to use should be introduced. To support both physical and social interaction between players, movement over a big space is recommended. With respect to that, tracking of the players in that space is required. However, we do not want to overwhelm the players with heavy equipment. Thus the tracking should be invisible to the players and the accessories of the system should be wireless in order to limit the hindrance on physical movement in the game space.

From the preliminary user study, we have identified adjustable game parameters as being an important factor in sustaining the players' interest. The older players emphasized that the game should not be too fast such that it would be tiring, nor too slow so that it would become boring.

7.4.3 Context of Use

The system is envisioned as being installed in the home setting. Given this constraint, the system dimensions should be reconfigurable according to the room size. We envisioned the floor platform to be constructed from blocks of square tiles to facilitate this. For example, in houses with more space available, we could construct a larger floor platform consisting of more tiles and fewer tiles for rooms with less space available.

Standard walking width as specified by a common standards handbook is best at 38 cm [29], so the 42 cm square is more than adequate to allow for this. It should be noted that these guidelines use a full-sized adult man as a reference and we understand that this size specification does not apply to all people. Another point to note is that the physical player in our game uses only one of her feet to register the position on the board, so if the player is not able to or feels more comfortable occupying more space, it is quite simple and comfortable to do so.

For parents to play the game remotely from their workspace, the game server is connected to the Internet so that virtual clients can join the game in real time.

7.4.4 Design Ideas Generation

In this step, we carried out brainstorming sessions. We explored popular card games, board games, and puzzle games that are popular in Singapore such as Mah Jong, memory card games, and Rush Hour. We also looked into music and dance games such as DDR.

We also explored popular arcade games such as Pacman and Space Invaders. We were inspired by Human Pacman, in which the players were transformed into characters of the game. We decided to bring Space Invaders out of its original arcade form, transforming grandparents and grandchildren into human space invaders characters, and enabling them to play the game harmoniously at home. Parents at work can also join in the game's virtual world remotely through the Internet browser, thus allowing all three generations to play together.

7.5 Prototype Iterations and System Description

7.5.1 Prototype Iterations

In this section we provide an overview of the prototype iterations from the first prototype which addressed more technical issues, through the more recently tested prototype, which allows for more complex game experiences.

Prototype 1 was a simple proof of concept system, which consisted of five floor blocks with LED display and built-in RFID readers for tracking of player's movements. The prototype confirmed that the players were comfortable moving on the platform and that their position could be registered by the system. The players also tried launching lasers using the customized space gun. This prototype aimed to verify that the system was usable and enjoyable to all the players. Two main issues were identified in this prototype. First, implementing the RFID readers on each blocks of the floor display would be very expensive when the system platform is expanded to a bigger room-sized grid. Second, the space guns used were not suitable for family interaction due to the implicit violence and were too large in size and too bulky to carry around during game sessions.

In prototype 2, we redesigned the RFID reader to be in a pouch strapped on the player's leg and the antenna placed inside the shoe. The RFID tags were placed on the floor grid. RFID tags were significantly cheaper than the reader, hence we could save huge costs using this new design. We also redesigned the space guns to be a simple handheld controller approximately the size of a mobile phone with a simple button to activate the laser beams. We have developed the online virtual player interface and most game functions were implemented. The virtual players can play with real players simultaneously over the Internet. In this prototype we have implemented two games: the Age Invaders and the Rush Hour puzzle game. Age Invaders was much more favored over the puzzle game, due to the physical nature of the game and fast tempo of the interaction.

In prototype 3, we redesigned the floor platform to be rearrangeable and flexible in the number of squares. We have also redesigned the smart slippers to have an embedded RFID antenna, so that the player has only to wear the slippers in order to start playing. This prototype is fully functional with the inclusion of sound in the game. We have carried out most of the in-depth user studies on this version of the system.

In the present prototype, based on the user studies results, we are improving on the smart slipper design, the handheld controller to include vibration and multicolor LED feedback, spatial sound effects, and the development of a toolkit to allow rapid prototyping and reprogrammability of the system in a relatively short time by artists and designers of various skill levels.

7.5.2 Current System Architecture

The system architecture is shown in Fig. 7.2, which consists of a home entertainment system and multiple 3D virtual online clients. The heart of the home entertainment

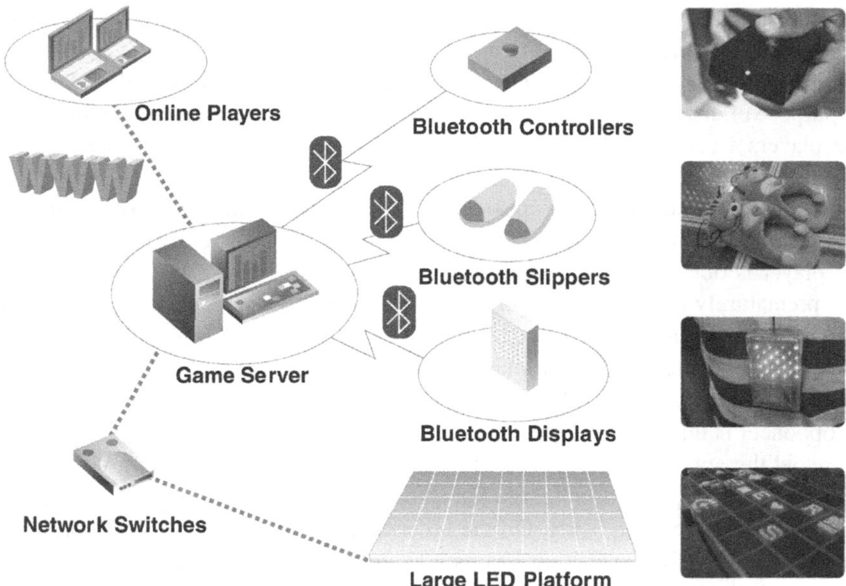

Fig. 7.2 Age Invaders system architecture

system is a game server, which is responsible for handling inputs and outputs of the system in real time. The game logic resides in the server. The game server is connected to the Internet to synchronize the game play between the home system and the virtual clients. Inputs of the system include wireless game controllers for triggering events in the game, wireless smart slippers with embedded RFID readers for tracking the position of the players, and control parameters from the virtual online clients. Outputs of the system include a large LED floor platform for displaying the objects and events of the game, wireless lanyard-style LED displays for displaying individual player's events, and a 3D virtual player interface for displaying the virtual world of the game. As the players move on the floor platform, their coordinates are tracked and translated to the virtual world in real time, creating a seamless link between physical and virtual worlds.

7.5.3 Game Play

The concept of the Age Invaders game is shown in Fig. 7.1. Two children are playing with two grandparents in the interactive physical space while up to two parents can join into the game via the Internet as virtual players, thus increasing the intergenerational interaction. The grandchildren form a team and the grandparents form another. The parents' role is to balance the game between the two teams. In the situation that not all family members are at home, it is possible to play the game with only two players (one in each team). Our study results suggest that users prefer four-player games because the games were more exciting by having a team member to engage in cooperative competition.

Grandparents and grandchildren wear lanyard-style Bluetooth LED displays for the purpose of displaying game events including loss of energy of their virtual avatar. The players wear special slippers with RFID tracking and a Bluetooth-enabled handheld controller device.

Each game session lasts for up to 2 min. The players gain points by picking up bonus items and avoiding laser beams. Each player starts off with five energy levels. The player is out of the game when his/her energy level drops to zero. The game ends prematurely if the energy level of both players of the same team became zero. Otherwise, at the end of 2 min, the team with the highest score wins.

During the game play, as the player presses a button on the handheld device, a laser beam image is displayed on the game board and heads toward the opponent. If the opponent is hit by the laser beam, she will lose one energy level. The opponent can avoid the approaching laser beam by hopping over it or simply moving to the adjacent squares. If the grandparent launches the laser, its speed is fast so that the grandchild has to react quickly. On the other hand, the grandparent has more time to react to the much slower laser beams launched by the grandchild. This balances the game difficulty between the ages.

In order to make the difficulty of the game balanced between the young and older people, Age Invaders imposes additional challenges in an innovative way for the invader players (the young and more dextrous). The invader footprint is one of these challenges. In the game, the invaders are presented with two squares that are adjacent to their current position to which they can move, as shown in Fig. 7.3. There is a timer which requires the advancement of steps each period of time, after which an energy level is deducted. This period is determined by the invader footprint speed which can also be adjusted by the virtual players at any time. To be fair to these players, they are rewarded with one bonus energy level by following the footprints correctly 10 times in a row.

The parents as virtual players can drag-and-drop barriers or energy power-ups in the shape of hearts on the virtual player interface and appear almost immediately on the physical game board rendered in patterns of lights. The physical players can pick up the energy power-ups to gain extra energy. The barriers will block laser beams. Parents can also adjust the game parameters as mentioned previously including the laser speed and the speed of the dance step patterns for the young players to follow. All the actions in the virtual environment are translated to the physical game board in real time. This provides a seamless game interaction between the real-world players and the parents in the virtual world.

The game play challenges and aids are summarized below:

Young Player

– Must follow the dance steps as they appear
– Speed of laser beam is slower

Fig. 7.3 The invaders have to follow the footprints on the floor during the game

– More difficult to collect power-ups unless intended for the player due to being restricted to their indicated squares

Older Player

– Can move freely on the game board
– Speed of laser beam is faster
– Power-up hearts can be collected easily

Virtual Player

– Placing power-ups and barriers
– Balancing the play experience by adjusting the step speed and laser speed

7.6 Intergenerational Player Study

7.6.1 Introduction

Initial study results were presented in [9] using prototype 2, where the players' enjoyment in the game was evaluated against the criteria highlighted in Penelope et al.'s game flow [30]. We have also carried out enjoyment and playability studies with younger players who have familiarity with contemporary electronic gaming, as presented in [10] using prototype 3. The aim is to improve the system from the usability and enjoyment standpoint, before engaging the older players. The younger more technology proficient players are also better able to overcome technological breakdowns of a prototype system and from our experience, are able to vocalize their internal state during the game play. This chapter presents subsequent studies using prototype 3 that looked into intergenerational playability and enjoyment issues.

7.6.2 Methods

In order to validate the enjoyment and playability issues when played according to the design goals, we conducted intergenerational studies as shown in Fig. 7.4, with the same users described in Section 7.3.2. The details of one such study helped to inform on the aspects of the game which were enjoyable and identified issues impeding the positive experience.

In order to determine their habits with their families, all players were surveyed using a paper questionnaire regarding their gaming activities including non-electronic or otherwise with their families. Sixty percent of the young players reported that they play some type of game, while only 30% of the older players

Fig. 7.4 Old and young players taking part in a game play session

reported playing games with their families. Those who do play games with their families reported similar types of games regardless of age. They reported playing chess, cards, board games, and scroll.

In order to "break the ice" and to get the two generations of players to interact and converse, players were organized into 5 teams of 4 players each with a total of 20 players. Each team was made up of two young players (between the ages of 10 and 12 years) and two older players (between the ages of 60 and 80 years). These players made name tags for each other, introduced their teams, and the children were designated as the scribes of the teams and would help the older players to fill out the questionnaires in English. Each team was also designated a game studies facilitator from our lab who helped to ensure that the questionnaires were filled out appropriately and honestly. The game sessions were conducted similar to the previous studies mentioned earlier. The results of the user studies are presented in the following sections organized into three sections, "physical interface design issues, physicality issues of the virtual and physical player roles, and focus group session with older players." Young and old, the players overall enjoyed the game experience with all respondents reporting a positive sentiment with nearly all respondents showing positive experiences and only one reporting a neutral experience. The results discussion is now provided.

7.6.3 Physical Interface Design Issues

In designing an interactive system for older people and children, we aim to have high levels of physical and social interaction among players on interfaces that are easy to use and at the same time require minimal wearable equipment. The large physical floor display replaces the need for head-mounted displays for playing mixed reality games. Virtual objects are displayed on the large display on the floor. The older users reported that they were able to recognize the virtual objects displayed on the floor display immediately and appreciated the bright, easy-to-understand symbols.

To be registered in the game, the players have to wear the smart slippers with a built-in RFID reader. The usability of the smart slippers presented a particular challenge to the older players, most likely due to their reduced mobility and dexterity. All of the adult players agreed that easily adjustable slippers are needed. One generally accepted feature change idea provided by the older players was to use an adjustable Velcro strap to adjust the tightness of fit.

On the other hand, all of the older people were able to understand that the game board was registering their physical steps. Using footsteps as a control mechanism in the game is intuitive for them. Most of the older people in our study recognized the floor platform as similar to the popular Dance Dance Revolution (DDR) dance platform, which they often see young children playing in arcade centers. It is possible that they have already developed a mental model of such a stepping interface, hence it may have increased their acceptance of our floor-sensing interface. Also, many of

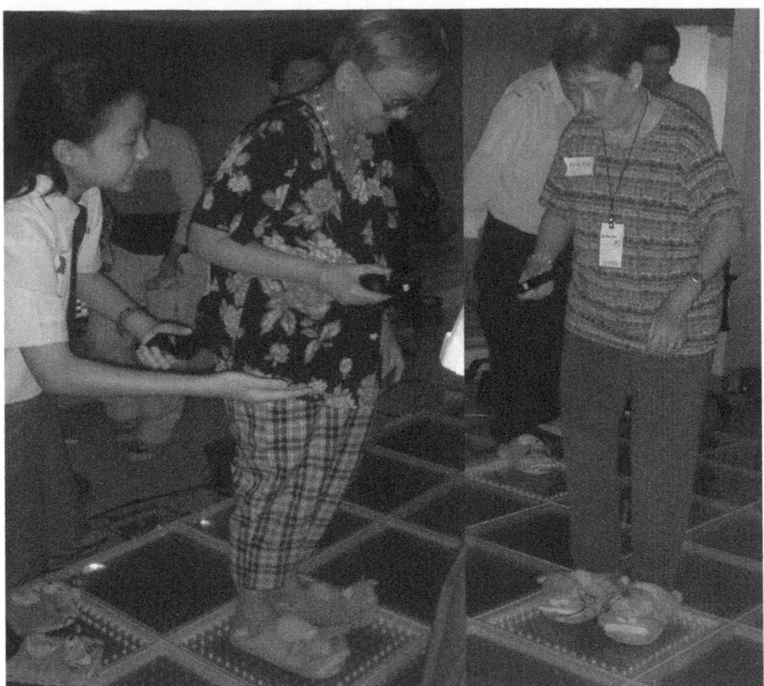

Fig. 7.5 Floor square lighted up when a player steps on it

the older players noted that when they stepped on a square, the light for that square lit up, as shown in Fig. 7.5. This gives immediate feedback to the users that their action is being registered by the system and it reinforces that they understood the purpose of this feature.

Eighty percent of the young players gave feedback that the handheld controller should have haptic feedback for the game events, for example, the reduction of an energy level. They explained that due to many tasks that they need to perform during the game, feedback that does not require their active awareness, for example vibration feedback, is much preferred. The group of older people did not have this concern. They may not have had exposure to this type of multi-modal experience in a game setting previously.

Each player wore a lanyard-style wearable LED display, which hung around their neck that lit up during game events, for example, when hit by a laser, collection of bonus items. None of the users in the study looked at their own display. We found out that it is not intuitive nor easy physically to have the users look at the display while playing the game. One suggestion is to integrate the display into the handheld controller. For future improvement, we will incorporate vibration feedback and an array of multicolor LEDs on the handheld controller as a form of feedback of game status and events.

7.6.4 Physicality Issues of the Virtual and Physical Player Roles

The Age Invaders platform involves the players in a physical game space arena focused on a room-sized game board with 45 tiles each representing a physical position the players can occupy. Physical players register their position in one square at a time since the size of the square is just large enough for one person standing in place. While occupying a square, it is reserved for their avatar in the virtual world enforced by the game logic.

The presence of the virtual player is felt on the physical game space by the evidence of their activities in the virtual game space including the placement of barriers and hearts or by changing the speed of the laser beams. The virtual player's activities were not easily understood by the physical players as being activity directed by the human player versus coming from the logic of the computer program.

We have identified a footprint timer range of 1–3 s to be the most exciting for the young players. Most young players felt the game was challenging because they have to take care of a few tasks at the same time, for instance, following the step patterns, avoiding the approaching laser beams, and trying to launch one. We observed that the footprint makes the game physically more interesting and challenging to the young and less demanding for the older people as they have the freedom to move to any position as they do not need to follow any sequence of steps. This matches the physical effort to the desired amount of movement that the adult prefers. Through the nature of the team competition, the adult is compelled to move into a position to take offensive action, but can easily reduce the amount of movement and play from a more defensive style.

Most players who had experienced the game play from the virtual player role expressed that they found the game play experience less enjoyable than the physical player role. This could have been for a number of reasons which might include the following:

- The physical players interact in a more social situation in which they see the other players
- Interaction in the physical space involves natural conversation and body language
- Interaction in the physical space adds the element of performing onstage for others, while the virtual player does not receive the same feedback
- The physical exertion of the virtual player is much less and involves small hand movements with the mouse and keyboard.

A possible avenue for future development could be to represent the virtual player's avatar in the physical space and participate as a player at the same level. This could allow for a virtual player that has to dodge laser beams and follow dance steps just like the physical player, as opposed to acting as a referee or just balancing the game play. This could be realized with a robot in the physical game space, which the virtual player could control. In place of a robot, a virtual character could be used which could be represented as a special avatar on the physical and virtual game space.

On the other hand, the interface for the virtual player could be modified to include a more physical interaction as well. For example, a DDR-style dance mat could be used to give the physical exertion component to the virtual player who is participating via the Internet and located far from the physical game space. However this feature may not be suitable for parents who are at work.

7.6.5 Focus Group Session with Older Players

Five weeks after we conducted the initial user study for the older and younger people, we went back to the senior center to conduct a follow-up focus group session with seven of the older players as shown in Fig. 7.6. Our aim was to investigate the longer lasting impact of the Age Invaders game. When prompted to describe the most memorable aspects about the game, all of them mentioned the launching of lasers, avoiding lasers, and chasing after the hearts on the game board. We identified that for the older players, the memorable actions in the game are physical in nature. The player has to press the physical button on the wireless controller to launch the virtual laser and in the cases of avoiding lasers and chasing after the hearts, the players have to physically move their bodies.

"This is a fresh idea and it was my first time playing" quoted by one of the older people, to which all agreed. They were all excited about this new entertainment platform. The older people have never performed any computer-related activities or played electronic games before and are afraid to attempt them. However, the players see this physical game system as being so different from traditional computer systems that not only were they comfortable to use the system but they were also having fun interacting with other players while playing.

When asked what skills were involved in playing the game and about the difficulty level, all agreed that the game was easy to learn and that the game speed was

Fig. 7.6 Focus group session with seven older players

fine. A few mentioned that the pace could be a little slower in order to play for a longer period of time. However, they emphasized that the game speed cannot be too slow, otherwise it would become boring. The current game pace is exciting for them. An interesting description was stated by one of the players, "The game gives me good exercise. When you see a heart, you have to run to collect it. If a laser is approaching, you have to avoid it quickly. The game is very engaging and can we play it again?" This supports the design goal of doubling the game as a form of exercise. We also noticed that the older people enjoy moderate physical activity that challenges their visual–motor coordination.

When asked about how much fun was the game as played, they all gave the maximum rating. "Thinking about it now, we can't wait to play again!" said one of them. It is obvious that the older players have enjoyed the game and have high motivation to play the game again. Of particular interest is the fact that the users do not see a strong connection between this system and traditional electronic gaming and computing in general. This high motivation level is valuable in and of itself as confirmation that older adults can be engaged in new technologies and have high enjoyment levels. Ongoing research is underway to understand the long-term use of the system.

7.7 Conclusion

We have presented our user-centered design process for intergenerational family entertainment. This chapter describes the design issues and decisions made during the development of a system with the goal of promoting social and physical interaction across the generations. We utilized the user-centered design approach of keeping the needs of the user central to the project development and constantly validating our assumptions with testing of incremental changes and later stage testing involving game sessions closer to the intended context of use. By following this method, we have been able to create a system, which not only meets the user needs for physical interactive entertainment but has also served to better understand user interaction in the mixed reality context. The extensive user studies helped to shape and construct the physical dimensions of the system beginning in the earlier stages including setting the size of the game squares and the handheld control device. Later refinements guided by the users included refinements to the virtual character role and also highlighted the key strengths of the game scenario. It was precisely the physical nature of the game system that presented the older players with a digital game experience they could easily understand. The older players, who normally express concern and apprehension about computers, were able to enjoy the interactive system and were anxious to try new games made for the platform. The social aspects of the game play were appreciated by two distinctly different groups of players who would not normally play together. Through the variable game parameters, the effort level for all players was set according to physical abilities, which ensured that all players were challenged physically, yet still fostered collaborative competitive play. According to our findings, when making design decisions in developing intergenerational family entertainment systems, the use of one portion of the user base, which is most proficient with technology before involving the novice users, should be considered. During the user studies, we noticed that the children assisted the older players to verbalize the situation and difficulties that they were facing with the game. This was found in our research to empower the novice users to accept digital technology and increased the playability of the game.

References

1. National Research Council USA. The aging population in the twenty-first century. 1998. *Virtual Reality*, 12(1):3–16, March 2008.
2. Bucar A and Kwon S. Computer hardware and software interfaces: Why the elderly are under-represented as computer users. *CyberPsychology & Behavior*, 2(6):535–543, December 1999.
3. Thomas KGF, Laurance HE, Luczak SE, and Jacobs WJ. Age-related changes in a human cognitive mapping system: Data from a computer-generated environment. *CyberPsychology & Behavior*, 2(6):545–566, December 1999.
4. Shneiderman B. Designing the user interface: Strategies for effective human-computer interaction. Addison-Wesley, New York 1998.
5. Jaycox K and Hicks B. Elders, students, and computers. University of Illinois, 1976.
6. Lazzaro N. Why we play games: Four keys to more emotion without story, March 8, 2004. http://www.xeodesign.com/whyweplaygames.html.
7. Granny got game? http://whatjapanthinks.com/2008/02/26/granny-got-game/.
8. Cheok AD, Goh K, Liu W, Farbiz F, Fong S, Teo S, Li Y, and Yang X. Human pacman: A mobile, wide-area entertainment system based on physical, social, and ubiquitous computing. *Personal and Ubiquitous Computing*, 8(2):71–81, May 2004.
9. Khoo ET, Cheok AD, Nguyen T, and Pan Z. Age invaders: Social and physical inter-generational mixed reality family entertainment. Virtual Reality, 12(1):3–16, March 2008.
10. Khoo ET, Merritt T, Cheok AD, Lian M, and Yeo K. Age invaders: User studies of inter-generational computer entertainment. *Entertainment Computing ICEC 2007*, 4740:231–242, 2007.
11. Christian H. An activity analysis of electronic game simulators. *Therapeutic Recreation Journal*, 12:21–25, 1978.
12. McGuire F. Improving the quality of life for residents of long term care facilities through videogames. *Activities, Adaptation and Aging*, 6:1–7, 1984.
13. Weisman S. Computer games and the frail elderly. *Gerontologist*, 23:361–363, 1983.
14. Whitcomb GR. Computer games for the elderly. *SIGCAS Computers and Society*, 20(3):112–115, 1990.
15. Matsuo M, Nagasawa J, Yoshino A, Hiramatsu K, and Kurashiki K. Effects of activity participation of the elderly on quality of life. *Yonago Acta Medica*, 17(46):17–24, 2003.
16. Babyak M, Blumenthal J, Herman S, Khatri P, Doraiswany M, Moore K, Craighead W, Baldewicz T, and Krishnan K. Exercise treatment for major depression: Maintenance of therapeutic benefit at 10 months. *Psychosomatic Medicine*, 62(5):633–638, 2000.
17. Bogost I. The rhetoric of exergaming. In *Proceedings of the Digital Arts and Cultures (DAC) Conference 2005*, December 2005.
18. Fuyuno I. Brain craze. *Nature*, 447:18–20, 2007.
19. Wii. http://en.wikipedia.org/wiki/Wii.
20. Gronbaek K, Iversen OS, Kortbek KJ, Nielsen KR, and Aagaard L. Igamefloor: A platform for co-located collaborative games. In *ACE '07: Proceedings of the international conference on Advances in computer entertainment technology*, pages 64–71, New York, NY, USA, 2007. ACM.

21. Mueller F, Agamanolis S, and Picard R. Exertion interfaces: Sports over a distance for social bonding and fun. In *CHI '03: Proceedings of the SIGCHI conference on Human factors in computing systems*, pages 561–568, New York, NY, USA, 2003. ACM.
22. Florian Mueller and Stefan Agamanolis. Exertion interfaces. In *CHI '07: CHI '07 extended abstracts on Human factors in computing systems*, pages 2857–2860, New York, NY, USA, 2007. ACM.
23. Florian Mueller and Stefan Agamanolis. Exertion interfaces. In *CHI '08: CHI '08 extended abstracts on Human factors in computing systems*, pages 3957–3960, New York, NY, USA, 2008. ACM.
24. Lena Mamykina, Elizabeth D. Mynatt, and David R. Kaufman. Investigating health management practices of individuals with diabetes. In *CHI '06: Proceedings of the SIGCHI conference on Human Factors in computing systems*, pages 927–936, New York, NY, USA, 2006. ACM Press.
25. Boehm BW. A spiral model of software development and enhancement. *Computer*, 21(5):61–72, May 1988.
26. Fallman D. Design-oriented human-computer interaction. In *CHI '03: Proceedings of the SIGCHI conference on Human factors in computing systems*, pages 225–232, New York, NY, USA, 2003. ACM Press.
27. Gulliksen J, Göransson B, Boivie I, Blomkvist S, Persson J, and Cajander Å. Key principles for user-centred systems design. *Behaviour & Information Technology*, 22(6):397–409, 2003.
28. State of the family in Singapore. http://fcd.ecitizen.gov.sg/CommitteeontheFamily/Research/Executive+Summary.htm.
29. Human factors/ergonomics handbook for the design for ease of maintenance. http://tis.eh.doe.gov/techstds/standard/hdbk1140/hdbk1140.html.
30. Sweetser P and Wyeth P. Gameflow: A model for evaluating player enjoyment in games. *Computers in Entertainment (CIE)*, 3(3):3, July 2005.

Chapter 8
Auditory-Induced Presence in Mixed Reality Environments and Related Technology

Pontus Larsson, Aleksander Väljamäe, Daniel Västfjäll, Ana Tajadura-Jiménez, and Mendel Kleiner

Abstract Presence, the "perceptual illusion of non-mediation," is often a central goal in mediated and mixed environments, and sound is believed to be crucial for inducing high-presence experiences. This chapter provides a review of the state of the art within presence research related to auditory environments. Various sound parameters such as externalization and spaciousness and consistency within and across modalities are discussed in relation to their presence-inducing effects. Moreover, these parameters are related to the use of audio in mixed realities and example applications are discussed. Finally, we give an account of the technological possibilities and challenges within the area of presence-inducing sound rendering and presentation for mixed realities and outline future research aims.

Keywords Presence · Auditory · Auralization · Sound · Acoustics · Virtual environments · Mixed reality · Augmented reality

8.1 Audio in Mixed Realities

As with virtual reality (VR) and virtual environment (VE), the concept of mixed reality (MR) has come to mean technologies that primarily concern various forms of visual displays. There is nonetheless a range of possibilities of using audio for the purpose of mixing realities and blurring the boundary between what is real and what is not. The purpose of integrating audio into the MR application is usually not only to add functionalities and alternative information presentation, but also to enhance the user experience.

P. Larsson (✉)
Volvo Technology Corporation, SE-405 08 Göteborg, Sweden
e-mail: pontus.larsson@chalmers.se

E. Dubois et al. (eds.), *The Engineering of Mixed Reality Systems*, Human-Computer Interaction Series, DOI 10.1007/978-1-84882-733-2_8,

A great advantage of audio compared to visual displays is that the mediation technology may be less visible and less obvious – for example, when using hidden loudspeakers or comfortable, open headphones. Compared to visual displays, mixing virtual and real audio is also relatively easy and cost-efficient: simply superimposing virtual sound on the real sonic environment using open headphones is usually sufficient for many applications (a technique comparable to optical mixing in visual displays) [1]. Using closed headphones with external microphones attached to mix virtual and real digitally is also possible and has been subject to some recent research [2]. This technique has the advantage of giving the possibility of efficiently attenuating certain sounds and letting others through but comes with a higher computational demand.

The extent to which audio is used in MR may of course vary and one may use audio for several different purposes, ranging from full-blown, entirely virtual 3D soundscapes with hundreds of sound sources and realistic room acoustic rendering seamlessly blended with the real-world acoustics, to very simple monophonic sounds produced via one loudspeaker (cf. Apple's Mighty Mouse™, which has a built-in piezoelectric loudspeaker producing click sounds). Different audio rendering techniques may of course also be combined in the same application.

It is rather straightforward to define different levels of reality mixing when talking about entirely visual stimuli/displays. One may distinguish four different distinct visual display cases along the virtuality continuum [3]: real environment (RE), augmented reality (AR), augmented virtuality (AV), and virtual environment (VE). The same cases may of course also be identified for auditory displays. Cases explaining auditory RE and VE are probably superfluous, but an AR audio application may for example be an interactive museum guide telling stories and augmenting sound to the different objects and artifacts as the museum visitor approaches them. Audio integrated in interaction devices and in such way increases the impression of the devices being a part of the mediation system could also be seen as audio AR. An example of using audio in interaction devices is the Nintendo Wii™ remote, which actually has a built-in loudspeaker which produces sound when the user, e.g., hits a virtual tennis ball or swings a virtual golf club. This audio augmentation thus provides a connection between the interaction device and the visual world – efficiently mixing the real and the virtual also across the displays.

The AV case, where a real object is mixed with the VE, is perhaps less distinguishable within the realm of auditory displays but could be exemplified by, e.g., systems where the user's own voice is integrated with the VE [4]. Another example is when the user's footsteps are amplified and presented within the VE to provide interaction feedback and enhance presence (see [5], although this study used synthetic generation of the footstep sounds).

In many cases when we discuss MR/VE audio, however, the sound is also accompanied by a visual display or visual information in some other form. For example, in our museum guide case above, the visitor not only hears the augmented audio but naturally also watches all the museum artifacts, reads signs and displays, and experiences the interior architecture visually. In more advanced systems, the auditory virtual information is also accompanied by digital visual information of some degree of virtuality. As such, the MR situation – or at least the taxonomy – becomes more complex; for audiovisual displays, there should exist at least 16 different distinct ways of mixing realities as shown in the table below.

As displayed in the table, the only cases which are *not* MR are the ones where we have real or virtual displays in both modalities at the same time, i.e., RE/RE and VE/VE – between these end points we have a continuous range of audiovisual reality mixing possibilities. It should be noted however that to be defined strictly as MR it seems reasonable that for cases where reality in one display is mixed with virtual information in another display, the content provided by reality should be *relevant* to the virtual environment. Thus, when we have a VE visual display and a real auditory environment (top right cell in Table 8.1), the auditory environment should contain information that is relevant to the visual environment for the system to be defined as an MR system. As an example, disturbing noise from projecting systems can probably not be classified as a relevant sound for the visual VE while the voice of a co-user of the VE most likely is a relevant and useful sound.

Regardless of the type of (audiovisual) reality mixing, the central goal of many MR systems is, or at least should be, to maximize the user experience. However, with added sensory stimulation and system complexity, measuring the performance of MR in terms of user experience is becoming more and more difficult. For this reason, the concept of presence (the user's perceptual illusion of non-mediation [6]) is important since it offers a common way of analyzing and evaluating a range of media technologies and content, regardless of complexity. Obtaining presence is also often a central goal of many mediation technologies such VR, computer games, and computer-supported communication and collaboration systems, and, as we will explain in the next section, sound and auditory displays have the potential of greatly enhancing presence.

Table 8.1 The 2D audiovisual reality–virtuality matrix. Only the cases in bold – REAL and VIRTUAL – can be considered as non-MR situations

Visual display (columns) / Auditory display (rows)

	Real Environment (RE)	Augmented Reality (AR)	Augmented Virtuality (AV)	Virtual Environment (VE)
RE	**aud: RE** **vis: RE** ***REAL***	aud: RE vis: AR *MIXED*	aud: RE vis: AV *MIXED*	aud: RE vis: VE *MIXED*
AR	aud: AR vis: RE *MIXED*	aud: AR vis: AR *MIXED*	aud: AR vis: AV *MIXED*	aud: AR vis: VE *MIXED*
AV	aud: AV vis: RE *MIXED*	Aud: AV vis: AR *MIXED*	aud: AV vis: AV *MIXED*	aud: AV vis: VE *MIXED*
VE	aud: VE vis: RE *MIXED*	Aud: VE vis: AR *MIXED*	aud: VE vis: AV *MIXED*	**aud: VE** **vis: VE** **VIRTUAL**

8.2 Presence and Auditory Displays

A common definition of presence which was first introduced by Lombard and Ditton [6] is "the perceptual illusion of non-mediation." The perceptual illusion of non-mediation occurs when the user fails to (perceptually) recognize that there is a mediation system between the user and the virtual world or object. There are several sub-conceptualizations of presence which apply to different areas of research and to different kinds of applications [6]. A representation of an avatar on an ordinary, small-sized computer screen, for example, may convey the sensation that the avatar is really there, in front of you, a sensation which may be termed "object presence." In the case of social interaction applications, the presence goal may be formulated as creating a feeling of being in the same communicative space as another, co-user of the virtual environment (termed social presence, "the feeling of being together"). For immersive single-user VEs, presence is most commonly defined as the sensation of "you being there," that is, a matter of you being transported to another, possibly remote, location – something which may be termed "spatial presence." As the concept of mixed reality (MR) spans the whole reality–virtuality continuum and may involve both user–user and user–virtual object/world interactions [5], all these presence conceptualizations may be useful when designing MR systems.

Although the conceptualizations are rather clear, the process of actually inducing and measuring these perceptual illusions efficiently is far from being fully understood. It is clear however that sound plays an important role in forming presence percepts [7, 8–10]. In fact, it has even been proposed that auditory input is crucial to achieving a full sense of presence, given that auditory perception is not commonly "turned off" in the same way as we regularly block visual percepts by shutting our eyes [7]. As Gilkey and Weisenberger [7] suggest, auditory displays, when properly designed, are likely to be a cost-efficient solution to high-presence virtual displays.

Auditory signals can have a strong impact on an overall presence response in a number of ways. First, although the visual system has a very high spatial resolution, our field of view is always limited and we have to turn our heads to sense the whole surrounding environment through our eyes [10]. The auditory system is less accurate than the visual one in terms of spatial resolution but on the other hand has the ability of providing us with spatial cues from the entire surrounding space at the same time. Moreover, the auditory system allows us to both locate objects, primarily by means of direct sound components, and feel surrounded by a spatial scene, by means of wall reflections and reverberation. Thus, sound should be able to induce both object presence ("the feeling of something being located at a certain place in relation to myself") and spatial presence ("the feeling of being inside or enveloped by a particular space") at the same time.

Second, while a visual scene – real or virtual – may be completely static, sound is by nature constantly ongoing and "alive"; it tells us that something is happening. This temporal nature of sound should be important for both object presence and spatial presence; the direct sound from the object constantly reminds us that it is actually there, and it is widely known that the temporal structure of reflections and reverberation highly affects the spatial impression. It has moreover been found that temporal resolution is much higher in the auditory domain than that in the visual domain, and it is likely that rhythm information across all modalities is encoded and memorized based on "auditory code" [11].

8.3 Spatial Sound Rendering and Presentation Technologies

Since the invention of the phonograph, made by Thomas A. Edison in 1877, sound recording and reproduction techniques have been continuously evolving. Preserving the spatial characteristics of the recorded sound environment has always been an important topic of research, a work that started already in 1930s with the first stereo systems that were made commercially available in 1960s. The aim of spatial sound rendering is to create an impression of a sound environment surrounding a listener in the 3D space, thus simulating auditory reality. This goal has been assigned many different terms including auralization, spatialized sound/3-D sound, and virtual acoustics, which have been used interchangeably in the literature to refer to the creation of virtual listening experiences. For example, the term auralization was coined by Kleiner et al. [12] and is defined as "...the process of rendering audible, by physical or mathematical modeling, the soundfield of a source in a space, in such way as to simulate the binaural listening experience at a given position in the modeled space."

One common criterion for technological systems delivering spatial audio is the level of perceptual accuracy of the rendered auditory environment, which may be very different depending on application needs (e.g., highly immersive VR or videoconferencing).

Apart from the qualitative measure of perceptual accuracy, spatial audio systems can be divided into head-related and soundfield-related methods. Interested readers can find detailed technical information on these two approaches in books by Begault [13] and Rumsey [14], respectively (see also the review by Shilling and Shinn-Cunningham [15]). The following sections will briefly describe current state-of-the-art technologies for reproduction of spatial audio and discuss their use in MR systems for presence delivery. One specific technology area not covered here is ultrasound displays which can provide a directed sound beam to a specific location (e.g., Audiospotlight http://www.holosonics.com; see more in [16]).

8.3.1 Multichannel Loudspeaker Reproduction

Soundfield-related or multichannel loudspeaker audio reproduction systems can give a natural spatial impression over a certain listening area – the so-called *sweet spot* area. The size of this sweet spot area mainly depends on the number of audio channels used. At present time, five- or seven-channel, often referred to as surround sound systems, has become a part of many audiovisual technologies and is a de facto standard in digital broadcasting and cinema domains. Such technologies have also been successfully used in various augmented reality applications, e.g., traffic awareness systems for vehicles [17], and are often an integral part of computer game and music applications.

Nonetheless, the next generations of multichannel audio rendering systems are likely to have a larger number of channels, as it is used in the technologies providing better spatial rendering such as 10.2-channel [18], vector-based amplitude panning – VBAP [19], ambisonics [20], or wave field synthesis – WFS [21, 22]. WFS can create a correct spatial impression over an entire listening area using large loudspeaker arrays surrounding it (typically > 100 channels). Currently the WFS concept has been coupled with object-based rendering principles, where the desired soundfield is synthesized at the receiver side from separate signal inputs representing the sound objects and data representing room acoustics [23].

8.3.2 Headphone Reproduction

Head-related audio rendering/reproduction systems, also referred to as binaural systems, are two-channel 3D audio technologies using special pre-filtering of sound signals imitating mainly the head, outer ears (the pinnae), and torso effects. These technologies are based on measuring the transfer functions, or impulse responses, between sound sources located at various positions around the head and the left and right ears of a human subject or an artificial dummy head. The measurement can be conducted using a small loudspeaker and miniature microphones mounted inside a person's or dummy head's left and right ear canal entrances. The loudspeaker is placed at a certain horizontal/vertical angle relative to the head, and the loudspeaker–microphone transfer functions or impulse responses are then measured using maximum length sequence (MLS), chirp, or similar acoustic measurement techniques from which the head-related transfer functions (HRTFs) or head-related impulse responses (HRIRs) can be calculated. When a soundfile is filtered or convolved with the HRTFs/HRIRs and the result is reproduced through headphones, it appears as if the sound is coming from the angle where the measurement loudspeaker was located. The measurement is then repeated for several other loudspeaker positions around the head and stored in an HRTF catalog which then can be used to spatialize the sound at desired spatial positions.

Currently most binaural rendering systems use generic HRTF catalogs (i.e., not the users' own set of HRTFs but a measurement using a dummy head or another human subject) due to the lengthy procedure of recording users' own HRTF; however, individualized catalogs are proven to enhance presence [24].

When generic HRTFs are used the most common problem is in-head localization (IHL), where sound sources are not externalized but are rather perceived as being inside the listener's head [25]. Another known artifact is a high rate of reversals in perception of spatial positions of the virtual sources where binaural localization cues are ambiguous (cone of confusion), e.g., front–back confusion [13]. Errors in elevation judgments can also be observed for stimuli processed with non-individualized HRTFs [26]. These problems are believed to be reduced when head-tracking and individualized HRTFs are used [25]. At the current time it is popular to use anthropometric data (pinnae and head measurements) for choosing "personalized" HRTFs from a database containing HRTF catalogs from several individuals [27]. However, as the auditory system expresses profound plasticity in the spatial localization domain, a person can adapt to localization with some generic HRTF catalog. One could see these processes as re-learning to hear with modified pinnae as was shown in [28]. This natural ability to adapt to new HRTF catalogs might be used when specifically modified, "supernormal" as termed by Durlach et al. [29], transfer functions are introduced in order to enhance localization performance, e.g., to reduce the front–back confusions [30].

Generally, binaural systems are used for sound reproduction over headphones, which make them very attractive for wearable AR applications (see the excellent review by Härmä et al. [31]). However, binaural sound can be also reproduced by a pair of loudspeakers if additional processing is applied (cross-talk cancellation technique), which sometimes is used in teleconferencing [32]. Three-dimensional audio systems are designed for creating a spatial audio impression for a single listener, which can be disadvantageous for applications where several users are sharing same auralized space and use it for communication, such as in CAVE simulations.

An alternative way of presenting sound for auditory MR/AR is by using bone conducted (BC) sound transducers [33]. BC sound is elicited by human head vibrations which are transmitted to the cochlea through the skull bones ([34]; for a recent review on BC see [35]). Most people experience BC sound in everyday life; approximately 50% of the sound energy when hearing one's own voice is transmitted through bone conduction [36]. It is important to note that binaural, spatial sound reproduction is also possible via BC sound if bilateral stimulation via two head vibrators is applied [37, 38].

Currently, the largest area of BC sound applications is in hearing acuity testing and hearing aids, where the transducer is either implanted or pressed against the skull. Recently, BC sound has proven interesting for communication systems as it facilitates the use of open ear canals. Such headphone-free communication not only allows for perception of the original surrounding environment but is also ideally suited for MR and AR applications [38]. First, additional sound rendering with open ear canals is ideally suited for speech translation purposes, where original language can by accompanied with synchronized speech of the translator. Another option is a scenario of interactive augmented auditory reality, where a voice rendered via BC sound is telling a story and the real sonic environment plays the role of a background. As a user can have several sensors providing the information about the environment such as in the "Sonic City" application by Gaye et al. [39], the BC sound-based narration can be dynamically changing to fit the user's environment. Finally, a combination of loudspeaker reproduction with BC sound can influence the perception of soundscape since sound localized close to the head serves as a good reference point for other surroundings sounds.

8.3.3 Presentation Systems – Design Considerations

When designing spatial sound presentation systems for MR one primarily needs to consider the following: (1) if the system is intended for sound delivery for a single point of audition or if the listener should be able to change his listening position without applying head-tracking and corresponding resynthesis of the sound scene (e.g., WFS with large listening area vs. Ambisonics with relatively small sweet spot); (2) how large listening area is required; (3) complexity and cost of the system; (4) if there are any undesirable acoustic properties of the room in which the system should be used (e.g., room native reverberation, external noise, etc.); and (5) what type of visual rendering/presentation system (if any) is to be used with the sound system.

Generally, stationary visual setups impose restrictions on the number and configuration of loudspeakers used (e.g., it might be difficult to use large loudspeaker arrays), thus significantly reducing the spatial audio system's capabilities. Headphone reproduction, on the other hand, clearly manifests a mediation device (i.e., the user knows for sure that the sound is delivered through the headphones). No direct comparison between effect of headphone and loudspeaker listening to spatial sound and presence has been carried out apart from the study by Sanders and Scorgie [40], who did not use proper binaural synthesis for headphone reproduction conditions and thus could not adequately access the importance of sound localization accuracy on auditory presence responses.

One would expect that the use of headphones (particularly the closed or insert types), which in principle leads to a heightened auditory self-awareness in a similar manner as earplugs do, would have a negative influence on the sense of presence ([24, 4] and see also Section 8.4). Binaural synthesis also can result in high auditory rendering update rates (this can be addressed by perceptually optimized auralization algorithms described in Section 8.3.4) and lower sense of externalization. Positive features of headphone reproduction are that they may be used for wearable applications such as AR and that the acoustic properties of the listening room are less critical. Depending on the application, indirect, microphone-based communication between users sharing ME can be considered as advantageous or not.

8.3.4 Virtual Acoustics Synthesis and Optimization

As spatial qualities and spaciousness are likely to influence presence to great extent, accurate synthesis of room acoustics is very important for spatial audio in MR applications. Moreover, adequate real-time changes of the auditory environment reflecting listener's or sound source's movement can be crucial for the sense of presence [41]. With the development of software implementations of different geometrical acoustics algorithms, high-accuracy computer-aided room acoustic prediction and auralization software such as CATT (www.catt.se) or ODEON (www.odeon.dk) have become important tools for acousticians but are limited in terms of real-time performance. Acoustic prediction algorithms simulating early sound reflections (< 100 ms) and the diffuse reverberation field in real time are often denoted virtual acoustics. Two different strategies for this real-time auralization are usually employed: (1) the physics-based approach, where geometrical acoustics techniques are adapted to meet low input–output latency requirements (e.g., [42]) or (2) the perceptual approach, where attributes of created listener impression, such as room envelopment, are of main concern (e.g., [43]). A second problem is how to accomplish optimal listening conditions for multiple listeners as optimization today only can be performed for a single sweet spot area.

Complex, high-quality room acoustics and whole auditory scene rendering in real time still require dedicated multiprocessor systems or distributed computing systems. The problem of efficiently simulating a large number of sound sources (> 60) in a scene together with the proper room acoustics simulation still remains the one big unsolved problem for virtual acoustics applications [41]. A common approach to adapt the synthesis resources is to employ automatic distance culling, which means that more distant sound sources are not rendered. However, audible artifacts can occur when a large number of sound sources are close to the listener, especially when these sources represent one large object, e.g., a car. Extending the philosophy of the perceptual approach and taking into account spatial masking effects of the auditory system [44, 45], only perceptually relevant information can be rendered thus supporting a vast number of sources [46].

8.4 Auditory Presence in Mediated Environments: Previous Findings

Despite the availability of a range of audio rendering and presentation technologies and the obvious advantages of using sound as a presence-inducing component in VEs and MRs, sound has received comparably little attention in presence research. There are still very few studies which explicitly deal with the topic of auditory presence in MRs, and the findings reviewed in this section may appear to concern only VEs. As indicated in Section 8.1 though, it is not obvious where the line between strictly VE and MR should be drawn when multiple modalities are involved. For example, an entirely virtual auditory environment combined with the real visual world should, according to our proposed taxonomy (shown in Table 8.1), be defined as MR. Some of the studies presented here are as such not conducted using entirely virtual environments and could easily be classified as MR studies, but we still chose to refer to them as VE studies for simplicity.

We will here provide a review of what we believe are the most important factors contributing to auditory or audiovisual presence experience. It is clear nonetheless that all the results cannot be generalized to all applications and cases of reality mixing, but are still believed to be useful as a starting point in the continued discussion on novel MR paradigms.

8.4.1 Presence and the Auditory Background

To examine the role of audition in VE's, Gilkey and Weisenberger [7] compared the sensation of sudden deafness with the sensation of using no-sound VEs. When analyzing the work of Ramsdell ([47], in [7]), who interviewed veterans returning from World War II with profound hearing loss, they found terms and expressions similar to those used when describing sensations of VEs. One of the most striking features of Ramsdell's article was that the deaf observers felt as if the world was "dead," lacking movement, and that "the world had taken on a strange and unreal quality" ([7], p. 358). Such sensations were accounted for the lack of "the auditory background of everyday life," sounds of clocks ticking, footsteps, running water, and other sounds that we often do not typically pay attention to [7, 47]. Drawing on these tenets, Murray et al. [24] carried out a series of experiments where participants were fitted with earplugs and instructed to carry out some everyday tasks during 20 minutes. Afterward, the participants were requested to account for their experience and to complete a questionnaire comprising presence-related items. Overall, support was found for the notion of background sounds being important for the sensation of "being part of the environment," termed by Murray et al. as environmentally anchored presence. This suggests that in augmented reality (AR) and MR applications, the use of non-attenuating, open headphones which allow for normal perception of the naturally occurring background sounds would thus be extremely important to retain users' presence in the real world. Open headphones also allow for simple mixing of real and virtual acoustic elements which of course may be a highly desirable functional demand of AR/MR applications.

Finally, the use of the earplugs also resulted in a situation where participants had a heightened awareness of self, in that they could better hear their own bodily sounds and which in turn contributed to the sensation of unconnectedness to the surround (i.e., less environmentally anchored presence). In addition to stressing the importance of the auditory background in mediated environments, Murray et al.'s study shows that the auditory self-representation can be detrimental to an overall sense of presence. This suggests that the use of closed or insert headphones, which in principle leads to a heightened auditory self-awareness in a similar manner as earplugs do, would not be appropriate for presenting VEs or MRs.

In a similar vein, Pörschmann [4] considered the importance of adequate representation of one's own voice in VEs. The VE system described by Pörschmann had the possibility of providing a natural sounding feedback of the user's voice through headphones by compensating for the insertion loss of the headphones. Furthermore, room reflections could be added to the voice feedback as well as to other sound sources. In his experiment, Pörschmann showed that this compensation of the headphones' insertion loss was more efficient in inducing presence than the virtual room acoustic cues (the added room reflections). That is, hearing one's own voice in a natural and realistic way may be crucial to achieving high-presence experiences which again stresses the importance of not using closed, sound muffling headphones (if the headphone effects cannot be compensated for).

8.4.2 Spatial Properties

Regarding spatial properties of sound and presence in VEs, Hendrix and Barfield [48] showed that sound compared to no sound increased presence ratings but also that spatialized sound was favored in terms of presence compared to non-spatialized sound. The effect was, however, not as strong as first suspected. Hendrix and Barfield suggested that their use of non-individualized HRTFs may have prevented the audio from being externalized (i.e., the sound appeared as coming from inside the head rather than from outside) and thus less presence enhancing than expected. Some support for this explanation can be found in the study by Väljamäe et al. [49], where indications of individualized HRTFs having a positive influence on the sensation of presence in auditory VE's were found.

In general, externalization is important for MR systems since it is likely to reduce the sensation of wearing headphones and thus also the feeling of unconnectedness to the surround [24]. Moreover, in MR systems which combine an auditory VE with a real visual environment, externalization potentially increases the perceived consistency between the auditory and visual environments. It is however possible that consistent visual information per se increases the externalization in these types of MEs and is not only dependent on HRTF individualization

Proper externalization can also be obtained by adding room acoustic cues [50]. In a study by Larsson et al. [51], anechoic representations of auditory-only VEs were contrasted with VEs containing room acoustic cues. A significant increase in presence ratings was obtained for the room acoustic cue conditions in this study, which was explained by the increased externalization. However, even if room acoustic cues are included, the reproduction technique still seems to influence the sense of presence. In a between-group study by Larsson et al. [52], stereo sound (with room acoustic cues) combined with a visual VE was contrasted to binaural sound (also with room acoustic cues) combined with the same visual VE. Here, it was shown that although room acoustic cues were present for both conditions, the binaural simulation yielded significantly higher presence ratings. Nonetheless, if virtual room acoustic cues are used in a ME, care should be taken to make them consistent with the visual impression and/or with the real room acoustic cues that possibly are being mixed into the auditory scene. Otherwise, it is likely that the user's sense of presence in the ME is disrupted due to the fact that perceptually different environments, spaces, are being mixed together [9].

Taking a broader perspective, Ozawa et al. [53] performed experiments with the aim to characterize the influence of sound quality, sound information, and sound localization on users' self-ratings of presence. The sounds used in their study were mainly binaurally recorded ecological sounds, i.e., footsteps, vehicles, doors, etc. In their study, Ozawa et al., found that especially two factors, obtained through factor analysis of ratings of 33 sound quality items, had high positive correlation with sensed presence: "sound information" and "sound localization." This implies that there are two important considerations when designing sound for MEs, one being that sounds should be informative and enable listeners to imagine the original/

intended or augmented scene naturally, and the other being that sound sources should be well localizable by listeners.

Spaciousness has since long been one of the defining perceptual attributes of concert halls and other types of rooms for music. For MR applications involving simulations of enclosed spaces, a correct representation of spaciousness is of course essential for the end user's experience. A "correct representation" would mean that the virtual room's reverberation envelops the listener in a similar manner as in real life. The potential benefits of adding spacious room reverberation have unfortunately been largely overlooked in previous research on presence, apart from the studies presented in [51–53]. Recently, however, subjective evaluation methods of spatial audio have employed a new spaciousness attribute termed "presence" similar to attributes used in VE presence research, defined as "...the sense of being inside an (enclosed) space or scene" ([54] and references therein), which promises future explorations of this subject.

8.4.3 Sound Quality and Sound Content

As suggested in the research by Ozawa et al. [53], the spatial dimension of sound is not the only auditory determinant of presence. In support of this, Freeman et al. [55] found no significant effect of adding three extra channels of sound in their experiment using an audiovisual rally car sequence, which was partly explained by the fact that the program material did not capitalize on the spatial auditory cues provided by the additional channels. On the other hand, they found that enhancing the bass content and sound pressure level (SPL) increased presence ratings. In a similar vein, Ozawa and Miyasaka [56] found that presence ratings increased with reproduced SPL for conditions without any visual stimulus, but that sensed presence in general was the highest for realistic SPLs when the visual stimulus was presented simultaneously with the auditory stimuli. In audiovisual conditions with an "inside moving car" stimulus, however, presence was the highest for the highest SPL, which was explained by the fact that increased SPL may have compensated for the lack of vibrotactile stimulation. A study by Sanders and Scorgie [40] compared conditions in virtual reality with no sound, surround sound, headphone reproduction, and headphone plus low-frequency sound reproduction via subwoofer. Both questionnaires and psychophysiological measures (temperature, galvanic skin response) were used to access affective responses and presence. All sound conditions significantly increased presence, but only surround sound resulted in significant changes in the physiological response followed by a marginal trend for the condition with headphones combined with a subwoofer.

From these studies one could draw the conclusion that it is important to calibrate both the overall SPL and the frequency response of an MR audio system so that it can produce a sound which is consistent with what the user sees. It is probably also important to calibrate virtually augmented sound with real sound sources so that a consistent mixed auditory scene is achieved and unwanted masking effects are avoided.

Another related line of research has been concerned with the design of the sound itself and its relation to presence [57, 58]. Taking the approach of ecological perception, Chueng and Marsden [58] proposed that expectation and discrimination are two possible presence-related factors; expectation being the extent to which a person expects to hear a specific sound in a particular place and discrimination being the extent to which a sound will help to uniquely identify a particular place. The result from their studies suggested that what people expect to hear in certain real-life situations can be significantly different from what they actually hear. Furthermore, when a certain type of expectation was generated by a visual stimulus, sound stimuli meeting this expectation induced a higher sense of presence as compared to when sound stimuli mismatched with expectations were presented along with the visual stimulus. These findings are especially interesting for the design of computationally efficient VEs, since they suggest that only those sounds that people expect to hear in a certain environment need to be rendered. The findings are also interesting for, e.g., an ME consisting of a real visual environment, an AR/AV auditory environment, since they imply that it might be disadvantageous to mix in those real sound sources, which, although they do belong to the visual environment, do not meet the expectations users get from the visual impression. In this case one could instead reduce the unexpected sound sources (by active noise cancellation or similar) and enhance or virtually add the ones that do meet the expectations.

8.4.4 Consistency Across and Within Modalities

An often reoccurring theme in presence research, which we already have covered to some extent, is that of consistency between the auditory and the visual display [4, 59, 55, 57, 58, 60]. Consistency may be expressed in terms of the similarity between visual and auditory spatial qualities [4, 59], the methods of presentation of these qualities [55], the degree of auditory–visual co-occurrence of events [57, 60], and the expectation of auditory events given by the visual stimulus [58]. Ozawa et al. [60] conducted a study in which participants assessed their sense of presence obtained with binaural recordings and recorded video sequences presented on a 50-inch display. The results showed an interesting auditory–visual integration effect; presence ratings were highest when the sound was matched with a visual sequence where the sound source was actually visible.

As discussed previously in Section 8.4.2, it is likely that proper relations between auditory and visual spaciousness are needed to achieve a high sense of presence. In an experiment by Larsson et al. [59], a visual model was combined with two different acoustic models: one corresponding to the visual model and the other of approximately half the size of the visual model. The models were represented by means of a CAVE-like virtual display and a multichannel sound system, and used in an experiment where participants rated their experience in terms of presence after performing a simple task in the VE. Although some indications were found supporting that the auditory, visually matched condition was rated as being the most presence-inducing one, the results were not as strong as predicted. An explanation to these findings, suggested by Larsson et al., was that, as visual distances and sizes often are underestimated in VEs [61, 62], it was likely that neither the "proper"-sized acoustic model nor the "wrong"-sized acoustic model corresponded to the visual model from a perceptual point of view. Thus, a better understanding of how visual "spaciousness" or room size is perceived would be needed to perform further studies on this topic.

It has been suggested that also the degree of consistency *within* modalities would affect presence [9]. In the auditory domain, an example of an inconsistent stimulus could be a combination of sounds normally associated with different contexts (e.g., typical outdoor sounds combined with indoor sounds), or simply that the SPL of a virtual, augmented sound source does not match the SPL of the real sound environment (as we discussed in Section 8.4.3 above). Another type of within-modality inconsistency could be produced by spatializing a sound using a motion trajectory not corresponding to that particular sound. Assume, for example, that we want to create the sensation of standing next to a road as a car passes by. This situation can be simulated by convolving a, preferably anechoic, car sound with HRTFs corresponding to the (time-varying) spatial locations of the virtual car. A within-modality inconsistency could then occur, e.g., if the sound of a car driving at low speed is convolved with an HRTF trajectory corresponding to a high-speed passage. In our experiments on auditory-induced self-motion sensation [49, 51], we observed that inconsistencies in the auditory scene had a considerable impact on presence and self-motion ratings. These inconsistencies included both artifacts from using the generic HRTFs (wrong motion trajectories) and more high-order effects caused by ecological inconsistency of the sound environment, for example, strange combinations of naturalistic stimuli representing concrete sound objects (e.g., the sound of dog or a bus) and artificial sounds (modulated tones). Therefore, one should be careful when creating virtual sound environments where ecological consistency and efficient spatial sound localization have to be assured. It is likely that a combination of both ambient and clearly localizable sounds should result in auditory-induced presence. It should be also noted that increased virtual sound environment complexity might create a reverse effect, as using too many sound effects will rather destroy the spatial sound image (see [63] for such effect in cinema sound design).

In sum, we see that a general understanding of various auditory display factors' contribution to the sense of presence begins to emerge. When designing audio for MR systems, it thus seems important not only to consider the spatial qualities (e.g., localization, externalization, and spaciousness) and general sound quality issues (e.g., low-frequency content), but one also has to assure that the sound's spatial and content qualities are consistent and match stimuli in other modalities. It is however clear that the findings presented above need further corroboration with different content and different measurement methodologies.

8.5 Example Scenario: The MR Museum of Music History

In this section we describe a scenario where several aspects of using audio in MR are exemplified. The example scenario furthermore suggests several different ways of mixing realities both across and within display types. The scenario which we call the MR museum of music history is yet only an imaginary product but believed to be a useful intellectual experiment showing both possibilities and challenges within the area of audio and audiovisual MR.

8.5.1 Displays and Interaction Devices

Upon entering the MR museum of music history, the visitors are provided with a wearable audiovisual MR system which is their primary interface to the museum experience. The interface consists of a see-through stereoscopic HMD which also doubles as stereoscopic shutter glasses, a position and orientation tracker, a binaural BC (bone conduction) headset, a microphone attached to the headset and a stylus-type interaction device with a few buttons, a tracking device, and a small built-in loudspeaker. The stylus' loudspeaker mainly provides feedback sounds when pressing the buttons or moving the stylus in interactive areas of the museum. A small electrodynamic shaker is also mounted inside the stylus to improve the sound and give some additional feedback if needed (in case the background level in the museum is high). Also stationary displays, visual and auditory, are located within the different sections of the museum.

The purpose of using BC technology in the audio headset is that the ear canals are completely open which allows the visitors to hear the real ambience and room acoustics and also simple mixing of the headset sound and external augmented/virtual sound sources. Moreover, being able to talk to fellow visitors is an important aspect of choosing the BC headset. The frequency range of BC technology may however be somewhat limited for, e.g., full-range music pieces, and here the stationary loudspeakers which are also part of the museum can extend the experience when needed. The stylus' loudspeaker has a clearly limited frequency response and the sounds emitted from this device have to be carefully designed to give the proper impression. To give an illusory enhancement of the stylus loudspeaker range at lower frequencies, the shaker can be activated.

8.5.2 Exhibition Displays

The main part of this imaginary museum consists of a large exhibition hall subdivided into sections covering the different periods of music history. Regular large-screen visual displays show general introductions to a certain period, famous composers and examples of different styles within that period. When the visitor walks up to such a display, the HMD is automatically switched into shutter glass mode (to provide stereoscopic depth in the picture) and a narrating voice starts. Music pieces are played with accurate spatial cues through the BC headset to exemplify the music of an era or a composer. The visitor may interactively control and navigate through the presentation via voice commands and the stylus which also presents different interaction sounds to aid this navigation.

This type of display exemplifies a combination which may appear on the limit of MR toward full VR. However, as the background ambience from the museum hall is mixed into the presentation and as the visual display is not fully immersive (rather a window to another reality) or may be used to present simple 2D images and text, we still can consider this as an audiovisual MR display example. The sounds emitted from the stylus could also be considered to be audio AR.

Another type of display in the museum is interactive exhibition cases showing musical instruments typical for the period. The visitor may walk up to the case and a virtual musician presented via the HMD introduces the visitor to the instrument. The HMD overlays visual information to guide the visitor through the interaction and allows changes in the appearance of the instrument (which is real). The visitor may chose to play the instrument using the stylus (e.g., bowing the string of a violin) which then provides feedback through the built-in shaker giving the visitor the impression of tactile feedback from the instrument. The virtual musician then appears to pick up the instrument to demonstrate how it is played.

This display can be considered to be an AR display regarding both audition and vision. Important to consider here is the addition of proper spatiotemporal and room acoustic cues to the sound of the instrument and to the narrating voice of the virtual musician. The cues should correspond to the location of the sound sources and to the actual acoustics of the museum hall so that the visitor experiences that the instrument and the musician are really emitting sound there, inside the museum hall. The spatial and room acoustic cues also externalize the sound so it is not perceived as coming from inside the visitor's head.

As a final example, the museum also features an MR concert hall which is a fairly large hall seating an audience of about 100 people and a stage. The walls and the ceiling of the hall are actually display surfaces onto which images can be projected to alter the visual appearance of the hall. In other words, the room is a CAVE-like visual display but with some real elements such as the audience seats and the stage. The surfaces of the room are furthermore completely sound absorbing and have a built-in, hidden 256-channel WFS loudspeaker system which is used to provide the acoustics of the displayed room. Here, music pieces from different periods played by a real orchestra can be enjoyed. The direct sound from the instruments is picked up by an array of microphones and virtual room acoustic cues added and distributed over the WFS system. The virtual interior is altered to give the historically correct acoustical and architectural setting for the music which the orchestra is playing.

This is an example of visual AV; real elements such as the audience seats and the orchestra are mixed with the virtual display of room architecture. The auditory display is more difficult to categorize; the sound is indeed generated by real instruments and augmented with room acoustics – but one could also see this as if the room acoustics presented through the WFS system is a virtual environment into which the real orchestra is mixed. Nonetheless, in this application it is extremely important to match auditory and visual spatial cues to obtain proper relations between auditory and visual spaciousness which in turn is necessary to achieve a high sense of presence. The WFS system is chosen to give full frequency range spatial sound which is necessary to give the high sound quality required by a music enthusiast which may be difficult to obtain with the BC headset. Also, with WFS it is possible to obtain a sweet spot area covering the whole audience area which is very difficult to obtain with other multichannel loudspeaker techniques.

8.6 Discussion

This chapter has shown how audio can be used in various MR displays and how various parameters, such as reverberation or sound quality, can influence presence. However, we can categorize these parameters and related technological challenges from a different perspective. One can think about three different levels of technological sophistication when building mixed or virtual auditory environments – physical, perceptual, and cognitive. On the *physical* level, there are several parameters of rendered sound scenes which when improved to perfection closely approach the physical properties of the real environment. Consider, for example, the latency between recording and playback in telepresence applications, the match between auditory and visual objects' positions or the quality of measured HRTFs for synthesis of virtual auditory spaces.

However, knowledge about auditory *perception* mechanisms allows for technical simplifications such as perceptual audio coding schemes, reduced temporal and spatial quality of recorded impulse responses, or acceptable latency in the system. It is important to note that the majority of studies on auditory perception rely on measurements obtained from stationary listeners in laboratory environments. On the other hand, in mixed reality environments users can be moving thus imposing different, often, higher thresholds for auditory perception (e.g., minimum audible angle for stationary vs. moving listener). Therefore, MR systems relying on spatial sound will most likely stimulate basic auditory perception research where users' locomotion will be taken to account.

Finally, the recent notion of ecological psychoacoustics [64] refers to the importance of *cognitive* aspects when creating auditory scenes. For example, a significant effect of expectation on the perception of sound objects' elevation was found by Hughes et al. [65] where ecological sounds "originating from above" (e.g., airplane, thunder) presented to the listeners at their head level were perceived at higher positions. Ecological validity of a simulated environment and its correspondence to the surrounding auditory and multisensory context may help to overcome both physical and perceptual imperfections of MR systems. In this perspective, vast empirical knowledge on sound design from radio, television, and cinema (e.g., [66] and references therein) should not be ignored when creating auditory MR but rather verified and extended.

From all this one may draw the conclusion that MR audio technology and design of auditory displays for MR systems involve several degrees of freedom and that the system/design parameters in turn affect the sense of presence in a number of ways. A main challenge is therefore to seek the relation between system/design parameters and sense of presence, in order to provide better and more efficient MEs, both in terms of end-user experience and computational costs. An ideal MR sound system should provide a maximum sense of presence at a minimal cost. It is important to highlight that auditory MR represents an ideal platform for prototyping other, more complex multisensory MR applications, given its cost and maturity of technologies involved.

Another challenge in MR is coherence across sensory modalities (e.g., combination of real visual objects with virtual auditory sounds) where real-time tracking should be involved and where presence can be reduced by spatiotemporally incoherent stimuli. However, such combinations also may benefit from multisensory optimization where multimodal perception properties can be successfully used to compensate for imperfections in certain modality [67]. For example, spatial resolution of auditory display can be reduced when combined with corresponding visual input [68] or lower visual frame rate can be applied when combined with sound providing temporal structure of events [69].

For the future outlook, it seems that head-related sound rendering methods will dominate MR applications. These may embed real-time processing of surrounding sounds and provide a combined soundscape where selected reality sounds will be mixed with other sound content (music, information tags, alarms, etc.). Processing of real soundscapes will probably include active noise canceling, enhancement and amplification of desired sounds, and adjusting acoustical properties (e.g., changing room acoustics to improve intelligibility). Thus, apart from presence-related research such as entertainment, training, and cybertherapy, auditory MR will have a number of support applications including navigation systems for blind and informational services. While this chapter provides some guidelines for development of such systems, exactly how the ideal system should be designed is as of yet far from fully understood and should be an issue for future research.

Acknowledgments The work presented in this chapter was supported by the EU FET Presence Research Initiative project POEMS (IST-2001-39223), the EU FET Integrated project PRESENCCIA (Project Number 27731), and the Swedish Science Council (VR). The first author thanks the Swedish Foundation for Strategic Research for its support. The second author thanks Alfred Ots' scholarship foundation. We would also like to thank Armin Kohlrausch for commenting on earlier drafts of this chapter.

References

1. Loomis, J.M., Klatzky, R.L., Golledge, R.G.: Auditory distance perception in real, virtual and mixed environments. In Y. Othta & H. Tamura (Eds.), Mixed reality: Merging real and virtual worlds. Ohmsha, Tokyo (1999)
2. Kyota, H., Takanobu, H., Asako, K., Fumihisa, S., Hideyuki, T.: Mixed reality system using audio and visual senses: Implementation of simultaneous presentation in both audio and visual MR. Proceedings of the Virtual Reality Society of Japan Annual Conference. 11, 2A2–3 (2006)
3. Milgram, P., Kishino, F.: A taxonomy of mixed reality visual displays. IEICE Transactions on Information Systems, E77–D(2), 1321–1329 (1994)
4. Pörschmann, C.: One's own voice in auditory virtual environments. Acta Acustica, 87, 378–388 (2001)
5. Nordahl, R.: Self-induced footsteps sounds in virtual reality: Latency, recognition, quality and presence. Proceedings of the Eight Annual International Workshop Presence, London, UK (2004)
6. Lombard, M., Ditton, T.B.: At the heart of it all: the concept of presence. Journal of Computer-Mediated Communication, 13(3) (1997)

7. Gilkey, R.H., Weisenberger, J.M.: The sense of presence for the suddenly deafened adult: implications for virtual environments. Presence: Teleoperators and Virtual Environments, 4(4), 357–363 (1995)
8. Ijsselsteijn, W.A.: Presence in depth. Doctoral dissertation, Eindhoven University of Technology, Eindhoven, The Netherlands (2004)
9. Slater, M: A note on presence terminology. Presence-Connect, 3(3), 1–5 (2003)
10. Pope, J., Chalmers, A.: Multi-sensory rendering: combining graphics and acoustics. Proceedings of the 7th International Conference in Central Europe on Computer Graphics, Czech Republic, 233–242 (1999)
11. Guttman, S.E., Gilroy, L.A., Blake, R.: Hearing what the eyes see: auditory encoding of visual temporal sequences. Psychological Science, 16(3), 228–235 (2005)
12. Kleiner, M., Dalenbäck, B-I., Svensson, P.: Auralization: an overview. Journal of the Audio Engineering Society, 41(11), 861–875 (1993)
13. Begault, D.R.: 3D sound for virtual reality and multimedia. Academic Press Professional, London (1994)
14. Rumsey, F.: Spatial audio. Focal Press Oxford; Boston (2001)
15. Shilling, R.D., Shinn-Cunningham, B.G.: Virtual auditory displays. In K.M. Stanney (Ed.), Handbook of virtual environments: Design, implementation, and applications (pp. 65–92). Lawrence Erlbaum Associates, London, Mahwah, NJ (2002)
16. Hughes, C.E., Stapleton, C.B., Hughes, D.E., Smith, E.M.: Mixed reality in education, entertainment, and training. IEEE Computer Graphics and Applications, 25(6), 24–30 (2005)
17. Jarlengrip, J.: Object detection system and method. International Patent no. WO/2007/049995. (2007)
18. Zimmermann, R., Kyriakakis, C., Shahabi, C., Papadopolous, C., Sawchuck, A.A., Neumann, U.: The remote media immersion system. IEEE MultiMedia, 11(2), 48–57 (2004)
19. Pulkki, V.: Virtual sound source positioning using vector base amplitude panning. Journal of the Audio Engineering Society, 45(6), 456–466 (1997)
20. Gerzon, M.A.: Ambisonics in multichannel broadcasting and video. Journal of the Audio Engineering Society, 33(11), 859–871 (1985)
21. Berkhout, A.J.: A holographic approach to acoustic control. Journal of the Audio Engineering Society, 36(12), 977–995 (1988)
22. Horbach, U., Corteel, E., Pellegrini, R.S., Hulsebos, E.: Real-time rendering of dynamic scenes using wave field synthesis. Proceedings of the IEEE International Conference on Multimedia and Expo (ICME '02), Lausanne, Switzerland, 1, 517–520. (2002)
23. Horbach, U., Boone, M.M.: Future transmission and rendering formats for multichannel sound. Proceedings of the AES 16th Conference on Spatial Sound Reproduction, Rovaniemi, Finland (1999)
24. Murray, C.D., Arnold, P., Thornton, B.: Presence accompanying induced hearing loss: implications for immersive virtual environments. Presence: Teleoperators and Virtual Environments, 9(2), 137–148 (2000)
25. Blauert, J.: Spatial hearing, revised edition. The MIT Press, Cambridge, MA (1997)
26. Wenzel, E.M., Arruda, M., Kistler, D.J., Wightman, F.L.: Localization using nonindividualized head-related transfer functions. Journal of the Acoustical Society of America, 94(1), 111–123 (1993)
27. Zotkin, D.N., Duraiswami, R., Davis, L.S.: Rendering localized spatial audio in a virtual auditory space. IEEE Transactions on Multimedia, 6(4), 553–564 (2004)
28. Hofman, P.M., Riswick, J.G.A., van Opstal, A.J.: Relearning sound localization with new ears. Nature Neuroscience, 1(5), 417–421 (1998)
29. Durlach, N.I., Shinn-Cunningham, B.G., Held, R.M.: Supernormal auditory localization. I. General background. Presence: Teleoperators and Virtual Environments, 2(2), 89–103 (1993)
30. Gupta, N., Barreto, A., Ordonez, C.: Spectral modification of head-related transfer functions for improved virtual sound spatialization. Proceedings of IEEE International Conference on Acoustics, Speech, and Signal Processing, Orlando, FL, 2, 1953–1956 (2002)

31. Härmä, A., Jakka, J., Tikander, M., Karjalainen, M., Lokki, T., Hiipakka, J., Lorho, G.: Augmented reality audio for mobile and wearable appliances. Journal of the Audio Engineering Society, 52(6), 618–639 (2004)
32. Evans, M.J., Tew, A.I., Angus, J.A.S.: Spatial audio teleconferencing: Which way is better?: Proceedings of the fourth International Conference on Auditory Display (ICAD '97), Palo Alto, California, 29–37 (1997)
33. Loomis, J.M., Golledge, R.G., Klatzky, R.L.: Navigation system for the blind: auditory display modes and guidance. Presence: Teleoperators and Virtual Environments, 7(2), 193–203 (1998)
34. Tonndorf, J.: Bone conduction. In J. Tobias (Ed.), Foundations of modern auditory theory (Vol. 2, pp. 197–237). Academic Press, New York (1972)
35. Stenfelt, S., Goode, R.L.: Bone conducted sound: physiological and clinical aspects. Otology & Neurotology, 26(6), 1245–1261, (2005)
36. Pörschmann, C.: Influences of bone conduction and air conduction on the sound of one's own voice. Acustica – Acta Acustica, 86(6), 1038–1045 (2000)
37. Snik, A.F.M., Bosman, A.J., Mylanus, E.A.M., Cremers, C.W.R.J.: Candidacy for the bone-anchored hearing aid. Audiology & Neurotology, 9(4), 190–196 (2004)
38. Väljamäe, A., Tajadura-Jiménez, A., Larsson, P., Västfjäll, D., Kleiner M.: Binaural bone-conducted sound in virtual environments: evaluation of a portable, multimodal motion simulator prototype. Journal of Acoustic Science and Technology, 29(2), 149–155 (2008)
39. Gaye, L., Mazé, R., Holmquist, L.E.: Sonic City: The urban environment as a musical interface. Proceedings of the 2003 Conference on New Interfaces for Musical Expression (NIME-03), Montreal, Canada, 109–115. (2003)
40. Sanders, R.D. Jr., Scorgie, M.A.: The effect of sound delivery methods on a user's sense of presence in a virtual environment. Master thesis Naval Postgraduate School, Monterey, CA (2002)
41. Durlach, N.I., Mavor, A.S.: Virtual reality scientific and technological challenges. National Academy Press, Washington, DC (1995)
42. Savioja, L., Huopaniemi, J., Lokki, T., Väänänen, R.: Creating interactive virtual acoustic environments. Journal of the Audio Engineering Society, 47(9), 675–705 (1999)
43. Jot, J.-M., Warusfel, O.: A real-time spatial sound processor for music and virtual reality applications. Proceedings of the 1995 International Computer Music Conference, Banff, AB, Canada, 294–295 (1995)
44. Faller, C., Baumgarte, F.: Binaural cue coding – Part II: schemes and applications. IEEE Transactions on Speech and Audio Processing, 11(6), 520–531. (2003)
45. Breebaart, J., van de Par, V., Kohlrausch, A., Schuijers, K.: Parametric coding of stereo audio. EURASIP Journal on Applied Signal Processing, 9, 1305–1322 (2005)
46. Tsingos, N., Gallo, E., Drettakis, G.: Perceptual audio rendering of complex virtual environments. INRIA technical report RR-4734, Feb. 2003, REVES/INRIA Sophia-Antipolis (2003)
47. Ramsdell, D.A.: The psychology of the hard-of-hearing and deafened adult. In H. Davis & S.R. Silverman (Eds.), Hearing and deafness (4th ed., pp. 499–510). Holt, Rinehart & Winston, New York (1978)
48. Hendrix, C., Barfield, W.: The sense of presence within auditory virtual environments. Presence: Teleoperators and Virtual Environments, 5(3), 290–301 (1996)
49. Väljamäe, A., Larsson, P., Västfjäll, D., Kleiner, M.: Auditory presence, individualized head-related transfer functions and illusory ego-motion in virtual environments. Proceedings of the Seventh Annual International Workshop Presence, Valencia, Spain, 141–147 (2004)
50. Begault, D.R., Wenzel, E.M., Anderson, M.R.: Direct comparison of the impact of head-tracking, reverberation, and individualized head-related transfer functions on the spatial perception of a virtual speech source. Journal of the Audio Engineering Society, 49(10), 904–916 (2001)
51. Larsson, P., Västfjäll, D., Kleiner, M.: Auditory information consistency and room acoustic cues increase presence in virtual environments. Acoustical Science and Technology, 29(2), 191–194 (2008)

52. Larsson, P., Västfjäll, D., Kleiner, M.: On the quality of experience: A multi-modal approach to perceptual ego-motion and sensed presence in virtual environments. Proceedings of the First ITRW on Auditory Quality of Systems, Akademie Mont-Cenis, Germany. (2003)
53. Ozawa, K., Chujo, Y., Suzuki, Y., Sone, T.: Psychological factors involved in auditory presence. Acoustical Science and Technology, 24(1), 42–44 (2003)
54. Rumsey, F.: Spatial quality evaluation for reproduced sound: terminology, meaning, and a scene-based paradigm. Journal of the Audio Engineering Society, 50(9), 651–666 (2002)
55. Freeman, J., Lessiter, J.: Here there & everywhere: The effects of multi-channel audio on presence. Proceedings of The Seventh International Conference on Audio Display, Helsinki, Finland, 231–234 (2001)
56. Ozawa, K., Miyasaka, M.: Effects of reproduced sound pressure levels on auditory presence. Acoustical Science and Technology, 25(3), 207–209 (2004)
57. Serafin, G., Serafin, S.: Sound design to enhance presence in photorealistic virtual reality. Proceedings of the 2004 International Conference on Auditory Display (ICAD '04), Sydney, Australia (2004)
58. Chueng, P., Marsden, P.: Designing auditory spaces to support sense of place: The role of expectation. Position paper for The Role of Place in On-line Communities Workshop, CSCW2002, New Orleans (2002)
59. Larsson, P., Västfjäll, D., Olsson, P., Kleiner, M.: When what you see is what you hear: Auditory-visual integration and presence in virtual environments. Proceedings of the 10th Annual International Workshop Presence, 11–18. Barcelona, Spain (2007)
60. Ozawa, K., Ohtake, S., Suzuki, Y., Sone, T.: Effects of visual information on auditory presence. Acoustical Science and Technology, 24(2), 97–99 (2003)
61. Knapp, J.M., Loomis, J.M.: Limited field of view of head-mounted displays is not the cause of distance underestimation in virtual environments. Presence: Teleoperators and Virtual Environments, 13(5), 572–577 (2004)
62. Thompson, W.B., Willemsen, P., Gooch, A.A., Creem-Regehr, S.H., Loomis, J.M., Beall, A.C.: Does the quality of the computer graphics matter when judging distances in visually immersive environments? Presence: Teleoperators and Virtual Environments, 13(5), 560–571 (2004)
63. 37Murch, W.: Dense clarity – Clear density. Paper delivered at the "Volume: Bed of sound" program/exhibition, PS1/MoMA, New York, NY. www.ps1.org/cut/volume/murch.html (2000)
64. Neuhoff, J.G: Ecological psychoacoustics: Introduction and history. In J.G. Neuhoff (Ed.), Ecological psychoacoustics. (pp. 1–13). Elsevier Academic Press, Amsterdam, Boston (2004)
65. Hughes, D.E., Thropp, J., Holmquist, J., Moshell, J.M.: Spatial perception and expectation: factors in acoustical awareness for MOUT training. Proceedings of Army Science Conference (ASC) 2004, Orlando, FL (2004)
66. Weiss, E., Belton J.: Film sound: Theory and practice. Columbia University Press, New York (1985)
67. Väljamäe, A., Tajadura-Jiménez, A., Larsson P., Västfjäll D., Kleiner M.: Handheld Experiences: Using Audio To Enhance the Illusion of Self-Motion, IEEE MultiMedia, vol. 15, no.4, pp. 68–75, 2008
68. Riecke B.E., Väljamäe, A., Schulte-Pelkum, J.: Moving sounds enhance the visually-induced self-motion illusion (circular vection) in Virtual Reality ACM Transactions on Applied Perception (TAP) Volume 6, Issue 2, Article No. 7 (2009)
69. Väljamäe, A., Soto-Faraco, S.: Filling-in visual motion with sounds. Acta Psychologica, 129(2), 249–254. (2008)

Chapter 9
An Exploration of Exertion in Mixed Reality Systems via the "Table Tennis for Three" Game

Florian 'Floyd' Mueller, Martin R. Gibbs, and Frank Vetere

Abstract Humans experience their physical and social environment through their bodies and their associated movement actions. However, most mixed reality systems approach the integration of the real with a virtual world from a computational perspective, often neglecting the body's capabilities by offering only limited interaction possibilities with a few augmented tangible objects. We propose a view on mixed reality systems that focuses on the human body and its movements, because we believe such an approach has the potential to support novel interaction experiences, as explored by a prototypal gaming system that was inspired by exertion actions exhibited in table tennis. "Table Tennis for Three" enables augmented bodily experiences while offering new opportunities for interaction, such as supporting three players simultaneously across geographical distances. This case study offers an exploration of the role of the human body and its associated movement actions in mixed reality systems, aiming to contribute toward an understanding of the use of exertion in such systems. Such an understanding can support leveraging the many benefits of exertion through mixed reality systems and therefore guide future advances in this research field.

Keywords Augmented reality · Videoconference · Table tennis · Ping pong · Exertion interface · Physical · Tangible · Sports · Proprioception · Social · Phenomenology · Body · Gross-motor interaction · Full-body interaction

---

F. Mueller (✉)
Interaction Design Group, Department of Information Systems, The University of Melbourne, Parkville, VIC, Australia
e-mail: floyd@floydmueller.com

E. Dubois et al. (eds.), *The Engineering of Mixed Reality Systems*, Human-Computer Interaction Series, DOI 10.1007/978-1-84882-733-2_9,

9.1 Introduction

Mixed reality systems aim to make use of the benefits of a virtual domain in combination with the advantages of a physical world. This is often achieved through visually augmenting tangible objects, meant to be grasped and manipulated with hands and fingers, in order to access the embedded digital information [1, 2, 15]. Such an interaction approach has been favored in many work-related scenarios in which the focus rests on the virtual content while the body's involvement is only dealt with peripherally. However, other scenarios exist in which the entire body and its movements play a significant role. For example, physical games such as sports put the human body and its capabilities for gross-motor interaction at the center of the experience. These physical games are important, as they have been attributed with social, physical, and mental health benefits [12, 13, 27, 33], in particular their potential for increasing the energy expenditure to address the obesity epidemic has been highlighted [12].

This potential of the human body, however, is not very prominent in many mixed reality systems, exemplified by the numerous mixed reality applications that feature tangible objects, which predominantly afford fine-motor interactions with hand and fingers [31]. Such augmented objects can facilitate enhanced experiences in terms of dealing with virtual information by allowing the user to grasp, examine, and rearrange them; however, their afforded interactions represent only a limited subset of expressive actions the human body supports, as people experience their environment through their bodies and interact with embodied others by utilizing their potential for action through movement [22].

In order to allow the body and its associated movement actions to take a more central role in mixed reality systems, the proposal is made here to reconsider the physical aspect of the real world in these systems and examine their potential for supporting the wide variety of bodily movements users can engage in. Focusing on the movements can allow for being sensitized to the affordances of the environment as well as artifacts to support bodily actions and allow for expressive interactions, which in turn could highlight opportunities for technological augmentation otherwise not readily evident. In order to advance the exploration of such an approach, we have developed a prototypal gaming system inspired by the exertion actions exhibited in table tennis. This investigation represents an approach to mixed reality systems in which the human body plays a central role in the design for the interaction. It is presented in the context of an exertion game, a game that requires intense physical effort from the player [25], in order to highlight the approach's potential to offer distinct benefits. The case study investigated describes "Table Tennis for Three," a physical game for three distributed players. It is aimed at telling a story of how a focus on the body and its movements relate to interaction design. The game development drew inspiration from table tennis, and the user plays with a real ball, bat, and table; however, the gameplay experience is quite different from traditional table tennis. The virtual augmentation utilizes a videoconferencing component to allow for distributed play while the affordances of tangible objects support movements that facilitate maintaining the benefits of physical play. This approach can facilitate novel user experiences such as supporting three geographically distant participants, contributing equally in the game, a scenario not easily achieved in traditional table tennis. Initial investigations with users have suggested that the game can facilitate engaging social interactions, similar to table tennis. The use of bat and ball has inspired to name the game "Table Tennis for three."

9.2 Related Work

The consideration of the human body in human–computer interactions can be grounded in prior work that goes beyond the immediate application in digital domains. Merleau-Ponty's phenomenology lays a foundation by introducing a perspective that the human body is mutually engaged with the mind and that this intertwined connection is the primary access to "being-in-the-world" and therefore determines how we perceive and interact with our environment and other embodied beings [22]. This "being-in-the-world" is derived from Heidegger's work, who stresses a role of the body and its actions within the environment in regard to the notion of meaning making, arguing that meaning only exists because humans act with their bodies and turn this action into meaning. Furthermore, humans live in a social world, which means these actions are not meaningful per se, but only meaningful through the social context, highlighting a social component.

Researchers that stress the role of the human body in a digital world draw on these philosophical investigations, for example Winograd et al. argues for a more nuanced view on the embodied user when interacting with computers [35]. McCarthy and Wright see technology as experience that is featured in an embodied world, arguing for an opportunity to positively influence the design [21]. Dourish identified an embodied view in the tangible and social computing systems developed in the 1990s [8]; he suggests combining their advantages because he believes that the features of technological systems are related to the features of social settings, following Merleau-Ponty's perspective. In sum, the interplay between the body and its movements in relation to the world humans interact in is grounded in early philosophical investigations and has been applied to interactions with computers recently, which drew attention to a social component that seems to be integral. The proposed work has been using this theoretical lens to investigate the phenomenon.

The relationship between physical affordances of the environment and engagement with technology as well as the role of the body in these experiences has been explored mainly in the context of games. Lindley et al. have found that the game's nature can change when players are involved in bodily actions, in contrast to button presses, from a traditional virtual game experience of "hard fun" to more social play [20]. De Kort et al. promote the consideration of embodied play because they believe that players have an intrinsic need to experience their physical environment kinesthetically [7]. They propose a relationship between physical environment and virtual gameplay while extending this view by proposing "sociality characteristics" for games, which includes a consideration of exertion actions, as they can "radically" impact social play [7]; however, the authors fall short in providing example applications for their claims. Moen [23] highlights the role of free-form movements in mixed reality settings and presents a framework for kinesthetic movement interaction, arguing that technological augmentation can support novel experiences, but the author concentrates on single-user interactions.

Fish'N'Steps is a social approach to combining physical bodily actions with virtual content to enhance a healthy activity. It is a mobile application that is aimed at encouraging participation in walking activities via means of social comparison [19]. The proposed system works in combination with a pedometer to motivate an increase in a participant's daily energy expenditure. It focuses on the users' everyday environment and their bodily actions in it, in contrast to dedicated exercise sessions. Furthermore, the system separates the physical activity from the social activity quite distinctly: only after the participants walked all day, they can share their progress through a fish tank metaphor displayed on a screen in an office, where their bodies rest while they assess their relative progress.

Consolvo et al. presents another distributed pedometer-based system implemented in a mobile phone [6]. Based on a study, the authors have identified design requirements that include aspects regarding the body, the users' environment, and the virtual augmentation. They found that combining the physical with the virtual world throughout the users' entire daily life is not necessary, but rather that this combination can offer benefits in time-specific situations, suggesting that a mixed reality approach could be suitable for dedicated exercise sessions.

Systems that combine real-world physical exertion with the virtual aspects of a videoconference have suggested the possibility of a social facilitation effect. For example, exercise bikes have been networked to allow for distributed races in a competitive environment. The bodily component suggests the use of physiological data to enhance the distributed experience, as participants reported that visualized heart rate from a remote rider motivated them to cycle faster [5]. The presence of a remote participant appears to affect the exertion performance; however, in exercise bike cycling the participants cannot interfere with one another physically, as for example in many team sports, in which players can actively prevent their opponents from achieving the game's goal [32]. This aspect of the shared experience is missing in networked bike riding; however, it has been explored in Breakout for Two [25]. Breakout for Two is a synchronous exertion game for two players with an integrated video communication channel, in which participants can chose between an active and passive style of playing. An evaluation showed that players were able to form a social bond between one another despite the geographical distance between them and that the exertion activity contributed to this outcome. What has yet to be explored is if the effect was specific to the type of exertion game and the two-location setup. Furthermore, it is still an unanswered question what role the mixed reality environment plays in these exertion activities.

The game of table tennis has inspired other research projects before, and a few approaches have presented a mixed reality approach around this sportive game [16–18, 36]. Most of these implementations focus on the demonstration of the technologies' capabilities, showcasing how mechanical and computational advances can simulate certain aspects of table tennis, for example force-feedback [17]. The outcomes of these projects suggest that simulating and recreating a traditional bodily game such as table tennis is still technologically challenging; a networked version that enables a recreation of a traditional table tennis experience might therefore currently not be feasible technically and financially.

In sum, research suggests that the consideration of the human body and its physically effortful interactions in interactive systems can facilitate beneficial experiences. Most utilized approaches are based on an embodied perspective that highlights the importance of the users' body being situated in a physical environment, interacting with other embodied beings. However, there is a limited understanding of what role a mixed reality environment plays when bodily actions are augmented with technology. The approach taken here is to advocate an appreciation of the physical environment for the support of the human body in order to identify opportunities for technical augmentation that provide a benefit to the experience. Through a case study, this notion of an increased focus on the body's actions and their use in a physical world while being engaged in an interactive experience is explored. The described investigation highlights the potential for novel experiences such as unique social support in terms of number and geographical location of participants, difficult to achieve without technological augmentation. Investigating this can contribute toward an understanding of the use of exertion in mixed reality systems, which can support the leveraging of the many benefits physical activity affords, guiding future advances in this research field.

9.3 Table Tennis for Three

The following section describes "Table Tennis for Three," our case study application that exemplifies a body-centric view of mixed reality approaches. Table Tennis for Three is a mixed reality game that draws inspiration from the exertion actions exhibited in table tennis. Its aim is to encourage players to be physically active and exert themselves, as research suggests that the involvement of the body in such gaming interactions can facilitate emotional and social experiences [4, 20]. The technological augmentation enables novel aspects not possible in traditional physical games such as table tennis: here it is the support of distributed users, as well as a scaling to three players who can participate equally in the gaming action.

As the game development drew inspiration from table tennis, and the user plays with a real ball, bat, and table, the name Table Tennis for Three was chosen; however, the gameplay experience is quite different from traditional table tennis. This novel gameplay demonstrates that enabling such enhanced experiences like supporting three geographical players equally does not necessarily require the full extent of computational augmentation, as prior simulation approaches might suggest. The described case study shows that thoughtful design can result in systems that enable novel and engaging experiences similar to – but not identical – traditional non-augmented experiences offering additional benefits. With our approach, we are aiming at inspiring future research in this area, while demonstrating that implementation is possible within the limits of current technology.

9.3.1 The Table Tennis for Three Experience

Fig. 9.1 Table Tennis for Three

The following describes the users' experience when playing Table Tennis for Three. Each player has a bat and a ball and steps up to the table. The table is set up so that the ball can be hit against the vertically positioned opposite half of the table (Fig. 9.1). This setup is familiar to table tennis players who practice on their own by playing the ball against the board. The vertical part of the table is painted white to also serve as projection surface for a videoconference of the other two players. Projected on top of the videoconference are eight semi-transparent targets that players have to hit with their ball (Fig. 9.2).

Fig. 9.2 The semi-transparent blocks overlaying the videoconferencing component

These targets, or blocks, "break" when hit by the players. The blocks are synchronized across the three tables, so the other players see the same block layout and the same block states (Fig. 9.3).

Fig. 9.3 The blocks are shared among the locations

If a block is hit once, it cracks a little. If it is hit again (regardless of by which player), it cracks more. If hit three times, it breaks and disappears, revealing the underlying videoconference completely: the player has broken through to the remote players. However, only the player who hits the block the third and final time makes it disappear and receives the point. This adds an element of strategy to the game: a player can try to snatch away points by hitting blocks that have already been hit twice by the other player. Each broken block scores one point, and once all blocks are cleared, the player with the most points wins the game.

9.4 Design of Table Tennis for Three

9.4.1 Choice of Tangible Equipment

Supporting exertion activities in interactive entertainment is often facilitated by a combination of interfaces that facilitate gross-motor actions and virtual game content. Gross-motor activities need to be not only afforded by the interface but also recognized by the computer in order to affect the gameplay and enable the interactive component. Table Tennis for Three uses a traditional table tennis bat and ball on a physical table as the interface to the virtual gameplay, supported by a detection system that detects the ball's impact. The following section justifies the choice of the tangible equipment in Table Tennis for Three.

9.4.1.1 Supporting Bodily Skill Training

The need to facilitate gross-motor actions to encourage exertion can be supported by tangible objects that afford certain movements known from traditional bodily interactions, such as the use of bats, racquets, and balls in sports: users are already familiar with the movements these objects are intended to support. Although most sports equipment appears to afford only a small subset of a person's entire range of movements, they can still require a lifetime of training to be mastered, for example a table tennis bat. This characteristic of facilitating the acquisition of bodily skills has been described as a key element of an exertion interface [25]. In addition to supporting bodily skill training, such sport equipment offers a familiarity that could reduce participants' hesitations to invest exertion during the activity.

9.4.1.2 Utilizing Existing Sport Advances

Using existing sports equipment such as the table tennis bat also utilizes the ergonomic and material advances years of sports research has produced in making such devices suitable and effective for athletic training and exercise. Due to these reasons, Table Tennis for Three uses a traditional table tennis bat that has not experienced any technical augmentation that would change its characteristics for the exertion activity.

9.4.1.3 Uncertainty of the Real World

Although several other augmented systems that are inspired by table tennis replace the ball with a virtual pendant [17, 36], Table Tennis for Three uses a real ball. Using a physical instead of a virtual ball enables a simplified ability to support a notion of uncertainty that is characteristic to sportive experiences. In sports activities that require a ball, the unpredictability of the ball is a significant element of what makes the game interesting. The ball might hit the edge of a racquet, fly off in unexpected ways, bounce off the top of a net in surprising ways, or dance around the rim of a basketball basket, creating sensations of anticipation within the players and the audience. The use of an oval ball in some sports such as rugby emphasizes this unpredictability by artificially increasing opportunities for uncertainty, instantiated through notions of surprise exhibited by the players. It should be noted, however, that the bounce of a ball could be predicted computationally, and is therefore not completely unpredictable. However, in the course of bodily actions in an exertion sports environment, the speed involved as well as the many other factors that influence what happens next makes many actions of the ball unpredictable for the players. Predicting a bounce is a skill player's practice over many years; however, small changes within the environment often create unpredicted situations that result in surprise, possibly affecting the outcome of the entire game. For example, one can imagine the unpredicted bounce of a ball off a defender in soccer, which leads to an own goal, resulting in a win of a team that was inferior. Such surprises are characteristic for sports and contribute to the fascination it has to so many people, as it can facilitate very emotional moments.

This notion of surprise has been acknowledged in traditional exertion activities [30] as well as augmented mixed reality systems [29]. Mixed reality systems, in contrast to exclusively virtual systems, are in a unique situation of being able to foster this notion because they are able to utilize the elements of the physical world that are often supporting this effect. In virtual gameplay, these surprise encounters need to be artificially introduced through deliberate programming, as an element of chance is required in most games. Game creators have to take special care in finding an engaging balance between believable chance and randomness as experienced by the players [28]. For example, in a game such as the Nintendo Wii Sports Tennis [34], the ball in the virtual world could be affected by a programmed element of chance; but such an approach might appear to be generic by the players, as the ball will never bounce off the physical environment that the users act in and experience with their bodies, enforcing the sense of a strict separation between the virtual and the physical world. The ball will also not bounce off the avatar's racquet frame in unexpected ways because the virtual world is programmed not to support this, but even if it would be accommodated for in the design, the experience will be "fundamentally different," as players might not believe the probability by which it occurs, and rather assume a bug in the software [11] than it being a core element of the game, possibly eliciting emotions of frustration rather than disappointment as a response to "bad luck." We believe that this concept of supporting uncertainty of the real world in virtual applications can contribute to the conceptual dissolving of the separation between the physical and the virtual world and see it within the tradition of Merleau-Ponty's stance of considering an embodied mind rather than a strict separation between the body and the mind.

The notion of uncertainty can also affect social aspects in mixed reality systems, important in the design of Table Tennis for Three, which supports audio and video communication between players. Gaver claims that the physical environment can provide affordances for social interaction [11], which might suggest that mixed reality systems have an advantage over purely virtual systems in terms of social support. Hornecker implies that "the richness of bodily movement" in combination with tangible objects is particularly beneficial for social interactions [14]. The afforded exertion activities in Table Tennis for Three are aimed to facilitate the probability of surprise occurring as well as to amplify the outcome of this uncertainty. Tangibility can support uncertainty without exertion; however, we believe the extensive, fast, and forceful movements exhibited in exertion activities enable as well as amplify these surprising moments. The social sharing of the resulting emotions might amplify their effects further, supporting the notion that there is a unique role for social support in mixed reality systems.

9.4.1.4 Supporting Proprioception and Force-Feedback

Physical exertion in Table Tennis for Three is achieved through the use of gross-motor activity. Although exertion can also be facilitated through non-physical, non-contact systems such as the Sony EyeToy [9], the utilization of tangible objects and the physical environment as proposed in mixed reality systems can offer unique benefits. Affordances of physical objects can support the users' sense of proprioception. This sense of proprioception is an important element in movement-based interaction [23]. For example, in a mixed reality environment, an extension of a player's arm, for example a racquet, affords the user with a different sense of where this extension is located in terms of his/her other body parts than in a virtual environment, as this mapping is achieved only through visual means. In an exclusively virtual environment misalignment between movement and object might occur, a problem particularly important in the context of fast sportive bodily actions. Furthermore, the use of physical objects enables an inexpensive use of feedback that is difficult to achieve with conventional force-feedback technology, as current developments indicate. For example, research has attempted to simulate the impact of a table tennis ball in a virtual environment [17], and the results show that simulating the variety and intensity of a ball and bat impact is not a trivial problem.

9.4.1.5 Avoiding Complex Equipment Such as Head-Mounted Displays

Solutions that utilize a virtual ball often require the user to wear a head-mounted display [17, 18]. Such a head-mounted display often includes a camera that enables the blending of the physical world with the virtual objects, setting the stage for a typical mixed reality system. These head-mounted displays suffer from technical limitations, such as limited resolution, viewing size, physical size, weight, and uncomfortable fit to the wearer's head [1]. In regard to exertion, it should be noted that these devices also possibly restrict the users in their bodily movements. Fast head movements might dislocate the device and lead to a misalignment of the viewing area. The cable providing power and video source data might limit the user's limb movements and might also restrict the action radius of the body to the length of the cable. Furthermore, the head-mounted display obscures the eyes of the users so they are not visible to their peers, limiting opportunities for eye contact as social cues. The use of a physical, instead of virtual, ball allows abdicating complex equipment such as head-mounted displays and their associated limitations.

9.4.2 Implementation

The implementation of the system can be described from three different perspectives: the detection mechanism, the social communication channel, and the gameplay. Detecting the outcomes of the bodily actions is facilitated by indirectly measuring the exertion activities. This is achieved by looking at the result of the exertion action applied to the ball. By measuring the location of the impact of the ball onto the vertical part of the table, an input mechanism based on exertion is facilitated to control the game. Social communication is enabled through a videoconference that includes an always-on audio channel, and the gameplay brings the remote stations together by enabling a shared space for all three players.

9.4.2.1 Impact Detection Mechanism

In any bodily game, there are two possible ways to detect and measure the exertion exhibited by the players. The exertion could be measured directly through physiological means, often acquired through equipment worn by the user. However, such an approach might restrict the players in their movements. Therefore, the exhibited exertion in Table Tennis for Three is measured indirectly: the outcome of the bodily activities is measured by sensing the results applied to the ball. Initial investigations examined tracking the ball with video capture technology; however, as table tennis balls can reach speeds around 100 km/h, conventional cameras with a frame rate of 25–30 frames per second (fps) were not fast enough to capture the balls. High-speed cameras were consequently used that captured up to 500 fps; however, the image analysis required CPU power that was beyond what the high end, but still commercially standard PCs we used were able to process with the amount of data generated. Furthermore, a high shutter speed of the cameras was required in order to acquire a sharp outline of the ball for easy segmentation by the algorithm. Unfortunately, bright illumination of the area above the table affects the videoconference projection, which benefits from a darker environment. The initial setup therefore required a balancing act between these various components. Although most of these restrictions are of a technical nature and might be addressed by advances in equipment, the initial vision-based system was limited by these compromises. Therefore, an alternative system that uses an audio-based approach was developed to overcome many of these restrictions.

The final design consists of eight piezoelectric sensors that are attached to the rear of the backboard in locations corresponding to the gameplay blocks projected on the front of the backboard (Fig. 9.4). The sensors detect the sound vibrations in the wooden board created by the ball striking it. This approach is similar to the system described by Ishii et al. [16]. In their system, any impact with the surface is located through interpolation. However, as this implementation is primarily used for visualization, any inaccuracy does not affect the interaction the same way as in the Table Tennis for Three game, where a false detection can determine the outcome of the game negatively and hence significantly impact upon the user's experience. Therefore, the number of sensors in the Table Tennis for Three game was increased to eight and their location was aligned to the game blocks projected on the front of the board to increase accuracy and detection rates.

It could be envisioned that this approach scales to accommodate more game "targets" to be sensed. However, an increase in piezoelectric sensors requires special data acquisition hardware, as most conventional boards only accept a limited number of analog signal inputs. The Table Tennis for Three system uses a commercial data acquisition board that accepts up to ten analog inputs; we have used eight, one for each target. Each of the eight inputs is sampled with 25 kHz, which provides an adequate resolution to reliably detect even fast hits. The sensor data are first squared to deal only with positive values and then filtered by custom-made software. This was necessary in order to eliminate other potential trigger sources such as reflecting noises from the edge of the board and impact sounds from the ball hitting the horizontal part of the table. The rigging of the vertical part of the table also affected the sound characteristics of the board as it dampened the sound distribution across certain parts. If the signal strength was above a certain threshold over a specified length of time, it was considered to be an impact. The sensor that first received the vibration signal then determined the location of the impact. Although the analysis did not consider an intensity value, it could be envisioned that the captured data could be used to also measure how hard the players hit the ball, similar to the approach described by Mueller [24].

Detecting the location of the impact with sensors attached to the back of the interaction surface shields the involved technology away from the exertion actions of the user. This has several advantages: the delicate sensor technology is not exposed to potential damage caused by the ball and the player is also not seeing possibly intimidating technological artifacts that might hinder the use of excessive force out of fear of breaking the equipment.

Fig. 9.4 Sensors attached to the back of the Table Tennis for Three system

9.4.2.2 Videoconferencing

The videoconferencing component, together with the gameplay implementation, comprises the virtual aspect of the Table Tennis for Three system. It is independent from the other technical aspects of the system, because developing a videoconferencing system is not a trivial task, and many commercial and research systems claim to offer the best compromise between bandwidth restrictions and image and audio quality. These implementations balance the most efficient compression codecs with en- and decoding CPU requirements, deal with varying network lags and congestions, provide circumventions for firewall issues, and aim to reduce noise and echo effects. In order to utilize the latest advances in videoconferencing technology, the videoconference implementation in Table Tennis for Three is a separate application that acts independently and is placed as a window behind the gameplay application that is half-transparent. The gameplay software is programmed with a transparent background, which allows the players to see the underlying videoconference.

In the current setup, the videoconference resolution is 640×480 pixels with 25 fps to support the fast-moving actions exhibited by the players during gameplay. The images are captured by consumer webcams. The audio is captured with Bluetooth headsets the players are wearing. Initial experiments with directional microphones did not achieve encouraging results as the impact noise of the table tennis ball was often captured on top of the players' voices. Furthermore, the bodily movements facilitated by the game resulted in the players changing their physical location much, so that talking when collecting balls behind the table or at the remote end of the room was barely picked up by stationary microphones. Therefore, players are asked to wear a Bluetooth headset, which acts as a low-cost wireless transmission device in Table Tennis for Three. Due to the fact that only the microphone functionality of the headset is used, the user can also wear the device on a shirt's collar, often preferred when compared to the time-consuming adjustment necessary if positioned on the ear. The sound effects of the game as well as the audio from the remote ends are sent to speakers located under the table in order to allow spectators to hear as well. This setup however often created echo issues, with the microphone picking up the audio coming from the speakers. An alternative setup would be to route the audio through the headset to avoid this issue. However, although several Bluetooth models were trialed, none were very suitable due to awkward fit to different ears, hence only the microphone functionality is used and users can choose to either wear the device on their ear or on their collar.

9.4.2.3 Gameplay

The game aspect of Table Tennis for Three is implemented as a separate application, which synchronizes its game state through a dedicated server component, programmed as a Windows XP application. Each playing station acts as a client in this star-shaped architecture, informing the server of any changes. The server is responsible for distributing the latest block states and score changes to all other clients. In the case of varying networking conditions that need to reach across various implementation restrictions, an HTTP fallback mechanism can be utilized in case certain network ports are blocked due to firewall settings. Although the system has not been tested across large distances, the aforementioned provisions make an Internet-based implementation feasible.

This implementation section showed that Table Tennis for Three exemplifies a mixed reality system, as it combines the advantages of the real world with the advantages of virtual objects. Designing for such mixed reality systems requires not only technical knowledge how these aspects can be implemented individually, but also how they can work together as the physical domain needs to be accessible to the virtual domain and vice versa. This bridging between the physical and virtual domains in Table Tennis for Three is facilitated by the gameplay: the detection mechanism that senses changes in the physical world triggers changes in the virtual world. In contrast to mouse- and keyboard-controlled interactive experiences, the focus in Table Tennis for Three lies on the significance of the user's actions in the physical world: the exertion the players invest is a significant contribution to the interaction with the system, and the gameplay needs to consider this. The invested exertion is not a by-product of the intention to control the system, it is an elementary part of the interaction experience: it is "the action."

By highlighting these three key design implementation elements of Table Tennis for Three, we aim to tell a story about exploring the role of the human body and its associated movement actions in mixed reality systems. We hope to inspire future developments that aim to utilize the benefits in novel ways, using Table Tennis for Three as an example of how such a mixed reality system can provide users with new experiences otherwise not available without augmentation.

9.5 Feedback from Users

A quantitative analysis with 41 players of Table Tennis for Three suggests that engagement can occur in this exertion game, even though the three players are in different locations (for more details see [10, 26]). The players reported that they had "fun" and found the game engaging. The evaluation using questionnaires and interviews indicated that the participants enjoyed playing the game and that they could see such a networked mixed reality game being helpful in facilitating rapport between people who are physically apart but want to stay in touch. In particular, they expressed a sense of "playing together" and commented on the fact that it "gave them something to talk about." Several players said that the game created a sense of social rapport, and that they were excited about being able to play together over a distance, wanting to play again. The affordance created by the shift toward the physical world in the design of the game appeared to support participants' engagement and interaction, and most players reported that they considered the activity a workout and that they forgot the world around them when playing, comparable with notions in traditional table tennis. The choice of table tennis equipment appeared to support bodily skill training, as three participants asked if they could practice on their own after the interview. During the interviews, players compared the game to their previous table tennis experiences, noting that they were able to use some of their skills; however, other requirements, such as playing the ball high to hit the upper blocks, require tactics different from traditional table tennis. The uncertainty of the real world was exemplified by many balls hitting the edge of the table or bat, flying off in unexpected ways, which facilitated laughter by the participants, contributing to a social atmosphere.

9.6 Future Work

The investigation of Table Tennis for Three is aimed at contributing to an understanding of what it means to focus on the human body and its movements in mixed reality systems, demonstrated by an example application. It is only an initial exploration that is intended to highlight certain aspects that such an approach can support. Further work is needed to generate a theoretical framework that frames this view in regard to other mixed reality approaches and identifies similarities and differences. For example, the benefits of focusing on the human body and its movements could be investigated empirically; this would provide insights into how mixed reality systems can be approached in terms of evaluation. Furthermore, future work could also detail the impact of such systems on embodied social experiences. The Table Tennis for Three game is also a demonstrator for the potential of mixed reality systems to support social interactions when geographically distant. Alternative scenarios could entail asynchronous instead of synchronous embodied experiences, another challenging area for future work. Further scaling of the approach beyond three participants could also shed light on the role of the body in massively large mixed reality systems. In such large environments the participants are likely to not simultaneously engage in bodily actions, and a spectator role might need to be considered, as exertion games can facilitate performance aspects [3]. Accommodating many participants and spectators can result in experiences similar to traditional sports events, and the role of augmenting movements made by thousands raises interesting questions for future mixed reality systems.

9.7 Discussion and Conclusions

With our work, we explored the role of the body and its associated movement actions in mixed reality systems through the use of a game named Table Tennis for Three. We have argued that when integrating the real world with the virtual world, the human body offers opportunities that should play significant roles to be considered in the design of such systems. By appreciating the body's movements when experiencing the environment, physical objects and other human beings, technological augmentation can facilitate novel experiences and support engaging interactions. To support this, we have proposed that the physical world aspects in mixed reality systems can take on a central role in supporting such embodied experiences, contrasting traditional development efforts that often start with a view on the virtual component. Our exploration suggests that a consideration of physical characteristics, for example through tangible equipment, can facilitate aspects such as bodily skill training, leverage existing sport advances, utilize uncertainties of the real world, support proprioception and force-feedback in a low-cost way, and reduce the need for complex equipment such as head-mounted displays, as featured in more traditional mixed reality systems. To demonstrate how such an approach can shape the design of systems, a prototypal game was presented that was built around exertion movements, inspired by the game of table tennis. The prototype does not aim to simulate a table tennis game as accurately as possible, but rather offers a unique experience for the participants, not achievable without augmentation. Table Tennis for Three explores how bodily movements can be supported by the physical environment and physical game objects and how technological augmentation can enable novel experiences, in this case the support of three players engaging in gameplay simultaneously while being in geographically distant locations. Furthermore, the system also explores how such an approach can have implications for an implementation process, as many traditionally difficult technical issues such as force-feedback and the overlaying of virtual content through head-mounted displays are circumnavigated through a focus on the embodied experience. Also, shielding the detection technology away from the user presents an approach specifically suitable for exertion actions, as the bodily movements could damage equipment as well as possibly influence users in their interaction intensity, important aspects for the design of future systems. Players of Table Tennis for Three reported that the game facilitated enjoyment and that they engaged in the gameplay with their partners despite the geographical distance. The focus on the physical world during the design process appeared to facilitate the positive responses of the participants; however, further evaluation work is needed to fully assess the impact mixed reality systems that aim to support exertion have on their users.

We hope the presented investigation can contribute to an understanding of mixed reality systems, in particular in the context of gaming where supporting bodily movements are believed to facilitate more emotional and more physically demanding experiences. Such an understanding can help create physical, mental, and social benefits; in particular an increase in fitness levels is currently often discussed in light of the obesity issue. It is believed that by delivering fitness benefits through gameplay, a wider audience could be reached. However, this does not mean that the exploration of a body-centric approach to mixed reality applications is limited to gaming applications. Future work will show if lessons learned from a game perspective can also be applied in other application domains, such as learning, training, and maintenance.

Mixed reality systems have come a long way in their short existence, and their potential to enhance human's everyday life through offering novel interaction experiences is manifold. The combination of the benefits of the physical world with the advantages of virtual augmentation holds a promise for many new applications yet to come. The body plays a central role in how humans experience their physical environment and embodied others, and by considering this body and its potential for movement in such mixed reality interactions, exciting new experiences can emerge that can contribute to the well-being of its users. With our work, we hope we have added toward an understanding how this future could evolve and how it could be shaped, and inspired an exciting outlook on the role of exertion in mixed reality systems.

Acknowledgments The development work for Table Tennis for Three was initially supported by The University of Melbourne and CSIRO Collaborative Research Support Scheme. We thank Frank Vetere, Shannon O'Brien, Matt Adcock, Bo Kampmann Walther, Keith Gibbs, Irma Lindt, the IDEAS Lab, the Interaction Design Group, and Ivo Widjaja. Thanks to Kerin Bryant for taking the pictures.

References

1. Azuma, R., Baillot, Y., Behringer, R., Feiner, S., Julier, S. and MacIntyre, B. Recent advances in augmented reality. *IEEE Computer Graphics and Applications, 21* (6), 34–47, 2001.
2. Azuma, R.T. A survey of augmented reality. *Presence, 6*, 355–385, 1997.
3. Behrenshausen, B.G. Toward a (Kin) aesthetic of video gaming: the case of dance dance revolution. *Games and Culture, 2* (4), 335, 2007.
4. Bianchi-Berthouze, N., Kim, W. and Patel, D. Does body movement engage you more in digital game play? and why? In *Affective Computing and Intelligent Interaction*, 102–113, 2007.
5. Bikeboard.at. http://nyx.at/bikeboard/Board/showthread.php?threadid=61242
6. Consolvo, S., Everitt, K., Smith, I. and Landay, J.A. Design requirements for technologies that encourage physical activity. *Proceedings of the SIGCHI Conference on Human Factors in Computing Systems*, 2006, 457–466.
7. de Kort, Y.A.W. and Ijsselsteijn, W.A. People, places, and play: player experience in a socio-spatial context. *Computers in Entertainment (CIE), 6* (2), 1–31, 2008.
8. Dourish, P. *Where the Action Is: The Foundations of Embodied Interaction*. Cambridge, MA: MIT Press, 2001.
9. EyeToy. http://eyetoy.com
10. Florian, M., Martin, G., Frank, V. and Stefan, A. Design space of networked exertion games demonstrated by a three-way physical game based on table tennis. *Computers in Entertainment, 6* (3), 2008.
11. Gaver, W.W. Affordances for interaction: the social is material for design. *Ecological Psychology, 8* (2), 111–129, 1996.
12. Graves, L., Stratton, G., Ridgers, N.D. and Cable, N.T. Comparison of energy expenditure in adolescents when playing new generation and sedentary computer games: cross sectional study. *BMJ, 335* (7633), 1282–1284, 2007.
13. Hobart, M. Spark: the revolutionary new science of exercise and the brain. *Psychiatric Services, 59* (8), 939, 2008.
14. Hornecker, E. Getting a grip on tangible interaction: a framework on physical space and social interaction. *Proceedings of the SIGCHI Conference on Human Factors in Computing Systems*. 437–446.
15. Ishii, H. and Ullmer, B. Tangible bits: towards seamless interfaces between people, bits and atoms. *Conference on Human Factors in Computing Systems*, Atlanta, USA, 1997, 234–241.
16. Ishii, H., Wisneski, C., Orbanes, J., Chun, B. and Paradiso, J. PingPongPlus: design of an athletic-tangible interface for computer-supported cooperative play. In *SIGCHI Conference on Human Factors in Computing Systems*, ACM Press New York, NY, USA, 1999, 394–401.

17. Knoerlein, B., Székely, G. and Harders, M., Visuo-haptic collaborative augmented reality ping-pong. In *International Conference on Advances in Computer Entertainment Technology*, ACM Press New York, NY, USA, 2007, 91–94.
18. Lawn, M. and Takeda, T., Design of an action interface with networking ability for rehabilitation. In *IEEE Engineering in Medicine and Biology Society*, Hong Kong, 1998.
19. Lin, J., Mamykina, L., Lindtner, S., Delajoux, G. and Strub, H. Fish'n'Steps: Encouraging Physical Activity with an Interactive Computer Game *UbiComp 2006: Ubiquitous Computing*, 2006, 261–278.
20. Lindley, S.E., Le Couteur, J. and Berthouze, N.L. Stirring up experience through movement in game play: effects on engagement and social behaviour. *Proceeding of the twenty-sixth annual SIGCHI Conference on Human Factors in Computing Systems*, ACM, Florence, Italy, 2008.
21. McCarthy, J. and Wright, P. *Technology as Experience*. Cambridge, MA: The MIT Press, 402–407, 2004.
22. Merleau, P. *Phenomenology of Perception (Routledge Classics)*. Routledge, London, 2007.
23. Moen, J. KinAesthetic movement interaction: designing for the pleasure of motion, Stockholm: KTH, Numerical Analysis and Computer Science, 2006.
24. Mueller, F. Exertion interfaces: sports over a distance for social bonding and fun, Massachusetts Institute of Technology, 2002.
25. Mueller, F., Agamanolis, S. and Picard, R. Exertion interfaces: sports over a distance for social bonding and fun *Proceedings of the SIGCHI Conference on Human Factors in Computing Systems*, ACM, Ft. Lauderdale, Florida, USA, 2003.
26. Mueller, F.F. and Gibbs, M.R. Evaluating a distributed physical leisure game for three players. *Conference of the Computer-Human Interaction Special Interest Group (CHISIG) of Australia on Computer-Human Interaction: OzCHI'07*, ACM, Adelaide, Australia, 2007.
27. Pate, R.R., Pratt, M., Blair, S.N., Haskell, W.L., Macera, C.A., Bouchard, C., Buchner, D., Ettinger, W., Heath, G.W. and King, A.C. Physical activity and public health. A recommendation from the Centers for Disease Control and Prevention and the American College of Sports Medicine. *JAMA, 273* (5), 1995.
28. Salen, K. and Zimmerman, E. *Rules of Play : Game Design Fundamentals*. Cambridge, MA: The MIT Press, 53–68, 2003.
29. Sharp, H., Rogers, Y. and Preece, J. *Interaction Design: Beyond Human Computer Interaction*. Wiley, New York, 2007.
30. The essence and importance of timing (sense of surprise) in fencing. http://www.mat-fencing.com/Akademia16.html
31. Ullmer, B., Ishii, H. and Glas, D., mediaBlocks: Physical containers, transports, and controls for online media. In *25th Annual Conference on Computer Graphics and Interactive Techniques*, ACM Press New York, NY, USA, 1998, 379–386.
32. Vossen, D.P. The nature and classification of games. *AVANTE, 10* (1), 2004.
33. Weinberg, R.S. and Gould, D. *Foundations of Sport and Exercise Psychology*. Human Kinetics, Champaign, IL, 2006.
34. Wii Sports. http://wii.nintendo.com/software_wii_sports.html
35. Winograd, T. *Understanding Computers and Cognition: A New Foundation for Design*. Addison-Wesley, Reading, MA, 1987.
36. Woodward, C., Honkamaa, P., Jppinen, J. and Pykkimies, E.P. Camball-augmented virtual table tennis with real rackets. *ACE Singapore*. 275–276.

Chapter 10
Developing Mixed Interactive Systems: A Model-Based Process for Generating and Managing Design Solutions

Guillaume Gauffre, Syrine Charfi, Christophe Bortolaso, Cédric Bach, and Emmanuel Dubois

Abstract Taking advantage of the physical objects surrounding the user and the human ability to manipulate them fosters the development of multiple, new and advanced interaction techniques, called mixed interactive systems (MIS). Much work has been done to address specific aspects of the development of MIS. However, there is still no unifying conceptual framework to link these contributions and that presents a global approach for the development of MIS. In this context, this chapter presents a domain-specific development process that goes beyond ad hoc approaches and attempts to overcome barriers between different types of developer expertise, through a set of connections between steps of the MIS development process. Furthermore, to facilitate iteration in the design, these connections are observable, thus allowing a designer to review their decisions. The development process is illustrated via a concrete museum application.

Keywords Mixed interactive systems · Design process · Model transformation · Mixed interaction design

10.1 Introduction

The past 10 years have seen a set of evolutions in terms of communication opportunities, sensing capabilities, device miniaturization and computational capacities. These improvements have played a large role in the ongoing migration of human–computer interaction from the mouse–screen–keyboard paradigm to advanced interactive techniques combining computational abilities of the digital world, physical resources present in the user's environment and the user's physical skills. This

G. Gauffre (✉)
University of Toulouse, IRIT, 118 route de Narbonne, 31062 Toulouse Cedex 9, France
e-mail: Guillaume.Gauffre@irit.fr

E. Dubois et al. (eds.), *The Engineering of Mixed Reality Systems*, Human-Computer Interaction Series, DOI 10.1007/978-1-84882-733-2_10,

new form of interactive system, hereafter referred to as a *mixed interactive system* (MIS), is no longer limited to dedicated application domains and is now emerging in mass-market contexts such as museums [30], games [25] and tourism [14]. However, such interactive systems are difficult to develop: there is a large heterogeneity among the types of data manipulated and the variety of sensors and effectors can be used to develop new MIS. Furthermore, the number of interaction objects and domain objects to take into consideration is far bigger than in a traditional interactive system. In addition, we have, so far, acquired only limited experience of the development of such systems. The challenge of building MISs is no longer limited to demonstrating the technical feasibility of interactive systems involving the fusion of the physical and digital worlds: it is now necessary to design and develop effective and suitably adapted mixed interactive systems. Technological approaches need to be complemented by more structured development approaches.

10.1.1 Existing MIS Development Support

Among the different forms of development support for MIS, three major types can be identified: low-level implementation support, prototyping support and, finally, design support. The aim of low-level implementation support is mainly to avoid the need to reprogram, for each new application, the wired or Wi-Fi communication path between a microcontroller mounted on a sensor and the rest of the application. As a result, a number of APIs have emerged, such as those for Phidgets [13] and Arduino [1]. Additional encapsulations have also been produced to extract physical data directly from sensors and to convert it into information relevant for an MIS. Examples of such toolkits include tag-based localization support [17] and audiovisual information associated with the physical environment [22].

These software improvements triggered the emergence of implementation frameworks, facilitating the reuse and assembly of software parts required in these complex systems. As a result, such frameworks contribute to the rapid prototyping of MIS, such as Studierstube [29], or provide packaged elements specific to MIS, such as marker-based tracking [11].

In parallel to this support for implementation, more formal and descriptive support has been proposed to provide ways for describing, comparing and generating MIS. Such approaches allow a more rationalized and systematic exploration of design solutions and help in reasoning about the design aspects of MIS without focusing on, or being influenced, either positively or negatively, by technological considerations. For example, describing an MIS with the RBI framework [16] highlights how some physical properties and pre-existing knowledge of the everyday life are encoded in the MIS. But the place and roles of the human body is also a source of variation in an MIS, as introduced in [18], as well as the characterization of resources in terms of metaphors [9]. Other dimensions have been identified and addressed in different models: the TAC paradigm [32] is centred on the relationship between physical objects involved in an MIS, ASUR [7] focuses on the description of the user's interaction with an MIS, MIM [5] describes the required modalities and Smith's flow nets [33] are used to describe haptic interactions.

Each of the design support techniques or tools described above deals with a specific subset of development issues. Comprehensive design approaches covering design and implementation have been proposed. On the one hand, some have addressed the links between human interaction capabilities, required devices and task models in order to check the adequacy of the different aspects [19]. On the other hand, DART illustrates the association of design and implementation approaches by trying to support a rapid transition from storyboards to working experience [23].

Such links between development phases thus constitute a solution that avoids the use of a unique and supposedly complete model of MIS. However, developing an MIS involves requirement analysis, interaction design, software design and implementation, while so far the proposed links cover only a limited part of the development process. Furthermore, the links between one model and another or with code usually consist of the elicitation of dependencies between elements of each model; how the translation must be performed is not clearly explained. Transformations are thus mostly influenced by the designer's perspective and not clearly documented: understanding design decisions almost always requires the presence of the designer to explain the reasoning.

10.1.2 Objective and Goal

The objective of our work is the articulation of the design resources required along the development process of a mixed interactive system. Our goal is twofold: we are aiming at articulating the steps that form the design process and explicitly documenting these articulations.

Indeed, developing an MIS requires one to reason about possible interaction techniques. This reasoning should be influenced by requirements imported from the results of a task analysis conducted in a preliminary requirement analysis step. Furthermore, the choices that lead to the designed interaction technique should be exported to the next steps, where the software architecture supporting the deployment of the technique is designed. Finally, based on this software architecture design, the MIS can be properly coded. Ensuring the links between these four steps constitutes our first goal. In addition, since developing an interactive system involves the repetitive involvement of different experts, it is anticipated that re-exploring design decisions is crucial and must be supported. Therefore, making the link between the four steps clearly observable, i.e. explicitly highlighting how one design consideration of one step generates a set of considerations in the next step, constitutes our second goal.

In Sections 10.2 and 10.3, we present these articulations and their limits and advantages. Section 10.4 discusses the role of this articulated process in an iterative design context, especially through the explicit documentation of the transformations. All through these sections, illustrations are provided based on a case study that we introduce in the following section.

10.1.3 A Case Study

As part of collaboration with the Museum of Toulouse, it is intended to explore the design of a mixed interactive experience to introduce cladistics, a new hierarchical classification of species. This classification is based on evolutionary ancestry, i.e. evolution of criteria rather than similarities between species [4]. Such classification is represented with trees of evolution called cladograms, represented in Fig. 10.1, in which leaves represent species and nodes represent criteria acquired during evolution. With this new representation, a valid group of species includes all the species that have one criterion in common. For example, the group represented on the tree is not a valid group in cladistics: the common ancestry is the red node; a valid group based on this node should thus also contain the viper, pigeon and crocodile.

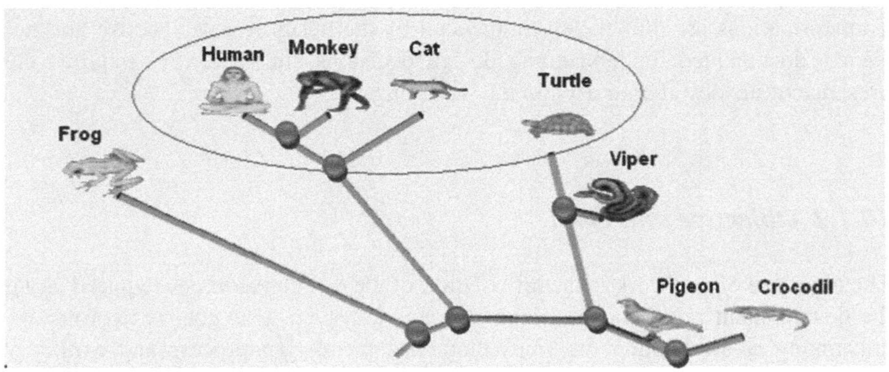

Fig. 10.1 A rearranged cladogram

The goal of the interactive experience is to explain why some of the previous groupings of species, such as fishes, are no longer valid in terms of cladistics. Traditionally, representing a group of elements consists of placing elements that share some similarities with one another spatially. In cladistics, spatially narrowing the species requires a manipulation of the tree structure: it consists of moving branches of the tree through rotations around one node. However, the species contained in the resulting group do not necessarily share the same evolutionary ancestry and therefore is not a valid group in cladistics. Provoking visitors to manipulate the cladogram structure is the pedagogical approach identified by the museum to bring the user's focus not only on the spatial group formed with species but also on the underlying articulated structure. As a result, the mixed interactive experience, which must be developed, will suggest that a cladistic group is fundamentally based on the structure, whatever be the position of the species.

10.2 Articulating MIS Task Analysis and Mixed Interaction Design

The two first steps of the MIS design process on which we focus are (1) the task analysis, which describes the global user activity and dynamic aspects of mixed interactive situations, and (2) the interaction design, which describes the mixed interaction in a way that takes into account the heterogeneity and richness of MIS. Several models exist for each of these two steps (e.g. sequence diagrams or task models for the former, and class diagrams or mixed interaction models for the latter). However, no clear links exist between them to ensure the transfer of design decisions and to help in maintaining coherence between the two steps. Some work in mixed interactive systems tries to link design and implementation steps by projecting scenarios on software architecture models [6, 27] or combining Petri Nets and DWARF components [15]. The rest of this section explores, characterizes and illustrates our approach for articulating MIS task analysis and interaction design.

10.2.1 Presentation of the Two Selected Models: K-MAD and ASUR

The articulation we propose is based on a task model (K-MAD [28]) and a mixed interaction model (ASUR [7]), which we briefly introduce in this section.

10.2.1.1 Task Analysis with K-MAD

K-MAD (Kernel of Model for Activity Description) [28] is centred on the *task* unit, which can be described according to two main aspects, the decomposition and the body.

The decomposition of a *task* unit of a given level gives place to several task units of lower level. The decomposition involves *operators* of synchronization, temporal and auxiliary scheduling. Figure 10.2 presents a K-MAD description of the task "Group" from our case study. The task "Group" is composed of two subtasks: "Manipulate Species" and "Describe Group".

The body supports the characterization of the *task* and consists of the *core*, the *state of the world* and the *conditions*:

- The *core* gathers the *type* of the task and a set of textual *attributes*. Type of task can be *unknown*, *abstract*, *system*, *user* or *interactive* task: this is when the *system* and the *user* together perform the *task*, such as the task "Group".
- The *state of the world* identifies the *objects* handled by the *task*; for example, the task "Construct Group" uses the object species and group.
- The *conditions* may be used to define a set of constraints on the objects used in the task.

10.2.1.2 Mixed Interaction Design with ASUR

The ASUR model (*Adapter*, *System*, *User*, *Real objects*) [7] adopts a user's interaction point of view on the design of mixed interactive systems. An ASUR model is composed of *participating entities* (PE) that can be either *digital entities* (S_{info}, S_{tool}, S_{object}), *physical entities* (R_{tool}, R_{object}), input or output *Adapters* (A_{in}, A_{out}) or a *User*.

Participating entities are not autonomous and need to communicate during task realization; such communication is modelled with ASUR *interaction channels* (IC). In addition, groups of *participating entities* and/or *interaction channels* have been included in the model in order to highlight the main data flow of the model (*interaction path*), a physical proximity of several *participating entities* (*physical proximity*), the fact that one physical (or digital) *participating entity* represents a given digital (or physical) *participating entity* (*representation group*), the need of coherence among a specific set of *participating entities* and *interaction channels*, etc.

Additional characteristics are used to refine this model. The main ones are the *medium* and the *representation* of an interaction channel, the *method of modification* and the *sensing mechanism* of the participating entities and the *intended user model* of the interaction path.

10.2.2 Articulation Between K-MAD and ASUR

As presented above, these two models express different aspects of the design of MIS. The articulation we propose is based on formal links established between elements of the two metamodels [2].

10.2.2.1 Task to Mixed Interaction Model Transformations

To link these two models, which do not share the same design goal and which are at different levels of abstraction, it is necessary to identify

1. when to pass from a task model, such as K-MAD, to a mixed interaction model, such as ASUR, and
2. how to perform the transition from the task model (K-MAD) to the mixed interaction model (ASUR).

In order to know when to adopt one or the other model, it is required to clearly characterize the border between these two models and the means to identify it.

Since ASUR considers that one *task* involves a unique *user* and a unique *object* of the *task*, we established two rules (Ri) to identify this border: R1 is related to the existence of a unique *user* and R2 is related to the existence of a unique *task object*.

In order to describe how to perform the transition between the two models, a study of the two metamodels emphasized articulatory elements between these metamodels. Some elements of the metamodels refer to the same concept and constitute direct links (L*i*) of the articulation:

- L1 is related to the concept of *task* and has been associated with a set of rules, named R3, to relate one or several ASUR models to a K-MAD task and identify ASUR *interaction channels.*
- L2 is related to the concept of *object* and has been associated with a set of rules, named R4, to describe how to transform K-MAD *objects* into physical or digital ASUR *participating entities*.
- L3 is related to the concept of *user* and has been associated with a set of rules, named R5, to describe how to transform a K-MAD *user task* in an ASUR *user* and additional properties: *sensing mechanism* and *method of modification* of the *user*.

The physical proximity group expressed in ASUR can be influenced by K-MAD conditions. Thus, we establish a last link L4 between the elements of metamodels related to the constraints. From this link, no generic transformation can be summarized in rules.

Beyond these links which ensure some coherence, additional elements of the metamodels are linked with three other set of rules:

- The K-MAD *system* (or *interactive*) task has been associated with a set of rules, named R6 (or R7), that describe how to transform a K-MAD *system* (or *interactive*) task in ASUR *participating entities* that complement the PE generated by R4 to represent K-MAD objects. Entities generated by R6 and R7 can be adapter, physical or digital *participating entities* required for the interaction.
- The *decomposition* and the *name* of a K-MAD task have been associated with a set of rules, named R3, that describe how to transform a K-MAD *decomposed task* in ASUR partial models and a K-MAD *name* task in ASUR *interaction channels* connecting *participating entities generated by* R4, R6 and R7.

10.2.2.2 Applying the Task to Mixed Interaction Model Transformations on the Case Study

As explained above, the use of articulation rules in a design context transforms a K-MAD tree into an ASUR model or a partial ASUR model, i.e. an incomplete ASUR model. To illustrate the rules, we consider the K-MAD description of our case study (Fig. 10.2). The K-MAD tree contains two interactive subtasks "Manipulate Species" and "Describe Group". For the purposes of this paper, we illustrate the rules on the less decomposed task "Describe Group" and we focus on the subtask "Construct Group" because "Provide Guidance" is secondary.

According to the Museum scenario, users have to "Describe Group" on the basis of species spatial proximity. Users thus have to alternatively "Move the Reference Point of Group", "Reduce" and "Enlarge" the group range.

In the subtask "Construct Group", the *user* is unique and the *task object* is the "Species" that the user wants to group. The rules R1 and R2 are checked and thus allow the use of the transformation rules.

First we apply a subpart of rules R4 which transform a K-MAD *object* into at least an ASUR *physical entity* (R) and/or a *digital entity* (S) on the whole subtask "Describe Group". We identify two objects: species and group. Each object can be physical, digital or a combination of physical and digital entities. "Species" is the object of the task: it can be a physical entity R_{object}, alone or can simultaneously have a digital representation S_{info}; it can also be a digital entity S_{object}, alone or can also have a physical representation R_{tool}. According to the same logic, we generate ASUR entities corresponding to the object Group. R4 provides 20 different ASUR partial models that represent different starting points for the interaction design. To completely explore the design space, every other rule must be applied to each of these 20 cases. In the rest of the paper, we limit the illustration to the ASUR partial model containing a S_{object} "Species" and a S_{tool} "Group". Figure 10.3 represents the ASUR model resulting from this illustration.

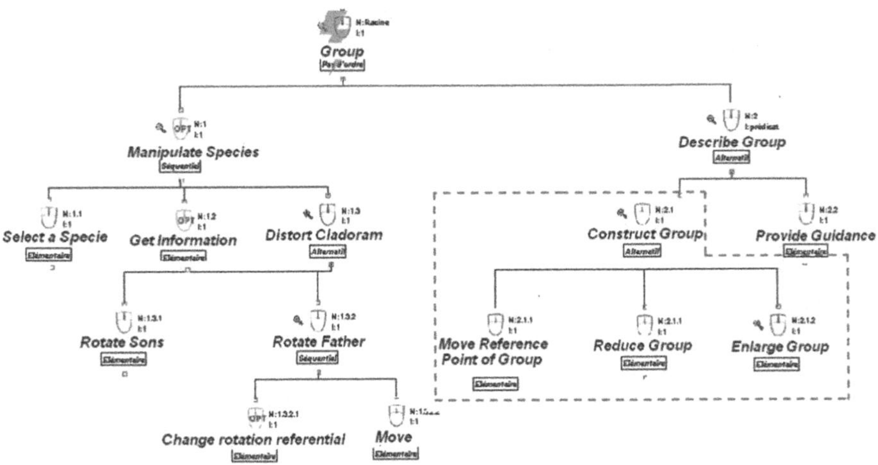

Fig. 10.2 K-MAD task "Group". The *dotted line* identifies the subtask illustrated in the paper

According to the rules R3 which transform a K-MAD *decomposed* task into several ASUR partial models, the equivalent ASUR partial model of "Construct Group" is the fusion of the ASUR partial models of its subtasks. We thus focus on the subtask "Reduce Group" since the approach is the same for transforming "Enlarge Group" and "Move Reference Point of Group".

The task "Reduce Group" is interactive, so we apply a subpart of rules R7 which transform a K-MAD *interactive* task in ASUR *PE*. Firstly, an R7 rule generates an ASUR *user*. Secondly, an R7 rule concerning a digital object, which is in our case

"Group", generates an *adapter* A_{in1} and an *adapter* $A_{\text{out1.1}}$ in charge of managing the input and the output of the interactive task, respectively. Thirdly, an R7 rule concerning a digital task object, which is in our case "Species", generates an *adapter* $A_{\text{out1.2}}$. Fourthly, the use of rules R7 implies the application of a subpart of rules R3 which create ASUR *interaction channels*. Regarding the digital object "Group", an R3 rule creates an *interaction channel* with the concept "Reduce" from the user to the "Group" through the adapter A_{in1} and an *interaction channel* from the "Group" to the user through the adapter $A_{\text{out1.1}}$. Regarding then the digital object "Species", an R3 rule constructs an *interaction channel* from "Species" to the user through the *adapter* $A_{\text{out1.2}}$.

Finally, we apply the same rules on the subtasks "Enlarge Group" and "Move Reference Point of Group" to complete the model. The rules generate two complementary sets of adapters (A_{in2}; $A_{\text{out2.1}}$; $A_{\text{out2.2}}$) and ($A_{\text{in3.}}$; $A_{\text{out3.1}}$; $A_{\text{out3.2}}$) and *interaction channels* connecting the *participating entities*.

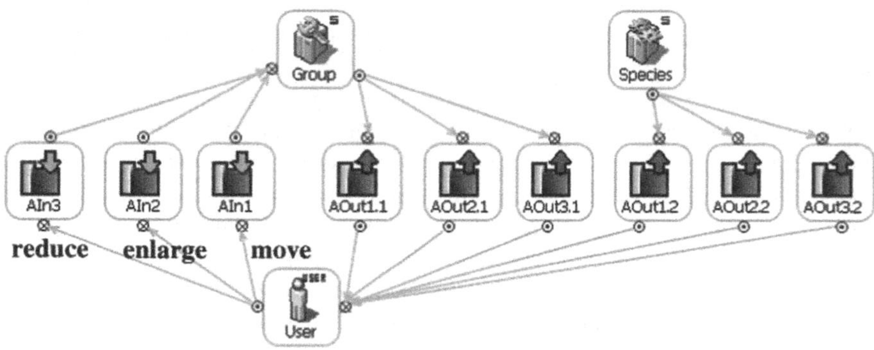

Fig. 10.3 An ASUR model generated by the rules from "Construct Group" task

The application of the rules, without making any other design choice, generates many different ASUR partial models constituting different starting points of the design of mixed interaction. The designer can choose one of these models to complete it. The next section motivates the choice of one solution and refines the generated starting point.

10.2.3 Designer and ASUR Refinement

Among the partial ASUR models generated, a first set involves a physical representation of the group and the second involves a digital representation. In this first iteration, we chose to work with the digital representation. The group is thus a digital entity that has an impact on the species: modifying the size of the group adds or removes species accordingly. In terms of ASUR, it must be an S_{tool}. For this reason, the partial ASUR model presented in Fig. 10.3 has been chosen as a starting point.

A second iteration or a parallel design process could focus on the design alternative based on the physical representation of the group.

To correctly match the museum expectations, it is now necessary to define a mixed interaction that is useful for performing this task. Figure 10.4 represents the refined model.

To refine the design interaction, we focused on the metaphor and technologies to use. As the "Group" has to be reduced and enlarged, and the application is dedicated to 14–40-year-old persons and has to be enjoyable, we decided to use a bubble metaphor. An *interaction channel* transfers information from the group, renamed "Bubble", to the "Species" to specify whether or not they are enclosed in it.

Exploring the ASUR characteristics associated with the *participating entities* and *interaction channels* constitutes an opportunity to refine the bubble metaphor design. The *medium*, an *interaction channel* property, expresses the means by which the information is transmitted. To enlarge and reduce the "Bubble", we used the metaphors of blowing up and deflating. The *medium* can be the gas. A second property is the *representation* which expresses the coding scheme used to encode information in the *medium*. In our case, it is a pressure value and its characteristic *language form* is weight.

Regarding the *participating entities*, the *sensing mechanism* is a property that expresses the processes used to capture the state or changes of the *medium*. In our case, the mechanism is pressure sensitive. A second property, the *method of modification*, refers to the method of affecting the *medium*. In our case, it will be gas compression. In order to modify the gas pressure by compression, we used a familiar object: an air pump represented in the ASUR model by a new R_{tool} manipulated by the user ("User" → "Air Pump"). As the tasks "Reduce Group" and "Enlarge Group" use the same *medium* and *sensing mechanism*, A_{in1} and A_{in2} are fused.

We use ASUR characteristics to refine the rest of the ASUR diagram. To avoid the multiplication of physical artefacts, the R_{tool} "Valve" attached to the R_{tool} "Air Pump" (double line) is used as a pointer and is manipulated by the user ("User" → "Valve") when moving the "Bubble". The role of "Ain3" is thus to detect the valve position. The *medium* of the incoming *interaction channel* is the light and its *language form* is the position. The *sensing mechanism* of "Ain3" is video sensitive. To complete the design, the MIS has to detect when the user grabs the air pump to begin the group construction. A new A_{in} is thus added and has light intensity sensitive as *sensing mechanism*. The "Ain4" is then embedded in the "Air Pump" (double line). Finally, according to the museum scenario, it is necessary to permanently display the cladogram structure. Therefore, an S_{info} "Cladogram Structure" is added and connected to the same A_{out} "Screen" resulting from the fusion of all A_{out}, as "Species" and "Bubble".

As a result, according to the museum context and the exploration of the ASUR characteristics, we obtain a complete solution: the cladogram is displayed on the screen; the user points to the screen using the valve and creates a group of species inside the bubble; to add or remove a species, the user pumps with the air pump to enlarge and reduce the bubble size accordingly.

10.2.4 Advantages and Limits of the Transformation Process

The multiplicity of rules and sub-rules to transform a K-MAD model into an ASUR model makes it hard to explore all the solutions. However, it ensures a systematic exploration of the possibilities or at least may help to keep a trace of alternatives that have not been explored, such as the use of a physical representation of the group.

So far this approach is limited to a specific task model (K-MAD) and a mixed interaction model (ASUR). But we believe that it would be of interest to apply a similar approach with different source and target models.

The application of the articulation rules generated different ASUR partial models, all of them involving every element expressed in the task model and relevant to the user's interaction. These ASUR models are in accordance with concepts expressed in the task model and represent a starting point for the design of a mixed interaction, by expressing design elements in terms of concepts of a specific model for mixed interaction: participating entities (user, physical and/or digital entities and adapters) and interaction channels connecting them. The resulting ASUR models are not totally defined: the designer has the possibility to refine many design aspects.

Finally, the link between these two steps (task and interaction) is clearly documented by the rules applied. The reasoning can be revisited later: reasons for identifying the different elements of the mixed interaction design are tightly coupled with decisions taken in the previous phase.

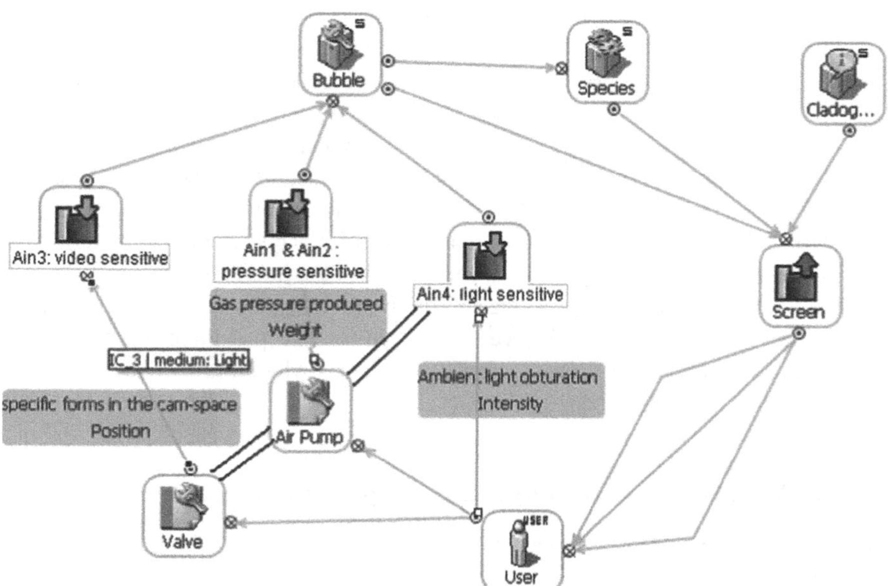

Fig. 10.4 Final ASUR model of museum scenario

10.3 Articulating Mixed Interaction Design with MIS Implementation

As illustrated in the previous section, an ASUR model captures several characteristics of a mixed interactive situation by defining each entity taking part in the interaction. The next goal of our approach, presented in this section, consists of linking these design results with the implementation of the software. In order to combine user-centred design requirements and software engineering requirements in the same design process, a software architecture model is used. Defining this model must set up some of the primary elements of the software architecture of an MIS, and in order to fit our approach, these elements must be derived from an ASUR model. To be efficient, this mechanism must consider not only some properties relevant for the design of interactive software architecture but also some properties inherent in the development context of MIS.

10.3.1 MIS Architecture Requirements

To enable the creation of the software architecture which will be used to implement the system, a generic software engineering approach could be used. For example, a notation like UML is able to describe this information. But such general purpose languages are too generic and as a result, profiles are often used for domain-specific developments [34]. To describe the software architecture independently of the UML notation, we preferred to adopt a model-driven engineering (MDE) approach [31]. It provides appropriate abstractions and notations to describe a particular domain: MIS development.

The field of HCI established several notions for defining a significant architectural model [24]: (1) the separation between functional core and interaction services, (2) the designation of roles for each software component involved in an interaction and (3) the definition of the communication between each of these components. The abstract model ARCH is an example of how a model can cover these aspects, in that case with a special interest in the designation of roles. This results in an additional consideration: the physical and logical separation of the interaction layer.

These four fundamental aspects are central in our design approach but to enhance the architecture modelling of MIS, we consider in the next part three supplementary properties characterized by [12] as internal properties, which improve the adequacy of the architecture in this context.

10.3.1.1 Modifiability, Portability and Development Efficiency

MIS are not well known and many challenges remain because the number of interaction possibilities is exploding. To enable the exploration of such possibilities, three main properties must be addressed during the development of mixed interactive systems:

- *Portability*, because devices and software libraries for interactive software are heterogeneous. The metamodel, presented in the next section, addresses this need for portability by adopting a platform-independent point of view as promoted by a model-driven architecture. A description of the way to instantiate the designed system on a runtime platform is presented in Section 10.3.3.
- *Development efficiency to enable rapid prototyping*. We choose an MDE approach to describe specification languages for each step of the development and to define rules for their articulation, as presented in Sections 10.3.2 and 10.3.3.
- *Modifiability to explore different design solutions*. This property is addressed via two aspects: modularity and reusability. The component-based architecture enhances the modularity. The designation of roles improves the reusability capacities, especially if we consider the distinction between input and output interaction, as expressed in MVC [20] and really pertinent for mixed interactive situations.

Considering these different aspects of modelling, the software architecture of interactive software and more specifically for supporting the development of MIS, the next section introduces the ASUR-IL metamodel [10] used in our process to describe an MIS architecture.

10.3.1.2 ASUR-IL Metamodel

The model can be seen as a combination of the abstract models ARCH and MVC. The PAC-Amodeus model [24] also extends ARCH but focuses on dialog control (due to its purpose, viz. multimodal systems) and does not treat the I/O distinction. The ASUR-Implementation Layer (ASUR-IL) describes an assembly of software components involved in the interaction and the different communications between them. Each *component* owns several *ports*, characterized by the kind of data supported, to enable *data flows* between them. As illustrated in Fig. 10.5, an ASUR-IL model is an *assembly* and contains several sub-assemblies.

Two types of sub-assemblies coexist in ASUR-IL:

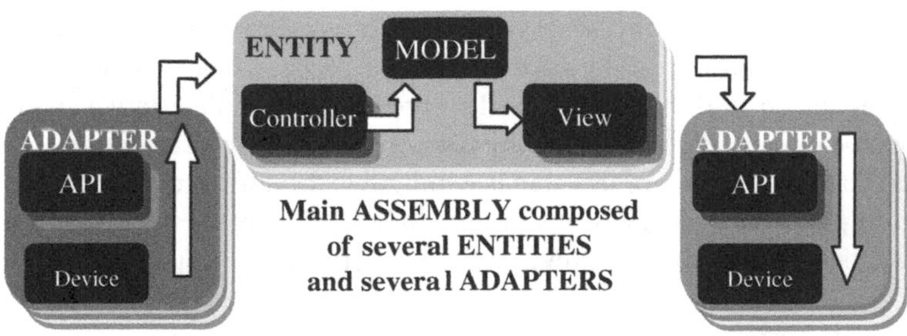

Fig. 10.5 The ASUR-IL metamodel – main components and information path

- *Adapters* group together *device* and *API* components and support the description of the different layers of the interaction (squares on the left and right of Fig. 10.5),
- *Entities* group together *model*, *view* and *controller* components and support the description of the domain objects (rectangle in the middle of Fig. 10.5).

For enabling the articulation with the models of other development steps, the ASUR-IL metamodel is described, with tools dedicated to the description of domain-specific languages.

10.3.1.3 Model-Driven Engineering Tools

As for ASUR we chose to express the metamodel using the tools of the Modeling Project [8] of the Eclipse Foundation. ASUR and ASUR-IL metamodels conform to the Ecore metametamodel and their manipulation is supported by the Eclipse Modeling Framework. These models can be edited by means of editors developed using the Graphical Modeling Framework. The main tool which supports the articulation of the two models is defined by using a transformation engine. This one is expressed with the Atlas Transformation Language [21], which combines two transformation approaches: declarative and imperative rules. This makes it possible to express the transformation required to link interaction design and architecture modelling.

10.3.2 ASUR to ASUR-IL Transformation Principles

As mentioned before, the principles of an articulation between the ASUR model and the ASUR-IL model need to be defined in order to link users' requirements and software design. To express the purpose of this transformation, the following subsections describe the different concepts of each correlated model and how they are linked during the transformation process.

10.3.2.1 Mixed Interaction to Software Architecture Model Transformation

As opposed to code generation, this transformation focuses on the translation of concepts that cannot be directly matched with a one-to-one cardinality. They are parts of different levels of abstraction of the development process. The source model does not contain all the information required to produce a complete target model and some target elements are conditioned by a combination of several source elements. In that context, the purpose of this step is to initialize the software architecture specification. It produces basic elements of an ASUR-IL model on the basis of design considerations expressed in the previous design step and more specifically

- the *digital entities* involved in the interaction with an MIS and their types
- the attributes of the *interaction channels* between each entity.

The target elements of this transformation are the main types of ASUR-IL assemblies, *adapters* and *entities*, which map the ASUR elements, *adapters* and *digital entities*, respectively.

When mapping ASUR *adapters*, the transformation identifies the different elements identified in ASUR to characterize the interaction. For each ASUR *adapter*, the *interaction channels* involved and their attributes (*medium* and *language form*) are the elements used to create the components and the communications of an ASUR-IL *adapter*. The basic behaviour consists of creating a *device* and several *APIs* to treat the different interaction forms (*medium* + *language form*) specified in the ASUR model. Another input model is used to identify these components: an ontology of devices and APIs organized using ASUR concepts. In this way, the ontology is used as a parameter of the rule; it draws links between existing ASUR-IL *devices* and *APIs* on the one hand and specific values of ASUR attributes on the other hand. The advantage is that the rule itself does not contain such information. The content of the ontology can be manually described by using an OWL editor like Protégé [26] or by storing the different developments made to enrich it. Without claiming to enable the creation of a complete classification of interaction devices, this ontology-based approach progressively constitutes a taxonomy of devices and software libraries, and offers a way to explore and compare different technologies for mixed interaction.

When mapping ASUR *digital entities*, the transformation identifies the different elements involved in the interaction and identified in ASUR, as well as their types (main object of the task – S_{object} – or the interaction tool – S_{tool} – for example); the result is the creation of *entity* sub-assemblies. An *entity* contains one *model* and several *views* and *controllers*; this is derived from the interaction forms associated with the *interaction channels* between the *digital entity* under consideration and the *adapter* used to affect (A_{In}) or reflect (A_{Out}) its state. *Views* and *controllers* are the components which link system-independent components (*devices* and interaction *APIs*) to the functional core components represented by the *model* component.

10.3.2.2 Applying the Mixed Interaction to Software Architecture Model Transformation on the Case Study

We applied these transformation principles to two *adapters* for input and two *digital entities* of our case study. The transformation produces one *sub-assembly* for each one and creates the different *data flows* between their components.

Creation of Adapter Sub-assemblies

Two rules based on the same mechanism are involved: one for *adapters* in charge of input interaction and one for *adapters* in charge of output interaction. These declarative rules create an *adapter* assembly for each ASUR *adapter*. In Fig. 10.6, the first ASUR *adapter* is used to get the gas pressure produced by the air pump and the second one is used to get the position of the valve. For the first adapter, the "GasPressureSensor" *device* is associated with the *medium* gas and the *language form* weight. The ontology revealed that the pattern Camera *device* + MarkerPoseEstimator *API* answers the need for position data sensed on the light *medium*. These *device* and *API* are thus instantiated in the ASUR-IL model of our case study. In the case where no matches are detected in the ontology, a *device* and an *API* are created with default attributes.

Finally, all *ports* are created with specified *data types* if the ontology describes them (numerical for gas pressure–numerical vector for position) and default values otherwise. The different *data flows* between these *ports* end the definition of the *adapter* sub-assemblies.

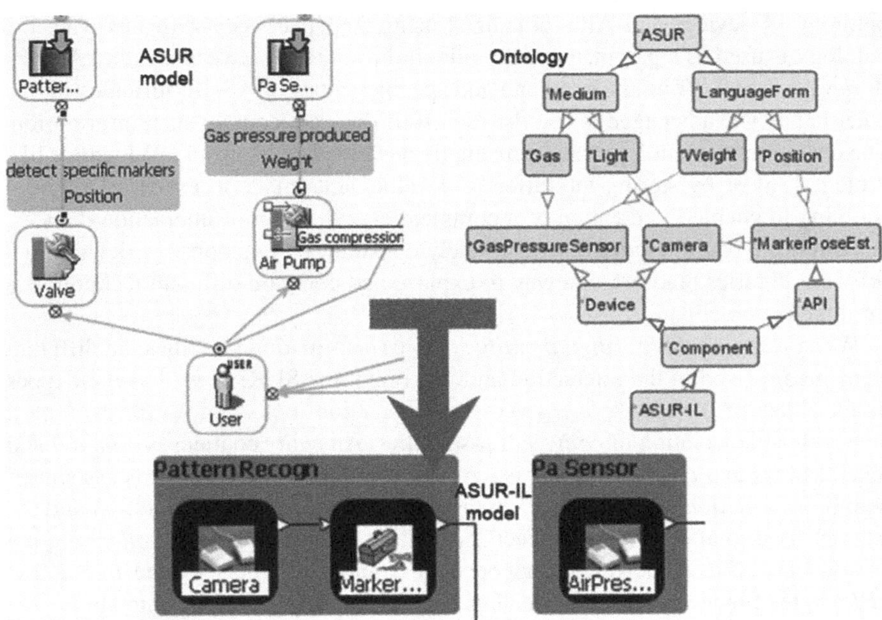

Fig. 10.6 Source (ASUR and ontology) and target (ASUR-IL) elements of the transformation of two adapters for input

Creation of Entity Sub-assemblies

The *entities* are the sub-assemblies which contain the components specific to the system currently developed. For each ASUR *digital entity*, the transformation rule associates one *entity* sub-assembly. In our example, Fig. 10.7, two sub-assemblies are thus created, the "Bubble" one and the "Species" one. Each of these two sub-assemblies contains one *model*. However, as mentioned above, the role of the ASUR *digital entity* to transform influences the definition of its ASUR-IL counterpart. In our case study, the *digital entity* S_{tool} (Bubble) interacts with the main object of the task S_{object} (Species); the *model* component of the bubble must be able to communicate with the *model* of the species (bold arrow in Fig. 10.7).

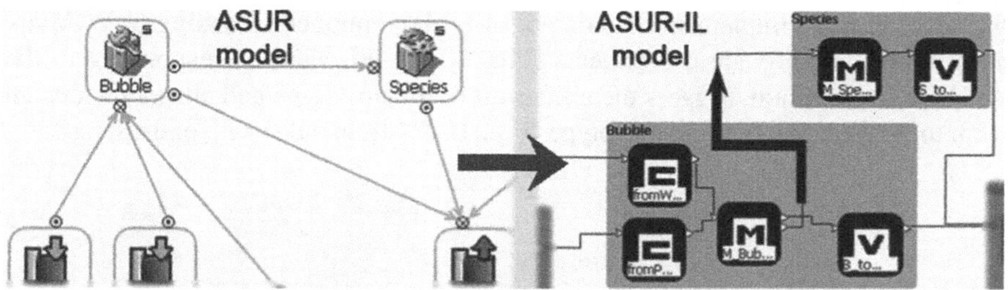

Fig. 10.7 Source and target elements of the transformation of two digital entities

Entity sub-assemblies also include *controller* and *view* components; identifying them relies on the *interaction channels* connected to the ASUR entity. In our example, the *digital entity* S_{tool} (Bubble) receives data from two *adapters* and with two distinct interaction forms. As a result, the ASUR-IL *entity* contains two *controllers* to compute the position and the gas pressure. Finally, this *entity* contains just one *view* to render its state. Concerning the *second digital* entity S_{object} (Species), apart from the S_{tool}, there are no data sent to this entity; as a result, this entity contains only one *model* component and one *view* to compute its representation. The view has to conform to the specified interaction form (3D rendering) to render its state.

10.3.3 From a Software Architecture Model for MIS to mplementation

The articulation of the different design models and transformations involved in the development process for MIS is based on the need to explore the different interactive solutions, given a set of requirements and the need to support the implementation step. The final step consists of mapping ASUR-IL architecture to a runtime platform to prototype and test the system. Another transformation has been developed to target the WComp metamodel, embedded in the WComp [3] rapid prototyping platform, developed on top of the .NET runtime. This platform has been chosen because of its simplicity of use and its small consumption of computational resources. WComp provides a graphical tool to instantiate components and to connect their ports at runtime. As opposed to specific platforms for MIS or interactive systems in general, the granularity of the component assemblies is not defined and thus offers a flexible platform.

To perform the mapping between ASUR-IL and WComp, we use the model-to-text transformation engine JET from the Modeling Project [8]. This engine is used to generate the C# code of the components' skeleton. The C# interfaces are thus generated if they do not exist at transformation time. A second effect is the production of an XML file describing a Wcomp assembly used to load and connect the different components. Each component has an ID which is generated or selected from a repository of existing components. Once the transformation is performed, the developer can implement the content of each component. Loading in WComp, an assembly of software components (Fig. 10.8 – left side) corresponding to the ASUR-IL description, triggers the execution of the prototype and allows the design team to evaluate the running prototype (Fig. 10.8 – right side) with end-users.

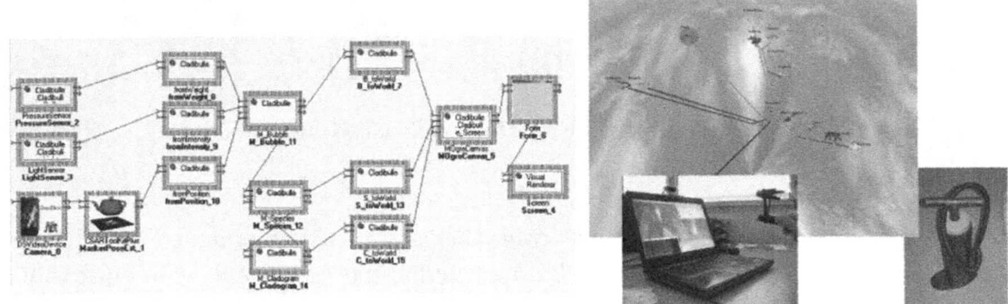

Fig. 10.8 WComp assembly and prototype captions

10.3.4 Limits and Interests of These Articulations

The transformations which linked the interaction model ASUR to the software architecture model ASUR-IL and ASUR-IL to the runtime platform WComp enable transitions between three development steps. It offers guidelines for taking decisions in terms of design choices at different levels of abstraction of the system: interaction design, software architecture specification and implementation.

This approach considers four properties of the engineering of interactive software (functional core and interaction service separation, role definition, communication description, physical and logical interaction distinction) and emphasizes three properties for the development of MIS. Development *efficiency* is supported by providing a transformation tool for each articulation. The positioning of the ASUR-IL model as an intermediate model before its transcription to a runtime platform is a way to ensure *portability* on different platforms. Finally, *modifiability* is addressed by promoting (1) the modularity of the system with a component-based model and (2) the reusability of components with the ontology as a parameter of the articulations.

But even if the content of the ontology provides a way to explore different MIS interaction techniques, this ontology is based only on ASUR concepts and thus cannot be claimed to be a classification of input and output interaction. Furthermore, ASUR does not provide enough information for characterizing other aspects of the system like the behaviour of the software components. It might thus be relevant to couple an ASUR-IL description to other models to interlace different aspects of software design.

Furthermore, using the ontology as a parameter of the transformation highlights a set of existing technologies that are relevant for the MIS under consideration. However, choosing one of the suggested solutions is left entirely to the designer.

Following this selection, the designer has to complete the description of the elements not characterized by the transformation. For example, it could be necessary to define the attributes of a new API. Another aspect of the design that requires editing concerns the different entities; the designer has to specify each port involved to qualify the communication between the interaction layers and the functional core. In that sense, we did not define this approach in order to support the automated development of an MIS. The goal is to provide a framework for covering the different steps of the development process. The next section presents the benefits found when iterating the process in order to refine the interaction technique and explore alternative design solutions.

10.4 Outcomes of the Design Process in an Iterative Development Context

Previous sections have described the sequencing of the different articulations to support the development of an MIS from task analysis to implementation. This organization of the different steps must be seen in an iterative development context. The use of models to support each step and established rules to switch from one to another therefore constitutes a list of potential targets to consider in further design refinements. The next sections illustrate the use of these steps in an iterative context. We illustrate how this process assists the design in

- highlighting the impact of one step on another,
- documenting the design decisions,
- suggesting different levels of refinement of the design.

Indeed, several kinds of problems can be discovered during evaluations, tests or user experiments of an intermediate version of an MIS. Given that each of the four models considered here (K-MAD, ASUR, ASUR-IL and WComp) covers a distinguishable aspect of system design, these problems can be associated with one of the models involved in our process. The definition of the process is thus helpful for several reasons: (1) it helps in locating where to start the redesign of the system for a given problem, indicating which parts of the decision can be kept; (2) it helps in finding new solutions by using the models; and (3) it helps in anticipating consequences of a redesign decision by highlighting which parts of the process will have to be re-executed and to what extent. We cannot yet provide a clear and complete set of rules to associate these problems with specific steps of our process nor offer a detailed and systematic result after a given refinement. However, we illustrate this mechanism below with a set of problems we encountered when developing the prototype presented in the previous sections.

10.4.1 K-MAD Level

Early user experiments revealed that after the use of the system, users were mainly focusing on the concept of group and not enough on the species themselves. This problem is not an interaction problem but rather linked to the definition of the task itself and the domain objects involved.

In order to focus the activity on the manipulation of species rather than only on the construction of a group, it was necessary to rethink the task structure. A modified version thus emphasized adding or removing of species to/from a group as shown in Fig. 10.9 instead of the positioning of a group zone (the Bubble).

The consequences in terms of development are that K-MAD to ASUR and ASUR to ASUR-IL transformations have to be reapplied with this new subtask. Coherence with other subtasks of the model also has to be studied.

Applying this redesign iteration leads to the identification of a fixed zone representing the group. It is therefore no longer manipulated and users can focus on species.

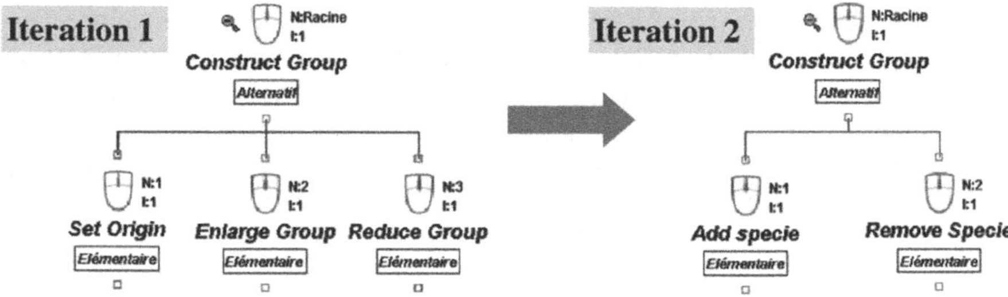

Fig. 10.9 Redesign of the subtask "Construct Group"

10.4.2 ASUR Level

Without the integration of this task redesign, the original system, as presented in Section 10.3.4, also revealed a difficulty in the simultaneous placement of the origin of the Bubble tool and the definition of its size.

The interaction forms used to perform these two actions are physical actions and are in conflict because the action on the air pump with one hand influences the precision of the other hand's position. This is clearly related to the interaction definition. Focusing on ASUR will be required to define an alternative solution.

Different improvements can solve this problem by acting on essential characteristics of the ASUR interaction channels and physical entities involved (cf. Fig. 10.10):

- modifying the ASUR representation of the information transmitted by the user to the air pump (reduction of the gesture's amplitude, of the physical force needed),

- choosing a different ASUR modification method to act on the air pump: using a foot motion instead of a hand motion, the force needed to act on it must be also reasonable to avoid the original conflict,
- letting the user directly act on the medium to modify the sensed data (gas pressure); thus, the air pump is no longer needed, the modification method is now to blow.

Each refinement impacts essentially on the design of the physical artefacts but produces minor effects on the design of the software components: ASUR to ASUR-IL transformation will not change the adapters used for input, the architecture remains unmodified, only the controller components must be updated to calibrate the data capture.

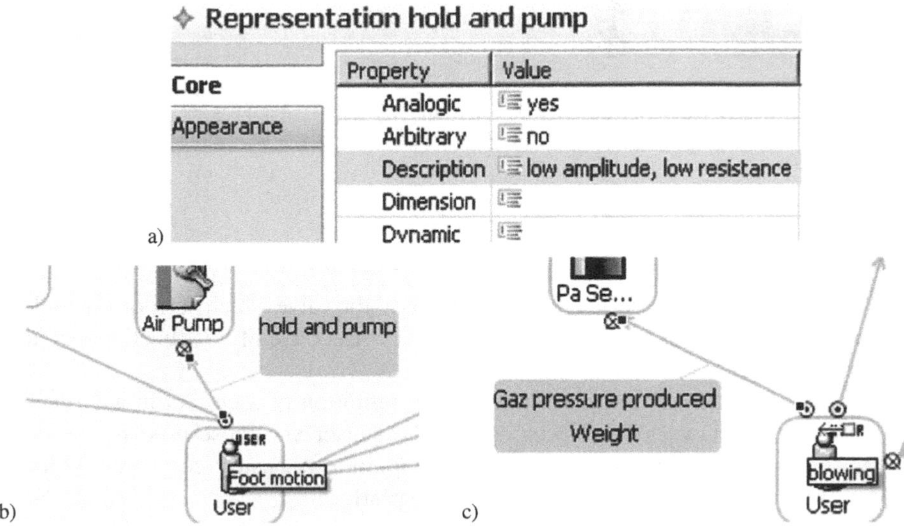

Fig. 10.10: Refinements (**a**) modifying the representation, (**b**) modifying the modification method, (**c**) removing the air pump

10.4.3 ASUR-IL Level

During the development, several improvements have been made at this level. The first prototype was developed using a tracking library to detect the position of the valve. But this solution was too sensitive to luminosity variations. The data produced, i.e. a three-dimensional position of the valve, were also too rich and not precise enough in our context.

The kind of device and API, and the data produced, are clearly some characteristics described in the ASUR-IL model. A way to improve the prototype is to change the content of the adapter and to use another data type for capturing a two-dimensional position only.

The new ASUR-IL model specifies an adapter which embeds a camera working in the infrared spectrum and an API for tracking infrared-sensitive markers. The kind of data on the outport of the API is now two-dimensional data.

As a result, another assembly has been generated using infrared tracking which offers a more robust tracking of the physical object valve. The modifications were performed on the definition of the adapter (Fig. 10.11) and on the controller component which now computes a two-dimensional position.

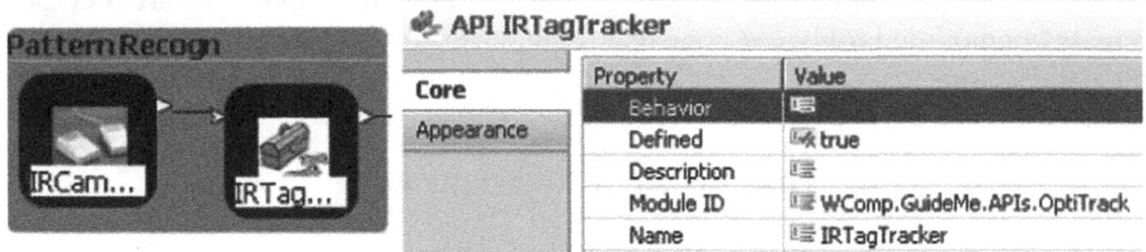

Fig. 10.11 Use of the infrared tracker instead of the marker-based tracker

10.4.4 WComp Level

Finally, experiments revealed that the rotation of the valve which performs the selection of an object was too limited. To enable a correct use of this functionality, this parameter had to be modified.

This adjustment is entirely linked to the definition of a correct transformation scale of data between those provided by the sensor and those used by the digital components coding the pointer. This adaptation is clearly correlated with the definition of the software components on the platform.

The advantage of the WComp platform, and also of the component-based platforms, is that we can act on component properties (i.e. C# language properties) at runtime. This has been used to calibrate some variables to refine the interaction, such as the degree of rotation, and also other variables, e.g. gas pressure and light threshold.

As this refinement is performed at runtime, it has no real impact; it is just a way to fine-tune the prototype. With WComp, it is possible to save an assembly in its current state, including the serialization of the properties' values. By this means, it is possible to test and store the prototype's configurations in different contexts (user abilities, light level, etc.).

10.5 Conclusions and Perspectives

This chapter introduced and illustrated an approach for articulating specification languages required to develop mixed interactive systems. Through this approach, four steps of the development are linked: task analysis, mixed interaction design, software architecture design and implementation. As a consequence, design choices elaborated in one step are linked to design or implementation aspects in subsequent steps. Moreover, each link explicitly details the source and target elements on the one hand and the translation process for effectively transforming the element on the other hand. Finally, this chapter also discussed the benefits of this approach in an iterative design context and especially highlighted the possibility of anticipating the amount of work when addressing a specific challenge: associating a problem to one step and even to a specific part of the element expressed in this step can contribute to the identification of the consequences it will have on the rest of the design.

Our approach can be considered as a set of vertical transformations that accompany the development process of MIS from the early phase of requirements analysis to the final implementation of the system. There are three forms of support provided by this approach: (1) helping the designer to take into consideration the multiple aspects relevant for the development of MIS: by covering the four major steps, the approach invites the designer to cover these points of view; (2) ensuring that design decisions taken in previous steps will not be forgotten: transformations enforce the presence of a set of elements; (3) facilitating a redesign of a system: following a first prototype, the design team will be able to revisit the design decisions by exploring the models established at each step and the detailed transitions between these models. In addition, the approach is a model-based approach, which involves models that are specific to MIS. Therefore, it contributes to the exploration of a wide set of possibilities in terms of the combination of physical and digital resources. In the end, our approach covers four major steps of the development process but is sufficiently flexible to allow one to start from the middle of the proposed process; for example, if the task analysis performed is not based on K-Mad but leads to the production of an ASUR model, the use of the current transformations is still possible. Consequently, this approach goes beyond ad hoc approaches and can break down barriers between different types of expertise.

However, our approach has been built and illustrated via application to a set of three well-known models and one prototyping platform. To generalize the approach, it would be necessary to be able to involve any design resources covering one of these four steps. An abstraction of the transformation rules would solve the problem and enable the specification of transformation rules for any model. Alternatively, a less ambitious solution would consist of building the appropriate transformations for each model that one would like to fit to this approach; this would be in line with the notions of domain-specific languages promoted by MDE [21].

A second limit of the current approach is that it generates a lot of design alternatives, especially the first transformation from task analysis to the mixed interaction model. An editing tool for managing the design streams corresponding to the different design solutions generated would, for example, keep track of the state of each design (totally, partially or not explored), allow the annotation of design streams, etc., and thus facilitate the systematic exploration of the different solutions. Furthermore, this tool would also constitute a potentially useful assistant to help find and explore the differences between different solutions: it could be in charge of highlighting, at each level of the development process, where differences exist and indicating the impact of these differences on the subsequent steps.

Currently, our approach does not provide any help for selecting one of the generated solutions. Being able to evaluate the quality of mixed interaction predictively in terms of usability, adequacy of the task or performance might rely on the models used in this process. However, in order to integrate this additional service into our approach, issues exist, in particular the need for identifying the relevant properties, the steps it affects and the mechanisms to ensure the preservation of these properties in further design refinement. We intend to explore this perspective through the expression of properties in terms of different models: ergonomic properties such as continuities have already been explored in MIS and could be partly associated with ASUR; properties linked to the software architecture will also be part of our next work.

Finally, the use of this approach in an iterative design context relies on an appropriate characterization of the identified problem. Currently the characterization process is left entirely to the designer's subjective interpretation. Identifying objective criteria in order to orient the focus of the upcoming design iteration is another challenge. In our future work, we will explore the possibility of using a set of ergonomic recommendations for MIS. An ergonomic recommendation would be targeted at a well-identified element in a given context and would suggest an interaction solution. Associating these descriptors with parts of the models used in our approach could help categorize the problems.

Acknowledgments This work has been done as part of a collaboration with the Museum of Toulouse. The authors wish to thank F. Duranthon for the Museum's involvement in the definition of the case study and subsequent design solutions. The work presented in the article is partly funded by the French Research Agency under contract CARE (Cultural experience: Augmented Reality and Emotion) – www.careproject.fr

References

1. Arduino: http://www.arduino.cc/, last access 2008/10/24.
2. Charfi S, Dubois E, Bastide R (2007) Articulating interaction and task models for the design of advanced interactive systems, TAMODIA, France: Springer, Berlin, pp. 70–83.
3. Cheung D F W, Tigli J Y, Lavirotte S, Riveill M (2006) WComp: A multi-design approach for prototyping applications using heterogeneous resources. In Proceedings of the 17th IEEE International Workshop on Rapid System Prototyping, Crete, pp. 119–125.
4. Cladistics Definition: http://en.wikipedia.org/wiki/Cladistic, last access 2008/10/24.
5. Coutrix C, Nigay L (2006) Mixed reality: A model of mixed interaction. In Proceedings of the Working Conference on Advanced Visual interfaces (Venezia, Italy, May 23–26, 2006). AVI '06. ACM, New York, NY, pp. 43–50.
6. Delotte O, David B, Chalon R (2004) Task modelling for capillary collaborative systems based on scenarios. In Proceedings of TAMODIA'04. ACM Press, NY, pp. 25–31.
7. Dubois E, Gray P D (2007) A design-oriented information-flow refinement of the ASUR interaction model, engineering interactive systems (EHCI-HCSE-DSVIS), Spain.
8. Eclipse Modeling Project, http://www.eclipse.org/modeling/, last access 2008/11/02.
9. Fishkin K P (2004) A taxonomy for and analysis of tangible interfaces. Personal and Ubiquitous Computing, 8 (5): Springer-Verlag, 347–358.
10. Gauffre G, Dubois E, Bastide R (2008) Domain-specific methods and tools for the design of advanced interactive techniques. In: H. Giese (Ed.): MoDELS 2007 Workshops, LNCS 5002, Springer, Heidelberg, pp. 65–76.

11. Gandy M, MacIntyre B, Dow S (2004) Making tracking technology accessible in a rapid prototyping environment. In Proceedings of the 3rd IEEE/ACM international Symposium on Mixed and Augmented Reality (November 2–5, 2004). Symposium on Mixed and Augmented Reality. IEEE Computer Society, Washington DC, pp. 282–283.
12. Gram C, Cockton G (1997) Design principles for interactive software. Chapman & Hall, Ltd., London, UK.
13. Greenberg S, Fitchett C (2001). Phidgets: Easy development of physical interfaces through physical widgets. In Proceedings of the ACM Symposium on UIST, USA, ACM, New York, NY, pp. 209–218.
14. Herbst I., Braun A, McCall R, Broll W (2008) TimeWarp: Interactive time travel with a mobile mixed reality game. In Proceedings of the ACM Conference on Mobile HCI, The Netherlands, pp. 235–244.
15. Hilliges O, Sandor C, Klinker G (2006) Interactive prototyping for ubiquitous augmented reality user interfaces. Proceedings of the 11th international conference on Intelligent user interfaces, ACM.
16. Jacob R J, Girouard A, Hirshfield L M, Horn M S, Shaer O, Solovey E T, Zigelbaum J (2008) Reality-based interaction: A framework for Post-WIMP interfaces. In Proceedings of the ACM conference on CHI'08, Italy, ACM, New York, pp. 201–210.
17. Kato H, Billinghurst M (1999) Marker tracking and HMD calibration for a video-based augmented reality conferencing system. In Proceedings of the 2nd International Workshop on Augmented Reality (IWAR 99). October, San Francisco, USA.
18. Klemmer S R, Hartmann B, Takayama L (2006) How bodies matter: Five themes for interaction design. In Proceedings of the 6th Conference on Designing interactive Systems (University Park, PA, June 26–28, 2006). DIS '06. ACM, New York, NY, pp. 140–149.
19. Klug T, Mülhauser M (2007) Modeling human interaction resources to support the design of wearable multimodal systems, in Proceedings of the ACM Conference on ICMI'07, Japan, pp. 299–306.
20. Krasner G E, Pope T (1988) A cookbook for using the model-view-controller user interface paradigm in Smalltalk-80. Journal of Object Oriented Programming, 1 (3): 26–49.
21. Kurtev I, Bézivin J, Jouault F, Valduriez P (2006) Model-Based DSL Frameworks. In Proceedings of OOPSLA '06. ACM, NY, pp. 602–616.
22. Liarokapis F, White M, Lister P (2004) Augmented reality interface toolkit. In Proceedings of the information Visualisation, Eighth international Conference (July 14–16, 2004). IV. IEEE Computer Society, Washington, DC, pp. 761–767.
23. MacIntyre B, Gandy M, Dow S, Bolter J D (2004) DART: A Toolkit for rapid design exploration of augmented reality experiences. In Proceedings of the ACM Symposium on UIST'04, USA, ACM, New York, pp. 197–206.
24. Nigay L, Coutaz J (1997) Software architecture modelling: Bridging two worlds using ergonomics and software properties. In P. Palanque and F. Paterno (Eds.) Formal methods in human–computer interaction, Springer-Verlag, Berlin, pp. 49–73.
25. Oda O, Lister L J, White S, Feiner S (2008) Developing an augmented reality racing game. In Proceedings of the 2nd international Conference on intelligent Technologies For interactive Entertainment, Mexico, pp. 1–8.
26. Protégé Tool, http://protege.stanford.edu/, last access 2008/11/02.
27. Renevier P, Nigay L, Bouchet J, Pasqualetti L (2004) Generic interaction techniques for mobile collaborative mixed systems. In Proceedings of CADUI'04. ACM, NY, pp. 307–320.
28. Scapin D L (2007) K-MADe, COST294-MAUSE 3rd International Workshop, Review, Report and Refine Usability Evaluation Methods (R3 UEMs) Athens, March 5.
29. Schmalstieg D, Fuhrmann A, Hesina G, Szalavári Z, Encarnação L M, Gervautz M, Purgathofer W (2002) The Studierstube augmented reality project. Presence: Teleoperators and Virtual Environments 11(1): (February 2002), 33–54.
30. Schmalstieg D, Wagner D (2007) Experiences with handheld augmented reality, 6th IEEE and ACM International Symposium on ISMAR 2007, Japan, pp. 3–18.

31. Schmidt D C (2006) Guest editor's introduction: model-driven engineering. Computer, 39(2): 25–31, February.
32. Shaer O, Leland N, Calvillo-Gamez E H, Jacob R J K (2004) The TAC paradigm: specifying tangible user interfaces. Personal and Ubiquitous Computing 8, 359–369.
33. Smith S P (2006) Exploring the specification of haptic interaction. In 13th International Workshop, DSVIS 2006, Ireland, LNCS vol. 4323, Springer, Berlin, pp. 171–184.
34. UML Profile Specifications, http://www.omg.org/technology/documents/profile_catalog.htm, last access 2008/11/02.

Part II
Software Design and Implementation

Chapter 11
Designing Outdoor Mixed Reality Hardware Systems

Benjamin Avery, Ross T. Smith, Wayne Piekarski, and Bruce H. Thomas

Abstract Developing usable and robust mixed reality systems requires unique human–computer interaction techniques and customized hardware systems. The design of the hardware is directed by the requirements of the rich 3D interactions that can be performed using immersive mobile MR systems. Geometry modeling and capture, navigational annotations, visualizations, and training simulations are all enhanced using augmented computer graphics. We present the design guidelines that have led us through 10 years of evolving mobile outdoor MR hardware systems.

Keywords Wearable computing · Mixed reality · Augmented reality · Input device · Hardware design

11.1 Introduction

Mixed reality (MR) is a term that encompasses augmented reality (AR), augmented virtuality, and virtual reality (VR). AR is the registration of projected computer-generated images over a user's view of the physical world. With this extra information presented to the user, the physical world can be enhanced or augmented beyond the user's normal experience. The addition of information that is spatially located relative to the user can help to improve their understanding of it. Early work in the field of MR relied on large and bulky hardware that required a user to utilize a tethered display. Users could not walk large distances and this restricted initial MR research. Desirable systems allow users to walk around and explore the physical world overlaid with computer-generated information without being tethered to a fixed location. In an early survey paper on AR, Azuma states that the ultimate goal

B. Avery (✉)
Wearable Computer Laboratory, University of South Australia, 5095 Mawson Lakes, SA, Australia
e-mail: ben@benavery.net

E. Dubois et al. (eds.), *The Engineering of Mixed Reality Systems*, Human-Computer Interaction Series, DOI 10.1007/978-1-84882-733-2_11,

of AR research is to develop systems that "can operate anywhere, in any environment" [1]. Our research has focused on aiming toward this goal by making systems that are portable and not limited to small areas.

A pioneering piece of work in mobile MR was the touring machine [5], the first example of a mobile outdoor system. Our group also produced some of the first outdoor prototypes, such as our early Tinmith systems [20]. Using new technology that was small and light enough to be worn, a whole new area of mobile MR research (both indoor and outdoor) was created (Fig. 11.1). While many research problems are similar to indoor VR and AR, there are unsolved domain-specific problems that prevent mainstream AR usage, particularly outdoors. For example, portable systems cannot use some of the more accurate tracking systems available in fixed indoor environments, limiting the fidelity and realism of the AR system.

The first outdoor MR systems were quite simple in that they relied only on the position and orientation of the user's head in the physical world as the user interface. The virtual environment could be indirectly adjusted via a keyboard or mouse. Without a user interface capable of interacting with the virtual environment directly, the user of these systems is limited to traditional 2D input techniques that are not natural when in an immersive 3D environment. Therefore, as part of our research, we have developed user interface techniques centered around pinch glove technologies [11, 13] that provide more natural interfaces for users. The hardware is a critical part of the design of user interfaces, since limitations of physical devices will affect user interactions.

Many of the hardware components needed to support interactions require miniaturization and concatenation in order to be used comfortably for mobile MR. For example, using an accurate global positioning system (GPS) unit requires a large antenna mounted on the user's head. But to naively mount the antenna would be too large and bulky. Components must be stripped of excess casings and carefully

Fig. 11.1 Tinmith outdoor wearable augmented reality computer

designed into a tightly integrated system. The immersion a user experiences is strongly reduced if the hardware interferes with the user. Much higher immersion can be achieved with a small wearable computer, by reducing the user's awareness of the devices worn.

Miniaturization, integration, and immersion are all related. For an experience to be natural and enjoyable, the hardware needs to be designed to support the user interface. This chapter focuses on the design of the hardware that is necessary to support mobile outdoor mixed reality systems. Research-based mobile MR systems built in the past used off-the-shelf components attached to a framework like a backpack or vest, allowing them to be easily built and modified [3]. However, these systems are cumbersome, heavy, and fragile. Currently there are no commercially available all-in-one systems available for mobile outdoor MR.

This chapter presents design guidelines we have developed for building outdoor mobile MR computers gained during our 10 years of experiencc [12, 20]. A history of our wearable mixed reality backpack computers is shown in Fig. 11.2. Readily available hardware such as GPS units, hybrid orientation tracking sensors, and laptop computers are combined using custom electronics allowing intuitive human–computer interactions to be performed. These design guidelines cater for systems to be robust, lightweight, and usable, but also take into account important practical considerations related to usability and debugging.

Fig. 11.2 1998–2007: 10 years of Tinmith outdoor wearable computers

11.2 Previous Work on Outdoor MR

While indoor examples are useful, the ultimate goal of MR research is to produce systems that can be used in any environment with no restrictions on the user. Mobile outdoor MR pushes the limits of current technology to work toward achieving the goal of unrestricted environments.

The Touring Machine, developed by Feiner et al. from Columbia University [5], is based on a large backpack computer system with all the necessary equipment attached. The Touring Machine provides users with labels that float over buildings, indicating the location of various buildings and features at the Columbia campus. Interaction with the system is achieved through the use of a GPS and head compass to control the view of the world. By gazing at objects of interest longer than a set dwell time the system presents additional information. The Touring Machine was then extended by Hollerer et al. for the placement of what they termed situated documentaries [8]. This system shows 3D building models overlaying the physical world, giving users the ability to see buildings that no longer exist on the Columbia University campus. Additional media features were added, such as the ability to view video clips, 360° scene representations, and information situated in space at the site of various events that occurred in the past.

The Naval Research Laboratory is investigating outdoor MR with a system referred to as the Battlefield Augmented Reality System (BARS), a descendent of the previously described Touring Machine. Julier et al. describe the BARS system [9] and how it is planned for use by soldiers in combat environments. In these environments, there are large quantities of information available (such as goals, waypoints, and enemy locations) but presenting all of these to the soldier can become overwhelming and confusing. The BARS system has also been extended to perform some simple outdoor modeling work [2]. For the user interface, a gyroscopic mouse is used to manipulate a 2D cursor and interact with standard 2D desktop widgets.

Nokia research has been performing research into building outdoor wearable MR systems, but with 2D overlaid information instead of 3D registered graphics. The Context Compass by Suomela and Lehikoinen [18] is designed to give users information about their current context and how to navigate in the environment. Two-dimensional cues are rendered onto the display. To interact with the system, a glove-based input technique named N-fingers was developed by Lehikoinen and Roykkee [10]. The N-fingers technique provides up to four buttons in a diamond layout that is used to scroll through lists with selection, act like a set of arrow keys, or directly map to a maximum of four commands.

More recently MR research has moved to include a strong focus on handheld devices. The advances in processing power and inclusion of built-in cameras on mobile phones have made it possible to render registered 3D augmentation on a mobile phone. Schmalsteig and Wagner extended their existing MR framework to create Studierstube ES, an MR framework and tracking solution for mobile phones and handheld devices [16]. Handheld devices are able to track the location of fiducial markers and display augmentations over a video image on the display. Devices were deployed at two museums with MR games and learning applications.

11.3 The Tinmith System

Tinmith is the software architecture that runs on our wearable MR systems. The Tinmith system supports a number of novel user interfaces that allow users to interact with their virtual surroundings. Tinmith was the first system developed with 3D interactions appropriate for an outdoor setting. Other backpack systems, such as the Touring Machine, focused on traditional 2D techniques. These other backpack systems employed 2D input devices (tablets and handheld trackballs) and used standard workstation mappings from 2D devices to 3D virtual data. Tinmith discarded the traditional desktop interaction metaphor (keyboard and mouse), instead designing the interface to take advantage of the 3D nature of the environment. An interface based on thumb-tracked pinch gloves uniquely combines command entry and dual cursor control to provide a complete user interface solution. Enabling users to gesture with their hands for pointing and selecting menu options is a more natural interface for outdoor interactions. The system supports creating 3D models of new and existing structures with a set of techniques termed construction-at-a-distance techniques. These techniques include AR working planes, infinite carving planes, laser carving, laser coloring, texture map capture, and surface of revolution. An overview of the Tinmith user interface is provided in this section. An in-depth presentation of the construction techniques is available in [13].

The user interface is made up of three components: a pointer controlled by the tracking of the thumbs with a set of gloves worn by the user; a command entry system where the user's fingers interact with a menu for performing actions; and an MR display that presents information back to the user [14]. The interface is shown in Fig. 11.3. The display for the interface is fixed to the head-mounted display (HMD) screen with menus on the lower left and right corners. The eight lower commands are mapped to the fingers and the user activates a command by pressing the appropriate finger against the thumb. When an option is selected, the menu refreshes with the next set of options that are available. Ok and cancel operations are activated by pressing the fingers into the palm of the appropriate hand and are indicated in the topmost green boxes of the menus.

The interaction cursors are specified using fiducial markers placed on the tips of the thumbs, visible in Fig. 11.6. The cursors can be used for manipulating virtual objects (a move operation on a virtual tree is being performed in Fig. 11.3). The user moves the cursor over a virtual object in the scene and selects the appropriate menu command to begin the move operation. The object is attached to that cursor and moved around freely by the user moving their hand. Another menu option is used to place the virtual object. More complex interactions are performed by using both the left and right thumb cursors simultaneously. Scaling of objects is achieved by moving the cursors closer together or further apart. Rotations are performed by moving one cursor in an arc around the second cursor.

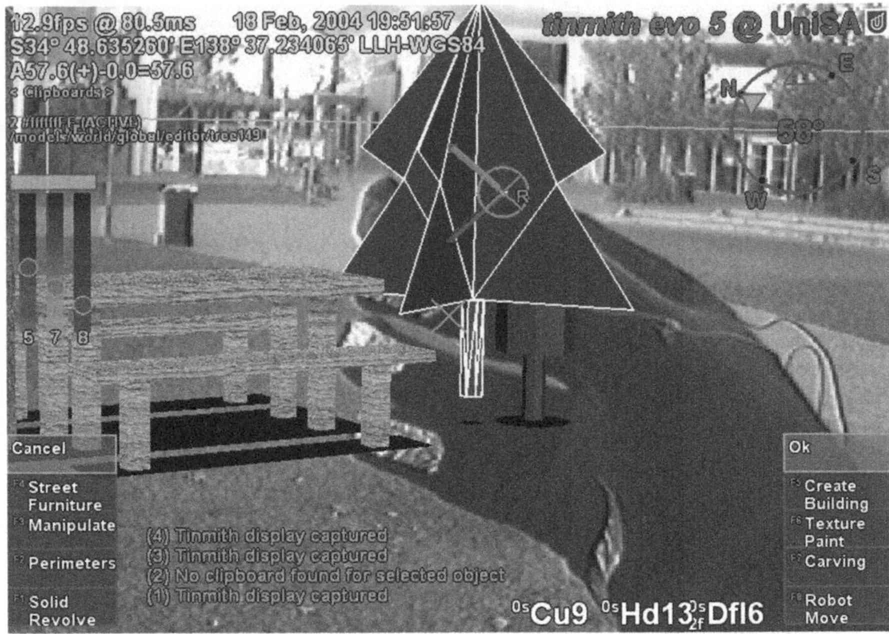

Fig. 11.3 The Tinmith user interface displays menus in the bottom corners of the screen. The user can move objects such as a virtual tree with tracked thumbs

The modeling and interaction techniques have to be strongly supported by the hardware. Tracking the location of the hands requires a high-quality camera for vision tracking and the modeling techniques require accurate tracking of the user location and orientation. At the same time the user needs to be sufficiently mobile to freely move around and perform the techniques. It is desirable for the MR system to be lightweight so it may be worn comfortably while performing tasks.

11.4 Hardware for Outdoor MR Systems

Outdoor MR is commonly performed in one of two ways, using handheld or immersive hardware technologies. Handheld MR is achieved by rendering a camera view and overlaid computer graphics on a handheld device such as a mobile phone or PDA. MR with an HMD allows images to be overlaid directly on the user's view of the world achieving a higher level of immersion. When used with a specialized wearable computer the user is able to freely walk around and explore a mixed reality environment. Recent trends have been moving toward the use of handheld over immersive hardware. And although we are investigating the use of handheld systems, currently we use immersive hardware as it provides greater flexibility and a more interactive experience. In particular both the user's hands remain free to support complex bimanual interactions. In comparison handheld systems tend to require the non-dominant hand to hold the hardware while the dominant hand interacts with the system [6].

Creating an MR overlay that is accurately registered to a user's view requires three primary devices: computer, display, and a tracker. The computer generates 3D graphics that are rendered to the display. The tracker is used to determine where the graphics are rendered to achieve correct registration.

When using HMDs for outdoor MR, video see-through and optical see-through are the two common techniques used to achieve the augmented environment. Video see-through uses a camera attached to the HMD to capture the real world view. The camera's video stream is combined with the virtual graphical objects with the graphics hardware and displayed on the HMD. Optical see-through instead uses a half-silvered mirror to combine the real world view and the computer display. Although current research is investigating techniques to improve the brightness of optical see-through displays, we have found the limited brightness does not provide a satisfactory image, particularly when using the system in bright sunlight. A notable exception is virtual retinal displays. To date this technology only produces a single color, red, with varying levels of intensity.[1]

The translation and orientation of the user's head needs to be accurately tracked. A wide variety of tracking technologies are available for indoor use including magnetic, vision based, inertial, or ultrasonic. However, the choices available when working outdoors are significantly more limited. Magnetic trackers such as those from Polhemus[2] or vision tracking algorithms such as the going out system by Reitmayr et al. [15] can be used outdoors but have very limited range and require preparation to make the area suitable for tracking (such as installing sensors or modeling the environment). GPS is the only suitable position tracking technology for use outdoors that supports an unlimited tracking area in open spaces and does not require previous preparation of the environment. We use survey-grade GPS units for position tracking, and an Intersense InertiaCube3 [3] for orientation tracking. The InertiaCube3 uses magnetometers, accelerometers, and a gyroscope to track position relative to magnetic north and gravity.

A common construction approach used when building wearable computer systems is to electrically connect off-the-shelf components and place them in a backpack or belt. This design method leads to cumbersome, bulky, and unreliable systems. An alternative approach is to remove the required electronic components from their casings and permanently install them into a single enclosure, hardwiring each of the components together. This increases robustness, decreases size and weight, and if carefully designed can maintain expandability. We currently have two generations of compact wearable MR systems, the 2005 and 2007 designs shown in Fig. 11.2.

[1] http://www.microvision.com

[2] http://www.polhemus.com

[3] http://www.intersense.com

This section discusses the components and construction required to achieve MR on mobile wearable computer system. First the head-mounted electronics that contains the display and trackers is presented, followed by discussion of the main enclosure that holds the computer and additional required electronics and battery requirements.

11.4.1 Head-Mounted Electronics

Many essential electronics in outdoor MR systems are mounted on the user's head. These components include the HMD, camera, GPS antenna (or entire GPS unit), orientation sensor, and often power regulation electronics. The tracking sensors need to be rigidly attached to the HMD to ensure correct registration of the MR graphics. We use a monoscopic HMD and single camera for a number of reasons. Stereo displays require two renders of the virtual scene, one for each eye display. For indoor systems this is possible by using a PC with multiple graphics cards; however, for a portable system this would add significant weight and complexity. Outdoor AR is often used for observing very large area visualizations such as entire buildings or annotations at a distance from the user. Stereoscopic HMDs only emulate some of the depth cues humans use to judge distance, and most of these fail to be effective beyond approximately 30 m [4]. These issues make stereoscopic HMDs not necessary for outdoor use.

Many different mounting systems may be used to attach electronics to user's head. The overall size of the electronics determines the support required from the mounting system. Readily available items such as skate or bike helmets (Fig. 11.4) or safety masks (Fig. 11.5a) can be adapted or modified to be suitable for holding electronic components. Alternatively, custom-designed mounting prototypes can be produced using a 3D printer (shown in Fig. 11.5b). This approach is more expensive but can provide more complex and aesthetically pleasing design that often appeals to those interested in commercial ventures. Figure 11.5c shows a military kevlar helmet modified to include MR hardware.

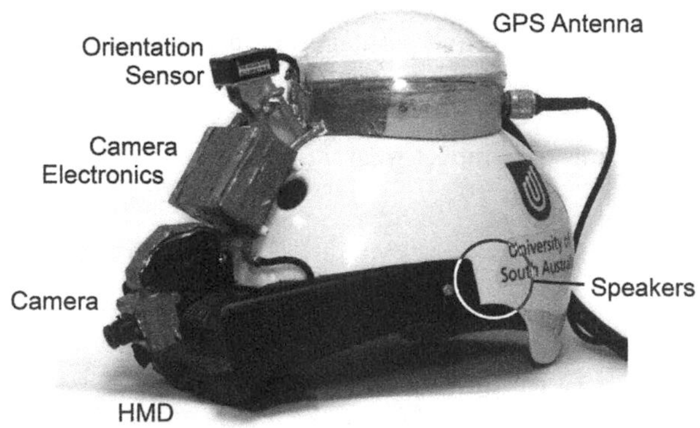

Fig. 11.4 Head-mounted electronics combines an HMD, camera and separate electronics, orientation sensor, GPS antenna, and speakers (internal)

In our 2005 backpack system we attached a Trimble GPS antenna, Intersense InertiaCube3, Point Gray Dragonfly camera, iGlasses HMD, and a number of power regulation circuits to a skate helmet (see Fig. 11.4). Securely mounting the HMD in front of the user's eyes is important to maintain correct. To achieve this we used a commercially available mount developed by iGlasses, with some modifications to finely adjust the mounting location. The camera is mounted as close as possible to the center of the user's eyes to reduce parallax effects. We mounted the camera using a custom mount that enables pitch adjustment to be easily configured for optimal user comfort and functionality. The total weight of the helmet and electronics is 1.5 kg.

More recently as the electronics have become smaller we reduced the overall size of the head-worn electronics. In our 2007 helmet design a head-worn safety shield with the visor removed was used as the main structure for attaching electronics. Although the design is very similar, the overall size and weight have been reduced. Significant size reductions were achieved by employing a smaller GPS antenna.

All of these devices require a communication bus to the computer. The tracking and camera signals are transmitted to the computer, and the appropriate graphics and audio data are computed and sent back to the display and speakers. There are a large number of signal and power wires connecting the head mount and backpack computer. Our current systems require a total of 19 wires: 3 for the orientation sensor, 2 for the antenna, 4 for the camera, 4 for the HMD S-video signal, 1 for HMD power control, 3 for stereo speakers, and 2 for power. One option is to run individual cables to each device. In practice this is inconvenient due to tangles and low flexibility of the cable bundle. We have used a large anti-kink single cable with 8 individually twisted, shielded pairs (contains 8 pairs with individual shields for a total of 24 signal wires). By using an individual large cable, a single plug can also be used to connect the head mount to the main enclosure. This makes the system more robust and easier to rapidly deploy. A LEMO[4] 20-way plug and socket was used allowing quick and reliable disconnection of the head mount and wearable computer.

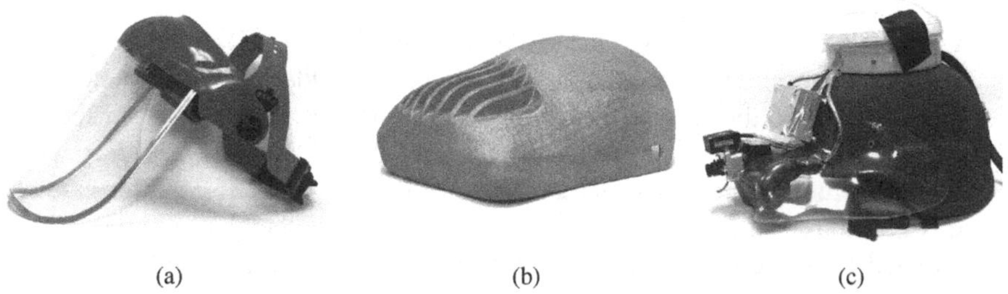

(a) (b) (c)

Fig. 11.5 Additional types of supports for the head-mounted electronics: (**a**) safety shield; (**b**) custom-designed visor; and (**c**) military kevlar helmet

[4] http://www.lemo.com

11.4.2 Main Enclosure

In addition to the head-mount electronics, the user carries a computer capable of generating the graphics. A number of additional support components are required to make a mobile system properly operate, also all carried by the user. We created a single enclosure containing the computer and all supporting peripheral components. By building a single-sealed enclosure there is less risk of components being moved or connectors disconnecting. A major advantage is that each component may be removed from its casing and only the internal electronics be carried allowing a significant reduction in size and weight. The weight of the enclosure and all components is 4 kg. Connections between components and the computer are hard-wired reducing the space taken up by connectors. While this approach reduces size and improves robustness, it makes the system more difficult to modify or upgrade. Through a long history of developing outdoor MR systems, we have selected what we feel are the best component choices and found that the size and robustness advantages prevail over the re-configurability restrictions.

The system does still support expansion through the use of external USB, power, and video plugs. Additional devices may be attached to the enclosure and powered by an external 12 V connector on the enclosure. An exposed USB connector allows devices (or hubs) to be connected to the computer as required.

The components included in the main enclosure are as follows:

- Laptop computer
- GPS processor
- Power regulators (12 V, 3.3 V)
- Hard disk drive
- Bluetooth module
- USB hub
- USB/RS-232 converter
- Wireless video transmitter
- Custom microcontroller electronics

A laptop computer is selected instead of an embedded PC given the 3D graphics acceleration requirements that are not available on embedded PCs. We found laptop computers provided the best performance in computation and graphics for the size. When the 2005 system was constructed we used a Toshiba Tecra M2 laptop with a 1.7 GHz Pentium M processor and a NVIDIA Geforce 5200Go graphics card. As there is no need for the keyboard, mouse, or screen on the laptop, the motherboard is extracted from the casing and this alone is mounted in the wearable computer enclosure.

The processor board for the GPS is also installed in the enclosure. We use the Trimble AG132 surveying grade GPS in our 2005 system, capable of differential updates to yield an accuracy of 50 cm. This GPS unit is much larger than those commonly embedded in mobile phones; however, it supports much higher accuracy. This increased accuracy is also achieved by using the large antenna on the head mount. In the 2007 system this unit was changed to the Novatel OEMV-1 which has a much smaller physical size.

Many of the components used in wearable systems have varying power requirements often with different operating voltages. Using a single battery source makes the system much easier to use and maintain compared with separate batteries for each device. The single battery reduces the overhead required to charge the system between uses. Because of these reasons, there needs to be a number of voltage regulators inside the enclosure to provide 3.3 V for our custom microcontrollers, 5 V for the USB devices, and 12 V for the HMD and laptop.

11.4.3 Batteries

With the many required components in a mobile mixed reality system there is a large power requirement. We use a single battery to power the entire system to avoid system failures when one device depletes before the others. Our system uses batteries placed in sealed aluminum enclosures making them very robust and able to be connected to the system with a single connector. The batteries are mounted separately to the main enclosure to allow hot swapping while the system is running supporting an unlimited run-time.

There are many battery technologies available including lead acid (Pb), nickel-metal hydride (NiMH), and a variety of lithium-based technologies, a popular one being lithium polymer (LiPo). We use NiMH and LiPo batteries to power the 2005 and 2007 systems, respectively. These technologies provide good capacity to weight ratios compared with the heavy lead acid battery technology. The NiMH batteries used on the system (shown in Fig. 11.1) supply 12 V with 8000 mAh capacity and weigh 2 kg each. Using a pair of these batteries allows the system to run for approximately 1 h. LiPo batteries are smaller than NiMHs of similar capacity. A disadvantage of LiPo batteries is the additional electronics required for monitoring and charging. The battery enclosures for LiPo batteries need to include load-balancing circuits for charging; however, the increased electrical density reduces the overall size and weight.

11.5 Input Devices

Interacting with a wearable computer is a well-established research problem [17]. The inability to use a regular keyboard or mouse when moving in an outdoor environment creates the need for alternative input devices and associated input metaphors within the mixed reality software. The primary input device we use for interacting with the mixed reality system is the user's hands, in the form of pinch gloves and tracked thumbs (see Fig. 11.6). These gloves control the menu system and direct manipulations as described previously. In addition to the gloves our system supports a button box and toy gun input devices.

11.5.1 Pinch Gloves

Pinch gloves provide the user with an intuitive method of operating menus within the mixed reality system by using simple pinch gestures. Our gloves are constructed using conductive fabric pads on the fingertips and palm and communicate wirelessly via Bluetooth [11]. Pinch gestures are made between the thumb and fingers or fingers and the palm. Attached to the back of the hand is an MSP430 microcontroller circuit. The microcontroller is attached to each of the fabric pads with conductive cotton that is sewn into the interior of the glove. This maintains flexibility of the glove and by hiding the wiring it decreases the chances of wires being caught or broken. The microcontroller detects pinch gestures by pulsing electrical signals to each of the fingers and palm pads looking for open and closed circuits. Attached underneath the circuit is an 850 mAh lithium polymer battery capable of running the gloves continually for over 30 days. The use of wireless technologies and removing the wires that tether the gloves to the rest of the system is important to make the gloves easier to put on and remove and reduce the restriction of the user's movements. Previous mobile mixed reality systems used wired gloves; we found them to be clumsy as the wires running along the arms to the hands easily got caught or tangled.

Fig. 11.6 Wireless pinch gloves allow the operation of menus using pinch gestures. The thumbs are tracked to provide 3D cursors for interaction

11.5.2 Button Box

The gloves are the primary input device to our system, donning gloves is not always appropriate or possible. We built an alternate handheld input device to emulate the operation of the gloves. We constructed a simple box with 12 push buttons (shown in Fig. 11.7b).

There are a number of advantages to using a button box as an alternative input device for a wearable MR system. By emulating the protocol and operation of the gloves, the user interface can remain consistent across the whole system. This decreases cognitive load for the user when switching between devices. Our button box is robust which is useful when testing the system or when operated by inexperienced users. The button box can be placed on the ground while adjusting the wearable computer with limited chance of breakage unlike pinch gloves. The button box may be used when instructing new users of the system. For example, while the new user is wearing the system the instructor can interact with the interface to demonstrate system operation. The button box can be easily handed between instructor and user. Alternatively the user can wear the gloves while the instructor uses the button box.

11.5.3 Additional Input Devices

Additional input devices may be used with the Tinmith system. We built a toy gun (shown in Fig. 11.7a) for controlling the ARQuake game [19]. The toy gun is based on a child's toy, which has had the internal components of a USB mouse integrated so that the trigger operates the mouse's left-click button. The gun's location is not tracked, but the simple act of pulling a trigger of a physical gun adds a sense of realism when playing the game. Hinkley et al. demonstrated that the use of physical props increases understanding when interacting with a computer compared to using generic input devices [7]. A USB trackpad can be attached to one of the batteries mounted to the belt but is not required to use the system. The system can be completely controlled from a custom manager daemon. This software starts immediately when the system boots and allows a user to use the wireless gloves or button box to perform a number of tasks including starting or terminating software, changing configurations, or setting up wireless networks .

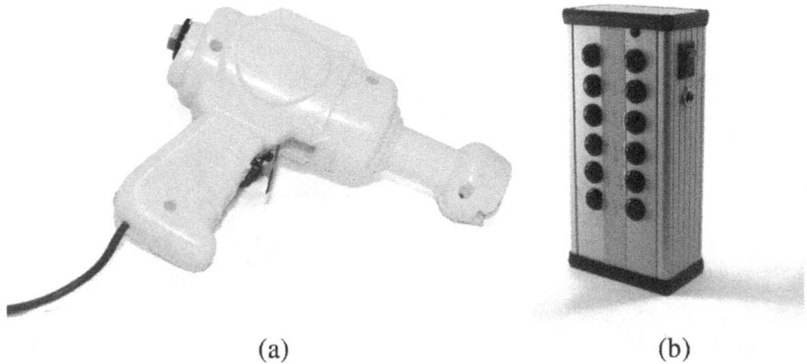

(a) (b)

Fig. 11.7 Additional input devices for mixed reality systems: (**a**) toy gun used with the ARQuake game and (**b**) wireless button box

11.6 Wearable Mixed Reality System Design

In our experience building wearable mixed reality systems, we have used a variety of designs and manufacturing processes. Here we summarize some guidelines specific to these design criteria.

11.6.1 Manufacturing Techniques

We employ computer numerically controlled (CNC) machining equipment to manufacture a variety of the parts required for wearable mixed reality systems. A milling machine uses a rotating cutter to shape metal and plastic parts. A CNC mill is controlled by a computer to quickly and accurately produce parts. We use a CNC mill for the creation of camera enclosures, main enclosure side panels, and cutouts required for connectors and switches. The use of precision machinery allows the components to be smaller and lighter, improving immersion of the MR system. Current 3D printer technologies provide an alternative to the use of a CNC mill for creating plastic parts. Currently cheaper 3D printers produce parts that are too brittle for our requirements. As these devices mature the quality of the parts they produce is improving. While more expensive 3D printers have overcome these limitations they are still not widely accessible. It is expected that as the demand for these devices increases, the cost will be reduced providing a highly accessible and promising manufacturing technique.

The PointGrey Firefly MV camera used in our system comes as a circuit board and sensor. We created a compact case for the camera, shown in Fig. 11.8. This allows the camera to be mounted close to the HMD reducing parallax effects. CNC milling is also used to cut out panels for electronics casings. The main enclosure has 17 connectors, switches, and LEDs that are exposed. The use of CNC machining aligns and cuts these very accurately. As seen in Fig. 11.9, connectors are mounted in the side panels, and in addition air vents have been cut to allow sufficient cooling.

Fig. 11.8 A CAD model of a camera enclosure and the CNC-machined final product

Fig. 11.9 Front and back panels of the main enclosure. A variety of connectors are available. Integrated fan grills provide airflow for cooling

We create a 3D design of the desired part in a computer-aided design (CAD) package, and then cut out the model with a CNC milling machine. We use Autodesk Inventor[5] for 3D design and SheetCAM[6] for generating the cutting paths for the CNC mill. The Taig Micromill[7] is controlled using Mach3.[8]

11.6.2 Belt vs. Backpack

In the past the components required for mobile outdoor mixed reality were mounted to a backpack. As can be seen in Fig. 11.2, backpacks can be large and bulky. The combination of components reducing in size as technology improves and our new construction techniques means we have moved away from backpacks. The main enclosure is now small enough to be mounted entirely on a belt. We believe that until computers can be integrated directly into the clothing, or are small enough to be placed in a pocket, that belt worn is a suitable middle ground. A case attached to the belt is easier to conceal behind clothing, and the user can move around more freely. Another benefit to a belt-worn computer is that it is easier for the user to reach behind and manipulate the system as required (e.g., to flip switches or remove plugs).

In our belt-worn system the batteries are attached to the belt using metal clips. The main enclosure is attached using bolts and spacers. Spacers are used to keep

[5] http://www.autodesk.com

[6] http://www.sheetcam.com

[7] http://www.taigtools.com

[8] http://www.machsupport.com

the enclosure slightly away from the body. This prevents heat transfer between the body and the enclosure and also improves ergonomics. If the enclosure were to be mounted rigidly to the belt then it would be comfortable against the user's back. The belt is attached to a large 20 cm high padding to make it more comfortable to wear on the waist. One limitation of a belt system is that until the system is extremely lightweight it can be cumbersome to attach and remove from the waist. We employ a military "webbing" belt for the system. Due to the nature of the padding on the belt, these systems have limited adjustability. To fit the range of people who have used our system, different size belts are available.

11.6.3 Electrical and Magnetic Interference

Electrical interference can be problematic when using modified consumer electronics in a confined space. These problems are often amplified when the original cases are removed. Many devices have shielding materials installed on their cases to block signals from both entering and escaping the device electronics. We have followed a number of simple procedures that significantly improved the performance of our wearable systems.

Our MR systems require many signal and power wires to pass through a single cable from the computer system to the head-worn electronics. Placing high-speed USB and firewire signal wires directly next to the GPS antenna cable caused significant tracking reliability problems. The GPS antenna signal was attenuated sufficiently to prevent GPS position lock. To overcome this problem we employ individually shielded twisted pairs for all the signal wires on the main communications cable. Each of the pairs is carefully chosen so the original manufacturer cable design is maintained using our cabling. Additionally, all wire lengths are kept to a minimum and strong solder joints are essential. Grounded copper shielding tape is used extensively both internally and externally on our backpack systems. Copper tape can be purchased with an adhesive backing allowing it to be easily and liberally applied to any questionable interference areas (an example of this can be seen in Fig. 11.4).

11.7 System Management

Engineering the wearable mixed reality system to be smaller and more compact has obvious advantages for mobility and robustness. It causes a number of new issues that are not present with ad hoc systems. These are primarily due to the inability to directly access components such as the laptop screen or individual connectors.

11.7.1 Power Management

With the large number of components embedded in wearable systems and no physical access, there is a need for a dedicated power management system.

A custom microcontroller is responsible for power management, voltage regulation, and software control of device power.

Software power control is needed to allow the user to manually specify when to power devices on and off. When all devices are embedded in the main enclosure, it is not possible to access power buttons or power sockets. For example, software control allows the user to turn the GPS off by selecting an appropriate menu option, without shutting down the entire system. This can also be exploited to save battery life, when certain components are not needed they are powered down, and also for initiating hardware resets of devices during debugging.

Certain devices will not turn on when the power is connected. One example is the IOGlasses HMD, for which the power button needs to be manually pressed to enable it after power is applied. The power management system has a control line attached to the HMD power button, allowing the microcontroller to detect that the system has been booted and automatically turning the HMD on. This makes the system much more automated and removed the need for the user to manually press multiple power buttons when turning the system on.

11.7.2 Configuration Selection

Wearable mixed reality systems operate with a variety of hardware configurations. As our system is currently a prototype, we require a greater number of configuration possibilities; however, even a commercial system would typically require different modes: a regular operation mode, a mode to download data, and a systems maintenance mode. Because there is no access directly to the computer display or input devices, this ultimately needs to be controlled from outside the regular operation of the system. We use a physical thumb-wheel encoder on the side of the main enclose to select from 10 preset configurations that are loaded when the system is booted. Using an external monitor and keyboard is an example of why this approach is required. If the system is taken outdoors and booted while configured to use an external monitor, nothing is output to the HMD. The system would be unusable and the user would have no display to alter the setup with. Making the user return to an external display to reconfigure the system is unrealistic. With our technique, the user can simply select the appropriate mode with the rotary dial and reboot the system.

Our technique uses a physical rotary encoder with selections 0–9. This component is monitored by the power management circuit. When the system is booted, the power management system reads the configuration selection and communicates the value to the operating system via the RS-232 serial connection. We have created a custom Linux boot script that is run early during the boot process that reads the device number from the power management unit and changes configuration files on the system accordingly.

Different configuration options we use include combinations of video output (VGA monitor vs. HMD), wireless networks, Bluetooth scanning modes, and different softwares loaded at startup.

11.7.3 Input Management

The glove and button-box input devices operate wirelessly using Bluetooth. Bluetooth is a suitable wireless standard for input devices due to relatively low power consumption, short range, small size of the hardware components, and ease of integration with existing software. A single USB-based Bluetooth receiver is capable of being shared to communicate with multiple devices. Modern operating systems such as Linux include support for communicating with Bluetooth devices. In the external hardware devices, we use Promi-ESD-02 Bluetooth modules,[9] pre-packaged Bluetooth wireless solution that is easily interfaced with existing and new circuit designs. They are small (20 mm × 18 mm), reliable, and come with a number of different antenna configurations depending on the range required. These modules support the RFCOMM standard, which is a simple interface allowing RS-232 communications over Bluetooth. On the PC end, no actual serial ports are needed, except for the interface provided by the single USB Bluetooth receiver.

To communicate with the devices in software, applications can open virtual serial ports or use RFCOMM directly via a Berkley Software Distribution sockets interface. The virtual serial port interface is a high-level abstraction, which limits its ability to indicate timeouts, wireless failures, or remote device failure. The direct RFCOMM interface allows finer-grained control over the device communications, allowing reconnects and other handling when necessary. Scanning for all RFCOMM devices and connecting is time consuming, and so typically the backpack system is pre-configured to maintain a list of active devices. To connect to new devices, the rotary encoder is dialed into Bluetooth scanning mode, the backpack then polls for devices, and records a list of those available. This way, if other devices are present or possibly paired up against other MR systems, there will be no conflict.

While Bluetooth has demonstrated itself to be reliable, it is mainly used for portable and optional input devices. These devices have low bandwidth requirements, and having cables would make them harder to use. System critical devices such as the rotary encoder must not be wireless, so that it can be used to configure the wireless system.

11.7.4 External Display

On our earlier backpack hardware systems, the laptop's screen was left open allowing people observing to see what the user of the system is experiencing (Fig. 11.2; 2001, 2002, 2004). This allowed us to perform demonstrations to a large audience using only one backpack system. This proved to be compelling and interactive for the observers; however, with the laptop attached to their back the user's movements became restricted. For example, when the user turns around the entire audience would shuffle around quickly to maintain a good view of the laptop's screen. To

[9] http://www.sena.com

overcome this problem, we have built an external display that is used to view what is currently being displayed on the HMD. This operates in one of two modes, wirelessly or via a cable. The HMD receives a PAL S-Video signal generated from the TV-Out of the integrated computer. A 1.2 GHz video transmitter is built into the main enclosure and connected to the S-Video signal using component-converting electronics. This transmits the video to our external display. The external display contains an LCD panel, battery, and video receiver. The display is shown in Fig. 11.10.

The external display can also be directly wired to the main enclosure with an RCA connector. The physical wired connection to the main enclosure is particularly useful to allow recording of videos of the system in operation. A handheld video camera is connected directly to the main enclosure and records a copy of the signal sent to the HMD. This allows videos to be recorded without interfering with the user's ability to operate the system.

The external display has a number of important uses. The first is for debugging the system. The HMD displays are small and although they operate at the same resolution as the external display, it can be difficult to read small text on the HMD. The external display is used if commands have to be manually entered into a Linux terminal. The other important use of an external display is when operating the system with other users. Those people not using the system are able to see what the operator is viewing. This is invaluable when training a new user, as the instructor can see exactly what they are viewing and instruct them accordingly. Similarly,

Fig. 11.10 External display containing an LCD panel and an integrated battery and wireless video receiver

when an expert user is operating the system, the display can be shown to other people for demonstrations or training. This display is often used when performing user evaluations to instruct and monitor study participants.

11.8 Conclusion

Developing mobile mixed reality systems requires unique interaction techniques and hardware systems. We have presented how interaction techniques and the mobile requirements of outdoor MR systems have directed the development of the hardware systems. Considerations such as user comfort, configurability, robustness have all contributed to the evolution of mobile mixed reality systems built over the last 10 years.

We have developed portable MR hardware systems and user interfaces that we found in practice to be significantly easier to use and more reliable than the previous bulky backpack designs. As the technology improves we will continue to refine and improve our design, aiming toward the goal of a completely immersive and ubiquitous system that a user wears and interacts with at all times. Our current system has many limitations that we are still investigating. These limitations are mainly based on the current state of the art in common off-the-shelf hardware components. While HMDs with a larger field of view are available, they are very bulky and not suitable for use outdoors. GPS devices can achieve accuracy to around 2 cm; however, this requires optimal conditions in an unobstructed environment – they do not work well under foliage, among buildings, on cloudy days and especially indoors. The overall system is still based on OEM components, which limits the overall size that is possible. The optimal solution is to design a single PCB with all of the components integrated. This is possible with large budgets and large quantities, something which is not practical in a research field like mixed reality yet.

Consideration needs to be made about the devices needed to create a mixed reality. Some components must be mounted directly on the user's head, but these components also need to communicate and be powered from the rest of the electronics. The size of the required components is no longer such that bulky backpacks need to be used as has been done in the past, but they are not yet small enough to be simply placed in a pocket. We used a belt-mounted design as a current middle ground, allowing the user to wear the system comfortably around the waist. The research described in this chapter is a work in progress that has evolved over many years, and we are continuing in our efforts to achieve improved performance and usability while at the same time reducing size and weight of our MR systems.

References

1. Azuma, R. T. The challenge of making augmented reality work outdoors. In *Mixed Reality: Merging Real and Virtual Worlds*, Ohta, Y. and Tamura, H., Editors, Springer-Verlag, Berlin, pp. 379–390, 1997.

2. Baillot, Y., Brown, D. and Julier, S. Authoring of physical models using mobile computers. In *5th Int'l Symposium on Wearable Computers*. pp. 39–46. Zurich, Switzerland 2001.
3. Behringer, R., Tam, C., McGee, J., Sundareswaran, S. and Vassiliou, M. A wearable augmented reality testbed for navigation and control, built solely with commercial-off-the-shelf (COTS) Hardware. In *3rd Int'l Symposium on Augmented Reality*. pp. 12–19. Munich, Germany 2000.
4. Cutting, J. and Vishton, P. Perceiving layout and knowing distances: The Integration, relative potency, and contextual use of different information about depth. In *Handbook of Perception and Cognition*, Epstein, W. and Rogers, S., Editors, Academic Press: San Diego, CA. pp. 69–117. 1995.
5. Feiner, S., MacIntyre, B. and Hollerer, T. A touring machine: Prototyping 3D mobile augmented reality systems for exploring the urban environment. In *1st Int'l Symposium on Wearable Computers*. pp. 74–81. Cambridge, MA 1997.
6. Guiard, Y. Asymmetric division of labor in human skilled bimanual action: The kinematic chain as a model. Journal of Motor Behavior, 1987, 19(4) pp. 486–517.
7. Hinckley, K., Tullio, J., Pausch, R., Proffitt, D. and Kassell, N. Usability analysis of 3D rotation techniques. In *10th Int'l Symposium on User Interface Software Technology*. pp. 1–10. Banff, Canada 1997.
8. Hollerer, T., Feiner, S. and Pavlik, J. Situated documentaries: Embedding multimedia presentations in the real world. In *3rd Int'l Symposium on Wearable Computers*. pp. 79–86. San Francisco, Ca 1999.
9. Julier, S., Lanzagorta, M., Baillot, Y., Rosenblum, L., Feiner, S. and Hollerer, T. Information filtering for mobile augmented reality. In *3rd Int'l Symposium on Augmented Reality*. pp. 1–10. Munich, Germany 2000.
10. Lehikoinen, J. and Röykkee, M.. N-fingers: A finger-based interaction technique for wearable computers. Interacting with Computers, 2001, 13(5) pp. 601–625.
11. Piekarski, W. and Smith, R. Robust gloves For 3D interaction in mobile outdoor AR environments. In *5th Int'l Symposium on Mixed and Augmented Reality*. pp. 251–252. Santa Barbara, USA 2006.
12. Piekarski, W., Smith, R. and Thomas, B. Designing backpacks for high fidelity mobile outdoor augmented reality. In *3rd Int'l Symposium on Mixed and Augmented Reality*. pp. 280–281. Arlington, VA, USA 2004.
13. Piekarski, W. and Thomas, B. Interactive augmented reality techniques for construction at a distance of 3D geometry. In *Immersive Projection Technology/Eurographics Virtual Environments*. pp. 19–28, Zurich, Switzerland 2003.
14. Piekarski, W. and Thomas, B. The tinmith system – Demonstrating new techniques for mobile augmented reality modelling. In *3rd Australasian User Interfaces Conference*. pp. 61–70. Melbourne, Vic 2002.
15. Reitmayr, G. and Drummond, T. W. Going out: Robust model-based tracking for outdoor augmented reality. In *5th Int'l Symposium on Mixed and Augmented Reality*. pp. 109–118. Santa Barbara, USA 2006.
16. Schmalstieg, D. and Wagner, D. Experiences with handheld augmented reality. In *6th Int'l Symposium on Mixed and Augmented Reality*. pp. 3–18. Nara, Japan 2007.
17. Starner, T. and Rhodes, B.. Wearable computers. In *Encyclopedia of Human-Computer Interaction*, Bainbridge, W., Editor, Berkshire Publishing: Great Barrington, MA 2004.
18. Suomela, R. and Lehikoinen, J. Context compass. In *4th Int'l Symposium on Wearable Computers*. pp. 147–154. Atlanta, GA 2000.
19. Thomas, B., Close, B., Donoghue, J., Squires, J., De Bondi, P., Morris, M. and Piekarski, W. ARQuake: An outdoor/indoor augmented reality first person application. In *4th Int'l Symposium on Wearable Computers*. pp. 139–146. Atlanta, GA 2000.
20. Thomas, B. H., Demczuk, V., Piekarski, W., Hepworth, D. and Gunther, B. A wearable computer system with augmented reality to support terrestrial navigation. In *2nd Int'l Symposium on Wearable Computers*. pp. 168–171. Pittsburg, PA 1998.

Chapter 12
Multimodal Excitatory Interfaces with Automatic Content Classification

John Williamson and Roderick Murray-Smith

Abstract We describe a non-visual interface for displaying data on mobile devices, based around active exploration: devices are shaken, revealing the contents rattling around inside. This combines sample-based contact sonification with event playback vibrotactile feedback for a rich and compelling display which produces an illusion much like balls rattling inside a box. Motion is sensed from accelerometers, directly linking the motions of the user to the feedback they receive in a tightly closed loop. The resulting interface requires no visual attention and can be operated blindly with a single hand: it is reactive rather than disruptive. This interaction style is applied to the display of an SMS inbox. We use language models to extract salient features from text messages automatically. The output of this classification process controls the timbre and physical dynamics of the simulated objects. The interface gives a rapid semantic overview of the contents of an inbox, without compromising privacy or interrupting the user.

Keywords Vibrotactile · Audio · Language model · Mobile

12.1 Motivation

We propose a multimodal interaction style where the user *excites* information from a device and then *negotiates* with the system in a continuous, closed-loop interaction. This draws upon the work of Hermann [5, 8, 7], who introduced model-based sonification. In [7], the authors state:

> ...why not sonify data spaces by taking the environmental sound production in our real world as a model. Nature has optimized our auditory senses to extract information from the auditory signal that is produced by our physical environment. Thus the idea is: build a virtual scenario from the data; define a kind of 'virtual physics' that permits vibrational reaction of its elements to external excitations; let the user interactively excite the system and listen.

J. Williamson (✉)
University of Glasgow, Glasgow, U.K
e-mail: jhw@dcs.gla.ac.uk

E. Dubois et al. (eds.), *The Engineering of Mixed Reality Systems*, Human-Computer Interaction Series, DOI 10.1007/978-1-84882-733-2_12,

In [22] we outline the basis of such a system along with some early prototypes and discuss a number of interaction scenarios; these include battery life monitoring and display of file system contents. In contrast to non-interactive displays, this *active perception* approach takes advantage of people's expectations about the evolution of dynamic systems. Feedback is tightly coupled to the input. This avoids interrupting or disturbing the user unnecessarily and opens up the potential for richer, more informative feedback. Users know what motions they have made and interpret the display in that context.

This chapter demonstrates how these rich physical models can be parameterized and then tightly coupled to inference mechanisms, to make artefacts imbued with apparent physical attributes which respond in an "intelligent" manner to changing contexts.

Impact perception is a task with which everyone is familiar; few people would have difficulty in distinguishing a hollow barrel from a full one after tapping it. Because such information is communicated primarily through the auditory and haptic channels, a completely non-visual interaction can be constructed. Given that mobile devices are often used where visual attention is inconvenient, the use of purely non-visual cues is a major advantage over visually dominated techniques. By taking a physical model and *overloading* its behaviour, information can be presented very rapidly, without disrupting human intuition about the evolution of physical systems.

The interaction is designed so that it can be used blindly; a user could pick up a phone from a nightstand in a dark room and shake it to get a sense of available messages without any visual attention. These interactions are short and simple, but can provide valuable summaries in a very compact manner.

The interfaces we have built use inertial sensing for natural motion sensing without any external moving parts; the user just shakes, tilts or wobbles the device to stimulate the auditory and vibrotactile feedback. This can either be an explicit action or occur as part of a user's background motion; walking, running, standing up or other everyday motions. This is similar in nature to the "virtual maracas" setup that Fernström proposes in [4] for displaying attributes of a system in an intuitive way. Shaking is a simple but rich motion; a single shake can convey far more information than a simple button press (as might be used in conventional interfaces), and repeated shaking motions are rapid, natural and expressive. The direction, intensity, acceleration profile and timing of motions can be sensed, and it is easy for humans to express themselves in these variables (as babies with rattles quickly learn).

In this chapter we demonstrate how automatic classification of text messages can be incorporated into such a system, allowing users to sense rich meta-data *about* the contents of their inboxes in an extremely rapid and natural manner. Each message is represented by a ball free to move within the device containing the information. This is combined with a directional filtering technique which provides simple ways of "sieving" the data during the interaction. This could obviously be extended to other collections of textual documents, although scaling the system beyond a few tens of items would require more refined input. Displaying email inboxes would be a trivial modification of the system, for example.

12.2 Background Review

Realistic synthesis of vibrotactile and audio sensations is key to building successful eyes-free interfaces. There has been a great deal of recent interest in physical models of contact sounds and associated vibration profiles. The model-driven approach is a fruitful design method for creating plausible and interpretable multimodal feedback without extensive ad hoc design. Yao and Hayward [23], for example, created a convincing sensation of a ball rolling down a hollow tube using an audio and vibrotactile display. A similar sonification of the physical motion of a ball along a beam is described in detail in [15]; subjects were able to perceive the ball's motion from the sonification alone. Hermann et al. [6] describe an interactive sonification based upon shaking a ball-shaped sensor pack instrumented with accelerometers. This excites data points in a high-dimensional space which are anchored via springs and produce impact sounds and vibrotactile feedback when they strike each other. The "material" of the objects is used to display the properties of the striking objects. These properties are derived from the geometric properties of the Voronoi tesselation of the data points.

Granular approaches to realistic natural sound generation were explored in [14], where contact events sensed from a contact microphone above a bed of pebbles drove a sample-based granular synthesis engine. A wide variety of sonorities could be generated as a result of physical interactions with the pebbles. This granular approach is used as the synthesis engine in our prototypes. A simple haptic "bouncing ball" on mobile devices was demonstrated by Linjama et al. [13], which used tap sensing to drive the motion of a ball; this, however, did not incorporate realistic dynamics or auditory feedback.

The authors discuss granular synthesis-based continuous auditory probabilistic displays in [21] and [20], where grain streams are reweighted according to model likelihoods. This work continues the theme of probabilistic display, but does so in a discrete, event-based context, where simplified representations of probability distributions (mode and entropy) are used to characterize the output of multi-model classifiers.

12.3 Inertial Sensing

Motion sensing is achieved by instrumenting mobile devices with tri-axis accelerometers. Accelerometers have previously been widely used for tilting-based interfaces (e.g. in [16] and [9]). In the present application, the linear acceleration component is more relevant than gravitational effects; the tilting is of less consequence than deliberate shaking motions. Accelerometer inputs are high-pass filtered (see Section 12.4) to eliminate the effects of slow tilt changes.

Prototypes of this system run on iPaq 5550 devices (see Fig. 12.1), using the MESH [11] device for inertial sensing and on-board vibrotactile display. The MESH's vibrotactile transducer is a VBW32 loudspeaker-style device. This device allows for the display of high-fidelity tactile sensations due to its large bandwidth and fast transient response. This is used in combination with the iPaq's internal

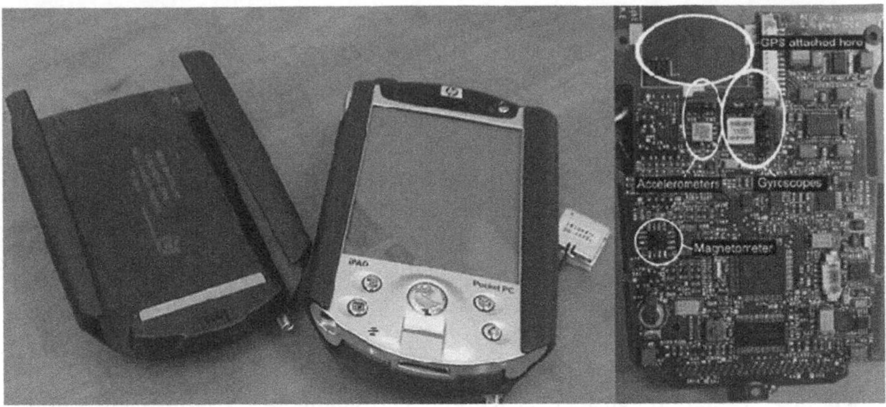

Fig. 12.1 The MESH expansion pack, with an iPaq 5550 Pocket PC. This provides accelerometer, gyroscope and magnetometer readings, as well as vibrotactile display

eccentric motor vibration unit, providing a lower frequency range of vibration sensations than achievable with the VBW32, like a woofer would in an audio system, at the cost of reduced temporal resolution. The accelerometers are used for sensing and are sampled at 100 Hz, with a range of approximately ± 2 g. The gyroscopes and magnetometers are not used. Capacitive sensing is used for tap detection (see Section 12.5.2.2).

Earlier versions of the "Shoogle" system [22] also run on standard mobile phones (such as the Nokia Series 60 devices), using the Bluetooth SHAKE inertial sensor pack (see Fig. 12.2). This provides accelerometer measurement and vibrotactile feedback in a matchbox-size wireless package, along with a range of other sensing functionality (gyroscopes, magnetometers and capacitive sensing). Work is underway in porting the automatic text message classification system to work transparently with real SMS inboxes on mobile phones, so that the system can be tested "in the wild".

Fig. 12.2 The wireless SHAKE sensor, shown with a 2 Euro piece and a Nokia 6660 for size comparison. This Bluetooth device comprises a complete inertial sensing platform with on-board vibrotactile feedback

12.4 Object Dynamics

The behaviour of the interface is governed by the internal physical model which defines the relation between sensed motions and the response of the component objects whose interactions generate feedback events. Here, the simulated physical system is based around objects bouncing around within a rectangular box whose physical dimensions *appear* to be the same as the true physical dimensions of the device. Each message in the inbox is mapped onto a single spherical object.

12.4.1 Accelerometer Mapping

The accelerations sensed by the accelerometers are used directly in an Euler integration model. This is quite sufficient given the relatively fast update rate and the non-stiffness of the dynamics; the feedback properties also mean that small numerical inaccuracies are imperceptible. The accelerations are high-pass filtered to remove components under ~ 0.5 Hz. This eliminates drifts due to changes in orientation and avoids objects becoming "stuck" along an edge. These accelerations are then transformed by an object-dependent rotation matrix (based on the message sender, see Section 12.5.2.1) and a scaling matrix which biases the objects along a specific axis:

$$\ddot{x}_i = [a_x\ a_y\ a_z] R_x(\theta_i) R_y(\phi_i) R_z(\psi_i) \begin{bmatrix} 1 \\ \alpha \\ 0 \end{bmatrix}, \qquad (12.1)$$

where a_x, a_y, a_z are the readings from the acclerometer; θ_i, ϕ_i; and ψ_i are the rotation angles for object i; and $0 < \alpha < 1$ is the direction-biasing term (see Fig. 12.3). As α decreases, the region of the state space which will activate the object becomes

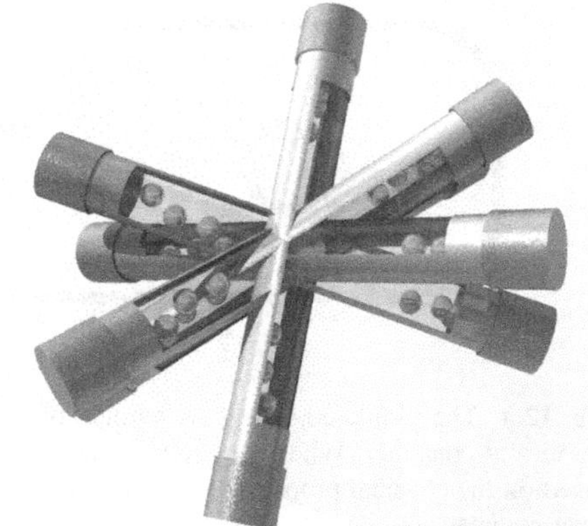

Fig. 12.3 The accelerations are transformed before application to the objects, such that each object "class" is excitable in a different direction. The cylinders here illustrate the different directions along which the device can be moved to excite different classes (although these are rather more oval shaped in the simulation). The cutaways show the virtual objects (ball bearings) within

smaller. Any other projection of the acceleration vector could be used; this could include more complex nonlinear projections. For example, the feature vector could be extended to include a quadratic basis while still using a simple linear projection matrix. The vector could also include estimated time derivatives of the acceleration measurements.

12.4.2 Friction and Stiction

Nonlinear frictional damping is applied to the motion of the objects. This eliminates rapid, small, irritating impacts caused by slight movements while remaining realistic and sensitive. The friction function is a piecewise constant function, so that

$$f = \begin{cases} f_s & (|\dot{x}| < v_c) \\ f_m & (|\dot{x}| \geq v_c) \end{cases}, \tag{12.2}$$

where f_s and f_m are the static and moving coefficients and v_c is the crossover velocity. These coefficients can be varied to simulate different lining materials within the box or different object surfaces (e.g. smooth plastic versus velvet balls).

12.4.3 Springs

When objects are created, they are attached to a randomly allocated position within the simulated box by a linear Hooke's law spring, such that

$$\ddot{x}_q = a_q + \frac{k(x_q - x_{q0})}{m}, \tag{12.3}$$

where x_{q0} is the anchor point (see Fig. 12.4). The spring coefficient k loosens or tightens the motion of the balls. Without this spring motion, the system can feel

Fig. 12.4 The simulated system. A number of balls, anchored via springs, bounce around within the virtual container. When they impact (as in the *top right*) sound and vibration are generated, based on the physical properties of the impact and the properties of the message with which they are associated

unresponsive as objects tend to cluster together as a consequence of the constraints created by walls. It is only through the spring force that the mass of the balls enters the dynamics calculations, although a more realistic system could include a mass term in the friction computation.

12.4.4 Impacts

Feedback events are generated only when the balls collide with the walls of the device "box". These impacts trigger sample playback on both the vibrotactile and audio devices. Inter-ball collisions are not tested for. Wall collisions are inelastic, transferring some kinetic energy to the wall, and the remainder to rebound. The rebound includes directional jitter – simulating a slightly rough surface – to reduce repetitive bouncing.

12.5 Message Transformation

Each of these impacts is intended to communicate information about the message with which it is associated. Due to the limitations of the haptic transducers, the vibrotactile feedback varies in a very limited way; it largely serves as an indicator of presence and gives an added degree of realism. The properties of each message are instead sonified, modulating the impact sounds to reveal meta-data. This meta-data is intended to summarize the contents of the inbox in a way which maintains user privacy (other listeners will not obtain significant personal information) and can be presented extremely rapidly.

Several transformations are used in the sonification process. The simplest transformation involves linking the mass of each ball to the length of the SMS message. Longer messages result in heavier balls with appropriate dynamics and suitably adjusted resonances. The most important feature is association of impact "material" to the output of a classifier which identifies language styles within the message. This is similar in nature to the language model-based sonifications used in the speed-dependent automatic zooming described in [3]. This aims to give an interacting user some sense of the content or style of the messages rapidly, without visual display or laborious text-to-speech output (which also has obvious privacy issues). The identity of the message sender and relative time of arrival of the messages are also displayed, by directional filtering and a rhythmic display, respectively. The impact sounds are also panned according to the site of the impact; however, this is useful only when the device is used with headphones.

12.5.1 PPM Language Model

The language modelling involves multiple partial-predictive-match (PPM) models [1, 2]. These code text very well, approaching the theoretical maximum compression for English texts (see [17]). Figure 12.5 gives an overview of the process. Each class

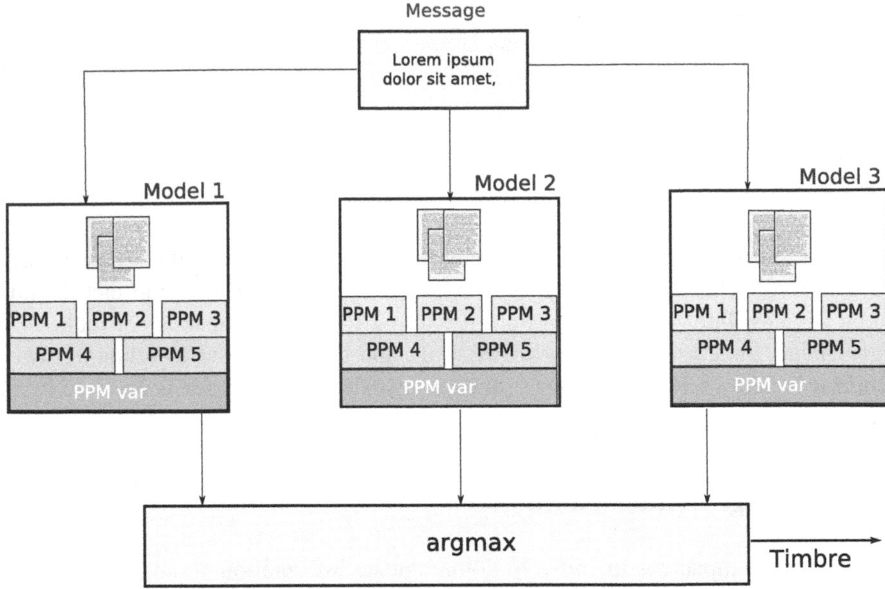

Fig. 12.5 The structure of the text classifier. Multiple models are run on incoming messages. Each of these models is composed of a number of weighted submodels. The index of the classifier with the highest posterior likelihood is used to select the impact timbre

of messages has a separate model θ_j and is trained on a corpus of messages in that style (e.g. in a particular language or in a specific vernacular).

The current implementation uses a hybrid structure, with one submodel trained with variable length prefix, running from the start of the word and terminating at the first non-letter character (which is particularly sensitive to keywords), combined with a smoothed fixed-length PPM submodel. This provides a measure of robustness in classification, especially where training texts are sparse.

The smoothed submodel combines weighted PPM models of different length (designated PPM_h for a length h model, with PPM_0 being the model trained with no prefix, i.e. the independent distribution of characters), up to a length 5 model

$$p(c|r_f) = \sum_{h=0}^{5} \lambda_h p(c|\mathrm{PPM}_h), \tag{12.4}$$

with the $\lambda_0 \dots \lambda_5$, $\sum_{h=0}^{5} \lambda_h = 1$ determining the weighting of the models. Symbols unseen in the training text are assigned a fixed probability of $\frac{1}{S}$, where S is the total number of possible symbols (e.g. all ASCII characters).

The fixed-length and word-length classifiers are used in a weighted combination, such that under each model θ_j, each character has a probability

$$p(c|\theta_j) = \lambda_q p(c|r_v) + (1 - \lambda_q) p(c|r_f), \tag{12.5}$$

where λ_q is a weighting parameter, r_v is the variable length model and r_f is the smoothed fixed-length model.

This smoothing ensures that when the variable length model abruptly fails to predict subsequent characters (e.g. when a word not seen in the training text appears), the system relaxes back to the fixed-length model, and the fixed-length model will, in the worst case, revert to the independent distribution of characters in the training text. For each model, a tree of probabilities are stored, giving $p(c|r)$, where c is the character predicted and r is the current prefix. The variable length model is pruned during training so that nodes with observation count below a certain threshold are cut off after a specified number of symbols have been seen. This reduces the size of the tree sufficiently that it can be used without excessive memory consumption. A section of an example tree is given in Fig. 12.6.

The likelihood of a message is then just

$$p(\theta_j|\text{text}) = \frac{p(\text{text}|\theta_j)p(\theta_j)}{p(\text{text})}. \tag{12.6}$$

Assuming constant prior for all models, and under the assumption that any message must belong to one of the initially trained classes, the model probabilities can be

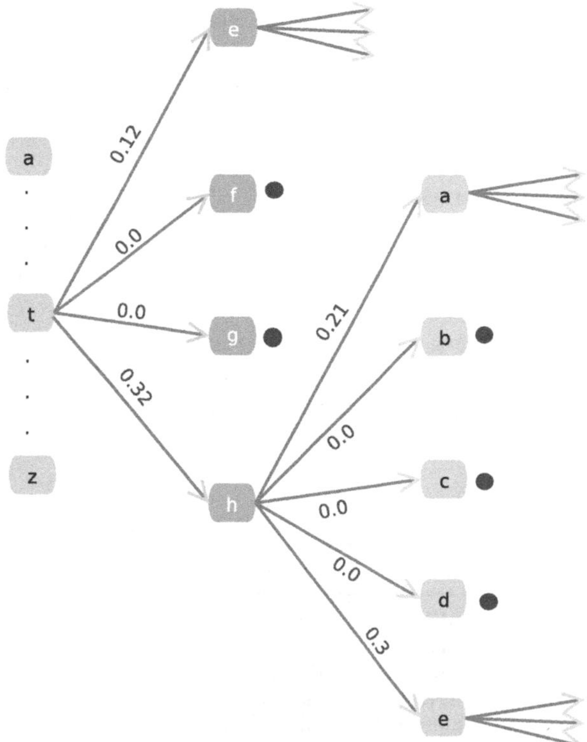

Fig. 12.6 A sample language model tree. The model is stored as a graph, with the edge weights being the probabilities of each transition, obtained from the normalized counts of that transition from the training corpus. *Solid circles* indicate no further transitions from this symbol. Each submodel has its own tree

normalized such that $\sum_{k=0}^{n} p(\text{text}|\theta_k) = 1$, i.e. the posterior likelihood becomes just

$$p(\theta_j|\text{text}) = \frac{p(\text{text}|\theta_j)}{\sum_{k=0}^{n} p(\text{text}|\theta_k)}. \tag{12.7}$$

For each model, we have

$$\log p(\text{text}|\theta_j) = \sum_{i=0}^{\text{END}} \log p(c_i|\theta_j). \tag{12.8}$$

Exponentiating and substituting (12.8) into (12.7), the model likelihoods are obtained.

12.5.1.1 Potential Enhancements

Although word-level models of text could be introduced, these have significant training requirements and require enormous storage for anything but the smallest corpora. Given the excellent compression capabilities of the PPM models and the good performance of the classifiers in the test scenarios (see Section 12.5.1.2), additional modelling is probably excessive for the current problem.

Ideally, each of these classes would be adapted online, with the user assigning incoming messages to particular classes, to cope with the various styles that user regularly receives. Although this is not currently implemented, it would be relatively simple to do so.

12.5.1.2 Test Model Classes

For testing, five language classes were created by selecting appropriate corpora. Due to the lack of suitable text message corpora in different styles, a number of artificial classes were created. Although these differences are exaggerated compared to the types of messages commonly received, they demonstrate the utility of the technique. Each of these was trained with a relatively small corpus, but this was sufficient given the very significant differences in language. Table 12.1 shows the test classes and their corresponding corpora.

Table 12.1 Test classes and the training texts used for them

Name	Corpus	Model
SMS	SMS messages (Singapore corpus [10])	θ_1
Finnish	Finnish poetry (Project Gutenberg)	θ_2
News	Collection of BBC News articles	θ_3
German	German literature (Project Gutenberg)	θ_4
Biblical	Old testament (KJV Genesis)	θ_5

Table 12.2 Test results with the five classifiers. These short texts were taken from documents not present in the training corpus. Zeros are shown where the probability is so close to 1 that the logarithm is not computed exactly. The entry with maximum probability for each row is highlighted in light grey. The class codes are as follows: SMS (θ_1); Finnish (θ_2); News (θ_3); German (θ_4); Biblical (θ_5)

Text	True	$\log_2 p(\theta_1)$	$\log_2 p(\theta_2)$	$\log_2 p(\theta_3)$	$\log_2 p(\theta_4)$	$\log_2 p(\theta_5)$	$H(\theta)$
"yo what up wit u the night. u going to the cinema?"	(θ_1)	-4.23×10^{-5}	−116.47	−18.98	−128.82	−15.15	$\mathbf{4.9 \times 10^{-4}}$
"Ken aina kaunis on, ei koskaan pöyhkä, Nopea kieleltänsä, mut ei röyhkä; Ken rik as on, mut kultiaan ei näytä; Tahtonsa saada voi, mut sit ei käytä."	(θ_2)	−233.32	0.0	−205.36	−186.36	−224.15	$\mathbf{1.47 \times 10^{-54}}$
"They are charged with crimes against humanity over a campaign against Kurds in the 1980s."	(θ_3)	−80.08	−233.69	0.0	−253.54	−77.39	$\mathbf{4.51 \times 10^{-22}}$
"Die Erde ist nicht genug, Mond und Mars offenbar auch nicht: Google will demnächst das gesamte Universum erfassen."	(θ_4)	−185.69	−213.26	−159.05	0.0	−178.71	$\mathbf{2.09 \times 10^{-46}}$
"Now after the death of Joshua it came to pass, that the children of Israel asked the LORD, saying, Who shall go up for us against the Canaanites first, to fight against them."	(θ_5)	−126.82	−438.91	−80.56	−484.06	0.0	$\mathbf{4.99 \times 10^{-23}}$

Table 12.2 shows testing results from these classifiers. The table shows example messages and their "true" class, along with the classifier probabilities and the classifier entropy. The classifier performs extremely well, even for the less well-distinguished categories.

12.5.1.3 Certainty Filtering

The timbre of the impact is always set to be the one associated with the most likely model (see Section 12.6.2), but the output of the classifiers is clearly uncertain; message classes can often be quite similar, and many messages may be either so short or so generic as to be indiscriminable. The system displays this uncertainty by manipulating the audio according to the entropy of the classifier distribution

$$H(\theta|\text{text}) = -\sum_{j=0}^{n} p(\theta_j|\text{text}) \log_2 p(\theta_j|\text{text}). \tag{12.9}$$

The entropy sonification is performed in two ways: first, when $H(\theta|\text{text})$ rises above some threshold H_{min}, the timbre associated with the message is set to be a special class representing a "general message"; second, when the entropy is below this threshold, a low-pass filter is applied to impact sound, with the cutoff inversely proportional to the entropy

$$c = \frac{z}{\varepsilon + H(\theta|\text{text})}, \tag{12.10}$$

for some constants z, ε. This dulls the sound as the entropy increases.

12.5.2 Exploration

The basic shaking system simply gives a sense of the numerosity and composition of the messages in the inbox. Two additional features extend the interaction to present other aspects of message content. These rely on the device being stimulated in different ways, rather than attempting to present more information in a single impact.

12.5.2.1 Identity Sieving

Identity sieving links the sender or sender group (e.g. family, friends, work) of the message (which can be obtained from the message meta-data) to a particular plane in space (see Section 12.4). These messages can be excited by moving the device in this plane; moving it in others will have less effect. A user can "sieve out" messages from a particular sender by shaking in various directions. The stiction model increases the selectivity of this sieving, so that objects who are free to move along other plains tend not to do so unless more violent motions are made. All objects can still be excited by making such vigorous movements.

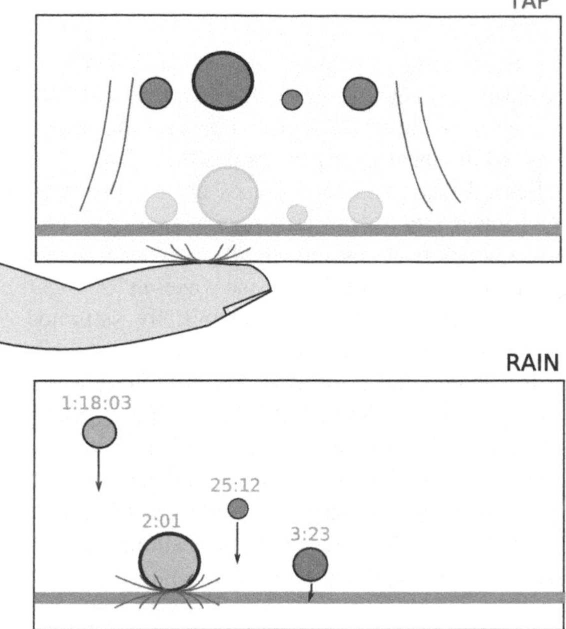

Fig. 12.7 Capacitive sensors detect tap motions on the case of the device. This causes the virtual objects to be launched up and then rain back down so that the timing of the impacts reveals the relative timing of the arrival of the associated messages. Here, the times shown in *light blue* are arrival times (the time since this message arrived), so that the newest message impacts first

12.5.2.2 Time-Sequenced "Rain"

An additional overview of the contents of the inbox can be obtained by tapping the device, causing the balls to shoot "upwards" (out of the screen) and then fall back down in a structured manner. Tapping is sensed independently using the capacitive sensors on the MESH device and is reliable even for gentle touches while being limited to a small sensitive area. The falling of the objects is linked to the arrival time of the messages in the inbox, with delays before impact proportional to the time gap between the arrival of messages. The rhythm of the sounds communicates the temporal structure of the inbox. Figure 12.7 illustrates this.

12.6 Auditory and Vibrotactile Display

The presentation of timely haptic responses greatly improves the sensation of a true object bouncing around within the device over an audio-only display. As Kuchenbecker et al. [12] describe, event-based playback of high-frequency waveforms can greatly enhance the sensation of stiffness in force-feedback applications. In mobile scenarios, where kinaesthetic feedback is impractical, event-triggered vibration patterns can produce realistic impressions of contacts when the masses involved are sufficiently small.

12.6.1 Vibrotactile Events

The vibrotactile waveforms sent to the VBW32 transducer on the MESH device are enveloped sine waves, with a frequency of 250 Hz. This is at both the resonant frequency of the transducer and around the peak sensitivity of the skin receptors involved in vibrotactile perception (Fig. 12.8).

Several basic envelope shapes are pre-programmed: simple impacts with very rapid linear attack and an exponential decay; sloshing-like vibrations with much longer attack portions and slightly varying frequencies; granular effects with sums of extremely short enveloped sine waves at random time delays; and heavier impacts with long ringing portions and initially saturated output. Figure 12.9 gives an overview of these waveforms.

To enhance the sensations, the vibrations from internal eccentric motor of the iPaq is layered with the VBW32 transducer. The short, high-frequency vibrations are sent to the smaller vibrator, with heavy, slow impacts routed to the motor-driven actuator. The greater power of the motor-driven actuator results in a more "solid" feel, but limited control restricts output to simple events played in conjunction with the high-frequency events (similar to the layering of sub-bass waveforms under Foley effects in film sound design).

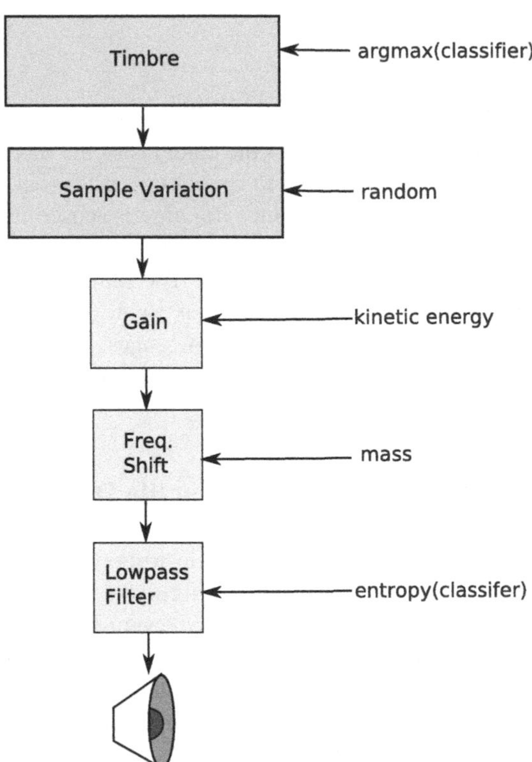

Fig. 12.8 The synthesis process. A wave is selected from the wavetable and then transformed according to the object properties

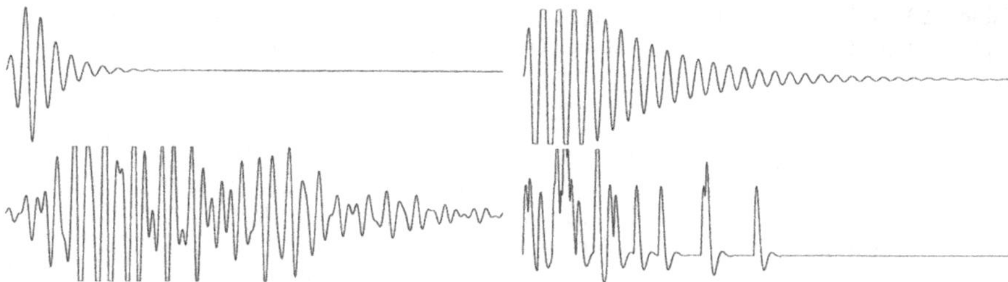

Fig. 12.9 Four different vibrotactile waveform types. *Left*-to-*right*, *top*-to-*bottom*: standard "light ball" impact; heavy, ringing impact; liquid sloshing; gritty, particulate impact. All of these have energy concentrated around the 250 Hz band

Even when the inbox is empty, gentle vibration feedback is produced by the internal vibration motor in response to movement to indicate that the system is "live" and sensing motion.

12.6.2 Audio Synthesis

The impact of the balls on the virtual box produces sound related to the physics of the collisions. Although ideally these sounds would be generated by a physical model (such as the general contact sound engine given by van den Doel et al. [18]), the limited computational power of many mobile devices – which lack efficient floating-point units – makes this difficult. Such techniques would, however, greatly increase the potential expressivity of the interface.

12.6.2.1 Sample Banks

Given these computational restrictions, the system instead relies on a granular technique, with wavetable playback for synthesis, combined with some simple signal post-processing. This gives a high degree of realism, but comes at the cost of significant effort in creating a sample library and limited flexibility.

A number of impact sounds (8–16) are pre-recorded for each of a number of impact types (wood on glass, for example). These slight variations are critical to avoid artificial sounding effects. On impact, a random sound from within this class is selected and mixed into the output stream. The audio output – which uses the FMOD library – mixes up to 32 simultaneous channels, to ensure that impacts do not cut off previous audio events in an unnatural manner.

A listing of some of the impact types which have been sampled is given in Table 12.3. These provide a wide range of natural sounding and easily distinguishable timbres, although the limited quality of the speakers on the iPaq introduces some unnatural artefacts. Humans are exceedingly adept at inferring the physical properties of materials from the sound of their physical interaction, and the realistic nature of the generated sounds makes the nature of the impact immediately obvious.

Table 12.3 A listing of some of the impact classes which have been sampled. Each of these impacts sampled numerous times so that the natural variations in the sounds are retained

Name	Description
Pingpong	Ping pong balls dropped onto a wooden board
Anvil	Miniature anvil struck with miniature hammer
Glass	Ordinary glasses struck with a wooden rod
Chime	Small metal chimes
Jar	Small hard candies hitting a glass jar
Water	Water drops in a cup
Slosh	Water sloshing in a glass
Bigslosh	Water sloshing in a large demijohn
Gravel	Gravel hitting gravel
Tick	Mechanical clock ticking
Klang	Long metal bar being struck
Metal	Metal radiator struck with a metal bar
Bubble	Bubbles formed by air blown in to water
Viscousbloop	Stones being dropped into a very viscous liquid
Keys	Keys jangling in a pocket
Didj	A didjeridoo being struck with a hand

Due to technical limitations of the implementation hardware, synchronization of audio with the vibrotactile is limited, with variable delays of up to 50 ms between the modalities. This does not, however, seem to reduce the subjective realism or quality of the interaction.

12.6.2.2 Audio Transformations

The samples are transformed based on the properties of each particular collision, to communicate as much information as possible given the limited processing capabilities and limited sample set. The gain of the impact sound is set to be proportional to the kinetic energy of the impact ($\frac{1}{2}mv^2$); this is essential for natural sounding effects. As described in Section 12.5.1.3, the entropy of the language class distribution is mapped to the cutoff of a simple one-pole IIR filter running on the impact sound, so that less certain classifications have a duller tone. The sample is also pitch shifted with a simple resampling process in proportion to the mass of the ball which impacted, so that large mass interactions produce lower sounds with deeper resonances than smaller ones. This transformation can only reasonably be applied to sound types which have clear resonances *in the object which impacts* – the effect is quite unnatural for sounds such as sloshing water, where pitch-shifted audio sounds like liquids of different viscosity in differently sized containers. Figure 12.8 gives an overview of the synthesis process.

Ideally there would be impulse responses for both the object and the container which would be convolved at runtime; pitch-shifting the object impact could independently change its perceived mass without interfering with the formants of the container impulse. However, this is computationally challenging with the current generation of mobile devices.

12.7 Further-Work – Active Selection

The current prototype has elementary "sieving" functions for sensing particular aspects of data within the device. More sophisticated selection methods, such as the active selection techniques described in [19], could be used to identify and select individual messages within the collection. This could involve modality scheduling, where the interaction moves from simple vibrotactile information (the presence of messages), through auditory display (the composition of the collection) and finally to visual display, for on-screen display of messages. Alternatively, speech synthesis could be applied in the final stage for an entirely non-visual message-browsing system. Such a system would be a significant step towards a usable non-visual, buttonless mobile platform.

12.8 Conclusions

This system extends our previous work on excitatory interfaces to include the sonifications based on the automatic classification of messages, as well as introducing the "sieving" metaphor to extend the display capabilities of the system. The automatic classification process could easily be extended to other data forms; music files could be linked to objects with properties obtained from the automatic classification of genres, for example.

The model-based interaction leads to an intuitive and compelling interface which is well suited to the physical manipulability of mobile devices. The metaphor of the mobile device as a physical container within which interaction can take place is one that can be extended to many other interaction scenarios. The interface is based on active sensing, where users drive the interaction at their own pace; the system does not interrupt of its own accord. The result is a rich multimodal display that can be used without visual attention, taking advantage of user's familiarity with the dynamics of processes in the physical world to present information in a natural and non-irritating manner.

Acknowledgments The authors are grateful for support from the IST Programme of the European Commission, under PASCAL Network of Excellence, IST 2002-506778; the IRCSET BRG project BRG SC/2003/271 Continuous Gestural Interaction with Mobile devices; HEA project Body Space; EPSRC project EP/E042740/1 and SFI grant 00/PI.1/C067. This publication reflects only the views of the authors. Audio examples and a video are available online at http://www.dcs.gla.ac.uk/ jhw/shoogle/

References

1. T. Bell, J. Cleary, and I. Witten. Data compression using adaptive coding and partial string matching. *IEEE Transactions on Communications*, 32(4):396–402, 1984.
2. J. Cleary, W. Teahan, and I. Witten. Unbounded length contexts for PPM. In DCC-95, pages 52–61. IEEE Computer Society Press, 1995.
3. P. Eslambolchilar and R. Murray-Smith. Model-based, multimodal interaction in document browsing. In *Multimodal Interaction and Related Machine Learning Algorithms*, 2006.

4. M. Fernström. Sound objects and human-computer interaction design. In D. Rocchesso and F. Fontana, editors, *The Sounding Object*, pages 45–59. Mondo Estremo Publishing, 2003.
5. T. Hermann. *Sonification for Exploratory Data Analysis*. PhD thesis, Bielefeld University, Bielefeld, Germany, 2002.
6. T. Hermann, J. Krause, and H. Ritter. Real-time control of sonification models with an audio-haptic interface. In R. Nakatsu and H. Kawahara, editors, *Proceedings of the International Conference on Auditory Display*, pages 82–86, Kyoto, Japan, 7 2002. International Community for Auditory Display (ICAD), ICAD.
7. T. Hermann and H. Ritter. Listen to your data: Model-based sonification for data analysis. In M. R. Syed, editor, *Advances in intelligent computing and mulimedia systems*, pages 189–194. Int. Inst. for Advanced Studies in System Research and Cybernetics, 1999.
8. T. Hermann and H. Ritter. Crystallization sonification of high-dimensional datasets. *ACM Transactions on Applied Perception*, 2(4):550–558, 2005.
9. K. Hinckley, J. Pierce, M. Sinclair, and E. Horvitz. Sensing techniques for mobile interaction. In *UIST'*2000, 2000.
10. Y. How and M.-Y. Kan. Optimizing predictive text entry for short message service on mobile phones. In *Human Computer Interfaces International*, 2005.
11. S. Hughes, I. Oakley, and S. O'Modhrain. Mesh: Supporting mobile multi-modal interfaces. In *UIST* 2004. ACM, 2004.
12. K.J. Kuchenbecker, J. Fiene, and G. Niemeyer. Improving contact realism through event-based haptic feedback. *IEEE Transactions on Visualization and Computer Graphics*, 12(2):219–230, 2006.
13. J. Linjama, J. Hakkila, and S. Ronkainen. Gesture interfaces for mobile devices - minimalist approach for haptic interaction. In *CHI Workshop: Hands on Haptics: Exploring Non-Visual Visualisation Using the Sense of Touch*, 2005.
14. S. O'Modhrain and G. Essl. Pebblebox and crumblebag: Tactile interfaces for granular synthesis. In *NIME*'04, 2004.
15. M. Rath and D. Rocchesso. Continuous sonic feedback from a rolling ball. *IEEE MultiMedia*, 12(2):60–69, 2005.
16. J. Rekimoto. Tilting operations for small screen interfaces. In *ACM Symposium on User Interface Software and Technology*, pages 167–168, 1996.
17. W.J. Teahan and J.G. Cleary. The entropy of English using PPM-based models. In *Data Compression Conference*, pages 53–62, 1996.
18. K. van den Doel, P.G. Kry, and D.K. Pai. Foleyautomatic: physically-based sound effects for interactive simulation and animation. In *SIGGRAPH '01*, pages 537–544. ACM Press, 2001.
19. J. Williamson. *Continuous Uncertain Interaction*. PhD thesis, University of Glasgow, 2006.
20. J. Williamson and R. Murray-Smith. Granular synthesis for display of time-varying probability densities,. In A. Hunt and Th. Hermann, editors, *International Workshop on Interactive Sonification*, 2004.
21. J. Williamson and R. Murray-Smith. Sonification of probabilistic feedback through granular synthesis. *IEEE Multimedia*, 12(2):45–52, 2005.
22. J. Williamson, R. Murray-Smith, and S. Hughes. Shoogle: Excitatory multimodal interaction on mobile devices. In *Proceedings of CHI 2007*, page In Press, 2007.
23. H.-Y. Yao and V. Hayward. An experiment on length perception with a virtual rolling stone. In *Eurohaptics 06*, 2006.

Chapter 13
Management of Tracking for Mixed and Augmented Reality Systems

Peter Keitler, Daniel Pustka, Manuel Huber, Florian Echtler, and Gudrun Klinker

Abstract Position and orientation tracking is a major challenge for mixed/augmented reality applications, especially in heterogeneous and wide-area sensor setups. In this chapter, we describe trackman, a planning and analysis tool which supports the AR-engineer in setup and maintenance of the tracking infrastructure. A new graphical modeling approach based on spatial relationship graphs (SRGs) eases the specification of known as well as the deduction of new relationships between entities in the scene. Modeling is based on reusable patterns representing the underlying sensor drivers or algorithms. Recurring constellations in the scene can be condensed into reusable meta patterns. The process is further simplified by semi-automatic modeling techniques which automize trivial steps. Data flow networks can be generated automatically from the SRG and are guaranteed to be semantically correct. Furthermore, generic tools are described that allow for the calibration/registration of static spatial transformations as well as for the live surveillance of tracking accuracy. In summary, this approach reduces tremendously the amount of expert knowledge needed for the administration of tracking setups.

Keywords Mixed/augmented reality · Spatial relationship graph · Tracking · Sensor fusion · Authoring · Calibration · Registration · Error analysis

13.1 Motivation

Tracking the position and orientation of users and objects in the scene is one of the most critical issues for mixed/augmented reality applications. A plethora of tracking methods based on various sensing technologies (e.g., optical, infrared, magnetic, ultrasonic, inertial) have been described for this purpose, all of them having their particular advantages and drawbacks [26]. Therefore, in order to achieve tracking

---

P. Keitler (✉)
Technische Universität München, München, Germany
e-mail: keitler@in.tum.de

E. Dubois et al. (eds.), *The Engineering of Mixed Reality Systems*, Human-Computer Interaction Series, DOI 10.1007/978-1-84882-733-2_13,

at the expected level of robustness, speed, and precision, rather complex tracking setups are often necessary, potentially requiring heterogeneous multi-sensor environments that include both mobile and stationary sensors of various modalities. In this respect, we expect increasing numbers of sensors, such as cameras as well as ubiquitously available RFID readers and-WiFi trackers, to become available in private and public buildings, coupled with increasing tracking and self-localization facilities in mobile devices. Until now there is no standardized way to accomplish the integration of such sensors into an application.

Typically, MR/AR applications have special solutions for special situations. This complicates the maintenance of tracking environments since changes in the infrastructure often require the source code of one or even several applications to be adapted, undermining system integrity. Developers of MR/AR applications, on the other hand, would rather focus on describing and modeling the application and its visualizations than on the tracking. Typically, applications only need to know the transformations between a few virtual or real-world entities. For them, it is not important how the tracking is achieved – as long as it is provided at expected quality levels. As a consequence, we expect a new breed of professionals, called *AR-engineers*, to emerge. They will be responsible for configuring and maintaining large, dynamically changing tracking setups. They will have general knowledge about trackers and the concept of spatial transformations, but neither will they be experts in all kinds of tracking systems nor will they be experts in conceiving and programming complex calibration or fusion algorithms.

13.1.1 Requirements

A number of requirements exist for an application-independent facility to allow AR-engineers to set up and maintain a tracking environment.

- **R1: Separation of tracking from applications** To support flexible use of tracking facilities across many applications, a common standard is needed for the specification of relationships between sensors and objects and the exchange of tracking data associated with them.
- **R2: Accuracy and performance** The standardization and abstraction must not lead to a degradation in tracking quality or speed, when compared to a hard-wired setup.
- **R3: Registration and calibration** Tools must be provided to register and calibrate the increasing number of sensors and objects in tracking environments efficiently, reliably, and precisely.
- **R4: Maintainability** The system should enable AR-engineers to describe and register new sensors and objects and to calibrate and continuously monitor them quickly and reliably. At any point in time, they need a clearly documented understanding of the current configuration. It should be impossible for AR-engineers to mistakenly configure physically impossible tracking setups.

13.1.2 Related Work

Many systems have been described which aim at the integration of multiple sensors and also at providing a layer of abstraction for the applications relying on them. However, they are mostly rather problem specific and do not follow a general-purpose approach, such as for example the perception and control techniques used in autonomous land vehicles [7, 24]. The architectures proposed for this field of application heavily rely on computer vision and make strong assumptions on the topology of the spatial relationships to be monitored [6, 1]. They were not designed with flexibility and maintainability in mind.

More generic architectures are based on so-called data flow networks, directed graphs whose nodes represent components for data acquisition from sensors or for data transformation. Components can be flexibly cross-linked, based on a small set of data types allowed on component inputs and outputs, such as 3 DoF position, 3 DoF orientation, or 6 DoF pose, a combination of both. Such data flow networks constitute one of the most important building blocks of ubiquitous tracking environments and provide the necessary transformation, synchronization, and network transport of tracking data.

In the domain of multimodal user interfaces, several component-based frameworks have been described that follow such a modular approach, though the processed data types differ, of course. They also feature graphical rapid prototyping environments to set up the data flow network [21, 14, 18].

For tracking, the two most prominent examples in the literature are *OpenTracker* [20] and *VRPN* [23]. Whereas *VRPN*, coming from the VR domain, focuses on how various sensors can be linked together and how tracking data can be synchronized and transferred via network, *OpenTracker* originated in AR and also includes rudimentary support for sensor fusion.

Also noteworthy is the *OSGAR* system [5]. It builds upon tracking data among others given by *VRPN* and models tracked, statically registered, or deduced spatial relationships in a scene graph [22]. Assumed tracking and registration errors can be propagated along its branches in terms of covariances, thereby providing the application with a measure of the expected tracking accuracy.

Modeling data flow networks using those systems is a great relief, compared to coding all drivers and algorithms from scratch. However, it is still a tedious task and maintainability (R4) is rather delimited by the fact that invalid data flows are not excluded conceptually. Furthermore, none of the described systems provides support for registration of statically aligned entities (R3), an obligation for real separation of tracking from the applications (R1).

13.1.3 The Ubitrack and trackman Approach

The *Ubitrack* tracking middleware adds a higher level of abstraction to the data flow concepts described above. AR-engineers can describe tracking setups as spatial relationships between sensors and objects. Corresponding data flow graphs are then generated partially or fully automatically. This higher level provides a more intuitive way of describing data flows. AR-engineers can focus on describing the physical sensor arrangements. Thereby, the risk of accidentally specifying physically impossible data flows is excluded conceptually. Spatial relationship graphs lend themselves to long-term documentation (and visualization) of the modeled sensor arrangement. To this end, the *trackman*[1] tool provides a graphical interface for the management, monitoring, and quality analysis of complex and heterogeneous tracking environments. Ubitrack provides the foundation for fulfilling requirements R1 through R4. This chapter focuses on the presentation of trackman and how the Ubitrack functionality is refined in order to accomplish the requirements fully.

13.2 The Ubitrack Framework

Before diving into the presentation of *trackman*, we provide an introduction to the basic concepts of spatial relationship graphs, data flow networks, and spatial relationship patterns. For more details, see [11, 15–19].

13.2.1 Spatial Relationship Graphs

The concept of *spatial relationship graphs* (SRGs) was proposed in [15]. A simple example is shown in Fig. 13.1a. SRGs are graphs which capture the structure of a tracking environment by describing the static and dynamic spatial properties of objects in the environment. The nodes of SRGs represent the local coordinate frames of real or virtual objects and sensors. Directed edges represent spatial relationships between nodes A and B, i.e., the pose (position and orientation, 6 DoF) of coordinate frame B relative to frame A. In Fig. 13.1a, the top node refers to a tracker that

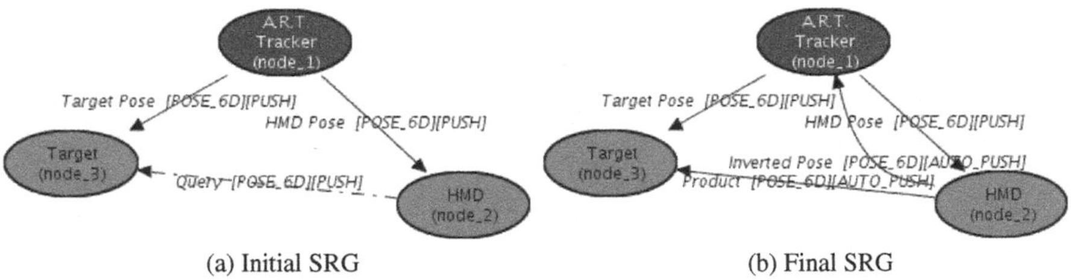

(a) Initial SRG (b) Final SRG

Fig. 13.1 (**a**) Exemplary SRG with a sensor tracking two targets. The *solid lines* depict tracking information that is continuously measured and updated. The *dashed line* depicts spatial information that can be derived from the tracking data. (**b**) Additional *solid lines* indicate the respective mathematical operations (inversion, concatenation) on the tracking data

---

[1]The Ubitrack runtime library and trackman can be downloaded from http://campar.in.tum.de/UbiTrack/WebHome

tracks the poses of two objects, represented by the bottom two nodes. The right one represents a head-mounted display and the left one refers to a generic target. For instance, the applications might want to render some virtual object on top of it. The directed solid edges represent the (dynamically changing) spatial relationships between the tracker and the two objects.

SRGs are similar to scene graphs in computer graphics [22]. Yet, in contrast to scene graphs, SRGs do not imply a predefined hierarchical ordering of the nodes. Applications can request any node in an SRG to assume the role of a root node, requiring the traversal through parts of the SRG from this node to a specified sink node. For a detailed comparison of scene graphs and SRGs, see [9].

The dashed edge in Fig. 13.1a describes a request to determine the spatial relationship between the tracked HMD and the tracked generic target. This relationship is not measured directly but can be derived by considering the known spatial relationships of both objects to the tracker. Figure 13.1b shows the resulting extended SRG. Two new edges have been added to the SRG: one reversing the spatial relationship between the tracker and the HMD and the other one replacing the dashed edge by concatenating the inverted edge from the HMD to the tracker with the edge from the tracker to the generic target.

13.2.1.1 Use of Cycles for Sensor Calibration and Object Registration

SRGs typically contain multiple edges between nodes, as depicted in Fig. 13.1b For example, if multiple independent trackers are tracking the same objects (and the transformations between those trackers are known), the SRG might contain multiple paths to determine the spatial relationship in question. Thus, as another difference to scene graphs, SRGs may contain cycles. These cycles are essential for exploiting redundancy in tracking setups. They provide a means to calibrate or register sensors or objects by using complementary tracking information (i.e., an alternate path in the graph). They also allow system monitoring and the detection of faulty (miscalibrated) sensors (in support of requirement R3).

13.2.1.2 Edge Characteristics

SRG edges represent a number of sensing characteristics. Most importantly, tracking information can have varying degrees of freedom (DoF), ranging from 2 or 3 translational DoF for wide-area sensors such as GPS or WiFi-based trackers, over 3 rotational DoF for mobile sensors such as gyroscopes and compasses, to full 6 DoF poses of high-precision trackers for small-area VR or AR setups [19]. Other edge characteristics involve the explicit modeling of sensing errors [2, 13].A third set of edge properties involves timing and synchronization issues with the special simple case of static edges [16]. The properties provide important criteria for selecting optimal (w.r.t. accuracy or speed) sensor arrangements when setups offer a multitude of options. They are essential to the derivation of good data flow networks (see below) and support requirement R2.

13.2.2 Data Flow Networks

SRGs are a descriptive rather than an operational specification of a certain setup and are not directly usable by an application. Rather, for efficient use by the Ubitrack runtime system that is included into the applications, they have to be converted into *data flow networks* (DFNs). DFNs consist of computational units that operate on tracking data.

DFNs are instances of *data flow graphs* (DFGs). DFGs are directed graphs and their nodes represent the components to be instantiated in the DFN. Edges represent the flow of tracking data between these components. Sources in a DFG generally represent sources of tracking data (i.e., tracking devices). Sinks correspond to interfaces to applications or to other data flow graphs.

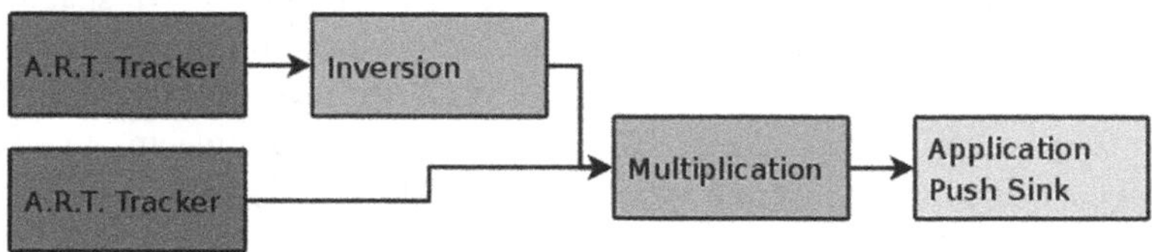

Fig. 13.2 Data flow network corresponding to the SRG shown in Fig. 13.1b. An inversion, followed by a multiplication, is needed to compute the *dashed edge* of Fig. 13.1a from the two *solid edges*

Figure 13.2 shows the data flow graph that computes the spatial relationship between the HMD and the target in the SRG of Fig. 13.1 The tracking data of the HMD are inverted and then concatenated with the tracking data of the target.

The Ubitrack runtime environment uses such data flow networks. At this level, Ubitrack is comparable to the approaches taken in other systems, such as OpenTracker [20]. In fact, we are able to export data flow networks that have been generated from SRGs into applications that use OpenTracker, using the Ubiquitous Tracking Query Language (UTQL) data exchange format [18, 14] (in support of R1).

13.2.3 Spatial Relationship Patterns

This section describes how SRGs can be transformed into DFGs. To this end, Pustka introduced the concept of *spatial relationship patterns* [17]. A pattern corresponds to a computational unit, i.e., a node, in a DFG. Tracking data are provided to the computational unit via inputs. It is transformed and then sent out via the output. Good examples are the inversion and multiplication nodes in the DFG of Fig. 13.2

13.2.3.1 Basic Concept

Spatial relationship patterns are depicted as template SRGs. They describe the effect of a computational unit on an SRG. For example, the inversion pattern in Fig. 13.3a

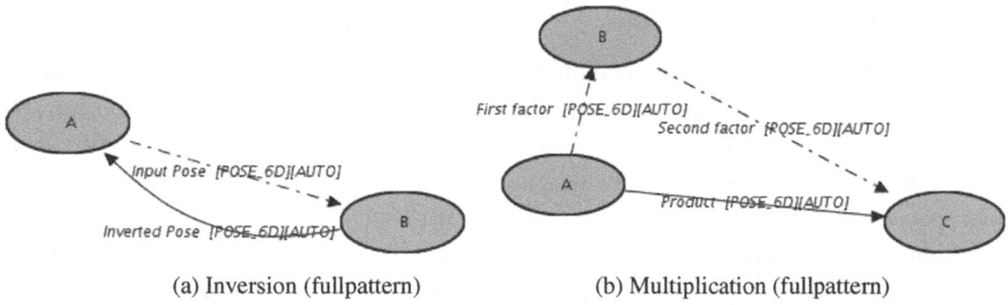

(a) Inversion (fullpattern) (b) Multiplication (fullpattern)

Fig. 13.3 Basic spatial relationship patterns for the inversion and multiplication of tracking data

states that, for a given SRG edge from node A to B, inversion adds a new edge to the SRG going in the reverse direction. Similarly, the multiplication pattern in Fig. 13.3b states that an SRG edge from A to B and an edge from B to C can be concatenated by multiplying the transformations. As a result, a new edge from A to C can be added to the SRG. Component inputs in the DFG correspond to *input edges* of the pattern. They are shown as dashed lines, and the associated *input nodes* as light gray ellipses. The resulting component output in the DFG corresponds to an *output edge* of the pattern. It is shown by a solid line and the associated *output nodes* by darker ellipses. If the input edges and nodes of a pattern match a part of an SRG, the output edges and nodes can be added to the graph. At the same time, the corresponding computational unit can be added to the DFG.

In addition to *full patterns* that have both input edges and output edges, there are *base patterns* that have only output nodes and edges, such as the tracker pattern in Fig. 13.4a Since it has an empty input section, it can be applied any time. It is used to add tracking devices as source computational units to the DFG.

Similarly, *query patterns* have only input nodes and edges (Fig. 13.4b). They connect the tracking setup to an application, in the form of a query for information about a specific spatial relationship in a scene. An example is the pose of the target relative to the HMD in Fig. 13.1a Generally, all base/query patterns have the same structure, an output/input edge with output/input source and sink nodes.

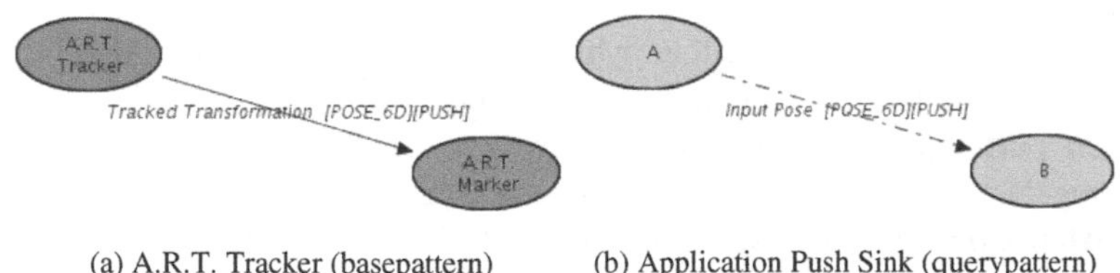

(a) A.R.T. Tracker (basepattern) (b) Application Push Sink (querypattern)

Fig. 13.4 Spatial relationship patterns for a tracking device and to connect the Ubitrack runtime system to an application

13.2.3.2 Synchronization Issues

To properly handle measurements that are generated asynchronously by independent sensors, each edge in an SRG is attributed with its synchronization mode, *push* or *pull*. *Pushed* measurements travel downward from source toward sink through a DFN, e.g., when a tracker such as a camera sends new data into the network at its own speed. *Pulled* measurements are pulled upward in a DFN. A pull operation may be initiated for example by an application requesting measurements with a specific time stamp via the Application Pull Sink component. Push as well as pull events are propagated recursively through the data flow network.

Synchronization problems occur when two or more unsynchronized inputs have to be combined by a computational unit, such as the multiplication component. The measurements then need to be valid for the same point in time. When a pull request occurs on the output, measurements have to be pulled for this time stamp on all inputs. When a push event occurs for one input edge, measurements for the same time stamp have to be pulled on the other inputs. The result can then be computed and pushed onward on the output. Generally, it is not possible to have more than one input in push mode, except when both measurements come from the same tracker or are otherwise synchronized in hardware. Therefore, all except one of them should be in pull mode. To this end, suitable conversion facilities must be included. The Buffer (constant interpolation), Linear Interpolation, and Kalman Filter components convert measurements from push to pull whereas the Sampler component converts from pull to push. Refer to [16] for more details.

13.2.3.3 Pattern Categories

A large number of patterns and associated computational units have already been integrated into Ubitrack [17]. For documentation purposes and for interactive use in trackman, they are categorized with respect to their structure (i.e., as base, full, and query patterns) and also with respect to their semantics:

- **Sensor patterns** describe how tracking data are provided to the data flow network. This mainly comprises driver components retrieving data from hardware.
- **Basic patterns** describe trivial transformation steps such as inversion or interpolation of a transformation or concatenation of two transformations.
- **Calibration patterns** represent algorithms such as the hand–eye calibration or absolute-orientation algorithm which are used to determine static spatial relationships under certain boundary conditions.
- **Fusion patterns** represent algorithms which can be used to somehow fuse tracking data to obtain a better, more accurate, or a more general result.
- **Persistence patterns** represent components that write tracking or calibration data to a file or read it from there.
- **Network patterns** represent components that send/receive tracking data to/from the network. They are needed to link independent DFNs.

- **Application patterns** represent components that transfer or receive tracking data to/from an application. This principally enables applications not only to consume tracking data but also to transform it somehow and reinject it into the data flow network. Other patterns in this category include render components, which create OpenGL-based 3D graphics output based on tracking data.

Table 13.1 presents a representative subset of patterns,[2] classified according to their structure and semantics. For the application and persistence patterns, there exist pairs of corresponding base and query patterns, such as Player and Recorder for logging and replaying tracking data or Calibration Reader and Calibration Writer maintaining the calibration or registration data of a static transformation in files.

The application source and sink patterns represent endpoints in the DFN which interface it to the application. The Application Pull Source is one of few data flow sources having type pull. It retrieves current tracking data at any time via a callback interface from the application. Similarly, the Application Push Sink pushes data into the application via a callback interface. In both cases, the DFN initiates the flow of tracking data. Application Push Source and Pull Sink, on the contrary, work without a callback mechanism and the application initiates the flow of tracking data. Some calibration patterns will be introduced in Section 13.5.1. For more details, refer to [17].

Table 13.1 Pattern categorization matrix showing a subset of the existing Ubitrack patterns. The transformation types are neglected for the sake of readability

		Syntax		
		Base pattern	Full pattern	Query pattern
Semantics	Sensor	A.R.T. tracker static transformation		
	Basic		Multiplication Inversion Buffer Interpolation Collector Gate Sampler	
	Calibration		Hand–eye calibration Absolute orientation Tip calibration	
	Fusion		Kalman Filter Functional fusion	
	Persistence	Player calibration reader		Recorder calibration Writer
	Network	Network source		Network Sink
	Application	Application Push Source Application Pull Source		Application Push Sink Application Pull Sink X3D object Background image

[2] A comprehensive reference is provided at http://campar.in.tum.de/UbiTrack/WebHome

13.2.4 SRG Design Activities

Pattern modeling consists of three major activities:

- **A1: Description of the tracking environment** All mobile and stationary sensors and all real and virtual objects are identified. Their known or tracked spatial relationships to one another are described. This activity mainly uses base patterns.
- **A2: Deduction of indirect spatial relationships** Full patterns are applied to suitable parts of an SRG either by an automatic pattern matching process or interactively by the AR-engineer.
- **A3: Definition of the runtime interface to the application** On the basis of query patterns, application interface(s) are inserted into the SRG.

trackman can assist AR-engineers in generating SRGs for a given tracking environment (A1 and A3). Ubitrack can use pattern matching techniques to automatically derive a DFG from a given SRG [11, 19] (A2). AR-engineers can influence the creation of DFGs manually in trackman, supporting requirements R2 and R4 (A2). The interactive variants of these activities are described in the subsequent sections.

13.3 trackman: Interactive Modeling of Spatial Relationships

trackman is a configuration and monitoring tool for tracking setups. It has a graphical interface, showing the current configuration of a setup in terms of both SRG and DFG. It also provides interactive means to access all patterns that are known to the Ubitrack runtime system and to integrate them into the current configuration.

13.3.1 System Architecture

In order to keep trackman independent from Ubitrack development and to ensure its compatibility with upcoming patterns, it was designed as a lightweight and generic tool. Architecturally, it is organized as a Ubitrack application.

trackman does not have special knowledge of patterns but rather imports the current set of available patterns from external description files that come with the Ubitrack runtime library. The description language is based on the UTQL[3] data exchange format [18]. In addition to the mere graph structure of the patterns, it also allows to specify important meta information. Type information for node/edge/pattern attributes (see Section 13.2.1.2 for the most important ones) as well as pattern documentation has to be provided. The resulting *pattern template specification language* XML schema[4] allows for the formal description of

[3]http://ar.in.tum.de/static/files/ubitrack/utql/utql.xsd

[4]http://ar.in.tum.de/static/files/ubitrack/utql/utql_templates.xsd, http://ar.in.tum.de/static/files/ubitrack/utql/utql_types.xsd

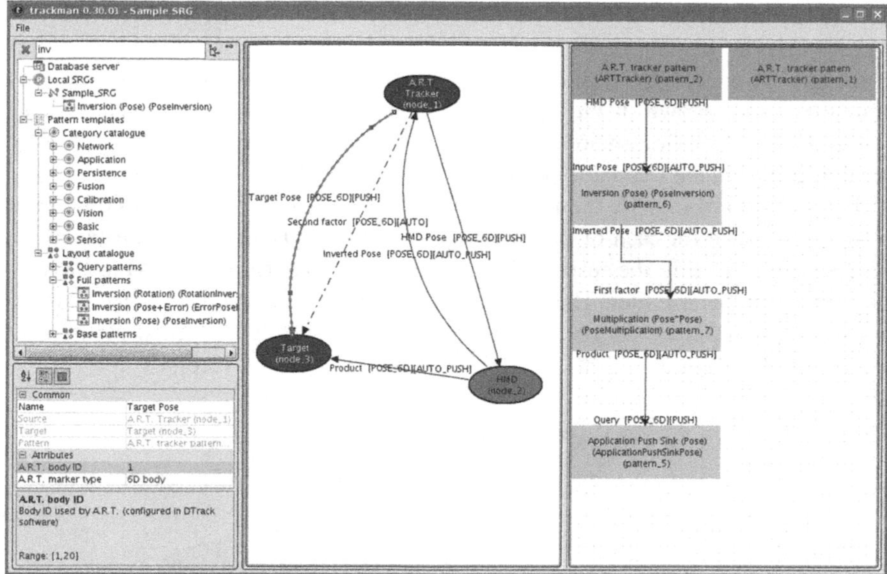

Fig. 13.5 The *trackman* graphical modeling tool for spatial relationship graphs

available patterns. trackman uses the meta information to allow for convenient configuration of node, edge, and pattern attributes in its property editor and to display documentation to the user, as can be seen in Fig. 13.5.

13.3.2 Graphical Layout

Figure 13.5 presents a screen dump of trackman showing the interactive construction of the SRG and DFG of Figs. 13.1 and 13.2. The tree on the left shows excerpts of the list of all patterns, accessible with respect to both semantic and structural (layout) categories. Below, the property editor allows to inspect and edit settings associated with the selected node, edge, or pattern. On the top left, a search facility allows the AR-engineer to restrict the displayed elements in the tree to only those patterns that contain all specified strings.

The central area is tiled, showing the current SRG and/or the DFG. In the DFG pane on the right, data sources (corresponding to base patterns, green) are the uppermost components, followed by intermediate computational units (full patterns, cyan), and finally the lowermost data sinks (query patterns, orange). The latter ones represent interfaces to applications. AR-engineers can alter the tracking setup in the SRG window. Resulting updates are automatically brought to the DFG window. At intermediate stages of the configuration process, not all nodes in the DFG window need to be integrated into the data flow network. For example, the right green node in Fig. 13.5 has not yet been connected to other modules.

13.3.3 Interactive SRG Generation

Starting with an empty work area in trackman, we use base and query patterns similar to those shown in Fig. 13.4 to describe the directly existing spatial relationships in the tracking environment and the application requests. To this end, they are dragged from the tree view on the left to the SRG editing workspace.

For the SRG in Fig. 13.1a, the A.R.T. Tracker pattern is dragged twice into the work area – once for each of the two targets. Names, IDs, and other attributes are modified by selecting the respective node, edge, or pattern and applying the settings in the property editor. The query pattern Application Sink is dragged into the workspace to describe the request that an edge be provided which describes the spatial relationship between the HMD and the target (see Fig. 13.6).

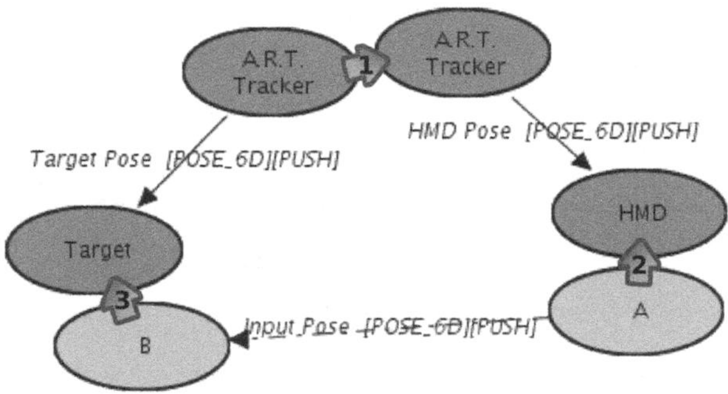

Fig. 13.6 Identification of coordinate systems via node unification. The indicated unification steps result in the SRG shown in Fig. 13.1a.

Using the *node unification* interaction scheme, all three patterns can be merged to form a single graph. To express that two nodes from different patterns are identical in the SRG, AR-engineers can drag one node on top of the other one. As a result of this operation, the subgraphs are merged at this node. Node unification can be applied to all combinations of input and/or output nodes. Nodes that result from unification of at least two output nodes are shown darker than normal output nodes and with a white label. Nodes within a single pattern cannot be unified (principle of pattern atomicity). Figure 13.6 shows the node unification steps which lead to the SRG shown in Fig. 13.1a.

13.3.4 Interactive Deduction of Spatial Relationships

Another interaction scheme is needed to let AR-engineers specify which operations should be applied to the tracking data such that additional spatial relationships can be derived. To this end, full patterns have to be integrated into the SRG, thereby adding further (deduced) edges in terms of their output edges.

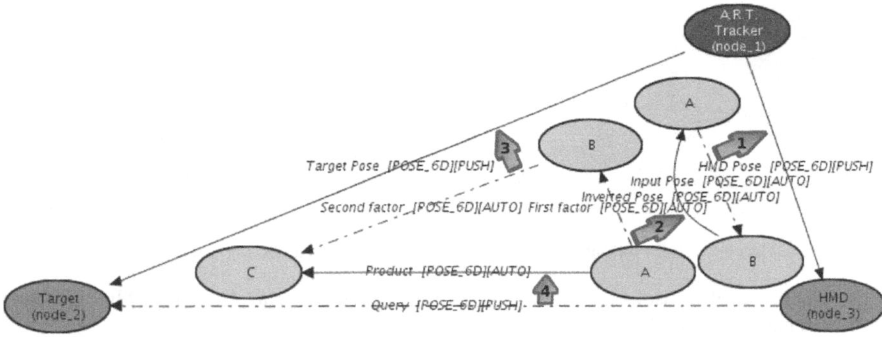

Fig. 13.7 Identification of data input and output of patterns via edge matching. The indicated matching steps result in the SRG shown in Fig. 13.1b

By *edge matching*, an edge from the input section of a new pattern is matched against an edge that exists already in the SRG or that is part of the output section of another pattern. The operation also immediately updates the corresponding DFG, linking the input of the computational unit with the output of another component.

The edge matching operation is performed by selecting the two edges, and then invoking the match operation from the menu. Both edges must have the same edge characteristics (according to Section 13.2.1) and illegal matchings are inhibited.

Edge-matching implies node unification on the source and sink nodes, respectively, if necessary. Edges belonging to the same pattern cannot be matched (again due to pattern atomicity). The edge-matching steps which lead to the SRG shown in Fig. 13.1b are depicted in Fig. 13.7.

trackman supports the analysis of synchronization issues. For many full patterns, it can perform the recursive propagation of synchronization mode flags on-the-fly (according to Section 13.2.3. For other full and query patterns that only allow for a specific constellation of mode flags, still a consistency check can be performed. Edge matchings with incompatible sync flags are inhibited. The conflict can be resolved manually by converting some push edges to pull mode.

13.3.5 More Modeling Functionality

With node unification and edge matching, SRGs can be constructed from scratch. Additional functionality is needed when dealing with existing SRGs. This is important for the maintenance of existing setups (R4) and also to recover from modeling mistakes. Therefore, trackman also provides the following interaction schemes.

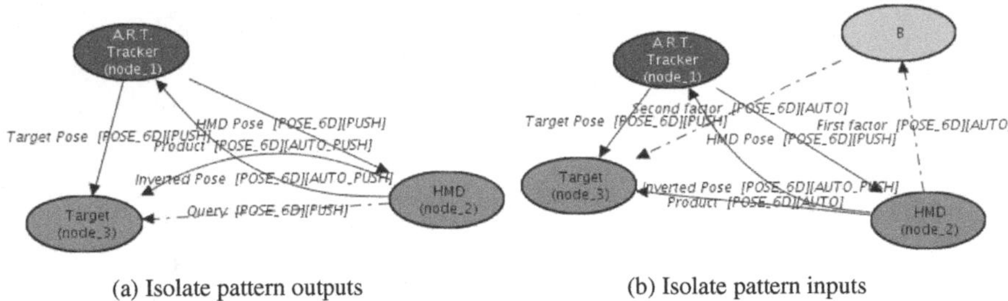

(a) Isolate pattern outputs

(b) Isolate pattern inputs

Fig. 13.8 Result of the isolate pattern output and input operations, invoked on the Multiplication pattern contained in Fig. 13.1b

- **Isolate Pattern Outputs**: trackman is able to separate the output edges of the pattern from connected nodes/edges in the input section of other patterns. The effect of this operation is shown in Fig. 13.8a. The output edge of the Multiplication pattern contained in the sample SRG (Fig. 13.1b) is isolated from matched input edges. Concretely, the matching step 4 of Fig. 13.7 is revoked.
- **Isolate Pattern Inputs**: To complement the previous scheme, trackman is also able to separate the input edges of a pattern from its context, effectively annulling all dependencies between these input edges and corresponding output nodes/edges of other patterns. Invoking this operation on the same Multiplication pattern results in Fig. 13.8b. The edge-matching steps 2 and 3 as depicted in Fig. 13.7 are revoked. This implies also the separation of those input nodes that are neither source nor sink of an output edge of the pattern, such as node "B" of the Multiplication pattern.
- **Isolate Entire Pattern**: This operation combines the two operations above and brings the pattern back to its atomic form.
- **Delete Pattern**: The pattern is removed from the current SRG. It does not matter whether the pattern was integrated in some larger SRG structure or existed in its atomic form. In the former case, an isolate pattern step is implicitly performed first.
- **Hide Pattern**: Parts of the SRG are hidden to provide an abstracted, clearer view of the SRG in the editor window. trackman provides this functionality on a per-pattern basis. This helps to maintain clarity in large SRGs such as the one shown in Fig. 13.12 which consists of approximately 100 patterns.

13.3.6 Ordering of Design Activities

It is up to the AR-engineer to decide about a suitable design approach. Patterns may be added to the SRG in any sequence. Furthermore, patterns may be combined using the node unification and edge-matching metaphors in any sequence. The output edge of a selected pattern may therefore be associated with a subsequent input edge even though it is currently unclear how the output edge can be deduced since the input edges of that pattern have not been matched yet. A valid DFG, of course, requires all input edges to have been matched properly.

The design process may therefore be started either with the environment, some basic fusion algorithm, or also the application interface. The first case might also be denoted as a *bottom-up approach* since the AR-engineer starts with physical entities (A1) and refines information step by step (A2), resulting in an application-level (A3) piece of information. In the opposite *top-down approach* the engineer could start with the application interface (A3) and drill down through various algorithms (A2) to finally reach real-world sensors and objects (A1). For clarification, going *up* according to the degree of abstraction from raw sensor measurements toward application-level data comes along with going *down* in the data flow from data sources to data sinks.

13.4 Advanced Interactive Modeling Concepts

This section describes two techniques which can further ease the SRG modeling process. Semi-automatic modeling automates simple operations and lets the user focus on the essential deduction steps. Meta patterns provide best-practice solutions to well-known problems, reducing the modeling problem to the addition of a few patterns only. Both techniques significantly reduce the amount of modeling operations that have to be performed manually.

13.4.1 Semi-automatic Modeling

Manual pattern matching can become a very tedious procedure. In more complex setups, the amount of patterns to be integrated in the SRG increases quickly. A concatenation of n edges requires $[n-1]$ applications of the Multiplication pattern. In addition to that, some edges have to be inverted. In practice, approximately half of all matchings of full patterns fall upon the Inversion and Multiplication patterns (e.g., 22 out of 42 in Fig. 13.12). Automatic pattern matching can relieve the user from the trivial aspects of these and other modeling operations. Figure 13.9 depicts

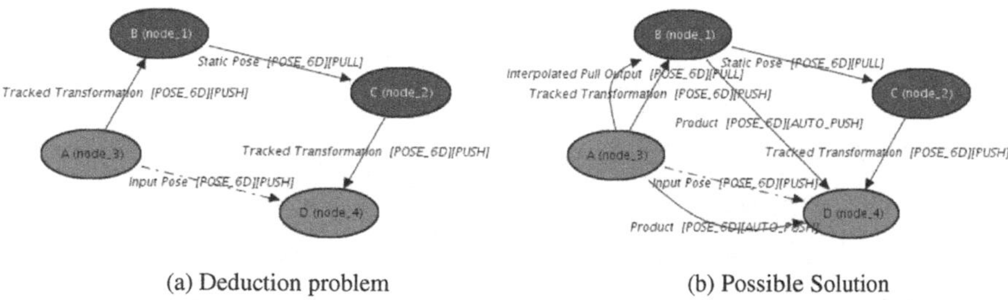

(a) Deduction problem (b) Possible Solution

Fig. 13.9 Typical modeling situation which requires many applications of full patterns

a typical modeling situation. The transitive transformation from A to D shall be deduced using known transformations from A to B, B to C, and C to D, respectively. Three full patterns are necessary to solve this simple problem and overall six solutions exist, one of which is shown in Fig. 13.9b. It first deduces a transitive transformation from B to D (Multiplication), then converts the mode of transformation A to B from push to pull, and finally concatenates both to the desired result.

On the opposite side of options, fully automatic pattern matching is also offered by Ubitrack [11]. Yet it has its limitations in selecting optimal patterns for every purpose. It is not easy to ensure that the chosen deduction steps meet the AR-engineer's notion of the solution. Particularly the many push/pull variations may require fine-tuning by the engineer, once the overall setup has been configured. Assuming that the two tracked edges in Fig. 13.9 offer comparable tracking quality at different frequencies, the position of the Interpolation influences the resulting quality and one would want to interpolate between measurements of the faster tracker. Differing tracking qualities between both trackers further complicates the consideration.

To exploit the best of both options, trackman provides semi-automatic modeling facilities. During manual operations, AR-engineers can enable automatic pattern matching for individual groups of patterns (e.g., for all variations of the Multiplication pattern or the Inversion pattern) while keeping other, more specialized patterns under strict manual control.

The automatic pattern matcher can be invoked in two ways. The first is to select the source and then the sink node of the transformation to be deduced and then to activate the matcher in the menu. The second method is to first insert a query pattern by unifying its source and sink nodes and then invoke the matcher on the corresponding input edge.

13.4.2 Meta Patterns

Another approach to simplify the modeling task is to provide template solutions for common, recurring problems in terms of *meta patterns*. Basically, they are incomplete SRGs and contain only those patterns that belong to the reusable core of the solution. Interchangeable parts such as the specification of a certain tracker are left open. A meta pattern can be embedded into an SRG like any other pattern.

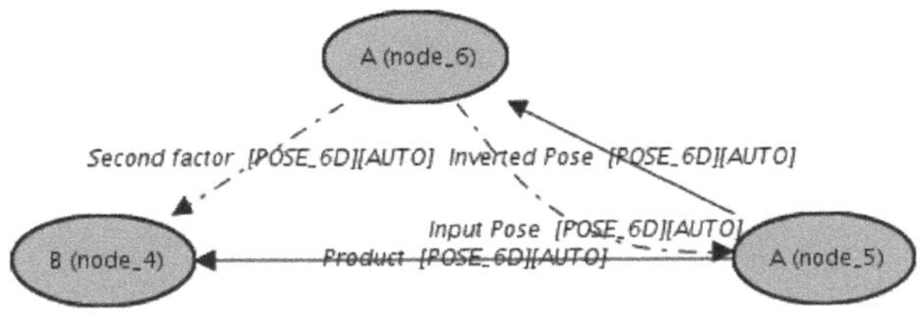

Fig. 13.10 Meta pattern describing the principal layout and application interface of the sample SRG in Fig. 13.1b

To illustrate the idea behind meta patterns, Fig. 13.10 shows the sample SRG from Fig. 13.1b with all base patterns removed, i.e., nodes are gray rather than black (see also Fig. 13.8). This meta pattern still conveys the basic structure of the sample application, with HMD and target being tracked by a single tracking system, as well as the application interface. It can be completed by simply matching an arbitrary tracker pattern (providing a push measurement of type 6 DoF pose) twice with the input edges of the meta pattern in order to obtain a valid data flow description again.

13.5 Tools to Analyze and to Interact with Data Flows

Sections 13.3 and 13.4 dealt with SRG modeling, showing how DFGs can be provided to applications using trackman. In addition to creating such data flows, a major task of AR-engineers involves the calibration of sensors and the registration of objects, i.e., the careful estimation of fixed spatial relationships between groups of sensors and/or objects. For example, in multi-sensor setups, the poses of all stationary sensors have to be determined. Similarly, groups of mobile sensors and objects that move together as a package need to describe their fixed spatial relationships to one another. AR-engineers need to measure these static relationships accurately during configuration time. Such relationships are represented by static edges in the SRG.

During daily use of the tracking setup, the engineers further have to monitor these relationships to determine whether changes due to wear and tear cause systematic errors that require re-registrations. Another concern is tracking accuracy. It is critical to be able to continuously evaluate a given sensor setup according to its current precision and accuracy [2] such that applications can deal appropriately with different levels of tracking quality.

This section presents the tools provided by trackman and Ubitrack to support these needs. In this respect, trackman behaves like any other application using Ubitrack. This implies that, in contradiction to Section 13.3.1, trackman needs to know some interface patterns that allow him to interact with the data flow. The implementation of this functionality in trackman still has a preliminary status. Yet, it already proved to be useful for several scenarios, e.g., [12, 13].

13.5.1 Tools for Calibration and Registration

trackman provides a generic means to carry out calibration procedures including the necessary user interactions. As a matter of principle, calibration does not differ from any other tracking application; it can be described fully by SRGs. They can be directly instantiated in trackman so that no additional implementation is necessary to solve the calibration problem.

In a typical calibration process, the AR-engineer has to move an object that is tracked by sensors in the environment. The tracking data of each sensor are stored, and the relative pose of the sensors can be determined from these data sets. Other processes require AR-engineers to align several objects (e.g., for HMD calibration) or to point with the tip of a tracked pointer at a specified location in the world. In both cases, the engineer has to signal when he is ready to take a measurement. When enough measurements are selected, the pose of the object can be registered.

Ubitrack provides a collection of patterns for state-of-the-art registration and calibration algorithms [17], among which are solutions for the absolute orientation [10], hand–eye calibration [25], and tip calibration (cf. Table 13.1). These patterns need to be embedded into an SRG context that supports capturing and recording of data as well as user interactions such as a button press event, as needed by the calibration task. trackman provides a generic user interface for this purpose.

When AR-engineers calibrate or register objects, tracking measurements are streaming (pushed) from one or more sensors into the DFN. They can be conditioned in three different ways before being passed to the registration or calibration algorithm:

- **Continuous Measurements**: Measurements are continuously collected. They can be either directly fed into the calibration algorithm or stored using the Collector and Calibration Writer patterns (cf. Table 13.1).
- **Discrete Measurements**: Samples are collected at regular time intervals. For this purpose, the collection mechanism for continuous measurements is extended by adding the Buffer (or another interpolation component) and Sampler components upstream in the data flow. The desired frequency can be specified as an attribute of the Sampler component.
- **User-Triggered Measurements**: Instead of sampling at regular time intervals, measurements are taken when the user presses a button. This asynchronous event triggers a gate to accept a suitable tracking measurement (either shortly before or after the button event). Typically, a number of user-triggered measurements, e.g., using calibration points, are collected. This setup uses the Gate pattern in combination with an Application Push Source pattern (for button events) upstream in the data flow. A button is provided by trackman to interact with the Application Push Source component.

Some calibrations (such as tip calibration or registering a tracker coordinate frame with a known CAD model) just need measurements from one tracking modality as input. Data can then flow directly from the data collection components to the parameter estimation components. This allows for *online incremental parameter estimation* as soon as the minimal number of measurements is provided. If desired, more measurements can be taken to incrementally improve the registration until the residual error is considered to be small enough.

In many calibration and registration processes, however, data streams of different trackers need to be associated with one another to obtain pairs of corresponding measurements. There are mainly two interaction methods for AR-engineers to establish such correspondences between measurements from several trackers:

- Use **simultaneous measurements** of the same entity, e.g., a pointing device, having the same time stamp. Both measurements can then be directly fed into the calibration pattern and one SRG is still sufficient to describe the entire calibration. This probably means running two tracking systems in parallel. Balancing the timestamps using interpolation might be necessary if the trackers are not synchronized in hardware. Using this solution, we can still benefit from online incremental parameter estimation.
- Exactly **reproduce the measurement**. This corresponds, for example, to conducting corresponding measurements (e.g., a set of points in space) sequentially using two different tracking systems. Thus, two SRGs are needed for the whole calibration step. The first SRG aggregates a list of measurements made by tracking modality A and stores it in a file (see above). In a second SRG, the actual calibration takes place, using both measurements from the file via the Calibration Reader pattern and measurements from tracking modality B. This method does not work well with the first and second methods of recording measurements described above since it is rather difficult to exactly reproduce a complete trajectory of an object, except if you have a robot at your disposal. Therefore, sets of corresponding pairs of measurements often have to be acquired manually.

Both of these approaches can be assembled from the meta patterns that gather continuous, discrete, or user-triggered data streams. At yet a higher level, they can be flexibly combined (loaded) with patterns to execute the mathematical calibration or registration algorithms. Altogether, trackman and Ubitrack thus provide a very flexible runtime environment within which different data collection routines can be bundled with mathematical algorithms as needed to quickly determine static relationships between objects and/or sensors in tracking environments. AR-engineers can perform this task in combination with their efforts toward configuring descriptions (SRGs and DFGs) of the tracking environment they are in charge of. They can also revisit and anew static spatial relationships during daily use whenever this deems necessary – as described next.

13.5.2 Tools for Online Analysis of Tracking Environments

The functionality provided in trackman for the direct instantiation of data flows is useful not only for registration steps but also for the live evaluation of application data flows and the comparison of different alternatives against a trusted reference When trackman is running during the daily use of a tracking environment, it can continuously audit any spatial relationship between some nodes A and B by issuing an Application Push Sink request with respect to that spatial relationship (dashed edge in Fig. 13.1a). Thus, trackman will be informed immediately of any new measurements for that edge. Measurements to be compared against the reference value are interfaced to trackman via the Application Pull Sink component; i.e., whenever a new reference measurement is pushed upon the application, alternative measurements of the same type w.r.t. other sensors are pulled. With this setup, it is possible to

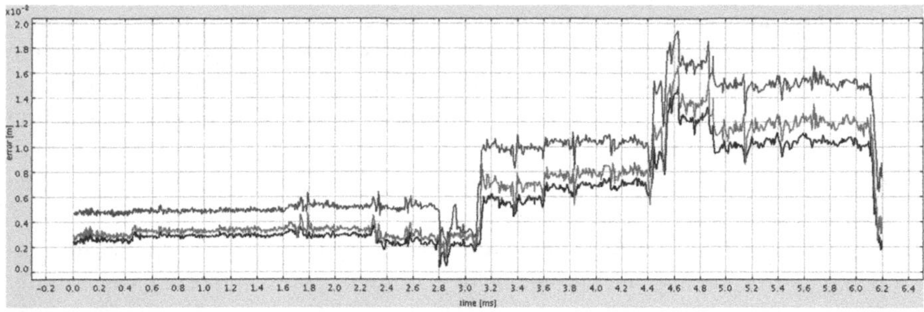

Fig. 13.11 Exemplary comparison plot showing deviations between four alternative measurements

observe in real time the deviations of position and orientation tracking, as estimated by the alternative data flows.

This online measurement tool has been very helpful in investigating tracking setups for several industrial AR applications [13, 12, 13]. Figure 13.11 shows an exemplary comparison. The *x*-axis of the plot represents time. The *y*-axis represents positional deviations (Euclidean distance) of three alternative tracking data flows relative to the reference data flow. Similarly, orientational deviations can be plotted.

13.6 Application Examples

trackman is actively used in our group for modeling and evaluation of tracking environments. Use cases range from rapid prototyping of small demo setups up to large-scale evaluations. We also used trackman for the evaluation of an indirect tracking setup [13, 12]. It consists of a static camera setup mounted to the ceiling of a room as well as a mobile stereo camera setup on a tripod which is tracked by the static setup. The mobile setup can be placed on-the-fly such that tracking is also possible in areas that are hidden from the static cameras. One might expect a strong degradation of tracking quality of the indirect tracking approach, as compared to direct tracking using only the cameras mounted to the ceiling. Our evaluation shows that the main source of error in this setup is the systematically wrong detection of the orientation of the mobile setup which propagates to large positional errors in the region of interest. The evaluation furthermore shows that by an appropriate error correction, indirect tracking can be almost as good as direct tracking. The used correction mechanism is based on common reference points in the scene which can be seen by both tracking systems.

At the moment, we are integrating a Faro arm[5] as a third tracking system, giving us reliable 3D point measurements as a reference. The corresponding SRG is depicted in Fig. 13.12. It consists of approximately 100 patterns whereas most of

---

[5]FARO Technologies Inc.

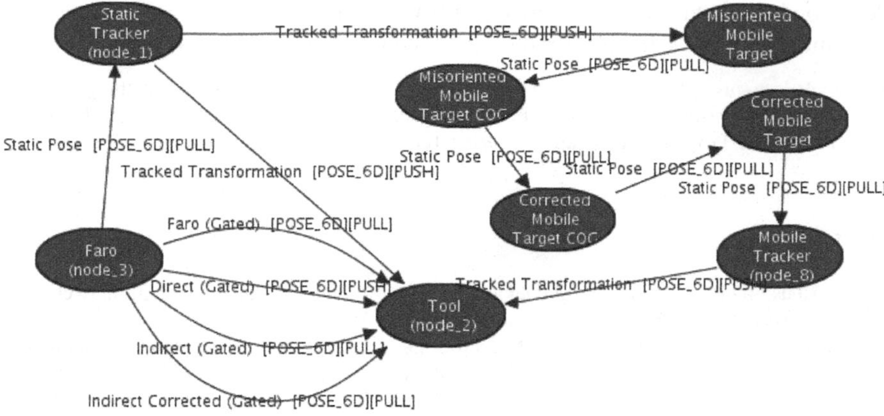

Fig. 13.12 SRG for comparison of accuracies resulting from different tracking approaches

them are hidden. It contains two static transformations that have to be calibrated, one between the "Mobile Target" and the "Mobile Tracker" and the other between the "Faro" node and the "Static Tracker" node. Both calibrations and the comparison itself were carried out completely in trackman, without support of additional tools, using just the methods described in Sections 13.5.1 and 13.5.2. The plot shown in Fig. 13.11 results from this comparison. Four edges exist between the "Faro" and "Tool" nodes, resulting in three deviations plotted relative to the reference measurement.

13.7 Conclusion

In Section 13.1.1, requirements on a tracking infrastructure have been stated. The "performance" requirement (R2) is clearly met by using the Ubitrack library. It provides state-of-the-art algorithms that can be linked and executed very efficiently. The other three requirements are somewhat interdependent. In a strict sense, "calibration" (R3) and "maintainability" (R4) are implications of the "separation of tracking from applications" (R1) requirement. The described graphical pattern modeling approach contributes a lot to the feasibility of these goals. Together with semi-automatic modeling and the meta-pattern concept, the preparation of appropriate application data flows is simplified a lot. At the same time, less expert knowledge is needed, due to the high-level graphical description and exclusion of semantically wrong data flows. Altogether, this has the potential to lower the inhibition threshold for the acquisition and productive operation of a tracking infrastructure. However, to achieve real separation of tracking from applications, tools to aid in administrative tasks are also needed. We showed the principal feasibility of generic solutions for the essential calibration and error analysis tasks. Nevertheless, there is still room for improvements, e.g., by integrating consistency checks and outlier detection into calibration procedures, by providing a more realistic 3D visualization of spatial coherences and other more intuitive operational concepts.

Acknowledgments This work was supported by the Bayerische Forschungsstiftung (project trackframe, AZ-653-05) and the PRESENCCIA Integrated Project funded under the European Sixth Framework Program, Future and Emerging Technologies (FET) (contract no. 27731).

References

1. J. Albus. 4D/RCS: a reference model architecture for intelligent unmanned ground vehicles. In *Proceedings of SPIE*, volume 4715, page 303. SPIE, 2002.
2. M. Bauer, M. Schlegel, D. Pustka, N. Navab, and G. Klinker. Predicting and estimating the accuracy of vision-based optical tracking systems. In *Proceedings of the IEEE International Symposium on Mixed and Augmented Reality (ISMAR)*, Santa Barbara, USA, October 2006.
3. B. Becker, M. Huber, and G. Klinker. Utilizing RFIDs for location aware computing. In *Proceedings of the 5th International Conference on Ubiquitous Intelligence and Computing (UIC'08)*, Oslo, Norway, 2008.
4. J. Bouchet, L. Nigay, and T. Ganille. ICARE software components for rapidly developing multimodal interfaces.In *Proceedings of the 6th International Conference on Multimodal Interfaces*, pages 251–258. ACM New York, USA, 2004.
5. E. Coelho, B. MacIntyre, and S. Julier. OSGAR: A scene graph with uncertain transformations. In *International Symposium on Mixed and Augmented Reality (ISMAR 2004)*, pages 6–15, 2004.
6. M. Darms, P. Rybski, C. Urmson, C. Inc, and M. Aubur. Hills. Classification and tracking of dynamic objects with multiple sensors for autonomous driving in urban environments. In *Intelligent Vehicles Symposium, 2008 IEEE*, pages 1197–1202, 2008.
7. E. D. Dickmanns. *Dynamic Vision for Perception and Control of Motion.* Springer Verlag, Berlin, 2007.
8. P. Dragicevic and J. Fekete. Input device selection and interaction configuration with ICON. In *People and Computer XV-Interaction Without Frontier (Joint proceedings of HCI 2001 and IHM 2001)*, pages 543–448, 2001.
9. F. Echtler, M. Huber, D. Pustka, P. Keitler, and G. Klinker. Splitting the scene graph - using spatial relationship graphs instead of scene graphs in augmented reality. In *Proceedings of the 3rd International Conference on Computer Graphics Theory and Applications (GRAPP)*, January. 2008.
10. B. Horn, H. Hilden, and S. Negahdaripour. Closed-form solution of absolute orientation using unit quaternions. *Journal of the Optical Society of America A*, 4(4):629–642, 1987.
11. M. Huber, D. Pustka, P. Keitler, E. Florian, and G. Klinker. A system architecture for ubiquitous tracking environments. In *Proceedings of the 6th International Symposium on Mixed and Augmented Reality (ISMAR '07)*, November 2007.
12. P. Keitler, M. Schlegel, and G. Klinker. Indirect tracking for on-the-fly elimination of occlusion problems. *Demonstration at IEEE International Symposium on Mixed and Augmented Reality (ISMAR '08)*, September 2008.
13. P. Keitler, M. Schlegel, and G. Klinker. Indirect tracking to reduce occlusion problems. In *Advances in Visual Computing, Fourth International Symposium, ISVC 2008 Las Vegas, USA, December 1–3*, volume 5359(2) of *Lecture Notes in Computer Science*, pages 224–235, Springer Berlin, 2008.
14. J. Newman, A. Bornik, D. Pustka, F. Echtler, M. Huber, D. Schmalstieg, and G. Klinker. Tracking for distributed mixed reality environments. In *Workshop on Trends and Issues in Tracking for Virtual Environments at the IEEE Virtual Reality Conference (VR '07)*, March 2007.

15. J. Newman, M. Wagner, M. Bauer, A. MacWilliams, T. Pintaric, D. Beyer, D. Pustka, F. Strasser, D. Schmalstieg, and G. Klinker. Ubiquitous tracking for augmented reality. In *Proceedings of the IEEE International Symposium on Mixed and Augmented Reality (ISMAR '04)*, Arlington, USA, November 2004.
16. D. Pustka. Construction of data flow networks for augmented reality applications. In *Proceedings of the Dritter Workshop Virtuelle und Erweiterte Realität der GI-Fachgruppe VR/AR*, Koblenz, Germany, September 2006.
17. D. Pustka, M. Huber, M. Bauer, and G. Klinker. Spatial relationship patterns: Elements of reusable tracking and calibration systems. In *Proceedings of the IEEE International Symposium on Mixed and Augmented Reality (ISMAR '06)*, October 2006.
18. D. Pustka, M. Huber, F. Echtler, and P. Keitler. UTQL: The Ubiquitous Tracking Query Language v1.0. Technical Report TUM-I0718, Institut für Informatik, Technische Universität München, 2007.
19. D. Pustka and G. Klinker. Integrating gyroscopes into ubiquitous tracking environments. In *Proceedings of the IEEE International Symposium on Mixed and Augmented Reality (ISMAR '08)*, September 2008.
20. G. Reitmayr and D. Schmalstieg. An open software architecture for virtual reality interaction. In *Proceedings of the ACM Symposium on Virtual Reality Software and Technology*, pages 47–54. ACM New York, USA, 2001.
21. M. Serrano, D. Juras, and L. Nigay. A three-dimensional characterization space of software components for rapidly developing multimodal interfaces. In *Proceedings of the 10th International Conference on Multimodal Interfaces*, pages 149–156. ACM New York, USA, 2008.
22. P. Strauss and R. Carey. An object-oriented 3D graphics toolkit. *Computer Graphics*, 26(2):341–349, July 1992. Siggraph '92.
23. R. M. Taylor, T. C. Hudson, A. Seeger, H. Weber, J. Juliano, and A. T. Helser. Vrpn: a device-independent, network-transparent vr peripheral system. In *Proceedings of the ACM Symposium on Virtual Reality Software and Technology*, pages 55–61. ACM Press, New York, USA, 2001.
24. S. Thrun, W. Burgard, and D. Fox. *Probabilistic Robotics (Intelligent Robotics and Autonomous Agents)*. MIT press, Cambridge, Massachusetts, USA, 2005.
25. R. Tsai and R. Lenz. Real time versatile robotics hand/eye calibration using 3D machine vision. In *IEEE International Conference on Robotics and Automation*, volum. 1, pages 554–561, 1988.
26. G. Welch and E. Foxlin. Motion tracking: No silver bullet, but a respectable arsenal. *IEEE Computer Graphics and Applications*, pages 24–38, 2002.

Chapter 14
Authoring Immersive Mixed Reality Experiences

Jan M.V. Misker and Jelle van der Ster

Abstract Creating a mixed reality experience is a complicated endeavour. From our practice as a media lab in the artistic domain we found that engineering is "only" a first step in creating a mixed reality experience. Designing the appearance and directing the user experience are equally important for creating an engaging, immersive experience. We found that mixed reality artworks provide a very good test bed for studying these topics. This chapter details three steps required for authoring mixed reality experiences: engineering, designing and directing. We will describe a platform (VGE) for creating mixed reality environments that incorporates these steps. A case study (EI4) is presented in which this platform was used to not only engineer the system, but in which an artist was given the freedom to explore the artistic merits of mixed reality as an artistic medium, which involved areas such as the look and feel, multimodal experience and interaction, immersion as a subjective emotion and game play scenarios.

Keywords Art · Mixed reality · Augmented reality · Authoring · Design tools · Immersion

14.1 Introduction

From a technical perspective the mixed reality concept is clearly becoming a possibility. Now is the time to pay more attention to making the technology accessible to a wider user group by offering mixed reality environments authoring tools to content creators. Artists and designers are among the key content creators we have identified. They play an important role in setting the standards for the immersive quality of a mixed reality environment, because they are trained to work with audiences

---

J.M.V. Misker (✉)
V2_ Institute for the Unstable Media, Rotterdam, The Netherlands
e-mail: jan@v2.nl

E. Dubois et al. (eds.), *The Engineering of Mixed Reality Systems*, Human-Computer Interaction Series, DOI 10.1007/978-1-84882-733-2_14,

and to incorporate participant's feedback throughout the whole design process. An extensive background on mixed reality in the arts is presented in Section 14.2.

In Section 14.4 the V2_Game Engine (VGE) is described, the platform we developed to engineer and author mixed reality environments. Furthermore, we summarise various techniques that, when implemented properly, can have a very large impact on the user experience.

We conclude with recommendations that represent the outcome of several case studies from our own practice. Our recommendations take the current technical state of affairs, including its shortcomings, as a given; in Sections 14.4.2 and 14.4.3 we suggest workarounds where needed in order to focus on the design issues and user experiences.

14.1.1 Definitions and Assumptions

In this section we explain some of the terminology and assumptions that are used throughout the chapter.

14.1.1.1 Mixed Reality

We define mixed reality as the mix of virtual content, visual or auditory, with the real world. The virtual content is created in such a way that it could be perceived as if it was real, e.g. contrary to applications in which information is overlaid using text or lines.

The visual virtual content can be projected over a video of the real world or on transparent displays, but in either case the virtual coordinate system is fixed with respect to the real-world coordinate system.

14.1.1.2 Immersion

In this context we define *immersion* as the (subjective) believability or engagement of the mix between real and virtual, combined with (objective) precision of measuring user state and (subjective + objective) visual similarity of real and virtual objects.

14.1.1.3 Absolute vs. Relative Coordinate Systems

The virtual content in mixed reality environments can be positioned absolutely or relatively with respect to the real world. Relative positioning means that virtual objects are aligned to markers, often 2D barcodes, although some projects are using computer vision to automatically recognise features in the real world to align and position the virtual objects [8]. A downside of this approach is that the markers or features have to be visible to a camera at all times and that the overlay of virtual content is done on the camera image. It is quite difficult to scale this approach to more viewpoints, because the coordinate systems of the different viewpoints all have to be aligned.

In an absolutely positioned system, sensors are used to fix the virtual coordinate system to the real world. This requires a multitude of sensors, as the positioning sensors often cannot be used for measuring orientation. The major benefit is that these systems can be made very robust, especially when fusing different sensor streams. A downside is that there needs to be an absolute reference coordinate system, usually "the world".

In our system and for our applications we chose to focus on creating an absolutely aligned coordinate system because it allows for more versatile systems; different types of mixed reality environments and perspectives can be explored for its artistic merits.

14.2 Background: Mixed Reality Environments in the Arts

Artistic use of mixed reality environments is an interesting application domain because the goal of an artwork is to change the perspective of the user/audience/spectator, by giving them a new experience. From a user-centred perspective it is obvious that the focus of the mixed reality environment is not on technology but on immersing the user or spectator in a mix of real and virtual worlds. We have created several mixed reality projects, which will be described in more detail.

14.2.1 Motivation for Using Mixed Reality in the Arts

Many artistic concepts revolve around realistic alternative realities, ranging from the creation of beautiful utopian worlds to making horrific confronting scenarios (refs). Whichever the artistic concept is, in general, the experience envisioned by the artist benefits from a high level of realism for the user (i.e. spectator). Such realism can be achieved by allowing the same sensory–motor relations to exist between the user and the alternative reality, as those which exist between a user and the real world.

In this light, mixed reality technology, when implemented successfully, provides the favoured solution, because the sensory–motor relations we use to perceive the real world can also be used to perceive the alternative reality. First of all because the alternative reality partly consists of real-world, real-time images. Second, the sensory changes resulting from a user's interaction with the virtual elements in the alternative reality are carefully modelled on those that would occur in the real world [18, 19].

14.2.2 Examples of Mixed Reality in the Arts

14.2.2.1 Example: Markerless Magic Books

The Haunted Book [15] is an artwork that relies on recent computer vision and augmented reality techniques to animate the illustrations of poetry books. Because there is no need for markers, they can achieve seamless integration of real and virtual elements to create the desired atmosphere. The visualisation is done on a computer screen to avoid head-mounted displays. The camera is hidden into a desk lamp for easing even more the spectator immersion. The work is the result of a collaboration between an artist and computer vision researchers.

14.2.2.2 Mixed Reality as a Presentation Medium

A noteworthy development is the increasing use of mixed reality techniques in museums. This makes it possible for the public to explore artworks in a new way, for example, by showing information overlaid on the work or by recreating a mixed reality copy that can be handled and touched in a very explorative manner. The museum context is used often in previous studies, but often mainly as a test bed for technological development [6]. Only recently has mixed reality started to be used outside of the scientific context for the improvements it can make to the museum visit, e.g. [12].

Another inspiring example of the use of mixed reality in a museum context is the installation *Sgraffito in 3D*,[1] produced by artist Joachim Rotteveel in collaboration with Wim van Eck and the AR Lab of the Royal Academy of Arts, The Hague. Sgraffito is an ancient decorative technique in which patterns are scratched into the wet clay. The artist has made this archaeological collection accessible in a new way using 3D visualisation and reconstruction techniques from the worlds of medicine and industry. Computed axial tomography (CAT) scans, as used in medicine, create a highly detailed 3D representation that serve as a basis for the visualisation and reconstruction using 3D printers. The collection is made accessible on the Internet and will even be cloned. The exhibition Sgraffito in 3D allowed the public to explore the process of recording, archiving and reconstruction for the first time, step by step. Video projections show the actual CAT scans. The virtual renderings enable visitors to view the objects from all angles. The workings of the 3D printer are demonstrated and the printed clones will compete with the hundred original Sgraffito objects in the exhibition.

14.2.2.3 Crossing Borders: Interactive Cinema

It should be noted that using and exploring a new medium is something that comes very natural to artists; one could argue that artists are on the forefront of finding innovative uses for new technology.

---

[1] http://www.sgraffito-in-3d.com/en/

An interesting recent development is the increasing use of interactive techniques to change the cinematic experience [2]. For example, in the BIBAP (Body in Bits and Pieces)[2] project a dance movie changes with respect to the viewers position in front of a webcam and the sound the viewer makes. We foresee that interactive cinema and mixed reality will merge sooner rather than later, opening up an entirely new usage domain.

14.3 Related Work: Authoring Tools

From the moment mixed reality evolved from a technology to a medium, researchers have stressed the need for properly designed authoring tools [10]. These tools would eliminate the technical difficulties and allow content designers to experiment with this new medium.

AMIRE was one of the earliest projects in which authoring for mixed reality environments was researched [1]. Within this project valuable design cycles and patterns to design mixed reality environments were proposed. However, the developed toolbox is mainly focused on marker-based augmented reality and has not been actively maintained.

DART is an elaborated mixed reality authoring tool creating a singular and unified toolbox primarily focusing on designers [11]. DART is in essence an extension of Macromedia Director, a media application that provides a graphical user interface to stage and score interactive programs. Programs can be created using the scripting language Lingo provided within Director. DART implements the ARToolKit[3] and a range of tracking sensors using VRPN[4] (virtual reality peripheral network) and interfaces them in Director. DART is closely interwoven with the design metaphors of Director and is designed to allow the users to design and create different mixed reality experiences. Images and content can be swapped, added and removed at run time. DART also includes some interesting design features. For instance it allows the designer to easily record and playback recorded data, e.g. video footage and movement of markers. The system has been constructed in such a way that the designer can easily switch between recorded and live data. Designers can work with this data to design mixed reality without mixed reality technology or having to move a marker or set up a camera frequently. Although DART provides an elegant and intuitive suite for editing mixed reality, we decided not to use it primarily because of the Shockwave 3D rendering engine. This engine does not provide the functionality and performance we desire for our applications.

Finally, existing mixed reality tools are primarily focused on creating mixed reality experiences that are based on relative alignment of a camera image with a virtual

---

[2] http://www.bibap.nl/

[3] http://www.hitl.washington.edu/artoolkit/

[4] http://www.cs.unc.edu/Research/vrpn/

image [5, 9]. Because we use an absolute coordinate system in our setup different design issues arise and need to be addressed.

14.4 Authoring Content for Mixed Reality Environments

We propose to distinguish three types of activities involved in authoring content for mixed reality environments.

- *Engineering* the underlying technology, which is included in this list because it provides crucial insight into the exact technical possibilities, e.g. the type and magnitude of position measurement errors.
- *Designing* the appearance of the real environment, virtual elements and the way they are mixed, as well as creating the sound.
- *Directing* the user experience, i.e. designing the game play elements and the activities a user/player can undertake when engaged in a mixed reality environment.

These activities can be compared to creating a movie or video game, for which many tools are available. However, these tools are not readily applicable to authoring content for mixed reality environments. For example, tools exist that allow an artist to mix video images with virtual images, e.g. Cycling '74 Max/MSP/Jitter[5] or Apple Final Cut Pro.[6] However, these are not designed to create complex game play scenarios or place a real-time generated 3D virtual object somewhere in 2D live streaming video image. There are tools that allow artists to design video games and create different game play scenarios, e.g. Blender[7] or Unity,[8] but these are focused on creating real-time 3D images and designing game play; they rarely incorporate streaming video images into this virtual world.

Even though mixed reality environments are becoming more accessible on a technological level, there are still many technical issues that have an immediate effect on the user experience. Artists and content designers should have a proper understanding of the technical limitations, but they should not have to fully understand them. The data recording and playback functionality of the DART system [11] is a good example of a user-friendly way to solve this issue. Currently no such functionality is included yet in our tool VGE, described in the following section.

14.4.1 Engineering and Authoring Platform: VGE

This section details the platform developed at V2_Lab for engineering and authoring of mixed reality environments.

[5] http://www.cycling74.com

[6] http://www.apple.com/nl/finalcutstudio/finalcutpro

[7] http://www.blender.org

[8] http://www.unity3d.com

14.4.1.1 Overall Architecture

During the earlier stages of our mixed reality environments development, the focus was on the technology needed for working prototypes, finding a balance between custom and off-the-shelf hardware and software tools. Based on our experiences in the case studies, we developed a more generic platform called V2_ Game Engine (VGE). We engineered the platform to enable artists and designers to create content for mixed reality environments.

On a technical level the platform allows for flexible combinations between the large amounts of components needed to realise mixed reality environments. We chose to work with as many readily available software libraries and hardware components as possible, enabling us to focus on the actual application within the scope of mixed reality. Figure 14.1 provides an overview of all components that are part of VGE.

The basis of VGE is the Ogre real-time 3D rendering engine.[9] We use Ogre to create the virtual 3D images that we want to place in our mixed reality environment. Next to Ogre we use OpenAL, the Bullet physics engine, SDL and several smaller libraries needed to control our sensors and cameras to create the final mixed reality result. Most of these available software libraries are written in C or C++, but in order to rapidly design programs and experiment with different aspects of these libraries we used Scheme as a scripting language to effectively glue these components together. Scheme wraps the various libraries and connects them in a very flexible manner, making it possible to change most aspects of the environment at run time. Not only parameters but also the actual routines being executed can be changed at run time. This allows for the engineers to rapidly test and prototype all parts of the mixed reality system. Components that run on different computers communicate using the Open Sound Control (OSC) protocol.

Artists and designers can use the Blender 3D authoring to model the geometry of the real space and add virtual objects to it. The OSC-based metaserver middleware makes it possible to feed these data into the VGE-rendering engine in real time, making it directly visible and audible to a user wearing a mixed reality system and vice versa. The measured position and orientation of the user can be shown in real time in the modelling environment. Because VGE can be controlled via the OSC protocol, it is relatively straightforward to control it from other applications, notably by the Max/MSP visual programming environment that is used extensively by artists and interaction designers.

14.4.1.2 Perspectives

As is clear from the case studies, our main research focus is on the first-person perspective, i.e. the player. But because all virtual content is absolutely positioned with respect to the real world, it is relatively easy to set up a third-person perspective.

---

[9] http://www.ogre3d.org

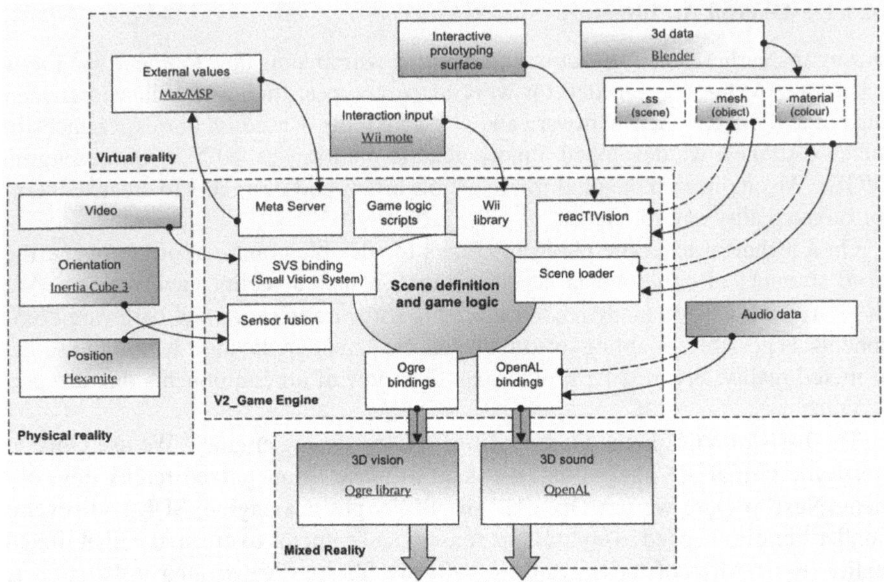

Fig. 14.1 Technical architecture of VGE

We experimented with this in the context of the *Game/Jan* project, an ongoing collaboration of theatre maker Carla Mulder with V2_Lab. The goal of this project is to create a theatre performance in which the audience, wearing polarised glasses, sees a mixed reality on the stage, in which a real actor is interacting with a virtual scene.

14.4.1.3 Sensors and Algorithms

As discussed earlier we want to create a virtual coordinate system that is fixed with respect to the real world. For positioning we employ off-the-shelf ultrasound hardware (Hexamite), for which we implemented time difference of arrival (TDoA) positioning algorithms [13]. Using TDoA eliminates the need to communicate the time stamp of transmission, increasing robustness and allows for a higher sampling rate up to an average of 6 Hz. The calculated absolute positions are transmitted via WLAN to the player-worn computer. The position measurements are fused with accelerometer sensor data using Kalman filters to produce intermediate estimates.

Orientation is measured using an off-the-shelf *Intersense InertiaCube3*, which combines magnetometers, gyroscopes and accelerometers, all in three dimensions. Together, this allows for 6 degrees of freedom.

14.4.2 Designing the Real World

Designing the appearance of the real world can be divided into two subtasks, first of all environmental models are needed, both geometrical as well as visual. Second, the actual appearance of the real world should be altered; in our case, we used lighting to achieve this.

14.4.2.1 Geometry and Visual Appearance

In mixed reality applications, knowledge of the geometry and visual appearance of the real world are of vital importance for the ability to blend in virtual content. A lot of research is targeted at building up an accurate model of the environment in real time, e.g. [8]. This research is progressing rapidly but the results are not yet readily available. For our type of applications we require high-quality models of the environment, so we chose to work in controlled environments that we can model in advance. We use two techniques for this: laser scanning and controlled lighting.

Laser scanning allows us to get a highly detailed model of the environment, in the form of a point cloud. For budgetary reasons, we developed our own laser scanner by mounting a SICK LMS200 2D laser scanner on a rotating platform. In one run this setup can generate about 400,000 points in a $360° \times 100°$ scan, at $0.36° \times 0.25°$ resolution, or 360,000 points in a $360° \times 180°$ scan, at $0.36° \times 0.5°$ resolution.

By making multiple scans of a space from different locations and aligning them to each other we can get a complete model of the environment. Based on this point cloud we can model the geometry of the environment, which we still do manually. The point cloud can be rendered in the mixed reality, as a way to trick the perception of the user into believing the virtual content is more stable than it really is.

14.4.2.2 Lighting

Taking control over the lighting of an environment provides two important features. First of all it is known in advance where the lights will be, making it possible to align the shadows of real and virtual objects. Second, changing the lighting at run time, synchronously in the real and virtual world, makes it still more difficult for users to discern real from virtual, enhancing the immersive qualities of the system. To incorporate this into our platform, we developed a software module that exposes a DMX controller as an OSC service.

14.4.3 Mixing Virtual Images

We want to blend a 2D camera image with real-time 3D computer-generated images. We are using these real-time images because this will allow us to eventually create an interactive game-like mixed reality experience. In our setup we created a video backdrop and placed the virtual objects in front of this camera image. In order to create a convincing mixed result, we need to create the illusion of depth in the 2D camera image. The virtual images need to look like they are somewhere in the camera image. We explored various known techniques [4] that create this illusion discussed in detail below:

- Stereo-pairs
- Occlusion
- Motion
- Shadows
- Lighting

These techniques can be divided in binocular depth cues and monocular or empirical depth cues. Binocular depth cues are hard wired in our visual system and only work because humans have two eyes and can view the world stereoscopically. Monocular depth cues are learned over time. We explored the effect these depth cues have on the feeling of immersion in our mixed reality environments when implemented flawless and flawed. We anticipated that we would not be using a flawless tracking system and we wanted to know how precise these techniques need to be implemented in order to create an immersive experience. The tests described below will explore these different aspects of mixing live camera images with 3D generated virtual images.

14.4.3.1 Test Setup

In order to experiment with various techniques, we created a test environment. In this environment we placed virtual objects, models of a well-known glue stick. We chose this object because everybody knows its appearance and dimensions.

In the test environment, we implemented scenarios in which virtual objects were floating or standing at fixed positions, orbiting in fixed trajectories (Fig. 14.2) and falling from the sky, bouncing from the real floor (Fig. 14.3). Note that each step involves more freedom of movement. Within these scenarios we experimented with various techniques described above.

Fig. 14.2 Virtual glue stick in orbit

Stereo-Pairs

Stereo-pairs is a technique to present the same or two slightly different images to the left and the right eye [16]. The difference between these two images corresponds with the actual difference between the left and right eye and thus creating a binocular rendering of a mixed reality scene. These binocular depth cues are preattentive;

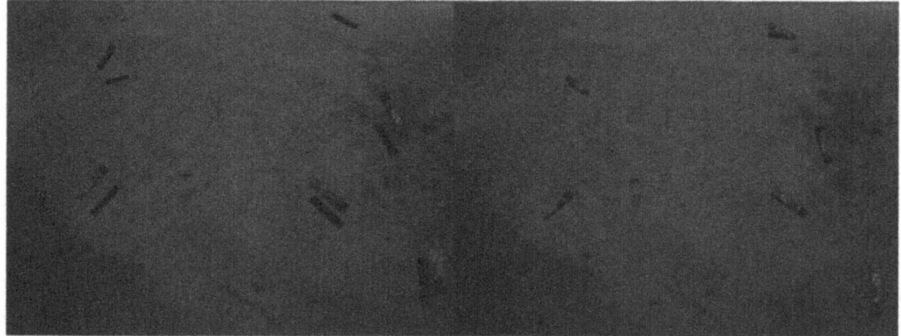

Fig. 14.3 Two frames showing virtual glue sticks in motion

this means viewers immediately see the distance between themselves and a virtual glue stick. When the same scene is rendered in monovision, there are no preattentive (binocular) depth cues in the virtual and real images thus one needs to judge the exact position of the virtual objects in the real scene. The preattentive depth cues in stereo-pairs greatly enhance the mix between both realities. One immediately believes the presented mixed realty to be one reality, e.g. the glue stick to be in the camera image. However, the error margin when rendering a mixed reality scene using stereo-pairs is much smaller than when rendering the same scene in mono-pairs. When the alignment of both worlds fails, it becomes impossible to view the stereo-paired scene as a whole. This is most likely because these depth cues are preattentive. Humans can accommodate their eyes to focus either on the virtual objects or on the real camera image but not on both. Mono-pair scenes can always be viewed as a whole.

Occlusion

Occlusion occurs when some parts of the virtual images appear to be behind some parts of the camera images. This monocular depth cue is great in fusing virtual and real images. You immediately believe a virtual object is part of the camera image if it appears from behind a part of the video backdrop. It does not matter if a glue stick is placed correctly from behind an object or flies through a wall. You will simply think that this just happened. The image will look unnatural not because the image seems to be incorrect but because you know it is unnatural for a glue stick to fly through a wall. This is true for a monovision setup. In a binocular setup this needs to be done correctly. You will perceive the depth of an object according to the binocular depth cues and not the way a scene in layered. If this is done incorrectly it will be impossible to focus the whole image. You will be able to see a sharp virtual object or the camera image but not both.

Camera Movement

Movement of the virtual and real camera will enhance the feeling of depth in your scene in mono- or stereo-pairs. The different speed of movement between objects placed in different positions, or parallax, is an important monocular depth cue. Movement of the virtual objects can also counteract the inaccuracy of the sensor system. When a virtual object is placed not exactly on a fixed position in the real space but moves around a bit, this movement will compensate for the inaccuracy of the tracking.

Shadows

Shadows are an important monocular depth cue. In the real world, shadows are always present, thus freely available in the camera images. Shadows are, however, not freely available in the virtual scene. Rendering real-time shadows adds complexity to a scene and slows down performance [14]. Virtual shadows do add an important monocular depth cue to the virtual scene. This enhancement outweighs the cost in performance. When combining virtual and real shadows they should be visually coherent, so that the angle and direction are the same. Casting shadows of virtual objects on objects in the real world and drawing shadows of real objects on virtual objects significantly improve the mix of these images. Especially casting virtual shadows on the real floor enhances the mixed reality. Shadows work both in mono- and stereo-pair scenes. Again the positioning of the shadows needs to be more accurate when using stereo-pairs than when using mono-pairs.

Lighting

Lighting is always present in the real world and this light needs to be mimicked in the virtual scene [3]. If there is no lighting present in the virtual scene, or worse, if the lighting is different, objects will look unnatural. Unlike shadows, lighting is easier to recreate in mixed reality. If the general direction is right the objects will look convincing.

Other Techniques

We explored other techniques including depth of field, general image blending and lens correction. When applied properly these techniques will enhance the final mixed reality, but we found they are of secondary priority for creating an immersive mixed reality experience.

14.4.4 Directing the User Experience

Because the user interface of a mixed reality system is in fact the world itself, we found that it is very important to design the experience in such a way that the user can behave in a natural way, or in other words is immersed. *Exercise in Immersion 4*, discussed below, was used as a test bed for measuring natural emotional speech [17], from which it can be concluded that users (players) were in fact feeling immersed in the environment.

By using a gaming metaphor, it is relatively straightforward to design an experience that the user can easily understand and follow. In the current version of VGE the game play is implemented in a scripting language, making it necessary to have a programmer assist the artist in implementing the game play. We are researching whether this can be improved.

14.4.4.1 Prototyping Tool: Interactive Table

In order to efficiently experiment with various usage scenarios, artist Jonas Hielscher collaborated with V2_Lab on using an interactive table as a prototyping tool. The table is comprised of a semi-transparent surface with a camera underneath. We employed the *reacTIVision* software [7] to track the position of markers placed on the surface. When the coordinate systems are aligned properly, this setup makes it possible to place virtual objects in the mixed reality environment, serving as a prototyping tool for directing user experiences.

In the experiment *Last Pawn*, a real table with a chess pawn stands in the middle of the room (Fig. 14.4). Around the table are three virtual windows hanging in the air and a virtual avatar stands in the middle of the room. When the participant moves the pawn on the table, the avatar walks to a position in space. If the avatar ends up in front of a window, he opens it and a new virtual space appears behind it. As such different spaces and atmospheres can be experienced. Additional real theatre light is controlled by the system to support the experience.

Fig. 14.4 *Last Pawn*, image courtesy Jonas Hielscher

In a second experiment, *Human Sandbox*, one participant equipped with the mixed reality system stands in the middle of the room, while another participant places several physical objects on the table (Fig. 14.5). They track and manipulate the virtual objects seen by the other participant. With this system we were able to test and experiment with different objects very easily. An interesting result with this

Fig. 14.5 *Human Sandbox*, image courtesy Jonas Hielscher

approach was that the game logic could be developed without having to program it, for example, users could play "Hide and Seek", just by putting and moving objects on the table.

14.4.5 Case Study: Exercise in Immersion 4

Exercise in Immersion 4 (EI4) is a co-production of artist Marnix de Nijs (NL) and V2_Lab. It is an art game that challenges how people perceive reality and questions their trust in virtual realities. The player is immersed more and more into a mixed reality world. The player wears a "classical", first-person augmented reality set, seeing the real world as video on a head-mounted display.

The experience is set up as a game in which the player passes several levels. In order to advance to the next level the player must move around and collect small virtual balls (bionts). These virtual balls respond on the real geometry by sticking on them. In the first level, the player only sees the video images with the added bionts. Moving around and collecting these balls gradually mix an exact point cloud scan of the same environment with the video images (Fig. 14.6). The player learns how the presented mixed reality reacts on his or her movement through the space and gets to trust the sensor system.

In the next levels we start to play with the trust gained in the previous level. First, virtual objects are fired towards the player to encourage him or her to move more quickly. The player is visually punished if a virtual object hits him. Every time a virtual object hits the player he or she loses some of the collected bionts. During this level the video image slowly faded away. The collected bionts still react on the real geometry and start to serve as an early warning system. They warn the player if he or she is nearing a physical object.

In the following level, we slowly start rotating the 3D scan to slowly disconnect the visual world from the physical world. Again the player needs to collect a number of bionts but is forced to trust his or her collected bionts to guide him or her through the real space. In the last level, the 3D scan is replaced by a scan of a different world. At this point there is no connection between the world the player is physically moving around and the world she or he visually sees.

Within these levels we want to experiment with different mixes of reality and see how people move around in this world. By letting them collect bionts, people are encouraged to move around in the virtual world at a speed that they would desire. By shooting objects towards the player, we encourage him or her to start moving quicker than he or she would actually want to. Next by rotating and finally replacing the world, we visually disconnect the virtual world from the physical world. Again we want to see how people move around when presented with this kind of mixed reality.

In the test we conducted at this point we found that people are very reluctant to move around quickly, even when only presented with a video image and no added virtual elements. Also players noted that visually mixing the two realities was more distressing than completely replacing the visual world. This shows that people are reluctant to trust the presented "reality", let alone go along with a mixed reality. This does not mean that people did not enjoy the experience of this mixed reality. This is what we set out to design, not to create the perfect mixed reality system but directing an intriguing experiment with mixed reality experiences.

Fig. 14.6 Screenshot of *Exercise in Immersion 4* showing the point clouds and the virtual bionts

14.5 Conclusions

We have described how VGE makes it easier to efficiently author mixed reality content. Three types of activities were described in detail: engineering, designing and directing. Using the VGE platform makes it possible to focus on the subjective aspects of the immersive quality of the experience. Content designers do not need to know how to set up a complex mixed reality system; instead they can focus on the content. We propose that not only artistic use of mixed reality systems can benefit from this approach, but that any system that has to be immersive, e.g. mixed reality training games, can benefit, because it will be easier to focus on the user aspects in an earlier stage of development.

We recommend that, when a mixed reality system is created, at a bare minimum, content designers should be able to work using their preferred tools, e.g. Blender3D or Max/MSP.

In future work we will further expand the VGE platform, focusing on the authoring aspects; we are currently investigating the merits of making the authoring environment an integrated part of the mixed reality environment.

Acknowledgments This research is part of the *MultimediaN* [10] project, a Dutch research programme in which partners from science, business and art collaborate on researching multimodal interaction. Parts of the artistic research were supported by the *Mondriaan Foundation* in the scope of the "Better than Reality" project. We thank our colleagues in the V2_Lab, especially Artm Baguinski, Stock, Andres Navarro and Chiel Vaessen, for their collaboration and hard work on the VGE platform, Michel van Dartel and Anne Nigten gave us very useful feedback throughout the project. Furthermore, we extend our deepest gratitude to all artists who collaborated with us on this exciting topic over the past years: Marnix de Nijs, Jonas Hielscher and Boris Debackere; they provided invaluable insights.

References

1. Abawi DF, Dörner R, Haller M, Zauner J (2004) Efficient Mixed Reality Application Development. In *Proc. 1st European Conference on Visual Media Production* (CVMP).
2. Altena A, Debackere B (eds.) (2008) *Sonic Acts XII: The Cinematic Experience.* Sonic Acts Press/Paradiso, Amsterdam, The Netherlands.
3. Birn J (2000) *Digital Lighting & Rendering* (2nd ed.). New Riders Press, Berkely, CA.
4. Bourke P (1999) Calculating Stereo Pairs. Accessed 17 December 2008 http://local.wasp.uwa.edu.au/~pbourke/projection/stereorender/
5. Geiger C, Stöcklein J (2005) Mixed Reality Authoring Using the MIREA Approach. In *Proc. International Conference on Humans and Computers* (HC 2005), Volume 8.
6. Grasset R, Woods E, Billinghurst M (2008) Art and Mixed Reality: New Technology for Seamless Merging Between Virtual and Real. *IMedia-Space Journal* (Issue 1).
7. Kaltenbrunner M, Bencina R (2007) reacTIVision: A Computer-Vision Framework for Table-Based Tangible Interaction. In *Proc. First International Conference on Tangible and Embedded Interaction* (TEI07) Baton Rouge, Louisiana.
8. Klein G, Murray D (2007) Parallel Tracking and Mapping for Small AR Workspaces. In *Proc. International Symposium on Mixed and Augmented Reality* (ISMAR'07).
9. Looser J, Grasset R, Seichter H, Billinghurst M (2006) OSGART – A Pragmatic Approach to MR. In *Proc. International Symposium on Mixed and Augmented Reality* (ISMAR'06).
10. MacIntyre B (2002) Authoring 3D Mixed Reality Experiences: Managing the Relationship Between the Physical and Virtual Worlds. At ACM SIGGRAPH and Eurographics Campfire: Production Process of 3D Computer Graphics Applications – Structures, Roles and Tools.

[10] http://www.multimedian.nl

11. MacIntyre B, Gandy M, Dow S, Bolter JD (2004) DART: A Toolkit for Rapid Design Exploration of Augmented Reality Experiences. In *Proc. Conference on User Interface Software and Technology* (UIST'04).
12. Miyashita T, Meier P, Tachikawa T, Orlic S, Eble T, Scholz V, Gapel A, Gerl O, Arnaudov S, Lieberknecht S (2008) An Augmented Reality Museum Guide. In *Proc. International Symposium on Mixed and Augmented Reality* (ISMAR'08).
13. Navarro A (2008) *Multisensor Data Fusion Applied to Augmented Reality*, M.Sc. thesis, Man-Machine Interaction group of Delft University of Technology.
14. Rost RJ, Kessenich JM, Lichtenbelt B, Malan H, Weiblen M (2006) *OpenGL Shading Language* (2nd ed.). Addison-Wesley, Reading, MA.
15. Scherrer C, Pilet J, Fua P, Lepetit V (2008) The Haunted Book. In *Proc. International Symposium on Mixed and Augmented Reality* (ISMAR'08).
16. Steinman SB, Steinman BA, Garzia RP (2000) *Foundations of Binocular Vision: A Clinical Perspective*. McGraw-Hill Medical, New York.
17. Truong KP, Neerincx MA, van Leeuwen DA (2008) Measuring Spontaneous Vocal and Facial Emotion Expressions in Real World Environments. In *Proc. 6th International Conference on Methods and Techniques in Behavioral Research*, Maastricht, The Netherlands.
18. van Dartel M (2009) Truth in New Media Art Through Sensory-Motor Coordination. In Brejzek T, Greisenegger W (eds.) *Monitoring scenography 2: Space and Truth*. Zürich University of the Arts, Zürich, Switzerland.
19. van Dartel M, Misker JMV, Nigten A, van der Ster J (2007) Virtual Reality and Augmented Reality Art Explained in Terms of Sensory-Motor Coordination. In Luciani A, Cadoz C. (eds.) *Proc. 4th International Conference on Enactive Interfaces*, Grenoble, France.

Chapter 15
Fiia: A Model-Based Approach to Engineering Collaborative Augmented Reality

Christopher Wolfe, J. David Smith, W. Greg Phillips, and T.C. Nicholas Graham

Abstract Augmented reality systems often involve collaboration among groups of people. While there are numerous toolkits that aid the development of such augmented reality groupware systems (e.g., ARToolkit and Groupkit), there remains an enormous gap between the specification of an AR groupware application and its implementation. In this chapter, we present *Fiia*, a toolkit which simplifies the development of collaborative AR applications. Developers specify the structure of their applications using the *Fiia* modeling language, which abstracts details of networking and provides high-level support for specifying adapters between the physical and virtual world. The *Fiia.Net* runtime system then maps this conceptual model to a runtime implementation. We illustrate *Fiia* via *Raptor*, an augmented reality application used to help small groups collaboratively prototype video games.

Keywords Augmented reality development · Groupware development · Model-based engineering · Electronic tabletop · Game sketching

15.1 Introduction

It is natural to use augmented reality (AR) to support collaboration. The combination of real and virtual information can help maintain group awareness and allows the use of tangible props to focus discussion. While there are numerous toolkits that help with parts of the development of augmented reality groupware systems (e.g., ARToolkit [12] and Groupkit [22]), there remains an enormous gap between the specification of a collaborative AR application and its implementation. Existing approaches are either high level, helping specify the systems conceptual architecture while giving little guidance for implementation, or low level, solving critical technical problems such as object tracking but giving little help for global structure.

C. Wolfe (✉)
School of Computing, Queen's University, Kingston, ONT, Canada
e-mail: wolfe@cs.queensu.ca

E. Dubois et al. (eds.), *The Engineering of Mixed Reality Systems*, Human-Computer Interaction Series, DOI 10.1007/978-1-84882-733-2_15,

In this chapter, we present *Fiia*, a toolkit which simplifies the development of collaborative AR applications by bridging the gap between high-level models and distributed AR implementations. Developers specify the structure of their applications using the *Fiia* modeling language, which abstracts details of networking and provides high-level support for specifying links between the physical and virtual worlds. The *Fiia.Net* runtime system then maps these conceptual models to runtime implementations. *Fiia* supports an end-to-end development process where designers specify their application in terms of a set of scenes expressed in the *Fiia* modeling language. Developers then code these scenes using *Fiia.Net*, directing the runtime system to implement the scenes themselves and the transitions between them. *Fiia* provides particularly high-level support for systems where some users have access to full AR technology and others do not, allowing easy development of different interfaces to the same system.

We illustrate *Fiia* via *Raptor*, a collaborative AR tool for prototyping video games. *Raptor* allows a small group of designers to collaborate on the design of a game, while others can play the game in real time as it is developed. Using Microsoft Surface [16], designers sketch out the games appearance and rules using a mix of physical and virtual objects. For example, a designer can specify the behavior of a car in a racing game by "stamping" a physical car on the track, placing a physical game controller on the table, and connecting virtual "pins" on the controller to pins on the virtual car (e.g., connecting a joystick to the car's steering function). Meanwhile, testers can play the game as it is being developed using purely virtual access via a game PC. This application shows the power of *Fiia*'s modeling and implementation capabilities, while showing the different roles and interaction styles of groupware AR applications.

The chapter is structured as follows. We first introduce *Raptor* as an example of a collaborative AR application. We then introduce the *Fiia* notation, showing how it can be used to model *Raptor*. We then discuss how the *Fiia.Net* toolkit automatically implements high-level *Fiia* diagrams. Finally, we discuss the implementation of the *Fiia.Net* toolkit itself and detail our experience with it.

15.2 Example: Collaborative Game Prototyping with Raptor

To motivate the concept of collaborative AR, we introduce *Raptor*, a tool supporting rapid prototyping of games. *Raptor* addresses the problem that games now cost tens of millions of dollars to build and involve teams often in excess of 100 people [10]. Given these costs, it becomes critically important to assess early in the development process whether the game will actually be fun to play. While other techniques (such as the use of design patterns [3]) may help, ultimately the fun can only be determined by building a game that people can play. *Raptor* allows groups of people to brainstorm around early game design. Designers use a tabletop surface to quickly sketch the game's appearance and play. Meanwhile, a player can test the prototype as it is being built. Designers can use *Raptor* as a "Wizard of Oz" [5] tool, mocking up game interaction in real time.

Unlike other game sketching tools [1], *Raptor* leverages modern interaction styles to support rapid interaction. The tabletop surface allows two or three people to closely collaborate in the design and provides rapid and tactile facilities for quickly testing game ideas. As seen in Fig. 15.1, small groups of people surround the table and work together in creating the game.

Designers use physical, virtual, and mixed reality objects. For example (somewhat similarly to *Build-It*[21]), physical objects can be used to add new instances of virtual objects into a scene. Figure 15.2 shows the addition of a car into a racing game by "stamping" a physical car onto the tabletop. The virtual car is added to the scene at the location where the physical car is stamped.

Similarly, physical objects can be *augmented* to show how they interact with the virtual world. In Fig. 15.1, a designer places an Xbox controller input device onto the table. A ring of "pins" surround the controller, representing the different input and output channels the controller provides (e.g., the different buttons and joysticks).

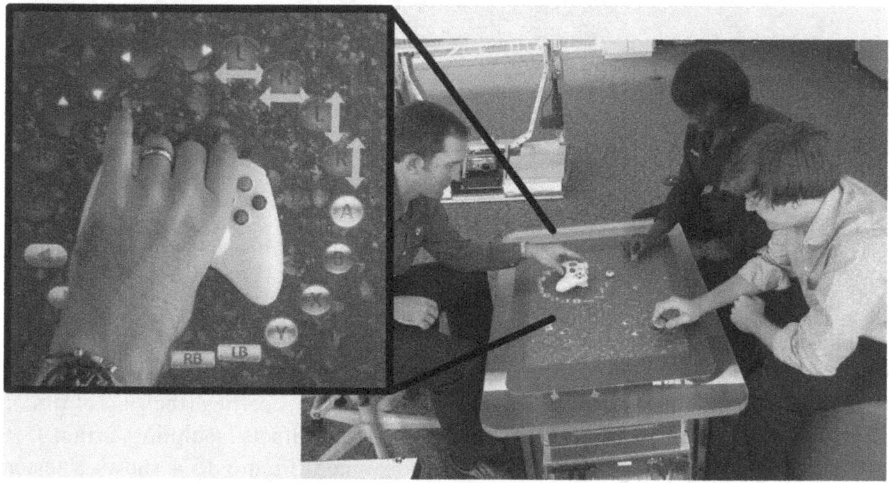

Fig. 15.1 Collaboratively designing a racing game using *Raptor*

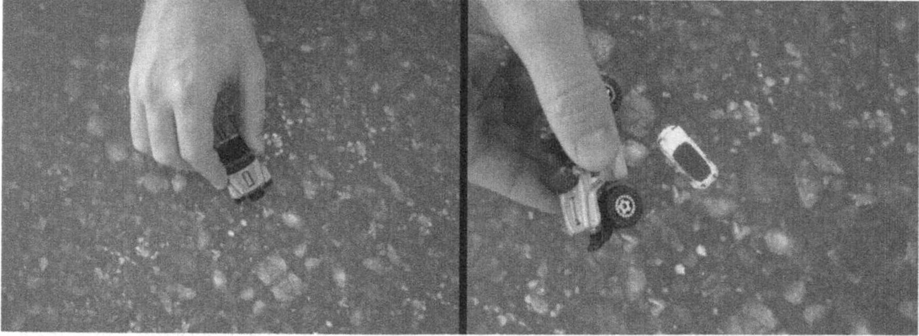

Fig. 15.2 Stamping a physical car on the table adds a virtual car into the game

As the controller is moved around the tabletop surface, the ring of pins moves with it, creating a truly mixed physical–virtual entity. The pins on the controller can be connected to pins on other objects; the designer attaches the "A" and "B" buttons to the car's gas pedal and brake pins, allowing these buttons to be used to accelerate and decelerate. To connect two pins, the designer touches the source pin and then touches the target pin. A line is drawn between them to show the connection.

Physical gestures can be used to manipulate the virtual game world; a scooping motion with the hands can be used to "drag" the terrain, creating a hill (Fig. 15.3). This style of input allows the designer to interact with virtual entities using physical actions.

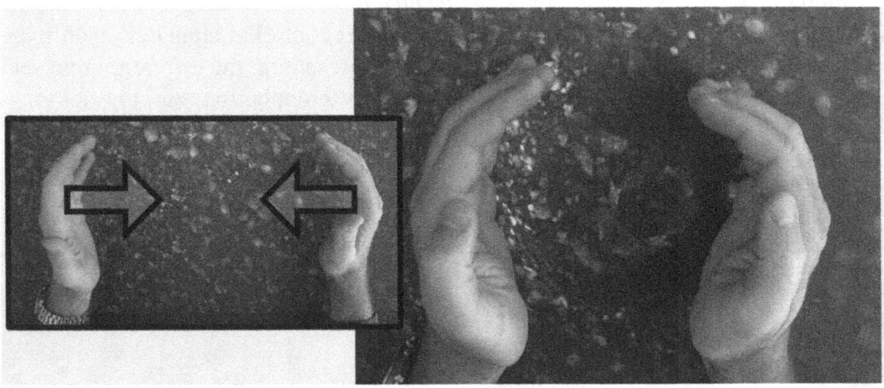

Fig. 15.3 Designers can manipulate the virtual terrain with physical gestures, e.g., using a scooping motion to create a hill

These examples show how the tabletop enables a fluid interaction between physical and virtual entities. These interactions include using physical artifacts as props (stamping); augmenting physical artifacts with virtual properties (the ring of pins); and using physical interactions to manipulate virtual artifacts (sculpting terrain.)

Testers can play the game as it is being designed. Figure 15.4 shows a tester sitting at a PC playing the game as the designers modify it. For example, if the designers are creating a racing game, then the tester immediately sees changes such as adding a new car to the game, repositioning an obstacle or modifying the terrain. Similarly, changes in *gameplay* are reflected immediately in the tester's view of the game: for example, the controls used to manipulate a car can be changed on the fly. This allows a "Wizard of Oz" style of gameplay testing, in which designers can simulate the game by manipulating objects on the table. This approach allows a tester to experience a game idea without the expense of fully implementing it.

Testers and designers have different viewpoints on the game. Designers have a top-down, two-dimensional view of the game world (Fig. 15.4), while testers see the game in a more traditional 3D form (Fig. 15.5).

Raptor shows the richness of interaction that can be achieved with collaborative augmented reality. As described above, the physical and virtual worlds can interact in a number of interesting ways, through the use of physical objects as props, the

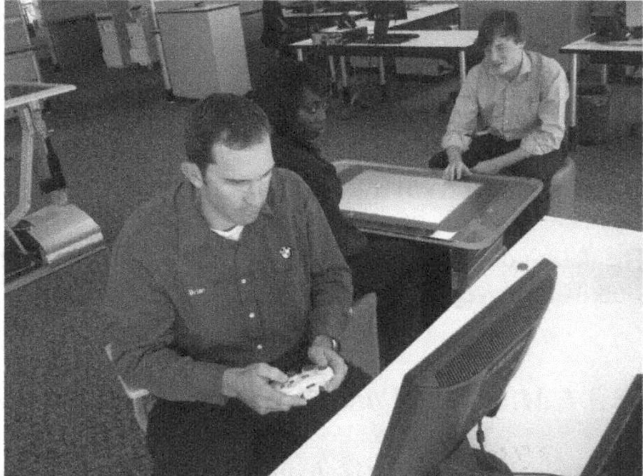

Fig. 15.4 Designers and testers collaborate using *Raptor*

Fig. 15.5 A tester can play a game as it is being created, creating a fluid testing process and supporting Wizard of Oz prototyping

augmentation of physical objects with virtual properties, and the use of physical gestures to manipulate virtual entities. Collaboration can be of the form of a group of designers around a table, using pointing, gesturing and speech to mediate their actions, or between testers and designers sitting at different locations in the room, interacting via different views of the same shared artifacts. A particular strength of *Raptor* is that not all users need to have hardware capable of delivering an AR experience. Here, the tester interacts with the game using a standard PC.

Initial tests with *Raptor* have shown that the tabletop-based AR interaction is natural, not unlike interaction between people sitting around a traditional table, and that the collaboration is fluid, with people easily shifting between roles of designer and tester.

This example illustrates many of the benefits of collaborative augmented reality. In the remainder of the chapter, we introduce the *Fiia.Net* toolkit, and illustrate how it was used to implement *Raptor*. We then discuss the implementation of the toolkit itself. First, we review other techniques for the design and implementation of collaborative AR applications.

15.3 Related Work

The design of *Fiia* draws from a wealth of prior research in modeling notations and toolkits for developing collaborative AR applications.

15.3.1 Modeling Collaborative Augmented Reality

The *Fiia* design notation is an *architectural style*, a visual notation from which software architectures for collaborative AR are constructed. Several other architectural styles have the goal of reducing the difficulty of programming *groupware* (collaborative applications) or augmented reality applications. To date, we are unaware of other architectural styles that attempt to provide support for both.

Architectural styles provide rules for decomposing groupware systems into components, allowing developers to use a "divide and conquer" development approach. For example, both the Clover Model [13] and PAC* [4] give advice on how to split up user interface and application, while supporting group tasks of production, communication, and coordination. These architectures are *conceptual*, meaning that they do not address the problems of how to implement them on distributed systems. Developers, therefore, face a significant task to convert them to running code. Phillips provides a detailed survey of conceptual architecture styles for groupware [19].

Among architectural styles for augmented reality applications, notable is ASUR [6]. Similarly to our own approach, ASUR allows applications to be modeled via scenarios, where ASUR diagrams consist of components and connectors. ASUR explicitly recognizes *adapters*, components that bridge between the physical and virtual worlds. ASUR is purely a modeling notation; while ASUR models form an excellent guide to developers, they are not themselves executable and must be converted by hand to code. ASUR does not provide explicit support for collaboration.

15.3.2 Toolkits for Collaborative AR

There exist numerous toolkits for developing groupware and several for writing AR applications. We are unaware of any toolkit that provides support for both.

Most groupware toolkits (such as Groupkit [22], ALV [11], and Clock [24]) require all users to interact with the application in the same way, and so could not be used to implement *Raptor*'s heterogeneous roles and platforms. The .Networking shared dictionary [15] does provide flexible support for heterogeneous clients.

Several groupware toolkits provide some support for dynamic adaptation, which could be used to implement transition between scenes. Schmalsteig et al. provide an approach for client migration in virtual reality applications [23]. A shared scene graph data structure is implemented via replication. The code and scene graph can be migrated to new client computers, providing a form of device adaptation. DACIA [14] is a middleware which provides support for component migration; it can be used to manually program adaptation at a level considerably higher than raw networking libraries. Genie [2] supports adaptivity by allowing the definition of distributed system configurations (including replication and caching strategies) and automatic migration between them.

Most toolkits for developing augmented reality applications address the specific problem of determining camera's position and orientation (or "pose") and determining the location of physical objects. An example of this problem is tracking the location of the physical Xbox 360 controller on the tabletop so that its pins can be drawn around it (Fig. 15.1); another example is determining the position and orientation of a head-mounted display. Augmented reality toolkits are typically presented as libraries that can be used from a range of host programming languages. For example, users of ARToolkit [12] and ARTag [7] attach patterned images (tags) to the environment. These are programmatically linked to entities in the virtual world. The pose of the camera in the physical world can be determined by analyzing the position of the tags in the image provided by the camera. GoblinXNA takes a similar approach, while providing integration with Microsoft's XNA studio game development environment [17]. Other problems addressed by toolkits can include localization, gesture recognition, and graphics [9].

While each of these approaches helps the problem of developing collaborative AR applications, work still remains to be done. The groupware approaches we have reviewed either (i) are high level but provide little support for the problems of distributed systems programming or (ii) provide programming help, but are not linked to a specific architectural style. Meanwhile, the augmented reality toolkits provide highly valuable libraries, but do not provide support at the architectural or design level. As we shall see, *Fiia* can be seen as a generalization of these approaches that provides far more flexibility at both the conceptual and distribution architectural levels, while providing necessary facilities for composing AR applications.

From this brief survey of related work, we can see the need for a toolkit like *Fiia* which allows high-level design of collaborative AR applications and provides highly flexible tool support for implementing those designs.

15.4 Fiia Notation

Fiia is a design notation for collaborative AR applications, supported by a toolkit (*Fiia.Net*) for realizing these designs as running applications. *Fiia* is a model-based approach, allowing a high-level conceptual model of the system to be automatically implemented as a distributed application involving both physical and virtual artifacts.

Compared to earlier approaches, *Fiia* makes three principal advances, providing

- a high-level notation for modeling both groupware and augmented reality, including features for data sharing and virtual/physical adapters;
- scenario-based design and implementation;
- easy transition from models to code.

We address each of these points in the following three sections.

15.4.1 Notation for Collaborative AR

Figure 15.6 shows an example *Fiia* diagram for *Raptor*. Designers interact with an *Editor*, which allows them to manipulate the scene, shaping the terrain, adding game elements (such as cars and controllers), and attaching behaviors to those elements. Elements are represented in the form of a "scene graph," a data structure capturing properties such as the elements' positions, geometry, and textures. The scene graph is stored in the *Scene* component. The *Editor* is an *Actor* (⟲) component, that is, a component capable of initiating action; *Scene* is a *Store* (⛁) component, i.e., a passive data store.

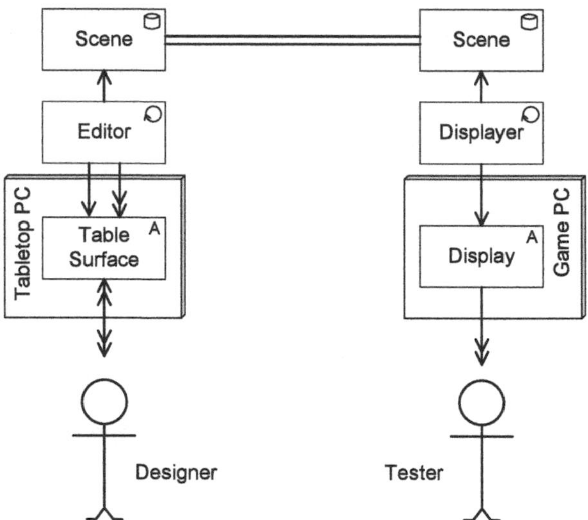

Fig. 15.6 *Fiia* model of *Raptor*'s initial scene

Designers interact with the *Editor* via a tabletop surface, represented by the *Table Surface* adapter component. The *Table Surface* provides input/output facilities for the physical tabletop (a Microsoft Surface [16]). The designer interacts with the *Table Surface* via a bi-directional flow of information. This is represented by a pair of *Fiia stream* connectors: ↠. (These connectors have been abbreviated in the figure as a double-ended stream.) The *Editor* polls the tabletop for its current state (via a *call* connector: →) and updates the table's display via a stream connector. In general, streams represent asynchronous dataflow and are useful for communicating discrete events or continuous media such as sound or video, while call connectors are used to represent traditional synchronous method calls.

Meanwhile, testers view the running game on a *Display*. A *Displayer* actor keeps the display up to date, responding to changes in the *Scene*. The tester and displayer's versions of the *Scene* are kept consistent via a *synchronization connector* (⟸). This connector is used to specify that two or more stores are to be maintained in a consistent state, so that changes in one are automatically reflected in the other.

Fiia diagrams are implemented as distributed systems. Here, at least two computers must be used: the computer running the tabletop surface (*Tabletop PC*) and the tester's computer (*Game PC*). *Fiia* diagrams, however, do not specify the details of this distribution. They abstract the allocation of components to computational nodes, the algorithms used to transmit data between nodes, and the consistency maintenance schemes used to implement data synchronization. As we will see in Section 15.6, the *Fiia.Net* toolkit automatically determines a distribution from the high-level *Fiia* diagram. This allows designers to concentrate on the function of their application without having to be mired in the details of their distributed implementation.

The symbols used in *Fiia* diagrams are summarized in Fig. 15.7. *Fiia* diagrams have two features that particularly help in the development of collaborative AR applications: *adapters* and *synchronization connectors*. We detail these features in the next two sections.

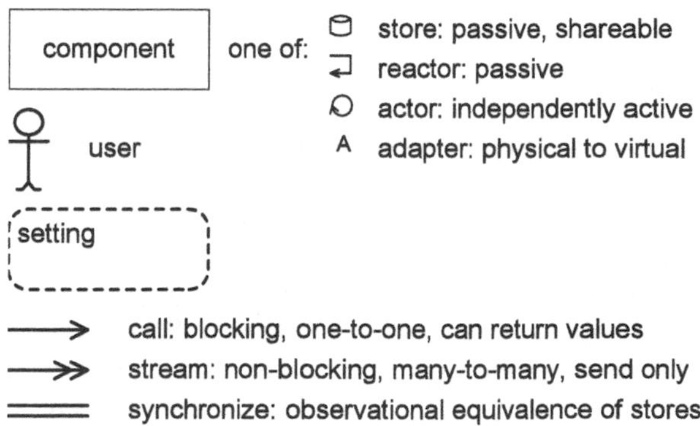

Fig. 15.7 The *Fiia* notation

15.4.1.1 Adapters

Dubois and Gray's *ASUR* notation first introduced the concept of adapters [6], software architectural components that bridge between the physical and virtual worlds.

Adapters can represent traditional devices (such as a keyboard or display) or more novel devices such as tabletop surfaces, accelerometers, cameras, or head-mounted displays. Adapters are core to the specification of augmented reality applications, as they clearly specify the interaction between the physical and virtual worlds.

Fiia's adapter ("**A**") components are similar in concept to those of ASUR, representing the boundary between the physical and virtual worlds. From the toolkit's perspective, adapters are actually software components that encapsulate the interface to an interaction device. For example, the *Table Surface* component implements the services required to interact with the tabletop surface, including object recognition, gesturing, and tabletop display. Specifically, the *Table Surface* contains functions to recognize the position and orientation of tagged physical artifacts (such as the car and controller) when they are placed on the surface. This allows implementation of *Raptor*'s "stamping" function (Fig. 15.2) and of the mixed reality controller (Fig. 15.1). The component is capable of interpreting multi-touch inputs as gestures, allowing implementation of gesture-based dragging and rotating of virtual game elements, as well as terrain sculpting (Fig. 15.3).

As illustrated by Fig. 15.6, adapters must be anchored to specific nodes, so that the *Fiia.Net* toolkit can determine which physical device is intended.

The *Fiia.Net* toolkit supports a variety of interesting adapters, including mouse, keyboard, Xbox 360 controller, video camera, microphone, speaker, and display. Adapters under development include Wii Remote and GPS. It is possible to create sophisticated applications through these rich adapters. For example, taking advantage of the fact that *Fiia* connectors can span node boundaries, a video broadcast can be created simply by connecting a camera in one location to a screen in another.

15.4.1.2 Data Sharing

The second way in which *Fiia* provides high-level support for collaborative AR is through the synchronization connector ("═"). This connector, first introduced as a notational convenience in Patterson's taxonomy of groupware architectures [18], specifies that two data stores are to retain *observational equivalence* throughout the execution of the program (or more simply, that the runtime system must make a best effort to ensure that both stores have the same value). Specifically, all requests to either store must return the same value, all updates to one store must be reflected in the other, and event streams originating from the stores must be equivalent.

Synchronization provides basis for implementing artifact sharing. Participants can access shared data, allowing customized interfaces. For example, the tester's display shows the game from a 3D perspective, while the designer sees the game top-down on a tabletop surface.

The power of *Fiia*'s data synchronization is that it does not require the designer to specify how the synchronization is to occur. The connector hides decisions of replication (centralized versus replicated data), networking algorithms, and consistency maintenance schemes.

15.4.2 Scenario-Based Design

The process of modeling with *Fiia* is high level, based on identifying and linking typical execution steps. Developers start by identifying scenarios of their system's use. From these scenarios, they determine example snapshots of the system in use. The developer then creates *Fiia* diagrams representing interesting situations and finally (as we shall see in Section 15.4.3) transforms them into code.

For example, in *Raptor*, the scenario begins (as shown in Fig. 15.6) with the designer manipulating the game and the tester viewing the results. In the second step (Fig. 15.8), the designer has "stamped" a car into the game and an Xbox 360 controller has been added, allowing the tester to drive the car. A new *Car* component is dynamically added to the *Fiia* architecture. This component contains all knowledge of the new car's behavior – how it responds to user inputs (e.g., that the "A" button causes the car to accelerate) and its physics (e.g., how acceleration affects speed). The car's behavior causes changes in the *Scene*, allowing the car to be rendered (by the *Editor* and *Displayer* components).

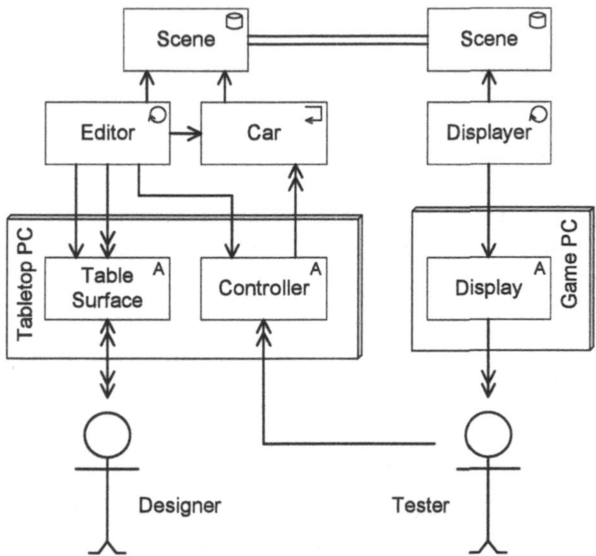

Fig. 15.8 Result of designer "stamping" a new car into the game

A new *Controller* adapter is added to the diagram, representing the physical Xbox 360 controller that will be used to manipulate the car. The tester provides this input. The *Car* polls the state of the controller during every new game frame, using the input to update the car's position.

The controller can be used by either the designer or tester, and in fact is frequently passed from one to the other during prototyping sessions. Controller inputs cause the position of the car to move both on the tabletop and on the game PC display. Despite the fact that the controller is shared, it must be explicitly anchored to either the tabletop PC or the game PC so that the runtime system can identify which controller is intended.

The *Fiia.Net* toolkit provides high-level operations for moving between stages of a scenario; e.g., adding and connecting new components can be carried out with one-line operations, even when those operations implicitly involve migrating data over a network.

Fiia diagrams such as those of Figs. 15.6 and 15.8 help in documenting how the collaborative AR application may change during execution. Developers must then write code using the *Fiia.Net* toolkit to render these scenes into code.

15.4.3 Mapping Fiia Diagrams to Code

As we have seen, *Fiia* diagrams follow naturally from scenarios. It is straightforward to map diagrams to code; the concepts from *Fiia* diagrams map one-to-one to C# code using the *Fiia.Net* toolkit. For example, the following code creates the *Scene* component for the designer and synchronizes it to the equivalent component for the tester:

```
Store scene = Fiia.NewStore<Scene>();

SyncConnector sync =
  Fiia.SyncConnect( "SceneSync", scene );
```

The *Scene* class is a standard C# class, providing operations for adding and editing elements of the game's scene graph. The following code creates the *Editor* and adds the call connector between it and the *Scene* store:

```
Actor editor = Fiia.NewActor<Editor>();

Fiia.CallConnect(
  editor.Property("Scene"),
  scene.Interface("IScene") );
```

The *Editor* is implemented by the C# *Editor* class. The call connection establishes its `Scene` property as a reference in the *scene* component; this reference enables inter-component calls using standard C# syntax, such as

```
scene.AddNode(...);
```

Streams are created similarly to call connectors, using either interfaces or C#'s standard delegate event handlers.

Adapters, like stores and actors, are created from C# classes. Rather than application code, they implement access to the physical device. The *Fiia.Net* toolkit provides a library of such adapters, ranging over standard devices such as mouse and keyboard to richer devices such as tabletop surfaces and game controllers. More adapters are being added to the toolkit regularly.

We see from these examples that mapping from *Fiia* diagrams to code is straightforward, as each element of the *Ffiia* diagram has a corresponding concept in the *Fiia.Net* API. The toolkit builds naturally on features familiar to C# programmers and has been integrated with Windows forms (for traditional graphical user interfaces) and XNA Studio (for 2D and 3D games and simulations). *Fiia.Net* runs on a wide variety of platforms, including PCs, Windows Mobile PDAs, and (forthcoming) the Xbox 360 game console.

15.4.4 Summing Up the Fiia Notation

As we have seen, the *Fiia* notation allows straightforward modeling of collaborative AR applications. The notation is high level, abstracting details of distributed systems, and non-traditional I/O devices. This allows developers to concentrate on the high-level structure of their application without having to be concerned with low-level implementation details. Two features of the *Fiia* notation particularly help with this: the *synchronization* connector allows data to be shared by different users of the system; and the *adapter* construct allows easy specification of the boundaries between the physical and virtual worlds.

The *Fiia.Net* toolkit automatically implements data synchronization, identifying appropriate replication, networking, and concurrency control algorithms. Similarly, *Fiia.Net* provides a library of adapters for a range of I/O devices including the table surface, Xbox 360 controller, and display used in this example.

The approach allows designers to sketch their application via a connected set of scenes, each expressed as a *Fiia* diagram. These diagrams are easily translated to code, as each of the diagram elements and diagram adaptations are directly represented in the *Fiia.Net* library.

15.5 The Fiia.Net Toolkit

As discussed in the previous section, *Fiia* diagrams abstract the details of application distribution and adapter implementation. This allows developers to concentrate on the functionality of their application rather than on low-level issues of network programming and image processing.

In this section, we show how *Fiia.Net* automatically maps *Fiia* diagrams to distributed systems, implements transitions between scenario steps, and realizes adapters. In Section 15.6, we provide a brief overview of how *Fiia.Net* itself is implemented.

15.5.1 Conceptual Framework

Figure 15.9 shows *Fiia.Net*'s conceptual organization. Programmers create a *Fiia* diagram (*f*) representing their scene, using the techniques described above. This diagram is automatically refined by *Fiia.Net* to a distribution architecture (*d*).

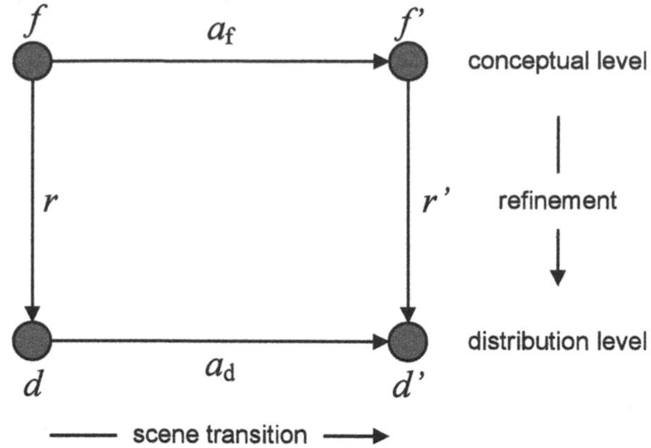

Fig. 15.9 *Fiia* framework

Runtime transitions may occur at both the *Fiia* level (change application, device, location, etc.) or at the distribution level (network or component failure). This leads to a new *Fiia* or distribution architecture (f' or d'). The toolkit then carries out necessary operations to reestablish consistency between the two levels. To our knowledge, *Fiia.Net* is unique in maintaining this two-level view of the system at runtime and in automatically maintaining consistency between the two views. This allows developers to enact runtime change using high-level *Fiia* scenes. It also allows developers the means to deal with partial failure at a high level. Rather than dealing with repair of broken sockets, programmers view failure as the disappearance of components and connectors, making it easier to respond to a failure in its broader context.

Having established this framework, we next examine the elements of *Fiia*'s distribution architecture and discuss how runtime adaptation is enacted. We then review the implementation of the *Fiia.Net* toolkit and present our experience with its use.

15.5.2 Distribution Architecture

Figure 15.10 shows the distribution architecture for the *Raptor* configuration that was shown in Fig. 15.8. This level of architecture pins down details of how the *Fiia* design is implemented as a distributed system. The distribution architecture is automatically generated by the *Fiia.Net* toolkit from the *Fiia* design provided by the programmer. As will be discussed, the distribution architecture is continuously updated at runtime in response to programmer-directed changes to the *Fiia* design and system-directed changes in the networking infrastructure.

Distribution architectures are expressed in terms of infrastructure components (Fig. 15.11). These include implementations of the components specified in the *Fiia*

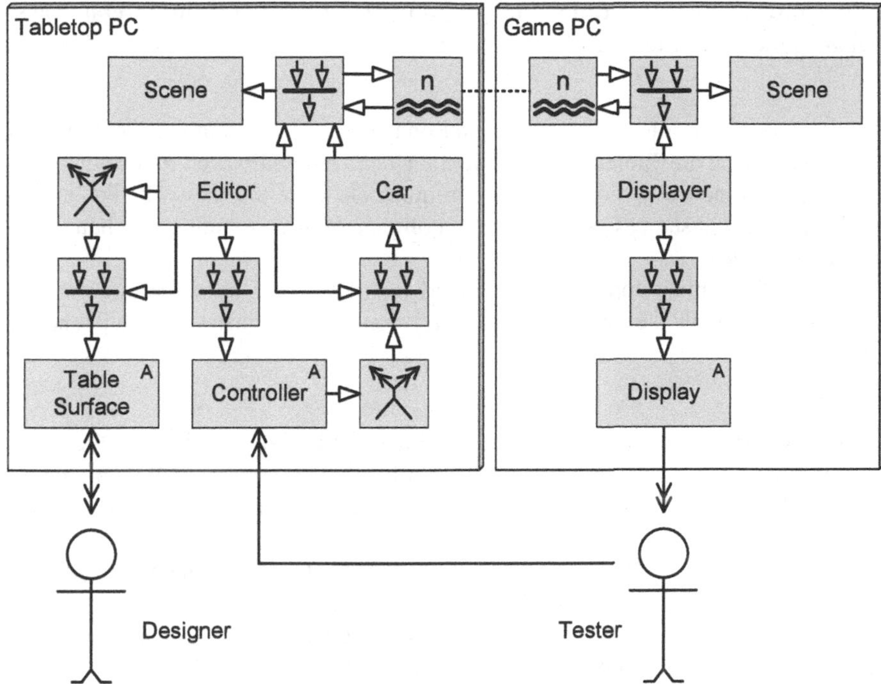

Fig. 15.10 Distribution architecture for the *Raptor* diagram of Fig. 15.8

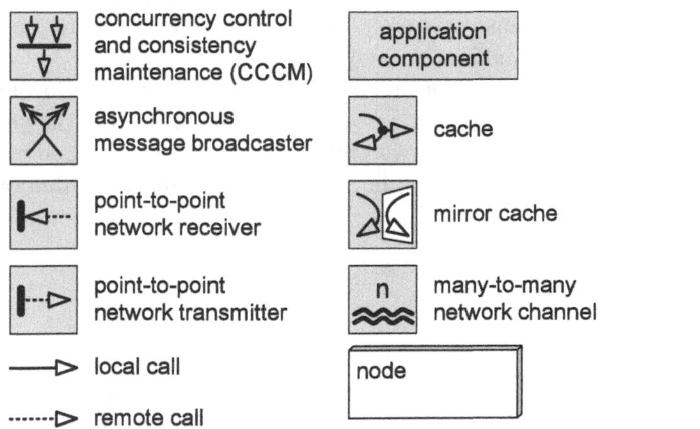

Fig. 15.11 Elements from which *Fiia* distribution architectures are constructed

design, as well as built-in components that handle issues such as caching, concurrency control, and communication. In effect, these components make up a machine language for distribution architectures, to which the *Fiia.Net* refinery compiles *Fiia* designs.

The distribution architecture differs from the *Fiia* design in several ways, including the following:

- Components are allocated to computational nodes. For example, the *Editor* is represented on the Tabletop PC, while the *Displayer* is allocated to the game PC.
- It is determined how components communicate over the network. For example, the two instances of the *Scene* component use a multicast channel to communicate.
- Support for replica consistency is added in the form of infrastructure components that provide a choice of concurrency control and consistency maintenance algorithms.

We now examine the specifics of this architecture in order to illustrate the range of issues that *Fiia* designs hide from the application programmer. We emphasize that Fig. 15.10 shows one of many possible distribution architectures for the *Fiia* design of Fig. 15.8.

The *Editor* and the *Displayer* each require access to data in the *Scene* component, which is replicated to both the tabletop and game PCs. Each instance of the *Scene* can be updated by both the local and remote user interfaces (in response to the designer and tester's inputs). Therefore, *Consistency Maintenance/Concurrency Control* (CCCM) components are required to ensure consistent execution of operations on the two replicas. CCCM's are shown visually as .

The CCCM components use an internal protocol based on message broadcasting to maintain the consistency of the replicas. The CCCMs communicate via a *channel* (), which provides multicast messaging.

In summary, the distribution architecture is a rich language allowing the expression of a wide range of distributed implementations. Not shown here is the range of implementations *Fiia.Net* provides for infrastructure components, which encapsulate, for example, choice of concurrency control algorithm or networking protocol.

15.5.3 Adapters

Fiia's adapters allow high-level specification of the points of transition between the physical and virtual worlds. *Fiia.Net* provides a library of reusable adapters. When these are used in *Fiia* diagrams, they can be automatically inserted as components into the runtime architecture. It is of course straightforward for developers to add custom adapters to the library. Adapters are typically built over existing libraries for common tasks such as interpreting gestures, object recognition, and camera pose.

As was seen in the *Fiia* diagrams of Fig. 15.6 and 15.8, adapters are explicitly anchored to a node. This allows *Fiia.Net* to determine which computer the adapter code is referencing.

An advantage of *Fiia*'s distribution independence is that adapters can be used by components on other nodes without requiring special network programming. For example, the *Editor* component does not need to be on the same node as the *Table Surface* adapter (although it happens to be in the refinement shown in Fig. 15.8.)

15.6 Implementing Fiia

In the previous section, we saw how the *Fiia.Net* runtime implements *Fiia* diagrams. The toolkit automatically handles distributed systems issues, such as component allocation, networking, and consistency maintenance, and provides implementations of common adapters, as well as providing high-level support for migration between scenes.

We now briefly review how *Fiia.Net* itself is implemented. Figure 15.12 shows the runtime architecture of the *Fiia.Net* system. Every node has a *Node Manager* component responsible for configuring local objects as directed by the *Refinery*. One "master" node has the special status of being responsible for storing the conceptual and distribution architectures (the *Architecture* component) and managing the consistency between them. The *Architect* carries out conceptual-level changes to the architecture (e.g, create a new workspace and adding components) and notifies the *Refinery*. The *Refinery* is a rule-based system responsible for mapping the *Fiia* architecture to a distributed implementation, taking into account any specified attributes.

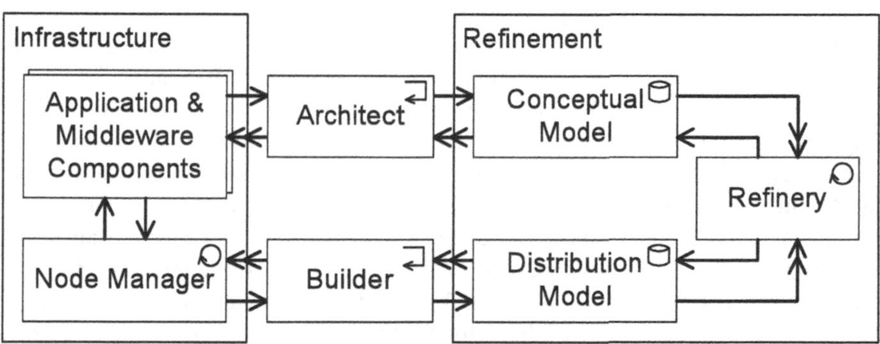

Fig. 15.12 Implementation of the *Fiia.Net* runtime system

Figure 15.13 shows an example of one of the refinery's rules, specifying how components are anchored to a node. Rules are written in Story Diagram notation [8]. This rule states that a *Fiia* component located within some setting may be anchored to any node that is contained within the same setting. The *Fiia.Net* runtime contains 34 rules. The refinery applies these rules repeatedly to the *Fiia* architecture until no more rules match. We have proven (via structural induction over the ruleset) that this process always terminates with a valid distribution architecture [20].

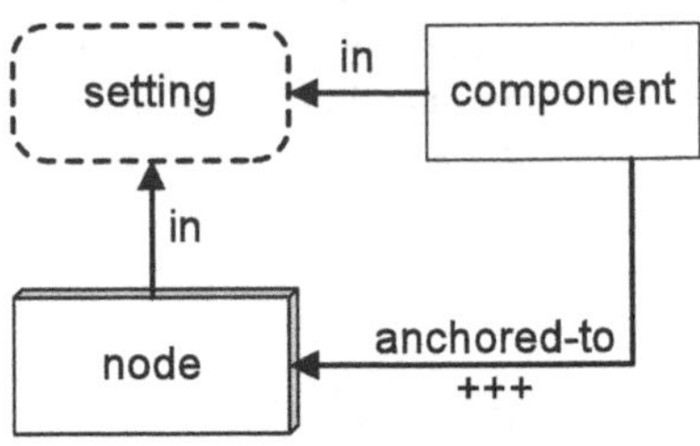

Fig. 15.13 The anchor rule

The chain of rule applications represents the refinement trajectory that we saw in Fig. 15.9. In the case of partial failure of the distributed system, any rule steps that are no longer valid are unwound, ultimately removing from the *Fiia* architecture any components or connectors that are no longer valid.

15.7 Experience

The *Fiia.Net* toolkit has been implemented and used to develop a range of applications. These include *Raptor* (as described in this chapter), a collaborative furniture layout program (involving tabletop design of the furniture layout, and interaction with the design by collaborators using PC and Smartphone), a distributed slide presentation system, an instant messaging system, and a voice over IP communication tool. These applications involve a wide range of interaction styles and devices.

We have found that developers require tutoring to understand how to structure applications around *Fiia* scenes, but are productive once they have learned the style. *Fiia* diagrams are significantly different from the UML class diagrams with which most developers are familiar. Class diagrams represent a general case, whereas *Fiia* diagrams represent a specific runtime snapshot of the system. Class diagrams focus on inheritance and aggregation structures, while *Fiia* diagrams represent communication patterns, data sharing, and interfaces between the physical and virtual worlds. (Class diagrams, of course, have no way of expressing runtime scenes or transitions between them and so are inadequate for modeling collaborative augmented reality.) Once developers have learned how to think of applications in terms of scenario steps linked by runtime transition, we have found them to be able to productively work with the *Fiia* notation.

The runtime performance of *Fiia.Net* applications is excellent, sometimes exceeding that of the standard *.Net* libraries. We implemented *Raptor* using both *Fiia* and standard *.Net Remoting*. In the *.Net* case, there was noticeable latency between the designer (tabletop) and tester (game PC) views. With the *Fiia* implementation, there was no perceptible delay. This shows that it is possible to implement applications using a conceptual model as abstract as *Fiia*'s, while winning excellent performance.

The speed of performing adaptations, however, is considerably slower. A single element can be added to the scene with only a slight delay as the *Fiia.Net* refinery computes and deploys the appropriate distribution architecture. However, when adding dozens of elements rapidly (with multiple designers repeatedly stamping as many new elements into the scene as quickly as they can), *Fiia.Net* can take as many as tens of seconds to refine the new architecture. We expect over time to dramatically improve this performance by deploying improved graph rewriting algorithms in the refinery.

Our next steps are to continue to improve the implementation of *Fiia*.net and to extend it to further platforms such as the Xbox 360 and the Microsoft Zune. Using the Mono implementation of Microsoft .Net, it should further be possible to extend *Fiia.Net* to other platforms such as the Macintosh and Linux.

15.8 Conclusion

In this chapter, we have introduced *Fiia*, a visual notation for expressing the design of collaborative AR applications. We have shown that *Fiia* allows applications to be specified at a high level reminiscent of scenarios. The *Fiia.Net* toolkit can then be used to implement these scenarios and the transitions between them. As we have shown, *Fiia.Net* resolves the issues of how applications are implemented as distributed systems involving a range of physical devices.

Acknowledgments This work benefitted from the generous support of the Natural Science and Engineering Research Council of Canada and NECTAR, the Network for Effective Collaboration Technologies through Advanced Research.

References

1. Agustin, M., Chuang, G., Delgado, A., Ortega, A., Seaver, J., Buchanan, J.: Game sketching. In: Proceedings of the Second International Conference on Digital Interactive Media in Entertainment and Arts, pp. 36–43 (2007)
2. Bencomo, N., Blair, G., Grace, P.: Models, reflective mechanisms and family-based systems to support dynamic configuration. In: MODDM '06, pp. 1-6. ACM Press (2006)
3. Bjork, S., Holopainen, J.: Patterns in Game Design. Charles River, Hingham, MA (2004)
4. Calvary, G., Coutaz, J., Nigay, L.: From single-user architectural design to PAC∗: A generic software architecture model for CSCW. In: Proc. CHI '97, pp. 242–249. ACM Press (1997)
5. Dahlbäck, N., Jönsson, A., Ahrenberg, L.: Wizard of Oz studies: why and how.In: IUI '93: Proceedings of the 1st International Conference on Intelligent User Interfaces, pp. 193–200. ACM (1993)
6. Dubois, E., Gray, P.: A design-oriented information-flow refinement of the ASUR interaction model.In: Engineering Interactive Systems. Springer LNCS (2007)
7. Fiala, M.: ARTag, a fiducial marker system using digital techniques. Computer Vision and Pattern Recognition, IEEE Computer Society Conference on **2**, 590–596 (2005)
8. Fischer, T., Niere, J., Torunski, L., Zündorf, A.: Story diagrams: A new graph rewrite language based on the Unified Modeling Language and Java.In: Proc. TAGT'98, pp. 296–309. Springer-Verlag (2000)
9. Fisher, S.S.: An authoring toolkit for mixed reality experiences. In: Proceedings of the International Workshop on Entertainment Computing (IWEC2002): Special Session on Mixed Reality Entertainment, pp. 487–494 (2002)

10. Graham, T.C.N., Roberts, W.: Toward quality-driven development of 3D computer games.In: Proceedings of the Thirteenth International Workshop on Design, Specification and Verification of Interactive Systems, pp. 248–261. Springer LNCS (2006)
11. Hill, R., Brinck, T., Rohall, S., Patterson, J., Wilner, W.: The *Rendezvous* language and architecture for constructing multi-user applications. ACM TOCHI **1**(2), 81–125 (1994)
12. Kato, H., Billinghurst, M.: Marker tracking and hmd calibration for a video-based augmented reality conferencing system. In: Proceedings of the 2nd International Workshop on Augmented Reality (IWAR 99) (1999)
13. Laurillau, Y., Nigay, L.: Clover architecture for groupware. In: CSCW '02, pp. 236–245. ACM Press (2002)
14. Litiu, R., Zeitoun, A.: Infrastructure support for mobile collaboration. In: HICSS '04. IEEE CS (2004)
15. McEwan, G., Greenberg, S., Rounding, M., Boyle, M.: Groupware plug-ins: A case study of extending collaboration functionality through media items. In: Proc. CollabTech 2006, pp. 42–47 (2006)
16. Microsoft: Surface.Http://www.microsoft.com/surface
17. Oda, O., Lister, L.J., White, S., Feiner, S.: Developing an augmented reality racing game.In: INTETAIN '08: Proceedings of the 2nd International Conference on INtelligent TEchnologies for interactive enterTAINment, pp. 1–8. ICST (Institute for Computer Sciences, Social-Informatics and Telecommunications Engineering) (2007)
18. Patterson, J.: A taxonomy of architectures for synchronous groupware applications. ACM SIGOIS Bulletin Special Issue: Papers of the CSCW'94 Workshops **15**(3), 27–29 (1995)
19. Phillips, W.G.: Architectures for synchronous groupware. Tech. Rep. 1999-425, Queen's University, Kingston, Ontario, Canada (1999)
20. Phillips, W.G.: The Workspace Model: Dynamic distribution of interactive systems. Phd thesis, Queen's University (2006)
21. Rauterberg, M., Fjeld, M., Krueger, H., Bichsel, M., Leonhardt, U., Meier, M.: BUILD-IT: a computer vision-based interaction technique for a planning tool. In: HCI'97, pp. 303–314. Springer-Verlag (1997)
22. Roseman, M., Greenberg, S.: Building real time groupware with GroupKit, a groupware toolkit. TOCHI **3**(1), 66–106 (1996)
23. Schmalstieg, D., Hesina, G.: Distributed applications for collaborative augmented reality. In: Proc. VR '02, pp. 59–67. IEEE CS (2002)
24. Urnes, T., Graham, T.C.N.: Flexibly mapping synchronous groupware architectures to distributed implementations. In: Proceedings of the Sixth Eurographics Workshop on Design, Specification and Verification of Interactive Systems (DSV-IS '99), pp.133–148 (1999)

Chapter 16
A Software Engineering Method for the Design of Mixed Reality Systems

S. Dupuy-Chessa, G. Godet-Bar, J.-L. Pérez-Medina, D. Rieu, and D. Juras

Abstract The domain of mixed reality systems is currently making decisive advances on a daily basis. However, the knowledge and know-how of HCI scientists and interaction engineers, used in the design of such systems, are not well understood. This chapter addresses this issue by proposing a software engineering method that couples a process for designing mixed reality interaction with a process for developing the functional core. Our development method features a Y-shaped development cycle that separates the description of functional requirements and their analysis from the study of technical requirements of the application. These sub-processes produce Business Objects and Interactional Objects, which are connected to produce a complete mixed reality system. The whole process is presented via a case study, with a particular emphasis on the design of the interactive solution.

Keywords Mixed reality · Interaction design · Model · Functional core · Process

16.1 Introduction

Mixed reality systems, which include tangible user interfaces, augmented reality, and augmented virtuality seek to smoothly merge physical and digital worlds to improve usability. Many prototypes in various domains [1–4] have been developed to demonstrate the technical feasibility and the interest of such interaction techniques. But developing mixed reality systems often remains based on the realization of ad hoc solutions, which do not facilitate the reusability of the systems and do not capitalize on previous solutions. It is now required to focus on design approaches rather than adopting technology-driven approaches only.

S. Dupuy-Chessa (✉)
Laboratory of Informatics of Grenoble, Grenoble Université, 38041 Grenoble Cedex 9, France
e-mail: Sophie.Dupuy-Chessa@imag.fr

E. Dubois et al. (eds.), *The Engineering of Mixed Reality Systems*, Human-Computer Interaction Series, DOI 10.1007/978-1-84882-733-2_16,

A design approach is based on the study of users' requirements in order to propose a suitable solution. It needs approaches, like models or processes, to reason about solutions, compare them, and choose the most appropriate one according to users' needs and good practice. However, good practice for mixed reality systems is still being identified. Existing knowledge and know-how must be exploited in order to be integrated into industrial practice. At the present time, software designers and developers tend to build graphical user interfaces, which are easy to develop, but which are not always adapted to the interaction situation. Therefore exploiting and spreading design knowledge and know-how about mixed reality systems design can be a way to facilitate the acceptance of mixed reality systems in industry.

The first step to make use of design knowledge is to integrate it into models. Given the particularities of the mixed reality systems domain, current design approaches in human–computer interaction (HCI) are no longer sufficient. Several proposals (for instance, by Dubois et al. [5] and by Coutrix and Nigay [6]) have been made for guiding the design of mixed reality systems. They provide a rationale for how to combine physical and digital worlds. They are used in addition to traditional user-system task description in order to identify physical and digital objects involved in interaction techniques and the boundaries between real and virtual worlds.

A second step in helping designers is proposing design processes. The lack of maturity of the mixed reality systems domain suggests processes based on experimentations, as presented by Kulas et al. [7], rather than models. Nevertheless the use of models and their associated processes, which has been described by Nigay et al. [8] or by Gauffre et al. [9], facilitates the link with classical software engineering (SE) practices and the integration of new interaction techniques into applications.

Our goal is to propose a design method based on models integrating both an SE method for the development of the functional core and HCI practices for designing the interaction. Compatibility between design methods for interactive systems and for the functional core is a recurring problem that has already been subject to specific studies by Tarby and Barthet [10] and Lim and Long [11]. In particular, Gulliksen and Göransson [12] and Sousa and Furtado [13] propose extending the Rational Unified Process with the design of interaction, in a user-centered approach. Constantine et al. [14] also describe a process unifying the design of interaction and that of the functional core but in a usage-centered approach. These studies illustrate an interest in considering both the interaction and functional aspects while designing a system. Nevertheless, none of these studies addresses mixed reality-specific aspects, such as the integration of interaction devices like head-mounted displays, positioning systems. Moreover, they offer a weak formalization of the proposed processes, which renders their application difficult for designers.

The second section introduces software engineering principles that are used as a foundation for the design of mixed reality systems and the Symphony Y-cycle software method [15] that we will use as a medium for integrating those principles. We then describe how a Y-shaped development cycle can be applied to the design of mixed reality systems by using specific models and processes. The functional aspects, which aim at designing a functional and interactive solution without considering the technical aspects, are described in Section 16.3. Then Section 16.4

describes the technical analysis that aims at choosing the most appropriate devices, software architectures, and platforms for supporting the mixed reality system under development. In Section 16.5, the junction of both concerns poses the challenge of merging technical choices with the models elaborated in the functional analysis. Finally, we conclude by considering lessons learnt from the use of the method. We also give details of evaluations of the method, both carried out and envisaged.

16.2 Extending an SE Method for Mixed Reality Systems

16.2.1 Extending Symphony for the Design of Mixed Reality Systems

Our approach is mainly based on the practices of the Rational Unified Process [16]. We apply three of them to the design of mixed reality systems:

- The process is *iterative*. Given today's sophisticated software systems, it is not possible to define the entire problem, design the entire solution, build the software, and then test the product at the end. An iterative approach is required for allowing an increasing understanding of the problem through successive refinements and for incrementally growing an effective solution over multiple iterations. Thus, we envisage building mixed reality systems incrementally and iteratively. Additionally, sub-processes are identified for allowing shorter iterations when the activities focus on crucial elements of the system, such as the design of the interaction.
- The Symphony process is driven by *use cases and scenarios* to manage requirements. We choose a compatible approach based on scenarios [7] to complement the process with design steps specific to the design of mixed reality systems (for instance, the choice of interaction devices or the design of interaction techniques). These scenarios are used as a pivot model for all specialists.
- The process uses *graphical models of the* software to capture the structure and behavior of components. Graphical models, such as UML diagrams, help to communicate different aspects of the software, enable a developer to see how the elements of the system fit together, maintain consistency between a design and its implementation, and promote unambiguous communication among developers. For the design of mixed reality systems, we complement classical HCI models like task trees [17] with specific models such as ASUR [5].

Additionally, the original Symphony method was centered on the early use of reusable and reused components. It provides a systematic approach for defining a solution using new and existing components. When the solution is precise enough to be described by computerized objects, we propose to structure the interaction space with Interactional Objects [18]. These constructs, which are specific to our approach, model user interface-oriented components. In parallel, the business is designed into components called Business Objects.

During the process, models and scenarios are continuously refined. SE and HCI-oriented activities are realized either in cooperation or in parallel, by design actors specialized either in SE and/or HCI. All actors collaborate in order to ensure consistency of adopted design options.

However mixed reality system design is not yet a fully mastered task. The design process needs to be flexible enough to evolve over time. Therefore, our Symphony method extended for mixed reality systems contains black box activities which correspond to not fully mastered practices: a black box only describes the activity's principles and its purpose without describing a specific process. In such a case, we let the designer use her usual practices to achieve the goal. For instance, "preparing user experiments" is a black box activity, which describes the desired goal without making explicit the way in which it is achieved.

The method also proposes extension mechanisms, in particular alternatives. Indeed, we can imagine alternatives corresponding to different practices. For instance, different solutions can be envisioned to realize the activity "analyzing users' tasks". They are specified as alternative paths in our process.

Additionally, Symphony is based on a Y-shaped development cycle (Fig. 16.1). It is organized into three design branches, similar to 2TUP [19]. For each iteration, the whole development cycle is applied for each functional unit of the system under development [15]:

- The *functional (left) branch* corresponds to the traditional task of domain and user requirements modeling, independently from technical aspects. Considering the design of a mixed reality system, this branch is based on an extension of the process defined by [8]. It includes interaction scenarios, task analysis, interaction modality choices, and mock-ups. This branch ends by structuring the domains with Interactional and Business Objects required to implement the mixed reality system.
- The *technical (right) branch* allows developers to design both the technical and software architectures. It also combines all the constraints and technical choices with relation to security, load balancing, etc. In this chapter, we limit the technical choices to those related to mixed reality systems support, that is, the choice of devices and the choice of the global architecture.
- The *central branch* integrates the technical and functional branches into the design model, which merges the analysis model with the applicative architecture and details of traceable components. It shows how the interaction components are structured and distributed on the various devices and how they are linked with the functional concepts.

In the rest of the chapter, the extended Symphony method and its design principles will be detailed in a case study, which concerns the creation of an inventory of premise fixtures.

16.2.2 Case Study

Describing the state of a whole premise can be a long and difficult task. In particular, real-estate agents need to qualify damage in terms of its nature, location, and extent when tenants move in as well as when they move out. Typically, this evaluation is carried out on paper or using basic digital forms. Additionally, an agent may have to evaluate changes in a premises based on someone else's previous notes, which may be incomplete or imprecise.

Identifying responsibilities for particular damage is yet another chore, which regularly leads to contentious issues between landlords, tenants and real-estate agencies.

In order to address these issues, one solution may be to consider improving the computerization of the process of making an inventory of premise fixtures. In particular, providing better ways to characterize damage and to improve the integration of the process into the real-estate agency's information system, as well as its usability, all of which could add considerable value to this activity.

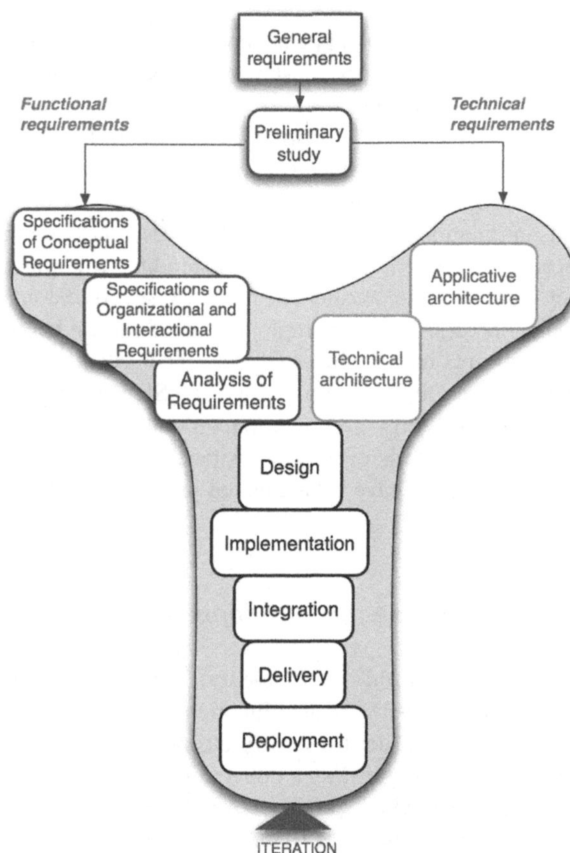

Fig. 16.1 Symphony design phases

In the following sections, we detail the application of our method to this case study.

16.3 The Functional Branch

16.3.1 Introduction

This section presents the development activities of the extended Symphony method's functional branch from the preliminary study to the requirements analysis.

In particular, the focus of our concern is on the collaborations that HCI specialists may have with SE experts. Therefore, we provide an excerpt of our development process centered on these aspects, in Fig. 16.2. Please note that, for the sake of conciseness, both the SE and HCI processes have been greatly simplified. For instance, we present collaborations between domains (i.e., a group of actors sharing the same concerns), not between the particular actors; in fact, several collaborations occur between the functional roles of each domain during the application's development cycle.

The activities that appear across the swimlanes correspond to cooperations: the development actors must work together to produce a common product. For instance, the "Description of weaving model between Business Objects and Interactional Objects" involves having both the HCI and SE experts identifying which Interactional Objects correspond to projections of Business Objects and laying this down in a specific model.

Coordination activities are not represented as such in the central swimlane because the experts do not need to produce a common product. On the contrary, they mustcompare products from their respective domains in order to validate their design choices. In our example, the coordination between the "Structuring of business concepts into Business Objects" and "Structuring of interaction concepts into Interactional Objects" implies that the SE and HCI experts identify whether they may need to modify their model in order to facilitate the ulterior weaving of the two models. The details of these activities, as well as the possible business evolutions they may trigger, have been covered in [20].

16.3.2 Initiating the Development

Before starting a full development iteration, a preliminary study of the business is realized. Its aim is to obtain a functional decomposition of the business as practiced by the client, in order to identify business processes and their participants. A business process is defined as a collection of activities taken in response to a specific input or event, which produces a value-added output for the process' client. For instance, our inventory of fixtures case study corresponds to a fragment of a larger

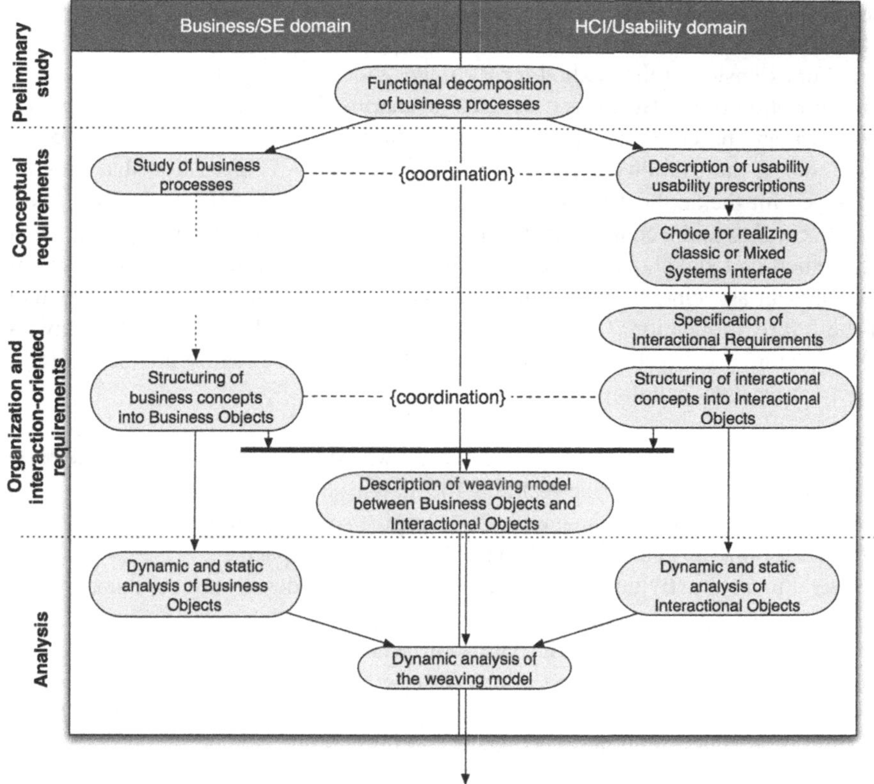

Fig. 16.2 Collaborations between the HCI and SE domains during the functional development

real-estate management business, in which several business processes can be identified: "management of tenants," "management of landholders," and "management of inventories of fixtures." An essential issue of this phase is therefore to identify the stakeholders' value for each process.

This study is described using high-level scenarios in natural language shared by all development specialists (including usability and HCI specialists), so as to provide a unified vision of the business, through the description of its constitutive processes.

In this phase, the usability specialist collaborates with the business expert for capturing prescriptions based on the current implementation of the business processes, as well as for defining a reference frame of the application's users, using the participants identified by the business specialist during the writing of the scenarios.

16.3.3 Conceptual Specifications of Requirements

In the original description of the Symphony method, this phase essentially comprises the detailing of the subsystems that constitute the different Business processes and of the actors that intervene at this level, in terms of sequence diagrams and scenarios.

In our extension of the method for HCI, we associate the usability specialist with the description of the Business processes' scenarios. In collaboration with the HCI specialist, and based on the scenarios and usability prescriptions (from the preliminary study), the usability expert determines the types of interaction that may be envisaged for the application, such as mixed reality, post-WIMP, or classical interfaces according to the context and needs. In collaboration with the other actors from the method and stakeholders, an estimation of the added value, cost, and risks of development associated with the interaction choice is realized, for each subsystem of the future application. Considering our example, the "Realization of an inventory of fixtures" subsystem is a good candidate for a mixed reality interaction for a variety of reasons including

- The case study typically features a situation where the user cannot use a desktop workstation efficiently while realizing the activity.
- Textual descriptions of damage are both imprecise and tedious to use, especially for describing the evolution of damage over time and space.
- Several manual activities are required for thoroughly describing the damage, e.g. taking measures, photographs.
- The data gathered during the inventory of fixtures cannot be directly entered into the information system (except if the user operates a wireless handheld device).
- Standard handheld device such as PDAs would only allow the use of textual, form-filling approaches, with the aforementioned limitations.

16.3.4 Organizational and Interaction-Oriented Specification of Requirements

Once the Business Processes are identified and specified, the organizational and interaction-oriented specification of requirements must determine the "who does what and when" of the future system. Concerning the business domain, the SE specialist essentially identifies use cases from the previous descriptions of business processes, and from there refines business concepts into functional components called Business Objects.

We have extended this phase to include the specifications of the interaction, based on the choices on the style of interaction made during the previous phase.

Three essential aspects are focused on in this phase: first, the constitution of the "Interaction Record" product, which integrates the synthesis of all the choices made in terms of HCI; second, the realization of prototypes, based on "frozen" versions of the Interaction Record; third, the elaboration of usability tests, which use the Interaction Record and the prototypes as a basis.

The design of these three aspects is contained as a sub-process within a highly iterative loop, which allows testing multiple interactive solutions, and therefore identifying usability and technological issues before the actual integration of the solution into the development cycle.

The construction of the Interaction Record is initiated by creating a projection of the users' tasks in the application under development: the HCI specialist describes "Abstract Projected Scenarios" [8], based on usability prescriptions proposed by the usability expert. However, at this point the description remains anchored in a business-oriented vision of the user task, as we can see in Table16.1.

Table 16.1 Abstract Projected Scenario for the "Create damage report" task

Theme(s)	{Localization, Data input}
Participant(s)	Inventory of Fixtures expert
Post-condition	The damage is observed and recorded in the Inventory of fixtures
(...) The expert enters a *room*. Her *position* is indicated on the *premises plan*. The past inventory of fixtures does not indicate any damage or wear-out (*damage*) that needs to be checked in this room. She walks around the room and notices a dark spot on one of the walls. She creates a new damage report, describes the observed damage, its position on the premise's plan and takes a *recording* (photograph or video) of the damage and its context (...).	

From this basis, the HCI specialist moves her focus to three essential and interdependent aspects of the future interaction: the description of interaction artifacts, interaction techniques, and the device classes for supporting the interaction. This latter activity is optional, given that it is only necessary when designing mixed reality interfaces. Additionally, this activity is undertaken in collaboration with the usability expert.

We expect the following types of results from these activities:

- A textual description of the interaction artifacts, including lists of attributes for each of these artifacts. A list of physical objects that will be tracked and used by the future system may also be provided (even though at this point we do not need to detail the tracking technology involved).
- Dynamic diagrams may be used for describing the interaction techniques. Both physical action-level user task models (e.g., ConcurTaskTrees [17]) and more software-oriented models (e.g., UML statecharts [16]) may be used. For instance, the following interaction technique for displaying a menu and selecting an option may be described using a task model: the expert makes a 1-s pressure on the Tactile input; a menu appears on the Augmented vision display with a default highlight on the first option; the expert then makes up or down dragging gestures to move the highlight; the expert releases the pressure to confirm the selection.
- Static diagrams for describing device and dataflow organization for augmented reality interactions, such as ASUR [5], complement the description of artifacts and interaction techniques. Figure 16.3 presents an example of such a diagram for the "Create a damage report" task.

The user, identified as the expert, is wearing an Augmented vision display ("==" relation), which provides information (→ relation symbolizes physical or numerical data transfer) about the marker and vocal note virtual objects. Additionally, the Mobile Display device, which is linked to the Tactile input ("==" relation), provides information about the marker, vocal note, and situational mesh (i.e., the 3D model of the premises) virtual objects. The marker is a numerical representation ("→" relation) of physical damage in the physical world. The expert can interact with the marker and situational mesh objects using Tactile input. She can interact with the vocal note using a Vocal Command input. The expert's position in the premises is deduced from the Positioning system, which sends information to the virtual objects for updating the virtual scene as the expert moves.

The descriptions of artifacts, interaction techniques, and classes of devices are then integrated into "Concrete Projected Scenarios" [8], which put into play all the concepts elaborated previously, as an evolution of the Abstract Projected Scenarios. An extract of Concrete Projected Scenario is presented in Table 16.2.

Finally, high-level user task models are deduced from the Concrete Projected Scenarios, both in order to facilitate the evaluation process and to validate the constructed models.

Following each iteration of the Interaction Record's development, we recommend the construction of paper and software prototypes (Flash or Powerpoint simulations, HCI tryouts...) putting into play the products of the interaction-oriented specifications. Beyond the advantage of exploring design solutions, the prototypes allow the usability expert to set up usability evaluations for validating the specifications. Figure 16.4 presents an early prototype for the Augmented Inventory of Fixtures application, with both the expert wearing an augmented vision device and the data displayed.

From these different products of the interface's design process, the usability expert compiles recommendations and rules for the future user interface, such as its graphic chart, cultural, and physical constraints. Based on the prototypes, the Interaction Record and the Concrete Projected Scenarios, the usability expert may start elaborating validation tests for all the products of the interaction-oriented specification. We use "Black box activities" for describing these steps, as described in Section 16.2.

Depending on the results of the usability tests, a new iteration of the specification of interaction-oriented requirements may be undertaken, returning to the Abstract Projected Scenarios if necessary.

Finally, once the interaction-oriented requirements are validated, the HCI expert proceeds with the elicitation of the Interactional Objects, deduced from the interaction concepts identified previously. The criteria for this selection are based on the concepts' granularity and density (i.e., if a concept is anecdotally used or is described by only a few attributes, then it may not be a pertinent choice for an Interactional Object).

As was mentioned in Fig. 16.2, a cooperation activity between HCI and SE experts aims at mapping these Interactional Objects to the Business Object they represent through a "represent" relationship. For instance, the "marker" Interactional

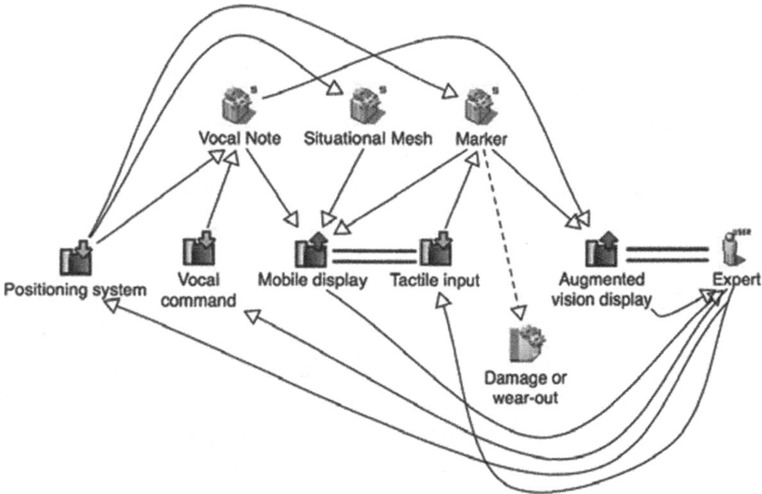

Fig. 16.3 ASUR model representing the "Create damage" task

Table 16.2 Concrete Projected Scenario for the "Create damage" task

Supporting device(s)	{Mobile tactile display, Augmented vision device, Vocal input device, Positioning system}
Interaction artifact(s)	{marker, situational mesh, vocal note}

(...) The Expert enters a *room*. Her *position* is indicated on the *situational mesh*, which is partially displayed on the *Mobile tactile display*. The past inventory of fixtures does not indicate any damage or wear (*marker object*) that needs to be checked in this room. She walks around the room, notices a dark spot on one of the walls. She creates a new *marker* and positions, orients and scales it, using the *Mobile tactile display*. Then she locks the *marker* and describes the damage by making a *vocal note with* the *Vocal input device* (...)

Fig. 16.4 Augmented Inventory of Fixtures prototype

Object is linked to the "Damage" object, through a "represent" relationship (see Fig. 16.5).

In the following section, we detail how the Symphony Objects that have been identified previously are refined and detailed.

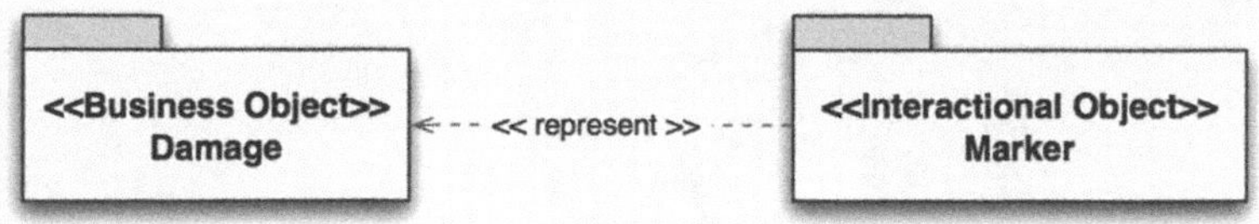

Fig. 16.5 "Represent" relationship between an Interactional Object and a Business Object

16.3.5 Analysis

This phase describes how the Symphony Objects are structured, in terms of services and attributes, and how they behave. The latter aspect is detailed in a dynamic analysis of the system, while the former is elaborated in a static analysis. Following these analyses, details of the communication between the business and interaction spaces, indicated by the "represent" relationship, are described.

Concerning the business space, the dynamic analysis consists of refining the use cases identified during the previous phase into scenarios and UML sequence diagrams, for identifying business services. These services are themselves refined during the static analysis into the Symphony tripartite structure (i.e. methods and attributes are identified, see Fig. 16.6). The left-most part describes the services proposed by the object, the central part describes the implementation of the services, and the right-most part (not used in this example) describes the collaborations the object needs to set up in order to function. A "use" dependency relationship allows Symphony Objects to be organized (e.g., the "Inventory of fixtures" depends on the "Damage" concept during its life cycle).

Concerning the interaction space, the dynamic analysis is similar to that of the business space, but based on the high-level user task models elaborated at the end of the specification of organizational and interaction-oriented requirements phase. They are complemented by UML statechart diagrams for describing the objects' life cycles. For instance, the "marker" Interactional Object can be described using a simple statechart diagram with two states: it may be "Locked" and immovable or "Unlocked" and moveable.

Similar to the business space, the static analysis refines these studies into tripartite components. We propose the same, model-oriented representation of Business Objects and Interactional Objects (i.e., "Symphony Objects") [17], in order to facilitate their integration into MDE tools, as well as their implementation.

At this point, both the business and interaction spaces have been described in parallel, from an abstract (i.e., from technological concerns) point of view. Now HCI and SE specialists need to detail the dynamic semantics of the "represent" relationships that were drawn during the Specification phases.

It is first necessary to identify the services from the interaction space that may have an impact on the business space. For instance, creating a "marker" object in the interaction space implies creating the corresponding "Damage" object in the business space. Second, the translation from one conceptual space to the next needs

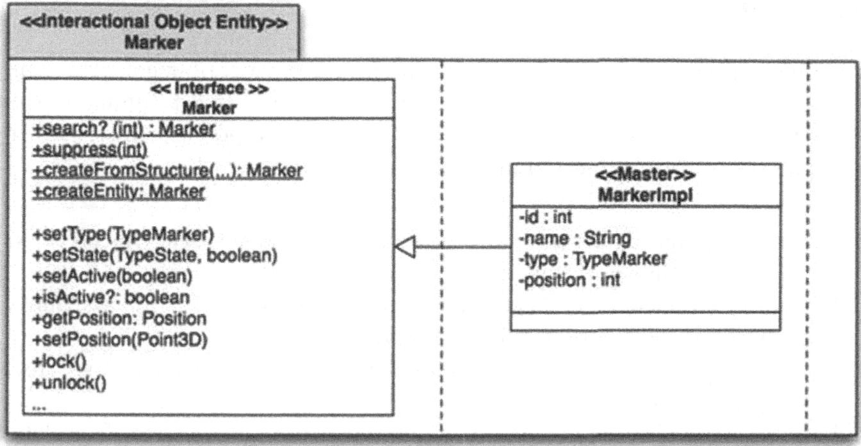

Fig. 16.6 Interactional Object example

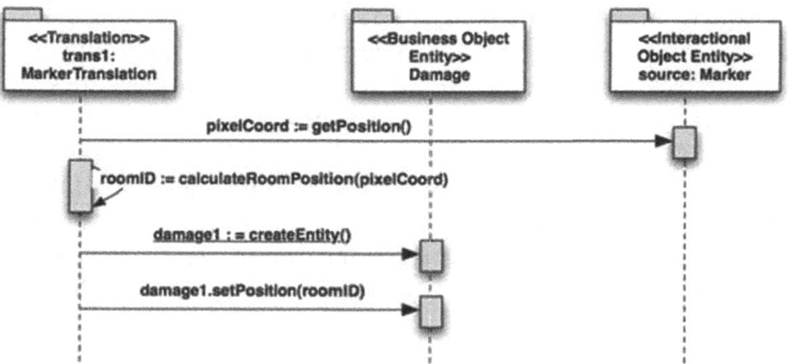

Fig. 16.7 Translation semantics corresponding to the "createMarker" event

to be described. In our example, it is necessary to convert the pixel coordinates of the "marker" into the architectural measures of the premises plan.

These translations from one conceptual space to another are managed by "Translation" objects. There is one instance of such object for each instance of connection between Interactional Objects and Business Objects. In the Analysis phase, the Translation objects are described using sequence diagrams for each case of Interactional–Business Object communication. Figure 16.7 illustrates the consequence of the "createMarker" interaction event in terms of its translation into the business space. Note that the reference to the marker object (i.e., the "source" instance) is assumed to be registered into the Translation object. Details of this mechanism are presented in Section 16.5.

16.3.6 Main Points Discussed

The extension of the Symphony method for the development of augmented reality systems capitalizes on the features we discussed in Section 16.2.1. Similar to what is achieved in terms of the business description, we have proposed the following principles for the development of the interaction space:

1. Early description of interaction components (i.e., "Interactional Objects"), during the specification of requirements.
2. Structuring of interaction components based on the same tripartite structure as the business components (i.e., "Business Objects").
3. Parallel and collaborative description of the business and interaction specifications and analysis.
4. Late connection between the business and interaction spaces, using Translation objects.

As we can see, principles 1 and 2 reproduce what was initially proposed for the business space. However, principles 3 and 4 aim at allowing HCI experts and usability experts to design ambitious interfaces early enough in the development cycle for permitting their integration into the final system. Additionally, the design of the user interface involves regular prototyping and evaluation activities, contained in a highly iterative sub-process, as recommended by ISO 13407 for UCD (user-centered design).

As a consequence of the application of these principles, the end of the development of the functional branch provides developers with two exhaustively detailed sets of products structuring the business and interaction spaces, as well as the necessary elements for realizing the junction between these spaces (i.e., the Translation classes).

Additionally, we have integrated regular collaborations between the HCI specialist and the usability expert during all the phases of the functional branch. The usability specialist herself involves future users in the design process (for instance through the observation of the business practices and the usability tests). These practices greatly increase the overall usability and efficiency of the future system. In this respect, we follow once again the indications of ISO 13407 for UCD.

16.4 The Technical Branch

The technical branch of the original Symphony method allows developers to design the applicative and technical architectures. Their goal is the analysis of all the constraints and technical choices related to security, pervasiveness, and load balancing, for example. We saw previously that in order to design mixed reality systems, our method considers the choice of techniques of interaction, interaction artifacts, and classes of devices. Consequently, this has led us to propose extensions for the technical branch.

The applicative architecture corresponds to the organization of technical and functional components among applicative tiers, as well as the description of the software architectures used for supporting the execution of Business and Interactional Objects detailed during the Analysis phase. Additionally, patterns and design rules are identified and defined for the applicative architecture. The technical architecture corresponds to the hardware and technology (e.g., frameworks) solutions that will allow the application to be run. Finally, note that both phases are realized concurrently with the functional requirements.

16.4.1 Description of the Applicative Architecture

The goal of this phase is to identify and describe the rationale concerning the selection of the software architecture, which must allow the integration of the technical and functional components. First, the distribution of components among applicative layers is described, before a software architecture for efficiently supporting the interaction is superimposed on the applicative layers.

Description of applicative layers. The original Symphony method recommends placing of the components in a five-tier architecture, for classic systems. The tiers are built following the Layer pattern [21], which enables designing, developing, and testing each tier independently from the others. The extension of the method preserves this decomposition of the information system and describes the distribution of Business Objects and Interactional Objects among the five layers. This applicative choice facilitates the maintenance, reuse, and evolution of future software.

Description of the software architecture. The original Symphony method recommends the MVC pattern for the design of the Presentation layer, which allows isolating the business concerns of the application from the interface's control and view concerns. However, this solution needs to be complemented for taking into account the distribution of Interactional Objects, as well as the technical constraints imposed by mixed reality systems, such as multimedia rendering loops. Figure 16.8 illustrates how we envisage this dispatch of components among the applicative tiers, using an adapted MVC software architecture:

- The Interactional Objects correspond to the abstract, logical part of the MVC's "View", while the "OpenGL Client" corresponds to the technical implementation of the Interactional Objects; the "Controller" is an adaptation of the View to the user input (e.g., pressing a given button triggers a notification, which allows matching this event with a given action).
- The Business Objects correspond to the "Model" part of the MVC pattern.
- The Translation objects correspond to facets of MVC's "Controller" in the sense that they manage the bridge between the "Model" and "View" aspects.

16.4.2 Description of the Technical Architecture

This section describes the technical analysis for choosing the most adequate devices and platforms for supporting mixed reality systems.

Choice of interaction devices. Once the need to develop a Mixed System (in this case, an augmented reality system) is identified (see Section 16.3.3), it is necessary to choose the most satisfactory interaction devices. This selection must be made on the basis of characteristics of the generic devices identified during the specification of organizational and interaction-oriented requirements (see Section 16.3.4).

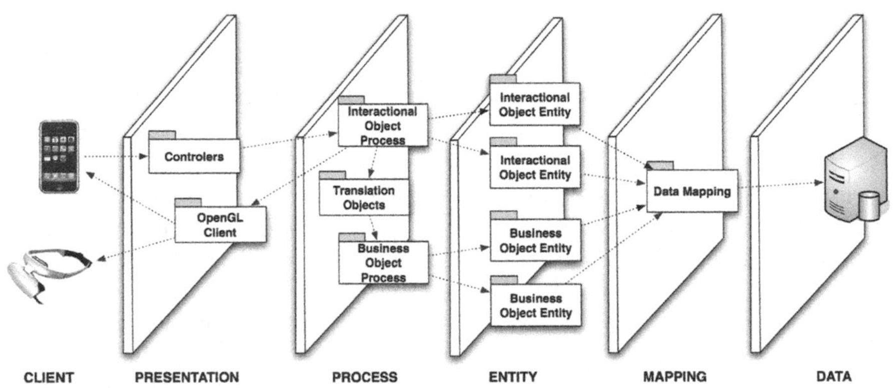

Fig. 16.8 Applicative architecture for mixed reality systems

Our method for facilitating the selection of devices is based on the QOC[1] notation [22]. It enables designers to classify and to justify the design decisions. In the context of the inventory of fixtures, the study of the interaction has determined the need for an augmented vision display, a tactile input and mobile display, a positioning system (i.e., orientation and localization), and a vocal command device (see Fig. 16.3). For the sake of conciseness, we will only present in Fig. 16.9 the selection of the augmented vision display.

Based on the QOC diagram, the usability expert has determined that the most adequate device for the inventory of fixtures is an HMD device: it allows user mobility; guarantees low energy consumption; and offers an acceptable image quality, low weight, and a wide space of visualization.

Description of the interaction's devices. This activity consists of detailing the technical specifications of each interaction device chosen during the previous activity. For instance, Table 16.3 shows the technical specifications of the HMD device.

---

[1] QOC: Questions, options, and criteria, is a semi-formal notation proposed by MacLean et al. This notation gives place to a representation as a diagram, which can decomposed into three columns, one for each element of the notation (questions, options, criteria) and links between the elements of these columns.

Table 16.3 Description of the interactive devices

Device	Technical specifications
HMD	Model AddVisor 150. Full color image on 1280 × 1024 pixels (SXGA), excellent image quality, high brightness, and contrast. Superposed image with up to 35% see-through or fully immersed. Designed for a 46° diagonal 100% overlap field of view. Low weight.

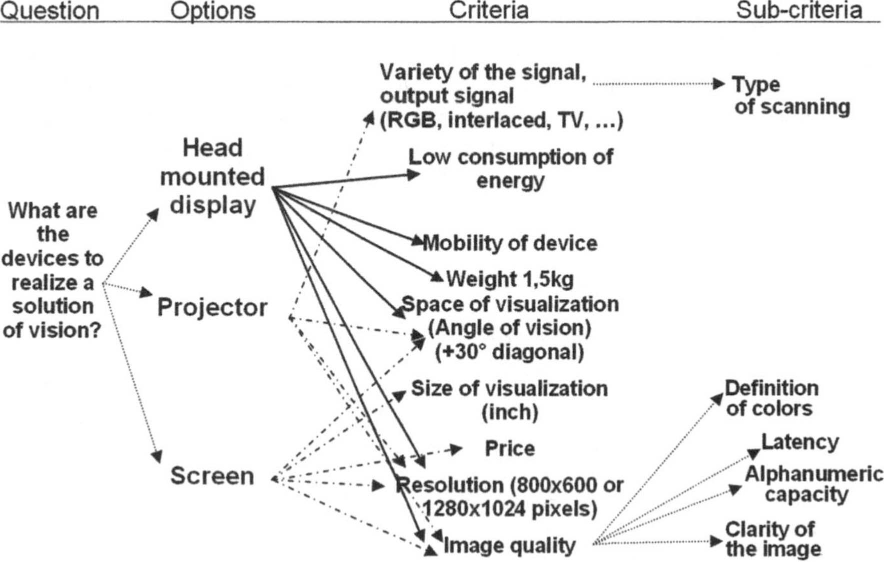

Fig. 16.9 Selection criteria for the vision support device

16.4.3 Main Points Discussed

In this section we have presented a methodological guide adapted to HCI concerns that aims at selecting the most adequate device, software architectures, and platforms to support the design of mixed reality systems, based on the use of principles underlying recognized software architectures. We use the QOC notation, which allows technical aspects to be organized and classified, for facilitating the choice of devices and software architectures adapted to mixed reality systems.

16.5 The Junction of the Functional and Technical Branches

16.5.1 Design

Two essential aspects need to be addressed at this point in the development cycle: the blending of the functional analysis with the technical choices (i.e., the organization of the functional and non-functional software components) and the deployment of these components on the technical infrastructure.

For the sake of conciseness, the latter point is not extensively discussed in this chapter: the choices made are in fact summarized in Fig. 16.10. We use a tactile smartphone device for running the application, which is linked to the real-estate agency's database through a wireless message bus. Additionally, the "Vocal Command" and "Positioning System" mentioned in Fig. 16.3 correspond to the internal microphone and Wi-Fi/accelerometers (used for position triangulation purposes) sub-devices of the smartphone. The "Tactile input" is managed by the "Tactile display" sub-device. An OpenGL client, which corresponds to a technical presentation component (c.f. Presentation tier in Fig. 16.8) managed by the Interactional Objects, manages the display of the adequate data for both the HMD and the Tactile display. Finally, note that the Interactional Objects, Business Objects and Translations are dispatched amongst the Process and Entity tiers.

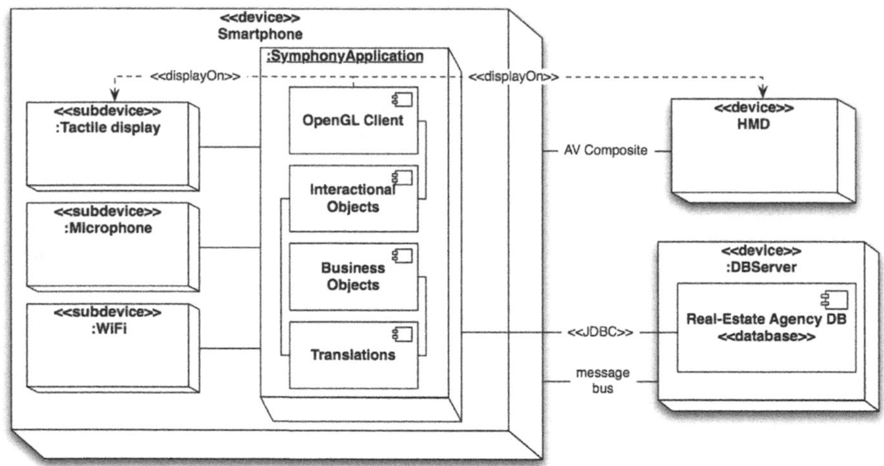

Fig. 16.10 Deployment diagram for the functional and technical components of the augmented inventory of fixtures application

The OpenGL client runs the main rendering loop of the 3D scene and dispatches user events to the Controller elements, while another thread loop taps into captured Wi-Fi and acceleration data in order to infer the user's location, which is then notified to the main loop. The initial position of the user in the premises is obtained using manual calibration (i.e., the user pinpoints her position in the premises on the smartphone before starting the inventory of fixtures).

We focus now on the design choices made for realizing the connection between Interactional Objects and Business Objects, via the Translation objects.

In the technical branch, we noted that the use of the MVC architectural style corresponds to the requirements for our Augmented Inventory of Fixtures. Consequently, we need to adapt the Analysis models concerning the structure and behavior of the Symphony Objects to this architectural style, while preserving the semantics of the functional services they provide.

As we saw previously, every collaboration between Symphony Objects (represented by "use" relationships in Section 16.3) occurs through a "Role" class (see the comments concerning Fig. 16.6).

In order to respect the MVC architectural style, we chose to overload the responsibilities of the "Role" classes with the management of the Interactional Object–Business Object (IO–BO) communications.

Concretely, when an event occurring in an Interactional Object needs to be reflected in the business space, the communications between the interaction space and the business space (identified by "represent" relationships in Section 16.3) occur through the "Role" classes. "Figure 16.11 presents an example of such a communication, where the Interactional Object that uses the "marker" object creates a new marker instance, through the "MarkerRole"object":

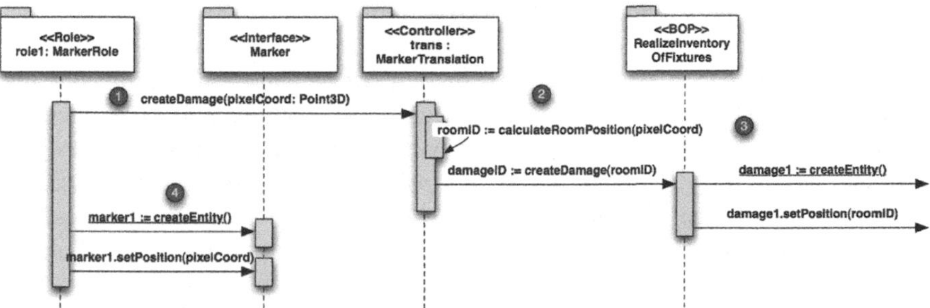

Fig. 16.11 Simplified view of the Interaction Object–Business Object connection at the design level

1. The "MarkerRole" object calls the "MarkerTranslation" object to create a new damage report in the business space.
2. The "MarkerTranslation" object translates the pixel coordinates of the marker into the corresponding position in the premises and calls the "RealizeInventoryOfFixtures" Business Object Process (which holds the applicative logic for creating damages).
3. The "RealizeInventoryOfFixtures" Business Object Process calls the Business Object Entity for creating the damage in the right room of the premises.
4. The "MarkerRole" calls the "marker" Interactional Object for creating a marker at the appropriate location in the 3D model of the premises (i.e., the "situational mesh" from Section 16.3).

Thus, all the occurrences of Interactional Object–Business Object (IO–BO) communications are concentrated into "Role" classes. Therefore, the coupling between the interaction and business spaces is limited to clearly identified entities.

16.5.2 Main Points Discussed

We saw in this section an overview of how the Symphony method realizes the blending of the functional analysis with the technical choices. After briefly showing how the functional (i.e., Symphony Objects) and technical components may be deployed, we studied how the organization between Symphony Objects and Translations (see Section 16.3) may be adapted to the MVC common architectural style.

Let us mention that the design solution that we provided in this section is in no way exclusive. Indeed, we will show in future work how other design solutions may be efficiently implemented, independently of the technical choices, provided that developers respect the structure of the Symphony models from the Analysis phase.

16.6 Conclusions and Future Work

The Symphony method extended for mixed reality systems permits a mixed reality system design to be considered in its entirety without neglecting either the functional or the interaction part. However, if it is clear that interaction cannot be designed without considering functionality, we have pointed out in [20] that the interaction choices also influence the functional part. Therefore the method needs to include cooperative activities in order to guarantee global design consistency, and also to maximize the benefits obtained from the analysis of each conceptual space.

The method also allows a clear separation of concerns, as well as design traceability for each domain. We focused in this chapter on how these properties are achieved in the interaction space.

The method has been applied to two case studies. Each study was realized by teams of three persons. These teams consisted of average and expert programmers, some of whom are authors of this chapter, others being interns in our research team.

The first application we developed concerned the simulation and evaluation of airport security. It had to respect precise requirements from another research team in our laboratory, and most particularly it had to fit into a large test workflow. Even though not strictly speaking a mixed reality system, the application nevertheless features a very complex interface (several windows, animated elements). It has met its requirements and is currently being transferred for actual deployment.

The other application (i.e., the mixed reality inventory of fixtures) is well advanced but still under development. At the current stage of development, screenshots are quite similar to the prototype presented in Fig. 16.4. Additionally, we are currently working on a robust localization system.

Even if these studies are not comparable to industrial designs, they forced us to define more precisely the design process and modify some of its steps.

However, we also noted that some developers and testers who intervened during the development or the evaluation of our method had trouble handling the volume of the specifications. Indeed, the amount of documentation produced during the development cycle is currently quite high (over 50 pages of specifications for a project of about 4000 lines of codes, for instance). This volume is generally necessary for allowing the integration of applications into large information systems (such as that of a real-estate agency) and for permitting the maintenance and evolution of the system. Nevertheless, extensive documentation is only necessary when the development team is not familiar with either the business domain or the interaction style. In more well-known contexts, large parts of the method may be either skipped or less strictly documented, thus making the development methodology more lightweight.

Finally, a large number of models are constructed during the development cycle of our mixed reality systems. Even though most of these models are either refinements of previous models or partially generated, we admit that the members of the development team currently spend too much time using a plethora of modeling tools for single iterations of their models, and not enough time discussing and iterating over these models.

Consequently, one of our long-term perspectives is to propose an open platform for supporting collaborative modeling activities and short iterations over these models. This platform may be based on the model-driven engineering approach (where models would be first-class elements). We hope that such support, coupled with our methodological guide, will facilitate the design of mixed reality systems.

Acknowledgments We are grateful to the Foundation "Gran Mariscal de Ayacucho, the university UCLA-Venezuela" for their financial support.

References

1. Wellner, P.: Interacting with Paper on DigitalDesk. Communications of the ACM (36)7, (1993), 87–96.
2. Müller, D.: Mixed Reality Learning and Working Environments – The MARVEL Approach. In Proceedings of the 12th European Conference for Educational and Information Technology (Learntec'04), Karlsruhe, Germany (2004).
3. Troccaz, J., Lavallée, S., Cinquin, P.: Computer Augmented Surgery. Human Movement Science 15, (1996), 445–475.
4. Ullmer, B., Ishii, H., Glas, D.: mediaBlocks: Physical Containers, Transports, and Controls for Online Media. In Proceedings of SIGGRAPH '98, Orlando, Florida USA, ACM Press (1998), 379–386.
5. Dubois, E., Gray, P., Nigay, L.: ASUR++: A Design Notation for Mobile Mixed Systems. Interacting with Computers 15(4), (2003), 497–520.
6. Coutrix, C., Nigay, L.: Mixed reality: A Model of Mixed Interaction. In: Proceedings of the 8th International Conference on Advanced Visual Interfaces AVI'2006, Venezia, ACM Press (2006) 43–50.
7. Kulas, C., Sandor, C., Klinker, G.: Toward a Development Methodology for Augmented Reality Users Interfaces. In Dubois, E, Gray, P., Nigay, L. (eds.): Proceedings of MIXER '04,

Exploring the Design and Engineering of Mixed Reality Systems, Proceedings of the IUI-CADUI'04 Workshop on Exploring the Design and Engineering of Mixed Reality Systems, Madeira (2004).
8. Nigay, L., Salembier, P., Marchand, T., Renevier, P., Pasqualetti, L.: Mobile and Collaborative Augmented Reality: A Scenario Based Design Approach. In Paterno, F. (ed.): Proceedings of the 4th International Symposium on Mobile HCI 2002, LNCS 2411, Springer, Pisa, Italy (2002) 241–255.
9. Gauffre, G., Dubois, E., Bastide, R.: Domain Specific Methods and Tools for the Design of Advanced Interactive Techniques, 3rd Workshop on Model Driven Development of Advanced User Interfaces at MoDELS'07, Nashville, TN – USA, CEUR-WS Proceedings (2007).
10. Tarby, J.C., Barthet, M.F.: Analyse et modélisation des tâches dans la conception des systèmes d'information: la méthode Diane+. In: Analyse et conception de l'IHM, Hermès (2001) 117–144 (In French).
11. Lim, K. Y., Long, J.: The MUSE Method for Usability Engineering, Cambridge University Press, Cambridge (1994).
12. Gulliksen, J., Göransson, B.: Usability Design: Integrating User-Centred Systems Design in the Systems Development Process. In Tutorial at CHI'2005, Portland, USA (2005).
13. Sousa, K., Furtado, E.: From Usability Tasks to Usable User Interfaces. In Dix, A., Dittmar, A., (eds.): TAMODIA '05: Proceedings of the 4th International Workshop on Task Models and Diagrams, New York, USA, ACM Press (2005) 103–110.
14. Constantine, L., Biddle, R., Noble, J.: Usage-Centered Design and Software Engineering: Models for Integration. In Harning, M.B., Vanderdonckt, J., (eds.): Proceedings of the IFIP TC13 Workshop on Closing the Gaps: Software Engineering and Human-Computer Interaction. (2003)
15. Hassine, I., Rieu, D., Bounaas, F., Seghrouchni, O.: Symphony: A Conceptual Model Based on Business Components. In: SMC'02, IEEE International Conference on Systems, Man, and Cybernetics. Volume 2. (2002)
16. Jacobson, I., Booch, G., Rumbaugh, J.: The Unified Software Development Process, Addison-Wesley, Reading, MA (1999).
17. Paterno, F.: ConcurTaskTrees: An Engineered Notation for Task Models. In: The Handbook of Task Analysis for Human-Computer Interaction, Lawrence Erlbaum Associates, Mahwah, NJ (2003) pp. 483–503.
18. Godet-Bar, G., Rieu, D., Dupuy-Chessa, S., Juras, D.: Interactional Objects: HCI Concerns In the Analysis Phase of the Symphony Method, Proceedings of the 9th International Conference on Enterprise Information System (ICEIS'2007), Madeira (2007).
19. Roques, P., Vallée, F.: UML2 en action, de l'analyse des besoins à la conception J2EE, collection Architecte Logiciel, Eyrolle, 2004 (In French).
20. Godet-Bar, G., Dupuy-Chessa, S., Rieu, D.: When interaction choices trigger business evolution, 20th International Conference on Advanced Information Systems Engineering (CAiSE'08), LNCS 5074, Springer, Montpellier, France, 16–20 June 2008, pp. 144–147.
21. Buschmann, F., Meunier, R., Rohnert, H., Sommerlad, P., Stal, M.: Pattern-Oriented Software Architecture – A System of Patterns. John Wiley and Sons, Chichester (1996).
22. Maclean, A., Young, R.M., Bellotti, V.M.E, Moran, T.P.: Questions, Options and Criteria: Element of Design Space Analysis. Human-Computer Interaction 6(3), (1991), 201–250.

Part III
Applications of Mixed Reality

Chapter 17
Enhancing Health-Care Services with Mixed Reality Systems

Vladimir Stantchev

Abstract This work presents a development approach for mixed reality systems in health care. Although health-care service costs account for 5–15% of GDP in developed countries the sector has been remarkably resistant to the introduction of technology-supported optimizations. Digitalization of data storing and processing in the form of electronic patient records (EPR) and hospital information systems (HIS) is a first necessary step. Contrary to typical business functions (e.g., accounting or CRM) a health-care service is characterized by a knowledge intensive decision process and usage of specialized devices ranging from stethoscopes to complex surgical systems. Mixed reality systems can help fill the gap between highly patient-specific health-care services that need a variety of technical resources on the one side and the streamlined process flow that typical process supporting information systems expect on the other side. To achieve this task, we present a development approach that includes an evaluation of existing tasks and processes within the health-care service and the information systems that currently support the service, as well as identification of decision paths and actions that can benefit from mixed reality systems. The result is a mixed reality system that allows a clinician to monitor the elements of the physical world and to blend them with virtual information provided by the systems. He or she can also plan and schedule treatments and operations in the digital world depending on status information from this mixed reality.

Keywords Mixed reality · Surgical sector · Location awareness

17.1 Health Care and Mixed Reality Systems

Physician and nursing staff in hospitals have a very high workload in general and they have to handle many different problems in a very short time. Digital assistance through software systems and electronic devices is able to reduce administrative

---

V. Stantchev (✉)
Public Services and SOA Research Group, Berlin Institute of Technology and Fachhochschule für Ökonomie und Management, Berlin, Germany
e-mail: vstantch@cs.tu-berlin.de

E. Dubois et al. (eds.), *The Engineering of Mixed Reality Systems*, Human-Computer Interaction Series, DOI 10.1007/978-1-84882-733-2_17,

workload and free physicians and nurses for their core competence, taking care of patients. Examples for such artifacts are hospital information systems (HIS) and electronic patient records (EPR) or electronic health records (EHR) [4] which simplify the access to patient data and medical information. Another artifact is devices which provide information about the location of patients, staff, and medical devices in the hospital. Such localization can be done via different technologies, for example, Ultra Wide Band (UWB), Bluetooth (BT), or Wireless LAN (WLAN) location applications.

Mixed reality systems can help fill the gap between highly patient-specific health-care services that need a variety of technical resources on the one side and the streamlined process flow that typical process supporting information systems expect on the other side. Thereby, elements of the physical world in the clinic (e.g., patients, devices, rooms, procedures and treatments) are combined with the digital world – the IT and IS infrastructure, including processing and data elements. Therefore, our development approach starts with an evaluation of existing tasks and processes within the health-care service and the information systems that currently support the service. Then we identify decision paths and actions that can benefit from mixed reality systems. The result is a mixed reality system that allows a clinician to monitor the elements of the physical world and to plan and schedule treatments and operations in the digital world. This scheduling is then used in the physical world to actually perform these actions, thereby integrating with computer-assisted medical interventions (CAMI) systems. According to the OPAS/ASUR design notation [18, 19], this system can be classified as an augmented reality (AR) system with general assumptions as follows: (i) objects (components R) are patients, clinicians, or medical devices; (ii) person (Component U) is the clinician in charge of planning and scheduling treatments; (iii) adapters (Components A) are WLAN and RFID tags; (iv) system (Component S) is the HIS system of the clinic.

To address typical design requirements of such systems (e.g., cooperating services, performance, and availability) we propose a service-oriented architecture (SOA) as software architecture and architectural translucency to provide stable QoS. Therefore, in the design and implementation phase of our approach, we evaluate related technologies and QoS assurance approaches and then present design principles for mixed reality systems. Furthermore, we present a clinical application scenario where we applied our approach and developed a mixed reality system that integrates the ASUR elements, implements the relationships between them, and supports the services provided by the clinic. It provides a fusion of the physical and digital worlds and thereby enables better handling of patients. Results demonstrated increased satisfaction among patients and clinicians, as well as significant cost savings.

17.1.1 Augmented and Mixed Reality

Azuma [2] defines augmented reality (AR) as a variation of virtual reality (VR). While VR technologies present to the user a completely synthetic environment without a relation to the real world (the users perceives only the virtual world), in an AR world the user can see the real world with its artifacts, together with virtual objects superimposed upon or composited with the real world. Obviously, AR supplements and enhances reality, rather than completely replacing it. Contrary to authors who interpret AR primarily in the context of a head-mounted display (HMD), Azuma defines three characteristics of AR systems:

- they combine real and virtual,
- they are interactive in real time, and
- they are registered in 3-D.

This definition of an AR system is extended by the definition of a mixed reality system as an interactive system combining physical and digital entities [19]. There is one important difference between these two definitions – while an AR system deals primarily with the output (e.g., visual, 2-D, 3-D) of a system, a mixed reality system deals also with inputs from the real world to the system (e.g., localization and context awareness). Therefore, a mixed reality system generally differentiates between input and output adapters. This is particularly true in our application scenario where we focus on localizers as input adapters that monitor proximity and exchange data with the system.

17.1.2 Usability Evaluation Techniques

"One of the basic lessons we have learned in human-computer interaction (HCI) is that usability must be considered before prototyping takes place" [23]. This statement is even more valid in life-critical applications such as health care. Nevertheless, usability studies are still not considered an obligatory part of design in this domain.

A comprehensive overview of usability evaluation techniques is presented in [23]. It differentiates between inspection methods (heuristic evaluation, cognitive walkthrough, and action analysis) and test methods (thinking aloud, field observation, and questionnaires). These techniques are categorized according to their applicability in different phases of the system development process, to their time requirements and the number of users, evaluators, and the complexity of equipment needed for the evaluation, as well as to their intrusiveness. A historic overview and recent developments in usability research of augmented and mixed reality specifically in the health-care domain is presented in [5].

Our approach considers intrusiveness as a particularly important aspect in health care; therefore, we apply cognitive walkthrough and action analysis as inspection methods. This requires high expertise from the evaluators, who are either clinicians themselves or design specialists with extensive domain knowledge. As test methods we use questionnaires and expert interviews.

17.1.3 Security Aspects

An overview of security aspects in ubiquitous computing in the health-care domain is presented in [41]. Authors start with the strict legal requirements for patient-related data and propose the usage of RFID tags for user authentication in mobile and ubiquitous scenarios deployed at Graz University Hospital. Important identified problems were security and privacy issues (protection precautions, confidentiality, reliability, sociability). The authors also pointed to the need of further psychological and technological research to address these problems.

Our approach follows these recommendations and incorporates security aspects at the hearth of the mixed reality system. It employs user proximity as an additional level of security and patient data protection besides state-of-the-art role-based security.

17.1.4 Work Structure

The rest of this chapter is structured as follows: in Section 17.2 we give an overview of the development approach. Section 17.3 describes a description of the case study and the scenario that underlies it. Furthermore, it defines critical aspects and design requirements for mixed reality systems in health care and describes how these were addressed within the case study. In Section 17.4 we assess our progress so far and outline our future research activities.

17.2 Overview of the Development Approach

Our development approach (see Fig. 17.1) is iterative and covers the following phases:

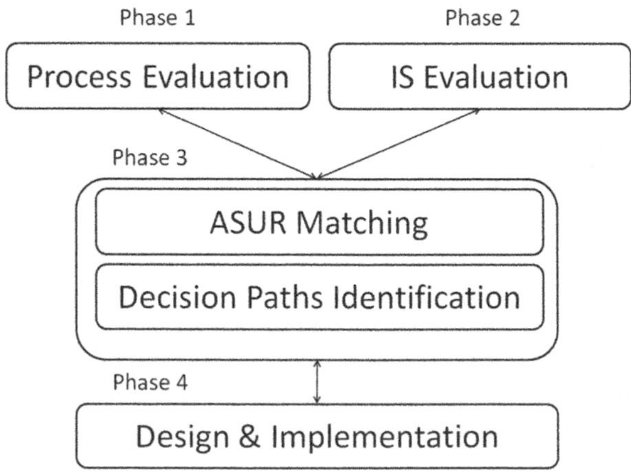

Fig. 17.1 Overview of the development approach

1. evaluation of existing tasks and processes within the health-care service;
2. evaluation of the information systems that currently support the service;
3. identification of decision paths and actions that can benefit from mixed reality systems; and
4. design and implementation of the mixed reality system, with focus on integration and NFPs.

The process is iterative, so that we go through these phases when new requirements need to be reflected by the system. The following sections will describe each of these phases in more detail.

17.2.1 Process Evaluation of the Health-Care Service

In order to capture the current state of the health-care service we use a standard process-oriented approach – system analysis [24]. It consists of several steps as depicted in Fig. 17.2 and is designed as a general blueprint for process optimization projects [24].

For the process evaluation of the health-care service, we focus on the situation analysis part of the approach. Here we use notations such as event-driven process chains (EPCs) and business process modeling notation (BPMN). We use usability evaluation techniques such as cognitive walkthrough, action analysis, field observation, and questionnaires [23]. Our user group were clinicians from hospitals with large surgical departments, as well as specialized clinics (e.g., in minimally invasive surgery).

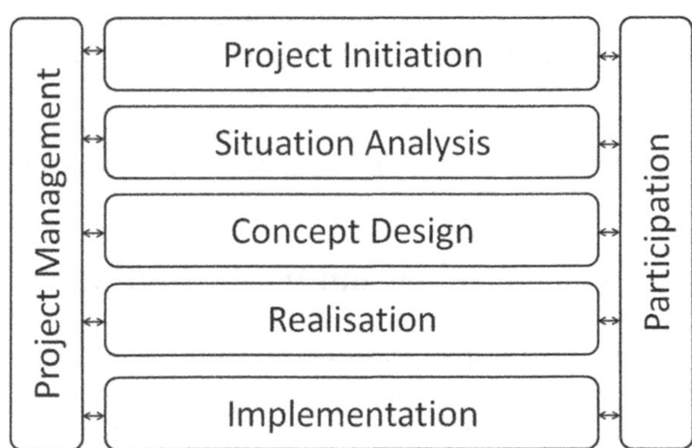

Fig. 17.2 Process model of system analysis

17.2.2 Evaluation of the Existing Information Systems

In this phase we focus on the evaluation of the information systems (IS) that currently support the service. This activity is the second main aspect of the situation analysis [24]. During this phase, we enhance the process models from Section 17.2.1 with information about the information systems used at every step of the process. This gives us a complete set of the current process activities, decision paths, and information systems, currently in use for the provision of the health-care service.

17.2.3 Identification of Decision Paths and Actions That Can Benefit from Mixed Reality Systems

The starting point for this phase is the complete set of activities, decision paths, and information systems that we compile in Section 17.2.2. We first classify them to map the ASUR-design approach. We then discuss with clinicians who fall in the user (Component U) category which decision paths and actions are currently underperforming and would benefit from a mixed reality system. Here we also identify relationships between the ASUR components ($\Rightarrow$, $\rightarrow$, $=$). The result is a list of decision paths and actions that will be addressed by the mixed reality system in the current iteration of the design and implementation process.

17.2.4 Implementation of the Mixed Reality System

We have already classified process attributes and information systems as ASUR components in Section 17.2.3. Furthermore, we have a list of decision paths and actions we want to address. In this phase our focus lies on the selection of proper adapters and the overall integration in the IS environment of the clinic. We use service orientation as an architectural model and the assurance of NFPs is a key aspect in such distributed loosely coupled environments.

We elaborate in the case study (Section 17.3) the steps of these development approach and how we apply them in the implementation of the system.

17.3 System Design and Implementation

Our application scenario focuses on the surgical sector – one of the largest cost factors in health care and at the same time a place where high creation of value takes place. For the effective utilization of the surgical sector pre- and postoperative processes are crucial. The surgery (equipments and specialists) is a fixed (and expensive) resource. So pre- and postoperative processes need to be aligned and provide for an optimized utilization of this resource. In this section, we show exemplary how we generate scenario descriptions as text, then convert them to the EPC notation, and use this EPC notation to create the ASUR model of the system.

17.3.1 Design of the System

There are many visions how to redesign and reorganize perioperative patient flow and work processes for maximum operating room productivity, which also bring changes in operating room architecture [32].

Figure 17.3 shows an overview of perioperative and postoperative processes in our application scenario. These were evaluated using our approach as described in Section 17.2 and the usability evaluation techniques described in Section 17.1.

The perioperative processes start with a notification from an operating room nurse or an anesthesia nurse that the clinical staff should transport the next patient to the operating room. This action takes place in the ward (location area 1). Then a transport service or a nurse moves the patient from the ward to the operating room

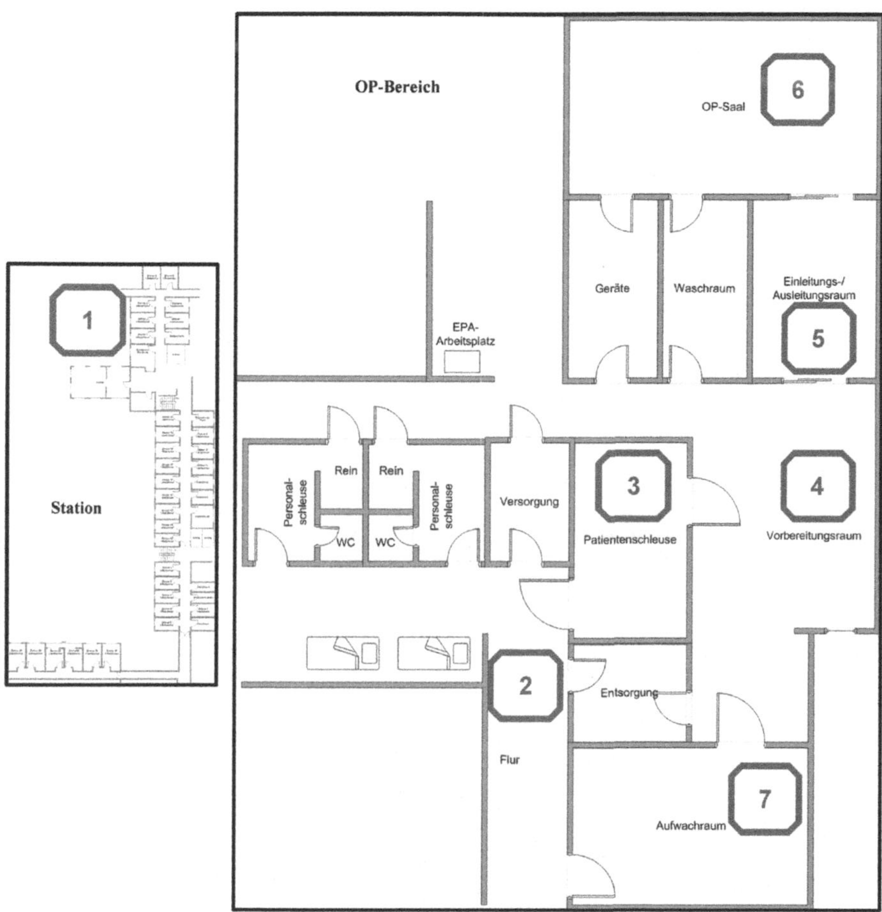

Fig. 17.3 Optimized process flow in surgery – the setting for the mixed reality system

area (location area 2). In the main registration area the clinicians transfer the patient from the ward bed to an operating room table (location area 3). Next, the staff moves the operating room table to the preparation room (location area 4), where the anesthesia nurse or the anesthetist prepares the patient for the operation. The stop that follows is in the induction area, where the patient is anesthetized (location area 5). Finally, the staff moves the patient to the operating room, where the preparation for

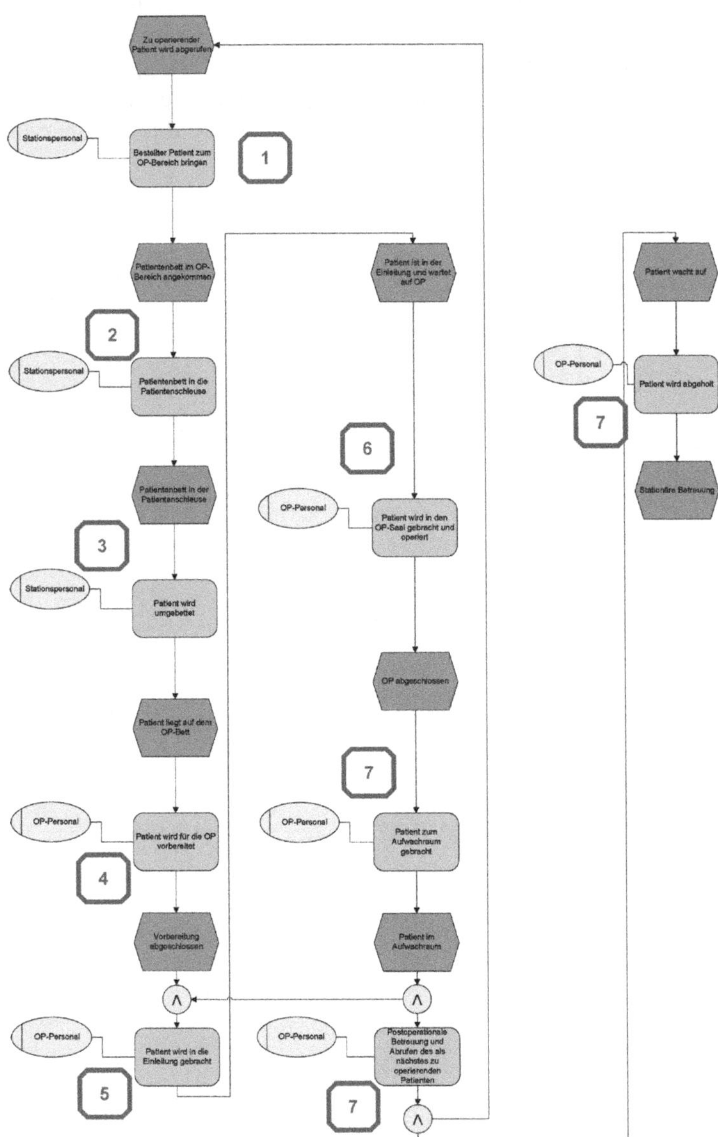

Fig. 17.4 A sample event-driven process chain within the application scenario

the operation starts, for example, operation-specific bedding, sterile coverage (location area 6). After the operation ends the patient is taken out of the operating room and back via the induction area (location area 5) and the preparation room (location area 4) to the recovery room (location area 7). The process ends with the transport of the patient back to the ward (location area 1).

The corresponding EPC model is shown in Fig. 17.4. It describes the sequence of the actions, together with possible decision paths. The location areas for every action are depicted with the same numbers as in Fig. 17.3.

An important prerequisite for a mixed reality system that supports this process is object and person location sensing. Such localization can be done via different technologies, for example, Ultra Wide Band (UWB), Bluetooth (BT), or Wireless LAN (WLAN) location applications. UWB has the advantage that it works independently of other systems, allows very precise location, and transmits with a very low signal strength. WLAN localization, on the other hand, can be done in existing WLAN networks and allows the localization of computers, such as handhelds and laptops. Hybrid approaches that use two or more such technologies typically provide higher precision and more robust position sensing [8]. Handhelds and laptops are widely used in hospital environments. They allow the access to hospital information systems and patient records. To improve the access to patient data the localization could be combined with the data from the HIS and EPR. While doing the ward round the laptop or handheld of the doctor could display only the patients of the room in which the doctor currently is located. This would prevent the physician from searching for the patient and therefore save time. Furthermore, such scenario would increase the overall security and privacy of the system by providing an additional layer of security to the role-based security model used in many existing health-care applications – the access is allowed only for those members of the security group (e.g., doctors) that are in physical proximity to the patient. We have described in detail the position sensing techniques we use in [38, 34].

17.3.2 ASUR Model of the System

As already stated in Section 17.2 we use process models such as EPCs and BPMN and then model their artifacts in the ASUR description [19]. The aim of our system is to allow a person to assess the overall process by blending the real world of a clinic with virtual information in a mixed reality system. Therefore, the adapters need to allow the person to control actual movement of the real objects by mapping it to the mixed reality system (see Fig. 17.5 for an overview and [34] for more details about the location aspects).

17.3.2.1 Real Objects (Components R)

Objects can generally be patients, clinicians, or medical devices. Patients or clinicians typically trigger the events that start an event-driven process chain. Therefore, they are mostly easily identifiable from the process models. Medical devices are

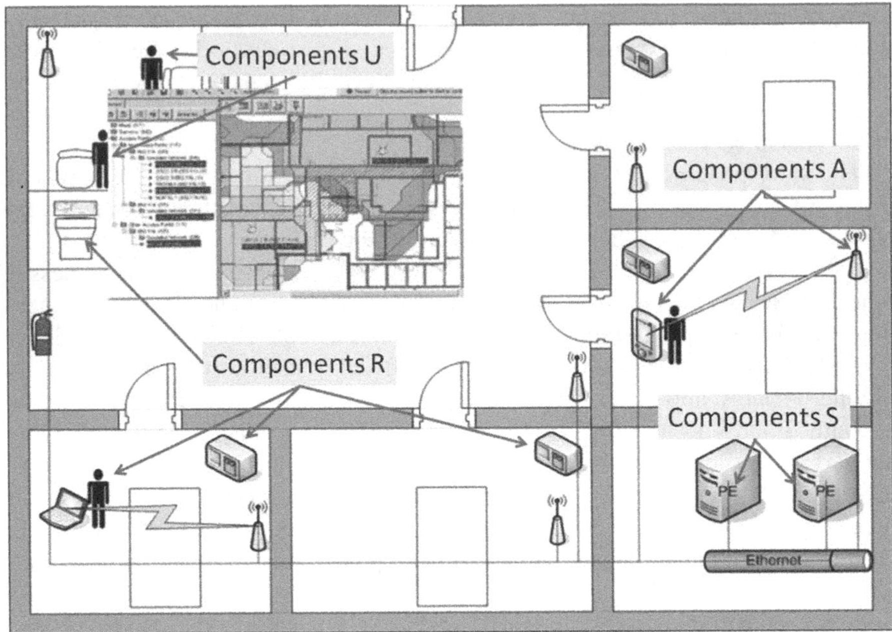

Fig. 17.5 Overview of the ASUR components in the mixed reality system

mostly reflected as "devices" that are needed to complete an action within the process chain. The completeness of the process model is therefore a key precondition to identify them correctly within the ASUR design model.

17.3.2.2 Person as User (Component U)

A person is generally a clinician. He or she can be in charge of planning and scheduling treatments, or more often this person is responsible for a function within the specific process. A key aspect is that this person is normally not the one that conducts the activities within the process chain where the information he needs originates, but is rather the one that is in charge of other following functions within the overall process.

17.3.2.3 Adapters (Components A)

The primary task of the adapters in our system is to map activities and movements of the objects in the real world into the mixed reality system. Here we use position-sensing techniques such as RFID and WLAN. These are input adapters, more specifically localizers as specified in [19]. Figure 17.6 shows two examples. The selection process for these localizers follows typical approaches for technology selection and is described in detail in [34].

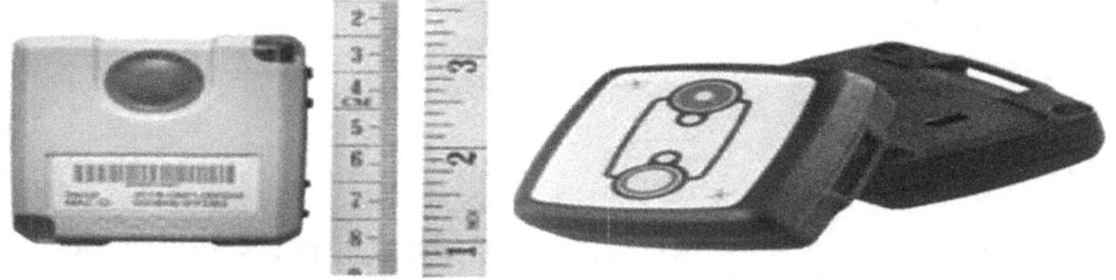

Fig. 17.6 Examples for localizers (courtesy of Ekahau)

17.3.2.4 Systems (Components S)

A typical system in our scenario is a HIS within the clinic which integrates with ERP systems (taking care of resource planning) and CAMI systems.

The result is a mixed reality system that allows a clinician to monitor the elements of the physical world and to blend them with virtual information provided by the systems. He or she can also plan and schedule treatments and operations in the digital world depending on status information from this mixed reality.

17.3.2.5 Relationships Between the ASUR Components of the System

A main objective of the mixed reality system is to use the existing infrastructure (WLAN, RFID, HIS) to allow for clinicians to access patient and process data in a context-aware way. These leads to several relationships between the ASUR components of the system. Table 17.1 shows a selection. It shows examples of the three kinds of relationships between ASUR components as defined in [19] – exchange of data, physical activity triggering an action, and physical colocation. In this case, a proximity of a patient object to a localizer adapter triggers exchange of data between the adapter and the system.

Table 17.1 Sample ASUR relations of the mixed reality system

Textual description	ASUR notation
Patient lies in bed (physical colocation)	$Robject_{Patient} = Rtool_{Bed}$
Patient closer than 1 m to localizer (physical activity triggering an action)	$Robject_{Patient} \Rightarrow A_{in}$
Localizer transmits data to the system (exchange of data)	$A_{in} \rightarrow S$

17.3.3 Addressing Critical Aspects of Mixed Reality Systems for Health-Care Services

Critical aspects of mixed reality systems for health-care services can be summed up as follows:

- context awareness,
- timeliness and high assurance,
- fault tolerance, and
- interoperability.

This section describes how we addressed these aspects in the design and implementation phase of our development approach.

17.3.3.1 Context Awareness

Only information that is relevant for the current specific task of the object (from the ASUR taxonomy as specified in this section: patient, clinician, device) should be provided.

This is an aspect that is often present in existing works, but is often not addressed sufficiently.

One application that uses location-aware access to HIS is described in [31]. It was implemented using agent-oriented middleware (SALSA) [39]. As the implementation is PDA based (device-based position calculation), neural networks were used to implement position sensing. A key shortcoming is the insufficient precision for delivering relevant patient information.

A concept of context-aware computing in health care is presented in [3]. It includes a scenario with scenes such as *Entering an Active Zone*, the *Context-aware Hospital Bed*, and the *Context-aware Hospital EPR*. Key lessons learned are the following:

- Context awareness can improve targeted data access to EPRs by clinicians.
- Access to physical things (e.g., container, x-ray image, wheelchair, bed) reveals activity. Based on information about this access, we can present proper data to support this activity.
- We can use context awareness to suggest courses of action, not to automatically react to context changes.

17.3.3.2 Timeliness and High Assurance

The general term that comprise both timeliness and high assurance is availability. There is no single agreed upon definition of this term. The historical view of availability has been as a binary metric that denotes whether a system is "up" or "down" at a single point of time. A well-known extension of this concept is to compute the percentage of time, on average, that a system is available during a certain period – this is how availability is defined when a system is described as having `99.99%` availability, for example.

There are several extended definitions of availability that address the inherent limitations of this definition – availability should be considered as a spectrum, rather as a binary metric, as systems can have various degraded, but still operational, states between "up" and "down." Furthermore, the definition does not consider QoS aspects. One possible extended definition proposes to measure availability by examining variations in system QoS metrics over time [7]. In our implementation we provide timeliness and high assurance using the concept of architectural translucency [35]. We presented details about the implementation of the concept and an evaluation in [36].

17.3.3.3 Fault Tolerance

Fault tolerance denotes the ability to provide a certain service even in the presence of faults [26]. Fault-tolerance guarantees require assumptions about possible failures and expected system load (load hypothesis). There exist a variety of fault models at the hardware level of computer systems (e.g., gate level or functional level) [16, 14, 13] that cannot be applied directly to service fault tolerance in the context of mixed reality systems, due to their higher complexity as compared to hardware-implemented functions. Furthermore, there are fault models that are defined at the component level of middleware environments such as CORBA [27, 21, 30]. This work uses the fault model also used in [30]. The model was originally proposed in [15] and extended in [25].

The fault model for our mixed reality system distinguishes the following fault classes:

- Crash fault: A service loses its internal state or halts. The processor is silent during the fault.
- Omission fault: A service fails to meet a deadline or to begin a task. This fault class includes the crash fault.
- Timing of performance fault: A service serves a request before or after its specified time frame of never. This fault class includes the omission fault.
- Incorrect computation fault: A service fails to produce a correct output in response to a correct input. This fault class includes the timing fault.
- Authenticated Byzantine fault: A service behaves in an arbitrary or malicious manner, but is unable to imperceptibly change an authenticated message. This fault class includes the incorrect computation fault.
- Byzantine fault: Every possible fault. This class includes the authenticated Byzantine fault.

The application and evaluation of this fault model is described in [33], its implementation in health-care scenarios – in [36].

17.3.3.4 Interoperability

We use SOA as architectural paradigm. Interoperability within an SOA at the level of the technical implementation is typically achieved by provision of service wrappers and their subsequent composition to applications. Composition of applications from web services is governed by different requirements than typical component-based software development and integration of binary components. Application developers and users do not have access to documentation, code, or binary component. Instead, they rely only on a rudimentary functional description offered by WSDL. Services execute in different contexts and containers, they are often separated by firewalls and can be located practically everywhere.

With the native capabilities of web services fully developed, several approaches for service composition started to emerge. The first-generation composition languages were Web Service Flow Language (WSFL) developed by IBM and Web Services Choreography Interface (WSCI) developed by BEA Systems. However, these proposals were not compatible with each other and this led to the development of second-generation languages. The most popular of them is BPEL4WS [1], which is a joint effort of IBM, Microsoft, SAP, Siebel, and BEA. It originates in the combination of first-generation languages (WSFL and WSCI) with Microsoft's XLANG specification. Regardless of that, there is still no generally accepted standard for the process layer comprising aggregation, choreography, and composition in the Web Service Architecture Stack (www.w3.org/2002/ws/).

We provide interoperability in two general ways:

- We use components that offer web service interfaces.
- We implement service wrappers for components that lack such interfaces.

For semantic interoperability we use concepts such as ontology mapping. A detailed discussion of our implementation regarding semantic interoperability is out of the scope of this work.

17.3.4 Addressing Software Design Requirements

Our implementation uses an SOA-based runtime infrastructure. The design principles presented in [3] for such kind of runtime infrastructure include

- distributed and cooperating services (e.g., an SOA),
- security and privacy,
- lookup and discovery (e.g., provided by foundation services in an SOA), and
- basic design principles such as performance and availability.

The rest of this section presents our design considerations that adhere to these principles. These considerations constitute the transition between the first and the second part of Phase 4 of our development approach (see Fig. 17.1).

17.3.4.1 Distributed and Cooperating Services

Services are autonomous, platform-independent entities. They can be described, published, discovered, and loosely coupled in standard ways. Services reflect a service-oriented approach to software engineering. It is a logical consequence of the COTS (commercial off-the-shelf) component integration. It lets organizations expose computing functionality programmatically over the Internet or various networks such as cable, the Universal Mobile Telecommunications System (UMTS), xDSL, and Bluetooth using standard XML-based languages and protocols and a self-describing interface [29].

Web services are currently the most promising service-oriented technology [40]. They use the Internet as the communication medium and open Internet-based standards, including the Simple Object Access Protocol (SOAP) [22] for transmitting data, the Web Services Description Language (WSDL) [12, 11] for defining services, and the Business Process Execution Language for Web Services (BPEL4WS) [1] for orchestrating services. These characteristics are generally well suited for our mixed reality system. Negative effects of the higher transmission overhead typically associated with the XML-based information interchange is compensated by our application of the architectural translucency approach (see Section 17.3.3).

17.3.4.2 Security and Privacy

There are a variety of security mechanisms that can be incorporated in web service architectures and that we considered for our mixed reality system. First, we can secure the transmission using general approaches for securing web content such as the Secure Socket Layer (SSL). We can use WS-Security [28] to secure SOAP messages and even extend this approach to complete BPEL compositions as proposed in [10]. Authentication in such approaches is best provided by integrated solutions for security credentials (e.g., Active Directory).

One successful approach for security in health-care applications is view-based security [6]. It allows the definition of security policies using two central concepts – a *view* (e.g., read diagnosis) and a *role* (e.g., a radiologist). The role gives the mapping between a view and a system *user* (e.g., Dr. X).

With context awareness as a critical aspect, we can provide an additional layer of security and privacy. This means that we introduce a location-based security model on top of the view-based security model.

By combining these three security approaches (web services-based, view-based, and location-based) we can guarantee appropriate security levels for different applications of our mixed reality system.

17.3.4.3 Lookup and Discovery

Lookup and discovery are a central part of every SOA infrastructure, as already described in this section. In our approach we use a COTS SOA suite such as the WebMethods suite from Software AG.[1] It allows us to account for all major aspects of service administration, lookup, and discovery, particularly when related with

[1] http://www.softwareag.com/de/products/wm/default.asp

security and privacy aspects. This means that our security model is enforced even before the search for dynamic service composition starts, thereby providing a list of possible services that are functionally compatible, on the one side, and are allowed for use by the specific role, on the other.

17.3.4.4 Performance and Availability

The use of an SOA suite and standard platforms for web services allows us to dynamically provide additional resources to a web service, or start multiple instances, if this is required at the current load of the service. Thereby, we can assure at runtime the service levels that are specified together with the service definition in the repository of the SOA suite. The approach is described in more detail in [37].

17.3.5 Technology Environment and Architectural Approach

Our WLAN positioning system is Ekahau [20], our HIS is FD Klinika [17], we are using Tablet PCs as mobile devices for the clinicians. Our architectural approach (see Fig. 17.7) is to use an SOA with wrappers that provide web service interfaces to the enterprise service bus (ESB) [9]. The AT engine implements the concept of architectural translucency in this scenario. It is responsible for service QoS assurance by monitoring and management. When it notices that, for example, a service is experiencing higher loads, it dynamically reconfigures the replication settings of

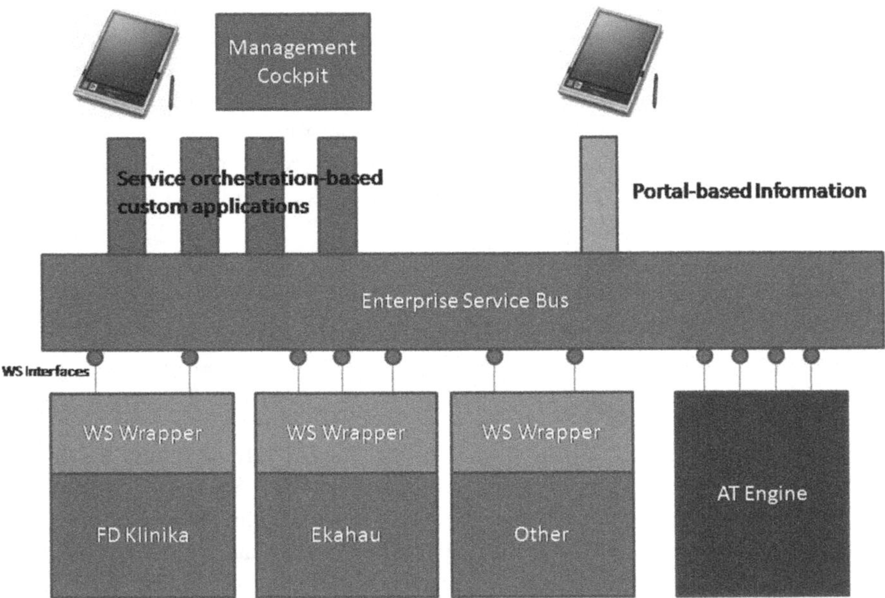

Fig. 17.7 Architectural approach

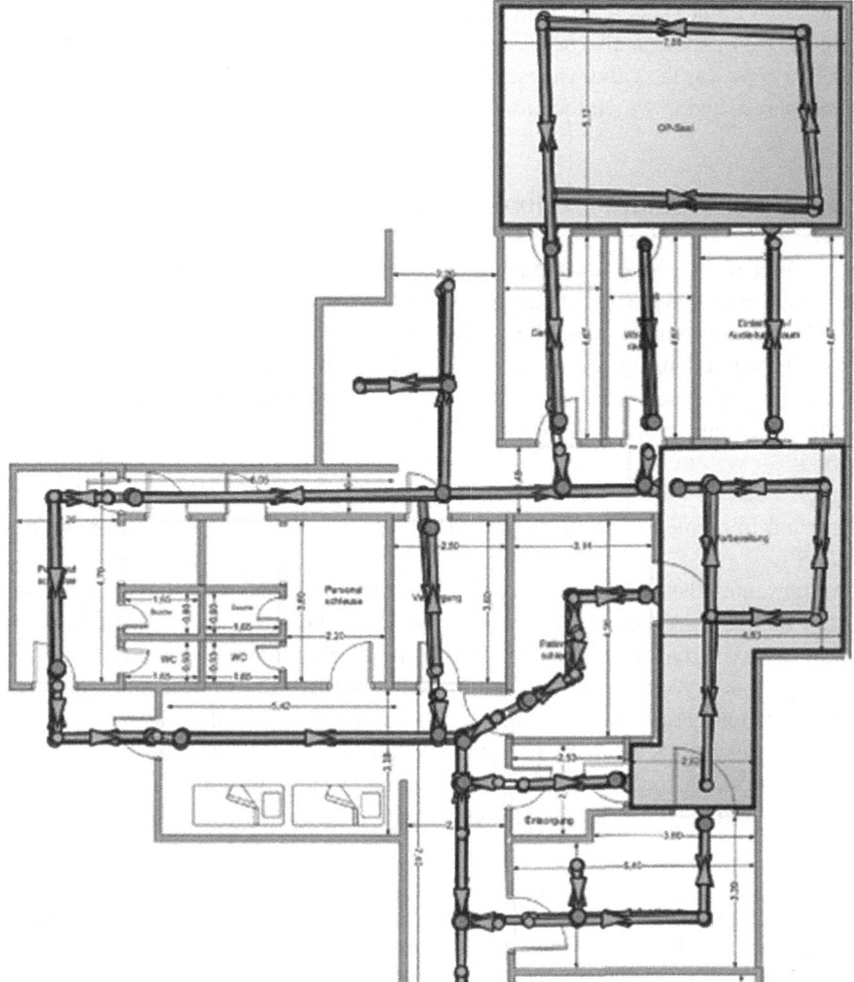

Fig. 17.8 Visualization of movement – tracking rails

the service to further provide the expected QoS. Integration of other systems (e.g., enterprise resource planning, external partner applications, health insurance systems). Representation and further information processing are depicted in the upper part of the figure. During the first stage (depicted green) we plan to provide portal-based access to EPRs that are extracted from the HIS and visualized on the Tablet PC depending on the current location of the Tablet PC, particularly other WLAN-enabled objects surrounding it (e.g., patient tags). During the second stage (depicted red) we are introducing more complex planning and evaluation functions. These are realized by composite services. Figure 17.8 shows an example – a clinician (e.g., an anesthetist or a surgeon) can follow the real movement of a patient and control whether particular steps have been executed in the preceding functions of the process flow. He or she can also access relevant patient data from these functions (e.g., when and how was the patient anesthetized, how were the vital parameters that were last measured, and at which location have they been measured).

17.4 Conclusion and Outlook

This chapter presented a development approach for enhancing health-care services with mixed reality systems. It integrates the ASUR design methodology to identify relevant components and their relations. The application of these concepts was demonstrated using a case study in a clinical environment. The presented development approach is iterative and covers the following steps: (i) evaluation of existing tasks and processes within the health-care service, (ii) evaluation of the information systems that currently support the service, (iii) identification of decision paths and actions that can benefit from mixed reality systems, as well as (iv) design and implementation of the mixed reality system, with focus on integration and NFPs.

We presented the ASUR components of the system and how we derive them from process models specified in EPCs and BPMN. Furthermore, we evaluated critical aspects of mixed reality systems that we had to address in our case study.

The case study described the application scenario, the architectural concept, and the technologies we employed. It demonstrated the feasibility of implementing mixed reality systems using the presented development approach.

Future work is focused primarily in the areas of definition of reference processes for certain health-care services and corresponding design and implementation guidelines.

Acknowledgments This work was developed in cooperation with several clinics where the field tests have been conducted. There were valuable evaluation contributions from a range of experienced clinicians. Finally, we would like to thank the anonymous reviewers and the editors of this book for their constructive criticism and valuable improvement suggestions.

References

1. T. Andrews, F. Curbera, H. Dholakia, Y. Goland, J. Klein, F. Leymann, K. Liu, D. Roller, D. Smith, S. Thatte, et al. Business Process Execution Language for Web Services (BPEL4WS) 1.1. *Online: http://www-106. ibm. com/developerworks/webservices/library/ws-bpel, May*, 139:140, 2003.
2. R.T. Azuma. A survey of augmented reality. *Presence: Teleoperators and Virtual Environments*, 6(4):355–385, August 1997.
3. J.E. Bardram. Applications of context-aware computing in hospital work: examples and design principles. In *SAC '04: Proceedings of the 2004 ACM Symposium on Applied Computing*, pages 1574–1579, New York, NY, USA, 2004. ACM.
4. R.J. Baron, E.L. Fabens, M. Schiffman, and E. Wolf. Electronic Health Records: Just around the Corner? Or over the Cliff? *Ann. Intern. Med.*, 143(3):222–226, 2005.

5. R. Behringer, J. Christian, A. Holzinger, and S. Wilkinson. Some usability issues of augmented and mixed reality for e-health applications in the medical domain. In *HCI and Usability for Medicine and Health Care*, volume 4799 of *Lecture Notes in Computer Science*, pages 255–266. Springer, 2007.
6. G. Brose. Manageable access control for corba. *J. Comput. Secur.*, 10(4):301–337, 2002.
7. A. Brown and D.A. Patterson. Towards availability benchmarks: A case study of software RAID systems. *Proceedings of the 2000 USENIX Annual Technical Conference*, 2000.
8. S. Bruning, J. Zapotoczky, Peter Ibach, and Vladimir Stantchev. Cooperative positioning with magicmap. *Positioning, Navigation and Communication, 2007. WPNC '07. 4th Workshop on*, pages 17–22, March 2007.
9. D. Chappel. *Enterprise Service Bus*. O'Reilly, 2004.
10. A. Charfi and M. Mezini. Using aspects for security engineering of web service compositions. In *ICWS '05: Proceedings of the IEEE International Conference on Web Services*, pages 59–66, Washington, DC, USA, 2005. IEEE Computer Society.
11. R. Chinnici, M. Gudgin, J.J. Moreau, J. Schlimmer, and S. Weerawarana. Web Services Description Language (WSDL) Version 2.0 Part 1: Core Language. *W3C Working Draft*, 26, 2004.
12. E. Christensen, F. Curbera, G. Meredith, and S. Weerawarana. Web Services Description Language (WSDL) 1.1, 2001.
13. J.A. Clark and D.K. Pradhan. Fault injection. *Computer*, 28(6):47–56, 1995.
14. F. Corno, G. Cumani, M.S. Reorda, and G. Squillero. An rt-level fault model with high gate level correlation. *hldvt*, 00:3, 2000.
15. F. Cristian, H. Aghili, R. Strong, and D. Dolev. Atomic broadcast: from simple message diffusion to byzantine agreement. *Inf. Comput.*, 118(1):158–179, 1995.
16. E.W. Czeck and D.P. Siewiorek. Effects of transient gate-level faults on program behavior. *Fault-Tolerant Computing, 1990. FTCS-20. Digest of Papers., 20th International Symposium*, pages 236–243, Jun 1990.
17. Fliegel Data. FD Klinika. http://www.fliegel-data.de/fd-online/, 2007.
18. E. Dubois, L. Nigay, J. Troccaz, O. Chavanon, and L. Carrat. Classification space for augmented surgery, an augmented reality case study. *Human-computer Interaction, INTERACT'99: IFIP TC. 13 International Conference on Human-Computer Interaction, 30th August-3rd September 1999, Edinburgh, UK*, 1999.
19. E. Dubois, Philip D. Gray, and L. Nigay. Asur++: A design notation for mobile mixed systems. In *Mobile HCI '02: Proceedings of the 4th International Symposium on Mobile Human-Computer Interaction*, pages 123–139, London, UK, 2002. Springer-Verlag.
20. Inc. Ekahau. *Ekahau Positioning Engine 3.1*. http://www.ekahau.com/file.php?id=129, 2005.
21. P. Felber and Priya. Experiences, strategies, and challenges in building fault-tolerant corba systems. *Transactions on Computers*, 53(5):497–511, May 2004.
22. M. Gudgin, M. Hadley, N. Mendelsohn, J.J. Moreau, and H.F. Nielsen. SOAP Version 1.2. *W3C Working Draft*, 2002.
23. A. Holzinger. Usability engineering methods for software developers. *Commun. ACM*, 48(1):71–74, 2005.
24. H. Krallmann, M. Schoenherr, and M. Trier. *Systemanalyse im Unternehmen - Prozessorientierte Methoden der Wirtschaftsinformatik*. Oldenbourg, 2007.
25. L.A. Laranjeira, M. Malek, and R. Jenevein. Nest: a nested-predicate scheme for fault tolerance. *Transactions on Computers*, 42(11):1303–1324, Nov 1993.
26. M. Malek. *Responsive Computing*. Kluwer Academic Publishers Boston, 1994.
27. E. Marsden, J.-C. Fabre, and Jean Arlat. Dependability of corba systems: Service characterization by fault injection. *srds*, 00:276, 2002.
28. A. Nadalin, C. Kaler, P. Hallam-Baker, R. Monzillo, et al. Web Services Security: SOAP Message Security 1.0 (WS-Security 2004). *OASIS Standard*, 200401, 2004.
29. M.P. Papazoglou, P. Traverso, S. Dustdar, and F. Leymann. Service-oriented computing: State of the art and research challenges. *Computer*, 40(11):38–45, Nov. 2007.

30. A. Polze, J. Schwarz, and M. Malek. Automatic generation of fault-tolerant corba-services. *tools*, 00:205, 2000.
31. M.D. Rodriguez, J. Favela, E.A. Martinez, and M.A. Munoz. Location-aware access to hospital information and services. *IEEE Transactions on Information Technology in Biomedicine*, 8(4):448–455, Dec. 2004.
32. W.S. Sandberg, B. Daily, M. Egan, J.E. Stahl, J.M. Goldman, R.A. Wiklund, and D. Rattner. Deliberate perioperative systems design improves operating room throughput. *Anesthesiology*, 103(2):406–18, 2005.
33. V. Stantchev. *Architectural Translucency*. GITO Verlag, Berlin, Germany, 2008.
34. V. Stantchev, T.D. Hoang, T. Schulz, and I. Ratchinski. Optimizing clinical processes with position-sensing. *IT Professional*, 10(2):31–37, 2008.
35. V. Stantchev and M. Malek. Architectural translucency in service-oriented architectures. *IEE Proceedings - Software*, 153(1):31–37, February 2006.
36. V. Stantchev and M. Malek. Translucent replication for service level assurance. In *High Assurance Service Computing (to appear)*, pages 127–148, Berlin, New York, 04 2009. Springer.
37. V. Stantchev and C. Schröpfer. Techniques for service level enforcement in web-services based systems. In *Proceedings of The 10th International Conference on Information Integration and Web-based Applications and Services (iiWAS2008)*, pages 7–14, New York, NY, USA, 11 2008. ACM.
38. V. Stantchev, T. Schulz, and T.-D. Hoang. Ortungstechnologien im op-bereich. In *Mobiles Computing in der Medizin (MoCoMed) 2007: Proceedings of the 7th Workshop on*, pages 20–33, Aachen, Germany, 2007. Shaker.
39. C. Varela and G. Agha. Programming dynamically reconfigurable open systems with salsa. *SIGPLAN Not.*, 36(12):20–34, 2001.
40. S. Weerawarana, F. Curbera, F. Leymann, T. Storey, and D.F. Ferguson. *Web Services Platform Architecture: SOAP, WSDL, WS-Policy, WS-Addressing, WS-BPEL, WS-Reliable Messaging and More*. Prentice Hall PTR Upper Saddle River, NJ, USA, 2005.
41. E. Weippl, A. Holzinger, and A.M Tjoa. Security aspects of ubiquitous computing in health care. *e & i Elektrotechnik und Informationstechnik*, 123(4):156–161, 2006.

Chapter 18
The eXperience Induction Machine: A New Paradigm for Mixed-Reality Interaction Design and Psychological Experimentation

Ulysses Bernardet, Sergi Bermúdez i Badia, Armin Duff, Martin Inderbitzin, Sylvain Le Groux, Jônatas Manzolli, Zenon Mathews, Anna Mura, Aleksander Väljamäe, and Paul F.M.J Verschure

Abstract The eXperience Induction Machine (XIM) is one of the most advanced mixed-reality spaces available today. XIM is an immersive space that consists of physical sensors and effectors and which is conceptualized as a general-purpose infrastructure for research in the field of psychology and human–artifact interaction. In this chapter, we set out the epistemological rational behind XIM by putting the installation in the context of psychological research. The design and implementation of XIM are based on principles and technologies of neuromorphic control. We give a detailed description of the hardware infrastructure and software architecture, including the logic of the overall behavioral control. To illustrate the approach toward psychological experimentation, we discuss a number of practical applications of XIM. These include the so-called, persistent virtual community, the application in the research of the relationship between human experience and multi-modal stimulation, and an investigation of a mixed-reality social interaction paradigm.

Keywords Mixed-reality · Psychology · Human–computer interaction · Research methods · Multi-user interaction · Biomorphic engineering

18.1 Introduction

The eXperience Induction Machine (XIM, Fig. 18.1) located in the Laboratory for Synthetic Perceptive, Emotive and Cognitive Systems (SPECS) in Barcelona, Spain, is one of the most advanced mixed-reality spaces available today. XIM is a human-accessible, fully instrumented space with a surface area of 5.5×5.5 m. The effectors of the space include immersive surround computer graphics, a luminous floor, movable lights, interactive synthetic sonification, whereas the sensors

U. Bernardet (✉)
SPECS@IUA: Laboratory for Synthetic Perceptive, Emotive, and Cognitive Systems, Universitat Pompeu Fabra, 08018 Barcelona, Spain
e-mail: bernuly@gmail.com

E. Dubois et al. (eds.), *The Engineering of Mixed Reality Systems*, Human-Computer Interaction Series, DOI 10.1007/978-1-84882-733-2_18,

include floor-based pressure sensors, microphones, and static and movable cameras. In XIM multiple users can simultaneously and freely move around and interact with the physical and virtual world.

Fig. 18.1 View into the eXperience Induction Machine

The architecture of the control system is designed using the large-scale neuronal systems simulation software *iqr* [1]. Unlike other installations, the construction of XIM reflects a clear, twofold research agenda: First, to understand human experience and behavior in complex ecologically valid situations that involve full body movement and interaction. Second, to build mixed-reality systems based on our current psychological and neuroscientific understanding and to validate these systems by deploying them in the control and realization of mixed-reality systems.

We will start this chapter by looking at a number of mixed-reality system, including XIM's precursor, "Ada the intelligent" space, built in 2002 for the Swiss national exhibition Expo.02.

XIM has been designed as a general-purpose infrastructure for research in the field of psychology and human–artifact interaction (Fig. 18.2). For this reason, we will set out the epistemological rationale behind the construction of a space like XIM. Here we will give a systemic view of related psychological research and describe the function of XIM in this context.

Subsequently we will lay out the infrastructure of XIM, including a detailed account of the hardware components of XIM, the software architecture, and the overall control system. This architecture includes a multi-modal tracking system, the autonomous music composition system *RoBoser*, the virtual reality engine, and the overall neuromorphic system integration based on the simulator *iqr*.

To illustrate the use of XIM in the development of mixed-reality experience and psychological research, we will discuss a number of practical applications of XIM: The persistent virtual community (Fig. 18.2), a virtual world where the physical world is mapped into and which is accessible both from XIM and remotely via a desktop computer; the interactive narrative "Autodemo" (Fig. 18.2); and a mixed-reality social interaction paradigm.

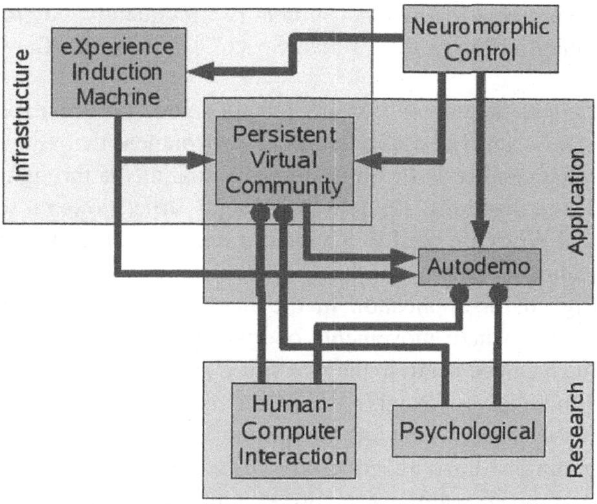

Fig. 18.2 Relationship between infrastructure and application. The eXperience Induction Machine is a general-purpose infrastructure for research in the field of psychology and human–artifact interaction. In relation to XIM, the persistent virtual community (PVC) is on the one hand an infrastructure insofar as it provides a technical platform, and on the other hand an application as it is built on, and uses, XIM. The project "Autodemo," in which users are guided through XIM and the PVC, in turn is an application which covers aspects of both XIM and the PVC. In the design and implementation both XIM and the Autodemo are based on principles and technologies of neuromorphic control. PVC and Autodemo are concrete implementations of research paradigms in the fields of human–computer interaction and psychology

18.1.1 Mixed-Reality Installations and Spaces

A widely used framework to classify virtual and mixed-reality systems is the "virtuality continuum" which spans from "real environment" via "augmented reality" and "augmented virtuality" to "virtual environment" [2]. The definition of mixed reality hence includes any "paradigm that seeks to smoothly link the physical and data processing (digital) environments." [3]. With this definition, a wide range of different installations and systems can be categorized as "mixed reality," though these systems fall into different categories and areas of operation, e.g., research in the field of human–computer interaction, rehabilitation, social interaction, education, and entertainment. Depending on their use and function, the installations vary in size, design, number of modalities, and their controlling mechanisms. A common denominator is that in mixed-reality systems a physical device is interfaced with a virtual environment in which one or more users interact. Examples of such installations are the "jellyfish party," where virtual soap bubbles are generated in response to the amount and speed of air expired by the user [4], the "inter-glow" system, where users in real space interact using "multiplexed visible-light communication technology" [5], and the "HYPERPRESENCE" system developed for control of multi-user agents – robot systems manipulating objects and moving in a closed, real environment – in a mixed-reality environment [6]. Frequently, tangible technology is used for the interface as in the “Touch-Space” [7] and the “Tangible Bits” [8] installations.

Many of the above-mentioned systems are not geared toward a specific application. “SMALLAB,” “a mixed-reality learning environment that allows participants to interact with one another and with sonic and visual media through full body, 3D movements, and vocalizations” [9], and the “magic carpet” system, where pressure mats and physical props are used to navigate a story [10], are examples of system used in the educational domain.

Systems designed for application in the field of the performing arts are the “Murmuring Fields,” where movements of visitors trigger sounds located in the virtual space which can be heard in the real space [11], and the “Interactive Theatre Experience in Embodied + Wearable mixed-reality Space.” Here “embodied computing mixed-reality spaces integrate ubiquitous computing, tangible interaction, and social computing within a mixed-reality space” [12].

At the fringe of mixed-reality spaces are systems that are considered “intelligent environments,” such as the “EasyLiving” project at Microsoft Research [13] and the “Intelligent Room” project, in which robotics and vision technology are combined with speech understanding systems and agent-based architectures [14]. In these systems, the focus is on the physical environment more than on the use of virtual reality. Contrary to this, are systems that are large spaces equipped with sophisticated VR displays such as the “Allosphere Research Facility,” a large (3-story high) spherical space with fully immersive, interactive, stereoscopic/pluriphonic virtual environments [15].

Examples of installations that represent prototypical multi-user mixed-reality spaces include Disney’s indoor interactive theme park installation “Pirates of the Caribbean: Battle for Buccaneer Gold.” In this installation a group of users are on a ship-themed motion platform and interact with a virtual world [16]. Another example is the “KidsRoom” at MIT, a fully automated, interactive narrative “playspace” for children, which uses images, lighting, sound, and computer vision action recognition technology [17].

One of the largest and most sophisticated multi-user systems, and the precursor of XIM, was “Ada: The Intelligent Space,” developed by the Institute of Neuroinformatics (INI) of the ETH and the University of Zurich for the Swiss national exhibition Expo.02 in Neuchâtel. Over a period of 6 months, Ada was visited by 560,000 persons, making this installation the largest interactive exhibit ever deployed. The goal of Ada was, on the one hand, to foster public debate on the impact of brain-based technology on society and, on the other hand, to advance the research toward the construction of conscious machines [18]. Ada was designed like an organism with visual, audio, and tactile input, and non-contact effectors in the form of computer graphics, light, and sound [19]. Conceptually, Ada has been described as an “inside out” robot, able to learn from experience, react in a goal-oriented and situationally dependent way. Ada’s behavior was based on a modeled hybrid control structure that includes a neuronal system, an agent-based system, and algorithmic-based processes [18].

The eXperience Induction Machine described in this chapter is an immersive, multi-user space, equipped with physical sensors and effectors, and 270° projections. One of the applications and platforms developed with XIM is the persistent virtual community (PVC), a system where the physical world is mapped into a virtual world, and which is accessible both from XIM and remotely via a desktop computer (see Section 18.3.1 below). In this way, the PVC is a venue where entities of different degrees of virtuality (local users in XIM, Avatars of remote users, fully synthetic characters) can meet and interact. The PVC provides augmented reality in that in XIM remote users are represented by a lit floor tile and augmented virtuality through the representation of users in XIM as avatars in the virtual world. XIM, in combination with the PVC, can be thus located simultaneously at both extremes of the "virtuality continuum" [2], qualifying XIM as a mixed-reality system.

18.1.2 Why Build Such Spaces? Epistemological Rationale

One can trace back the origins of psychology as far as antiquity, with the origins of modern, scientific psychology commonly located in the installation of the first psychological laboratory by Wilhelm Wundt in 1879 [20]. Over the centuries, the view of the nature of psychology has undergone substantial changes, and even current psychologists differ among themselves about the appropriate definition of psychology [21]. The common denominator of the different approaches to psychology – biological, cognitive, psychoanalytical, and phenomenological – is to regard psychology as the science of behavior and mental processes [20]. Or in Eysenck's words [21], "The majority believe psychology should be based on the scientific study of behavior, but that the conscious mind forms an important part of its subject matter."

If psychology is defined as the scientific investigation of mental processes and behavior, it is in the former case concerned with phenomena that are not directly measurable (Fig. 18.3). These non-measurable phenomena are hence conceptual entities and referred to as "constructs" [22]. Typical examples of psychological constructs are "intelligence" and the construct of the "Ego" by Freud [23]. Scientifically, these constructs are defined by their measurement method, a step which is referred to as operationalization.

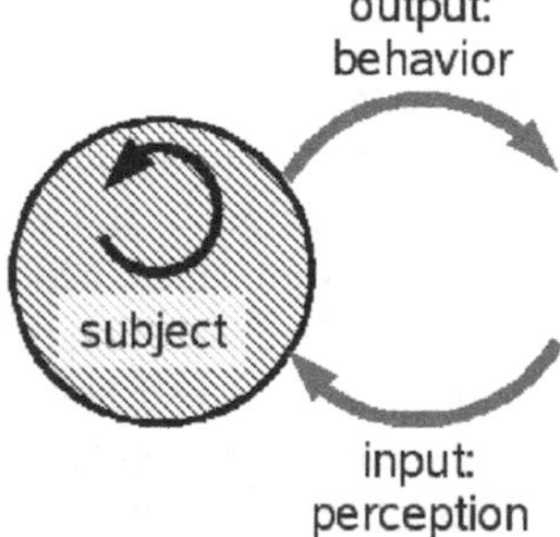

Fig. 18.3 The field of psychology is concerned with behavior and mental processes, which are not directly measurable. Scientific research in psychology is to a large extent based on drawing conclusions from the behavior a subject exhibits given a certain input

In psychological research humans are treated as a "black box," i.e., knowledge about the internal workings is acquired by drawing conclusions from the reaction to a stimulus (Fig. 18.3; input: perception, output: behavior). Behavior is here defined in a broad sense, and includes the categories of both directly and only indirectly measurable behavior. The category of directly observable behavior comprises, on the one hand, non-symbolic behavior such as posture, vocalization, and physiology and, on the other hand, symbolic behavior such as gesture and verbal expression. In the category of only indirectly measurable behavior fall the expressions of symbolic behaviors like written text and non-symbolic behaviors such as a person's history of web browsing.

Observation: With the above definition of behavior, various study types such as observational methods, questionnaires, interviews, case studies, and psychophysiological measurements are within the realms of observation. Typically, observational methods are categorized along the dimension of the type of environment in which the observation takes place and the role of the observer. The different branches of psychology, such as abnormal, developmental, behavioral, educational, clinical, personality, cognitive, social, industrial/organizational, or biopsychology, have in common that they are built on the observation of behavior.

Experimental research: The function of experimental research is to establish the causal link between the stimulus given to and the reaction of a person. The common nomenclature is to refer to the input to the subject as the independent variable, and to the output as dependent variable. In physics, the variance in the dependent variable is normally very small, and as a consequence, the input variable can be changed gradually, while measuring the effect on the output variable. This allows one to test a hypothesis that quantifies the relationship between independent and dependent variables. In psychology, the variance of the dependent variable is often rather large, and it is therefore difficult to establish a quantification of the causal connection between the two variables. The consequence is that most psychological experiments take the form of comparing two conditions: The experimental condition, where the subject is exposed to a "manipulation," and the control condition, where the manipulation is not applied. An experiment then allows one to draw a conclusion in the form of (a) manipulation X has caused effect Y and (b) in the absence of manipulation X effect Y was not observed. To conclude that the observed behavior (dependent variable) is indeed caused by a given stimulus (independent variable) and not by other factors, so-called confounding variables, all conditions are kept as similar as possible between the two conditions.

The concepts of observation and experiment discussed above can be captured in a systemic view of interaction between the four actors: subject, social agent, observer/investigator, and environment (Fig. 18.4). "Social agent" here means other humans, or substitutes, which are not directly under investigation, but that interact with the subject. Different research configurations are characterized by which actors are present, what and how is manipulated and measured. What distinguishes the branches of psychology is, on the one hand, the scope (individual – group), and, on the other hand, the prevalent measurement method (qualitative–quantitative), e.g., in a typical social psychology experimental research configuration, what is of interest is the interaction of the subjective with multiple social agents. The subject is either manipulated directly or via the persons he/she is interacting with.

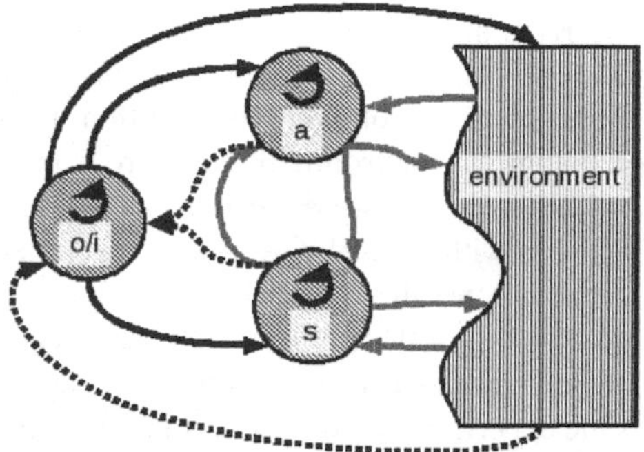

Fig. 18.4 Systemic view of the configuration in psychological research. S: subject, A: social agent, O/I: observer, or investigator (the implicit convention being that if the investigator is not performing any intentional manipulation, he/she is referred to as an "observer"). The subject is interacting with social agents, the observer, and the environment. For the sake of simplicity only one subject, social agent, and observer are depicted, but each of these can be multiple instances. In the diagram *arrows* indicate the flow of information; more specifically, *solid black lines* indicate possible manipulations, and *dashed lines* possible measurement points. The investigator can manipulate the environment and the social agents of the subject, and record data from the subject's behavior, together with the behavior of other social agents, and the environment

The requirement of the experimental paradigm to keep all other than the independent variable constant has as a consequence that experimental research effectively only employs a subset of all possible configurations (Fig. 18.4): Experiments mostly take place in artificial environments and the investigator plays a non-participating role. This leads to one of the main points of critique of experiments, the limited scope and the potentially low level of generalizability. It is important to keep in mind that observation and experimental method are orthogonal to each other: In every experiment, some type of observation is performed, but not in all observational studies two or more conditions are compared in a systematic fashion.

18.1.3 Mixed and Virtual Reality as a Tool in Psychological Research

Gaggioli [24] made the following observation on the usage of VR in experimental psychology: "the opportunity offered by VR technology to create interactive three-dimensional stimulus environments, within which all behavioral responses can be recorded, offers experimental psychologists options that are not available using traditional techniques." As laid out above, the key in psychological research is the systematic investigation of the reaction of a person to a given input (Fig. 18.4).

Consequently, a mixed-reality infrastructure is ideally suited for research in psychology as it permits stimuli to be delivered in a very flexible, yet fully controlled way, while recording a person's behavior precisely.

Stimulus delivery: In a computer-generated environment, the flexibility of the stimulus delivered is nearly infinite (at least the number of pixels on the screen). This degree of flexibility can also be achieved in a natural environment but has to be traded off against the level of control over the condition. In conventional experimental research in psychology the environment therefore is mostly kept simple and static, a limitation to which mixed-reality environments are not subject, as they do not have to trade off richness with control. Clearly this is a major advantage which allows research which should generalize better from the laboratory to the real-world condition. The same rationale as for the environment is applicable for social interaction. Conventionally, the experimental investigation of social interaction is seen as highly problematic, as the experimental condition is not well controlled: To investigate social behavior, a human actor needs to be part of the experimental condition, yet it is very difficult for humans to behave comparably under different conditions, as would be required by experimental rigor. Contrary to this, a computer-generated Avatar is a perfectly controllable actor that will always perform in the same way, irrespective of fatigue, mood, or other subjective conditions. A good example of the application of this paradigm is the re-staging of Milgram's obedience experiment [25]. The eXperience Induction Machine can fulfill both roles; it can serve as a mixed-reality environment and as the representation of a social agent (Fig. 18.5). Moreover the space can host more than a single participant, hence allowing an expansion from the advantages of research in a mixed-reality paradigm to the investigation of groups of subjects.

Recording of Behavior: To draw conclusions from the reaction of persons to a given stimulus, the behavior, together with the stimulus, needs to be measured with high fidelity. In XIM, the spatio-temporal behavior of one or more persons can be recorded together with the state of the environment and virtual social agents. A key feature is that the tracking system is capable of preserving the identity of multiple users over an extended period of time, even if the users exhibit a complex spatial behavior, e.g., by frequently crossing their paths. To record, e.g., the facial expression of a user during an experiment in XIM, a video camera is directly connected to the tracking system, thus allowing a videorecording of the behavior to be made for real-time or post hoc analysis. Additionally, XIM is equipped with the infrastructure to record standard physiological measures such as EEG, ECG, and GSR from a single user

Autonomy of the environment: A unique feature of XIM is the usage of the large-scale neuronal systems simulator *iqr* [1] as "operating system." The usage of *iqr* allows the deployment of neurobiological models of cognition and behavior, such as the distributed adaptive control model [26] for the real-time information integration and control of the environment and Avatars (Fig. 18.5, spirals). A second application of the autonomy of XIM is the testing of a psychological user model in real time. Prerequisite is that the model is mathematically formulated as is, e.g., the "Zurich model of social motivation" [27]. In the real-time testing of a model,

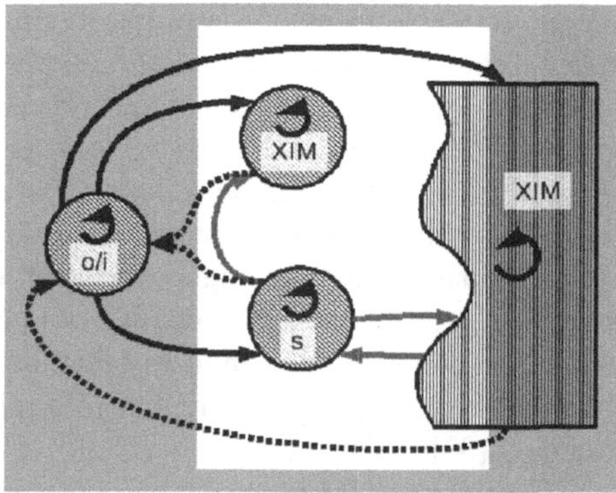

Fig. 18.5 Systemic view of the role on the eXperience Induction Machine (XIM) in psychological research. XIM is, on the one hand, a fully controllable dynamic environment and, on the other hand, it can substitute social agents. Central to the concept of XIM is that in both roles, XIM has its own internal dynamics (as symbolized by spirals). The *shaded area* demarcates the visibility as perceived by the subject; while XIM is visible as social agent or as environment, the investigator remains invisible to the subject

predictions about the user's response to a given stimulus are derived from the model and instantly tested. This allows the model to be tested and parameters estimated in a very efficient way.

18.1.4 Challenges of Using Mixed and Virtual Realities in Psychological Research

As in other experimental settings, one of the main issues of research using VR and MR technology is the generalizability of the results. A high degree of ecological validity, i.e., the extent to which the setting of a study is approximating the real-life situation under investigation, is not a guarantee, but a facilitator for a high degree of generalizability of the results obtained in a study. Presence is commonly defined as the subjective sense of "being there" in a scene depicted by a medium [28]. Since presence is bound to subjective experience, it is closely related to consciousness, a phenomenon which is inherently very difficult, if not even impossible, to account for by the objective methods of (reductionist) science [29]. Several approaches are pursued to tackle the presence. One avenue is to investigate determinants of presence. In [30] four determinants of presence are identified: The extent of fidelity of sensory information, sensory–motor contingencies, i.e., the match between the sensors and the display, content factors such as characteristics of object, actors, and events represented by the medium, and user characteristics. Alternatively, an operational definition can be given as in [31], where presence is located along the two dimensions of "place illusion," i.e., of being in a different place than the physical location, and the plausibility of the environment and the interactions, as determined by the plausibility of the user's behavior. Or, one can analyze the self-report of users when interacting with the media. In the factor analysis of questionnaire data [32] found four factors: "engagement," the user's involvement and interest in the experience; "ecological validity," the believability and realism of the content; "sense of physical space," the sense of physical placement; and "negative effects" such as dizziness, nausea, headache, and eyestrain. What is of interest here is that all three approaches establish an implicit or explicit link between ecological validity and presence; the more ecologically valid a virtual setting, the higher the level of presence experienced. Conversely, one can hence conclude that measures of presence can be used as an indicator of ecological validity. A direct indicator that indeed virtual environments are ecologically valid, and can substitute reality to a relevant extent, is the effectiveness of cybertherapy [33].

As a mixed-reality infrastructure, XIM naturally has a higher ecological validity than purely virtual environments, as it includes "real-world" devices such as the light emitting floor tiles, steerable light, and spatialized sound.

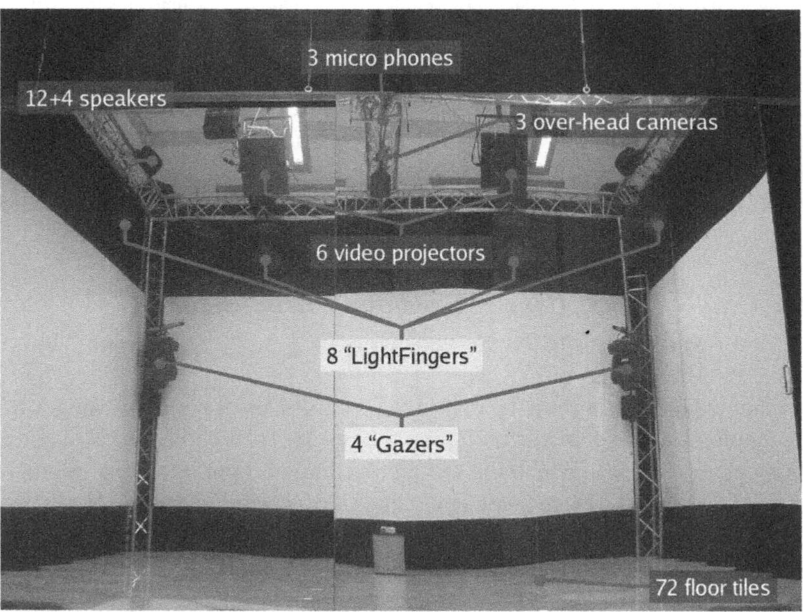

Fig. 18.6 The eXperience Induction Machine (XIM) is equipped with the following devices: three ceiling-mounted cameras, three microphones (Audio-Technica Pro45 unidirectional cardioid condenser, Stow, OH, USA) in the center of the rig, eight steerable theater lights ("LightFingers") (Martin MAC MAC250, Arhus, Denmark), four steerable color cameras ("Gazers") (Mechanical construction adapted from Martin MAC250, Arhus, Denmark, camera blocks Sony, Japan), a total of 12 speakers (Mackie SR1521Z, USA), and sound equipment for spatialized sound. The space is surrounded by three projection screens (2.25 × 5 m) on which six video projectors (Sharp XGA video projector, Osaka, Japan) display graphics. The floor constitutes 72 interactive tiles [49] (Custom. Mechanical construction by Westiform, Niederwengen, Switzerland, Interface cards Hilscher, Hattersheim, Germany). Each floor tile is equipped with pressure sensors to provide real-time weight information, incorporates individually controllable RGB neon tubes, permitting to display patterns and light effects on the floor

A second issue with VR and MR environments is the limited feedback they deliver to the user, as they predominantly focus on the visual modality. We aim to overcome this limitation in XIM by integrating a haptic feedback device [34]. The conceptual and technical integration is currently underway in the form of a "haptic gateway into PVC," where users can explore the persistent virtual community not only visually but also by means of a force-feedback device.

Whereas today's application of VR/MR paradigms is focusing on perception, attention, memory, cognitive performance, and mental imagery [24], we strongly believe that the research methods sketched here will make significant contributions to other fields of psychology such as social, personality, emotion, and motivation.

18.2 The eXperience Induction Machine

The eXperience Induction Machine covers a surface area of $\sim 5.5 \times \sim 5.5$ m, with a height of 4 m. The majority of the instruments are mounted in a rig constructed from a standard truss system (Fig. 18.6).

18.2.1 System Architecture

The development of a system architecture that provides the required functionality to realize a mixed-reality installation such as the persistent virtual community (see below) constitutes a major technological challenge. In this section we will give a detailed account of the architecture of the system used to build the PVC, and which "drives" the XIM. We will describe in detail the components of the system and their concerted activity

XIM's system architecture fulfills two main tasks: On the one hand, the processing of signals from physical sensors and the control of real-world devices, and, on the other hand, the representation of the virtual world. The physical installation consists of the eXperience Induction Machine, whereas the virtual world is implemented using a game engine. The virtual reality part is composed of the world itself, the representation of Avatars, functionality such as object manipulation, and the virtual version of XIM. As an integrator the behavior regulation system spawns both the physical and the virtual worlds.

18.2.1.1 Design Principles

The design of the system architecture of XIM is based on the principles of distributed multi-tier architecture and datagram-based communication.

Distributed multi-tier architecture: The processing of sensory information and the control of effectors are done in a distributed multi-tier fashion. This means that "services" are distributed to dedicated "servers," and that information processing

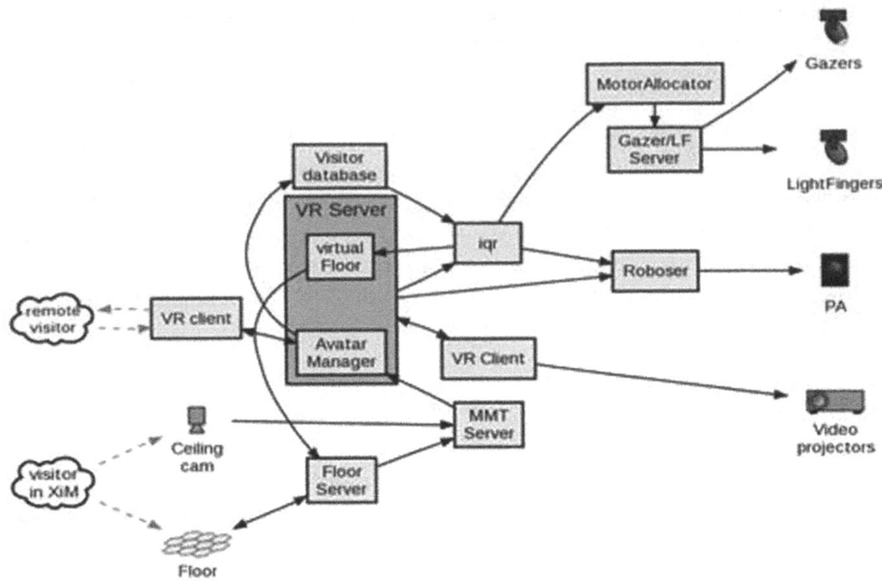

Fig. 18.7 Simplified diagram of the system architecture of XIM. The representation of the mixed-reality world ("VR Server") and the behavior control ("iqr") is the heart of the system architecture. Visitors in XIM are tracked using the pressure-sensitive floor and overhead cameras, whereas remote visitors are interfacing to the virtual world over the network by means of a local client connecting to the VR server

happens at different levels of abstraction from the hardware itself. At the lowest level, devices such as "Gazers" and the floor tiles are controlled by dedicated servers. At the middle layer, servers provide a more abstract control mechanism which, e.g., allows the control of devices without knowledge of the details of the device (such as its location in space). At the most abstract level the neuronal systems' simulator iqr processes abstract information about users and regulates the behavior of the space.

Datagram-based communication: With the exception of the communication between iqr and RoBoser (see below), all communication between different instances within the system is realized via UDP connections. Experience has shown that this type of connectionless communication is reliable enough for real-time sensor data processing and device control, while providing the significant advantage of reducing the interdependency of different entities. Datagram-based communication avoids deadlocking situations, a major issue in connection-oriented communication.

18.2.1.2 Interfaces to Sensors and Effectors

The "floor server" (Fig.18.7) is the abstract interface to the physical floor. The server, on the one hand, sends information from the three pressure sensors in each of the 72 floor tiles to the multi-model tracking system and, on the other hand, handles requests for controlling the light color of each tile. The "gazer/LF server" (Fig. 18.7) is the low-level interface for the control of the gazers and LightFingers. The server listens on a UDP port and translates requests, e.g., for pointing position to DMX commands, which then sends to the devices via a USB to DMX device (open DMX USB, ENTTEC Pty Ltd, Knoxfield, Australia). The "MotorAllocator" (Fig. 18.7) is a relay service which manages concurrent requests for gazers and LightFingers and recruits the appropriate device, i.e., the currently available device, and/or the device closest to the specified coordinate. The MotorAllocator reads requests from a UDP port and sends commands via the network to the "gazer/LF server."

Tracking of visitors in the physical installation: Visitors in XIM are sensed via the camera mounted in the ceiling, the cameras mounted in the four gazers, and the pressure sensors in each of the floor tiles. This information is fed into the multi-model tracking system (MMT, Fig. 18.7) [35]. The role of the multi-modal tracking server (MMT server) is to track individual visitors over an extended period of time and to send the coordinates and a unique identifier for each visitor to the "AvatarManager" inside the "VR server" (see below).

Storage of user-related information: The "VisitorDB" (Fig. 18.7) stores information about physically and remotely present users. A relational database (mySQL, MySQL AB) is used to maintain records of the position in space, the type of visitor, and IDs of the visitors.

The virtual reality server: The virtual reality server ("VR server," Fig. 18.7) is the implementation of the virtual world, which includes a virtual version of the interactive floor in XIM, Avatars representing local and remote visitors, and video displays. The server is implemented using the game engine Torque (GarageGames, Inc., OR, USA). In the case of a remote user ("remote visitor," Fig. 18.7), a client instance on the user's local machine will connect to the VR server ("VRClient"), and by this way the remote visitor will navigate though the virtual environment. If the user is locally present in XIM ("visitor in XIM," Fig. 18.7), the multi-modal tracking system (MMT) sends information about the position and the identity of a visitor to the VR server. In both cases, the remote and the local user, the "Avatar Manager" inside the VR server is creating an Avatar and positions the Avatar at the corresponding location in the virtual world. To make the information about remote and local visitors available outside the VR server, the Avatar Manager sends the visitor-related information to the "visitor database" (VisitorDB, Fig. 18.7). Three instances of VR clients are used to display the virtual environment inside XIM. Each of the three clients is connected to two video projectors and renders a different viewing angle (Figs. 18.1 and 18.6).

Sonification: The autonomous reactive music composition system RoBoser (Fig. 18.7), on the one hand, provides sonification of the states of XIM and, on the other hand, is used to playback sound effects, such as the voice of Avatars. For the sonification of events occurring in the virtual world, RoBoser directly receives information from the VR server. The current version of the music composition system is implemented in PureData (http://puredata.info).

Sonification: The autonomous reactive music composition system RoBoser (Fig. 18.7), on the one hand, provides sonification of the states of XIM and, on the other hand, is used to playback sound effects, such as the voice of Avatars. RoBoser is a system that produces a sequence of organized sounds that reflect the dynamics of its experience and learning history in the real world [36, 37]. For the sonification of events occurring in the virtual world, RoBoser directly receives information from the VR server. The current version of the music composition system is implemented in PureData (http://puredata.info).

System integration and behavior regulation: An installation such as the XIM needs an "operating system" for the integration and control of the different effectors and sensors, and the overall behavioral control. For this purpose we use the multi-level neuronal simulation environment iqr developed by the authors [1]. This software provides an efficient graphical environment to design and run simulations of large-scale multi-level neuronal systems. With iqr, neuronal systems can control real-world devices – robots in the broader sense – in real time. iqr allows the graphical online control of the simulation, change of model parameters at run-time, online visualization, and analysis of data. iqr is fully documented and freely available under the GNU General Public License at http://www.iqr-sim.net.

The overall behavioral control is based on the location of visitors in the space as provided by the MMT and includes the generation of animations for gazers, LightFingers, and the floor. Additionally a number of states of the virtual world and object therein are directly controlled by iqr. As the main control instance, iqr has a number of interfaces to servers and devices, which are implemented using the "module" framework of iqr.

18.3 XIM as a Platform for Psychological Experimentation

18.3.1 The Persistent Virtual Community

One of the applications developed in XIM is the persistent virtual community (PVC, Fig. 18.2). The PVC is one of the main goals of the PRESENCCIA project [38], which is tackling the phenomenon of subjective immersion in virtual worlds from a number of different angles. Within the PRESENCCIA project, the PVC serves as a platform to conduct experiments on presence, in particular social presence in mixed reality. The PVC and XIM provide a venue where entities of different degrees of virtuality (local users in XIM, Avatars of remote users, fully synthetic characters controlled by neurobiologically grounded models of perception and behavior) can meet and interact. The mixed-reality world of the PVC consists of the Garden, the Clubhouse, and the Avatar Heaven. The Garden of the PVC is a model ecosystem, the development and state of which depends on the interaction with and among visitors. The Clubhouse is a building in the Garden, and houses the virtual XIM. The virtual version of the XIM is a direct mirror of the physical installation: any events and output from the physical installation are represented in the virtual XIM and vice versa. This means, e.g., that an Avatar crossing the virtual XIM will be represented in the physical installation as well. The PVC is accessed either through

XIM, by way of a Cave Automatic Virtual Environment (CAVE), or via the Internet from a PC.

The aim of integrating XIM into PVC is the investigation of two facets of social presence. First, the facet of the perception of the presence of another entity in an immersive context, and second, the collective immersion experienced in a group, as opposed to being a single individual in a CAVE. For this purpose XIM offers a unique platform, as the size of the room permits the hosting of mid-sized groups of visitors. The former type of presence depends on the credibility of the entity the visitor is interacting with. In the XIM/PVC case the credibility of the space is affected by its potential to act and be perceived as a sentient entity and/or deploy believable characters in the PVC that the physically present users can interact with. In the CAVE case, the credibility of the fully synthetic characters depends on their validity as authentic anthropomorphic entities. In the case of XIM this includes the preservation of presence when the synthetic characters transcend from the virtual world into the physical space, i.e., when their representational form changes from being a fully graphical humanoid to being a lit floor tile.

18.3.2 A Space Explains Itself: The "Autodemo"

A fundamental issue in presence research is how we can quantify "presence." The subjective sense of immersion and presence in virtual and mixed-reality environment has thus far mainly been assessed through self-description in the form of questionnaires [39, 40]. It is unclear, however, to what extent the answers that the users provide actually reflect the dependent variable, in this case "presence," since it is well known that a self-report-based approach toward human behavior and experience is error prone. It is therefore essential to establish an independent validation of these self-reports. Indeed, some authors have used real-time physiology [41, 42, 43, 44], for such a validation. In line with previous research, we want to assess whether the reported presence of users correlates with objective measures such as those that assess memory and recollection.

Hence, we have investigated the question whether more objective measures can be devised that can corroborate subjective self-reports. In particular we have developed an objective and quantitative recollection task that assesses the ability of human subjects to recollect the factual structure and organization of a mixed-reality experience in the eXperience Induction Machine. In this experience – referred to as "Autodemo" – a virtual guide explains the key elements and properties of XIM.

The Autodemo has a total duration of 9 min 30 s and is divided into four stages: "sleep," "welcome," "inside story," and "outside story." Participants in the Autodemo are led through the story by a virtual guide, which consists of a prerecorded voice track (one of the authors) that delivers factual information about the installation and an Avatar that is an anthropomorphic representation of the space itself. By combining a humanoid shape and an inorganic texture, the Avatar of the virtual guide is deliberately designed to be a hybrid representation.

After exposure to the Autodemo, the users' subjective experience of presence was assessed in terms of media experience (ITC-Sense of Presence Inventory – [32]). As a performance measure, we developed an XIM-specific recall test that specifically targeted the user's recollection of the physical organization of XIM, its functional properties, and the narrative content. This allowed us to evaluate the correlations between the level of presence reported by the users and their recall performance of information conveyed in the "Autodemo" [45].

Eighteen participants (6 female, 12 male, mean age 30±5) took part in the evaluation of Autodemo experience. In the recall test participants on average answered 6 of 11 factual XIM questions correctly (SD = 2) (Fig. 18.8a). The results show that the questions varied in difficulty with quantitative open questions being the most difficult ones. Questions on interaction and the sound system were answered with most accuracy, while the quantitative estimates on the duration of the experience and the number of instruments were mostly not answered correctly. From the answers, an individual recall performance score was computed for each participant.

Ratings of ITC-SOPI were combined into four factors and the mean ratings were the Sense of Physical Space 2.8 (SE = 0.1), Engagement – 3.3 (SE = 0.1), Ecological Validity 2.3 (SE = 0.1), Negative Effects 1.7 (SE = 0.2) (Fig. 18.8b). The first three "positive presence-related" scales have been reported to be positively inter-correlated [32]. In our results only Engagement and Ecological Validity were positively correlated, ($r = 0.62$, $p < 0.01$).

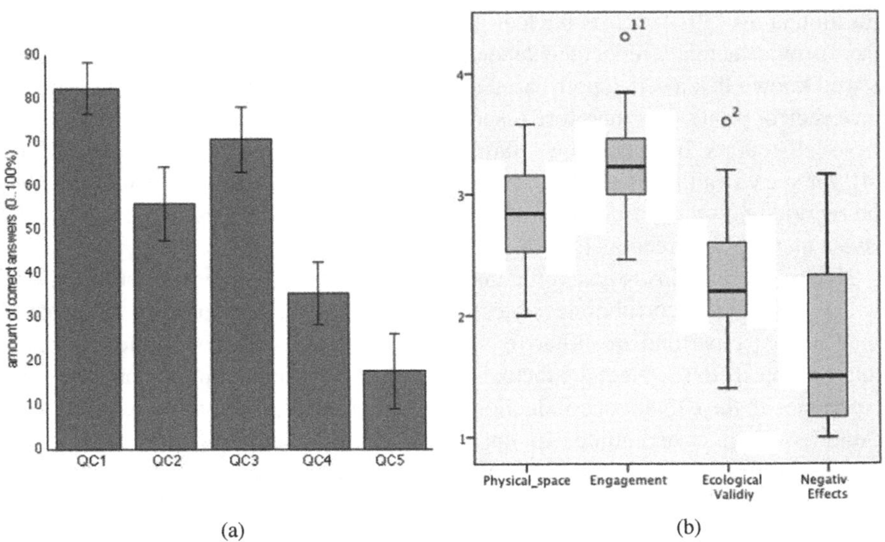

Fig. 18.8 (**a**) Percentage of correct answers to the recall test. The questions are grouped into thematic clusters (QC): QC1 – interaction; QC2 – persistent virtual community; QC3 – sound system; QC4 – effectors; QC5 – quantitative information. *Error bars* indicate the standard error of mean. (**b**) Boxplot of the four factors of the ITC-SOPI questionnaire (0.5 scale)

We correlated the summed recall performance score with the ITC-SOPI factors and found a positive correlation between recall and Engagement: $r = 0.5$, $p < 0.05$. This correlation was mainly caused by recall questions related to the virtual guide and the interactive parts of the experience. Experience time perception and subject-related data (age, gender) did not correlate with recall or ITC-SOPI ratings.

In the emotional evaluation of the avatar representing the virtual guide, 11 participants described this virtual character as neutral, 4 as positive, and 2 as negative.

The results obtained by ITC-SOPI for the Autodemo experience in XIM differ from scores of other media experiences described and evaluated in [32]. For example, on the "Engagement" scale, the Autodemo appears to be more comparable to a cinema experience (M=3.3) than to a computer game (M=3.6) as reported in [32]. For the "Sense of Physical Space" our scores are very similar to IMAX 2D displays and computer game environments but are smaller than IMAX 3D scores (M=3.3).

Previous research indicated that there might be a correlation between the users' sensation of presence and their performance in a memory task [46]. The difference between our study and [46] is that we have used a more objective evaluation procedure by allowing subjects to give quantitative responses and to actually draw positions in space. By evaluating the users' subjective experience in the mixed-reality space, we were able to identify a positive correlation between the presence engagement scale and factual recall. Moreover, our results indicated that information conveyed in the interactive parts of the Autodemo was better recalled than those that were conveyed at the moments that the subjects were passive. We believe that the correlation between recall performance and the sense of presence identified opens the avenue to the development of a measure of presence that is more robust and less problematic than the use of questionnaires.

18.3.3 Cooperation and Competition: Playing Football in Mixed Reality

Although the architectures of mixed-reality spaces become increasingly more complex, our understanding of social behavior in such spaces is still limited. In behavioral biology sophisticated methods to track and observe the actions and movements of animals have been developed, while comparably little is known about the complex social behavior of humans in real and mixed-reality worlds. By constructing experimental setups where multiple subjects can freely interact with each other and the virtual world including synthetic characters, we can use XIM to observe human behavior without interference. This allows us to gain knowledge about the effects and influence of new technologies like mixed-reality spaces on human behavior and social interaction. We addressed this issue by analyzing social behavior and physical actions of multiple subjects in the eXperience Induction Machine. As a paradigm of social interaction we constructed a mixed-reality football game in which two teams of two players had to cooperate and compete in order to win [47]. We hypothesize that the game strategy of a team, e.g., the level of intra-team cooperation while competing with the opposing team, will lead to discernible and invariant behavioral patterns. In particular we analyzed which features of the spatial position of individual players are predictive of the game's outcome.

Overall 10 groups of 4 people played the game for 2 min each (40 subjects with an average age of 24, SD = 6, 11 women). All subjects played at least one game, some played two ($n = 8$). Both the team assignment and the match drawing process were randomized. During the game the players were alone in the space and there was no interaction between the experimenter and the players

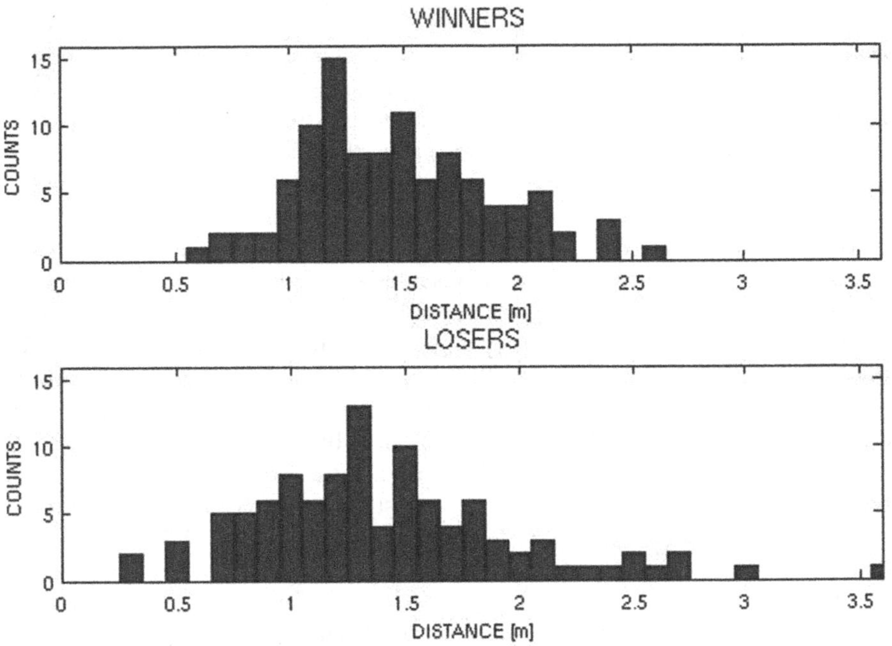

Fig. 18.9 Distribution of the inter-team member distances of winners and losers for epochs longer than 8s

We focused our analysis on the spatial behavior of the winning team members before they scored and the spatial behavior of the losing team members before they allowed a goal. For this purpose, for all 114 epochs, we analyzed the team member distance for both the winning and losing teams. An epoch is defined as the time window from the moment when the ball is released until a goal is scored. For example, if a game ended with a score of 5:4, we analyzed, for every one of the nine game epochs, the inter-team member distances of the epoch winners and the epoch losers, without taking into account which team won the overall game. This analysis showed that the epoch winners and epoch losers showed significantly different moving behavior, for all epochs that lasted longer than 8 s (Fig. 18.9). In this analysis epoch-winning teams stood on average 1.47 ± 0.41 m apart from each other, while epoch-losing teams had an average distance of 1.41 ± 0.58 m to each other

(Fig. 18.9). The comparison of the distributions of team member distance showed a significant difference between epoch-winning and epoch-losing teams ($P = 0.043$, Kolmogorov–Smirnov test).

The average duration of an epoch was 12.5 s. About 20.3% of all epochs did not last longer than 4 s. The analysis of the distributions of inter-team member distances for all epoch winners and epoch losers did not reach significance (Kolmogorov–Smirnov test, $P = 0.1$). Also we could not find a statistical significant correlation between game winners and the number of scored goals or game winners with the inter-team member distance regulation. Winning teams that chose an inter-team member distance of 1.39 ± 0.35 m scored on average 6 ± 2 goals. Losing team members scored 3 ± 1.5 goals and stood in average 1.31 ± 0.39 m apart from each other. The trend that winners chose a bigger inter-team member distance than losers shows no significant differences.

Our results show that winners and losers employ a different strategy as expressed in the inter-team member distance. This difference in distance patterns can be understood as a difference in the level of cooperation within a team or the way the team members regulate their behavior to compete with the opposing team. Our study shows that in long epochs, winners chose to stand farther apart from each other than losers. Our interpretation of this behavioral regularity is that this strategy leads to a better defense, i.e., regulating the size of the gap between the team members with respect to the two gaps at the sideline. Long epoch-winning teams coordinated their behavior with respect to each other in a more cooperative way than long epoch-losing teams.

The methodological concept we are proposing here provides an example of how we can face the challenge of quantitatively studying complex social behavior that has thus far eluded systematic study. We propose that mixed-reality spaces such as XIM provide an experimental infrastructure that is essential to accomplish this objective. In a further step of our approach we will test the influence of virtual players on the behavior of real visitors, by building teams of multiple players, where a number of player's of the team will be present in XIM and the others will play the game over a network using a computer. These remote players will be represented in XIM in the same way as the real player, i.e., an illuminated floor tile and virtual body on the screen. With this setup we want to test the effect of physical presence versus virtual presence upon social interaction.

18.4 Conclusion and Outlook

In this chapter we gave a detailed account of the immersive multi-user space eXperience Induction Machine (XIM). We set out by describing XIM's precursors Ada and RoBoser, and followed with a description of the hardware and software infrastructure of the space. Three concrete applications of XIM were presented: The persistent virtual community, a research platform for the investigation of (social) presence; the "Autodemo," an interactive scenario in which the space is explaining itself that is used for researching the empirical basis of the subjective sense of presence; and finally, the application of XIM in the quantification of collaboration and competition based on spatio-temporal behavior of users in a mixed-reality variation of the classical computer game pong. The methodological concepts proposed here provide examples of how we can face the challenge of quantitatively studying human behavior in situations that have thus far eluded systematic study.

We have tried to elaborate in some detail the epistemological rationale behind the construction of a mixed-reality space such as XIM. We did so because we are convinced that mixed and virtual reality infrastructures such as XIM represent the psychological research platform of the future. Part of this process will be that research is moving beyond the currently predominant investigations of human–computer interaction, which focuses on the media itself, into a wider investigation of the human psyche, e.g., the fields of personality, motivational and emotional psychology.

Ecological validity is often seen as one of the pivotal aspects and shortcomings of current VR and MR environments. Yet the ecological validity will undoubtedly increase with advancements in the field of computer graphics and developments of new and better feedback devices. What is frequently neglected, though, is the importance of plausibility in the interaction of the user with the virtual environment and virtual actors inhabiting it. We believe that a high level of plausibility can only be achieved by employing a bio-inspired AI system for the control of environments and virtual characters, equipping them with an appropriate level of autonomy. This is the rational why we are using the large-scale neuronal system simulator as an "operating system" in XIM. It is in this vein that we see our engagement in the field of interactive narratives and performance arts, like the interactive real-time performance re(PER)curso staged in 2007 [48].

Acknowledgments This work was carried out as part of the PRESENCCIA project, an EU-funded Integrated Project under the IST programme (Project Number 27731). The Original Floor System was developed by Institute of Neuroinformatics of ETH Zurich and of University of Zurich.

References

1. U. Bernardet, M. Blanchard, and P.F.M.J. Verschure, "IQR: A Distributed System for Real-Time Real-World Neuronal Simulation," *Neurocomputing*, vol. 44–46, Jun. 2002, pp. 1043–1048.
2. P. Milgram and F. Kishino, "A Taxonomy of Mixed Reality Visual Displays," *IEICE Transactions on Information Systems*, vol. E77–D, Dec. 1994, pp. 1321–1329.
3. C. Coutrix and L. Nigay, "Mixed reality: a model of mixed interaction," *Proceedings of the Working Conference on Advanced Visual Interfaces*, Venezia, Italy: ACM, 2006, pp. 43–50.
4. Y. Okuno, H. Kakuta, T. Takayama, and K. Asai, "Jellyfish party: blowing soap bubbles in mixed reality space," *Proceedings. The 2nd IEEE and ACM International Symposium on Mixed and Augmented Reality,* 2003, pp. 358–359.
5. T. Narumi, A. Hiyama, T. Tanikawa, and M. Hirose, "Inter-glow," *ACM SIGGRAPH 2007 Emerging Technologies*, San Diego, California: ACM, 2007, p. 14.
6. D. Tavares, A. Burlamaqui, A. Dias, M. Monteiro, V. Antunes, G. Thó, T. Tavares, C. Lima, L. Gonçalves, G. Lemos, P. Alsina, and A. Medeiros, "Hyperpresence – An application environment for control of multi-user agents in mixed reality spaces," *Proceedings of the 36th Annual Symposium on Simulation*, IEEE Computer Society, 2003, p. 351.

7. A.D. Cheok, X. Yang, Z.Z. Ying, M. Billinghurst, and H. Kato, "Touch-Space: Mixed Reality Game Space Based on Ubiquitous, Tangible, and Social Computing," *Personal and Ubiquitous Computing*, vol. 6, Dec. 2002, pp. 430–442.
8. H. Ishii and B. Ullmer, "Tangible bits: towards seamless interfaces between people, bits and atoms," *Proceedings of the SIGCHI Conference on Human Factors in Computing Systems*, Atlanta, Georgia, United States: ACM, 1997, pp. 234–241.
9. D. Birchfield, B. Mechtley, S. Hatton, and H. Thornburg, "Mixed-reality learning in the art museum context," *Proceeding of the 16th ACM International Conference on Multimedia*, Vancouver, British Columbia, Canada: ACM, 2008, pp. 965–968.
10. V.B.D. Stanton and T. Pridmore, "Classroom collaboration in the design of tangible interfaces for storytelling," *CHI '01: Proceedings of the SIGCHI Conference on Human Factors in Computing Systems*, New York, USA: ACM, 2001, pp. 482 489.
11. W. Strauss, M. Fleischmann, M. Thomsen, J. Novak, U. Zlender, T. Kulessa, and F. Pragasky, "Staging the space of mixed reality – Reconsidering the concept of a multi user environment," *Proceedings of the Fourth Symposium on Virtual Reality Modeling Language*, Paderborn, Germany: ACM, 1999, pp. 93–98.
12. A.D. Cheok, W. Weihua, X. Yang, S. Prince, F.S. Wan, M. Billinghurst, and H. Kato, "Interactive theatre experience in embodied + wearable mixed reality space," *Proceedings of the 1st International Symposium on Mixed and Augmented Reality*, IEEE Computer Society, 2002, p. 59.
13. B. Brumitt, B. Meyers, J. Krumm, A. Kern, and S. Shafer, "EasyLiving: Technologies for Intelligent Environments," *Null*, 2000, pp. 12–29.
14. R.A. Brooks, "The intelligent room project," *Proceedings of the 2nd International Conference on Cognitive Technology (CT '97)*, IEEE Computer Society, 1997, p. 271.
15. T. Höllerer, J. Kuchera-Morin, and X. Amatriain, "The allosphere: a large-scale immersive surround-view instrument," *Proceedings of the 2007 Workshop on Emerging Displays Technologies: Images and Beyond: The Future of Displays and Interacton*, San Diego, California: ACM, 2007, p. 3.
16. M. Mine, "Towards virtual reality for the masses: 10 years of research at Disney's VR studio," *Proceedings of the Workshop on Virtual Environments 2003*, Zurich, Switzerland: ACM, 2003, pp. 11–17.
17. A.F. Bobick, S.S. Intille, J.W. Davis, F. Baird, C.S. Pinhanez, L.W. Campbell, Y.A. Ivanov, A. Schutte, and A. Wilson, The KidsRoom: A Perceptually-Based Interactive and Immersive Story Environment," *Presence: Teleoperators & Virtual Environments*, vol. 8, 1999, pp. 369–393.
18. K. Eng, A. Baebler, U. Bernardet, M. Blanchard, M. Costa, T. Delbruck, R.J. Douglas, K. Hepp, D. Klein, J. Manzolli, M. Mintz, F. Roth, U. Rutishauser, K. Wassermann, A.M. Whatley, A. Wittmann, R. Wyss, and P.F.M.J. Verschure, "Ada – intelligent space: An articial creature for the Swiss Expo.02," Proceedings of the 2003 IEEE International Conference on Robotics and Automation (ICRA 2003), Sept. 14–19, 2003.
19. K. Eng, R. Douglas, and P.F.M.J. Verschure, "An Interactive Space that Learns to Influence Human Behavior," *Systems, Man and Cybernetics, Part A, IEEE Transactions on*, vol. 35, 2005, pp. 66–77.
20. R.L. Atkinson, R.C. Atkinson, and E.E. Smith, *Hilgards Einführung in die Psychologie*, Spektrum Akademischer, Verlag, 2001.
21. M. Eysenck, *Perspectives On Psychology*, Psychology Press, Routledge, London, 1994.
22. H. Coolican, *Research Methods and Statistics in Psychology*, A Hodder Arnold Publication, London, 2004.
23. S. Freud, Das Ich und das Es: Metapsychologische Schriften., Fischer (Tb.), Frankfurt, 1992.
24. A. Gaggioli, "Using Virtual Reality in Experimental Psychology," *Towards Cyberpsychology*, Amsterdam: IOS Press, 2001, pp. 157–174.

25. M. Slater, A. Antley, A. Davison, D. Swapp, C. Guger, C. Barker, N. Pistrang, and M.V. Sanchez-Vives, "A Virtual Reprise of the Stanley Milgram Obedience Experiments," *PLoS ONE*, vol. 1, 2006, p. e39.
26. P.F.M.J. Verschure, T. Voegtlin, and R. Douglas, "Environmentally Mediated Synergy Between Perception and Behaviour in Mobile Robots," *Nature*, vol. 425, 2003, pp. 620–624.
27. H. Gubler, M. Parath, and N. Bischof, "Eine Ästimationsstudie zur Sicherheits- und Erregungsregulation während der Adoleszenz," *Untersuchungen zur Systemanalyse der sozialen Motivation (III)*, vol. 202, 1994, pp. 95–132.
28. W. Barfield, D. Zeltzer, T. Sheridan, and M. Slater, "Presence and Performance Within Virtual Environments," *Virtual Environments and Advanced Interface Design*, Oxford University Press, Inc., Oxford, 1995, pp. 473–513.
29. T. Nagel, "What Is It Like to be a Bat?," *Philosophical Review*, vol. 83, 1974, pp. 435–450.
30. W.A. IJsselsteijn, H. de Ridder, J. Freeman, and S.E. Avons, "Presence: Concept, Determinants, and Measurement," *Human Vision and Electronic Imaging V*, San Jose, CA, USA: 2000, pp. 520–529.
31. M. Slater, "RAVE Manifesto," Barcelona, 2008.
32. J. Lessiter, J. Freeman, E. Keogh, and J. Davidoff, "A Cross-Media Presence Questionnaire: The ITC-Sense of Presence Inventory," *Presence: Teleoperators & Virtual Environments*, vol. 10, 2001, pp. 282–297.
33. G. Riva, C. Botella, P. Legeron, and G. Optale, Cybertherapy: Internet and Virtual Reality As Assessment and Rehabilitation Tools for Clinical Psychology and Neuroscience, IOS Press, 2004.
34. A. Frisoli, F. Simoncini, M. Bergamasco, and F. Salsedo, "Kinematic Design of a Two Contact Points Haptic Interface for the Thumb and Index Fingers of the Hand," *Journal of Mechanical Design*, vol. 129, May. 2007, pp. 520–529.
35. Z. Mathews, S. Bermúdez i Badia, and P.F.M.J. Verschure, "A novel brain-based approach for multi-modal multi-target tracking in a mixed reality space," *Proceedings of 4th INTUITION International Conference and Workshop on Virtual Reality 2007*, Athens: 2007.
36. J. Manzolli and P.F.M.J. Verschure, "Roboser: A Real-World Composition System," *Computer Music Journal*, vol. 29, 2005, pp. 55–74.
37. K. Wassermann, J. Manzolli, K. Eng, and P.F.M.J. Verschure, "Live Soundscape Composition Based on Synthetic Emotions," *IEEE Multimedia*, vol. 10, 2003, pp. 82–90.
38. M. Slater, A. Frisoli, F. Tecchia, C. Guger, B. Lotto, A. Steed, G. Pfurtscheller, R. Leeb, M. Reiner, M.V. Sanchez-Vives, P. Verschure, and U. Bernardet, "Understanding and Realizing Presence in the Presenccia Project," *Computer Graphics and Applications, IEEE*, vol. 27, 2007, pp. 90–93.
39. T.W. Schubert, "The sense of presence in virtual environments: A three-component scale measuring spatial presence, involvement, and realness," *Zeitschrift für Medienpsychologie*, vol. 15, 2003, pp. 69–71.
40. B.G. Witmer and M.J. Singer, "Measuring Presence in Virtual Environments: A Presence Questionnaire," *Presence: Teleoperators & Virtual Environments*, vol. 7, 1998, pp. 225–240.
41. A. Brogni, V. Vinayagamoorthy, A. Steed, and M. Slater, "Variations in physiological responses of participants during different stages of an immersive virtual environment experiment," *Proceedings of the ACM Symposium on Virtual Reality Software and Technology*, Limassol, Cyprus: ACM, 2006, pp. 376–382.
42. P.M. Emmelkamp and M. Felten, "The process of exposure in vivo: cognitive and physiological changes during treatment of acrophobia," *Behaviour Research and Therapy*, vol. 23, 1985, pp. 219–223.
43. M. Meehan, B. Insko, M. Whitton, and J. Frederick P. Brooks, "Physiological measures of presence in stressful virtual environments," *Proceedings of the 29th Annual Conference on Computer Graphics and Interactive Techniques*, San Antonio, Texas: ACM, 2002, pp. 645–652.

44. M. Slater, "How Colorful Was Your Day? Why Questionnaires Cannot Assess Presence in Virtual Environments," *Presence: Teleoperators & Virtual Environments*, vol. 13, 2004, pp. 484–493.
45. U. Bernardet, M. Inderbitzin, S. Wierenga, A. Väljamäe, A. Mura, and P.F.M.J. Verschure, "Validating presence by relying on recollection: Human experience and performance in the mixed reality system XIM," *The 11th Annual International Workshop on Presence, October 25–27*, 2008, pp. 178–182.
46. H. Dinh, N. Walker, L. Hodges, C. Song, and A. Kobayashi, "Evaluating the importance of multi-sensory input on memory and the sense of presence in virtual environments," *Virtual Reality, 1999. Proceedings, IEEE*, 1999, pp. 222–228.
47. M. Inderbitzin, S. Wierenga, A. Väljamäe, U. Bernardet, and P.F.M.J. Verschure, "Social cooperation and competition in the mixed reality space eXperience Induction Machine.," *The 11th Annual International Workshop on Presence, October 25–27*, 2008, pp. 314–318.
48. Anna Mura, B. Rezazadeh, A. Duff, J. Manzolli, S.L. Groux, Z. Mathews, U. Bernardet, S. Wierenga, S. Bermudez, S., and P. Verschure, "re(PER)curso: an interactive mixed reality chronicle," *ACM SIGGRAPH 2008 talks*, Los Angeles, California: ACM, 2008, pp. 1–1.
49. T. Delbrück, A.M. Whatley, R. Douglas, K. Eng, K. Hepp, and P.F.M.J. Verschure, "A Tactile Luminous Floor for an Interactive Autonomous Space," *Robotics Autonomous System*, vol. 55, 2007, pp. 433–443.

Chapter 19
MyCoach: In Situ User Evaluation of a Virtual and Physical Coach for Running

Margit Biemans, Timber Haaker, and Ellen Szwajcer

Abstract Running is an enjoyable exercise for many people today. Trainers help people to reach running goals. However, today's busy and nomadic people are not always able to attend running classes. A combination of a virtual and physical coach should be useful. A virtual coach (MyCoach) was designed to provide this support. MyCoach consists of a mobile phone (real time) and a web application, with a focus on improving health and well-being. A randomised controlled trial was performed to evaluate MyCoach. The results indicate that the runners value the tangible aspects on monitoring and capturing their exercise and analysing progress. The system could be improved by incorporating running schedules provided by the physical trainer and by improving its usability. Extensions of the system should focus on the real-time aspects of information sharing and "physical" coaching at a distance.

Keywords Running · Exercising · Virtual coach · Physical coach · Mobile device · Web application · User evaluation

19.1 Introduction

Running is an enjoyable exercise for many people today. People join running clubs or start individual exercise to improve their fitness level, enhance their health status or simply enjoy exercising and physical challenges [1]. Trainers help people to achieve their goals, to provide a training scheme and to motivate and stimulate people to exercise. However, a trainer requires people to train at specific moments, and at specific locations, which conflicts with today's nomadic lifestyle.

As runners increasingly carry digital devices during exercise, like running watches and heart rate belts, the idea of a virtual coach was born. The resulting

M. Biemans (✉)
Novay, PO. Box 589, 7500 AN Enschede, The Netherlands
e-mail: Margit.Biemans@novay.nl

E. Dubois et al. (eds.), *The Engineering of Mixed Reality Systems*, Human-Computer Interaction Series, DOI 10.1007/978-1-84882-733-2_19,

virtual coach is a combination of a mobile phone and a web-based application. The mobile phone monitors physical (e.g. speed) and physiological (e.g. heart rate) information during a training and coaches by providing auditory feedback during the exercise. After the training, the information collected during a session is automatically uploaded to the web application. The information is used to manage exercises, to monitor progress and fitness level and to advise on forthcoming activities and training.

The focus of this chapter is not so much on designing a virtual trainer, but on evaluating the use of a virtual trainer, or to be more specific, the focus is on the evaluation of a combination of a physical and virtual trainer: mixed realities!

This chapter starts with a description of existing virtual trainer/coach systems for running. Then the MyCoach system is described, consisting of a mobile device, and a web application. The mixed reality (combination of a virtual and physical trainer) is tested in a randomised controlled experiment with 210 runners using the system over 3 months. The experimental design and the combination of quantitative and qualitative measurement methods are described. The latter sections describe the results of the pre-trial, during trial and post-trial measurements. Based upon the results, conclusions are drawn about specific features of the MyCoach system, the tangibility of results which improves motivation and the importance of a personal goal-oriented training scheme. Moreover, enhanced services of the MyCoach system are identified for further research.

19.1.1 Virtual Trainer/Coach

Users like to make their exercise more tangible by measuring and monitoring efforts during and after exercise, and recording contextual data like weather conditions. Collecting and sharing information on routes and running experiences via the Internet is common practice [2, 3]. Next to recording and analysing exercise data, mobile systems are emerging that provide coaching during exercise [4]. To provide an optimal user experience Nike works together with Apple on the Nike + iPod Sport Kit [5] pedometer that fits in a dedicated Nike shoe and a receiver (the iPod nano needs a dedicated receiver in the shoe and the iPod touch can serve as a receiver itself), connecting to an iPod. More traditional watch manufacturers have also identified sports business as relevant areas for development [6].

The new kinds of running information systems aim not only at capturing and analysing user data but also at providing motivational support and navigation. Motivational support is especially important when people are mainly extrinsically motivated, for example aiming at an increased fitness level. For example, the Houston system is a prototype mobile phone application for encouraging activity by sharing step count with friends [7]. They found four key design requirements for such applications, i.e. give users proper credit for activities, provide personal awareness of activity level, support social influence and consider the practical constraints of users' lifestyle. Navigational support for recreational activities can be provided in several ways, usually consisting of map-based information and auditory cues. Abel is an example of a personal enhanced navigational device for cycling and walking in The Netherlands and Germany [8]. Additional features may include virtual competition and emergency options that enhance the sense of safety during exercise.

In the next section, our virtual system "MyCoach" will be described. MyCoach consists of a combination of a mobile phone (with real-time functionality) and a web-based application, the entire application focusing on the health and well-being of runners.

19.2 MyCoach

The MyCoach system consists of three pieces of hardware: (1) a lightweight mobile device with Bluetooth and GPRS/UMTS capabilities, (2) an arm strap to wear the mobile on the lower or upper arm and (3) a breast strap with heart rate sensor for measuring heart rate. The breast strap also contains a GPS chip for location determination. Finally, the breast strap has Bluetooth functionality to allow for heart rate data and GPS data to be transmitted to the mobile device, where it is stored and further processed.

The MyCoach system has two clients. The mobile client runs on the mobile phone, and is capable of collecting, storing and interpreting work-out data (see Fig. 19.1) during exercise. This involves the heart rate and location data as well as derived data like covered distance, current location and speed. All this information can be viewed on the mobile's display in real time during exercise. The information provides runners with insights in their performance and/or progress. Moreover, the current location and covered track can be displayed on a map in

Fig. 19.1 Mobile client

real time as well. The mobile client also has coaching functionality, which provides real-time advice and alerts on speed and/or heart rate. The advice is presented in a multimodal fashion, i.e. coaching messages are shown on the mobile's display (see Fig. 19.1) but can also be received in audio format using the mobile's loud speaker or via ear plugs. The coaching functionality supports optimal training effort and may safeguard against overtraining. Finally, an obvious but important feature of the system is that it allows for emergency calls, as it is running on a connected device, i.e. a mobile phone. For this experiment, the mobile client ran on the Sony Ericsson W880i.

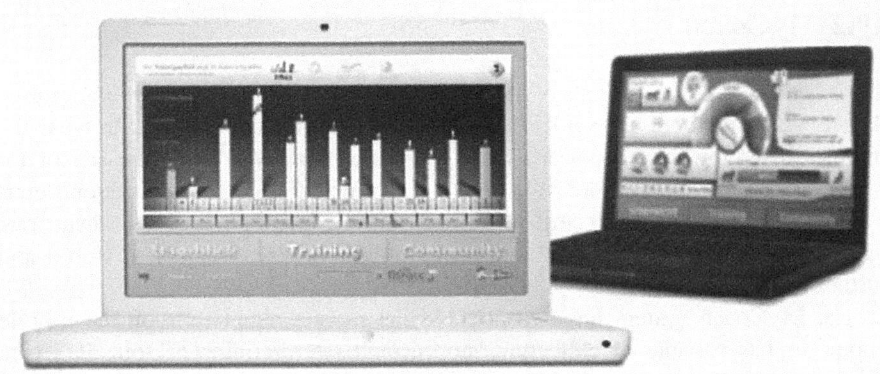

Current workload, training progress, workout history and many other things ...

Fig. 19.2 Overview of personal web site

The second client of the MyCoach system is a personal web site on which all exercise data are collected and visualised (see Fig. 19.2). When a user has finished a training exercise, all the recorded data on the mobile are sent automatically and wirelessly to a central database. The web client of the MyCoach system provides secured access to the database in the form of a personal web site where all recorded exercise data can be visualised (see Fig. 19.2). The user can generate various statistics that display individual exercises as well as aggregated results. Individual exercises may be completely replayed, i.e. the exercise is displayed on a map while simultaneously the instantaneous heart rate and speed are shown in graphs. On an aggregate level a user may display their development in terms of average speed, heart rate or covered distance to assess progress. The web site also provides advice on training schedules based on current fitness levels. The fitness level is visualized playfully by slower and faster animals like a snail or dolphin. Each fitness level is associated with an animal. Users are both stimulated and rewarded via these fitness indicators. As such the current schedules and coaching functionality focus on a healthy lifestyle rather than on goal-oriented schedules that aim for a particular achievement.

19.3 User Experiment

In order to evaluate the differences between physical and mixed realities coach a randomised controlled trial was performed. Two different groups were involved: one experimental group running exercise training with both a physical and a virtual coach (MyCoach = mixed realities group) and one control group running exercise training with only a physical coach. Both groups trained for 3 months and several pre- and post-measurements were conducted.

With mixed reality we mean the integration of the physical and digital worlds in a smooth and usable way. This is for example provided by the context-aware and real-time features that MyCoach provides during exercise. The most prominent mixed reality feature of MyCoach is virtual coaching. Virtual coaching is generated in real time and based on the user's current context (location, speed, and heart rate) and on the user's profile (current fitness level and desired fitness level). MyCoach merges virtual coaching with the real world via auditory feedback during exercise. The advice by the virtual coach should be consistent with and complement the (physical) human coach.

19.3.1 Runners

The overall user trial aimed to evaluate the overall MyCoach system. Runners from various backgrounds and various experience levels were asked to participate in the trial (Fig. 19.3). A specific subset of the trial and its results were used for this chapter on training aspects, a form of a mixed reality system.

The runners were selected by means of three channels: a group invitation to people who subscribed for a specific running event, an advertisement on the National Athletics Union web site and an invitation letter (e-mail) and telephone call to people who showed interest by the previous channels. In total 200 people were selected to participate; we equipped 91 of them with the MyCoach system and 119 people participated in the control group. The people in the MyCoach group kept running in their normal training group with their original trainer during the experiment.

After 3 months, 24 people in the MyCoach group had quit the trial, i.e. they were excluded from the post-survey. The main reason for that is that some participants did not actively participate, i.e. they had not registered on the MyCoach web site or they had not made any uploads. The reasons for not being active participants are mainly as follows: (1) injuries keeping people from training, (2) people cannot cope with the technology and (3) failing technology. People who did not use the system frequently were excluded from the post-survey because they could not provide enough experience-based information. From the control group 25 people quit the trial, i.e. they did not fill in the post-survey. From these people no information is available on why they quit.

So, in total 67 people participated in the MyCoach group (mixed realities) and 94 people in the control group (physical trainer only).

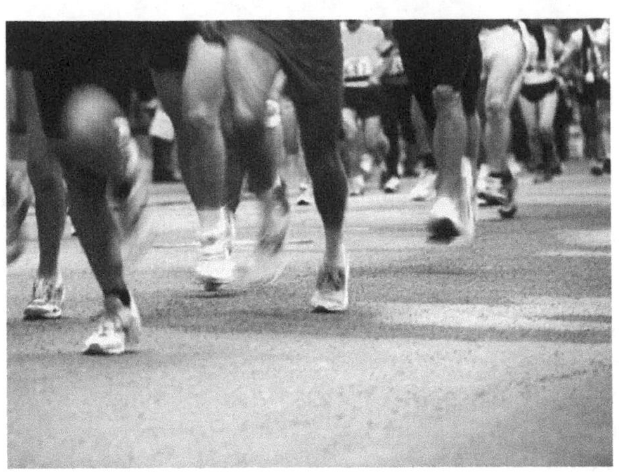

Fig. 19.3 Running

19.3.2 Measurement

The measurements combined qualitative methods such as focus group discussions and quantitative methods such as surveys and loggings of system usage. Information was gathered at three moments in time, i.e. pre-trial, during the trial and post-trial.

Pre-trial: Four focus group discussions with trainers and runners (seven to eight participants, duration of 2 h) were conducted to identify relevant training information and motivational aspects and to explore other relevant issues about running. A semi-structured focus group discussion protocol was used to address all relevant topics, to maintain sufficient exploratory flexibility and to allow for communicative validation [9]. To ensure reliability, the focus group discussions were attended by a second researcher. As is common in qualitative research, participants were selected on the basis of diversity and maximum representativeness within normal populations of runners, in relation to age and running level (characteristics that may affect an individual's experience of, and attitudes towards, a particular phenomenon) [10–12]. The focus group discussions took about 2 h and were tape recorded. Before and during analysis, coding frameworks were constructed based on the research objectives, the focus group discussion protocol and relevant data.

The results of the focus group discussions were also used to design the pre-survey. The pre-survey was constructed with Survey World and sent out by e-mail. After 2 weeks, the non-respondents got a reminder to complete the survey. At the start of the experiment, all participants provided their e-mail account to the researchers. Whether they had daily and personal access to a PC was unknown. However, having an e-mail address might indicate that they had access to and used a PC before.

The pre-survey asked about people's running and training habits and motivation for running based on existing scales for intrinsic and extrinsic motivation [13].

During the trial: Usage information (log data) from the web application was analysed, and netnography data were used. The log data consisted of both the amount of sessions people conducted on the web sites and the amount of uploads. Netnography refers to ethnographic data derived from Internet sites [14]. In this case, a Google search revealed that three people who participated in the MyCoach group posted information about the MyCoach system on their personal web sites or weblogs. These postings and the corresponding comments were also gathered and analysed.

Post-trial: Focus group discussions were conducted. Two focus group discussions were held with seven to eight participants. For some people who could not attend the focus group discussions, interviews were conducted. The focus group discussions and interviews aimed at experiences of the participants on running with and without MyCoach. The post-survey was also constructed with Survey World and aimed at the running experiences of MyCoach. It measured changes in motivation and considered experiences, opinions and preferences regarding the virtual training system.

19.4 Results

In the MyCoach group (mixed realities) 67 people participated (38 male and 29 female) and in the control group (physical trainer) 94 people participated (62 male and 32 female). People in the MyCoach group were on average 44.1 years old (SD = 9.4) and had on average 6.0 years of running experience (SD = 4.9). People in the control group were on average 44.5 years old (SD = 8.5) and had 7.0 years of running experience (SD = 4.4).

19.4.1 Pre-trial Results: Running and Training Habits

Pre-trial information was gathered about running and training habits by focus groups and surveys. First, four focus group sessions with six to eight participants (runners and trainers) each were conducted to discuss running and training habits [9]. Based upon these insights, the surveys were designed. The surveys provide the quantitative information (what happens), whereas the focus groups provide more detailed qualitative information (why does it happen).

First, we were interested in why people like to exercise or train. From the focus groups it became clear that many people have different reasons to go running or to keep running: “healthcare reasons”, “I run to lose weight” “because my kids run”, “running provides me with a feeling of freedom”, etc. In the pre-survey, these questions were posed, based upon the Motives for Physical Activities Measure – Revised (MPAM-R) [13]. Ryan et al. [13] identified five main constructs of intrinsic motivation and exercise adherence: social, appearance, enjoyment, competence and fitness. People had to score 30 questions on these constructs on a 7-point Likert scale (see Fig. 19.4). The results reveal that fitness (health and well-being), competence and enjoyment were found most important, while social aspects (group) and appearance (the looks) were found less important (although a score around average). Experienced runners score higher on interest/enjoyment, i.e. a higher intrinsic motivation, while fitness is especially important for beginning runners. The results suggest that a successful training system should preferably aim at fitness, competence and enjoyment, and less at social aspects and appearance.

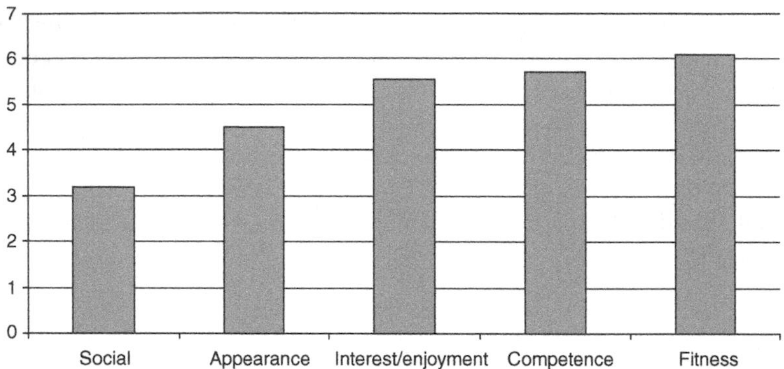

Fig. 19.4 Reasons why people exercise (1–7 Likert scale)

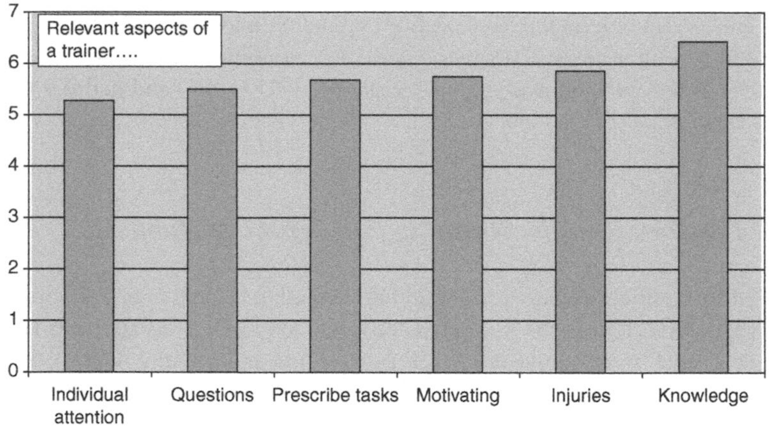

Fig. 19.5 Results on the relevance of a trainer (1–7 Likert scale)

Next to why people like to train or exercise, we were also interested in what people want or expect from a (physical) trainer (Fig. 19.5). Based upon the aspects mentioned in the focus groups and interviews, six aspects were identified. Again, people had to score the relevance of each aspect on a 7-point Likert scale. The identified aspects were "a trainer should" motivate and stimulate, answer questions, prescribe running tasks, prevent injuries and overtraining, pay individual attention and should be knowledgeable about all kinds of running aspects. The results reveal that people found all aspects relevant for a trainer (scores above 5) and that being knowledgeable was found most important.

We were also interested in the kinds of aspects people pay attention to during training. Hence, these are the aspects trainers should focus on or at least pay attention to (Fig. 19.6). Again, based upon the information gained in the focus group discussions, the following aspects were identified: running technique, breathing technique, heart rate, speed, elapsed time, adherence to scheme or nothing. Remarkably, people indicate that most attention is paid during training to the one aspect that cannot be taken care of by a system so far, i.e. running technique.

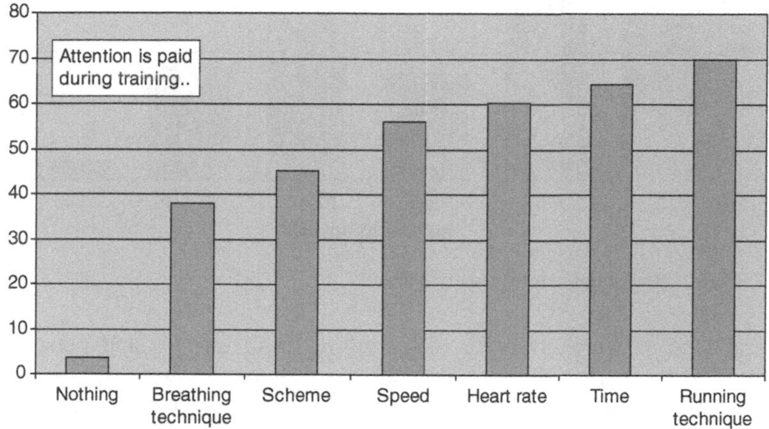

Fig. 19.6 Overview of relevant aspects during training

Next to these trainer and training-related aspects, we were interested in the devices people carry with them during running.

Half of the people (50%) wear a watch and heart rate device during running, around 25% carries a mobile phone and less than 10% uses a GPS system. The heart rate devices are mostly used by experienced and intrinsically motivated runners.

19.4.2 During Trial Results: Use of the MyCoach System

During the trial we could observe the use of MyCoach by logging of data. Next to the analysis of usage data, netnography (Online ethnography) [7] information was available. During the trial, a Google scan showed that three people who participated in the trial blogged about it on their personal web sites. We followed and analysed these discussions on their web sites, without intervening. First, the results of the usage data are described, next the nethography.

19.5 Usage Data

First, we were interested in whether people really used the MyCoach system. Therefore, we looked at the amount of times people uploaded their exercise data to the system (see Fig. 19.7). This figure indicates that about 20% of the people were not able to upload exercise information at all.

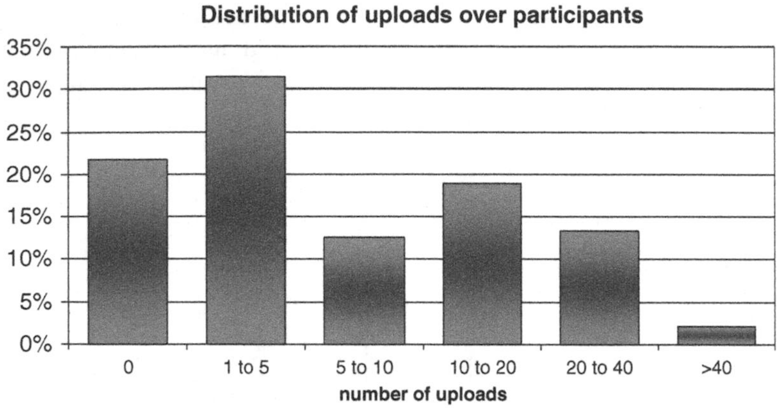

Fig. 19.7 Distribution of uploads over participants

Several reasons were given for this, ranging from injuries and personal circumstances to not being able to cope with the technology, usability aspects and, mostly reported, failing technology (see Fig. 19.8). As stated in the previous section, people who did not make any upload were excluded from the trial. However, problems with usability are a valuable result for our evaluation. A detailed analysis showed that people having affinity with mobile technology, measured by the

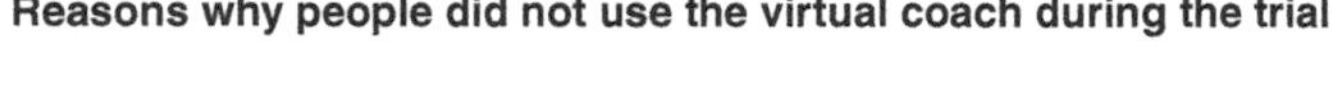

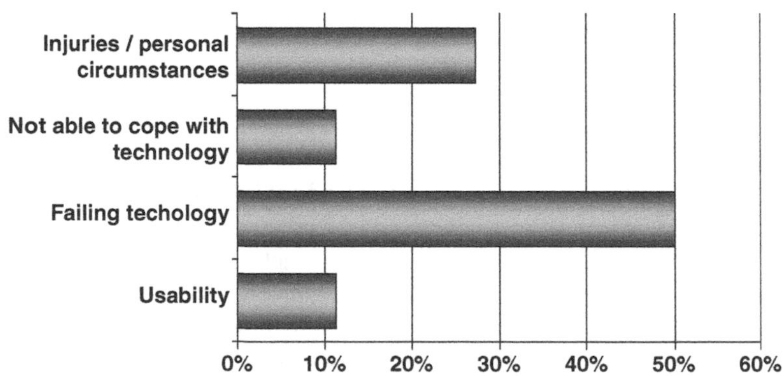

Fig. 19.8 Reasons for not uploading exercise data during the trial period

personal innovativeness scale [15], value MyCoach consistently higher on functionality, usability and fun. Around 80% of the people managed to upload exercise information at least once. Studying those figures in depth indicated that 35% of the original 91 people used the system two to three times a week.

Failing technology and not being able to cope with the technology were important reasons for not using the system. Therefore, we asked people how often the system worked properly for them (Fig. 19.9). From these results it can be derived that some affinity with (mobile) technology is required for MyCoach; people with more affinity with (mobile) technology report a higher success rate. And, there is a large variation in the opinions of the functioning of the system. About 50% of the people found it to function well, while the other 50% indicated that it did not function properly.

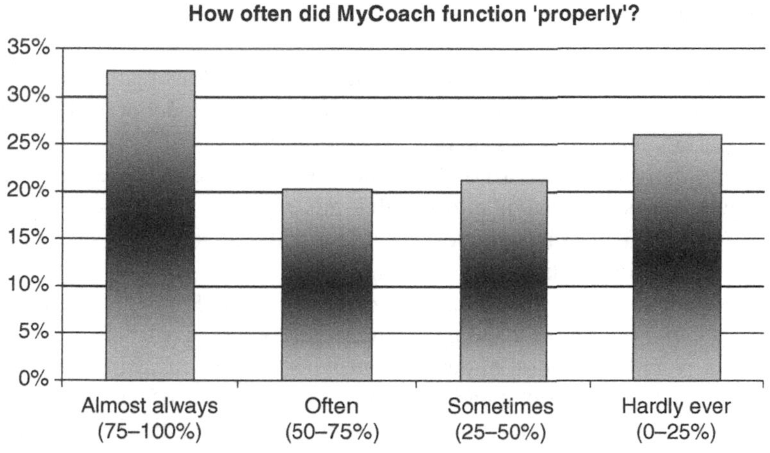

Fig. 19.9 Opinions about technical functioning of MyCoach

19.6 Netnography

In their weblogs, three people reported about using MyCoach. The information they provided was rather fact based, fewer subjective experiences were described. They reported that they were participating in the trial and what the mobile phone and web application looked like (pictures): "this is an example of the starting screen", "the training button provides you detailed information about the selected training", "before you arrive at home, the data is on the web-site", "it is easier to see data on a watch than on a mobile phone" and "Personally, I am more focused on running technique than on performance data". They also reported that the system did not always work properly: "the connection with the chest band has been broken". Many people – from outside the trial – commented to the postings and compared it to their own wearable devices (Garmin) ("this interface looks nicer than my boring Garmen"). The trend in this data was that they were curious about the system, so the

Web-Logger uploaded some more pictures. After a while, using the system was not new anymore, so they did not report on it anymore and continued with their normal postings.

So, in general it can be said from the nethography study that a lot of people – outside the trial – were curious about the system; it looks new and fancy and sometimes it does not work properly. Real conclusions or other observations cannot be derived.

19.6.1 Post-trial: Evaluation of MyCoach

From the perspective of the MyCoach system, the main difference between the physical trainer and the mixed reality system is that the mixed reality group got additional information about exercising. The additional information was available at three moments:

Before the training: MyCoach (Web application) provides suggestions on when and how long to exercise. This information was based on a model of healthiness and not on a goal-oriented training scheme.

During training: MyCoach (mobile phone client) makes performance measures more tangible, measuring and monitoring all kinds of physical (e.g. speed) and physiological (e.g. heart rate) information. Besides, multimodal (visual and auditory) coaching information can be provided to the runner.

After training: MyCoach (Web application) provides all kinds of information on monitoring, capturing exercise and analysing progress (tangible).

First, the overall perception of the MyCoach system was measured on a 7-point Likert scale (1–7). In general, it can be seen that the opinions of people differ a lot, as standard deviations are rather high (Fig. 19.10). Obviously, the ease of use score is rather low. This is in agreement with earlier observations of problems using the system. The Mann–Whitney test of independent samples of non-parametric data showed that experienced runners value usefulness and ease of use significantly higher ($p<0.1$)!

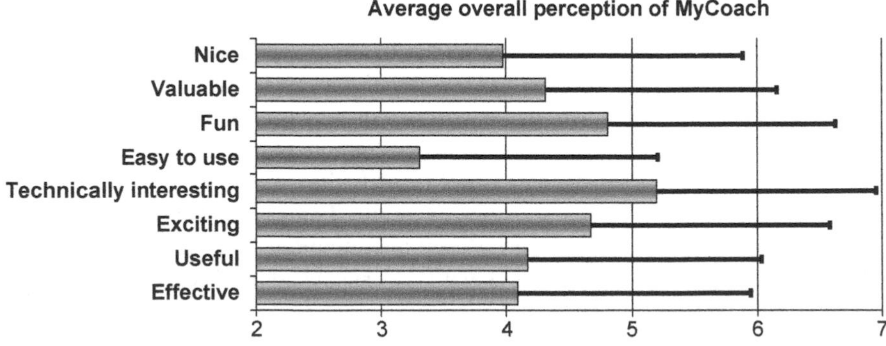

Fig. 19.10 Overview of perceptions of MyCoach

Next, the value of the provided exercise information during training was measured on a 7-point Likert scale. Speed and calorie information are perceived as less valuable. All other kinds of information are perceived as rather valuable, time and heart beat as most valuable. Figure 19.11 provides an overview of the perceived values during training.

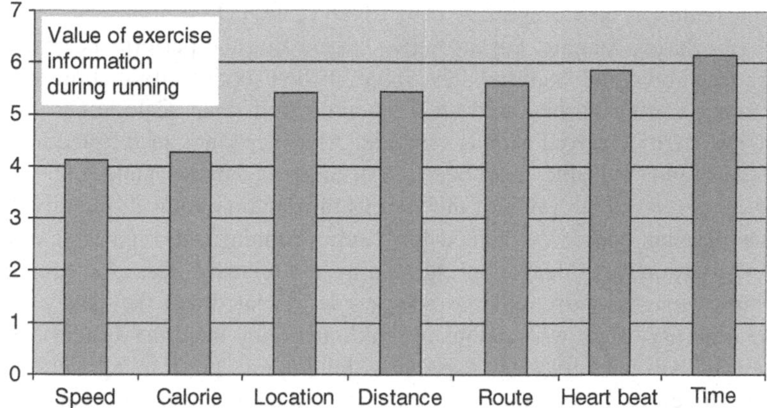

Fig. 19.11 Perceived values of exercise information *during* training (1–7 Likert scale) (mobile phone)

During running, auditory coaching information was available. Although all participants got the same manual at the start of the experiment, this functionality was known by 70% of the participants after the trial; only 26% of them stated that they used it. From the focus group discussions it became clear that the main reason for not using it was that the coaching information delivered by the system did not adhere

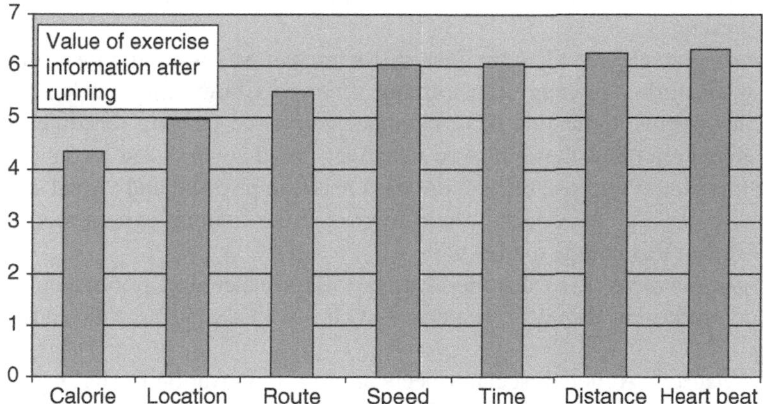

Fig. 19.12 Perceived values of exercise information *after* training (1–7 Likert scale) (Web application)

to their training scheme, delivered by their physical trainer. So, it could provide conflicting information. They would like to stick to their old scheme and thus not use the system. On the other hand, other people said that they often run too fast, so they liked the "slow down, slow down" advice of MyCoach; in this way they were able to keep a good and stable pace. Another person said during the focus group discussions: "The virtual coach was very motivating and handy." The appreciation (N = 62) of this feature is on average 2.97 (1–7 Likert scale) (SD = 1.98).

Not only during running, but also after having run, the performance measures could be monitored and analysed. The value of the exercise information provided after training was again measured on a 7-point Likert scale. Calorie and location information were perceived as less valuable. All other kinds of information were perceived as rather valuable, heart beat and distance as most valuable (Fig. 19.12).

Runners perceived the value of the various information items differently during and after running: speed was valued low during running and high after running. Route information was valuable during running and relatively less after running.

During focus group discussions some people indicated that they had problems with the usability of the web application, although they liked the system concept: "the web site was not very clear, especially the graphics per training were hard to interpret. Therefore, I focused on the distance. You could easily see your progress. That is what I really liked about the system. I use to write down my distances and time. The system makes it easier to see things."

Motivation is a crucial aspect of a trainer. The motivation scores between the mixed reality and the control group were pre- and post-trial measured and compared. The Mann–Whitney test of independent samples of non-parametric data showed no differences between the motivation scores of both groups ($p \geq 0.013$). This means that MyCoach system has no effect on the motivation of the runners.

In short, the results of the evaluation are categorised:

Tangible aspects: MyCoach captures and measures performance data during (mobile phone) and after running (web application). These aspects are valued and appreciated by the runners. In this way, effort and progress can be viewed, during and after exercise.

Care aspects: People liked the idea that someone was watching them or could follow them during running. The training scheme is now based on healthy and well-being aspects. Extending this to competence-based training schedules would be valuable. Preferably, these training schedules could be uploaded by the physical trainer; this should improve the coordination between physical and virtual coach.

Fun aspects: The MyCoach system improved the running experience, as it is state-of-the-art technology to play with.

Competition aspects: At this moment, the performance data provide opportunities to compete with oneself. Comparison with others should be a nice additional feature.

Share aspects: Although social aspects are not a motivation to start exercising, when people are used to running, they like the idea of sharing information. Real-time information sharing provides the idea that people are not alone. Sharing schedules and performance data with others could be a valuable enhanced feature once the basic features covering the tangible aspects are satisfactorily realised.

Stay in touch aspects: The real-time aspect of the mobile phone provides a nice feeling of safety. One safety button on the phone could improve this feeling. Being always online and location sharing with others should be a nice additional feature.

19.7 Conclusions

A randomised controlled trial was performed to evaluate the differences between a physical and a mixed reality running coach. Two different groups were involved: one experimental group running exercise training with both a physical and a virtual coach (MyCoach = mixed reality group) and one control group running exercise training with only a physical coach. Both groups trained for 3 months and several pre- and post-measurements were conducted.

Our findings underline the relative value that users place on various support features. We found that users' primary concern is about monitoring and capturing their exercise and analysing progress. The "tangibility" of exercise has a positive influence on the motivation to exercise. However, the lack of usability of the mobile client and the web application could have a negative effect on this. When comparing the features of MyCoach with the key design requirements mentioned in [7] for encouraging physical activity, we note that MyCoach focuses mainly on providing awareness of activities. Some credit for reaching a higher level of fitness is also given. Social support currently mainly comes from the physical coaching, while future enhanced features of MyCoach will focus also on social aspects like sharing data and routes. Finally, the combination of a physical and virtual coach takes practical constraints of runners for exercising into account.

Coaching is most valued when it is coupled to a personal goal-oriented training schedule. At this moment, this means that the mixed reality system is preferred: a coach provides a training scheme and focuses on running technique, and the MyCoach system provides exercise data to monitor and analyse performance. The specific real-time and sharing options of this particular virtual coaching system could be of crucial importance to integrate the physical and virtual coach to become a mixed reality system.

19.8 Further Development of MyCoach

Obvious extensions of the MyCoach system focus on the real-time aspect of the system. Sharing – real-time – information with others is the most obvious one. For personal coaches, real-time performance information could be useful to monitor and coach the individual runner at a distance. In this way, the trainer can coach several people at the same time, without physical location borders. Moreover, sharing exercise data like heart rate or speed with "running buddies" in a community can evolve into a real competitive system. Anderson et al. [16] found that such awareness of the activities of others encourages reflection on, and increases motivation for, daily activity. Moreover, competition could be included by uploading exercise data back to the mobile and comparing it in real time with a current exercise. In this way, people are – asynchronously – running against each other. Finally, exercise information could be shared in real time with friends of family members. For the last group, for example, real-time location information might be comforting. Figure 19.13 provides a visual overview from the basic to the enhanced services of the MyCoach system.

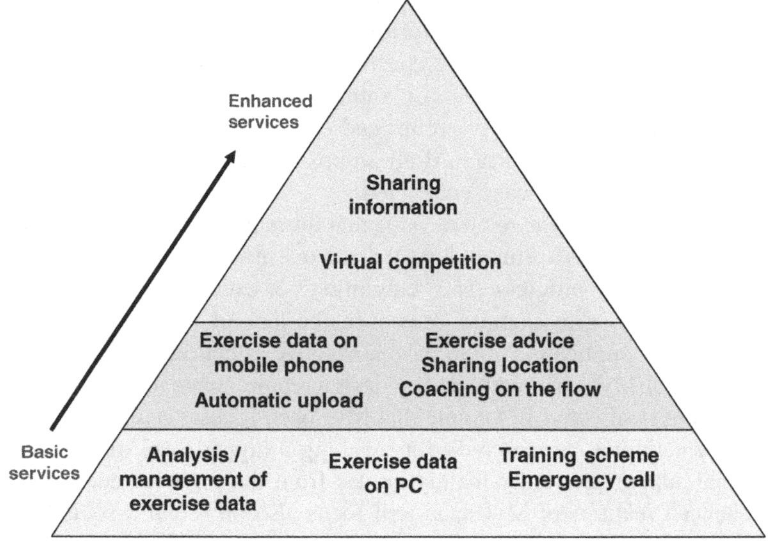

Fig. 19.13 Overview from basic till enhanced services of MyCoach

References

1. Van Bottenburg, M. (2006). *De tweede loopgolf.* (In Dutch; The Second Running Wave) W.J.H. Mulier Instituut, 's-Hertogenbosch. [retrieved from the Internet on 18 November 2008]
2. http://www.polar.fi [retrieved from the Internet on 18 November 2008]
3. http://www.suunto.com [retrieved from the Internet on 18 November 2008]
4. Buttussi, F., Chittaro, L., and Nadalutti, D. (2006). 'Bringing mobile guides and fitness activities together: a solution based on an embodied virtual trainer', *Proceedings of MOBILE HCI 2006: 8th International Conference on Human-Computer Interaction with Mobile Devices and Services,* ACM Press, New York, September 2006, pp. 29–36.
5. http://www.apple.com/ipod/nike [retrieved from the Internet on 18 November 2008]
6. http://www.timextrainer.com [retrieved from the Internet on 18 November 2008]
7. Consolvo, S., Everitt, K., Smith, I., and Landay, J. A. Design requirements for technologies that encourage physical activity. In, *CHI'06: Proceedings of the SIGCHI conference on Human Factors in computing systems*, pp. 457–466, ACM (New York, USA).
8. http://www.uitmetabel.nl/ [retrieved from the Internet on 18 November 2008]
9. Flick, U. (2002). *An Introduction to Qualitative Research.* London: Sage.

10. Patton, M. Q. (1990). *Qualitative Evaluation and Research Methods* (2nd edn.). Newbury Park, CA: Sage Publications, Inc.
11. Mays, N. and Pope, C. (1996). Rigour in qualitative research. In: Mays N. and Pope C. editors. *Qualitative Research in Health Care*. London: BMJ Books.
12. Silverman D. (2001). *Interpreting Qualitative Data: Methods for Analyzing Talk, Text and Interaction* (2nd edn.). London: Sage.
13. Ryan, R. M., Frederick, C. M., Lepes, D., Rubio, N., and Sheldon, K. M. (1997). Intrinsic motivation and exercise adherence. *International Journal of Sport Psychology*, 28, pp. 335–354.
14. Kozinets, R. V. (2002). "The field behind the screen: Using netnography for marketing research in online communities." *Journal of Marketing Research,* 39, pp. 61–72.
15. Lua, J., Yaob, J., and Yu, C. (2005). 'Personal innovativeness, social influences and adoption of wireless internet services via mobile technology'. *Journal of Strategic Information Systems,* 14, pp. 245–268.
16. Anderson, I., Maitland, J., Sherwood, S., Barkhuus, L., Chalmers, M., Hall, M., Brown, B., and Muller, H. (2007). Shakra: tracking and sharing daily activity levels with unaugmented mobile phones. *Mobile Networks and Applications,* 12(2–3), pp. 185–199.

Chapter 20
The RoboCup Mixed Reality League – A Case Study

Reinhard Gerndt, Matthias Bohnen, Rodrigo da Silva Guerra, and Minoru Asada

Abstract In typical mixed reality systems there is only a one-way interaction from real to virtual. A human user or the physics of a real object may influence the behavior of virtual objects, but real objects usually cannot be influenced by the virtual world. By introducing real robots into the mixed reality system, we allow a true two-way interaction between virtual and real worlds. Our system has been used since 2007 to implement the RoboCup mixed reality soccer games and other applications for research and edutainment. Our framework system is freely programmable to generate any virtual environment, which may then be further supplemented with virtual and real objects. The system allows for control of any real object based on differential drive robots. The robots may be adapted for different applications, e.g., with markers for identification or with covers to change shape and appearance. They may also be "equipped" with virtual tools. In this chapter we present the hardware and software architecture of our system and some applications. The authors believe this can be seen as a first implementation of Ivan Sutherland's 1965 idea of the ultimate display: "The ultimate display would, of course, be a room within which the computer can control the existence of matter . . ." (Sutherland, 1965, Proceedings of IFIPS Congress 2:506–508).

Keywords Mixed systems · Robotics · RoboCup · Physical control

20.1 Introduction

In the RoboCup robotics conference and challenge [2], there are two domains that can be easily distinguished – the virtual-robot simulation leagues and real robot leagues. In the simulation leagues, typically complex scenarios are implemented

---

R. Gerndt (✉)
University of Applied Sciences Braunschweig/Wolfenbuettel, Wolfenbuettel, Germany
e-mail: r.gernd@fh-wolfenbuettel.de

E. Dubois et al. (eds.), *The Engineering of Mixed Reality Systems*, Human-Computer Interaction Series, DOI 10.1007/978-1-84882-733-2_20,

and often a large number of virtual "robots" or agents are used. The 2D soccer simulation league, which is the only league playing soccer with a full team size of 11 players, may serve as an example of where game strategies for an entire team can be evaluated. The other extreme is the teen-size humanoid league, with real humanoid robots. These complex robots with many degrees of freedom are hard to control, considerably expensive and a large field, or environment, is required, making it much more difficult to move beyond basic ball handling and self-balancing skills.

There have been numerous initiatives trying to combine the better of the two scenarios such as in [3, 4]. The RoboCup mixed reality system bridges the gap between virtual and real robot leagues [5–8]. It allows for complex scenarios and real devices in a same system. See Fig. 20.1 for a typical example of our system in use.

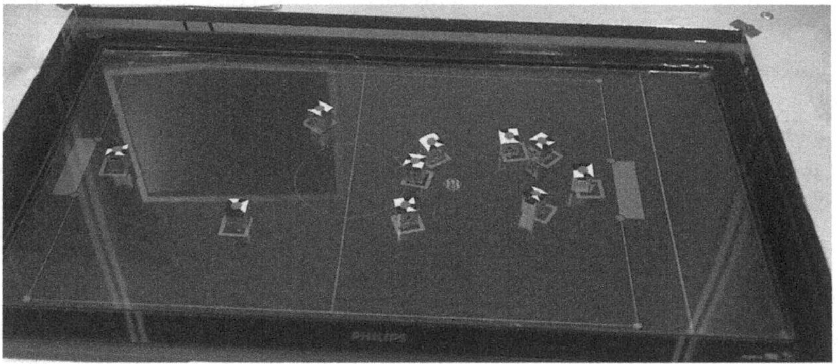

Fig. 20.1 Mixed reality five versus five real robots soccer game on a 42" display with virtual ball

There are taxonomies to classify mixed reality systems. However, we believe that the general nature of the presented system framework requires to relate the classification to specific applications. The micro-robot soccer with augmentation of the robots may be located in the augmented reality domain of the reality–virtuality continuum as presented in [9]. However, if the robots are used to augment some virtual objects, this may be located in the augmented virtuality domain.

For our mixed reality system we differentiate objects according to two bipolar criteria: we distinguish whether an object is static or dynamic and whether it is real or virtual. We consider all four types of objects to be possibly controlled by the real world or the computer. First, there are *static, virtual objects*, e.g., the soccer goals, which in our soccer application are virtual and do not change. These objects may have properties that are relevant for the application, as a ball in the goal is relevant for the scoring in a soccer game. Second, there are *static, real objects*, e.g., the physical boundaries of the display, or possibly any other real unmovable object, placed within these boundaries. The static objects do not change in position, orientation, or appearance during system lifetime. The real, static objects do have real and virtual properties, which may differ. A solid, physical obstacle may, for example, be "tunneled" by a virtual object but not by a physical one. Third, there are *dynamic, virtual objects*, e.g., the soccer ball used in our typical soccer application. They can change position, orientation, appearance, and so on. Lastly, there are the *dynamic, real objects*, which in our system are typically the robots or other devices controlled by the real world or real physics, like a real soccer ball, for instance. Properties of these objects may differ, depending on the control applied by the system, if any. Robots, e.g., may behave according to virtual limitations, such as having a maximum speed lower than physically possible.

There have been proposals for active, physical objects in mixed reality systems before, e.g., like the "propelled bricks" or a "magnetic puck" [10, 11]. However, unlike the previous proposals, the use of possibly autonomous robots offers higher flexibility. The system allows to control position, orientation, and possibly additional properties of a large number of robots independently of each other and independently of their position with respect to each other and on the screen.

The target domain for the RoboCup mixed reality system is research and edutainment. Education is addressed by an easy access to the programming and low costs of the overall system with a considerably high number of robots occupying minimal space. The use of real robots makes the system much more attractive for students than the typical pure virtual multi-agent frameworks without bringing much additional burden in terms of hardware complexity or difficult programming frameworks. The system has also been used in introductory programming experience in undergraduate courses and it demonstrated extreme effectiveness in the motivation of the students, who, based on prepared templates, were able to program soccer playing behavior despite their limited experience and novice status [12, 13]. Specific applications, e.g., like soccer can also be used for entertainment. Then users may, for example, take control of some robots via gamepads.

Possible research scenarios span from typical simulation-only robotic multi-agent systems to applications, only possible in real multi-robot systems. They include the fields that emerge from the interaction of real and virtual worlds. Examples include soccer, but also traffic simulation [14], human coaching, automated role assignment, multi-robot learning strategies, and swarm applications based on local on-robot sensing and actuation. Moreover, because the robots are so small, new applications become also possible, such as the use of the micro-robots and the entire mixed reality system in insect mixed society experiments (Fig. 20.2).

As also shown in the European LEURRE project [15], insects can be deceived to "believe" the robots are members of their group. This allows the programming of exhaustively long behavioral experiments that only robots can perform.

Our first mature benchmark application combining research, education, and entertainment aspects was a two versus two robotic soccer game performed on a 20'' display. The current benchmark is a five versus five game on a 42'' display. In the future, with even larger screens, 11 versus 11 is targeted. Aside from robotic soccer there already are numerous other applications that explore research, education, and entertainment in a well-balanced way. This includes a Pacman-like game with real "Pacman" and virtual ghosts, an ice hockey game, where real robots have been "equipped" with virtual hockey sticks and a virtual ice hockey puck with "virtual" physics different from a soccer ball. In this chapter we will present a racing

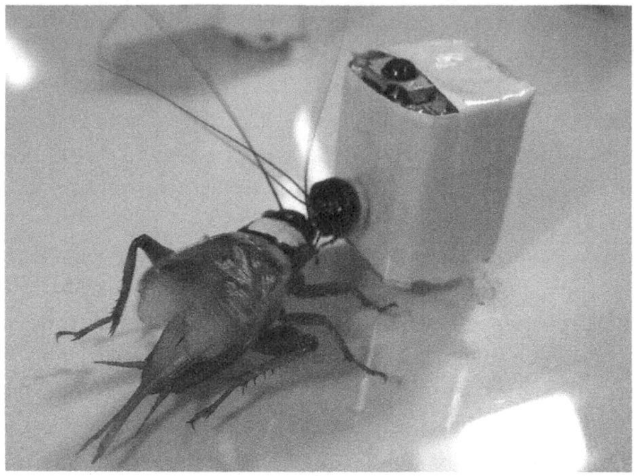

Fig. 20.2 Mixed society experiment where the head of a cricket was attached to a robot, thus deceiving real crickets because of pheromone signatures

game with virtual and real obstacles, illustrating the traveling salesman and similar problems. All applications can be implemented on the same system framework.

The basic hardware setup of the RoboCup mixed reality system consists of a horizontally mounted display and a set of micro-robots. The left part of Fig. 20.3, marked "real," sketches the hardware setup. A camera that is mounted above the

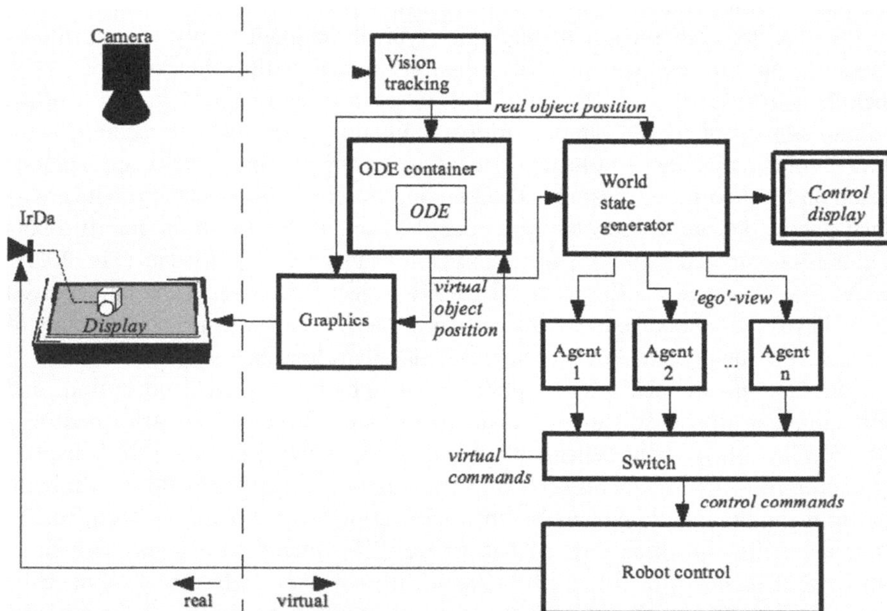

Fig. 20.3 Structure of RoboCup mixed reality system

screen captures the scene with all virtual and real objects. Vision tracking allows determining the position and orientation of the robots and other real objects on the screen. For identification, each robot can be equipped with an individual marker. The number of individually distinguishable robots depends on the markers used and on the resolution of the camera. The robots can move freely on the screen. Individual software agents control the robots. An IrDa link is used for wireless data exchange.

The right part of Fig. 20.3, marked "virtual," shows the structure of the software. There is an overall framework with a number of modules for input and output, simulation and control. The vision-tracking module captures the camera output and provides information on positions and poses of the robots and possibly other real objects to the other software modules. The world state generator generates an individual view for every single robot in the system. A control display can be attached for debugging and development purposes. The individual views are then communicated to the agents that control the robots. There is one individual agent module for every robot. The switch module separates the commands issued by the agents into commands that affect virtual objects, like kicking a virtual ball and control of real robots. The robot control module takes care of interfacing and communicating with the robots. The ODE container wraps the Open Dynamics Engine (ODE) [16] physics engine and takes care of simulation of the virtual objects. It processes data of real objects, like position and space occupied, and commands that affect virtual objects. It outputs information on new poses and positions of the virtual objects. The graphics module displays all virtual objects on the screen.

In our chapter, we will present the overall hardware and software architectures of the RoboCup mixed reality system. We will then present the results of the developments based on the system, done by a still increasing community from academia all over the world and present plans for future developments and some conclusions.

20.2 Hardware Architecture

The hardware architecture of the system is composed of four main components and their accessories, namely the micro-robots, the augmented reality display, one or multiple tracking cameras, and a computer.

20.2.1 Micro-Robots

The micro-robots are small differentially driven mobile vehicles with an approximate dimensions of a 2.5 cm cube (Fig. 20.4). The envisaged target cost for the micro-robots for series production is less than 20 •. The cube body is composed of a few milled aluminum parts screwed together and internal batteries. The only moving parts are the drives and the wheels. The diameter of the wheels and the size of the robot were designed so as to find the best balance of torque and velocity, while keeping space for batteries so as to ensure maximum autonomy and minimum weight. The metallic wheels have their axis of rotation just slightly below the

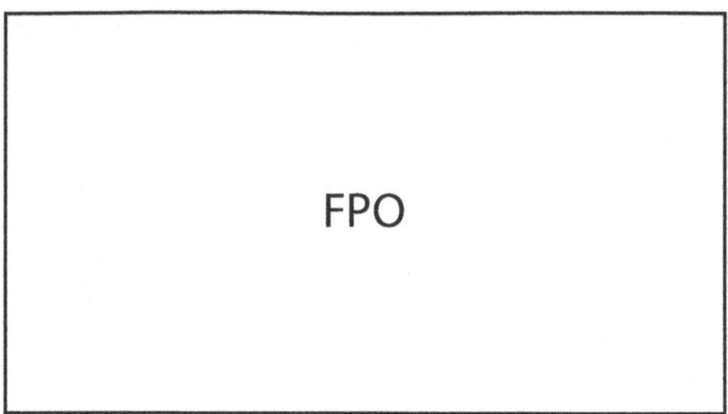

Fig. 20.4 Most recent generation of micro-robots

geometric center of the body, with the largest diameter possible so as to occupy both lateral faces almost entirely.

Designed with expandability in mind the accompanying controller board features an expansion bus and a power processor allowing the stacking of custom-designed circuit boards on top of it. Both the front and the back of the body have six extra screw holes distributed in a pattern similar to the six faces of a dice. These holes allow the attachment of external devices such as sensors, actuators, or even adjacent circuits. There are extra mounting holes for the motors allowing the wheels to be optionally assembled with their axis near the bottom edge of the body (Fig. 20.5). Four more holes are located on the bottom surface allowing the attachment of devices on the bottom of the robot.

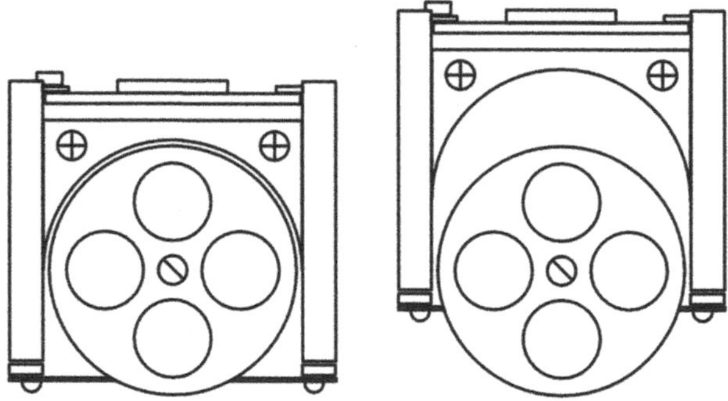

Fig. 20.5 Two types of wheel placement are possible

The robot is equipped with two micro-stepper motors (Fig. 20.6), specially modified for achieving higher torques and bi-directional actuation. These motors were originally designed for automatically adjusting the focus of the lenses of micro-cameras in mobile phones and other miniature devices. The wheels have no encoder, but approximate velocity can be managed obtained through the control of the stepping signals (Table 20.1).

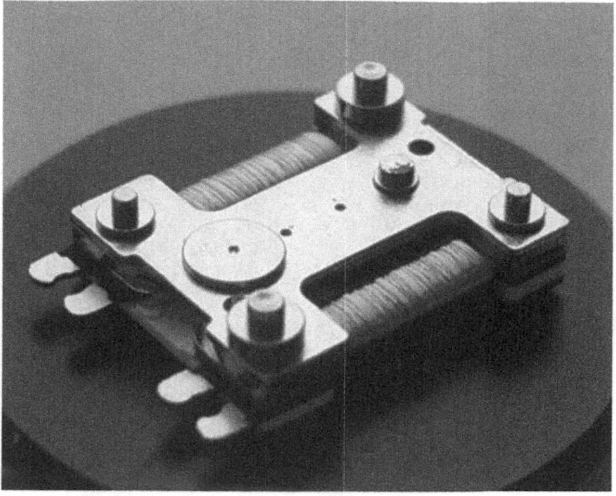

Fig. 20.6 Close-up macro-picture of the micro-stepper motor

Table 20.1 Stepper motor specification [17]

Feature	Value
Size w, d, h (mm)	7.0, 8.5, 1.9
Configuration	2 coils, 1 rotor
Gear ratio	1:240
Torque at 2.8 V (g cm)	2.0–4.0
Power consumption at 200 rps (mA)	4–12
Max. rotation speed (rpm)	12,000
Direction	Bidirectional

The detachable controller on the top of the robot (Fig. 20.7) consists of a board with a crystal, a voltage regulator, an IrDA transceiver, a connector and it contains a 32-bit ARM as the main microcontroller and an 8-bit AVR microcontroller as its slave, the later being mainly dedicated to the control of the stepper motors. Table 20.2 summarizes the main features of bothprocessors.

Table 20.2 Controller specification

Feature	Master processor	Slave processor
Architecture	ARM	AVR
Type	AT91SAM7 × 256	Atiny84
Flash memory size (kb)	256	8
RAM (kb)	65	0.5
Frequency (MHz)	48	8
Compiler	GCC	GCC
Uploading interface	JTAG, USB, Serial	SPI

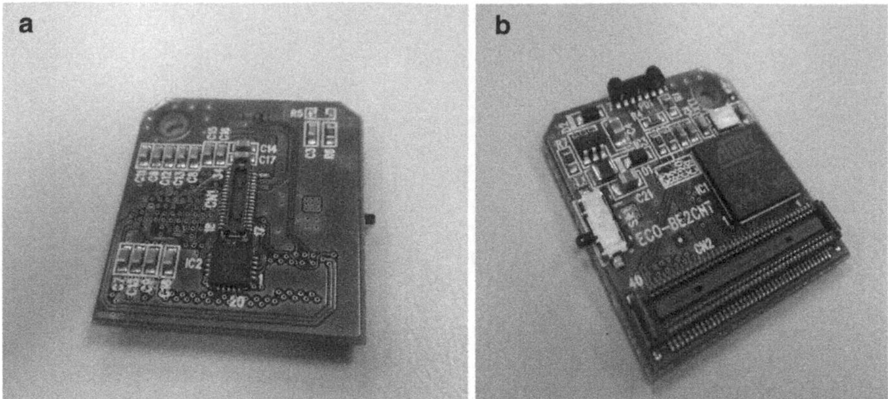

Fig. 20.7 Micro-robot:(**a**) controller board bottom view and (**b**) controller board top view

The controller itself does not come equipped with any sensors, actuators, or other specialized hardware except for the IrDA transceiver. Most pins of the ARM processor and some of the pins of the AVR processor are available on the 80-pin top connector. This means one can easily stack a peripheral board on that connector, adding extended functionality to the robot. The ARM processor has a high-performance 32-bit architecture, with periodic interval and real-time timers, 62 I/O lines, built-in communication interfaces, four 16-bit PWM channels, two-wire interface, 8-channel 10-bit AD converter, and much more. This allows the support for a myriad of features requiring only a minimum number of external components. Such features include microphone and speaker support, micro-SD card support, wireless Ethernet, LCD output, USB support, relays, DC motor controlling, and the connection of intelligent sensors, such as gyroscopes, accelerometers, and others capable of communicating through SPI or CAN ports. The ARM microcontroller controls the AVR microcontroller over one of its SPI interfaces.

In order to use the robots three additional accessories were also designed: a USB-to-infrared transmitter, a firmware uploading interface board, and a battery charger.

20.2.1.1 Battery Charger

The battery charger device consists of a platform on which six robot bodies can be attached upside down for simultaneous recharging. Each robot contains two internal lithium-ion polymer cells, with 190 mA h each. Tests show this is enough for at least 4 h of continuous operation or even more if alternating between idle and moving states, as it happens in several applications. The terminals of the two internal batteries are made available in the body's top connector in a way to allow the

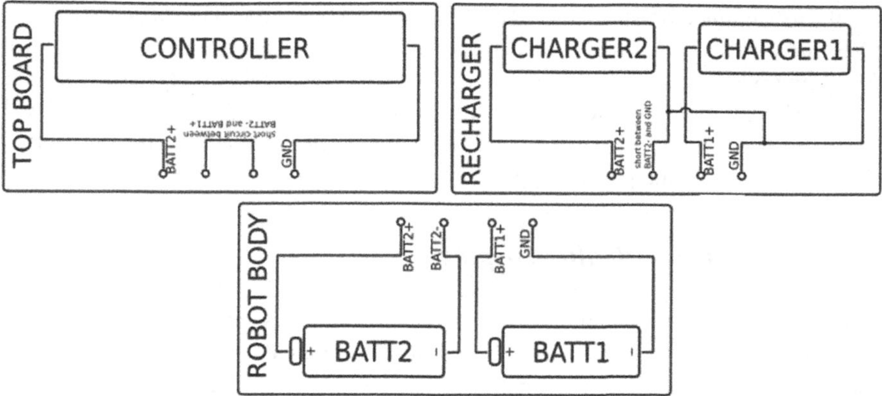

Fig. 20.8 Serial versus parallel battery configuration in operation versus charging

serial connection of the cells when robot body is attached to the microcontroller and parallel charging with two individual charging circuits when the body is connected to the charger (Fig. 20.8).

20.2.1.2 Infrared Transmitter

The infrared transmitter consists of a USB-to-serial chip converter, connected to an IrDA modulator and a FET amplifier circuit for boosting the range of the transmitted signal. Data are sent directly from the computer through the USB port and converted into short pulses in four high-power infrared LEDs distributed on each of the four corners of the field. The whole perimeter of the field is framed with reflective walls that act like mirrors so as to reflect the transmitted signal, thus widening otherwise restrict angle of coverage of the LEDs and also avoiding possible occlusions because of obstacles or other robots in the way.

20.2.1.3 Firmware Uploading Interface Board

The firmware uploading interface board is the device that allows the use of full-sized standard connectors with the small robots for programming and debugging. The board consists of a platform in which a robot body can be attached upside down and a robot controller can be attached just next to it. The connections are routed to full-sized connectors and to debugging LEDs through jumpers. The full-sized connectors include industry standard JTAG and SPI headers as well as a legacy serial DB9 connector and a type-B USB device connector. The firmware of the AVR microcontroller can be uploaded and debugged through the SPI. For low-level debugging one has the option to either use the LEDs or a robot body. The firmware of the ARM microcontroller can be uploaded via USB or via JTAG. The ARM supports step-by-step debugging. The robot body can be powered by its internal batteries or by external power supply.

20.2.2 Augmented Reality Display

One of the original characteristics of the system and an essential part of the mixed reality environment is the horizontally mounted augmented reality display. Objects and robots can be placed on the screen with the display of virtual objects. If required, virtual objects can be virtually attached to the robots.

Some brands of LCD screens were found to emit infrared light, thus causing interference with the IR control signals. To avoid this and also reduce reflections of ceiling lights, polarizing and other optical filter sheets can be used.

Polarizing filters are also used for facilitating the automatic detection of unknown artefacts that can be randomly placed over the screen. By mode of operation, all light emitted by an LC display has the same polarization angle. Therefore, a polarization filter in front of the camera lens can be adjusted to prevent all light emitted by the display from reaching the camera. This technique helps separating virtual objects from real objects in the image processing (Fig. 20.9).

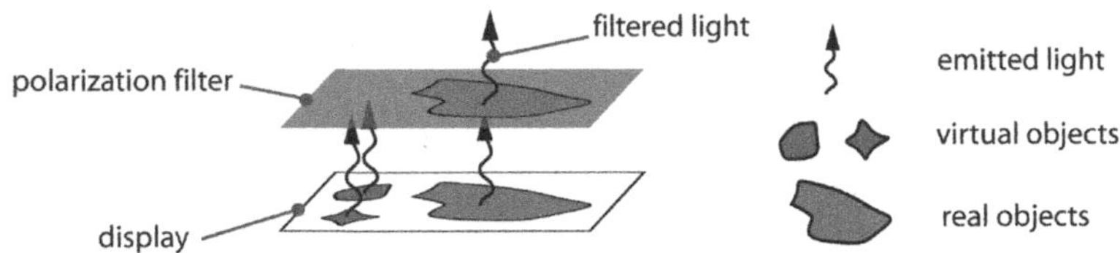

Fig. 20.9 Use of polarizing filter distinguishes between real and virtual objects on the display

20.2.3 Tracking Camera

A high-resolution tracking camera is responsible for the capturing of the detailed images necessary for the feedback of robot's position and orientation and other real objects on the screen as well as their identification (Fig. 20.10).

For sufficient accuracy the camera image has to be calibrated, in order to compensate distortion that may result from misalignment of camera and display. Initially a rectangular grid displayed on the LCD had to be matched with a checkerboard by manually adjusting the intersections of the grid. If markers with colors are used, a color calibration by manual teach-in is required in order to adopt the system to the ambient light. For future use, automated schemes have been proposed. With proper calibration of the display, static offsets are neglectable. However, the limited frame

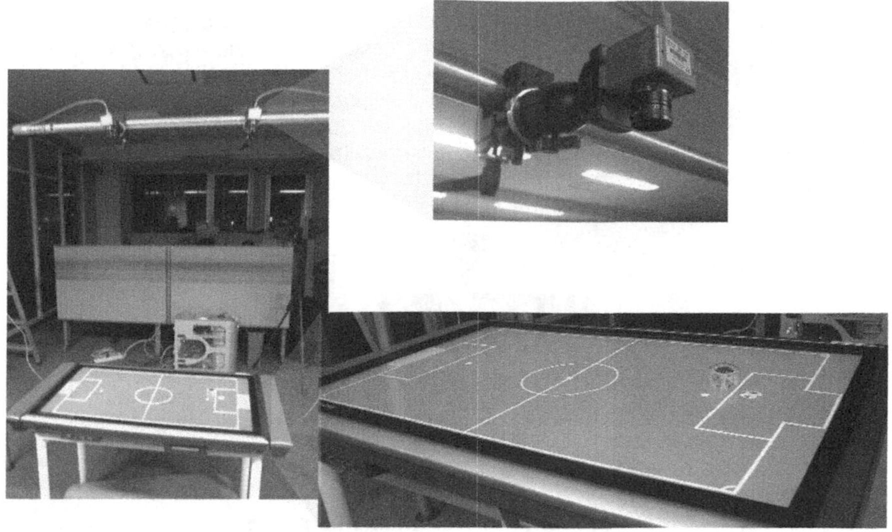

Fig. 20.10 Camera – display setup

rate of the camera and the image processing may result in a dynamic offset between moving real objects and attached virtual tools or augmentation.

Currently, the typical setup consists of a high-resolution IEEE 1394 firewire camera capable of at least 15 fps at 1280 × 1024 or even higher rate and resolution industrial Gigabit Ethernet camera. Current prices for these cameras typically are in the range of 800 • and more. With respect to increased field size, use of multiple cameras and combining their pictures into a single image may become necessary, as indicated in the left part of Fig. 20.10. With reduction of overall costs in mind, using multiple low-cost web cams has been proposed.

20.2.4 Computer

The computer server is a central part of the system. The basic requirements are as follows: multiple core CPU with performance of a Core 2 Duo 2.3 GHz or superior, hardware OpenGL accelerated GPU for the rendering of graphics on the augmented reality display, 2 GB of RAM, port for the connection of the camera(s), and network interface for connection of clients into the system.

20.3 Software Architecture

The software architecture comprises five domains to be possibly maintained independently. These domains are vision tracking, graphics, application, robot control, and agents (Fig. 20.11). XML structures were specified to define the UDP datagram communication over Ethernet within the framework. XML was chosen as the data

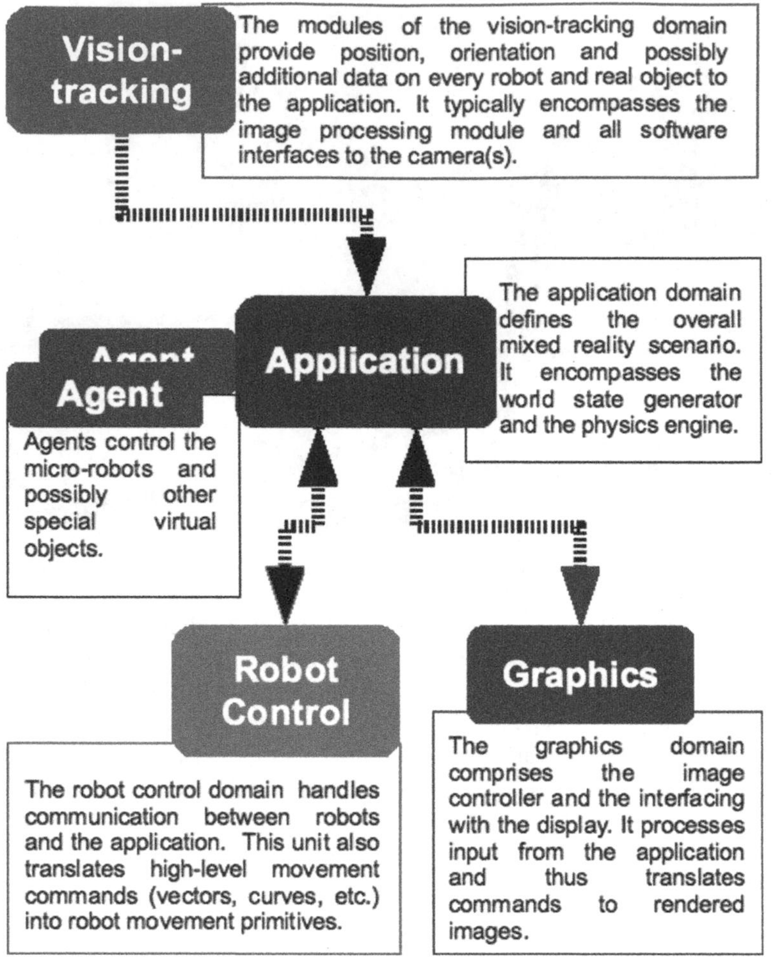

Fig. 20.11 Software domains overview

format for its suitability to encode any kind of information, human readability, and broad availability of tools to parse and validate files. UDP was chosen as a transport protocol for its simplicity and speed. Communicating over Ethernet allows the modules to run on different computers in the network.

On startup, the modules may exchange initialization data, as often needed for correct collaboration. For example, the application module might send the dimensions of the mixed reality display in millimeters to the graphics module (Listing 1).

"<type>" and "<protocol_version>" are required. The former describes the type of communication and the latter defines the protocol version. In this example "<screen_dimension>" is an extension of the basic specification that is required when the application module connects to the graphics module. Different mixed reality applications may need to exchange different data with other modules. For

```
<connect>
    <type>Graphics</type>
    <protocol_version>1.0</protocol_version>
    <screen_dimensions>
        <width>400</width>
        <height>300</height)
    </screen_dimensions>
</connect>
```

Listing 1 XML initialization example

example, the mixed reality soccer application module may want to send information about the state of the game (running, paused, kick-off, penalty, half-time) to the client module. This information is specific to soccer only. Therefore, applications may extend the basic XML specification with application-specific conventions.

20.3.1 Vision-Tracking Module

The vision-tracking module is responsible for tracking all real objects on the field. It retrieves images from the camera above the field. Two separate image-processing algorithms then extract information. The marker detection algorithm extracts the ID, position, and orientation of all markers, placed on micro-robots or other real objects. The real-object tracking algorithm extracts the ID, position, and outline of all real objects (including the robots) on the field. The real-object tracking algorithm relies on a polarization filter placed in front of the camera lens, adjusted so that all light emitted by the mixed reality LC display is absorbed.

In a first step the captured image is subtracted from a given background image, smoothed and turned into a binary image through a threshold filter (Fig. 20.12). In a second step the Teh-Chin chain approximation algorithm is applied to the binary image, resulting in a list of all contours in the binary image. This list is reduced to a reasonable amount of contour points per object, which is eight points by default.

The results of both tracking algorithms are merged, encoded in XML, and sent to the application modules. Listing 2 shows an example of an XML file, containing a list of an object and a robot. Each object is identified by its ID and shape. A shape consists of a number of x-, y-coordinates. A robot is defined by its ID, orientation, and center point.

20.3.2 Application Modules

The application modules are the central hub of the software stack. They form the core of the mixed reality server and are responsible for managing connections to all other modules and providing the mixed reality functionality. The application

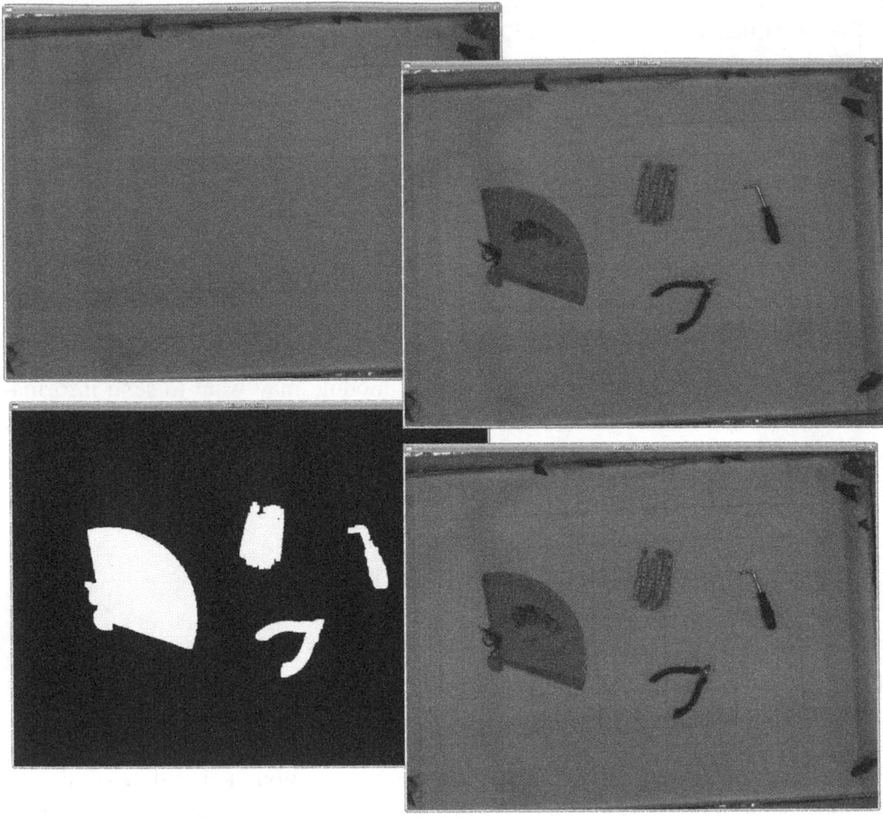

Fig. 20.12 Vision tracking: (*upper left*) background image, (*lower left*) image as seen by the camera, (*upper right*) shapes of artifacts, and (*lower right*) image with identified real objects

```
<worldData>
    <object>
        <id>42</id>
        <shape>
            <pos><x>156</x><y>349</y></pos>
            <pos><x>207</x><y>291</y></pos>
            <pos><x>199</x><y>325</y></pos>
        </shape>
    </object>
    <robot>
        <id>7</id>
        <orientation>180</orientation>
        <pos><x>146</x><y>120</y></pos>
    </robot>
</worldData>
```

Listing 2 Example XML description of object and robot

modules receive the real-object information from the vision-tracking module. They then merge information of real and virtual objects and forward this combined world data to the agent modules in the clients' domain. They also send commands to the graphics modules to display the virtual objects. Further on, they process control commands from the client modules that affect virtual objects or forward them to the robot control module.

Two implementations of the application modules exist. The first implementation is a mixed reality soccer server and the second is a generic C++ framework that provides developers with an API to develop any type of mixed reality application.

20.3.3 Graphics Module

The graphics module is a 3D hardware accelerated, generic module used to display any kind of information on the mixed reality display. It is separated into two threads: The first thread listens for incoming XML files from the application modules and translates them into a list of primitives that are to be drawn. The second thread constantly iterates over the latest list of drawing commands and translates them into OpenGL calls. The available primitives are as follows: 2D lines, polygons, textures, text, 3D objects, light sources, and sound files. For playing sound files, the OpenAL library is used. Each graphical command consists at least of the name of the object to be displayed and the 2D position on the screen. The name of the object refers to the name given in the theme pack. A theme pack is an archive containing a set of primitives. As the graphics module is intended to be generic, applications can transmit theme packs to the graphics module. After activation, all primitives from the theme pack are available for display. Some parameters are only relevant for certain types of primitives, such as the pitch for sound files. Other parameters are optional, such as the layer. The graphics module subdivides the 3D space provided by OpenGL into 1000 2D layers.

The UDP protocol used to transmit the XML files gives no guarantee that every file is transmitted. Therefore, the graphics module was designed to be stateless. This means that each XML file has to contain a complete list of all objects that are to be drawn. If there were commands to enable/disable the display of objects this could lead to accumulation errors if some XML files are lost in transmission.

20.3.4 Robot Control Module

The robot control module receives high-level control commands for the micro-robots from the application module. It translates these commands into low-level commands for the micro-robots and sends them via USB to the IrDA transmitter.

The robots may be addressed individually or in a broadcast mode. The commands are composed of one mandatory command keyword and multiple optional arguments for that command. Commands are sent to the robot separated by commas. A command can be wrapped within parenthesis, and this itself can be used as an argument, allowing the sending of nested commands. The format of the robot commands can better be understood through the following examples:

Example 1, command 'go forward with speed 10':

```
fw,0a
```

Example 2, nested commands:

```
lst,(fw,14),(slps,01),stop
```

Example 3, loop command:

```
lp,03,(lst,(fw,14),(slps,01),stop,(slps,01))
```

In Example 1, the command takes one argument (a number in hexadecimal notation). Other commands, e.g., the "stop" takes no argument. The command in Example 3 allows a list of commands to be executed in sequence. The command line of Example 3 is a nested loop command. The first argument tells how many times to run the loop and the second argument is the command to be executed in the loop. This command makes the robot go forward for 1 s, stop for 1 s, and repeat that three times.

All the examples previously described are broadcasted and executed by all robots. In order to control the robots independently, the robots need to be addressed by their IDs. There are two types of IDs in the robots, a fixed firmware ID (fid) and a software ID (sid) that can be changed dynamically. Both can be used for addressing the robots. The following examples show some examples:

Example 4:

```
fid,00,(fw,14)
```

Example 5:

```
sid,00,(chsid,01)
```

Example 6:

```
sbkt,(fw,14),stop,(sl,14),(bw,05)
```

Example 4 shows the usage of the firmware ID 00. Example 5 shows how to change the software ID of a specific robot. Example 6 shows the software ID bucket command, by which one can send several different commands to different robots in a single message. When this command is issued, all robots of ID 00 will execute the first argument, robots with ID 01 will execute the second argument, and so on.

The command-parsing infrastructure was designed for usability and expandability. Commands are implemented as simple C functions using the same argument passing convention as the typical main function of a console application. The following line shows a typical example of one such function prototype for a firmware program:

```
int cmd_set_forwardvelocity(int argc, char **argv)
```

The returning integer indicates error if different than 0 and the arguments are passed as a pointer to char strings and an integer saying how many arguments are there.

20.3.5 Agents

The agents implement the artificial intelligence that impersonates the micro-robots. Several instances of the agents may connect to the application module, depending on how many micro-robots are part of the application. Each agent typically only issues commands for its specific robot. However, they may also take control of virtual objects. For example, there is a kick command to kick the virtual ball, if the robot is close enough and there are move commands to control virtual tools, like a virtual hockey stick.

20.4 Experience

20.4.1 Development Process

Currently the RoboCup mixed reality robots are in their third generation. Around year 2005 it started with a small cube robot for demonstration purpose. From this demonstrator the second generation of mixed reality robots, with all necessary support circuitry, like charger, was developed in 2006. They had dimensions of about 1×1 cm and a height of 2.5 cm. Different from the current third-generation robots, used since the beginning of 2008, they only had a single processor to handle IR communication and the stepper drives. Batteries also were smaller, as were the wheel diameters. The second-generation robots have been used for a series of tournaments and development contests all over the world. Eventually a redesign with a number of improvements was carried out, leading to the current robot generation. As with the software development, the hardware development work also was shared among the teams of the RoboCup mixed reality community.

Initially a software framework with basic features and an example agent was provided to the teams. Similar to an open-source approach the software was developed by cooperation. However, this did not include the agents that control the robots, since they represent the intelligence of the soccer robot teams, which were to play each other during the RoboCup soccer tournaments.

20.4.2 Soccer System

Different soccer scenarios have been implemented, all of them were making use of the mixed reality features of the system. The basic system has been described throughout this chapter. It makes use of a virtual soccer field and a virtual soccer ball that are virtually "kicked" by real robots. The robots are controlled by software agents, which implement different behaviors and strategies. Among others, test with dynamically changing goalkeepers against a team with fixed behavior in a two versus two robots soccer game has been carried out. Human player have been asked to control individual robots via game pads, playing with and against computer-controlled robots.

There have also been tests with a real ball and real goals. However, with a real ball, control became very cumbersome. Only very short "kicks" with a high degree of inaccuracy were possible.

20.4.3 Racing Application

In order to introduce static real objects to our mixed reality system, we developed a mixed reality racing game called beRace! (Fig. 20.13). In this application, random everyday objects are placed on the display. The game then generates a virtual racing track around these obstacles. The track consists of a number of checkpoints. Each checkpoint is a line drawn between two real objects. Depending on the game mode, the goal for the robots is to pass through these checkpoints in a predefined order. Some real objects might be light enough for the robots to move them. In this case, the virtual racing track will be adjusted to the change in reality.

To introduce further interaction between real and virtual objects we place virtual items on the screen that can be picked up by the robots by driving over them. Items are virtual rockets, mines, boosters, and oilcans. Items can be used and may change the properties of the robots. For example, a robot may lay down a puddle of oil. If another robot passes through this puddle, any incoming steering commands for this robot will be exaggerated for 3 s to simulate slipperiness.

This application demonstrates how real objects (robots, obstacles) and virtual objects (racing track, items) can interact with each other in various ways. Virtual rockets may explode upon impact with real obstacles and upon impact with virtual mines. Real robots may move real and virtual obstacles but are temporarily disabled when touching virtual mines.

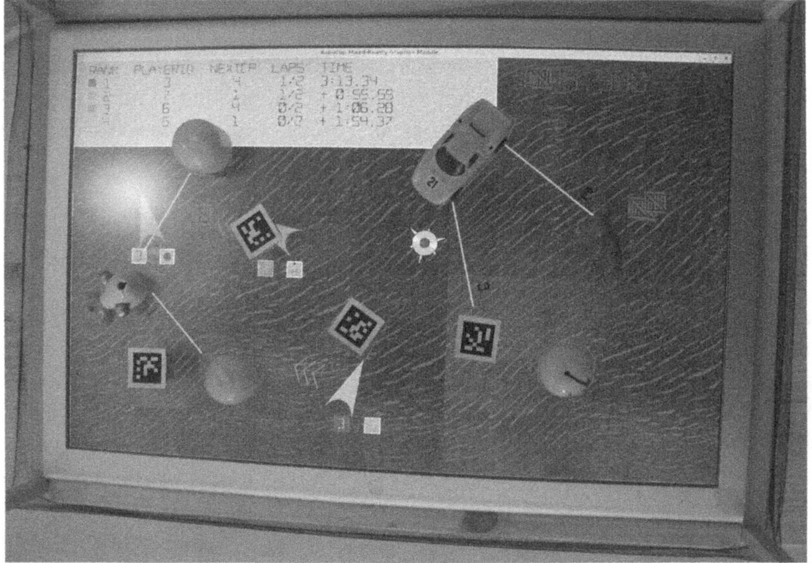

Fig. 20.13 beRace! Application, markers done with ARToolKit [18]

20.4.4 Future Developments

A number of ideas for further improvements have been presented during the RoboCup mixed reality tournaments. With low system costs as major objective, a number of concepts have been presented to overcome the problem of the still considerably expensive camera. One approach has been to use a number of low-cost webcams instead of the expensive Firewire or Ethernet cameras. Using a number of webcams not only alleviate the cost problem but also widens the area that can be used as a mixed reality arena. However, there still are a number of technical challenges, like combining the individual images into an overall picture and sustaining a sufficiently high frame rate. Another approach, going even further, was making use of low-cost cameras that are mounted to the robots. The cameras will provide an egocentric view of the robots and may be combined with the images from static cameras. However, this may lead to an incomplete coverage of the arena, e.g., if all mobile robot cameras point into a certain direction.

Aside from cameras, robots may be equipped with other sensors and actuators, e.g., to serve as tangible interfaces, which not only allow a physical input to a system but also, by moving on the screen, a physical output of a system. Further actuators may allow to change color or shape, thus allowing a true two-way interaction between virtual and real world.

20.5 Summary and Conclusions

In this chapter we presented a hardware and software architecture, suitable for a mixed reality system with far-reaching two-way interaction with multiple dynamic real objects. We gave a detailed description of the hardware architecture and of the robots, which are the key components to allow the mixed reality system to physically interact with the real world and of the software architecture. We provided real-world examples to illustrate the functionality and limitations of our system.

We showed how the overall system is structured in order to allow students to easily gain access to programming of robots and implementing artificial intelligence applications.

The RoboCup mixed reality system was used for education and for research, even in non-technical domains like traffic control. A system with tangible components as well as a virtual part offers an ideal platform for the development of future user interfaces for a close and physical interaction of computer and user.

References

1. Sutherland I E (1965) The Ultimate Display. Proceedings of IFIPS Congress 2:506–508.
2. The RoboCup in the Internet: www.robocup.org
3. Boedecker J, Guerra R da S, Mayer N M, Obst O, Asada A (2007) 3D2Real: Simulation League Finals in Real Robots. Lecture Notes in Computer Science 4020:25–34.

4. Boedecker J, Mayer N M, Ogino M, Guerra R da S, Kikuchi M, Asada M (2005) Getting Closer: How Simulation and Humanoid League Can Benefit from Each Other. Symposium on Autonomous Minirobots for Research and Edutainment 93–98.
5. Guerra R da S, Boedecker J, Mayer N M, Yanagimachi S, Hirosawa Y, Yoshikawa K, Namekawa K, Asada M (2008) Introducing Physical Visualization Sub-League. Lecture Notes in Computer Science.
6. Guerra R da S, Boedecker J, Yanagimachi S, Asada M (2007) Introducing a New Minirobotics Platform for Research and Edutainment. Symposium on Autonomous Minirobots for Research and Edutainment, Buenos Aires.
7. Guerra R da S, Boedecker J, Asada M (2007) Physical Visualization Sub-League: A New Platform for Research and Edutainment. SIG-CHALLENGE Workshop 24:15–20.
8. Guerra R da S, Boedecker J, Mayer N M, Yanagimachi S, Hirosawa Y, Yoshikawa K, Namekawa M, Asada M (2006) CITIZEN Eco-Be! League: Bringing New Flexibility for Research and Education to RoboCup. SIG-CHALLENGE Workshop 23:13–18.
9. Milgram P, Takemura H, Utsumi A, Kishina F (1994) Augmented Reality: A class of displays on the reality-virtuality continuum Paper presented at the SPIE, Telemanipulator and Telepresence Technologies, Boston.
10. Fitzmaurice G W (1996): Graspable User Interfaces. PhD at the University of Toronto.http://www.dgp.toronto.edu/~gf/papers/PhD%20-%20Graspable%20UIs/Thesis.gf.html.
11. Pangaro G, Maynes-Aminzade D, Ishii H (2002) The Actuated Workbench: Computer-Controlled Actuation in Tabbletop Tangible Interfaces. In Proceedings of UIST'02, ACM Press, NY, 181–190.
12. Guerra R da S, Boedecker J, Mayer N M, Yanagimachi S, Ishiguro H, Asada M (2007) A New Minirobotics System for Teaching and Researching. Agent-based Programming. Computers and Advanced Technology in Education, Beijing.
13. Guerra R da S, Boedecker J, Ishiguro H, Asada M (2007) Successful Teaching of Agent-Based Programming to Novice Undergrads in a Robotic Soccer Crash Course. SIG-CHALLENGE Workshop 24:21–26.
14. Dresner K, Stone P (2008) A Multiagent Approach to Autonomous Intersection Management. Journal of Artificial Intelligence Research, March 2008, 31:591–656.
15. Caprari G, Colot A, Siegwart R, Halloy J, Deneubourg J -L (2004) Building Mixed Societies of Animals and Robots. *IEEE Robotics & Automation Magazine*.
16. Open Dynamics Engine (ODE) in the Internet: www.ode.org.
17. Guerra R da S, Boedecker J, Yamauchi K, Maekawa T, Asada M, Hirosawa T, Namekawa M, Yoshikawa K, Yanagimachi S, Masubuchi S, Nishimura K (2006) CITIZEN Eco-Be! and the RoboCup Physical Visualization League. Micromechatronics Lectures – The Horological Institute of Japan.
18. ARToolKit. In the Internet: http://www.hitl.washington.edu/artoolkit.

Chapter 21
Mixed-Reality Prototypes to Support Early Creative Design

Stéphane Safin, Vincent Delfosse, and Pierre Leclercq

Abstract The domain we address is creative design, mainly architecture. Rooted in a multidisciplinary approach as well as a deep understanding of architecture and design, our method aims at proposing adapted mixed-reality solutions to support two crucial activities: sketch-based preliminary design and distant synchronous collaboration in design. This chapter provides a summary of our work on a mixed-reality device, based on a drawing table (the Virtual Desktop), designed specifically to address real-life/business-focused issues. We explain our methodology, describe the two supported activities and the related users' needs, detail the technological solution we have developed, and present the main results of multiple evaluation sessions. We conclude with a discussion of the usefulness of a profession-centered methodology and the relevance of mixed reality to support creative design activities.

Keywords Virtual desktop · Sketching tools · Creative design · User-centered design

21.1 Introduction

Cutting-edge technologies, like the ones involved in mixed reality, are often designed by engineers focusing primarily on technological aspects, without directly involving the end-users. The user of the final product will often thus have to learn and to adapt to the new concepts this new technology will bring. The fact that precise user's needs are not at the heart of the initial phase of design can create a gap between these needs and the solution offered. This sometimes leads to the failure of the project, as the user may find it difficult to adapt to new ways of working.

We propose a different approach, based on a multidisciplinary way of working. Our methodology is rooted in a user-centered design approach and based on a thorough analysis of a dedicated domain's field and market.

S. Safin (✉)
LUCID-ULg: Lab for User Cognition Innovative Design, University of Liège, Liège, Belgium
e-mail: Stephane.Safin@ulg.ac.be

E. Dubois et al. (eds.), *The Engineering of Mixed Reality Systems*, Human-Computer Interaction Series, DOI 10.1007/978-1-84882-733-2_21,

This methodology has been applied by the LUCID-ULg Lab in the computer-aided architectural design field. Based on a deep knowledge of the architectural project workflow, and thanks to a close collaboration with "real" architects, we have identified two specific activities that would benefit from the support of mixed-reality environments.

The first activity we want to support is the early design phase of a project. Despite the vast offer in CAD tools, the preferred support for this phase is still the traditional pen-and-paper. Even in domains where design constitutes only a part of the whole process (as for instance building or naval engineering, architecture, industrial design, or town planning), there are great ideas that emerge from quick drawings made on the corner of a napkin! We will discuss in detail the many reasons for this situation. We have come to realize that, for supporting this crucial phase, an immersive and non-intrusive environment must be designed. We will present the Virtual Desktop environment and the EsQUIsE software as solutions for this problem.

The second activity is about distant and synchronous collaborative design. Despite the many communication tools available, and the existence of some shared drawing applications, the industry has not adopted tools for such activity. Design is a very complex creative task. It can take a long time for the ideas to emerge and to mature. Collaborative design requires intimate and trustful communication, so that partners can share and discuss complex and fuzzy ideas during long creative sessions. If the communication media introduces even a small bias, it might ruin the whole process, as the different actors will spend most of their effort in making sure the information is properly transmitted instead of focusing on the creative part. We will introduce the combination of the Virtual Desktop and the SketSha software to support this activity and discuss how this immersive environment brings the distant partners as if they were in the same room.

We first present our methodology. We then explain the context of architectural design and the needs of the two considered situations. We detail the technological tools we have implemented to respond to these issues. We will then present the promising results of the multiple experiments we have conducted to validate our two immersive systems. We will discuss the issues they raise, their adequacy to the aimed situations, and the way we envision their future. We then conclude on the usefulness of the user-centered design and the profession-centered methodology, and the potential of mixed-reality paradigm to support creative design activities.

21.2 Profession-Centered Methodology and User-Centered Design

Even if the importance of the user is more widely recognized in software engineering domains, many complex IT projects are still driven primarily by technical issues. The question of the user and his/her activities may then be treated as secondary issues. This can lead to ill-adapted applications or environments. This technology-driven way of working can be contrasted with an anthropocentric way of designing mixed-reality systems [33, 34]. This approach grounds project development in the context of real activities, based on user needs identified by activity analysis.

We can distinguish several methods to involve users in the software development cycle. Each of them has several advantages and disadvantages. Norms and guidelines (see for example Bastien and Scapin [3]) are a way to represent the users' capabilities and cognitive constraints. They are easy to use, practical, and cheap, but they only represent static knowledge about human beings and fail to take into account the specific contexts of human activities. Personas [32] are a means of representing potential users and contexts of use in the development process. They may help designers focus on the concrete end-users in the process, but only represent a small part of the reality. Activity analysis can offer a deep understanding of user needs and the processes and context of their activities, but it is costly and time consuming, especially for high-expertise activities, which may be very difficult to understand and describe fully. User-centered methodologies [31], with iterative usability testing, are a way to check the relevance of the concepts or prototypes. It is also very expensive, as it requires several iterations and the development of several functional prototypes, although it gives strong insight into software development. Finally, participative design [40] is a way to involve users in the development process, putting the users in a decision role. It gives a lot of guarantees about the relevance of the product and greatly favors its acceptability. But it requires the availability of end-users in the framework of an institutional context, allowing them to assume a decision role. Furthermore, those methods are often used after the definition of the project, and the design of new software or environments are thus not strongly anchored in a need analysis.

The approach we propose in this chapter is a mixture of these methods. We extend them thanks to a strong anchoring in the professional domain and in the market. Collaborating closely with the architectural domain allows our development team to anticipate users' needs and to design adapted responses to them.

The way we define needs is based on a multidisciplinary approach. The competencies involved can be defined along three axes, working together on development projects to enrich their mutual reflections:

- *The domain axis*, composed of architects, building designers, or structure engineers. This axis holds all the technical knowledge of the architecture domain. They know the practices, the tools, and the issues related to the domain. But they do not constitute a group of users, being inserted in a research context and not in a professional or industrial context.
- *The usage axis*, with ergonomists and work psychologists. This axis has the responsibility to lead the participative design process, to gather information about real activities of architects, and to manage the ergonomics aspects of the user interfaces.
- *The development axis*, with computer scientists and computer graphics designers. This axis has the responsibility to design and develop applications based on the identified needs and requirements from the other actors.

These three axes collaborate on application development in the following way (Fig. 21.1): the domain axis and the usage axis work together to feed the development axis, which will design the application. This application (being in a concept stage, a prototype, or a final product) is tested with real users. This leads to a new development cycle which in turn is tested, forming an iterative process.

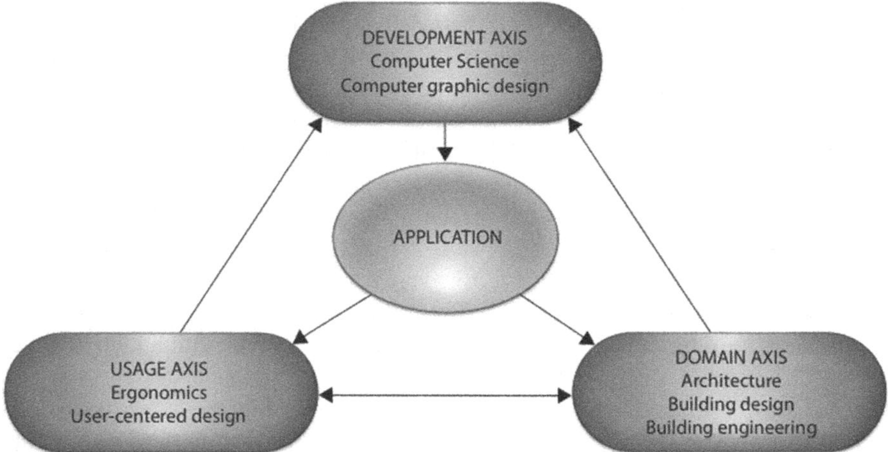

Fig. 21.1 Multidisciplinary methodology

Concretely, this means several steps and methods for each research or development project:

- *Formation of a user group*. This group will follow the project from its beginning to its end. These users are architects in professional situations. They are selected for the diversity of their practices: size of their office, type of architecture, background, age, etc. They meet together on a regular basis, to be informed of the development of the project and to react to some concepts and ideas. Furthermore, this group will provide users for interviews, observations, and application testing.
- *Project meetings*. Each time decisions have to be made, members of the three axes are involved. The development axis will handle the technical constraints; the usage axis will deal with the constraints linked to usability and the context of use; and the domain axis will bring issues about the meaning and the utility of the concepts discussed. This separation of concerns supports an integrated reflection that will lead to solutions that take into account the functional, technical, and cultural points of view on the development.
- *Focus groups*. The user group meets regularly to respond to specific questions on which the project team has no definitive answer. Concepts and ideas from the project team will also be validated with focus groups.
- *Evaluations*. At key moments, the prototypes will be evaluated. These tests bring the strongest feedback on the efficiency of the solution. These evaluations take place in a setting as natural as possible – from realistic tasks to the placement in the user's office.

- *Industrial partnership.* In addition, all the projects are followed by industrial partners. They are informed of the developments, participate in key meetings, and ensure the feasibility of the development.
- *Many demonstrations and close relationships with the industrial actors.* Apart from the user group and the industrial partners, the lab tries to communicate widely with the domain actors, by making regular prototype demonstrations. This helps to have informal feedback on the development, anchored in very diverse realities. This also helps to anticipate future needs and identify related domains.

This approach is interesting because it guarantees the involvement of the users (or at least some domain experts) at each step of the development process, starting with the definition of global objectives. It allows a deep understanding of complex high-level activities, as creative design and architecture, and the co-construction and exploitation of knowledge about these activities. The close cooperation between the three axes and informal communication enable a strong reactivity at each step of the development. This reactivity allows the development team to discuss each aspect of the application throughout as a negotiation between the three axes, in real time. The whole approach is designed to guarantee the adjustment of our solutions not only to the cognitive processes of potential single users, but also to the needs of the market. The everyday focus on the usefulness of the application and its usability, strongly anchored to the domain, may lead to a great enhancement of the user acceptance.

21.3 Context and Needs

21.3.1 Architectural Design

An architectural project is a long process characterized by several steps, several actors, and several tools. An architect's work begins by determining the client's needs and ends with the construction or renovation of a building. The architectural project, which may last several weeks or several years, currently suffers from a fragmented approach. This breakdown stems from different legal responsibilities at the various phases. It results in various sorts of representations that may or may not make use of computer tools (Fig. 21.2).

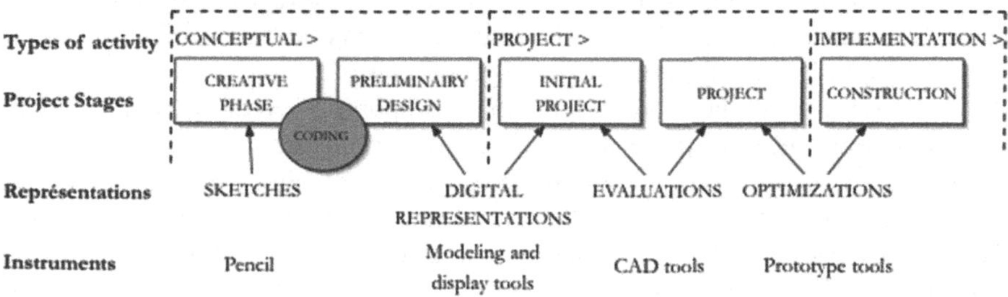

Fig. 21.2 Phases of an architectural project

The first phase is the creative process during which the architect generates ideas and gradually recognizes constraints and criteria involved in the project undertaken [21]. While the subsequent phases of the project are largely supported by information technology, this initial phase is essentially a pencil and paper exercise. After making sketches, the architect has to go through the fastidious step of encoding the sketches on the computer, which is necessary to study the feasibility of the contemplated solution. Next, there are a number of production phases that precisely define all aspects of the building. These phases include comprehensive geometric resolution and complete parameterization of the architecture in order to draw up plans that are communicated to the various parties involved in the project. Finally, in the construction phase, the architect supervises the project. The distinction between creative design and engineering activities is relevant because different types of instruments are used, different cognitive processes are brought into use, and different types of representations are involved.

All these activities are becoming progressively more collective. The architect does not own all the necessary technical knowledge, and several experts (structure, acoustics, energy needs, etc.) have to intervene based on the plans. The different collaborators sometimes work together from the beginning of the design. The conceptual design becomes collective. Moreover, those collaborators are usually working in different places, sometimes quite distant from each other. In these cases, meetings can be very expensive and time consuming.

In this context, and based on our observations and knowledge of the trade, we can identify two different technological gaps, i.e., two activities that are not currently supported by information technologies: real-time collaboration at a distance and the preliminary conceptual sketch-based design stage.

Many CAD tools already allow ideas to be designed and directly manipulated digitally. However, these tools fail to help the designer in the initial design phases, i.e., when the broad outlines of the project must be defined and the crucial option chosen [2, 12, 42]. One of the explanations for this failure relates to the user interface: these tools require painstaking coding of precise data which is only possible once the project has largely been defined [23]. Moreover these systems place users in a circumscribed space. Their movements are reduced to mouse shifts and clicks, and their sensory interactions are limited to passive visual and auditory simulation. A second reason is related to the sketches widely used at the start of the design process. The sketch is used as a graphic simulation space [18]: basic elements of the project set down in the earliest drawings are progressively transformed until a definitive resolution is achieved. Each sketch represents an intermediate step from the first rough sketch to the definitive design solution.

In the same way, there are several tools supporting remote communication, becoming over time more powerful, less expensive, and easier to handle. For example, email is a great asynchronous communication tool. Online exchange databases allow the easy sharing of large files for cooperation. Video-conferencing is a powerful tool for real-time collaborative discussion. But these tools fail to really support collaboration during the creative design process in architecture: there is a need to share in real time the products of the early design, the sketches.

In the following sections we describe these two issues more deeply.

21.3.2 Sketch-Based Preliminary Design

The sketching phase, one of the first steps in an architectural project, represents an important part of the process. It is usually described as a trial-and-error process. Errors are very common and they are quite cheap to recover from. The sketching phase, in case of huge errors, allows the designer to start the design again "from scratch" and change the concepts. Errors can also be very productive, but, as the process goes further, remaining errors become considerably more expensive and their recovery becomes more difficult. In the production phases of design, it is not possible to change concepts but only to correct them (and sometimes not completely). This emphasizes the need to assist designers to detect and correct their errors during the sketching phase, in order to detect them before it is too late (when the price of design is already too expensive).

In current design practice, preliminary drawings are essentially produced on paper before being converted into a representation in a computer-aided design (CAD) system. Why do designers still prefer hand-drawn sketches to computer-assisted design tools at the beginning of the design process? According to McCall et al. [28], there are three reasons: first of all, the pen-and-paper technique leads to abstraction and ambiguity which suit the undeveloped sketch stage. Digital pictures, hard edged, are judged more finite and less creative than traditional sketches, fuzzy, and hand-drawn. Designers need freedom, speed, ambiguity, vagueness to quickly design objects they have in mind [1]. Second, it is a non-destructive process – successive drawings are progressively transformed until the final solution is reached – whereas CAD tools are used to produce objects that can be manipulated (modification, destruction, etc). Third, sketching produces a wide collection of inter-related drawings, while CAD systems construct a single model isolated from the global process. Moreover, the sketch is not simply an externalization of a supposed designer's mental image; it is also a heuristic field of exploration in which the designer discovers new interpretations of his/her own drawing, opening up a path to new perspectives for resolution [11, 22].

Whereas digital representations are by nature unequivocal, the sketch is sufficiently equivocal to produce unanticipated revelations [44]. Sketches, externalizations of the designer's thoughts, allow the designer to represent intermediate states of the architectural object. In addition to this function of presenting and saving information, sketches play a role as mediator between the designer and his/her solution. They are cognitive artifacts in Norman's [29] sense of the term, enabling the individual to expand his/her cognitive capacities. They are rich media for creativity: the ambiguity of the drawing enables new ideas to emerge when old sketches are getting a second look. The architect voluntarily produces imprecise sketches in order to avoid narrowing too rapidly to a single solution and to maintain a certain freedom in case of unexpected contingencies during the process.

Scientific studies of the sketch identify the operations that emerge from producing a series of sketches, in particular the *lateral transformations* where the movement involves passing from one idea to another slightly different idea as well as *vertical transformations* where the one idea moves to another more detailed version of the same idea [10]. Goel also shows that through their syntactic and semantic density, as well as their ambiguity, freehand sketches play an important role in exploratory activity. He suggests that the properties of freehand drawing facilitate lateral transformations and prevent early fixations.

The conceptual sketch has different graphical characteristics than digital representations produced by CAD software [21, 22]. There is not much variation in the lines used for the sketch (types of dotted lines, colors, thicknesses, etc.) and the lines are very imprecise. The drawing is incomplete and shapes often begin to emerge from an accumulation of lines, sometimes redundant. A number of solutions may coexist on the same sketch. This type of drawing is extremely personal, which limits understanding by another person. On the contrary, the clean plans produced using CAD tools are complete and precise. They provide a single and unique representation of the architectural object. A variety of highly codified lines are used. There is no difficulty communicating these plans to someone else and they are produced with exactly this objective in mind.

Therefore, a system that aims to support the graphic conceptual activity should satisfy the following requirements:

- Allow the *natural* drawings of sketches that are the primary ways of thinking.
- Do not interrupt the designer's flow of thinking.
- Allow multiple representations.
- Allow incomplete description of the architectural object.
- Allow the use of imprecise descriptions of the architectural object.
- Help to broaden the point of view of the designer to help him/her produce transformations.

21.3.3 Distant Collaborative Design

In a wide range of types of activity, collaboration has intensified, notably in the design domain. Collective work is increasingly organized simultaneously, rather than sequentially as it used to be in the past. Moreover, design teams are often spatially distributed, and the need for distant real-time interaction is consequently emerging. A lot of effective systems are available for sharing information, but most of them are asynchronous (e.g., databases, email) or allow only partial interaction (e.g., phone).

Therefore, a tool to support distant sharing must respond to the following needs:

- Provide a natural pen-based environment, without wires, mouse, or keyboard to support normal drawing. Moreover, working together on a shared space generates the need for a wide space, to express various and different points of view on a same subject. This environment must therefore have a large size (comparable to a drawing table), but also the right level of resolution in order to provide the requested drawing precision.

- Support freehand sketches, drawn from distant locations on a shared workspace in real time. The method of sketching must be as close as possible to the "classic" face-to-face drawing session, with a shared sheet of paper. Designers thus can express more ideas, concepts, and alternatives than in long-distance asynchronous collaborations, which inevitably and obviously provoke delays, misunderstanding, hazardous interpretations, loss of documents, and coordination problems [13].
- Provide an awareness of the situation (who is around and what is happening) by supporting, in real time, a global and multimodal overview of the context.
- Support the integration of additional reference material (notes, plans, manuals, etc.) generally required for collaborative work.

21.3.4 Why Mixed Reality Should Be a Good Way of Responding to These Needs

Virtual reality is a promising way to respond to the challenges of changes linked to collaborative design and sketch-based design in organizations and processes. The aim of mixed reality is to enhance the individual capabilities (mainly in terms of information perception) without cutting him/her off from the real world, i.e., breaking the frontier between the real and the virtual while helping the user to complete a task [8]. Yet that is the main problem identified in the needs discussed above: designers, in order to benefit from virtual tools, have to deviate from their natural way of working. Evaluating the performance of a building implies switching from creative sketches to formal CAD drawings, and communicating at a distance implies switching from rich multimodal communication in meetings to single-channel or asynchronous communication.

The LUCID-ULg Lab proposes a system for sketch-based multimodal interaction based on the paradigm of the *invisible computer* [30]. Instead of requiring designers to change their way of conceiving a design, we propose to support one of the most usual ways of collaborating: freehand sketching, which plays an important role, especially in the initial stages of design.

As we show below, our response involves a system where there is a mixture of realities, allowing for interactions between the real environment (the table, the pencil, and the colleagues) and the virtual environment (the virtual shared sketches, the interpretation and evaluation of the building). The frontier between reality and virtuality is particularly obvious in the series of graphic representations produced by the architect. Our solution as part of the "invisible technology" movement is to emphasize seamlessness between real and virtual worlds [30, 34]. When applied to architecture, the concepts of *simplicity* (complexity should be a characteristic of the task not the tool), of *versatility* (the apparatus should be designed to encourage new and creative interactions), and of *pleasure* (the tools should be pleasant and amusing) take on a particular significance. We have attempted to infuse these concepts into the prototype that we are presenting here.

21.4 Technological Solutions

21.4.1 Introduction

This section describes the hardware and software implementation we have built to produce an immersive environment for architect and designers. This environment consists of a Virtual Desktop on which two different systems are running. There were some general requirements that we constantly kept in mind, in order to guide our technological choices, including

- Follow the "disappearing computer" paradigm. It means the software we need should reproduce the usual environment and working habits of the user as closely as possible.
- Provide a large working area. Usually, architects are used to working on large drawing boards (typically, around 1.5 large $\times$ 0.6 m depth).
- Pen-based interaction. Architects and designers are very much used to drawing (while most mechanical engineers, for instance, have much less experience of drawing).
- Augmented sheets of paper. It imitates traditional paper (layers with transparency support, graph paper), with augmented capabilities (very large size, zoom, scale, and rotation functions, and customable transparency).
- Allow traditional interaction. Real drawing tools, like rulers, will be allowed. Also, the digital table can be used as a real table (on which to place tools, real paper documents, or a coffee mug).
- The compatibility with real paper documents should be supported (typically by importing them as JPEG in our stack of virtual sheets).
- Provide a good level of resolution for the drawing.

21.4.2 The Virtual Desktop

The Virtual Desktop (Fig. 21.3) is the hardware part of our mixed-reality immersive environment. It is made up of three main core elements (the computer, the digital table, and projectors encased in a suspended ceiling), and a few additional extensions (a video camera for gesture recognition and a videoconference system for collaboration).

The computer we have chosen offers two DVI (video) outputs, in order to connect to the two parallel projectors. It is linked to the table through a USB connection. It runs the dedicated applications, but is also responsible for managing calibration (synchronization between the digital table coordinates and "screen" coordinates). The digital table offers a comfortable drawing area, with its A0 dimension. The suspended ceiling is a work of joinery, built in wood, and specifically designed for our research needs. It stores the two projectors, and possibly the computer and the video camera.

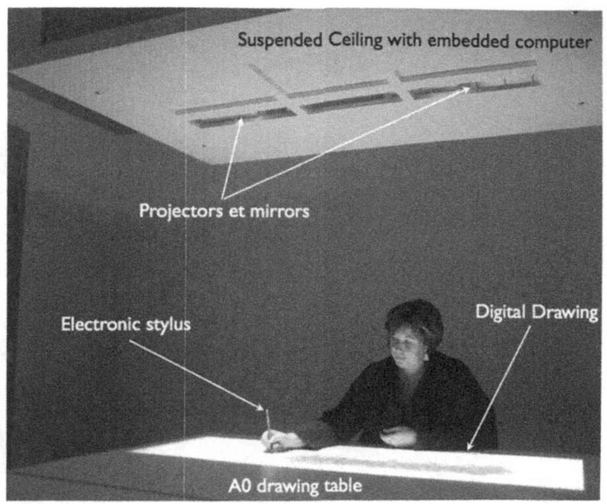

Fig. 21.3 Virtual Desktop

The disposition of the table and the projectors has required some adjustment. The first idea was to project the working space from below a table. Tests have showed that this projector encumbrance under the table made the designer's leg position uncomfortable (which does not suit long working sessions), did not respect the disappearing computer criterion, and constrained the designer's freedom of movement. Inclined worktables are not suitable for design because the designer usually needs to work with a lot of paper sheets. It also becomes uncomfortable to work on such a table after several working hours. So we preferred a simple horizontal whiteboard with a projection from above.

In the first release of the Virtual Desktop, a projector was placed in a suspended ceiling with a classical mirror. To obtain a larger work surface and to increase the precision (the target was 4 pts/mm^2), a second projector was later added to the Virtual Desktop. This change required the resolution of a technical challenge: to manage one screen with two projectors and obtain precise lines efficiently.

In order to clear shadows arising from projection from the ceiling, projectors and mirror were installed to make the projection inclined, so that the user sits out of the projection beam (Fig. 21.4).

The first release of the desktop was realized with a pen-positioning system based on infrared and ultrasound triangulation. Two problems lead us to replace it. On the one hand, the pointer, bigger than usual drawing tools, is quite difficult to handle and adds shadow areas on the drawing. On the other hand, the system has a centimetric precision which is much too low for architectural sketching.

In the second release, a selenoid digital pen has been chosen with several benefits: it has much finer precision and does not add large shadow areas; it does not need a power source which makes it lighter and less bulky; it is more stable and easier to handle; it is also more accurate than the infrared pen. It perfectly matches the characteristics of a usual pen.

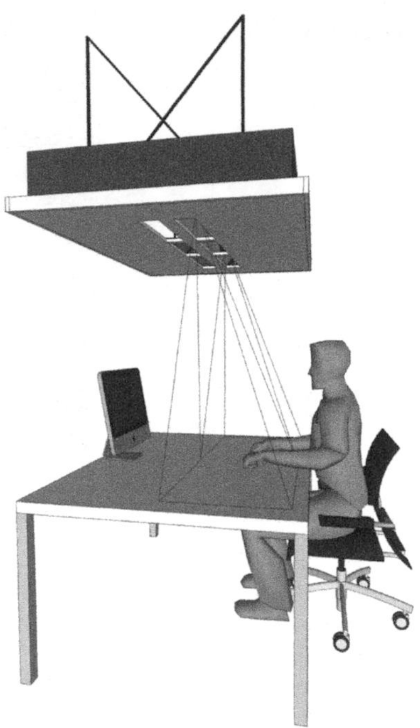

Fig. 21.4 User's position related to projection cone

Projection from above allows the coexistence of real and virtual drawings and a simple integration of pen-and-paper drawings in the system: the user can highlight real documents with the electronic pen, retracing the drawing to import it into the virtual world.

If we compare our Virtual Desktop with the Microsoft Surface table, for instance, we can easily show that the latter is not suitable for long working sessions, as the user cannot put his/her knees below the table. Another well-known smart surface is the DiamondTouch table, produced by Circle Twelve Inc. It uses a similar projection from above like the Virtual Desktop, but with only a single projector, reducing the available working area. Also, these two systems primarily aim at finger manipulation, and do not offer pen support. They target more general applications, while the Virtual Desktop mainly focuses on designers' applications.

Additional components can enhance the Virtual Desktop. A webcam on a 24-inch screen computer offers the ideal extension to support a video-conference session when remote collaboration is needed. We have also added a video camera in the suspended ceiling: through image processing, we can evaluate gesture recognition as an extended interaction modality. Currently, we are able to transmit "finger pointing" to the partners in a collaborative session (see [43]). In the near future, we hope the system will react to hand movements, so that the user can organize his/her sheets of digital paper more naturally with simple gesture.

21.4.3 EsQUIsE

21.4.3.1 Introduction

EsQUIsE is an application dedicated to the early stages of design in architecture. The user simply draws his/her sketches as he/she would do with normal paper. This way, his/her creative process is not disturbed by the application, because he/she does not have to explicitly declare his/her intentions to the system.

EsQUIsE assists the user by providing relevant information (3D model, topological model, and energetic needs) on the building being designed. The software architecture consists of three modules (Fig. 21.5): the entry module, the interpretation module, and the evaluation module(for more detail see [14, 15, 19, 20, 23]).

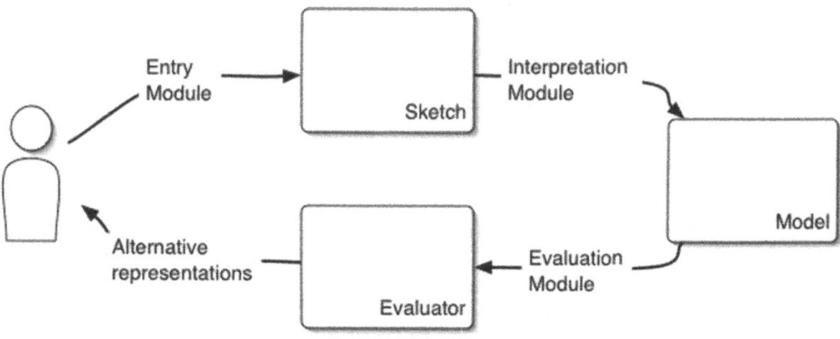

Fig. 21.5 EsQUIsE architecture

21.4.3.2 The Entry Module

The role of the entry module consists of analyzing sketches in order to construct a geometrical model of the drawing, i.e., the significant graphic elements and the relationships they maintain. The principal constraint on such a system is obviously the requirement that it should work in real time. Analysis therefore takes place in two phases. While the electronic stylus is being moved over the pad, the system captures the designer's movements. Then, as soon as a line is finished, the system takes advantage of the time lapse available before the start of the next line to run all the procedures to synthesize and analyze the layout. The synthesis module consists of successive filters intended to extract the essential characteristics of the lines, reducing as much as possible the amount of information to be processed while conserving as faithfully as possible the appearance of the original line. To ensure that the sketch retains its "triggering potential" this step is carried out transparently for the user, who only ever works on his/her initial drawing, unaware of any interpretation being made by the system.

Once the strokes have been individually processed, EsQUIsE captures the relationships between them by using a combined technique of segmentation (to differentiate and to compose sets of lines which "work together") and of classification (grouping lines according to their characteristic criteria). To reach that goal, we have implemented a multi-agent system, which allows the system to consider multiple scenarios at the same time, until enough information is available for a classification decision. Beyond some particular symbols (hatching, blackening, dotted lines, underlining, etc.), the system also focuses on the identification of the written captions which it identifies and situates on the sketch. The aim of the analysis of the drawing is to weave the network of relationships between the different graphic objects it contains. Relationships include, for example, inclusion, intersection, proximity, and superposition of lines and contours. Because the sketch is imprecise, we have developed a "fuzzy graphics" approach that takes into account a considerable margin of error in the identification of points, lines, and intersections. Outlines, for example, do not need to be fully closed-off in order to be recognized; by analyzing the proximity of the ends of the lines, EsQUIsE is able to identify an imprecise outline.

21.4.3.3 The Interpretation Module

The role of the interpretation module is to translate the geometrical information, produced by capturing the sketch, into a functional model of the planned architectural object. This model is generated from collected semantic properties. Lines make outlines which are translated as rooms. Other lines are recognized as letters forming parts of legends. Those are completed by implicit information known by the system. For example, the word "bath"» translates on the sketch the function that the designer gives to the designated space. The outline in which this word appears becomes a function-space in the architectural model with characteristics for this room: a 24° C temperature, a high humidity level, and an average noise level. Those parameters, given with any designer's intervention, are used by the system to fix technological choices: the lines separating the outlines are interpreted as walls separating the rooms. Those, being characterized, are able to find their own technological composition in order to modulate heating and humidity flows passing by the walls. Operating in the same way with the geometrical characteristics of the rooms (ceiling height, for example) the system is able to compose in real time, a complete and cogent (coherent) model of the building being designed, from some sketches drawn by the designer. This whole process is carried out in the background, without requesting the user to declare his/her intention explicitly, so that he/she can truly focus on his/her creative task.

21.4.3.4 The Evaluation Module

This building's model may therefore be used as a source for several evaluations. The main one is the production of the 3D model through which the designer can virtually walk and that allows him/her to check the representation of the dimensions and spaces he/she thought of. EsQUIsE is also able to use this model to estimate the energy performance of the future building and so gives the designer a good idea of his/her options. Simulating the solar source, knowing the desired temperatures for each room and each wall's composition, this second module may estimate the needs in heating or cooling the building.

Figure 21.6 shows the latest version of the software interface, which is purposely kept as simple and uncluttered as possible.

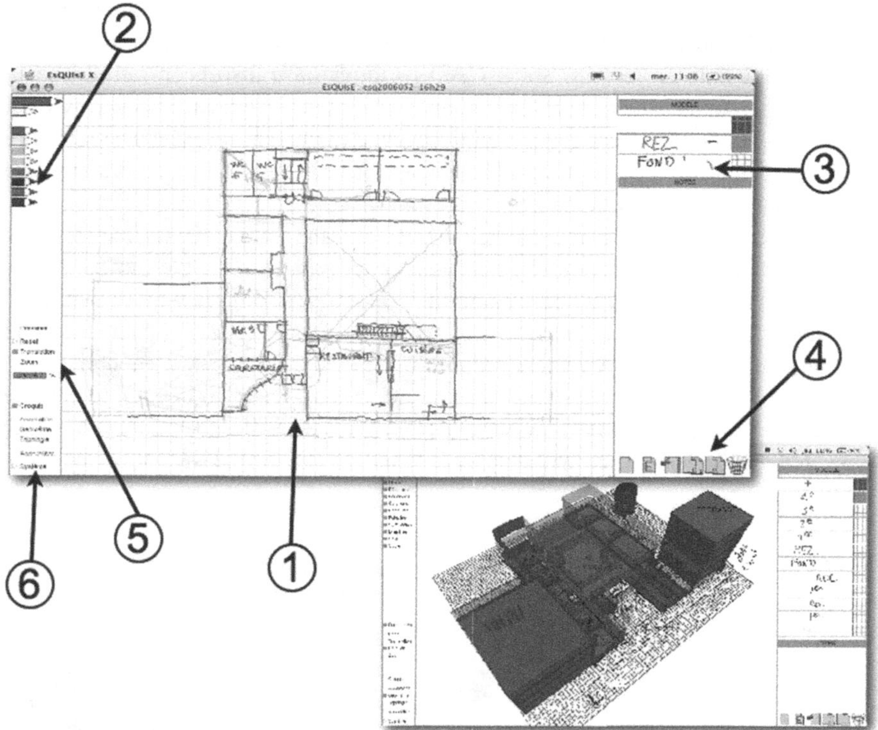

Fig. 21.6 EsQUIsE interface

In EsQUIsE, all the operations are driven by a single stylus. A large area (1) is available for drawing virtual sketches using a palette of virtual pencils and erasers (2). Each sheet of tracing paper is indicated by a tab (3). The user can name these tabs. He/she can also arrange them, by simply dragging and dropping virtual sheets of tracing paper to superpose them within the model. The user clicks on editing icons (4) to create, delete, or duplicate each sheet of tracing paper. Tracing sheets are handled (rotation, shifting places, and zoom) using tools available in the image handling area (5) and parameters can be set for the level of transparency of the tracing paper. The option area (6) enables the user to pass from one mode to another (sketch mode, 3D mode, other digital architectural evaluators, preferences, etc.). The building designer can sketch freely on the virtual tracing paper with digital pens that can draw in different colors. EsQUIsE only interprets black lines in making a model of the building. Other colors are used for idea sketches and annotations. The tracing sheets are semi-transparent and can easily be arranged in relation to one another.

21.4.4 SketSha

The SkeSha software offers a shared drawing environment. It allows several remote workstations to be connected to the same drawing space, in order to support collaborative design. The application captures the strokes that compose the sketch, shares them between the different distant locations (through a classic Internet connection), and transmits the whole information in real time on the active boards through video-data projectors. Some CAD facilities have also been introduced in the prototype, such as the possibility to manage different layers and sheets of virtual paper, to delete or reproduce them, and to manage their transparency. The software also allows the import of plans and images. Pointing, annotating, and drawing are possible thanks to the electronic pen.

The system is completed by a 24-inch display and an integrated camera that allow the participants to see and talk to each other in an almost 1/1 scale during a real-time conference. This integrated camera is in fact a very simple way to avoid the deviation of the look when talking to the interlocutor(s) (see Fig. 21.7 for the whole environment). Moreover, a gesture recognition module based on computer vision is currently being developed. In the near future, this system will be able to capture gestures and finger pointing on a Virtual Desk and send the information to other connected desks, which then will display a "hand avatar" of the distant partner.

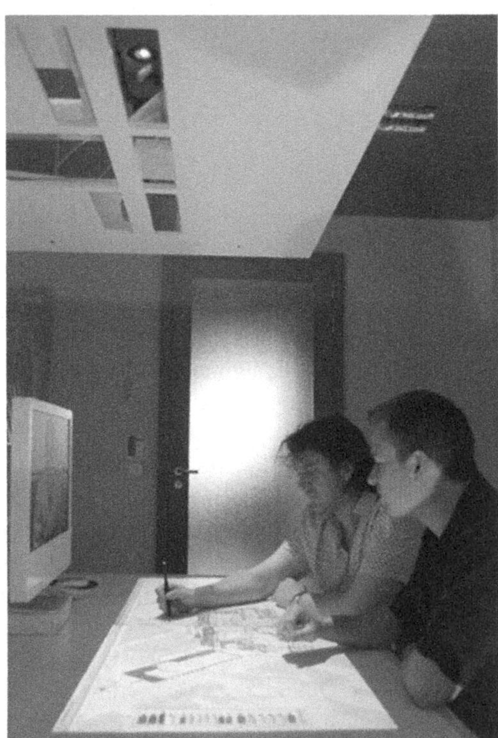

Fig. 21.7 Distributed collaborative design studio

The application structure can be seen as two separate modules: the graphical interface designed to be as natural and friendly as possible and an efficient network layer.

The graphical interface is composed of four elements (Fig. 21.8):

- The main drawing area, designed to cover the whole surface of the Virtual Desktop.
- The pen toolbar, where the user can select a pen (with a specific color or thickness) or the eraser.
- The "pages" toolbar where the user can create new sheets of paper, duplicate and delete some, or reorder them as he/she wishes in a layered stack.
- The navigation widget, dedicated to our pen-based environment. Because of the large working area, the widget is called with a simple "press and wait" operation with the pen. Once it is under the pen, the user can control the view with the classical "translate," "rotate," and "zoom" operation.

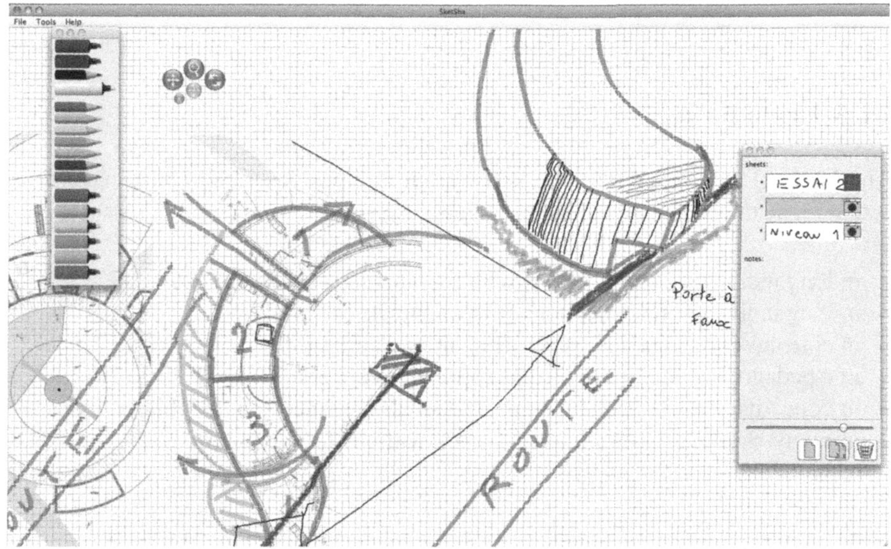

Fig. 21.8 SketSha interface

The network layer is responsible for distributing the different actions from/to all users. It has been designed with the following requirements in mind:

- The project view must be exactly the same for all the users (if the screens have different sizes, the center point of the view is shared). If a user changes the sheet order or changes the current active sheet, it will impact all the users.

- The drawing must be in real time: if the network fails to provide proper bandwidth, a stroke that is being drawn should not be affected (the local rendering must happen as fast as possible whatever the network).
- We want the system to support multiple clients. Tests have been successfully conducted up to five users in the same session.
- We want an optimized use of the network capabilities. If multiple view changes are queued somewhere in the network flow, they can be reduced to a single one. This process is called "coalescence."

There is an apparent paradox between the real-time requirement ("process my data first") and the sharing of the same view ("process everybody's data in the same order for every client"). To solve this problem, we have chosen to encode the multiple actions as messages transmitted over the network to a central server (one client is responsible for acting as the server). The server puts all these messages in a single queue to order them, then redispatches them in that order to all the clients. These messages have properties to describe their "coalescing" behavior or "real-time" behavior. Thanks to these qualifications, we can properly process the messages to reach the given goals.

21.5 Evaluations

The Virtual Desktop and the two software prototypes described above have been tested many times, in a wide range of situations:

- in long individual work sessions with students in architecture course [7, 35–39];
- in long individual work sessions with architects [6, 24–27];
- in collective sessions with students in architecture [4, 5];
- in a pedagogical long-term distant collaborative work setting [9, 16, 17];
- in collective work sessions with professionals (engineers and architects); and
- in many short demonstrations and trials with professionals from various industries.

Most of these evaluations and tests have been videotaped (Fig. 21.4) and analyzed by ergonomists. These studies had different goals from each other, and therefore the observations were based on different evaluation criteria. But they shared some common topics:

- the usability of the system and the way they are handled,
- the expressive power of sketches to support the activities,
- the immersive aspect of the Virtual Desktop, and
- the influence of the technology on the quality of the design process.

In this section we synthesize the main results of these studies.

21.5.1 Usability

In all the tests we have made, the most interesting result may be the simplicity of the systems: it takes very little time for any user to completely master them (less than half an hour for EsQUIsE and less than 10 m for SketSha). Furthermore, in long sessions, the systems seem to disappear from the consciousness of the users.

If we investigate each function separately, we can draw the following conclusions:

- The navigation widget is a very powerful tool. It is perfectly assimilated by the users and allows flexible manipulation. In comparison with EsQUIsE menu setting, the manipulations done with the widget are more accurate, more precise, and above all much faster.
- The principle of overlays is very efficient: icons are well understood, the transparency setting is often used, and editing functions seems to appear quite useful. Therefore, it allows the same kind of use as conventional tracing paper, being augmented by the ease of management (calibration from one layer to another is automatic) and the editing functions. But, it has a limitation: the layers cannot be moved independantly in the horizontal plan, they are always grouped. This function could be useful in order to change the point of view of the designer and to be flexible.
- The pen-based interface is easy to handle. But the current technology raises quite an annoying problem: only a single stylus can be used at a time on a single table. Therefore real-time collaboration is much more efficient in distant situations than in co-present situations.

They also show the richness of the interactions supported by our collaboration system. They demonstrate its ability to support distant collaboration as if the users were co-present. The long-term sessions have also shown that the system was an efficient cooperation tool for concrete projects.

21.5.2 Sketches

We have shown [37] that the sketches on EsQUIsE, although being less precise than paper sketches, contain the same quantity of information than the latter. But we also have shown previously [39] that using the system implies an interesting diversification of sketches: in EsQUIsE, the user separates the "rough" sketches from the "clean" sketches in different virtual sheets. This differs from traditional pen-and-paper drawings, where a single sheet may contain both rough and clean sketches. We explain this difference with the modalities of construction of the 3D self-generated model. It illustrates the distinction between two types of graphic output in the creative stage of conceptual research for an architectural project (Fig. 21.9):

- *Simulation sketch.* An architect must have the necessary conceptual tools at his/her disposition to allow for a flexible and unlimited search for solutions

[18]. Rough drafts spontaneously produced by building designers fulfill this function. These drawings are characterized by a high level of ambiguity and personalization, as well as by a proliferation of graphic solutions to architectural problems. This is what makes it difficult, if not impossible, for these sketches to be understood and used by another person.

- *Synthetic sketch.* This sketch results from finishing activities. A unique solution is represented and emerges from a choice of structuring lines selected from among the large number of lines present in the simulation sketches. The drawing is less ambiguous and more conventional than the simulation sketches. The synthetic sketch can be largely interpreted by another architect.

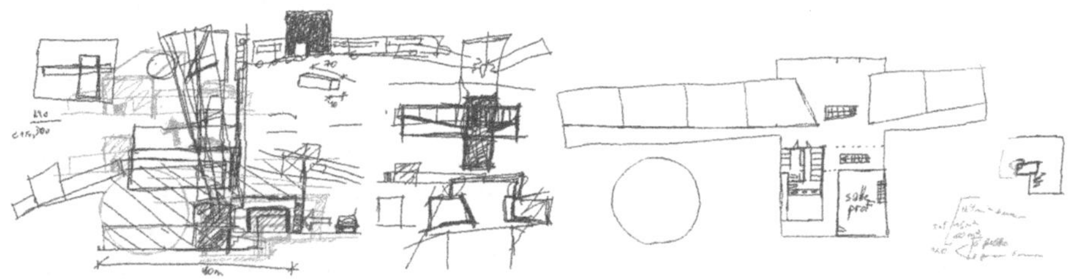

Fig. 21.9 Simulation sketch (*left*) and synthetic sketch (*right*) for the same building design

EsQUIsE and the Virtual Desktop are therefore capable of hosting the multiple sorts of drawings that occur in the preliminary phase of architectural design, all being involved in the man–machine dialogue. But this also shows that these two kinds of drawings are voluntarily separated in EsQUIsE. Therefore, we think that the model of "comprehensive interpretation" is a bit of an illusion. If the objective is to interpret conceptual sketches, we think that the simulation sketch is and should remain personal. Its very ambiguous and idiosyncratic nature lends itself to a difficult computer (or even human) interpretation. On the other hand, the finished drawing or synthetic drawing can be interpreted and contains all the information necessary to make a model of the building.

21.5.3 Immersion

An essential point of interest of the Virtual Desktop, in comparison with classical pen-and-paper activities, lies in the methods of sketch exploration. The exploration of drawings is indeed an important element of the architectural conception. Having new points of view on the drawing provides the emergence of unexpected discoveries [41] and of what Goel [10] calls "lateral transformations", i.e., the movement from an idea to another.

During the design, the sketches are explored by the architects. There are movements on the paper sheet, allowing explorations for the formalization and the expression of the non-graphic ideas and expression of some intentions, especially in terms of circulation of people and space dynamics. In classical pen-and-paper activities, the sketches are explored with the pen: some elements are pointed to bring them to the fore in the architect's reasoning and the pen is often in movement to explore the circulation in space or some other dynamic concepts (see Fig. 21.10).

Fig. 21.10 Exploration by pointing on paper/pen

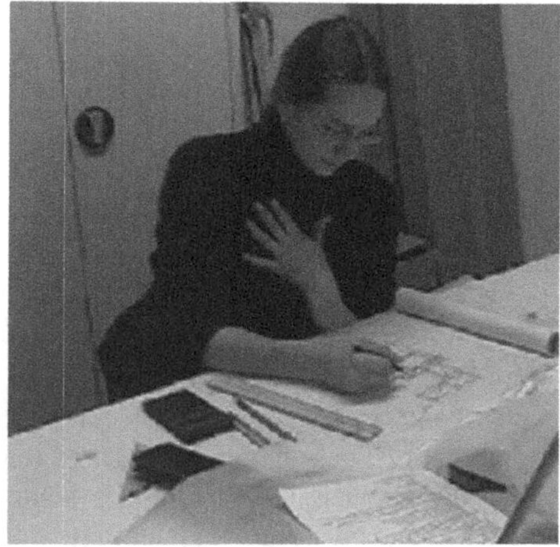

In Virtual Desktop activity, even though these methods of exploration are present, we also notice a bigger physical investment in the drawing: several times, the whole hand allows the expression of a movement and the use of the two hands allows a space delimitation or an intention expression related to a surface (see Fig. 21.11). This can be explained not only by the bigger size of the drawing on the Virtual Desktop, but also by the immersive aspect of the system. In fact, several factors facilitate the immersion in the Virtual Desktop:

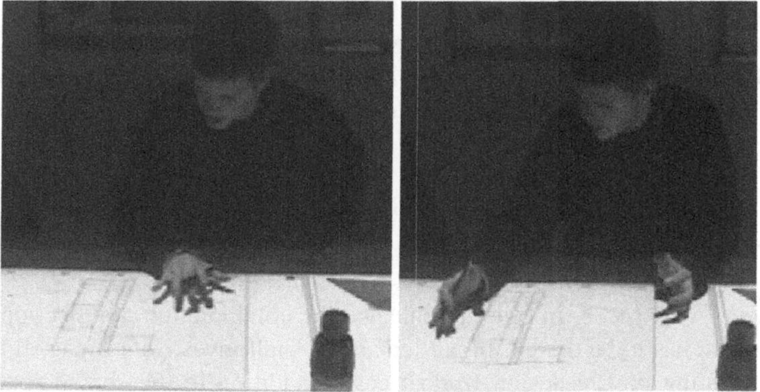

Fig. 21.11 Exploration by hand movement and space delimitation with two hands in the Virtual Desktop

- The luminosity of the work surface contrasts with the darker environment of the room.
- The environment's "embodying aspect" places the designer between the table and the suspended ceiling, in a delimited space and explicitly dedicated to the design.
- The presence of a large and colored dynamic 3D model contributes to workspace specialization and keeps the user's attention on the system.

21.5.4 Design Process

Long-term evaluations of EsQUIsE have shown the following results (for more details, see [39]):

- The 3D model is a good tool for evaluating building volumes, used at some key moments to check the effectiveness and the esthetics of the design. But it does not allow the direct expression of three-dimensional ideas, which is an important function of the volumetric drawings (e.g., perspective drawings). Furthermore, the 3D model is used mainly by students. Professional architects seem to be more confident in the volumetric aspects of their design, and thus do not need to evaluate and continually check their building's volume.
- The 3D model and the interaction modalities of EsQUIsE confer a structuring impact on the design process. The designer's way of drawing is directed toward the definition of an efficient model. It seems to have an influence on design strategies, promoting, for instance, reflection on coherence between the different floors.
- This structuring aspect leads to a spontaneous differentiation of sketches in the system, as explained earlier. The users seem to differentiate their own personal drawings (simulation drawings) and the drawings they keep for communicating in a less ambiguous way with the computer (synthetic drawings), as they would do with other human partners. They use different virtual sheets for these different kinds of drawings. We interpret this observation as an intention to hide a part of their design from the system's interpretation. They want to keep their simulation drawings uninterpreted. New tools should be implemented to allow the coexistence of the different drawings and to communicate which sketches have to be interpreted.

About SketSha, the system seems to enhance the quality of collaboration. But it raises several issues:

- *Design of workspace*. In order to enhance the collaboration, a reflection on the workspace has to be driven. In particular, we shall investigate the usefulness of implementing private design workspaces in addition to the shared space. The orientation of the drawings may also be studied: the distant table could share the same orientation or the drawing can be inverted to simulate a face-to-face arrangement.

- *Integration in industrial practice.* As the system seems to be really useful in experimental settings or for pedagogical purposes, how can it impact professional industrial practices? The first comments from our industrial partners indicate that the system would not replace all needs for real meetings, but can support day-to-day collaboration, and indeed enhance trust between distant partners and provide organizational communication.
- *Ownership of information.* In a design project, the different partners may have different responsibilities. If the whole information is shared, it may cause trouble for keeping track of the decisions, and thus for keeping track of responsibilities. Modalities of information tracking and labeling should be designed.
- *Ways of collaborating.* Will the system radically change the way designers collaborate? Or will it need the definition of particular roles? Future long-term studies will inform us about the way people organize their work according to the possibilities of the system.
- *Additional modules.* SketSha is designed so that external modules can easily be plugged in. We foresee many possible developments: automated collaboration analysis, or domain-specific helpers, for instance. The integration of such additional tools and their impact on the collaboration has still to be studied.

21.6 Characterization of These Mixed-Reality Systems

The whole system consists of a particular way of mixing real and virtual. Dubois [8] describes a taxonomy of mixed-reality environment, depending on two main criteria: the nature of the object being augmented (augmented reality and the augmented virtuality) and the type of augmentation (execution of a task or helps for evaluation).

The main issue here is to define what the task is and what the object is. The Virtual Desktop, in this taxonomy, can be considered as an augmented virtuality execution device; the target of the activity is a virtual sketch that is augmented by natural pen-based interaction. Therefore it aims at giving normal ways of interacting with the computer, i.e., natural ways to draw the digital sketch being processed. It helps the drawing and therefore the execution of a task. It also allows a quick integration of real drawings in a virtual world, by highlighting real pen-and-paper drawings in the Virtual Desktop with the electronic pen.

The EsQUIsE system can be considered as augmented reality evaluation software. It gives calculation and information on a sketch. The object of the activity is the graphical description of the building or even the building itself. This sketch is real, although it has been drawn on the Virtual Desktop: it is more than a simple image because it contains not only the graphical, topological, and technical descriptions of the building, but also the history of the design process and thus offers a reflexive aspect. As we have shown above, the drawing produced with the system shares the most common characteristics with pen-and-paper sketches. The key issue is that the object of the activity is *the activity* itself (the reflexive conversation between an architect and his/her drawings). EsQUIsE provides digital alternative representations of the building, in order to help the designer to evaluate the performance of his/her process and the solution being designed. This has been previously referred to as the augmented sketch [21], which offers assistance in the heart of the design process.

According to the same taxonomy, SketSha could be considered as augmented reality task execution software. The collaboration situation is real, based on speech, gesture, and sketches. The environment helps designers to execute collaborative tasks at a distance, providing them with rich multimodal and creative interaction. This can place them in a situation close to co-present collaboration.

The whole system proposed here is designed to give a smooth integration between reality and virtuality. The drawing, although virtual, is based on a real activity that is important in the design process. The movement real–virtual–real is facilitated by several augmentations: pen-based interaction constitutes a natural way to communicate with a system, the multimodality supports rich real meetings, and the software components give external representations to carry potential insight for the design. Therefore, the whole system is a mixed augmentation (augmenting real and virtual parts of the activity) which supports execution of the drawing via a natural interface and the evaluation of the solution and the design.

21.7 Discussions

The mixed-reality environment we designed is used for two purposes, responding to two metaphors:

- The first application (EsQUIsE) considers the Virtual Desktop as a metaphor for the traditional architect's drawing table. Recognizing the importance of sketches for preliminary design, while identifying the limits of existing computer systems in this context, we have designed an environment where the architect is able to draw freehandedly while the system interprets the sketches and provides him/her with feedback (a 3D model of the building and an assessment of its energy needs). In this "augmented sketch" environment, the architect is also able to integrate its other productions (paper sketches and digital plans) through different importing and processing modules.
- The second application (SketSha) uses the Virtual Desktop as a remote meeting table, allowing collaborative design at a distance. Indeed, an increasing number of teams must collaborate remotely while existing CAD tools mostly only allow for partial and asynchronous interaction. This setup is a combination of a Virtual Desktop, a standard video-conference system, and networked, real-time, collaborative drawing software. The solution as a whole is multimodal in essence (gestures, speech, drawing, etc.) supporting remote collaborative design.

Thanks to their transparent interfaces, these two settings are designed to soften the link between real world and virtual world. The interaction modalities with the virtual sketches are comparable to the drawing modalities in a normal pen-and-paper environment. The intent is to support *natural* pen-based interaction while *augmenting* the drawing (by its interpretation for the first case and by its distant sharing in the second case). The idea is for the device to disappear from the consciousness of its user in order to let him/her focus on his/her actual task (i.e., designing). Mixed reality is therefore a powerful way to create complex environments, in which the user feels "at home."

The several evaluations presented in this chapter, made in different contexts and with different kinds of users, have shown the relevance of the concepts implemented. We have shown that the Virtual Desktop provides an immersive environment: it allows a natural way of working through flexible interactions to support design activity which is known as a high-level activity. The concept of *invisible computer* supported by a mixed-reality environment seems pertinent in the particular context of creative design tasks. This mixed-reality paradigm is a strong way to support natural interaction, to insert the technology in current practices and environments in a smooth way and to support flexibility, multimodality and richness of interaction, invisible interface and augmented drawing, and a "soft" link between real world and virtual world.

Finally, the profession-centered approach and user-centered design offer a way to address the particularities of situations. They allow the design of adapted technologies, responding to real needs, useful in real situations. The simplicity and the specialization of the technology are the keys to the success of tomorrow's technologies, in opposition to the extreme complexity usually encountered in IT solutions [30]. Placing the users at the heart of the development is the required condition to design simple and specialized applications.

References

1. Aliakseyeu, D.(2002) Direct manipulation interface for architectural design tools. Conference on Human Factors in Computing Systems, CHI '02 Extended Abstracts on Human Factors in Computing Systems. Minneapolis, Minnesota, USA, pp. 536–537.
2. Aliakseyeu, D. and Martens, J.-B. (2001). Physical paper as the user interface for an architectural design tool. In: Proceedings of INTERACT 2001, Tokyo, Japan, July, pp. 680–681.
3. Bastien, C. and Scapin, D. (1993). Ergonomic Criteria for the Evaluation of Human-Computer Interfaces. Rapport de l'INRIA: Institut National de Recherche en Informatique et en Automatique.
4. Burkhardt, J.-M., Détienne, F., Moutsingua-Mpaga, L., Perron, L., Safin, S. and Leclercq, P. (2008) Multimodal collaborative activity among architectural designers using an augmented desktop at distance or in collocation. Proceedings of ECCE 2008: European Conference on Cognitive Ergonomics. 16–19 September – Madeira, Portugal.
5. Burkhardt, J.-M., Détienne, F., Moutsingua-Mpaga, L., Perron, L., Safin, S. and Leclercq, P. (2008) Conception architecturale collaborative avec un « bureau augmenté »: une étude exploratoire de l'effet de la distance et de la co-localisation. Actes de SELF 2008: 43ème congrès de la Société d'Ergonomie de Langue Française. 17–19 septembre 2008 – Ajaccio.
6. Darses, F., Mayeur, A., Elsen, C. and Leclercq, P. (2008). Is there anything to expect from 3D views in sketching support tools? DCC'08, Proceedings of the 3rd International Conference on Design Computing and Cognition, Atlanta, USA.
7. Decortis, F., Safin, S. and Leclercq, P. (2005). A role for external representations in architectural design? The influence of a virtual desk and an early 3D view on the design activity.

Proceedings of International Workshop on Understanding Designers'05. Aix-en-Provence, France, October.

8. Dubois, E. (2001) Chirurgie Augmentée, un Cas de Réalité Augmentée; Conception et Réalisation Centrées sur l'Utilisateur. Thèse de doctorat, université Joseph Fourier, Grenoble I.
9. Elsen, C. and Leclercq, P. (2008). A sketching tool to support collaborative design. CDVE'08, 5th International Conference on Cooperative Design, Vizualisation and Engineering, Mallorca, Espagne.
10. Goel, V. (1995). *Sketches of Thought.* Bradford-MIT Press, Cambridge.
11. Goldschmidt, G. (1991). The Dialectics of Sketching. Design Studies, 4, 123–143.
12. Gross, M. (1996). The Electronic Coktail Napkin, Working with Diagrams. Design Studies, 17, 53–69.
13. Gül, L. and Maher, M.L. (2006). The impact of virtual environments on design collaboration. In: 24th eCAADe Conference on Communicating Space(s), pp. 74–80.
14. Juchmes, R., Leclercq, P. and Azar, S. (2004). A multi-agent system for architectural sketches interpretation. Proceedings of Eurographics Workshop on Sketch-Based Interfaces and Modeling, Grenoble, France, pp. 53–62.
15. Juchmes, R., Leclercq, P. and Azar, S. (2005). A Freehand Sketch Environment for Architectural Design Supported by a Multi-Agent System. Special Issue of Computers and Graphics on Calligraphic Interfaces, 29(6), 905–915.
16. Kubicki, S., Bignon, J.-C., Lotz, J., Gilles, H.G., Elsen, C. and Leclercq, P. (2008). Digital cooperative studio. ICE 2008 14th International Conference on Concurrent Enterprising, Special Session ICT-supported Cooperative Design in Education, Lisboa, Espagne.
17. Kubicki, S., Bignon, J.-C., Gilles, H.G., and Leclercq, P. (2008). Cooperative digital studio IT-supported cooperation for AEC students. CIB-W78 25th International Conference on Information Technology in Construction, Santiago de Chile, Chili.
18. Lebahar, J. (1983). *Le dessin d'architecte. Simulation graphique et réduction d'incertitude.* Editions Parenthèses, Paris.
19. Leclercq, P. (1999). Interpretative tool for architectural sketches. In *Visual and Spatial Reasoning in Design*, Gero, J. and Tversky, B. (Eds.), Key Centre of Design Computing and Cognition, Sydney, Autralia, pp. 69–80.
20. Leclercq, P. (2004). Invisible Sketch Interface in Architectural Engineering. *Graphic recognition, recent advances and perspectives, Lecture Notes in Computer Science*, LNCS 3088, Springer Verlag, Berlin, 353–363.
21. Leclercq, P. (2005) Le concept d'esquisse augmentée. Actes de SCAN'05: Séminaire de Conception Architecturale Numérique. Paris, Ecole Nationale Supérieure d'Architecture de Paris-Val de Seine, France.
22. Leclercq, P. and Elsen, C. (2007). Le croquis synthé-numérique. Actes de SCAN 07: Séminaire de conception architecturale numérique, Liège, Belgique.
23. Leclercq, P. and Juchmes, R. (2002). The Absent Interface in Design Engineering. AIEDAM Artificial Intelligence in Engineering Design and manufacturing. Special issue: Human Computer Interaction in Engineering Contexts, 16(5), Cambridge university Press, November 2002.
24. Leclercq, P., Mayeur, A. and Darses, F. (2007). Production d'esquisses créatives en conception digitale. Actes d'IHM'07, 17e conférence francophone sur l'Interaction Homme Machine, ICAM, Paris.
25. Mayeur, A., Darses, F. and Leclercq, P. (2008). Contributions of a 3D numerical environment for architectural sketches. Proceedings of the 8th International Symposium on Smart Graphics, Rennes, France. Lecture Notes in Computer Science, Springer.
26. Mayeur, A., Darses, F. and Leclercq, P. (2007). Apports de la visualisation de maquettes virtuelles 3D en phase d'esquisse architecturale. Actes d'Epique'07, Congrès de la Société Française de Psychologie, UFR de Psychologie, Université de Nantes.
27. Mayeur, A., Darses, F. and Leclercq, P. (2007). Evaluation ergonomique d'une tablette graphique d'aide à la conception architecturale. Actes de SELF'07, 42ème congrès de la Société d'Ergonomie de Langue Française, St-Malo.

28. McCall, R., Ekaterini, V. and Zabel, J. (2001). Conceptual design as hypersketching. In Proceedings of the 9th Int. Conference CAAD Futures, Kluwer Academic Publishers, Dordrecht, The Netherlands, pp. 285–298.
29. Norman, D.A. (1991). Cognitive artifacts. In *Designing interaction: Psychology of the Human-Computer Interface*. J.M. Carroll (Ed.). Cambridge University Press, New York.
30. Norman, D.A. (1998). *The Invisible Computer*, MIT Press, Cambridge University Press, Cambridge MA.
31. Norman, D.A. and Draper, S.W.(1986). *User Centered System Design*. Hillsdale, NJ: Lawrence Erlbaum.
32. Pruitt, J. and Grudin, J. (2003) Personas: practice and theory. Proceedings of the 2003 Conference on Designing for User Experiences. pp. 1–15. San Francisco, California.
33. Rabardel, P. (1995). Les Hommes et les Technologies. Approche Cognitive des Instruments Contemporains. Armand Colin, Paris.
34. Russell, D.M., Streitz, N.A. and Winograd, T. (2005). Building Disappearing Computers. A Special Issue of Communications of the ACM on The Disappearing Computer, a Vision of Computing that is Truly Unremarkable, 48(3), 42–49.
35. Safin, S., Boulanger, C. and Leclercq, P. (2005) Premières évaluation d'un Bureau Virtuel pour un processus de conception augmenté. Proceedings of IHM 2005. Toulouse, France: ACM Press, pp. 107–111.
36. Safin, S., Boulanger, C. and Leclercq, P. (2005). A virtual desktop's first evaluation for an augmented design process. Proceedings of Virtual Concept 2005. Biarritz, France, November
37. Safin, S., Juchmes, R. and Leclercq, P. (2008) Du crayon au stylo numérique: influences des interprétations numériques sur l'activité graphique en tâches de conception. Proceedings of IHM08: Conférence francophone sur l'interaction homme-machine. Metz, septembre 2008.
38. Safin, S., Leclercq, P. and Decortis, F. (2006) Understanding and supporting collaborative design using an horizontal tabletop display. Proceedings of IEA2006. 16th World Congress on Ergonomics. Maastricht, The Netherlands, July.
39. Safin, S., Leclercq, P. and Decortis, F. (2007) Impact d'un environnement d'esquisses virtuelles et d'un modèle 3D précoce sur l'activité de conception architecturale. Revue d'Interaction Homme-Machine, 8(2), 65–98.
40. Schuler, D. and Namioka, A. (Eds.) (1993). *Participatory Design. Principles and Practices*. Hillsdale, NJ: Lawrence Erlbaum.
41. Suwa, M., Gero, J.C. and Purcell, T. (2000). Unexpected Discoveries and S-invention of Design Requirements: Important Vehicles for a Design Process. Design Studies, 21, 539–567.
42. Suwa, M. and Tverski, B. (1996). What architects see in their design sketches: implications for design tools. In Proceedings of ACM Conf. On Human Factors in Computing Systems CHI'96, ACM Press, New York, pp. 191–192.
43. Vandamme, J.-F., Safin, S. and Leclercq, P. (2007). Modalités d'interaction sur interface gestuelle: première évaluation des usages spontanés. *Workshop sur les tables collaboratives, conférence IHM07: Conférence francophone sur l'interaction homme-machine*. Paris, novembre 2007.
44. Verstijnen, I.M., van Leeuwen, C., Goldschmidt, G., Hamel, R. and Hennessey, J.M. (1998). Sketching and Creative Discovery. Design Studies, 19(4), 519–546.

Index

E. Dubois et al. (eds.), *The Engineering of Mixed Reality Systems*, Human-Computer Interaction Series, DOI 10.1007/978-1-84882-733-2,